P9-BZW-553

ΕΙΔΕΤΙCΑΓΝΟΕΙ
ΓΝΟΕΙΤΑΙ
ωCΤΕΛΛΕΦΟΙΜΥ
ΖΗΛΟΥΤΕΤΟΠΡΟ
ΦΗΤΕΥΕΙΝΚΑΙΤΟ
ΛΑΛΕΙΝΜΗΚωΛΥ
ΕΤΑωCCΛCΙΠΑΝ
ΤΑΔΕΕΥCΧΗΜΟ
ΝωCΚΑΙΚΑΤΑΤΑΞΙ
ΓΙΝΕCΘω
ΓΝωΡΙΖωΔΕΥΜΙ
ΑΔΕΛΦΟΙΤΟΕΥΑΓ
ΛΙΟΝΟΕΥΗΙΤΕΝ
CΑΜΗΝΥΜΙΝΟΚ
ΠΑΡΕΛΑΒΕΤΕΕΝ
ΚΑΙΕCΤΗΚΑΤΕΔΙ
ΚΑΙCωΖΕCΘΕΤΙΝΙ
ΛΟΓωΕΥΗΓΓΕΛ·Α
ΜΗΝΥΜΙΝΕΙΚΑΤ
ΧΕΤΕΕΚΤΟCΕΙΜΗ
ΕΙΚΗΕΠΙCΤΕΥCΑΤ
ΠΑΡΕΔωΚΑΓΑΡΥΜΙ
ΕΝΠΡωΤΟΙCΟΚΑΙ
ΠΑΡΕΛΑΒΟΝΟΤΙ
ΑΠΕΘΑΝΕΝΥΠΕΡ
ΤωΝΑΜΑΡΤΙωΝ
ΗΜωΝΚΑΤΑΤΑΓΡΑ
ΦΑCΚΑΙΟΤΙΕΤΑΦ
ΚΑΙΟΤΙΕΓΗΓΕΡΤΑΙ
ΤΗΗΜΕΡΑΤΗΤΡΙΤ
ΚΑΤΑΤΑCΓΡΑΦΑC
ΚΑΙΟΤΙωΦΘΗΚΗ
ΦΑΕΙΤΑΤΟΙCΙΒ
ΕΠΕΙΤΑωΦΘΗ
ΠΑΝωΠΕΝΤΑΚ
CΙΟΙCΑΔΕΛΦΟΙC
ΕΦΑΠΑΞΕΞωΝΟΙΠ
ΟΝΕCΜΕΝΟΥCΙΝ
ΕωCΑΡΤΙΤΙΝΕCΔ
ΕΚΟΙΜΗΘΗCΑΝ
ΠΕΙΤΑωΦΘΗΙΑ
ΚωΒωΕΠΕΙΤΑΤ
ΑΠΟCΤΟΛΟΙCΠΑ
ΕCΧΑΤΟΝΔΕΠΑΝ
ωCΠΕΡΕΙΤωΕΚ
ΜΑΤΙωΦΘΗΚΑΜ
ΕΓωΓΑΡΕΙΜΙΟΕΛΑ
ΧΙCΤΟCΤωΝΑΠ

ΛωΝΟCΟΥΚΙΜΙΙ
ΚΑΝΟCΚΑΛΕΙCΘ
ΑΠΟCΤΟΛΟCΔΙΟ
ΠΕΔΙωΞΑΤΗΝΕΚ
ΚΛΗCΙΑΝΤΟΥΘΥ
ΧΑΡΙΤΙΔΕΘΥΕΙΜΙΟ
ΕΙΜΙΚΑΙΗΧΑΡΙC

ΚΑΙΕΓΕΝΕCΘΕΕΝ
ΤΑΙCΑΜΑΡΤΙΑΙCΥ
ΜωΝ·

ΑΡΑΚΑΙΟΙΚΟΙΜΗ
ΤΕCΕΝΧωΑΠωΛ
ΤΟΕΙΕΝΤΗΖωΗ
ΤΗΝΕΝΧωΗΛΠΙΚ
ΤΕCΕCΜΕΝΜΟΝ
ΕΛΕΕΙΝΟΤΕΡΟΙ
ΠΑΝΤωΝΑΝωΝ

CΑΝΤΟCΑΥΤωΤΑ
ΠΑΝΤΑΤΟΤΕΚΑΙΑΥ
ΤΟCΟΥΙΟCΥΠΟΤΑΓ

CΕΤΑΙΤωΥΠΟΤΑΞ
ΤΙΑΥΤωΤΑΠΑΝΤΑ
ΙΝΑΗΟΘCΤΑΠΑΝ
ΤΑΕΝΠΑCΙΝ
ΕΠΕΙΤΙΠΟΙΗCΟΥCΙ
ΟΙΒΑΠΤΙΖΟΜΕΝΙ
ΥΠΕΡΤωΝΝΕΚ
ΕΙΟΛωCΝΕΚΡΟΙ
ΚΕΓΕΙΡΟΝΤΑΙΤΙΚΑΙ
ΒΑΠΤΙΖΟΝΤΑΙΥΠ
ΑΥΤωΝΤΙΚΑΙΗΜ
ΚΙΝΔΥΝΕΥΟΜΕΝ
ΠΑCΑΝωΡΑΝ
ΚΑΘΗΜΕΡΑΝΑΠΟ
ΟΝΗCΚωΝΗΤΗΝ
ΥΜΕΤΕΡΑΝΚΑΥΧΗ
CΙΝΑΔΕΛΦΟΙΗΝ
ΕΧωΕΝΧωΙΥΤω
ΙΜωΝΕΙΚΑΤΑΑΝ
ΡωΠΟΝΕΘΗΡΙω
CΗCΑΕΝΕΦΕCω
ΤΙΜΟΙΤΟΟΦΕΛΟC
ΕΙΝΕΚΡΟΙΟΥΚΕΓΙ
ΡΟΝΤΑΙΦΑΓωΜ
ΚΑΙΠΙωΜΕΝΑΥΡΙ
ΟΝΓΑΡΑΠΟΘΝΗCΚΟΜΕΝ
ΜΗΠΛΑΝΑCΘΕΦ
ΡΟΥCΙΝΗΘΗΧΡΗCΘ
ΟΜΙΛΙΑΙΚΑΚΑΙΕΚ
ΝΗΨΑΤΕΔΙΚΑΙωC
ΚΑΙΜΗΑΜΑΡΤΑΝ
ΑΓΝωCΙΑΝΓΑΡΘΥ
ΤΙΝΕCΕΧΟΥCΙΝ
ΠΡΟCΕΝΤΡΟΠΗΝΥ
ΜΙΝΛΑΛω
ΑΛΛΕΡΙΤΙCΤΙCωCΕΓΙ
ΡΟΝΤΑΙΟΙΝΕΚΡΟΙ
ΠΟΙωΔΕCωΜΑΤΙ
ΚΟΝΤΑΙ
ΑΦΡωΝCΥΟCΠΙΡ
ΟΥΖωΟΠΟΙΕΙΤΑΙ
ΤΗΝΕΑΝΜΗΑΠΟ
ΝΗΚΑΙΟCΠΙΡΕΙCΥ
ΤΟCωΜΑΧΙΟΤΕΝΗ
ΜΕΝΟΝΑΛΛΑΓΥΜ
ΚΟΚΚΟΝΕΙΤΥΧΟΙ
ΤΟΥΗΤΙΝΟCΤωΝΛ

**Hermeneia
—A Critical
and Historical
Commentary
on the Bible**

Old Testament Editorial Board

Frank Moore Cross, Jr., Harvard University, chairman
Klaus Baltzer, University of Munich
Paul D. Hanson, Harvard University
S. Dean McBride, Jr., Yale University
Roland E. Murphy, O. Carm., Duke University

New Testament Editorial Board

Helmut Koester, Harvard University, chairman
Eldon Jay Epp, Case Western Reserve University
Robert W. Funk, University of Montana
George W. MacRae, S.J., Harvard University
James M. Robinson, Claremont Graduate School

1 Corinthians

A Commentary on
the First Epistle
to the Corinthians

by Hans Conzelmann

Translated by
James W. Leitch

Bibliography and References by
James W. Dunkly

Edited by
George W. MacRae, S.J.

1975

Fortress Press

Philadelphia

Translated from the German *Der erste Brief an die
Korinther* by Hans Conzelmann (1st edition).
Kritisch-Exegetischer Kommentar über das Neue
Testament begrundet von Heinrich August Wilhelm
Meyer, Fünfte Abteilung—11. Auflage. © Vanden-
hoeck & Ruprecht, Göttingen, 1969.

© 1975 in the English translation
by Fortress Press

All rights reserved. No part of this publication may
be reproduced, stored in a retrieval system, or transmitted in any form or by any means, electronic,
mechanical, photocopying, recording, or otherwise,
without the prior permission of the copyright owner.

Library of Congress Catalog Card Number 73–88360
ISBN 0–8006–6005–6

20–6005 Printed in the United States of America

Type set by Maurice Jacobs, Inc., Philadelphia

1328

FÜR ELISABETH

2 June 83

66769

The Author

Hans Conzelmann, born in 1915, served on the theological faculties at Tübingen, Heidelberg, and Zürich
before assuming his present position on the theological
faculty at Göttingen. He is well known in English for *The
Theology of St. Luke* (1960), *An Outline of the Theology of
the New Testament* (1969) and *Jesus* (1973). He has also
contributed to Kittel's *Theological Dictionary of the New
Testament*, *Religion in Geschichte und Gegenwart*, *Das Neue
Testament Deutsch*, the *Handbuch zum Neuen Testament*, and
the *Meyer Kommentar*. His thorough revision of Martin
Dibelius' *The Pastoral Epistles* has already appeared
in *Hermeneia*.

Contents

The name *Hermeneia*, Greek ἐρμηνεία has been chosen as the title for the commentary series to which this volume belongs. The word *Hermeneia* has a rich background in the history of biblical interpretation as a term used in the ancient Greek-speaking world for the detailed, systematic exposition of a scriptural work. It is hoped that the series, like the name, will carry this old and venerable tradition forward. A second, entirely practical reason for selecting the name lay in the desire to avoid a long descriptive title and its inevitable acronym or worse, an unpronounceable abbreviation.

The series is designed to be a critical and historical commentary to the Bible without arbitrary limits in size or scope. It will utilize the full range of philological and historical tools including textual criticism (often ignored in modern commentaries), the methods of the history of tradition (including genre and prosodic analysis), and the history of religion.

Hermeneia is designed for the serious student of the Bible. It will make full use of ancient Semitic and classical languages; at the same time English translations of all comparative materials, Greek, Latin, Canaanite, or Akkadian, will be supplied alongside the citation of the source in its original language. The aim is to provide the student or scholar in so far as possible with the full critical discussion of each problem of interpretation and with the primary data upon which the discussion is based.

Hermeneia is designed to be international and interconfessional in the selection of its authors, and is so represented on its board of editors. On occasion, distinguished commentaries in languages other than English will be published in translation. Published volumes of the series will be revised continually, and eventually new commentaries will be assigned to replace older works in order that the series can be open-ended. Commentaries are also being assigned for important literary works falling in the categories of apocryphal and pseudepigraphical works of the Old and New Testament, including some of Essene or Gnostic authorship.

The editors of *Hermeneia* impose no systematic-theological perspective (directly or indirectly by the selection of authors) upon the series. It is expected that authors will struggle fully to lay bare the ancient meaning of a biblical work or pericope. In this way its human relevance should become transparent as is the case always in competent historical discourse. However, the series eschews for itself homiletical translation of the Bible.

The editors are under a heavy debt to Fortress Press for the energy and courage shown in taking up an expensive and long project the rewards of which will accrue chiefly to the field of biblical scholarship. The translator of this volume is the Reverend Dr. James W. Leitch of Basel, Switzerland. Mr. James W. Dunkly of Weston College, Cambridge, Massachusetts, is responsible for all bibliographic and reference materials in the footnotes, Reference Codes, and final Bibliography. His diligence in seeking out translations of ancient and modern literature and in verifying citations has been of great assistance to the Volume Editor.

The editor responsible for this volume is George W. MacRae, S.J., of Harvard University.

November 1974

Frank Moore Cross, Jr.
For the Old Testament
Editorial Board

Helmut Koester
For the New Testament
Editorial Board

1. Abbreviations

Abbreviations used in this volume for sources and
literature from antiquity are the same as those used
in the *Theological Dictionary of the New Testament*,
ed. Gerhard Kittel, tr. Geoffrey W. Bromiley, vol. 1
(Grand Rapids, Michigan, and London: Eerdmans,
1964), xvi–xl. Some abbreviations are adapted from
that list and can be easily identified.

In addition, the following abbreviations have
been used:

AAG	Abhandlungen der Gesellschaft der Wissenschaften zu Göttingen (Philologisch–historische Klasse)
AAM	Abhandlungen der geistes– und sozialwissenschaftlichen Klasse der Akademie der Wissenschaften und der Literatur in Mainz
Achil. Tat., *Clit. et Leuc.*	Achilles Tatius, *Clitophon et Leucippus*
Act. Joh.	*Acta Johannis*
Act. Paul. et Thecl.	*Acta Pauli et Theclae*
ad loc.	*ad locum*, at the place or passage discussed
Agathias, *Hist.*	Agathias, *Historia*
AGSU	Arbeiten zur Geschichte des späteren Judentums und des Urchristentums
AJPh	*American Journal of Philology*
ANF	*The Ante–Nicene Fathers: Translations of the Writings of the Fathers Down to A.D. 325*, ed. Alexander Roberts and James Donaldson (Buffalo: Christian Literature Publishing Company, 1885–97; Grand Rapids: Eerdmans, 1951–56), 10 vols.
AnzAW	Anzeige der Akademie der Wissenschaften in Wien (Philosophisch–historische Klasse)
Apollod., *Bibl.*	Apollodorus, *Bibliotheca*
Apollon. Dyscol., *Constr.*	Apollonius Dyscolus, *De constructione*
APOT	*The Apocrypha and Pseudepigrapha of the Old Testament in English, with Introductions and Critical and Explanatory Notes to the Several Books*, ed. Robert Henry Charles (Oxford: Clarendon, 1913), 2 vols.
Apul., *Apol.*	Apuleius, *Apologia* (= *Pro se de Magia*)
ARGU	Arbeiten zur Religionsgeschichte des Urchristentums
Aristob., *fr.*	Aristobulus, *fragmenta*
Aristot., *Ath. resp.*	Aristotle, *Atheniensium respublica*
ASNU	Acta Seminarii Neotestamentici Upsaliensis
AThANT	Abhandlungen zur Theologie des Alten und Neuen Testaments
Athen., *Deipnosoph.*	Athenaeus, *Deipnosophistae*
Athenag., *Res. mort.*	Athenagoras, *De resurrectione mortuorum*
Aug., *Trin.*	Augustinus, *De trinitate*
BBB	Bonner Biblische Beiträge
Ber.	*Berakoth*, tractate of Mishnah, Tosefta, and Talmud
BEvTh	Beiträge zu *Evangelische Theologie*
BHTh	Beiträge zur Historischen Theologie
BJRL	*Bulletin of the John Rylands Library*
BKT	*Berliner Klassikertexte* (Berlin: Königliche Museen zu Berlin, 1904–23), 7 vols.
BZNW	Beiträge zur *Zeitschrift für die neutestamentliche Wissenschaft*
CAH	*The Cambridge Ancient History*, ed. J. B. Bury *et al.* (Cambridge: University Press, 1923–39), 12 vols.
Caius, *Inst.*	Caius, *Institutiones*
CD	The Cairo Genizah Damascus Document
cf.	*confer*, compare
Charit., *Chaer. et Call.*	Chariton, *Chaereas et Callirhoe*
Chrys., *Hom. in Epist. I ad Cor.*	Johannes Chrysostomus, *Homiliae in Epistula I ad Corinthios*
Cic., *Acad.* *Cluent.*	Cicero, *Academica* *Pro Cluentio*
CIJ	*Corpus Inscriptionum Iudaicarum*, ed. Jean–Baptiste Frey (Rome: Pontificio Istituto di Archeologia Cristiana, 1936–52), 2 vols.
CN	*Coniectanea Neotestamentica*
col.	column(s)
Corp. Herm. *Ascl.*	*Asclepius* in *Corpus Hermeticum*

DBS	*Dictionnaire de la Bible, Supplément*, ed. F. Vigouroux (Paris: Letouzey & Ané, 1926–).	Luc., *Anach.*	Lucian, *Anacharsis*
		Cyn.	*Cynicus*
		Dial. meretr.	*Dialogi meretricii*
Dig.	*Digesta Iustiniani*	*Dial. mort.*	*Dialogi mortuorum*
Dio C.,	Dio Cassius,	*Fug.*	*Fugitivi*
Hist. Rom.	*Historia Romae*	*Halc.*	*Halcyon*
DJD	Discoveries in the Judaean Desert	*Imag.*	*Imagines*
ed.	editor, edited by	*Ver. hist.*	*Verae historiae*
[Ed.]	Editor of this volume of Hermeneia	Lucan,	Lucan,
Ep. Ap.	*Epistula Apostolorum*	*Bell. civ.*	*Bellum civile (Pharsalia)*
6 Esdr.	*6 Esdras*	Lyc., *Leocr.*	Lycurgus, *Leocrates*
ET	English translation	*MAMA*	*Monumenta Asiae Minoris Antiqua*, ed. William M. Calder (Manchester: Manchester University Press; London: Longmans, Green, 1928–62), 8 vols.
Ev. Phil.	*Evangelium Philippi*		
Ev. Th.	*Evangelische Theologie*		
Ev. Thom.	*Evangelium Thomae*		
Ev. Ver.	*Evangelium Veritatis*	Manil.,	Manilius,
4 Ezra	*4 Ezra (= 2 Esdras)*	*Astronom.*	*Astronomicon*
f (ff)	and the following	Mart.,	Martial,
FRLANT	Forschungen zur Religion und Literatur des Alten und Neuen Testaments	*Epigr.*	*Epigrammata*
		M. Aur.	Marcus Aurelius Antoninus,
GCS	Die Griechischen Christlichen Schriftsteller	Ant.,	
		Medit.	*Meditationes*
Ginza L, R	*Ginza* Left, Right	Max. Tyr.,	Maximus Tyrius,
HAT	Handbuch zum Alten Testament	*Diss.*	*Dissertationes*
Herm.,	Hermas,	*Milet*	*Milet. Ergebnisse der Ausgrabungen und Untersuchungen seit dem Jahre 1899*, ed. Theodor Wiegand (Berlin: Reimer, 1906–).
Mand.	*Mandata* (in *Pastor Hermae*)		
Sim.	*Similitudines* (in *Pastor Hermae*)		
Vis.	*Visiones* (in *Pastor Hermae*)		
Hesych.,	Hesychius, *Lexicon*	Min. Fel.,	Minucius Felix,
Lex.		*Oct.*	*Octavius*
Hipp.,	Hippolytus,	MM	James Hope Moulton and George Milligan, *The Vocabulary of the Greek Testament Illustrated from the Papyri and Other Non–Literary Sources* (London: Hodder & Stoughton, 1930)
In Dan.	*Commentarius in Danielum*		
HNT	Handbuch zum Neuen Testament		
Horat.,	Horatius,		
Carm.	*Carmina*		
Ep.	*Epistulae*	MT	Masoretic text.
HTR	*Harvard Theological Review*	*MThZ*	*Münchener Theologische Zeitschrift*
HZ	*Historische Zeitschrift*	n. (nn.)	note(s)
ibid.	*ibidem*, in the same place	*NAG*	*Nachrichten von der Akademie der Wissenschaften in Göttingen* (= *NGG* after 1940)
ICC	International Critical Commentary		
idem	the same (person)	NIC	New International Commentary
Iren., *Haer.*	Irenaeus, *Adversus haereses*	no(s).	number(s)
item	the same (thing)	*NovTest*	*Novum Testamentum*
j.	Jerusalem (Palestinian) Talmud, followed by abbreviated title of tractate	NPNF	*A Select Library of Nicene and Post–Nicene Fathers of the Christian Church*, ed. Philip Schaff (New York: Christian Literature Company, 1887–1900; Grand Rapids: Eerdmans, 1952–55), 28 vols. in 2 series
JAC	*Jahrbuch für Antike und Christentum*		
JBR	*Journal of Bible and Religion*		
Jos. et As.	*Joseph et Aseneth*		
Jub.	*Jubilees*		
KEK	Kritisch–exegetischer Kommentar über das Neue Testament, begründet von Heinrich August Wilhelm Meyer		
		n.s.	new series
		NtlAbh	Neutestamentliche Abhandlungen
		NTS	*New Testament Studies*
KNT	Kommentar zum Neuen Testament, ed. Theodor Zahn	NTTS	New Testament Tools and Studies
(Zahn)		*OCD*[1]	*The Oxford Classical Dictionary*, ed. Max Cary *et al.* (Oxford: Clarendon, 1948)
KuD	*Kerygma und Dogma*		
LCC	Library of Christian Classics	*OCD*[2]	*The Oxford Classical Dictionary*, ed. N. G. L. Hammond and H. H. Scullard (Oxford: Clarendon, [2]1970)
Liv.,	Titus Livius,		
Urb. cond.	*Ab urbe condita*		
Loeb	Loeb Classical Library	*Od. Sal.*	*Odae Salomonis*

Orig., *Cat.* Origen, *Catenae*
  Comm.   *Commentarius in Matthaeum*
  in Matt.
Oros., *Hist.* Orosius, *Historia*
  contra pag.   *contra paganos*
Ovid., *Am.* Ovidius, *Amores*
  Ars am.   *Ars amatoria*
  Met.   *Metamorphoses*
  Tr.   *Tristia*
p. (pp.) page(s)
Paus., *Descr.* Pausanias, *Descriptio Graecae*
P. Berol. Berlin Papyri, esp. *Papyri graecae bero-*
  linenses, ed. Wilhelm Schubart (Bonn:
  Marcus & Weber, 1911)
PGM *Papyri Graecae Magicae*, ed. and tr. Karl
  Preisendanz (Leipzig and Berlin:
  Teubner, 1928–31), 2 vols.
P. Grenf. I, *An Alexandrian Erotic Fragment and*
  Other Greek Papyri, chiefly Ptolemaic, ed.
  Bernard P. Grenfell (Oxford: Claren-
  don, 1896). II, *New Classical Fragments*,
  ed. Bernard P. Grenfell and Arthur S.
  Hunt (Oxford: Clarendon, 1897).
Phaedr., Phaedrus,
  Fab.   *Fabulae*
Philodem. Philodemus
Philos., Philosophus,
  Lib.   Περὶ παρρησίας *Libellus*
Plaut., Plautus,
  Pseudol.   *Pseudolus*
Plin., Pliny the Younger,
  Panegyr.   *Panegyricus*
Plut., Plutarch,
  Amic. mult.   *De amicorum multitudine*
  Fort. Rom.   *De fortuna Romanorum*
  Herod.   *De malignitate*
   malign.   *Herodoti*
  Num.   *Numa*
  Quaest.   *Quaestiones*
   Plat.   *Platonicae*
  Virt. doc.   *An virtus doceri possit*
Pol., *Phil.* Polycarp, *Epistula ad Philippenses*
Polyb., *Hist.* Polybius, *Historia*
Pomp. Mel., Pomponius Mela,
  Chor.   *De chorographia*
Ps.– Pseudo–Callisthenes,
  Callisth.,
  Hist. Alex.   *Historia Alexandri Magni*
  Magn.
Ps.–Cl., Pseudo–Clement,
  Hom.   *Homiliae*
  Recog.   *Recognitiones*
Ps.– Pseudo–
  Demetr.,   Demetrius,
  Eloc.   *De elocutione*
  Form. ep.   *De forma epistularum*
PSI *Pubblicazioni della Società Italiana: Papiri*
  Greci e Latini, vols. 1–11 (1912–35),
  14 (1957)

Ps.–Lib., Pseudo–Libanius,
  Charact. ep.   *De charactere epistularum*
Ps.–Philo, Pseudo–Philo,
  Ant. bib.   *Liber antiquitatum biblicarum*
Ps.–Phocy- Pseudo–Phocylides,
  lides,
  Poema   *Poema admonitorum*
  adom.
Ps. Sal. *Psalmi Salomonis*
Ptol., *Ep. ad* Ptolemaeus (Gnosticus), *Epistula ad*
  Flor.   *Floram*
Q Qumran documents:
  1Q27 (=
   1QMyst) Book of Mysteries
  1QH Hodayot, the Psalms of
    Thanksgiving
  1QM Milḥamah, the War Scroll
  1QpHab Habakkuk Pesher
  1QS Manual of Discipline, Rule of the
    Community
  1QSa,
   1QSb adjuncts to the Rule
  4QDb Damascus Document fragments
  4QFlor Florilegium
  4QpNah Nahum Pesher
  4QTest Testimonia
Quint. Curt. Quintus Curtius Rufus,
  Ruf.,
  Hist. Alex.   *Historia Alexandri*
RAC *Reallexikon für Antike und Christentum*,
  ed. Theodor Klauser (Stuttgart:
  Hiersemann, 1950–)
RB *Revue Biblique*
RechBibl Recherches Bibliques
RechSR *Recherches de Science Religieuse*
rev. revised by
RevBén *Revue Bénédictine*
RGG³ *Die Religion in Geschichte und Gegenwart:*
  Handwörterbuch für Theologie und Reli-
  gionswissenschaft, ed. Kurt Galling *et al.*
  (Tübingen: J. C. B. Mohr [Paul
  Siebeck], 1957–62), 7 vols.
RHE *Revue d'Histoire Ecclésiastique*
RHPhR *Revue d'Histoire et de Philosophie Reli-*
  gieuses
RSV Revised Standard Version of the Bible
RThPh *Revue de Théologie et de Philosophie*
SAKDQ Sammlung Ausgewählter Kirchen-
  und Dogmengeschichtlicher Quellen-
  schriften
Sallust., *Iug.* Sallust, *Bellum Iugurthinum*
Sallust. Sallustius Neoplatonicus,
  Neoplat.,
  Deis   *De deis et mundo*
  et mund.
SANT Studien zum Alten und Neuen Testa-
  ment
SBT Studies in Biblical Theology
SBU Symbolae Biblicae Upsalienses

ScEccl	Sciences Ecclésiastiques
SEÅ	Svensk Exegetisk Årsbok
Sen., Const.	Seneca, De constantia sapientis
Ep.	Epistulae morales
Herc. fur.	Hercules furens
Ir.	De ira
Prov.	De providentia
Quaest. nat.	Quaestiones naturales
Sext. Emp.,	Sextus Empiricus,
Math.	Adversus Mathematicos
Arith.	Adversus arithmeticos (Math. 4)
Astrol.	Adversus astrologos (Math. 5)
Dogm.	Adversus dogmaticos (Math. 7–11)
Eth.	Adversus ethicos (Math. 11, Dogm. 5)
Geom.	Adversus geometras (Math. 3)
Gramm.	Adversus grammaticos (Math. 1)
Log. 1, 2	Adversus logicos (Math. 7, 8; Dogm. 1, 2)
Mus.	Adversus musicos (Math. 6)
Phys. 1, 2	Adversus physicos (Math. 9, 10; Dogm. 3, 4)
Rhet.	Adversus rhetores (Math. 2)
Sext., Sent.	Sextus, Sententiae
SGV	Sammlung gemeinverständlicher Vorträge und Schriften aus dem Gebiet der Theologie und Religionsgeschichte
Shab.	Shabbat, tractate of Mishnah, Tosefta, and Talmud
SHT	Studies in Historical Theology
Simpl.	Simplicius,
Comm. in Epict. Ench.	Commentarius in Epicteti Enchiridionem
SNovTest	Supplements to Novum Testamentum
SNTS Monograph Series	Studiorum Novi Testamenti Societas Monograph Series
Strabo,	Strabo,
Geog.	Geographia
StudTh	Studia Theologica
Suet., Claud.	Suetonius, Claudius
Vitell.	Vitellius
Sukk.	Sukka, tractate of Mishnah, Tosefta, and Talmud
SUNT	Studien zur Umwelt des Neuen Testaments
Supp. Epigr.	Supplementum Epigraphicum Graecum, ed. J. J. E. Hondius (Leiden: Sijthoff, 1923–)
s.v. (vv.)	sub voce (vocibus), under the entry (entries)
TDNT	Theological Dictionary of the New Testament, ed. Gerhard Kittel, tr. Geoffrey W. Bromiley (Grand Rapids: Eerdmans, 1964–73)
Tert., Apol.	Tertullian, Apologia
Cor.	De corona militum
Prax.	Adversus Praxean
Res.	De resurrectione carnis
Test. Jobi	Testamentum Jobi
Test. Sal.	Testamentum Salomonis
Tg. Is.	Targum to Isaiah
Tg. Ps.	Targum to the Psalms
Tg. Zech.	Targum to Zechariah
Thdrt.,	Theodoret,
Interp. Epist. I ad Cor.	Interpretatio Epistulae Primae ad Corinthios
Theogn., El.	Theognis, Elegiae
ThF	Theologische Forschung
ThHK	Theologischer Hand–Kommentar
ThQ	Theologische Quartalschrift
ThRund	Theologische Rundschau
Thuc., Hist.	Thucydides, Historia
ThZ	Theologische Zeitschrift
tr.	translated by
[Trans.]	translator of this volume of Hermeneia
TThZ	Trierer Theologische Zeitschrift
v (vv)	verse (verses)
Val. Max.,	Valerius Maximus,
Fact. et dict. mem.	Factorum ac dictorum memorabilium libri IX
VD	Verbum Domini
Vett. Val.,	Vettius Valens,
Anthol.	Anthologia
VigChr	Vigiliae Christianae
v.l.	varia lectio, variant reading
vol.	volume
Vulg.	Vulgate
WMANT	Wissenschaftliche Monographien zum Alten und Neuen Testament
WuD	Wort und Dienst. Jahrbuch der Theologischen Schule, Bethel
WUNT	Wissenschaftliche Untersuchungen zum Neuen Testament
WZ (Halle)	Wissenschaftliche Zeitschrift (Halle)
ZKTh	Zeitschrift für Katholische Theologie
ZRGG	Zeitschrift für Religions– und Geistesgeschichte

2. Short Titles of Commentaries, Studies, and Articles Often Cited

Commentaries on 1 Corinthians as well as a few basic reference works are cited by author's name only. Additional short titles are used within a specific sequence of footnotes for works cited only with reference to a single passage; full bibliographical information accompanies the first citation. Where English translations of modern works exist primary page references are to the English followed by page references to the original in square brackets.

Allo
E.–B. Allo, *Première Épître aux Corinthiens*, Études Bibliques (Paris: Gabalda, 1934).

Bachmann
Philipp Bachmann, *Der erste Brief des Paulus an die Korinther*, with additions by Ethelbert Stauffer, KNT (Zahn), 7 (Leipzig and Erlangen: Deichert, ⁴1936).

Barth, *Resurrection*
Karl Barth, *The Resurrection of the Dead*, tr. H. J. Stenning (New York: Revell, 1933).
Die Auferstehung der Toten (Munich: Kaiser, 1924)·

Bauer
Walter Bauer, *A Greek–English Lexicon of the New Testament and Other Early Christian Literature*, tr. William F. Arndt and F. Wilbur Gingrich (Chicago: University of Chicago Press; Cambridge: University Press, 1957).
Griechisch–Deutsches Wörterbuch zu den Schriften des Neuen Testaments und der übrigen urchristlichen Literatur (Berlin: Töpelmann, ⁴1949–52, ⁵1958).

Bengel, *Gnomon*
Johann Albrecht Bengel, *Gnomon of the New Testament*, tr. Charlton T. Lewis and Marvin R. Vincent (Philadelphia: Perkinpine & Higgins; New York: Sheldon, 1864), 2 vols.
Gnomon Novi Testamenti (Stuttgart: Steinkopf, ⁸1887).

Betz, *Eucharistie*
Johannes Betz, *Die Eucharistie in der Zeit der griechischen Väter*, vol. 2, part 1 (Freiburg: Herder, 1961).

Betz, *Lukian*
Hans Dieter Betz, *Lukian von Samosata und das Neue Testament*, TU, 76 (Berlin: Akademie–Verlag, 1961).

Blass–Debrunner
Friedrich Blass and Albert Debrunner, *A Greek Grammar of the New Testament and Other Early Christian Literature*, tr. and rev. Robert W. Funk (Chicago: University of Chicago Press; Cambridge: University Press; Toronto: University of Toronto Press, 1961). Cited by section rather than page.

Blinzler, *Aus der Welt und Umwelt des NT*
Josef Blinzler, *Aus der Welt und Umwelt des Neuen Testaments. Gesammelte Aufsätze 1* (Stuttgart: Katholisches Bibelwerk, 1969).

Bömer, *Untersuchungen*
Franz Bömer, *Untersuchungen über die Religion der Sklaven in Griechenland und Rom*, AAM, 1957, 7; 1960, 1; 1961, 4; 1963, 10 (Wiesbaden: Steiner, 1957–63), 4 vols.

Bonsirven, *Exégèse*
Joseph Bonsirven, *Exégèse rabbinique et exégèse paulinienne* (Paris: Beauchesne, 1939).

Bornkamm, *Early Christian Experience*
Günther Bornkamm, *Early Christian Experience*, tr. Paul L. Hammer (London: SCM; New York: Harper & Row, 1969). Translations from *Das Ende des Gesetzes* and *Studien*.

Bornkamm, *Das Ende des Gesetzes*
Günther Bornkamm, *Das Ende des Gesetzes. Gesammelte Aufsätze Band I*, BEvTh, 16 (Munich: Kaiser, ⁵1966).

Bornkamm, *Geschichte und Glaube* 1, 2
Günther Bornkamm, *Geschichte und Glaube. Erster Teil. Gesammelte Aufsätze Band III*, BEvTh, 48 (Munich: Kaiser, 1968).
Günther Bornkamm, *Geschichte und Glaube. Zweiter Teil. Gesammelte Aufsätze Band IV*, BEvTh, 53 (Munich: Kaiser, 1971).

Bornkamm, *Studien*
Günther Bornkamm, *Studien zu Antike und Urchristentum. Gesammelte Aufsätze Band II*, BEvTh, 28 (Munich: Kaiser, ²1963).

Bornkamm, *Vorgeschichte*
Günther Bornkamm, *Die Vorgeschichte des sogenannten Zweiten Korintherbriefes*, SAH 1961, 2 (Heidelberg: Winter, 1961).

Bousset
Wilhelm Bousset, "Der erste Brief an die Korinther," in *Die Schriften des Neuen Testaments*, ed. Wilhelm Bousset and Wilhelm Heitmüller, vol. 2 (Göttingen: Vandenhoeck & Ruprecht, ³1917), 74–167.

Bousset, *Hauptprobleme*
Wilhelm Bousset, *Die Hauptprobleme der Gnosis*, FRLANT, 10 (Göttingen: Vandenhoeck & Ruprecht, 1907).

Bousset, *Kyrios Christos*
Wilhelm Bousset, *Kyrios Christos*, tr. John E. Steely (New York and Nashville: Abingdon, 1970).
Kyrios Christos, FRLANT, 22 (Göttingen: Vandenhoeck & Ruprecht, 1913, ²1921, ⁵1965).

Bousset, *Schulbetrieb*
Wilhelm Bousset, *Jüdisch–christlicher Schulbetrieb in Alexandria und Rom*, FRLANT, 23 (Göttingen: Vandenhoeck & Ruprecht, 1915).

Bousset–Gressmann, *Die Religion des Judentums*
Wilhelm Bousset, *Die Religion des Judentums*, rev. Hugo Gressmann, HNT, 21 (Tübingen: J. C. B. Mohr [Paul Siebeck], ⁴1966).

Bouttier, *En Christ*
Michel Bouttier, *En Christ. Étude d'exégèse et de*

théologie pauliniennes, Études d'Histoire et de
Philosophie Religieuse, 54 (Paris: Presses Universitaires, 1962).

Brandenburger, *Adam und Christus*
Egon Brandenburger, *Adam und Christus*,
WMANT, 7 (Neukirchen: Neukirchener Verlag,
1962).

Braun, *Gesammelte Studien*
Herbert Braun, *Gesammelte Studien zum Neuen
Testament und seiner Umwelt* (Tübingen: J. C. B.
Mohr [Paul Siebeck], 1962).

Braun, *Qumran*
Herbert Braun, *Qumran und das Neue Testament*
(Tübingen: J. C. B. Mohr [Paul Siebeck], 1966),
2 vols.

Bultmann, *Exegetica*
Rudolf Bultmann, *Exegetica*, ed. Erich Dinkler
(Tübingen: J. C. B. Mohr [Paul Siebeck], 1967).

Bultmann, *Faith and Understanding* 1
Rudolf Bultmann, *Faith and Understanding*, vol. 1,
tr. Louise Pettibone Smith, ed. Robert W. Funk
(London: SCM; New York: Harper & Row,
1969).
Glauben und Verstehen, vol. 1 (Tübingen: J. C. B.
Mohr [Paul Siebeck], 1933, ⁶1966).

Bultmann, *Primitive Christianity*
Rudolf Bultmann, *Primitive Christianity in Its Con-
temporary Setting*, tr. Reginald H. Fuller (Cleve-
land and New York: World/Meridian, 1956).
Das Urchristentum im Rahmen der antiken Religionen
(Zurich: Artemis, 1949, ²1954).

Bultmann, *Stil*
Rudolf Bultmann, *Der Stil der paulinischen Predigt
und die kynisch–stoische Diatribe*, FRLANT, 13
(Göttingen: Vandenhoeck & Ruprecht, 1910).

Bultmann, *Theology*
Rudolf Bultmann, *Theology of the New Testament*,
tr. Kendrick Grobel (London: SCM; New York:
Scribner, 1951–55), 2 vols.
Theologie des Neuen Testaments (Tübingen: J. C. B.
Mohr [Paul Siebeck], ⁶1968).

von Campenhausen, *Aus der Frühzeit*
Hans von Campenhausen, *Aus der Frühzeit des
Christentums* (Tübingen: J. C. B. Mohr [Paul
Siebeck], 1963).

von Campenhausen, *Begründung*
Hans von Campenhausen, *Die Begründung kirchlicher Entscheidung beim Apostel Paulus*, SAH 1957,
2 (Heidelberg: Winter, 1957).

von Campenhausen, *Ecclesiastical Authority*
Hans von Campenhausen, *Ecclesiastical Authority
and Spiritual Power in the Church of the First Three
Centuries*, tr. John A. Baker (London: Black;
Stanford: Stanford University Press, 1969).
*Kirchliches Amt und geistliche Vollmacht in den ersten
drei Jahrhunderten*, BHTh, 14 (Tübingen: J. C. B.
Mohr [Paul Siebeck], ²1963).

von Campenhausen, *Tradition and Life*
Hans von Campenhausen, *Tradition and Life in the

Church*, tr. A. V. Littledale (Philadelphia: For-
tress, 1968).
Tradition und Leben (Tübingen: J. C. B. Mohr
[Paul Siebeck], 1960).

Cerfaux, *Christ*
Lucien Cerfaux, *Christ in the Theology of St. Paul*,
tr. Geoffrey Webb and Adrian Walker (Freiburg
and New York: Herder & Herder, 1959).
Le Chrsit dans la théologie de saint Paul, Lectio
Divina, 6 (Paris: Cerf, ²1954).

Cerfaux, *Church*
Lucien Cerfaux, *The Church in the Theology of Saint
Paul*, tr. Geoffrey Webb and Adrian Walker (New
York: Herder & Herder, 1959).
La théologie de l'église suivant saint Paul, Unam
Sanctam, 54 (Paris: Cerf, ²1948).

Cerfaux, *Recueil*
Lucien Cerfaux, *Recueil Lucien Cerfaux. Études
d'exégèse et d'histoire religieuse*, Bibliotheca Ephem e-
ridum Theologicarum Lovaniensium, 6–7; 18
(Gembloux: Duculot, 1954–62), 3 vols.

Chadwick
Origen, *Contra Celsum*, tr. Henry Chadwick (Cambridge: University Press, ²1965).

Charles, *APOT*
*The Apocrypha and Pseudepigrapha of the Old Testa-
ment in English*, ed. Robert Henry Charles
(Oxford: Clarendon Press, 1913), 2 vols.

Colpe, *Religionsgeschichtliche Schule*
Carsten Colpe, *Die religionsgeschichtliche Schule*,
FRLANT, 78 (Göttingen: Vandenhoeck &
Ruprecht, 1961).

Cramer, *Catenae*
Catenae graecorum patrum, ed. J. A. Cramer (Oxford: University Press, 1844), 8 vols.

Cullmann, *Early Church*
Oscar Cullmann, *The Early Church*, ed. A. J. B.
Higgins (London: SCM, 1956).

Cumont, *Oriental Religions*
Franz Cumont, *The Oriental Religions in Roman
Paganism* (Chicago: Open Court, 1911; New
York: Dover, 1956).
Les religions orientales dans le paganisme romain,
Annales du Musée Guimet, Bibliothèque de
vulgarisation, 24 (Paris: Leroux, ³1929).

Danby
The Mishnah, tr. Herbert Danby (London: Oxford
University Press, 1933).

Daube, *NT and Rabbinic Judaism*
David Daube, *The New Testament and Rabbinic
Judaism*, School of Oriental and African Studies,
University of London, Jordan Lectures in Com-
parative Religion, 2 (London: Athlone, 1956).

Davies, *Paul and Rabbinic Judaism*
W. D. Davies, *Paul and Rabbinic Judaism* (London:
SPCK, ²1955).

Deissmann, *Light*
Adolf Deissmann, *Light from the Ancient East*, tr.
Lionel R. M. Strachan (New York and London:

Hodder & Stoughton, [2]1911).

Licht vom Osten (Tübingen: J. C. B. Mohr [Paul Siebeck], [4]1923).

Deissmann, *Paul*

Adolf Deissmann, *Paul*, tr. William E. Wilson (New York: Harper's, [2]1957).

Paulus (Tübingen: J. C. B. Mohr [Paul Siebeck], [2]1925).

Delling, *Studien*

Gerhard Delling, *Studien zum Neuen Testament und zum hellenistischen Judentum*, ed. Ferdinand Hahn *et al.* (Göttingen: Vandenhoeck & Ruprecht, 1970).

Diels, *Fragmente*

Hermann Diels, *Die Fragmente der Vorsokratiker*, rev. Walther Kranz (Berlin: Weidmann, [7]1954), 3 vols.

Dinkler, *RGG*[3]

Erich Dinkler, "Korintherbriefe," *RGG*[3] 4:17–23.

Dinkler, *Signum Crucis*

Erich Dinkler, *Signum Crucis* (Tübingen: J. C. B. Mohr [Paul Siebeck], 1967).

Dupont, *Gnosis*

Jacques Dupont, *Gnosis. La connaissance religieuse dans les épîtres de S. Paul*, Universitas Catholica Lovaniensis, Dissertationes in Facultate Theologica, 2, 40 (Louvain: Nauwelaerts, [2]1960).

Dupont–Sommer

André Dupont–Sommer, *The Essene Writings from Qumran*, tr. Geza Vermes (Oxford: Blackwell; Cleveland and New York: World/Meridian, 1961).

Ellis, *Paul's Use of the OT*

E. Earle Ellis, *Paul's Use of the Old Testament* (Edinburgh: Oliver & Boyd; Grand Rapids: Eerdmans, 1957).

Eltester, *Eikon*

Friedrich Wilhelm Eltester, *Eikon im Neuen Testament*, BZNW, 23 (Berlin: Töpelmann, 1958).

Epstein

The Babylonian Talmud, ed. Isidore Epstein (London: Soncino, 1936), 35 vols.

Feuillet, *Le Christ Sagesse*

André Feuillet, *Le Christ Sagesse de Dieu d'après les Épîtres pauliniennes*, Études Bibliques (Paris: Gabalda, 1966).

Fowler, *Corinth*

Corinth, ed. H. N. Fowler (Athens: American School of Classical Studies, 1929–   ), 16 vols. to date.

Freedman–Simon

Midrash Rabbah, tr. H. Freedman and Maurice Simon (London: Soncino, 1939), 10 vols.

Georgi, *Gegner*

Dieter Georgi, *Die Gegner des Paulus im 2. Korintherbrief*, WMANT, 11 (Neukirchen–Vluyn: Neukirchener Verlag, 1964).

Gerhardsson, *Memory and Manuscript*

Birger Gerhardsson, *Memory and Manuscript*, tr.

E. J. Sharpe (Lund: Gleerup; Copenhagen: Munksgaard, 1961).

Grant

Theophilus of Antioch, *Ad Autolycum*, ed. and tr. Robert M. Grant, Oxford Early Christian Texts, 1 (Oxford: Clarendon, 1970).

Grass, *Ostergeschehen*

Hans Grass, *Ostergeschehen und Osterberichte* (Göttingen: Vandenhoeck & Ruprecht, [2]1962).

Grobel

The Gospel of Truth, tr. Kendrick Grobel (New York and Nashville: Abingdon, 1960).

Grosheide

F. W. Grosheide, *Commentary on the First Epistle to the Corinthians*, NIC (Grand Rapids: Eerdmans, 1953).

Guillaumont *et al.*

The Gospel According to Thomas, ed. and tr. A. Guillaumont *et al.* (Leiden: Brill; New York: Harper & Row, 1959).

Güttgemanns, *Der leidende Apostel*

Erhardt Güttgemanns, *Der leidende Apostel und sein Herr*, FRLANT, 90 (Göttingen: Vandenhoeck & Ruprecht, 1966).

Harris–Mingana

The Odes and Psalms of Solomon, ed. and tr. James Rendel Harris and Alphonse Mingana (Manchester: Manchester University Press; London: Longmans, Green, 1916–20), 2 vols.

Heinrici

C. F. G. Heinrici, *Der erste Brief an die Korinther*, KEK, 5 (Göttingen: Vandenhoeck & Ruprecht, [8]1896).

Hennecke–Schneemelcher–Wilson

New Testament Apocrypha, ed. Edgar Hennecke, rev. Wilhelm Schneemelcher, tr. ed. Robert McL. Wilson (London: Lutterworth; Philadelphia: Westminster, 1963–65), 2 vols.

Héring

Jean Héring, *The First Epistle of Saint Paul to the Corinthians*, tr. A. W. Heathcote and P. J. Allcock (London: Epworth, 1962).

La première Épître de Saint Paul aux Corinthiens, Commentaire du Nouveau Testament, 7 (Neuchâtel: Delachaux et Niestlé, 1949, [2]1959).

Hermann, *Kyrios und Pneuma*

Ingo Hermann, *Kyrios und Pneuma*, SANT, 2 (Munich: Kösel, 1961).

Holl, *Aufsätze* 2

Karl Holl, *Gesammelte Aufsätze zur Kirchengeschichte. II: Der Osten* (Tübingen: J. C. B. Mohr [Paul Siebeck], 1928).

Hurd, *Origin*

John C. Hurd, Jr., *The Origin of I Corinthians* (London: SPCK; New York: Seabury, 1965).

Jacoby, *FGH*

Felix Jacoby, *Die Fragmente der griechischen Historiker* (Leiden: Brill, 1957–64), 25 vols.

James

The Biblical Antiquities of Philo, tr. Montague R. James, Translations of Early Documents, Series I, Palestinian Jewish Texts (Pre-Rabbinic), 13 (London: SPCK, 1917).

Jeremias, *Abba*
Joachim Jeremias, *Abba* (Göttingen: Vandenhoeck & Ruprecht, 1966).

Jeremias, *Eucharistic Words*
Joachim Jeremias, *The Eucharistic Words of Jesus*, tr. Norman Perrin (London: SCM; New York: Scribner, 1966).
Die Abendmahlsworte Jesu (Göttingen: Vandenhoeck & Ruprecht, [4]1967).

Jervell, *Imago Dei*
Jacob Jervell, *Imago Dei. Gen 1,26f. im Spätjudentum, in der Gnosis und in den paulinischen Briefen*, FRLANT, 76 (Göttingen: Vandenhoeck & Ruprechert, 1960).

Jonas, *Gnosis* 1
Hans Jonas, *Gnosis und spätantiker Geist*, vol. 1 (Göttingen: Vandenhoeck & Ruprecht, [3]1964).

Jonas, *Gnosis* 2.1
Hans Jonas, *Gnosis und spätantiker Geist*, vol. 2, pt. 1 (Göttingen: Vandenhoeck & Ruprecht, [2]1966).

Käsemann, *Essays on NT Themes*
Ernst Käsemann, *Essays on New Testament Themes*, tr. W. J. Montague, SBT, 1, 41 (London: SCM, 1964).
Exegetische Versuche und Besinnungen, vol. 1 (Göttingen: Vandenhoeck & Ruprecht, [2]1960).

Käsemann, *NT Questions of Today*
Ernst Käsemann, *New Testament Questions of Today*, tr. W. J. Montague (London: SCM; Philadelphia: Fortress, 1969).
Exegetische Versuche und Besinnungen, vol. 2 (Göttingen: Vandenhoeck & Ruprecht, [2]1965).

Käsemann, *Leib*
Ernst Käsemann, *Leib und Leib Christi*, BHTh, 9 (Tübingen: J. C. B. Mohr [Paul Siebeck], 1933).

Käsemann, *Perspectives on Paul*
Ernst Käsemann, *Perspectives on Paul*, tr. Margaret Kohl (London: SCM; Philadelphia: Fortress, 1971).
Paulinische Perspektiven (Tübingen: J. C. B. Mohr [Paul Siebeck], 1969).

Klein, *Die zwölf Apostel*
Günter Klein, *Die zwölf Apostel*, FRLANT, 77 (Göttingen: Vandenhoeck & Ruprecht, 1961).

Kramer, *Christ, Lord, Son of God*
Werner Kramer, *Christ, Lord, Son of God*, tr. Brian Hardy, SBT, 1, 50 (London: SCM, 1966).
Christos Kyrios Gottessohn, AThANT, 44 (Zurich: Zwingli, 1963).

Kümmel, *Introduction*
Paul Feine and Johannes Behm, *Introduction to the New Testament*, rev. Werner Georg Kümmel, tr. A. J. Mattill, Jr. (New York and Nashville: Abingdon, 1966).

Einleitung in das Neue Testament, rev. Werner Georg Kümmel (Heidelberg: Quelle & Meyer, [14]1965).

Kümmel, *Heilsgeschehen und Geschichte*
Werner Georg Kümmel, *Heilsgeschehen und Geschichte* (Marburg: Elwert, 1965).

Kümmel, *Kirchenbegriff*
Werner Georg Kümmel, *Kirchenbegriff und Geschichtsbewusstsein in der Urgemeinde und bei Jesus*, SBU, 1 (Uppsala: Seminarium Neotestamenticum Upsaliense; Zurich: Niehaus, 1943).

Lauterbach
Mekilta de–Rabbi Ishmael, ed. and tr. Jacob Z. Lauterbach (Philadelphia: Jewish Publication Society of America, 1933–35), 3 vols.

Legge
Hippolytus, *Philosophumena*, tr. F. Legge, Translations of Christian Literature, Series I (London: SPCK, 1921), 2 vols.

Lidzbarski, *Mandäische Liturgien*
Mark Lidzbarski, *Mandäische Liturgien*, AGG, n.s. 17, 1 (Berlin: Weidmann, 1920).

Lietzmann, *Mass and Lord's Supper*
Hans Lietzmann, *Mass and Lord's Supper*, tr. Dorothea H. G. Reeve (Leiden: Brill, 1953–).
Messe und Herrenmahl, Arbeiten zur Kirchengeschichte 8 (Bonn: Marcus & Weber, 1926).

Lietzmann–Kümmel
Hans Lietzmann, *An die Korinther*, rev. Werner Georg Kümmel, HNT, 9 (Tübingen: J. C. B. Mohr [Paul Siebeck], [4]1949). Note: Either "Lietzmann" or "Kümmel" may stand alone occasionally, signifying that the one (but not the other) expresses *ad loc.* the opinion in question.

Lindars, *NT Apologetic*
Barnabas Lindars, *New Testament Apologetic* (London: SCM; Philadelphia: Westminster, 1961).

Littérature et théologie pauliniennes
Littérature et théologie pauliniennes, RechBibl, 5 (Bruges: Desclée de Brouwer, 1960).

Lohse, *Märtyrer*
Eduard Lohse, *Märtyrer und Gottesknecht*, FRLANT, 64 (Göttingen: Vandenhoeck & Ruprecht, [2]1963).

Lohse, *Texte*
Die Texte aus Qumran, ed. and tr. Eduard Lohse (Darmstadt: Wissenschaftliche Buchgesellschaft, 1964).

Lührmann, *Offenbarungsverständnis*
Dieter Lührmann, *Die Offenbarungsverständnis bei Paulus und in paulinischen Gemeinden*, WMANT, 16 (Neukirchen–Vluyn: Neukirchener Verlag, 1965).

Lutz
Musonius Rufus "the Roman Socrates," ed. and tr. Cora E. Lutz (New Haven: Yale University Press; London: Oxford University Press, 1947).

Mattern, *Verständnis*
Lieselotte Mattern, *Das Verständnis des Gerichtes bei*

Paulus, AThANT, 47 (Zurich and Stuttgart: Zwingli, 1966).

Michaelis, *Einleitung*
Wilhelm Michaelis, *Einleitung in das Neue Testament* (Bern: Haller, ³1961).

Michel, *Paulus und seine Bibel*
Otto Michel, *Paulus und seine Bibel*, BFTh, 2, 18 (Gütersloh: Bertelsmann, 1929).

Moore, *Judaism*
George Foot Moore, *Judaism in the First Three Centuries of the Christian Era* (Cambridge, Mass.: Harvard University Press, 1927–30), 3 vols.

Moulton–Howard–Turner, *Grammar 1*
James Hope Moulton, *A Grammar of New Testament Greek*, vol. 1, *Prolegomena* (Edinburgh: T. & T. Clark, ³1919).

Moulton–Howard–Turner, *Grammar 2*
James Hope Moulton and Wilbert Francis Howard, *A Grammar of New Testament Greek*, vol. 2, *Accidence and Word–Formation* (Edinburgh: T. & T. Clark, 1929).

Moulton–Howard–Turner, *Grammar 3*
James Hope Moulton, *A Grammar of New Testament Greek*, vol. 3, *Syntax*, by Nigel Turner (Edinburgh: T. & T. Clark, 1963).

Munck, *Paul*
Johannes Munck, *Paul and the Salvation of Mankind*, tr. Frank Clarke (London: SCM; Richmond: John Knox, 1959).
Paulus und die Heilsgeschichte, Acta Jutlandica, 26, 1 (Aarhus: Universitetsforlaget; Copenhagen: Munksgaard, 1954).

Neuenzeit, *Herrenmahl*
Paul Neuenzeit, *Das Herrenmahl*, SANT, 1 (Munich: Kösel, 1960).

Neugebauer, *In Christus*
Fritz Neugebauer, *In Christus. ΕΝ ΧΡΙΣΤΩΙ. Eine Untersuchung zum paulinischen Glaubensverständnis* (Göttingen: Vandenhoeck & Ruprecht, 1961).

Nilsson, *Geschichte*
Martin Nilsson, *Geschichte der griechischen Religion*, Handbuch der Altertumswissenschaft, 5 (Munich: Beck, ²1955–61), 2 vols.

Nock–Festugière
Corpus Hermeticum, ed. Arthur Darby Nock and tr. André–Jean Festugière (Paris: Les Belles Lettres, 1938–54), 4 vols. (vols. 1–2, ²1960).

Norden, *Agnostos Theos*
Eduard Norden, *Agnostos Theos. Untersuchungen zur Formengeschichte religiöser Rede* (Leipzig and Berlin: Teubner, 1913).

Pascher, *Königsweg*
Joseph Pascher, *Η ΒΑΣΙΛΙΚΗ ΟΔΟΣ. Der Königsweg zu Wiedergeburt und Vergottung bei Philon von Alexandreia*, Studien zur Geschichte und Kultur des Altertums, 17, 3–4 (Paderborn: Schöningh, 1931).

Paulusbild

Das Paulusbild der neueren deutschen Forschung, ed. Karl Heinrich Rengstorf, Wege der Forschung, 24 (Darmstadt: Wissenschaftliche Buchgesellschaft, ²1969).

Peterson, Εἶς Θεός
Erik Peterson, Εἶς Θεός: *Epigraphische, formgeschichtliche und religionsgeschichtliche Untersuchungen*, FRLANT, 41 (Göttingen: Vandenhoeck & Ruprecht, 1926).

Peterson, *Frühkirche*
Erik Peterson, *Frühkirche, Judentum und Gnosis* (Rome, Freiburg and Vienna: Herder, 1959).

Poland, *Geschichte des griechischen Vereinswesens*
Franz Poland, *Geschichte des griechischen Vereinswesens*, Preisschriften–gekrönt und herausgegeben von der Fürstlich Jablonowskischen Gesellschaft zu Leipzig, Historisch–nationalökonomischen Sektion, 38, 23 (Leipzig: Teubner, 1909).

Radermacher, *Grammatik*
Ludwig Radermacher, *Neutestamentliche Grammatik*, HNT, 1, 1 (Tübingen: J. C. B. Mohr [Paul Siebeck], ²1925).

Reitzenstein, *Mysterienreligionen*
Richard Reitzenstein, *Die hellenistischen Mysterienreligionen nach ihren Grundgedanken und Wirkungen* (Stuttgart: Teubner, ³1927).

Reitzenstein, *Poimandres*
Richard Reitzenstein, *Poimandres* (Leipzig and Berlin: Teubner, 1904).

Reitzenstein–Schäder, *Studien*
Richard Reitzenstein and Hans Heinrich Schäder, *Studien zum antiken Synkretismus aus Iran und Griechenland*, Studien der Bibliothek Warburg, 7 (Leipzig and Berlin: Teubner, 1926).

Riesenfeld, *The Gospel Tradition*
Harald Riesenfeld, *The Gospel Tradition*, tr. E. Margaret Rowley and Robert A. Kraft (Philadelphia: Fortress, 1970).

Robertson–Plummer
Archibald Robertson and Alfred Plummer, *A Critical and Exegetical Commentary on the First Epistle of St Paul to the Corinthians*, ICC (Edinburgh: T. &. T. Clark, ²1914).

Rohde, *Psyche*
Erwin Rohde, *Psyche*, tr. W. B. Hillis (London: Kegan Paul, Trench, Trubner; New York: Harcourt, Brace, 1925).
Psyche. Seelencult und Unsterblichkeitsglaube der Griechen (Tübingen: J. C. B. Mohr [Paul Siebeck], ⁶1910), 2 vols. in 1 (separately paged).

Roller, *Formular*
Otto Roller, *Das Formular der paulinischen Briefe*, BWANT, 58 (Stuttgart: Kohlhammer, 1933).

Schlatter
Adolf Schlatter, *Paulus der Bote Jesu* (Stuttgart: Calwer, ²1956).

Schlier, *Christus und die Kirche*
Heinrich Schlier, *Christus und die Kirche im Epheserbrief*, BHTh, 6 (Tübingen: J. C. B. Mohr [Paul

Siebeck], 1930).

Schlier, *Eph.*
Heinrich Schlier, *Der Brief an die Epheser* (Düsseldorf: Patmos, ⁵1965).

Schlier, *Die Zeit der Kirche*
Heinrich Schlier, *Die Zeit der Kirche* (Freiburg: Herder, 1956).

Schmidt–Till, *Koptisch–gnostische Schriften* 1
Carl Schmidt, *Koptisch–gnostische Schriften*, vol. 1, rev. Walter Till, GCS, 45 (Berlin: Akademie–Verlag, ²1954).

Schmiedel
Paul W. Schmiedel, *Die Briefe an die Thessalonicher und an die Korinther*, Hand–Commentar zum Neuen Testament, 2, 1 (Tübingen: J. C. B. Mohr [Paul Siebeck], ²1892).

Schmithals, *Gnosticism in Corinth*
Walter Schmithals, *Gnosticism in Corinth*, tr. John E. Steely (New York and Nashville: Abingdon, 1971).
Die Gnosis in Korinth, FRLANT, 66 (Göttingen: Vandenhoeck & Ruprecht, 1956, ²1965, ³1969).

Schmithals, *The Office of Apostle*
Walter Schmithals, *The Office of Apostle in the Early Church*, tr. John E. Steely (New York and Nashville: Abingdon, 1969).
Das kirchliche Apostelamt, FRLANT, 79 (Göttingen: Vandenhoeck & Ruprecht, 1961).

Schmithals, *Paul and the Gnostics*
Walter Schmithals, *Paul and the Gnostics*, tr. John E. Steely (New York and Nashville: Abingdon, 1972).
Paulus und die Gnostiker, ThF, 35 (Hamburg: Reich, 1965).

Schweizer, *Neotestamentica*
Eduard Schweizer, *Neotestamentica* (Zurich and Stuttgart: Zwingli, 1963).

Schwyzer, *Grammatik* 1
Eduard Schwyzer, *Griechische Grammatik*, vol. 1: *Allgemeiner Teil, Lautlehre, Wortbildung, Flexion*, Handbuch der Altertumswissenschaft, 2, 1 (Munich: Beck, 1939).

Schwyzer, *Grammatik* 2
Eduard Schwyzer, *Griechische Grammatik*, vol. 2: *Syntax und syntaktische Stilistik*, ed. Albert Debrunner, Handbuch der Altertumswissenschaft, 2, 1 (Munich: Beck, 1950).

Scott
Hermetica, ed. and tr. Walter Scott (Oxford: Clarendon, 1924), 4 vols.

von Soden, "Sakrament und Ethik"
Hans von Soden, "Sakrament und Ethik bei Paulus," in *Marburger theologische Studien (Rudolf–Otto Festgruss)*, ed. H. Frick, vol. 1 (Gotha: Klotz, 1931), 1–40.

von Soden, *Urchristentum und Geschichte* 1
Hans von Soden, *Urchristentum und Geschichte*, vol. 1, ed. Hans von Campenhausen (Tübingen: J.C.B. Mohr [Paul Siebeck], 1951).

Spicq, *Agapé*
Ceslaus Spicq, *Agapé dans le Nouveau Testament*, Études Bibliques (Paris: Gabalda, 1958–59), 3 vols.

Staab, *Pauluskommentare*
Karl Staab, *Pauluskommentare aus der griechischen Kirche aus Katenenhandschriften*, NtlAbh, 15 (Münster: Aschendorff, 1933).

Stengel, *Die griechischen Kultusaltertümer*
Paul Stengel, *Die griechischen Kultusaltertümer*, Handbuch der klassischen Altertumswissenschaft, 5, 3 (Munich: Beck, ³1920).

Studia Paulina
Studia Paulina in honorem Johannis de Zwaan septuagenarii (Haarlem: Bohn, 1953).

Studiorum Paulinorum Congressus
Studiorum Paulinorum Congressus Internationalis Catholicus 1961, Analecta Biblica, 17 (Rome: Biblical Institute Press, 1963), 2 vols.

Thyen, *Homilie*
Hartwig Thyen, *Der Stil der Jüdisch-Hellenistischen Homilie*, FRLANT, 65 (Göttingen: Vandenhoeck & Ruprecht, 1955).

Ulonska, *Paulus und das Alte Testament*
Herbert Ulonska, *Die Funktion der alttestamentliche Zitate und Anspielungen in den paulinischen Briefe* (dissertation, Münster, 1963).

Vielhauer, *Aufsätze*
Philipp Vielhauer, *Aufsätze zum Neuen Testament*, Theologische Bücherei, 31 (Munich: Kaiser, 1965).

Volz, *Eschatologie*
Paul Volz, *Die Eschatologie der jüdischen Gemeinde im neutestamentlichen Zeitalter* (Tübingen: J. C. B. Mohr [Paul Siebeck], 1934).

Wegenast, *Verständnis der Tradition*
Klaus Wegenast, *Das Verständnis der Tradition bei Paulus und in den Deuteropaulinen*, WMANT, 8 (Neukirchen–Vluyn: Neukirchener Verlag, 1962).

Weiss
Johannes Weiss, *Der erste Korintherbrief*, KEK, 5 (Göttingen; Vandenhoeck & Ruprecht, ⁹1910, ¹⁰1925).

Weiss, *Rhetorik*
Johannes Weiss, *Beiträge zur paulinischen Rhetorik* (Göttingen: Vandenhoeck & Ruprecht, 1897).

Wendland, *Literaturformen*
Paul Wendland, *Die urchristlichen Literaturformen*, HNT, 1, 3 (Tübingen: J. C. B. Mohr [Paul Siebeck], ³1912). Usually bound with his *Die hellenistisch–römische Kultur* (HNT, 1, 2) and paged continuously with it, i.e., pp. 257–448.

Wetter, *Charis*
Gillis Petersson Wetter, *Charis. Ein Beitrag zur Geschichte des ältesten Christentums*, UNT, 5 (Leipzig: Hinrichs, 1913).

Wilckens, *Weisheit und Torheit*
Ulrich Wilckens, *Weisheit und Torheit*, BHTh, 26

(Tübingen: J. C. B. Mohr [Paul Siebeck], 1959).

Wiles, *The Divine Apostle*
Maurice F. Wiles, *The Divine Apostle* (Cambridge: University Press, 1967).

Williams
Justin Martyr, *The Dialogue with Trypho*, tr. A. Lukyn Williams, Translations of Christian Literature, Series I—Greek texts (London: SPCK; New York and Toronto: Macmillan, 1930).

Wilson
The Gospel of Philip, tr. Robert McL. Wilson (London: Mowbray, 1962).

Winer–Moulton, *Grammar*
Georg Benedikt Winer, *A Treatise of the Grammar of New Testament Greek*, tr. and rev. William F. Moulton (Edinburgh: T. & T. Clark, [3]1882). *Grammatik des neutestamentlichen Sprachidioms* (Leipzig: Vogel, 1867).

Zuntz, *Text*
Günther Zuntz, *The Text of the Epistles*, Schweich Lectures, 1946 (London: British Academy/ Oxford University Press, 1953).

The English translation of First Corinthians at the head of each section of this Commentary is an original one produced from the Greek text by the translator and the editor of the volume, with a view to reflecting the exegetical options followed in the Commentary. The author's German translation was consulted throughout. Wherever possible, all other biblical translations follow the RSV, the source being indicated in each case.

For the most part, translations from ancient Greek and Latin texts are taken from the *Loeb Classical Library* and are identified by volume and page numbers in that series. The sources of all other translations are indicated.

Modern scholarly literature is cited according to published English translations whenever these are available, but for the convenience of the reader reference is made in brackets also to the original. For those works listed in the Short Title list, only the page numbers of the original are included within square brackets. An exception to this policy is the *Theological Dictionary of the New Testament/Theologisches Wörterbuch zum Neuen Testament*; since the pagination of *TDNT* is normally almost identical with that of *TWNT*, the German page references are omitted.

The Bibliography has been expanded to include a larger number of works frequently cited in the Commentary itself, but no attempt has been made to add literature that has appeared since 1969.

The endpapers are photographed from the excellent facsimile of Codex **א**: *Codex Sinaiticus Petropolitanus: The New Testament, The Epistle of Barnabas and the Shepherd of Hermas*, ed. Helen and Kirsopp Lake (Oxford: Clarendon, 1911). The front endpaper is folios 72v and 73r, containing 1 Cor 11:15—14:5, the back endpaper folios 73v and 74r, containing 1 Cor 14:5—15:37. Page v shows a detailed enlargement.

Introduction[1]

1. The Text[2]

The first letter to the Corinthians has been preserved on papyrus;[3] Papyrus 46 (Chester Beatty) contains the whole epistle.[4]

The position in regard to the transmission of the text is inherently the same as in the rest of the Pauline epistles. There are three well-known textual types: (1) the "Egyptian" or "Alexandrian," which is represented above all by p[46] and p[11] (in both cases with certain limitations), by the majuscules ℵ B C, by the minuscules 33 and 1739;[5] (2) the "Western," represented by D F G, the Old Latin, the Church Fathers;[6] (3) the "Byzantine," also called "Koine" or "Reichstext."

Special significance attaches to the oldest witness, p[46].[7] It belongs to the Alexandrian type, but displays also Western readings which have in part been corrected in terms of the Alexandrian type. This proves the early existence of these types in Egypt and the early rise of textual criticism there. In addition there are occasional Byzantine readings.

For the establishing, not of the original text, but of the archetype Zuntz develops the following principles.

The compass of the Western text is to be defined narrowly: the text of D and G and citations by the early Latin Fathers. This Zuntz regards as the unedited text of the second century. In criticism, we have to note that there are assimilations in this text.[8]

From the Alexandrian text Zuntz separates a "proto-Alexandrian" group: p[46],[9] B, 1739, Coptic, Clement of Alexandria, Origen. Between the two types there is no direct relationship. Where they agree, therefore, they take us back to a very early stage. The resulting rules are (numbered by me):

1. Agreement between the proto-Alexandrian and Western texts, which is almost always genuine.

2. Western alone, which is hardly ever genuine.

---

1   *Introduction to the New Testament*, founded by Paul Feine and Johannes Behm, re-ed. Werner Georg Kümmel, tr. A. J. Mattill, Jr. (New York and Nashville: Abingdon, 1966), 198–205 [198–206]. In addition to the literature listed there, see also Bruce M. Metzger, *Index to Periodical Literature on the Apostle Paul*, NTTS, 1 (Leiden: Brill; Grand Rapids: Eerdmans, 1960).

2   For bibliography on the text see the following: Kurt Aland *et al.* (eds.), *The Greek New Testament* (Stuttgart: United Bible Societies, 1966, ²1968), xlix–lv; Hans Lietzmann, *An die Römer*, HNT, 8 (Tübingen: J. C. B. Mohr [Paul Siebeck], ⁴1933), 1–18; G. Zuntz, *The Text of the Epistles*, Schweich Lectures, 1946 (London: Oxford University Press, 1953), 765–769; Heinrich Vogels, *Handbuch der Textkritik des Neuen Testaments* (Bonn: Hanstein, ²1955); Jean Duplacy, *Où en est la critique textuelle du Nouveau Testament?* (Paris: Gabalda, 1959); Frederic G. Kenyon, *The Text of the Greek Bible*, Studies in Theology (London: Duckworth, ²1949); Bruce M. Metzger, *The Text of the New Testament* (New York and London: Oxford University Press, ²1968); Kurt Aland, *Studien zur Überlieferung des Neuen Testaments und seines Textes*, Arbeiten zur neutestamentlichen Textforschung, 2 (Berlin: de Gruyter, 1967).

3   Parts of 1 Cor are contained in seven papyri, among them two early ones; see Aland, *Studien*, 95. For an overview of the texts from 1 Cor, see *ibid.*, 97. Aland dates p[46] *ca.* 200 and p[15] in the third century (*ibid.*, 104f, 112, 124).

4   N. B. p[11] and p[68], *ibid.*, 137–154 (text). p[11] contains 1:17–20, 20–22; 2:9f, 11f, 14; parts of chaps. 3, 4, 5, 6, 7. In addition, p[14] (from the same papyrus as p[11]?) has 1:25–27; 2:6–8; 3:8–10, 20. p[68] has 4:12–17 and 4:19—5:3. The other papyri are p[34] and p[61].

5   1739 is notable for having preserved in Rom the text of Origen.

6   Metzger, *Text*, 214, includes the Greek Fathers to the end of the third century and the Syrian Fathers to *ca.* 450.

7   Examples of the noteworthy peculiarities of p[46]: (1) abbreviations in 8:1–6: p[46] omits $\tau\iota$ in v 2 with Tert Orig Ambst Hil; $\tau\grave{o}\nu\ \theta\epsilon\acute{o}\nu$ in v 3 with Cl; $\dot{\upsilon}\pi'\ \alpha\dot{\upsilon}\tau o\hat{\upsilon}$ in the same verse with Cl ℵ* 33; $\dot{\alpha}\lambda\lambda'$ in v 6 with B.

(2) 13:4f reads: $\dot{\eta}\ \dot{\alpha}\gamma\acute{\alpha}\pi\eta\ \mu\alpha\kappa\rho o\theta\upsilon\mu\epsilon\hat{\iota}\ \chi\rho\eta\sigma\tau\epsilon\acute{\upsilon}\epsilon\tau\alpha\iota$
$\dot{\eta}\ \dot{\alpha}\gamma\acute{\alpha}\pi\eta\ o\dot{\upsilon}\ \zeta\eta\lambda o\hat{\iota}\ o\dot{\upsilon}\ \pi\epsilon\rho\pi\epsilon\rho\epsilon\acute{\upsilon}\epsilon\tau\alpha\iota$
$\dot{\eta}\ \dot{\alpha}\gamma\acute{\alpha}\pi\eta\ o\dot{\upsilon}\ \phi\upsilon\sigma\iota o\hat{\upsilon}\tau\alpha\iota\ o\dot{\upsilon}\kappa\ \epsilon\dot{\upsilon}\sigma\chi\eta$-
$\mu o\nu\epsilon\hat{\iota}$
$\mu\grave{\eta}$
$o\dot{\upsilon}\ \zeta\eta\tau\epsilon\hat{\iota}\ \tau\grave{o}\ \dot{\epsilon}\alpha\upsilon\tau\hat{\eta}\varsigma$

(3) 15:2 reads: $\delta\iota\ o\upsilon\ \kappa\alpha\iota\ \sigma\omega\zeta\epsilon\sigma\theta\epsilon\ \tau\iota\nu\iota\ \lambda o\gamma\omega\ \epsilon\upsilon\eta\gamma/$
$\gamma\epsilon\lambda\iota\sigma\alpha\mu\eta\nu\ \ddot{\upsilon}\mu\epsilon\iota\nu\ /\ \dot{\kappa}\dot{\alpha}\dot{\tau}\dot{\epsilon}\dot{\chi}\epsilon\iota\nu\ \epsilon\iota\ \kappa\alpha\tau\epsilon\chi\epsilon\tau\epsilon\ \epsilon\iota\ \mu\eta\ /$
$\epsilon\iota\kappa\eta\ \epsilon\pi\iota\sigma\tau\epsilon\upsilon\sigma\alpha\tau\epsilon$. This is a mixture of $\epsilon\dot{\upsilon}\eta\gamma\gamma\epsilon\lambda\iota$-$\sigma\acute{\alpha}\mu\eta\nu\ \dot{\upsilon}\mu\hat{\iota}\nu\ \dot{o}\phi\epsilon\acute{\iota}\lambda\epsilon\tau\epsilon\ \kappa\alpha\tau\acute{\epsilon}\chi\epsilon\iota\nu$ and $\epsilon\dot{\upsilon}\eta\gamma\gamma\epsilon\lambda\iota\sigma\acute{\alpha}\mu\eta\nu$ $\dot{\upsilon}\mu\hat{\iota}\nu\ \epsilon\dot{\iota}\ \kappa\alpha\tau\acute{\epsilon}\chi\epsilon\tau\epsilon$.

8   Kümmel, *Introduction*, 384f [404].

9   p[46] is highly valued despite its errors.

3. Individual Egyptian texts and Western, which is hardly ever genuine.
4. Byzantine texts, which can be genuine when their reading is anticipated in p[46], B, or the Western text.
5. The number of genuine readings which are represented solely by p[46] and Egyptian texts is not very large.[10]

Despite this noteworthy methodological approach, we abide by the wise old policy that the procedure in individual cases will be eclectic.

2. The Position of 1 Corinthians in the Corpus Paulinum[11]

In the Muratorian Canon the two epistles to the Corinthians stand at the head of the Pauline epistles.[12] Harnack considers this to be the original position.[13] It is said that the collection took shape in Corinth,[14] and that later, for understandable reasons, Romans was set in the forefront.[15]

In actual fact we know nothing about the collecting and editing of the epistles.[16] The only certain fact is that Marcion knows them.[17] And we can detect faint traces of elementary stages: *1 Clement* knows (Romans and) 1 Corinthians,[18] while Ignatius mentions a collection of Pauline epistles (Ign. *Eph.* 12:2), as does also 2 Pet (3:15f); cf. also Pol. *Phil.* 3:2.

3. Authenticity, Unity, Date of Composition

1. Authenticity and Unity

The authenticity of the epistle is universally recognized.[19] On the other hand, it is frequently doubted whether the composition, as it stands at present, is original. Literary criticism is aroused not so much by the loose construction (the latter can be explained; it is partly the result of entering into questions asked in a letter to Paul from Corinth, 7:1) as by the observation of breaks and joins. It becomes convincing, to be sure, only if it can be

---

10   Zuntz, *Text*, 64.
11   Adolf von Harnack, *Die Briefsammlung des Apostels Paulus* (Leipzig: Hinrichs, 1926); Thomas Walter Manson, "The Corinthian Correspondence," in his *Studies in the Gospels and Epistles*, ed. Matthew Black (Manchester: Manchester University Press, 1962), 190–209 (I), 210–224 (II), first published in the series "St. Paul in Ephesus," *BJRL* 26 (1941–42): 101–120, 327–341; Edgar J. Goodspeed, "The Editio Princeps of Paul," *JBL* 64 (1945): 193–204; John Knox, "A Note on the Format of the Pauline Corpus," *HTR* 50 (1957): 311–314; C. Leslie Mitton, *The Formation of the Pauline Corpus of Letters* (London: Epworth, 1955); Jack Finegan, "The Original Form of the Pauline Collection," *HTR* 49 (1956): 85–103; Nils A. Dahl, "Welche Ordnung der Paulusbriefe wird vom Muratorischen Kanon vorausgesetzt?" *ZNW* 52 (1961): 39–53; Walter Schmithals, *Paul and the Gnostics*, tr. John E. Steely (New York and Nashville: Abingdon, 1971), 253–274 [185–200].
12   Many would infer that this was also Tertullian's order, cf. Schmithals, *Paul and the Gnostics*, 254 [186]; *contra* Dahl, "Welche Ordnung," 41f.
13   Theodor Zahn, *Geschichte des Neutestamentlichen Kanons*, vol. 2, pt. 1 (Erlangen and Leipzig: Deichert, 1890), 344–364: the compiler of the Canon found this arrangement in his scroll and inferred that this was the chronological order. Dahl's comment on this, "Welche Ordnung," 41f, is as follows. The arrangement in the Muratorian Canon is in fact intended to be chronological. But the compiler did not find it in any manuscript. In the manuscripts

and other lists of the Canon there is no trace of this order. On the contrary, the epistles to the Corinthians, Galatians, and Romans were set at the head because their "chronological" order is not identical with their canonical arrangement.
14   According to Knox and Mitton, in Ephesus. According to Goodspeed, Ephesians is a compilation from the other epistles, made with the intention of forming an introduction to the published collection.
15   According to Schmithals, if Rom (and in p[46] Heb) is removed from the head, then the epistles to the Corinthians everywhere come at the beginning. This is true also of *1 Cl.* 47:1f. But the removal of Rom is a postulate, the whole argument is circular, and the reference to *1 Cl.* 47 is grotesque.
16   Kümmel, *Introduction*, 338f [353f].
17   Without the Pastorals.
18   35:5f; cf. 37:5; 47:1–3 (the singular is used: *1 Cl.* apparently knows of *one* epistle of Paul to Corinth); 49:5.
19   For earlier attacks, see Paul W. Schmiedel, *Die Briefe an die Thessalonicher und an die Korinther*, Hand–Commentar zum Neuen Testament, 2, 1 (Freiburg: J. C. B. Mohr [Paul Siebeck], [2]1892), 47–94.

shown not merely that there are sudden transitions of thought,[20] but that different situations must be presupposed for different parts of the epistle.[21]

Examples of breaks are: (a) 10:1–22(23) fits badly into its context. Before and after this section, Paul upholds in principle our freedom to eat; here, on the contrary, he abrogates it by pointing to the sacrament. If the section is removed, then we have a unified complex of thought. (b) Chap. 13 interrupts the continuity between chaps. 12 and 14. The two brackets in 12:31 and 14:1 are badly constructed.

Moreover, differences in the situation, it is believed, can be observed:[22] In 1:10ff, it is held, Paul is better informed about conditions in Corinth than in 11:18ff. The latter section, it is argued, must accordingly belong to an earlier letter. In addition, in 1:11 Paul names as his informants the people of Chloe; according to 16:17 he has with him three men from Corinth. There is no mention on either occasion of the other group. This is the more striking for the fact that "the household" of one of those named in 16:17 is mentioned in 1:16.[23] In chap. 9 Paul has to defend his standing as an apostle. In chaps. 1–4 there is no trace of this. Does chap. 9 represent a later development?

For a reconstruction, account must be taken of the references to further letters, both from Paul to Corinth (5:9) and from Corinth to Paul (7:1), as also of the further correspondence that can be gathered from 2 Corinthians. Hand in hand with the literary reconstruction there must go historical reconstruction, the establishing of what happened between Paul and the community.

Examples of Hypotheses:

J. Weiss:

a) Literary: Within 1 Corinthians he distinguishes parts of three letters.

Letter A: 10:1–23; 6:12–20; 11:2–34 (2 Cor 6:14—7:1).[24]

Letter B: 7:1—9:23; 10:24—11:1; 12—15; 16.

Letter C: 1:1—6:11.[25]

b) Historical:[26]

1. Letter A.
2. Letter from Corinth.
3. Letter B 1 (= B above).
4. News from Macedonia; the sending of Titus (2 Cor 8).
5. Chloe's people reach Paul.
6. Letter B 2 (= C above).
7. Bad news brought by Timothy.
8. Intermediate journey.
9. Letter C: 2 Cor 2:14—6:13; 7:2–4; 10—13.
10. Arrival of Titus.
11. Letter D: 2 Cor 1:1—2:13; 7:5—16; 9.

W. Schmithals:

a) Literary:

Letter A: 2 Cor 6:14—7:1; 1 Cor 9:24—10:22; 6:12–20; 11:2–34; 15; 16:13–24.

Letter B: 1:1—6:11; 7:1—9:23; 10:23—11:1; 12:1—14:40 (with the reversal of chaps. 13 and 14); 16:1–12.

b) Historical:

1. Visit to Paul by the people mentioned in 16:17.
2. Letter A, presumably brought by Stephanas.

---

20 These can be explained by pauses in dictation, etc.

21 In this connection it has to be borne in mind that the composing of the letter was spread over a certain period of time; see 16:16f.

22 Schmithals, *Paul and the Gnostics*, 115–118 [84–86], with reference to Johannes Weiss, *Der erste Korintherbrief*, KEK, 5 (Göttingen: Vandenhoeck & Ruprecht, ⁹1910, ¹⁰1925), xxxix–xliii.

23 This of course can also be explained by the suggestion that Stephanas happens to be present at the moment in question. The difference between 4:19 (Paul will come soon) and 16:3ff (he will delay for some time yet) is not important.

24 Further, according to Johannes Weiss, *The History of Primitive Christianity*, tr. ed. Frederick C. Grant (New York: Wilson-Erickson, 1937), reprinted as *Earliest Christianity* (New York: Harper, 1959), 1:341 (*Das Urchristentum* [Göttingen: Vandenhoeck &

Ruprecht, 1917], 271f): 16:7 ?; 16:8f; 16:20f?

25 Further hypotheses of the literary critics:
Maurice Goguel, *Introduction au Nouveau Testament*, vol. 4, pt. 2 (Paris: Leroux, 1926), 86:
A: (2 Cor 6:14—7:1); 6:12–20; 10:1–22.
B: 5:1—6:11; 7:1—8:13; 10:23—14:40; 15; 16:1–9, 12.
C: 1:10—4:21; 9:1–27; 16:10f.
Erich Dinkler, "Korintherbriefe," *RGG*³, 4:18:
A: 6:12–20; 9:24–27; 10:1–22; 11:2–34; 12—14.
B: 1:1—6:11; 7:1—9:23; 10:23—11:1; 15—16.
For further examples see Kümmel, *Introduction*, 203–205 [204f].

26 Weiss, *Earliest Christianity*, 1:341 [271f].

3. The sending of Timothy, about the same time (4:17).

4. A letter from Corinth to Paul (7:1), brought by Chloe's people (1:11), perhaps already sent before the arrival of Stephanas in Corinth, but more probably soon after his arrival.

5. Letter B.

6. Return of Timothy.

7. Intermediate visit, etc.

There is no conclusive proof of different situations within 1 Corinthians. The existing breaks can be explained from the circumstances of its composition. Even the complex that gives the strongest offense, chaps. 8—10, can be understood as a unity.[27]

2. The Date of Composition

a) The tradition of the early church.[28] The Vulgate MSS include prologues to the epistles of Paul.[29] The prologue to 1 Corinthians runs:[30]

Corinthii sunt Achaei. et hi similiter ab apostolis audierunt verbum veritatis et subversi multifarie a falsis apostolis, quidam a philosophiae verbosa eloquentia, alii a secta legis Iudaicae inducti. hos revocat ad veram et evangelicam sapientiam scribens eis ab Epheso per Timotheum, "The 'Corinthians' are Achaeans. And they, likewise, heard the word of truth from the apostles and were perverted in manifold ways by false apostles, some being seduced by the verbose eloquence of philosophy, others by the sect of the Jewish Law. These he recalls to the true wisdom of the gospel, writing to them from Ephesus by the hand of Timothy" [Trans.].

b) The real facts can be derived from the epistles of Paul and the narrative of Acts.

The reason for writing is a letter from Corinth (7:1). Paul is in Ephesus (16:8).[31] He has sent Timothy to Corinth (4:17; the latter is accordingly not the bearer of the letter).

The events subsequent to the writing are these: Paul travels from Ephesus to Corinth ("intermediate visit") and afterwards writes a letter "with many tears" (2 Cor 2:4). He sends Titus to Corinth and he himself travels to Macedonia, where he meets Titus on the latter's return (2 Cor 2:12f; 7:5ff).[32]

Titus again goes to Corinth. Paul follows him. This is his last visit (Acts 20:1–3). During it the epistle to the Romans is written. Then he travels (with the offering collected for the primitive community, 16:1–4) to Jeru-

---

27 See esp. Hans von Soden, "Sakrament und Ethik bei Paulus," in *Marburger theologische Studien* (*Rudolf–Otto Festgruss*), ed. H. Frick, vol. 1 (Gotha: Klotz, 1931), 1–40; reprinted in his *Urchristentum und Geschichte*, ed. Hans von Campenhausen, vol. 1 (Tübingen: J. C. B. Mohr [Paul Siebeck], 1951), 238–275.

28 On the Muratorian Canon, see §2.

29 For the text of the "Marcionite Prologues," see Erwin Preuschen, *Analecta*, vol. 2, Sammlung ausgewählter kirchen– und dogmengeschichtlicher Quellenschriften, 1, 8 (Tübingen: J. C. B. Mohr [Paul Siebeck], ²1910), 85–88. For their Marcionite character, see D. De Bruyne, "Prologues bibliques d'origine Marcionite," *RevBén* 24 (1907): 1–16; P. Corssen, "Zur Überlieferungsgeschichte des Römerbriefes," *ZNW* 10 (1909): 1–45, 97–102 (esp. 37–45); Adolf von Harnack, "Der marcionitische Ursprung der ältesten Vulgata–Prologe zu den Paulusbriefen," *ZNW* 24 (1925): 204–218; Harnack, "Die marcionitischen Prologe zu den Paulusbriefen, eine Quelle des muratorischen Fragments," *ZNW* 25 (1926): 160–163. For a different approach, see W. Mundle, "Die Herkunft der 'marcionitischen' Prologe zu den paulinischen Briefen," *ZNW* 24 (1925): 56–77; Marie–Joseph Lagrange, "Les prologues prétendus marcionites," *RB* 35 (1926): 161–

173. The prologue to Rom reads as follows: *Romani sunt in partibus Italiae. hi praeventi sunt a falsis apostolis et sub nomine domini nostri Jesu Christi in legem et prophetas erant inducti. hos revocat apostolus ad veram evangelicam fidem scribens eis a Corintho*, "The 'Romans' live in the regions of Italy. These were reached beforehand by false apostles, and under the name of our Lord Jesus Christ had been introduced to the Law and the Prophets. The Apostle recalls them to the true evangelical faith, writing to them from Corinth" [Trans.].

30 See previous note.

31 It makes little difference whether he is in the city itself or in the immediate neighborhood (in view of 15:32?). In Asia there are already a considerable number of communities, 16:19. So he has obviously been working there for a longish time, cf. 4:18f: he had not been in Corinth for a long time. He is writing in the spring (16:8), *ca.* A.D. 55. The chronological relationship between 1 Cor and Gal cannot be established with certainty.

32 For his travel plans, their alterations and their execution, see on 16:3ff.

salem. There he is arrested.

A piece of internal evidence for the placing of 1 Corinthians is provided by the epistle to the Romans. The whole surviving correspondence of Paul with the Corinthian community lies temporally close together, and Romans also belongs in proximity to it.

Now the latter coincides closely in certain sections with 1 Corinthians; compare

1 Corinthians	Romans
1:18ff	1:18ff
8—10	14:1—15:6
12	12:3ff
15:19, 44–49	5:12ff

The statements in 1 Corinthians are thoroughly practical, those in Romans more thematic. The latter gives the impression in these sections of being a theoretical further development of the former.[33] Thus help can be gained from Romans for the exegesis of 1 Corinthians (and vice versa).[34]

4. The Language[35]

The epistle displays the well–known characteristics of the language of Paul.[36] Elements of the higher Koine (and the classical language[37]) stand side by side with elements of colloquial speech.[38] On the average, we have (elevated) Koine[39] combined with elements of the LXX.[40]

As stylistic elements, Paul, like the diatribe, makes use of dialogical terms,[41] 15:35; 7:21, and the figures of rhetoric: the stringing together of rhetorical questions (with anaphora), 4:7;[42] 9:1;[43] antistrophe, 13:11; asyndetic addition of new paragraphs (the figure $\dot{\epsilon}\xi$ $\dot{\alpha}\pi o\sigma\tau\acute{\alpha}\sigma\epsilon\omega s$, "with a gap"), 5:9; 6:1, 12,[44] and rhetorical asyndeton in general, 7:27; cf. vv 18, 21;[45] parallelism, 1:25ff; 7:29–31; 15:47ff; antithesis, 4:10f; 15:42ff; with paranomasia, 7:32–34; chiasmus, 5:2–6; 7:1–7; the spinning out of catchwords, 10:1ff; 11:29ff; the stringing together of illustrations, 9:7ff; from the world of sport, 9:24ff;[46] the customary metaphors of the diatribe, 3:2; 9:11; 13:11.

---

33 Rom 5:12ff is indeed a veritable commentary on 1 Cor 15:19, 44–49. In 1 Cor 8—10 the critical principle is $\sigma vv\epsilon\acute{\iota}\delta\eta\sigma\iota s$, "conscience"; in Rom 14f it is $\pi\acute{\iota}\sigma\tau\iota s$, "faith."

34 J. R. Richards, "Romans and I Corinthians: Their Chronological Relationship and Comparative Dates," *NTS* 13 (1966–67): 14–30, vainly seeks to reverse the order of 1 Cor and Rom.

35 Archibald Robertson and Alfred Plummer, *A Critical and Exegetical Commentary on the First Epistle of St Paul to the Corinthians*, ICC (Edinburgh: T. & T. Clark, ²1914), xlvi–liv; E.–B. Allo, *Première Épître aux Corinthiens*, Études Bibliques (Paris: Gabalda, 1934), liii–lxxv; Blass–Debrunner, Index *s.v.* "Paul"; Johannes Weiss, *Beiträge zur paulinischen Rhetorik* (Göttingen: Vandenhoeck & Ruprecht, 1897); Rudolf Bultmann, *Der Stil der paulinischen Predigt und die kynisch–stoische Diatribe*, FRLANT, 13 (Göttingen: Vandenhoeck & Ruprecht, 1910); Ernst von Dobschütz, "Wir und ich bei Paulus," *ZSTh* 10 (1932–33): 251–277; W. F. Lofthouse, " 'I' and 'We' in the Pauline Letters," *ExpT* 64 (1952–53); 241–245; David G. Bradley, "The Topos as a Form in the Pauline Paraenesis," *JBL* 72 (1953): 238–246; Nils Wilhelm Lund, *Chiasmus in the New Testament* (Chapel Hill: University of North Carolina Press, 1942); Joachim Jeremias, "Chiasmus in den Paulusbriefen," *ZNW* 49 (1958): 145–156, now also in his *Abba* (Göttingen: Vandenhoeck & Ruprecht, 1966), 276–290.

36 Blass–Debrunner §3: "Paul exhibits a good, sometimes even elegant, style of vulgar Greek." The listing of (Pauline or NT) *hapax legomena* (Robertson and Plummer, xlixf) has little bearing on the verdict. The choice of words is governed partly by the object ($\ddot{\alpha}\gamma\alpha\mu os$ in chap. 7), by rhetoric and even simply by chance, by natural changes in linguistic usage, etc.

37 This of course is not surprising. After all, the Koine is the descendant of Attic Greek. An example is the use of the substantivized neuter adjective for the abstract, Blass–Debrunner §263(2) (classical Greek and higher Koine).

38 Rhetorical use of the first person, 10:30; Blass–Debrunner §281.

39 Words: temporal $\dot{\omega}s$ $\ddot{\alpha}v$, 11:34 (LXX, papyri); Blass–Debrunner §455(2). Hellenistic forms: $\ddot{\eta}\mu\eta v$, 13:11; $\ddot{\iota}v\alpha$ with future indicative, 9:19f, etc.

40 E.g., the use of the genitive of the substantivized infinitive. The use of this form is not in itself nonclassical, but what certainly are so are its frequency and the freedom in its use, both of which point to the LXX: Ludwig Radermacher, *Neutestamentliche Grammatik*, HNT, 1, 1 (Tübingen: J. C. B. Mohr [Paul Siebeck], ²1925), 189; Blass–Debrunner §400.

41 Bultmann, *Stil*, 64–74. Examples galore in Epictetus.

42 Cf. Philo, *Leg. all.* 3.58.

43 Epict., *Diss.* 3.22.48.

44 Blass–Debrunner §463.

45 Blass–Debrunner §494.

46 Particularly popular in the diatribe: Epict., *Diss.* 3.25.2–5. Paul differs from the diatribe in that he never works out the pictures, but is content to indicate them.

With regard to vocabulary, the fact that many words are especially frequent in 1 Corinthians or used in it alone must not mislead us into drawing far–reaching conclusions. In the other epistles the situation is similar. Nor does the choice of words allow of direct conclusions in regard to the terminology of the partners in Corinth. That can also be determined by the environment in which Paul is composing his letter. The epistle to the Romans does not reflect the language of the Roman Christian community (which Paul does not know), but what was at that time the language of the Pauline school.[47]

5. The Form of the Epistle[48]

Deissmann[49] has suggested differentiating between a "letter," i.e., a real letter in actual correspondence, and an "epistle," i.e., an artificial letter in which the garb of a letter is a mere form and serves to dress up a treatise. This differentiation is heuristically useful, but if taken as a hard and fast alternative, it does not apply to the epistles of Paul.[50] These contain on the one hand genuine correspondence (1 Corinthians being a peculiarly striking example), and on the other hand expositions of a fundamental kind which go far beyond the immediate occasion (chap. 13). Besides, Paul writes not as a private individual but as an apostle.

Certain formalities of epistolary style are observed: the opening (see on 1:1–3) with a fixed basic form and variations of it in individual cases; the proemium (see on 1:4–9); the concluding greeting. The structure in between is free, more especially in 1 Corinthians. Galatians and Romans are constructed according to a homiletic schema: (a) dogmatic teaching; (b) paraenesis.[51] The buildup of 1 Corinthians, on the other hand, does not follow any rule.[52] A considerable part of it consists of answers to questions which had been addressed to Paul in a letter from Corinth (7:1). He does not attempt to arrange them in a systematic order. Plainly, he simply follows the order of the Corinthian letter. The systematic element does not lie in the outward arrangement, but in the fact that Paul relates one topic after another to the basis of existence, to faith: the form of the community (formation of groups), the theme of freedom (sexual ethics, the attitude to idols and to sacrificial food), the structure of divine service (the situation of women, the Lord's Supper, pneumatic utterance), the attitude of the

47 Furthermore, the Corinthians learned their mode of expression from Paul.

48 Paul Wendland, *Die urchristliche Literaturformen*, HNT, 1, 3 (Tübingen: J. C. B. Mohr [Paul Siebeck], ³1912), 342–381, 411–417; Otto Roller, *Das Formular der paulinischen Briefe*, BWANT, 58 (Stuttgart: Kohlhammer, 1933); Wilhelm Michaelis, *Einleitung in das Neue Testament* (Bern: Haller, ³1961), 144–149; Kümmel, *Introduction*, 176–179 [173–175]; Béda Rigaux, *The Letters of St. Paul: Modern Studies*, ed. and tr. Stephen Yonick and Malachy J. Carroll (Chicago: Franciscan Herald, 1968), 115–146 (*Saint Paul et ses lettres: État de la question*, Studia Neotestamentica, Subsidia 2 [Paris and Bruges: Desclée de Brouwer, 1962], 163–199); Heikki Koskenniemi, *Studien zur Idee und Phraseologie des griechischen Briefes bis 400 n. Chr.*, Annales Academicae Scientiarum Fennicae, B, 102, 2 (Helsinki: Suomalainen Tiedeakatemia, Akateeminen Kirjakauppa; Wiesbaden: Harrassowitz, 1956).

49 Adolf Deissmann, *Bible Studies*, tr. Alexander Grieve (Edinburgh: T. & T. Clark, 1901), 9f (*Bibelstudien* [Marburg: Elwert, 1895], 196).

50 This is true also of others. Wendland, *Literaturformen*, 378: *1 Cl.* is "a thoroughly artistic product, whose literary character no one can deny, and yet it is a real letter."

51 The schema is taken over in Col and Eph. The inference is that it was practiced in the "school." In content it corresponds to the relationship observed already at the pre–Pauline stage between the "indicative" (of the saving event) and the "imperative" (of the paraenetic consequences).

52 Weiss (xliii) is too much under the influence of rhetoric when he avers (assuming that the unity is recognized) that a clever hand has been at work in the arrangement. The parts are nicely divided: A. 1:10—4:21 on the parties; B. 5—6 on moral disorders; C. 7:1—11:1 on matters of moral doubt; D. 11:2—14:40 on disorders in the assemblies; E. 15 on the resurrection; the conclusion, 16. The schema a b a prevails: "The way in which the digressions in 2:6–16; 6:1–11; chaps. 9 and 13 are inserted into their context leads us to infer a firm principle of arrangement."

But this is to attribute too much whether to Paul or to an editor.

52a John C. Hurd, Jr., *The Origin of I Corinthians* (London: SPCK; New York: Seabury, 1965).

individual in relation to himself and to the community (charismata), hope.

An original hypothesis designed to cast light on the origin and structure of the epistle is developed by J. C. Hurd.[52a] He distinguishes two groups of paragraphs: emotional ones, which are based on information received by word of mouth, and calm ones, which take up the letter of the Corinthians (who naturally drew a not unfavorable picture of themselves). Note here that the letter from Corinth for its part takes up the earlier letter of Paul. The resulting picture is as follows:

1. Sections of Criticism: 1:10—4:21; 5:1–8; 6:1–11; 9:3–27; 11:17–34.

2. Discussion. The exchange can be reconstructed.[53] Paul wrote, for example: Christians should marry because of the danger of πορνεία, "sexual immorality." The Corinthians object. They hold to the position which Paul himself had once taught them: Better not to touch a woman at all! Paul: No dealings with fornicators! The Corinthians: That is impossible. Paul: No meat that has been sacrificed to gods! The Corinthians: We see nothing wrong in that; there are of course no gods. Paul: Women should cover themselves. The Corinthians: Our custom has always been different. Paul: No enthusiasm! The Corinthians: But you appeared yourself in the role of a pneumatic. Paul: Do not mourn for the dead. They will rise again. The Corinthians: That is not a spiritual idea.

Paul occasionally quotes sentences from their letter—6:12; 10:23; 6:13; 7:1; 8:1, 4, 5f, 8; 11:2[54]—in order to criticize it. The criticism does not refer to former behavior, but looks forward. Paul cites authorities: Jesus, the Bible, custom, his own commission.

Many sections, it is true, cannot be pressed into this schema.[55] On the one hand Hurd knows too much. On the other, he leaves certain facts out of account, e.g., that Paul can work with prescribed material (§6).[56]

6. Methods of Presentation and and Argumentation[57]

The more Paul's position is attacked, the more firmly must he ground his statements.

He appeals to traditional authorities, to the *Bible*.[58] He can quote it more or less exactly (1:19) or freely vary it and work it into his own formulations (14:21; 15:25, 27). He can add an exegesis (9:9f), expand the text in Targum fashion (15:45), combine passages together (15:45f). On one occasion he writes a sort of midrash on the Exodus (10:1ff).[59] A *word of Jesus* is unconditionally valid (7:10), as is also the *example of the Lord* (11:1) to which he can

---

53 The topic is in agreement with the apostolic decree. Under the influence of the latter Paul changed his mind.

54 Many exegetes assume this of these sentences: 6:12, most exegetes; 6:13, Weiss, Allo; 7:1, Robertson and Plummer, xxv, Jeremias, *Abba*, 273; 8:1, all exegetes; 8:4, Hans Leitzmann, *An die Korinther*, rev. Werner Georg Kümmel, HNT, 9 (Tübingen: J. C. B. Mohr [Paul Siebeck], ⁴1949), Weiss, Robertson and Plummer, Allo, Jeremias; 8:5f, F. W. Grosheide, *Commentary on the First Epistle to the Corinthians*, NIC (Grand Rapids: Eerdmans, 1953); 8:8, C. F. G. Heinrici, *Der erste Brief an die Korinther*, KEK, 5 (Göttingen: Vandenhoeck & Ruprecht, ⁸1896), and Jeremias.

55 E.g., 6:12–20 is "a transitional passage," Hurd, *Origin*, 89.

56 E.g., 7:1f does not provide any evidence that Paul had already decreed in an earlier letter that between married people normal sexual relationships should prevail.

57 Wilhelm Bousset, *Jüdisch–christlicher Schulbetrieb in Alexandria und Rom*, FRLANT, 23 (Göttingen: Van-denhoeck & Ruprecht, 1915); Hartwig Thyen, *Der Stil der jüdisch–hellenistischen Homilie*, FRLANT, 65 (Göttingen: Vandenhoeck & Ruprecht, 1955); Hans von Campenhausen, *Die Begründung kirchlicher Entscheidung beim Apostel Paulus*, SAH, 1957, 2 (Heidelberg: Winter, 1957), now in his *Aus der Frühzeit des Christentums* (Tübingen: J. C. B. Mohr [Paul Siebeck], 1963), 30–80.

58 Otto Michel, *Paulus und seine Bibel*, BFTh, 2, 18 (Gütersloh: Bertelsmann, 1929), reprinted (Darmstadt: Wissenschaftliche Buchgesellschaft, 1972); Joseph Bonsirven, *Exégèse rabbinique et exégèse paulinienne* (Paris: Beauchesne, 1939); E. Earle Ellis, *Paul's Use of the Old Testament* (Edinburgh: Oliver & Boyd; Grand Rapids: Eerdmans, 1957); Barnabas Lindars, *New Testament Apologetic* (London: SCM; Philadelphia: Westminster, 1961); Hans von Campenhausen, The Formation of the Christian Bible, tr. J. A. Baker (Philadelphia: Fortress, 1972) (*Die Entstehung der christlichen Bibel*, BHT, 39 [Tübingen: J. C. B. Mohr (Paul Siebeck), 1968]).

59 Cf. 2 Cor 3:7–18.

link a reference to himself as example. Naturally, the *Church* is an authority and at the same time an intrinsic norm (3:16). All this points back to the ultimate authority, the event of salvation, the determination of existence "in Christ" (6:11; 8:11). A factor in the actualizing of the event of salvation is the established tradition of the Church (5:7; 11:2, 23; 15:3).

The result of relating these authorities back to the work of salvation is that they do not remain in the formal sphere. They are immediately understandable in the existence of the Church and of the believers.[60]

Alongside this there is a group of arguments of, in my opinion, a completely different kind. To this group there belong set forms of paraenesis, such as the catalogues of virtues and vices, and specific ideas of theological cosmology, that is to say, elements of a speculative religious world–picture: 11:2ff. Maxims of a proverbial kind appeal to the "wisdom" of the readers (5:6); Paul claims immediate support from the power of discernment, from experience, from valid custom (10:15; 11:13).

In the case of these arguments, too, whether and how they are incorporated in the totality of the understanding of God, world, man, salvation in Christ must be asked.

Now it is clear that *in general* the paraenesis is derived from the work of salvation (as the slogan has it: the imperative comes from the indicative).[61] This was the case already before Paul, but is thought through and given concrete shape by him. What, then, is the relation between this and the nontheological arguments (on grounds of reason, custom)?

In Paul's sense they are not "nontheological." The truth is that faith leads to freedom, and the latter is freedom for the renewal of conduct. His injunctions are instructions on the practical exercise of freedom. They agree in content with morality of a Jewish and universal bourgeois kind. For the Christian factor does not lie in a new moral conceptuality, but in the relating of morals to faith.

The structure of his thought can be grasped still more precisely, and here indeed we have the help of a literary observation. There are certain sections which are more or less independent of their context and which, better than others, can be interpreted on their own. They display a great many similarities to each other and also to Hellenistic Jewish writings. They give the impression of having been already formed, at least in outline, before their present application in the epistle. Their content is wisdom teaching. It is plain that here we have traces of the heritage of Jewish schooling which Paul brought with him into Christianity.[62] In addition to this, they give us an insight into the studies which Paul, as a Christian theologian, now pursues into the way in which he theologically works over his Jewish world–picture. The signs are plainest in the sections 2:6–16; 10:1–13; 11:2–16, and the foundations of chap. 13.[63] Typical characteristics are these: the two–tier framework of the esoteric schools, which derives from a specific type of Jewish wisdom speculation (and has long been united with mystery elements),[64] namely, that on hidden wisdom.[65] Another type is vanished wisdom. It provides the motif for 1:18ff.[66] This section furnishes an outstanding example of the Christological style of the adaptation of the

60 Hans von Campenhausen, *Begründung*, 29: "Everything that Paul desires, demands and recommends in the way of definite order and definite judicial rulings in the community, is to be understood as the necessary expression—the development and confirmation—of that which is immediately effectually given with the essential new being, with the reality of the church and the Christian standing of each individual Christian. . . . According to the specific context Paul then lays particular stress on the new fellowship with Christ, the membership of all Christians in one body, the leading of the Holy Spirit, or the unequivocal separation from the world, its idols and its sins. However the particular case may be, again and again there emerges in the background the uniqueness of the Christian 'calling,' of the being of the church in Christ. . . ."

61 Rudolf Bultmann, *Theology of the New Testament*, tr. Kendrick Grobel (London: SCM; New York: Scribner's, 1952–55), 1:100–106, 332f [102–107, 334f.]

62 Cf. the educational enterprise of the Therapeutae (Philo, *Vit. cont.* 25–33).

63 Cf. also the foundations of 15:35ff. From other epistles: 2 Cor 3:7–18; Rom 1:18–32; 4; 5:12ff; 7:7ff; 10:4–8; 12:3ff. Heb, too, largely rests upon school learning (so Bousset, Windisch).

64 Philo, *Leg. all.* 3.219, etc.; Heb 5:11ff; Jn 3:1ff; see on 1 Cor 2:6ff.

65 Job 28; Bar 3:9ff; André Feuillet, *Le Christ Sagesse de Dieu d'après les épîtres pauliniennes*, Études Bibliques (Paris: Gabalda, 1966), 47–57.

66 The third type, the wisdom that is nearby, emerges in Rom 10:4ff. On the typology, see Burton L. Mack,

material. Wisdom teaches that God is wise, and that wisdom is his, i.e., that man can receive wisdom only from him. Out of this Paul constructs the insight of faith, that *Christ* is the wisdom of God—Christ, moreover, understood in the sense of the theology of the cross.[67]

Jewish wisdom had already eliminated the time factor from the wisdom school's treatment of Israel and its history.[68] This approach, too, Paul makes use of for soteriology. An objectifying treatment of the course of history is of no interest to him. The past is at any given moment immediately behind me. It is the realm within which I understand myself on the basis of faith.

Hence it is immediately bound up with the present on the ground of which I can understand my future.

Talk of God and his nature and ways is consistently transformed into statements on his saving act, which took place "in Christ" and actualizes itself in the gospel, the "word of the cross."

7. The Theological Character of the Epistle

1. 1 Corinthians has already been criticized as "that unit among the major Pauline letters which yields the very least for our understanding of the Pauline faith," as being poor in doctrinal content.[69] This criticism misjudges both the character of the epistle and the character of Paul's theology. It understands by theology merely the theoretical development of doctrine. The latter is of course *also* a part of the theologian's work. But Paul's approach is in the first instance a different one. Theology is for him primarily the exposition of the event of salva-

tion that is doctrinally formulated in the creed and actualized in the gospel; that is to say, it expounds the self-understanding of the faith which has its object in the work of salvation. In Romans Paul provides a commentary on faith[70] by showing the justification of the sinner to be the fruit of the death of Christ and describing the existence of the justified sinner in the world and in its relation to the future. The great attraction of 1 Corinthians, however, lies in the fact that here Paul is practicing applied theology, so to speak. This is not to say he is doing anything substantially different from what he does in Galatians and Romans, but he does it in a different way. Theology is here translated into an illumination of the existence of the church and of the individual Christian in it. And conversely, since for Paul theology is not an application of timeless principles but the understanding of the situation in which man finds himself at the moment in which grace reaches him through the word, he can therefore spotlight the church and the individual in the concrete position of the moment. The "strong" man, the freeman, the married man—each remains where he stands; for he is called as what he is. The new element is given in the fact that he is now free, etc., "in Christ." *Here* is *one* body (12:13). This does not mean that all are the same, but that in their very differences—individual, psychological, social, cultural—they are one. Here lies the truth of the eschatological ὡς μή, "as though . . . not" (7:29–31). Here the slave who is called in Christ is the Lord's freeman, and the freeman who is called is the Lord's slave (7:22).[71]

Logos und Sophia: Untersuchungen zur Weisheitstheologie im hellenistischen Judentum, SUNT, 10 (Göttingen: Vandenhoeck & Ruprecht, 1973). [See also B. L. Mack, "Wisdom Myth and Mytho-logy: An Essay in Understanding a Theological Tradition," *Interpretation* 24 (1970): 46–60—Trans.].

67 The style of the theological transplanting emerges still more clearly when it is observed that Paul takes up a further idea of wisdom teaching, that of the overthrow of the lofty and the exaltation of the humble by God; see on 1:18ff.

68 Sirach; see on 10:1ff. Paradigm: Rom 7:7ff, where Paul sets the Ego in the place of Adam (this, too, following the Jewish example).

69 Walter Bauer, *Orthodoxy and Heresy in Earliest Christianity*, tr. ed. Robert A. Kraft and Gerhard Krodel (Philadelphia: Fortress, 1971), 219 (*Rechtgläubigkeit und Ketzerei im ältesten Christentum*, ed. Georg Strecker,

BHT, 10 [Tübingen: J. C. B. Mohr (Paul Siebeck), ²1964], 221f). Bauer arrives at this verdict in the context of the question why *this* letter in particular (and not, e.g., the theologically weighty epistle to the Romans) was so highly valued in early times (*1 Cl.*, Ignatius, Polycarp); *1 Cl.* was able to use it as a first-rate weapon against the goings-on in Corinth. Then it was given a wider circulation, starting from Rome.

70 Repeatedly taking up traditional formulas: 3:24ff; 4:25, etc.

71 The understanding of the saving event and of ethics in terms of history is brilliantly presented by H. von Soden, "Sakrament und Ethik."

Excursus:
Paul and the Ethics
of the Stoics and
Cynics[72]

In the Stoa, as in Paul, the individual man as such forms a prominent theme, and the understanding of man is very closely bound up with an understanding of the world. Freedom is freedom over against the world, and therewith at the same time over against oneself. It is freedom toward death.

Despite all the associations, there are no indications that Paul studied philosophy.[73] The points of agreement[74] do not go beyond the terms and ideas of popular philosophy with which it was possible for any and everyone to be acquainted. Moreover, it has to be borne in mind that Hellenistic Judaism had taken over philosophic ideas and in the course of its thinking had transformed them in terms of the Jewish understanding of God and the world.

The style of thought is fundamentally different. In Paul there is no trace of a thematic exposition of the sort of picture of man and the world which in philosophy forms the foundation and framework of ethics.[75] He does not take his bearings on the data which I can grasp by the use of reason, on the distinction between $\tau\grave{\alpha}$ $\grave{\epsilon}\phi$' $\dot{\eta}\mu\hat{\iota}\nu$, "things in our power," and $\tau\grave{\alpha}$ $o\grave{\upsilon}\kappa$ $\grave{\epsilon}\phi$' $\dot{\eta}\mu\hat{\iota}\nu$, "things not in our power." The individual is not a worldly being, contrasted as such with the world as conceived in terms of a world-picture. His standing as an individual is determined by the event of salvation: he is sinful

and justified. He is not on the move toward himself, but knows himself related to the Lord in faith. His self–understanding, his "wisdom" accrues to him in recognizing the foolishness of the cross. It does not become his "own" wisdom, of which he could boast. The world is not theoretically analyzed. It is measured: it is hastening to its end. Nor is God's lordship over the world proved by worldly factors (the orderly arrangement of nature, etc.), but on the ground of the cross God's action upon the guilty world is proclaimed. Death is not a natural fate, but the wages of sin.[76] While the philosopher seeks to gain the mastery of time by means of training, Paul holds that the life of the believer stands under the determination of the cross and will be led not out of suffering, but through suffering to hope (Rom 5:3ff).

The isolation into which faith leads is not a universal characteristic of existence. It is the actualization of the freedom of grace, which creates the freedom of faith. The place of the latter is in the community, for it is existent only "in Christ."

To the act of salvation corresponds faith's reference to the future, the resurrection. While the wisdom teacher's ideal is to be no longer dependent on hope, for Paul hope is the *conditio sine qua non* for the mastering of life in the world (chap. 15). Incidentally, this hope is not grounded on any (apocalyptic) world–picture, but presented in terms of the understanding of the event of salvation.[77]

---

72 Weiss, *passim*; Max Pohlenz, "Paulus und die Stoa," *ZNW* 42 (1949): 69–104, reprinted separately (Darmstadt: Wissenschaftliche Buchgesellschaft, 1964) and in *Das Paulusbild in der neueren deutschen Forschung*, ed. Karl Heinrich Rengstorf, Wege der Forschung, 24 (Darmstadt: Wissenschaftliche Buchgesellschaft, ²1969), 522–564; Rudolf Bultmann, *Primitive Christianity in Its Contemporary Setting*, tr. Reginald H. Fuller (Cleveland and New York: World, 1956), 135–145, 185–188 [127–137, 172–175]; Herbert Braun, "Die Indifferenz gegenüber der Welt bei Paulus und bei Epiktet," in his *Gesammelte Studien zum Neuen Testament und seiner Umwelt* (Tübingen: J. C. B. Mohr [Paul Siebeck], 1962), 159–167; J. N. Sevenster, *Paul und Seneca*, SNT, 4 (Leiden: Brill, 1961); Wolfgang Schrage, "Die Stellung zur Welt bei Paulus, Epictet und in der Apokalyptik: Ein Beitrag zu 1 Kor 7,29–31," *ZNW* 61 (1964): 125–154.

73 Say, in his home town of Tarsus, which was celebrated for its philosophical, and in particular its Stoic, schools.

74 On the trend of the ideas of popular philosophy, see

Jacques Dupont, *Gnosis: La connaissance religieuse dans les épîtres de Saint Paul*, Universitas Catholica Lovaniensis, Dissertationes in Facultate Theologica, 2, 40 (Louvain: Nauwelaerts, ²1960), *passim*.

75 See esp. Pohlenz, *Paulus und die Stoa*. When $\phi\acute{\upsilon}\sigma\iota\varsigma$, "nature," and $\nu\acute{o}\mu o\varsigma$, "law," stand together for once (Rom), then it is in a completely non–Stoic sense. Nature in Paul is not a factor on its own, and law is the law revealed by God, which can be read in the OT. Paul does not play off an unwritten law against the written one, but asserts that it is made known by God also to the heathen, through conscience.

76 The Stoic makes death a matter of no consequence. By this means he can turn death into an act of his own: Ernst Benz: *Das Todesproblem in der stoischen Philosophie*, Tübinger Beiträge zur Altertumswissenschaft, 7 (Stuttgart: Kohlhammer, 1929), 85f. For Paul, death remains our enemy until it is annihilated as the last enemy; see on 15:26.

77 The *peccavimus omnes* of the Stoics has no bearing upon the future that lies before me at any given moment.

2. The loose structure of 1 Corinthians can mislead us into believing that its subject matter, too, is loose and arbitrary. This opinion is rightly rejected by Karl Barth. He does not dispute "the haphazard character of the series of subjects dealt with in 1 Cor. i.–xiv." nor "the lack of connexion by which 1 Cor. xv., with its new theme, is at first joined to this series. But the question arises: first, whether Paul's *reflections* upon the subject dealt with in 1 Cor. i.–xiv. are as disparate as these subjects themselves, or rather whether a thread cannot be discovered which binds them internally into a whole; and, secondly, whether 1 Cor. xv. is merely to be comprehended as one theme by the side of many others, or rather whether the thread hitherto followed does not at this point become visible, so that this theme, however much externally it is one theme by the side of many others, fails to be recognized at the same time as the Theme of the Epistle."[78] Barth's thesis is, in fact, that the "last things" form *the* theme of the epistle, the one that holds all the other themes together.[79] This thesis rightly brings out the fact that the position of chap. 15 at the end of the epistle is no accident. It is in harmony with the general scheme that was widely employed for the presenting of Christian teaching.[80] Paul brings to consciousness what was contained from the start in the hope of resurrection; it is not something other than soteriology, that is, Christology. The hope is true because and insofar as the creed is true. For the latter's statements on Christ contain, as such, statements on the believer. In the presentation of this hope the general direction of Paul's theological thinking again comes to light; here, too, it stands out with peculiar sharpness as a result of the antithesis to the direction of thought prevailing in Corinth.[81]

The concept of the "cross" predominates in 1 Corinthians over that of justification, which was the prevailing concept in Galatians and Romans, but has in substance no other intention than the latter, namely, to present the ideas of *sola gratia—sola fide*, of the destruction of human καύχησις, "boasting," and of the transportation into the freedom of faith.

8. The Milieu: the City of Corinth[82]

The ancient and powerful commercial city on the Isthmus, which owed its wealth[83] to its position on "two seas,"[84] had been destroyed by the Romans in 146 B.C.[85] Caesar founded it anew as a Roman colony in 44 B.C.,[86]

---

78 Karl Barth, *The Resurrection of the Dead*, tr. H. J. Stenning (New York: Revell, 1933), 6 [1f]; see Bultmann's review in *ThBl* 5 (1926): 1–14, now in his *Faith and Understanding*, tr. Louise Pettibone Smith (London: SCM; New York: Harper & Row, 1969), 1:66–94, esp. 66f [38–64, esp. 38f].

79 Bultmann, *Faith and Understanding*, 1:80 [51], agrees in principle, but his view of eschatology differs from Barth's. He believes that eschatology, contrary to Paul's own intention, does not attain to pure expression in chap. 15, where he finds that speculative elements have intruded, but in chap. 13, in the presentation of love as the eschatological possibility.

80 Cf. the position of the topic "The Last Things" in 1 Thess, in Mk, in Q, in the discourses in Mt, in the *Didache*. We have here a scheme of presentation that has catechetical character.

81 This is true independently of the disputed question whether Paul's evaluation of the Corinthians' eschatology is correct in detail. Whether he saw through its enthusiastic character or regarded it as pure scepticism, either way he saw it as falling under the heading of the "human" (cf. 3:1ff).

82 Pauly–W., *Suppl.* 4:991–1036; 6:182–199. For the American excavations (with illustrations, inscriptions, coins, and reprints of the most important literary sources), see H. N. Fowler (ed.), *Corinth* (Athens: American School of Classical Studies, 1929–), and Henry S. Robinson, "Excavations at Ancient Corinth, 1959–1963," *Klio* 46 (1965): 289–305.

83 ἀφνειός, "rich," is a standard attribute on the basis of Hom., *Il.* 2.569, cited by Strabo, *Geog.* 8.377; cf. Thuc., *Hist.* 1:13; Ael. Arist., *Or.* 3.23.

84 Lat. *bimaris*: Horat., *Carm.* 1.7.2; Ovid, *Met.* 5.407. Roughly 2 kilometers from the city lies the harbor of Lecheion on the Gulf of Corinth; roughly 10 kilometers to the East lies the harbor of Cenchreae (Rom 16:1; Acts 18:18) on the Saronic Gulf. The trade route via the Isthmus (by unloading the goods or transporting the ships on the "diolkos") was attractive, because the voyage round the Peloponnesus (Cape Malea) was feared (Strabo, *Geog.*, 8.378).

85 Strabo, *Geog.*, 8.361, 381; Paus., *Descr.* 2.1.2.

86 Strabo, *Geog.*, 8.381; cf. Paus., *Descr.* 2.1.2; Dio C., *Hist. Rom.* 43.50.

Laus Julia Corinthiensis.[87] It quickly began to flourish again and in 27 B.C. became the seat of the governor of the province of Achaea (southern and central Greece); this became a senatorial province in A.D. 44.

The "city of Aphrodite"[88] had a reputation for vice; the Athenians in particular assiduously cultivated this reputation.[89] The proverb warns us: οὐ παντὸς ἀνδρὸς ἐς Κόρινθον ἔσθ' ὁ πλοῦς, "Not for every man is the voyage to Corinth."[90]

With regard to religion, the literary and archaeological sources display the absolutely normal picture of a Roman Hellenistic city. There are naturally a few sanctuaries of foreign gods;[91] Isis,[92] Serapis, the Mother of the gods. This is the usual thing; compared with other places the findings are modest.

This is not to deny that the harbors[93] were frequented by a motley throng, and that the picture of the lowest social class,[94] from which the greater part of the Christians derived (1:26ff), was different from that of the official

Corinth as presented in its buildings and inscriptions. On the other hand, the stability of the Greek and Roman religious tradition is not to be underestimated.[95]

Incidentally, the often–peddled statement that Corinth was a seat of sacred prostitution (in the service of Aphrodite)[96] is a fable. This realization also disposes of the inference that behind the Aphrodite of Corinth lurks the Phoenician Astarte.[97]

The presence of Jews is documented by an inscription: συν]αγωγὴ Ἑβρ[αίων, "synagogue of Hebrews."[98]

9. Chronology

According to Acts 18:12 Paul's sojourn in Corinth takes place during the proconsulship of Gallio.[99] The latter can be fairly exactly dated thanks to an inscription on the famous "Gallio stone" in Delphi.[100]

The only number preserved there is 26. It refers to the number of the preceding acclamations addressed to Claudius as Emperor. The date can be calculated from

87   Fowler, *Corinth* 8, pt. 3, no. 130.

88   Ael. Arist., *Or.* 3.23.

89   Κορινθία κόρη, Plato, *Repub.* 404d; Aristophanes (writing during the Peloponnesian War) coins the word κορινθιάζεσθαι (fr. 354). Κορινθιαστής is a title of comedies, Athen., *Deipnosoph.* 7.313c; 13.559a.

90   Strabo, *Geog.* 8.378 (Loeb 4:191), repeated in 12.559 (on Comana in Pontus); Latin form in Horat., *Ep.*, 1.17.36. Strabo propounds the fable that the city owed its wealth largely to the servants of Aphrodite. That the city can also be spoken of in very different terms is shown by Ael. Arist., *Or.*, 3.23f.

91   Paus., *Descr.* 2.

92   Cf. the description of the Isis festival in Apul., *Met.* 11.

93   Christians in Cenchreae: Rom 16:1.

94   Alciphr., *Ep.* 3.60: οὐκ ἔτι εἰσῆλθον εἰς τὴν Κόριν-θον· ἔγνων γὰρ ἐν βραχεῖ τὴν βδελυρίαν τῶν ἐκεῖσε πλουσίων καὶ τὴν τῶν πενήτων ἀθλιότητα, "I did not enter Corinth after all; for I learned in a short time the sordidness of the rich there and the misery of the poor" (Loeb 209).

95   For the participation of the populace in the cultus, see Kern, *Inschr. Magn.*, no. 100; Martin Nilsson, *Geschichte der griechischen Religion*, vol. 2, Handbuch der Altertumswissenschaft, 5, 2 (Munich: Beck, 1961), 83.

96   Alone of the Greek cities!

97   The fable is based on Strabo, *Geog.* 8.378: the temple of Aphrodite, he says, was so rich that it had more than a thousand ἱεροδούλους ἑταίρας, "prostitutes in the temple service." Strabo, however, is not speak-

ing of the present, but of the city's ancient golden period. As far as the present is concerned, he knows only of a "little temple" of the goddess on Acrocorinth. Pausanias knows nothing at all of the matter. As for the other passages which are used as evidence (esp. Pind., fr. 107; along with further information in Athen., *Deipnosoph.* 13.573f), not a single one of them speaks of sacred prostitution, but only of the participation of the Corinthian courtesans in the service of their patron. Incidentally, Strabo's assertion is not even true of the ancient Corinth. Reminiscences like the one that originated with Pindar have been mixed up in his mind with his own knowledge of the temple cities of Asia Minor (esp. Comana in Pontus). See Hans Conzelmann, "Korinth und die Mädchen der Aphrodite," *NAG* 8 (1967–68): 247–261.

98   Fowler, *Corinth* 8, pt. 1, no. 111; illustrations in Adolf Deissmann, *Light from the Ancient East*, tr. Lionel R. M. Strachan from 2nd German ed. (New York and London: Hodder & Stoughton, ²1911), 13 [13]. Philo includes Corinth in his long list on the dispersion of the Jews, *Leg. Gaj.* 281f.

99   L. Junius Gallio Annaeanus (*IG* 7:1676) is the younger brother of the philosopher Seneca; originally his name was M. Annaeus Novatus; he was adopted by L. Junius Gallio.

100 There are four fragments. Illustrations in Deissmann, *Paul: A Study in Social and Religious History*, tr. William E. Wilson (New York: Harper & Row, ²1957), plate 1; and L. Hennequin in *DBS* 2:355–373. Reconstructions in Deissmann, *Paul*, 261–286

further inscriptions. According to *CIL* 3: 1977, the 24th acclamation took place in the 11th tribunate of Claudius (identical with the year of his reign), i.e., 25 January 51 to 24 January 52. According to *CIL* 6: 1256, the 27th acclamation was in the 12th year, and in fact before 1 August 52. For the inscription was prepared for the inauguration of an aqueduct, and we learn from Frontinus, *De aquis* 13, that the inauguration took place on 1 August. An inscription from Caria[101] contains a combination of the 12th tribunate and the 26th acclamation. Thus the 26th acclamation lies between 25 January and 1 August 52. At this time Gallio is in office in Achaea. The only remaining question is whether the term is 51/52 or 52/53.[102] In favor of the earlier date is the fact that the proconsuls enter their office in the spring.[103] Now the inscription in Delphi contains the Emperor's answer to a report of Gallio's, which in turn had been preceded by the laying of information before Gallio and an investigation by him. Then the report went from Greece to Rome, was dealt with by the authorities, and came back again. For this, the time from the beginning of May (arrival) to 1 August is decidedly short. Hence Gallio would presumably have entered on office already in the spring of 51. The later date, however, cannot be excluded with certainty.

For Paul's sojourn, there remains a further uncertainty in that we do not know how far it overlaps with Gallio's. If we assume that Paul was brought before him only after a certain measure of success in his labors, then his sojourn will fall roughly in the period A.D. 49/51 or 50/52.

A further orientation point is provided by the mention of Aquila and Prisc(ill)a (16:19; Rom 16:3; Acts 18:2, 18, 26). According to Acts 18:2 this couple had come from Rome to Corinth shortly before the arrival of Paul; they had been expelled from the city by an edict of Claudius against the Jews. This edict is confirmed by Suetonius, *Claudius* 25: *Judaeos impulsore Chresto assidue tumultuantis Roma expulit*, "Since the Jews constantly made disturbances at the instigation of Chrestus, he [Claudius] expelled them from Rome."[104] Orosius dates it A.D. 49.[105]

[212–229]; Ditt., *Syll.* 2:493f (no. 801D); Edmund Groag, *Die römischen Reichsbeamten von Achaia bis auf Diocletian*, Akademie der Wissenschaften in Wien, Schriften der Balkankommission, Antiquarische Abteilung, 9 (Vienna and Leipzig: Hölder–Pichler–Tempsky, 1939), 32–35.

101 Georges Cousin and Gaston Deschamps, "Emplacement et ruines de la ville de Κυς en Carie," *BCH* 11 (1887): 305–311 (inscription, 306f).

102 Generally the proconsuls reside for a year; two years are possible: Theodor Mommsen, *Römische Staatsrecht*, Handbuch der römischen Altertümer, 1–3 (Leipzig: Hirzel, ³1887), 2:254–257; reprinted (Graz: Akademische Druck– und Verlagsanstalt, 1952–53) and (Darmstadt: Wissenschaftliche Buchgesellschaft, 1971). In Gallio's case it is readily pointed out that he was not in good health. After his consulship he made a recuperative journey to Egypt, Pliny, *Hist. nat.* 31.33. And he took ill in Achaia, Sen., *Ep.* 104.1: *illud mihi in ore erat domini mei Gallionis, qui cum in Achaia febrem habere coepisset, protinus navem ascendit clamitans non corporis esse sed loci morbum,* "For I remembered my master Gallio's words, when he began to develop a fever in Achaia and took ship at once, insisting that the disease was not of the body but of the place" (Loeb 3:191).

103 According to an edict of Claudius they have to leave Rome before mid–April, Dio C., *Hist. Rom.* 60.17.3.

104 Loeb 2:53. This does not mean that *all* the Jews were banished. Dio C., *Hist. Rom.* 60.6.6 (in the report on the year A.D. 41): τούς τε Ἰουδαίους πλεονάσαντας αὖθις, ὥστε χαλεπῶς ἂν ἄνευ ταραχῆς ὑπὸ τοῦ ὄχλου σφῶν τῆς πόλεως εἰρχθῆναι, οὐκ ἐξήλασε μέν, τῷ δὲ δὴ πατρίῳ βίῳ χρωμένους ἐκέλευσε μὴ συναθροίζεσθαι, "As for the Jews, who had again increased so greatly that by reason of their multitude it would have been hard without raising a tumult to bar them from the city, he did not drive them out, but ordered them, while continuing their traditional mode of life, not to hold meetings" (Loeb 7:383). There follow other measures of a similar kind: dissolution of the brotherhoods, closing of the καπηλεῖα, "shops."

105 *Anno eiusdem nono expulsos per Claudium urbe Iudaeos Iosephus refert,* "In the ninth year of the same reign, Josephus reports, the Jews were expelled from the City by Claudius" [Trans.]. Orosius, *Hist. contra Pag.* 7.6.51f (tr. Roy J. Deferrari ["The Fathers of the Church," 50 (Washington: Catholic University of America Press, 1964), p. 297]). On the error in regard to Josephus, see Eduard Meyer, *Ursprung und Anfänge des Christentums*, vol 3 (Stuttgart and Berlin: Cotta, 1923), 38, n. 1; reprinted (Darmstadt: Wissenschaftliche Buchgesellschaft, 1962).

10. The Community in Corinth

Who or what is it that Paul has to combat here? At first sight, his foe is moral and religious disorders, such as sexual freedom or the degeneration of the Lord's Supper. Now these conditions are bound up in a significant way with religious enthusiasm. Plainly in the mind of the Corinthians the two are a unity: their conduct is grounded on a freedom principle (6:12; 10:23); this in turn rests upon "knowledge" (8:1), and the latter derives from experience of the Spirit (12:4ff). Their freedom is accordingly not moral indifference, but represents a speculative position. The reconstruction of this position is one of the essential tasks of an exposition of the two epistles to the Corinthians. That is difficult, especially as in Corinth also various views are intermingled. Chap. 1 mentions three or four groups, 11:18 σχίσματα, "divisions." Chaps. 8—10 give indications of controversies on fundamental questions regarding the relation to the world. On the other hand it is not possible to determine the differences between the groups mentioned in chap. 1. And, when all is said and done, the community still forms a unity. As such it addresses itself to Paul with questions (7:1) and delegations (16:13), and Paul writes to the whole community. The Lord's Supper, for all the disorders, is celebrated by the community, not by the groups (11:17ff). Since Paul does not enter into any special opinions on the part of the groups, it is impossible for specific positions which Paul combats to be assigned to any specific group.[106]

Thus we can only attempt to trace out general characteristics of Corinthian thought and life. The difficulty of this task is increased further by the problem of how far it is permissible to draw upon 2 Corinthians: Has Paul to do with the same opponents there as in 1 Corinthians (Schmithals), or has a new group found its way into the community (Georgi, Bornkamm)?

The investigations of recent times took their start from F. C. Baur.[107] In keeping with his picture of the history of the apostolic age he defines the opponents as Judaists.

This thesis breaks down in face of the text, however: in 1 Corinthians it is not necessary to guard against any Judaistic demands.[108]

Lütgert[109] put forward the counter-thesis that the opponents are hyper-Paulinists, pneumatics, Gnostics. The Christ party with its slogan of freedom seeks to outdo Paul. It is against this party that Paul's attack is directed.

To Lütgert's credit, he inquires into the part that had been played in the developments in Corinth by Paul's own preaching, and by the way it had been received and assimilated by his hearers. But it is arbitrary to attribute to a specific "party" the views thus inferred.

Reitzenstein[110] turns the question the other way about: he derives from the epistle a picture of *Paul* as a Gnostic. From this there arises the picture, so widespread today, that the Corinthians are Gnostics. Paul, himself also subject to the influence of Gnostic ideas, asserts against them his theology of the cross, if also at times only brokenly, for he himself verges on the enthusiasm he attacks (see on 2:6ff). Schmithals in particular maintains the thesis that in Corinth there prevailed not only an enthusiasm of a general kind, but also a thoroughly worked out mythological Gnosticism: the σάρξ, "flesh," of Jesus is rejected in dualistic terms (12:1–3). The doctrine of Christ is only a special case of anthropology. The Gnostics are themselves χριστοί, "christs."[111] The dualism determines the libertinistic theory and the practical behavior resulting therefrom: the latter is not arbitrary, but is strictly related to the annihilation of the σάρξ and of idols.

106 E.g., to ascribe the wisdom combated in chaps. 1–3 to the Apollos group or to the Christ group. There is nothing that we can infer of the Peter group either, more especially since the theology of Peter is unknown.

107 Ferdinand Christian Baur, "Die Christuspartei in der korinthischen Gemeinde," *Tübinger Zeitschrift für Theologie* 5 (1831): 61–206; now in his *Ausgewählte Werke in Einzelausgaben*, ed. Klaus Scholder, vol. 1 (Stuttgart and Bad Canstatt; Frommann [Holzboog], 1963), 1–146.

108 The demand to abstain from sacrificial meat is, to be sure, fundamentally Jewish. But it would be Judaistic only if it were grounded upon the validity of the Mosaic Law for the Christian.

109 Wilhelm Lütgert, *Freiheitspredigt und Schwarmgeister in Korinth*, BFTh, 12, 3 (Gütersloh: Bertelsmann, 1908). Modified by Adolf Schlatter, *Die korinthische Theologie*, BFTh, 18, 2 (Gütersloh: Bertelsmann, 1914).

110 Richard Reitzenstein, *Die hellenistischen Mysterienreligionen*, (Leipzig: Teubner, ³1927) 75–79, 333–396, reprinted (Darmstadt: Wissenschaftliche Buchgesellschaft, 1967).

111 Walter Schmithals, *Gnosticism in Corinth*, tr. John E. Steely (New York and Nashville: Abingdon, 1971),

The view that Corinthian libertinism has its own specific content is correct. This is the result of its speculative foundation. Only there is no need of a fully developed Gnostic myth to account for it; nor are there any traces of such a myth in Corinth. We do not require this hypothesis to enable us to explain the text.

We have to make a methodical distinction between ideas and concepts which *in themselves* are Gnostic and those which may have been taken over by Gnosticism but were of earlier origin and arose in a totally different speculative context.[112] The concepts and motifs in 1 Corinthians belong without exception to the second group.

That there were no champions of a dualistic Christology in Corinth emerges from 15:1ff: faith's assertion that the death of Christ is an act of salvation is not called in question. On the contrary, it can be used by Paul as a universally accepted basis for his argument.

The position in Corinth cannot be reconstructed on the basis of the possibilities of the general history of religion. Certainty attaches only to what we can learn from the text. Hypotheses are admissible only so far as they are essential for the interpretation of the text. The question accordingly is: Does the obvious structural unity of the manifold phenomena—Christology, enthusiasm, sacramentalism, the catchwords of knowledge and freedom—require the acceptance of a mythological Gnostic system to make them understandable? The answer is in the negative. The unity is completely explained by the agreement between exaltation Christology and enthusiasm.

We are merely being superficial if in terms of historical causality we trace out external "influences" of syncretistic, Gnostic movements and seek to explain the developments in Corinth thereby. For of course with regard to these "influences" the counter-question must be asked at once: We have here to do with people who have only recently become Christians; what were the ideas they brought with them into the community? What effect has their Christian faith on these ideas? What course is now given to their previous thinking? And if indeed there are "influences," how are these possible on the basis of faith? How does the latter work as a principle of appropriation and selection? We have to bear in mind that of course it expresses itself in the thought-forms of the moment. Thus the act of "taking over" is an element that is given with faith itself. The decisive question is then that of the criteria. This is the question Paul addresses to the Corinthians.[113] Compared with it, the question of the thought material, and its more or less syncretistic or Gnostic character, is only a part of the foreground. Moreover, we must not seek to define this material too precisely. Ideas of Jewish and Greek origin (popular philosophy), such as could be picked up on the streets,[114] traditional views of Greek religion, products of the mysteries (initiations, ecstasies)—all these are present and cannot be neatly separated. There are also isolated traces of the beginnings of the formation of what later presented itself as "Gnosticism," that is, Gnosticism *in statu nascendi*. The Corinthians could be described as proto-Gnostics.[115]

When we attempt to follow out the situation in Corinth from the Pauline beginnings onward, we can detect a few clear lines of development. The first and most important factor[116] is the summing up of the "gospel" in the creed: Christ died and rose again. This formula can be interpreted in the sense that death is nullified, so to speak, and that faith has now to focus solely on the exalted Lord.[117] Faith then becomes the movement of spiritual ascent along with the Redeemer. This move-

---

377, n. 248 (to p. 207) [355 (n. to p. 195A)].

112 A prime example is the principle "like by like" (see on 2:10f); further, a statement like 2:9, or the correspondence between knowing and being known (8:2f).

113 Helmut Koester, "Paul and Hellenism," in *The Bible in Modern Scholarship*, ed. J. Philip Hyatt (New York and Nashville: Abingdon, 1965), 187–195: "It is not the occurrence of such terms, concepts, myths, and theological doctrines, but only the movement of interpretation of such traditional language, together with the quest for the criteria and for the direction of Paul's interpretation, that will inform us

about Paul's thought and about his understanding of Christian existence, even if he shares the theological terminology of his opponents" (193).

114 "The wise man is king." "To the wise man all things belong." "Knowledge makes free."

115 In many respects the findings are the same as in Philo.

116 Designated as such by Paul himself, 15:1–3.

117 An analogous possibility can be derived from the view of baptism as dying and rising again with Christ (Rom 6). The formula "Christ died and rose again" invites the establishing of a direct analogy between Christ and the believer: "We have died and risen

ment can find confirmation in experiences inaugurated in Corinth by Paul himself, experiences of the Spirit in an ecstasy in which the pneumatic is caught up out of the world into heaven. Then the Spirit is no longer the criterion and ἀρραβών, "guarantee," upholding me as a believer in the world and leading me here to a new way of life. Experience of the Spirit becomes experience of the self, and Christ becomes a cipher for this experience.

The catchwords "wisdom" and "freedom," which Paul had introduced, can also be felt to lead in the same direction. When understood in terms of the pneumatic experience of the self, the freedom of faith is transformed into a speculative principle whose purpose is to bring about the detachment of the pneumatic from the world.[118]

This transformation by which the faith that is related to the word is turned into spiritual experience of the self accounts for all the phenomena encountered in 1 Corinthians, as also for the way in which Paul enters the lists. He consistently opposes the movement of spiritual ascent and reverses the direction of thought, and thus uses his theology of the cross to bring out more clearly than in any other epistle the historic character of faith.

---

again with Christ." This Paul rules out by speaking of *our* resurrection consistently in the future tense. Col (2:9ff) and Eph (2:5ff) then use the aorist also of believers and thereby enter, formally speaking, into the immediate vicinity of enthusiasm (cf. 2 Tim 2:18). They then ward off the latter in their own way.

118 The direction in which the influence of Apollos led is at best a matter of conjecture.

1

The Opening

1 Paul, called to be an apostle of Christ Jesus[1] by the will of God,[2] and the brother Sosthenes, 2/ to the church of God that is in Corinth,[3] to those sanctified in Christ Jesus, those called to be saints,[4] together with all who call upon the name of our Lord Jesus Christ in every place, theirs and ours (or: their [Lord] and ours[5]): 3/ grace be with you and peace from God our Father and the Lord Jesus Christ.

The opening has the twofold form which Paul continually uses.[6] It is derived from the oriental epistolary formula, but has been developed further.[7] Regular parts are:

superscriptio, adscriptio, salutatio.

■ **1** After his name Paul regularly states his official position:[8] ἀπόστολος, "an apostle." For him this title is

---

1 The order "Christ Jesus" with p[46] B D G, against ℵ A and the majority of the MSS; see the exposition.

2 κλητός, "called," can be taken along with διὰ θελήματος θεοῦ, "by the will of God" (Kümmel); cf. Gal 1:15. But κλητὸς ἀπόστολος, "called to be an apostle," is a standard term (Rom 1:1), and διὰ θελήματος θεοῦ can replace κλητός (2 Cor 1:1). διὰ θελήματος θεοῦ will accordingly relate to the concept κλητὸς ἀπόστολος as a whole. In this very way the fact that A D delete κλητός can be explained as a simplification of the overloaded expression (see Lietzmann).

3 With τῇ οὔσῃ compare Acts 13:1, ἡ οὖσα ἐκκλησία, "the one there existent"; cf. also Acts 5:17; we have here a term taken from official language, see Edwin Mayser, *Grammatik der griechischen Papyri aus der Ptolomäerzeit*, vol. 2, pt. 1 (Berlin: de Gruyter, 1934), 347f. Paul does not make the same technical use of it as we find in Acts.

4 Lietzmann takes ἡγιασμένοις adjectivally; the saints sanctified and called. But "the sanctified" and "the saints" rather give the impression of being parallel expressions.

5 Schmiedel and Lietzmann favor the second rendering. But the listener would not pick up this connection; κυρίου ἡμῶν, "our Lord," is too far away.

6 Likewise also the other NT letters, with the exception of Jas and the two fictitious letters in Acts 15:23; 23:26, the latter addressed by a Roman officer to his superior; the form in *1 Cl.* and Pol. *Phil.* is also twofold. For the twofold form cf. Dan 4:1 Θ (=3:31 Aram.): Ναβουχοδονοσορ ὁ βασιλεὺς πᾶσι τοῖς λαοῖς, φυλαῖς καὶ γλώσσαις τοῖς οἰκοῦσιν ἐν πάσῃ τῇ γῇ· εἰρήνη ὑμῖν πληθυνθείη, "King Nebuchadnezzar to all peoples, nations, and languages, that dwell in all the earth: Peace be multiplied to you!" (cf. 1 and 2 Pet; *1 Cl.*). *S. Bar.* 78:2: "Thus saith

Baruch the son of Neriah to the brethren carried into captivity: 'Mercy [cf. 1 and 2 Tim; 2 Jn; Pol. *Phil.*] and peace'" (Charles, *APOT* 2:521). Literature: Hans Lietzmann, *An die Römer*, HNT, 8 (Tübingen: J. C. B. Mohr [Paul Siebeck], [4]1933), *ad* Rom 1:1; Wendland, *Literaturformen*, 411–417; Roller, *Formular*, 56–65, 78–85; Ernst Lohmeyer, "Probleme paulinischer Theologie: I. Briefliche Grüssüberschriften," *ZNW* 26 (1927): 158–173, now in his *Probleme paulinischer Theologie* (Stuttgart: Kohlhammer, n.d.), 7–29; the correction of the latter by Gerhard Friedrich, "Lohmeyers These über das paulinische Briefpräskript kritisch beleuchtet," *ThLZ* 81 (1956): 343–346; Otto Eissfeldt, *The Old Testament: An Introduction*, tr. Peter R. Ackroyd (Oxford: Blackwell; New York: Harper & Row, 1965), 22–24 (*Einleitung in das Alte Testament* [Tübingen: J. C. B. Mohr (Paul Siebeck), [3]1964], 29–31).

7 See the previous note. On the order of sender and receiver, see Godfrey R. Driver, *Aramaic Documents of the Fifth Century, B.C.* (Oxford: Clarendon, [2]1957), 41f. Examples of the naming of the receiver first are to be found in oriental and Greek letters: Murabba'at no. 48 (*DJD* 2:167f); *P. Oxy.* 246, in Deissmann, *Light*, 172f [139]. On the development of the oriental formula: originally the introductory formula is not a part of the letter at all, but a dictation formula (as indicated by K. Galling), cf. Driver, *Aramaic Documents*, 13f. (Letter III, 11.1f): "From 'Aršam to 'Artawant: I send thee much greetings of peace and prosperity." This characteristic of the letter introduction is still maintained down to Ben Kosba: Murabba'at nos. 42–44, 46 (*DJD* 2:155–166), of which nos. 43 and 44 are by Ben Kosba: מן...ל...שלום.

8 The detail in which he does so is unusual; see Roller, *Formular*, 57 (and n. 244 on pp. 431–433). The offi-

not yet restricted to the "Twelve" (that is, with the addition of Paul himself; see on 9:5 and 15:7). And it is linked not to the historical Jesus, but to the commission of the risen Lord,[9] and indeed to a specific act of calling. This immediacy in the relationship to God is a mark of freedom from any other commissioning body and underlines the authority of the apostolate.[10] The process of the calling (on the Damascus road) is merely indicated by the word κλητός, "called." It is never *recounted* by Paul.[11] The relation between God and Christ as the authors of the call is explained by Gal 1:1–5, 11–16: it takes place through Christ according to the will of God. It is for this reason that Paul is an apostle "of Christ Jesus." The fact that he points back from Christ to God as the original author is typical of his thinking (see on 3:23).

Christ and God are differentiated as persons. But their working is a perfect unity.

A fellow writer is mentioned by Paul elsewhere also.[12] The introduction of Sosthenes[13] as a "brother" accords with the customary designation used by the Christians for each other, but also hints at the distance between him and the "Apostle."[14] The word order "Christ Jesus" is found only in the genitive and after the preposition ἐν, "in," but not when the Kyrios title is also used.[15] There is no difference of meaning between "Jesus Christ" and "Christ Jesus."[16]

■ **2** The *adscriptio*. As in the *superscriptio*, so also here we have an abundance of definitions. On the text: in p⁴⁶ B D* G the words τῇ οὔσῃ ἐν Κορίνθῳ are placed after ἡγιασμένοις ἐν Χριστῷ Ἰησοῦ. This is to be re-

cial position is meant also in Phil 1:1, where Paul designates himself along with Timothy as δοῦλοι Χριστοῦ Ἰησοῦ, "slaves of Christ Jesus"; see the commentaries *ad loc.*

9 Hans von Campenhausen, "Der urchristliche Apostelbegriff," *StudTheol* 1 (1948): 96–130; also his *Ecclesiastical Authority and Spiritual Power in the Church of the First Three Centuries*, tr. John A. Baker (London: Black; Stanford: Stanford University Press, 1969), 30–54 [32–58]; on the concept in general see Lucien Cerfaux, "Pour l'histoire du titre *Apostolos* dans le Nouveau Testament," *RechSR* 48 (1960): 76–92, now in *Recueil Lucien Cerfaux. Études d'exégèse et d'histoire religieuse*, Bibliotheca Ephemeridum Theologicarum Lovaniensium, 6–7, 18 (Gembloux: Duculot, 1954–62), 3:185–207. Literature and surveys of research: E. M. Kredel, "Der Apostelbegriff in der neueren Exegese: Historisch–kritische Darstellung," *ZKTh* 78 (1956): 169–193, 257–305; Günter Klein, *Die zwölf Apostel: Ursprung und Gehalt einer Idee*, FRLANT, 77 (Göttingen: Vandenhoeck & Ruprecht, 1961) (against the derivation from the Jewish institution of *šaliᵃḥ*). The derivation from Gnosticism is impossible, contrary to Schmithals, *The Office of Apostle in the Early Church*, tr. John E. Steely (New York and Nashville: Abingdon, 1969); see on 15:9.

10 But also its limitations. These arise from the definition of the office in terms of the theology of the cross, a definition unfolded especially in 2 Cor; see Ernst Käsemann, "Die Legitimität des Apostels," *ZNW* 41 (1942): 33–71, now published separately in the series Libelli (Darmstadt: Wissenschaftliche Buchgesellschaft, 1956) and in *Paulusbild*, 475–521. The idea of office is constructed on the basis of the word–character of the saving event: there is a correspondence between καταλλαγή, λόγος τῆς καταλλα-

γῆς, and διακονία τῆς καταλλαγῆς, "reconciliation, message of reconciliation, and ministry of reconciliation" (2 Cor 5:18f). This connection is constitutive of the actualizing of the event of salvation in the church through preaching.

11 Unlike Acts. On the essential significance of Paul's calling for his self–understanding, see Bultmann, "Neueste Paulusforschung," *ThRund* n.s. 6 (1934): 229–246; Ulrich Wilckens, "Die Bekehrung des Paulus als religionsgeschichtliches Problem," *ZThK* 56 (1959): 273–293.

12 2 Cor; Phil; Phlm; 1 Thess (two). The fellow–writer is not a fellow–author; cf. the singular in v 4.

13 Timothy is not present, 4:17; 16:10. It is idle to speculate on the identity of Sosthenes with the Sosthenes of Acts 18:17. The name is widespread.

14 Only in Phil does Paul grant the fellow–writer the same title as himself, but there it is δοῦλοι, "slaves."

15 An exception is Rom 8:34 (text uncertain), perhaps 2 Cor 4:5 (text uncertain). For the word order see Lietzmann on Rom 1:1. He rightly observes that this word order still allows a glimpse of the fact that Χριστός, "Christ" = "anointed one," was originally an appellative.

16 Cerfaux, *Christ in the Theology of St. Paul*, tr. Geoffrey Webb and Adrian Walker (Freiburg and New York: Herder & Herder, 480–485 [361–381], seeks to distinguish between: (*a*) Jesus Christ, meaning Jesus whom the Father raised from the dead and for whom he secured recognition as Christ, and (*b*) Christ Jesus, meaning the preexistent Christ who manifested himself in the man Jesus. The interpretation is impossible for the simple reason that here Paul's use of the Christological titles is completely misunderstood; for the actual use made of them, see Werner Kramer, *Christ, Lord, Son of God*, tr. Brian Hardy, SBT, 1, 50 (London: SCM, 1966).

garded, with Lietzmann, as a long–established error on the part of the Western text, and one that arose in Egypt at an early stage. The transposition is stylistically intolerable. τῇ οὔσῃ . . . cannot be separated from ἐκκλησίᾳ (cf. 1 Thess 2:14). Certainly the original form also gives the impression of being overloaded (ἡγιασμένοις, "sanctified," alongside κλητοῖς ἁγίοις, "called to be saints"). Should ἡγιασμένοις ἐν Χριστῷ Ἰησοῦ, "sanctified in Christ Jesus," be deleted as a gloss, especially as the form ἡγιασμένοις is not found elsewhere in Paul?[17] In content, to be sure, the passage is good Pauline theology (cf. 6:11); it gives expression to the character of sanctification as being a matter of grace. Holiness is received, not achieved.

The phrase ἐν Χριστῷ Ἰησοῦ[18] is not to be understood in mystico–spatial terms ("in the pneumatic Christ" or "in the Christ–body"). ἐν can merge into the instrumental sense (διά). The expression refers to the objective work of salvation which God accomplishes "in Christ": "in" him he shows his love (Rom 8:39). 2 Cor 5:17ff can serve as a standard of reference: in Christ God has reconciled the world to himself. In Christ we are justified (cf. 2 Cor 5:21 with Rom 5:9 and 1 Cor 6:11).

The reference is accordingly to the Christ *extra nos*. The work of salvation is the presupposition for the converse statement that Christ is in us. The idea of reciprocality (he in me—I in him), in itself fully in accord with mystical thinking, is in Paul's case understood from first to last in terms of his *theologia crucis* and is governed by the concept of faith (Gal 2:19–21).[19] Our "being"[20] in Christ does not abrogate the eschatological proviso, the futurity of the resurrection (Rom 6:1–11).[21] The phrase can be applied to many situations and modes of conduct and used to characterize them as "Christian" or churchly.[22] In this context there are nuances in the use of the various Christological titles, without it being possible to detect any consistent schema.[23]

The choice of the word ἐκκλησία, "church,"[24] as the most important self–designation of the Christian community is usually traced back to the example of the Old Testament קָהָל.[25] This derivation, however, has

---

17 Weiss; Zuntz, *Text*, 91f.
18 Kramer, *Christ, Lord, Son of God*; Fritz Neugebauer, *In Christus* (Göttingen: Vandenhoeck & Ruprecht, 1961); Michel Bouttier, *En Christ*, Études d'histoire et de philosophie religieuses, 54 (Paris: Presses Universitaires de France, 1962).
19 Similarly, the parallel interchange, I in the Spirit—the Spirit in me (Rom 8:9), is not intended in a mystical sense.
20 The use of the verb εἶναι is of no significance.
21 This is brought out particularly clearly by a comparison with the phrase σὺν Χριστῷ (κυρίῳ), "with Christ [the Lord]." The sense of this expression is on the one hand eschatological (1 Thess 5:10) and on the other hand sacramental (Rom 6:1ff).
22 Paul has become the community's father in Christ, 4:15; our labor is not in vain in the Lord, 15:58; his imprisonment is made known in Christ, Phil 1:13. The churches which are in Christ are the "Christian" churches, 1 Thess 2:14; Gal 1:22. Specially characteristic of the wide area of application is Rom 16:1ff.
23 Fritz Neugebauer, *In Christus* (cf. his résumé, "Das paulinische 'in Christo,' " *NTS* 4 [1957–58]: 124–138), is all too schematic in positing the distinction: (*a*) ἐν Χριστῷ, "in Christ," is used in conjunction with concepts of salvation, with the church, or with

the apostles; (*b*) with ἐν κυρίῳ, "in the Lord," the prevailing idea is that of the createdness of man, both in the indicative and also in the imperative sense. But he must himself concede that there are exceptions: 1 Cor 7:22; Rom 16:11, 13. In Rom 16 no difference at all can be ascertained. Cf. further 1 Cor 9:1 with 4:15; Rom 9:1 with 14:14; cf. also the use with σύν, "with."
24 Literature: Bauer and *TDNT*, *s.v.* ἐκκλησία; Cerfaux, *The Church in the Theology of Saint Paul*, tr. Geoffrey Webb and Adrian Walker (New York: Herder & Herder, 1959); Bultmann, *Theology* 1:92–109, 306–314 [94–109, 306–315].
25 Leonhard Rost, *Die Vorstufen von Kirche und Synagoge im Alten Testament*, BWANT, 24 (Stuttgart: Kohlhammer, 1938).

recently been called in question on good grounds.[26] Either way, it is plain that the sense of the term is related to the realms of salvation history and especially of eschatology; ἐκκλησία belongs to the same context as other Christian self–designations like ἅγιοι, "saints," and ἐκλεκτοί, "elect."[27] These concepts characterize the Christians as the assembly of the saints of the last days. This is further underlined by the genitive τοῦ θεοῦ, "of God."[28] There has been much discussion of the question whether ἐκκλησία is primarily the individual congregation (as the assembled eschatological com-

munity) or the whole "church."[29] Paul uses the singular and the plural (11:16; 1 Thess 2:14), and accordingly employs the word for both.[30] The underlying idea here is that the church manifests itself in the individual congregation.[31]

κλητοῖς ἁγίοις, "called to be saints": the subject of their calling is not the Apostle, but God or Christ, cf. v 9; Rom 8:30; 9:24f. "Called" has the same eschatological sense as "holy,"[32] which in the Old Testament–Jewish tradition is a cultic–eschatological concept. The ethical significance is secondary.[33] Holiness is not a

---

26 Wolfgang Schrage, " 'Ekklesia' und 'Synagoge': Zum Ursprung des urchristlichen Kirchenbegriffs," *ZThK* 60 (1963): 178–202, asks why the Christians chose ἐκκλησία and not συναγωγή. This choice cannot be explained from the LXX, since there is there no essential difference between the two words, and since the LXX expression ἐκκλησία κυρίου is not found in the NT. Schrage thinks that in the light of the LXX συναγωγή would indeed have lain nearer to hand, since the word has eschatological significance in later passages: Isa 56:8 (J. Y. Campbell is also against a derivation from the LXX: "The Origin and Meaning of the Christian Use of the Word ΕΚΚΛΗΣΙΑ," *JThSt*, o.s. 49 [1948]: 130–142). An explanation with the help of the Qumran texts also fails: עדה could very well be rendered by συναγωγή. Schrage presumes that συναγωγή was too closely bound up with the Law, and that therefore the Jerusalem Hellenists chose ἐκκλησία for the very reason that it was a profane political term. It was from this quarter, he thinks, that it first gained entry into conservative Jewish Christianity (Mt). The source material, to be sure, is not sufficient to justify these conclusions. For example, we do find ἐκκλησία linked with criticism of the Law in Gal 1:12f; but this criticism has no connection with ἐκκλησία as a *concept*. And the linguistic usage of the Jerusalem Hellenists is unknown.

27 Werner Georg Kümmel, *Kirchenbegriff und Geschichtsbewusstsein in der Urgemeinde und bei Jesus*, SBU 1, (Zurich: Niehans; Uppsala: Seminarium Neotestamenticum Upsaliense, 1943), now reprinted (Göttingen: Vandenhoeck & Ruprecht, 1968), 16–19; Cerfaux, *Church*, 106–114 [90–97], according to whom ἐκκλησία means "les convoqués saints," the LXX κλητὴ ἁγία; see below, n. 32.

28 Cf. 10:32; 11:22; 15:9; Gal 1:13; τοῦ Χριστοῦ, Rom 16:16 (plural). For Paul's theology as a whole, to be sure, the definition of the church as ἐκκλησία is not sufficient. It is supplemented by describing it as the body of Christ; see on 10:14ff and 12:12ff.

29 Since the celebrated controversy between R. Sohm

and A. Harnack; Rudolf Sohm, *Kirchenrecht*, vol. 1, Systematisches Handbuch der deutschen Rechtswissenschaft, 8, 1 (Leipzig: Duncker & Humblot, 1892); Adolf von Harnack, *The Constitution and Law of the Church in the First Two Centuries*, tr. F. L. Pogson, ed. M. D. A. Major, Crown Theological Library, 31 (London: Williams & Norgate; New York: Putnam, 1910) (*Entstehung und Entwicklung der Kirchenverfassung und des Kirchenrechts in den ersten zwei Jahrhunderten* [Leipzig: Hinrichs, 1910]); Karl Holl, "Der Kirchenbegriff des Paulus in seinem Verhältnis zu dem der Urgemeinde," *SAB* 86 (1921): 920–947, now in his *Gesammelte Aufsätze zur Kirchengeschichte*, II: *Der Osten* (Tübingen: J. C. B. Mohr [Paul Siebeck], 1928), reprinted (Darmstadt: Wissenschaftliche Buchgesellschaft, 1965), 44–67, and in *Paulusbild*, 144–178; Bultmann, *Theology* 2:95–118 [446–470].

30 "Church": 6:4; 12:28; this meaning is disputed by Cerfaux (in reference to 11:16), *Church*, 113 [96]: "The Church of God is the organization in which the needy Christians are involved, and this is not the universal Church."

31 Karl Ludwig Schmidt, *TDNT* 3:506; Bultmann, *Theology* 1:92–108, 306–314 [94–109, 306–315]. But this sense cannot already be pressed out of the expression τῇ οὔσῃ . . ., "which is . . ."; the latter is harmless (cf. Phil 1:1).

32 Cf. 1:24. Called: 1QM IV, 10 קרואי אל, following קהל אל, "company of God"; CD IV, 4: those called by name (cf. also ἐκλεκτός, "chosen," as an eschatological term, Mk 13:20; Rom 8:33, etc.). Apocalyptic: *Eth. En.* 50:1; 100:5. There is a tendency to derive the expression κλητοὶ ἅγιοι from מקרא קדש, "holy convocation" (Exod 12:16, etc.); rendered in the LXX by κλητὴ ἁγία; see Otto Procksch, *TDNT* 1:107. It may be that this OT expression also plays a part. Yet we have to bear in mind both the independent significance which κλητός, "called," and ἅγιος, "holy," each have on their own, and also their close conjunction in eschatological Judaism.

33 "Holy" is applied in the OT to Israel as the chosen

quality of the individual, but a communal state in which we are placed by baptism. Paul never uses the word in the singular of the individual Christian.[34]

The "ecumenical" outlook in v 2b is felt by many expositors to be a difficulty. Weiss would delete it (along with 4:17; 7:17; 11:16; 14:33) as an interpolation. He holds that it derives from the editor of the *corpus Paulinum*, at the head of which 1 Corinthians originally stood, and that 2 Cor 1:1 has been drawn upon for it. But the expression must not be pressed, and we cannot argue that Paul surely could not write a greeting to all Christians. He is using a full–hearted expression in the sense of the idea of the universal church.[35] "Call upon the name of the Lord" is an expression from the (Greek) Old Testament.[36] The Christians reinterpret it in terms of the

$\kappa \acute{\upsilon} \rho \iota o s$ Jesus instead of $\kappa \acute{\upsilon} \rho \iota o s$ as Yahweh; it even becomes a technical expression for "Christians."[37] It shows how faith is understood, as acclamation addressed to the Lord (in the assembly). From this in turn it can be seen how the Kyrios title is understood.[38] The expansion of the greeting to all places[39] is explained by Lietzmann as deriving from Jewish liturgical custom.[40]

■ **3** The *salutatio* is ceremonious, in threefold form.[41] The basis is the Hebrew "peace" greeting (see notes 6, 7,

---

people: Exod 19:6, then to the "remnant": Isa 4:3; 62:12; cf. further Dan 7:18; 8:25; *1 Macc.* 1:46; 10:39; *Pss. Sol.* 17:26. The eschatological sense emerges in apocalyptic: *Eth. En.* 1:9 (the holy as heavenly beings); 48:7, etc., and in the Qumran scrolls: 1QM III, 5; VI, 6, etc.

34 The self–designation of Christians as $\mathring{\alpha} \gamma \iota o \iota$ can be traced back to the primitive church; cf. the application of the concept to the latter in Rom 15:25f; 1 Cor 16:1; 2 Cor 8:4; 9:1, 12. But it cannot be proved that the primitive church claimed the title for itself in an exclusive sense (with Kümmel, *Kirchenbegriff*, 16, against Holl).

35 Cf. the (admittedly more narrowly restricted) outlook in 2 Cor 1:1.

36 Ps 98:6 (99:6); Joel 3:5, taken up in Rom 10:13; Acts 2:21. The expression accordingly has its roots in Hellenistic–Jewish Christianity. For "calling upon" as acclamation, see the context of Rom 10:12f; Kramer, *Christ, Lord, Son of God*, 78f [74f]; Philipp Vielhauer, "Ein Weg zur neutestamentlichen Christologie?" *EvTh* 25 (1965): 24–72, now in his *Aufsätze zum Neuen Testament*, Theologische Bücherei, 31 (Munich: Kaiser, 1965), 141–198.

37 Acts 9:14, 21; 2 Tim 2:22.

38 It is the acclamation in divine worship that is in mind; see on 12:3. It should be noticed that this "calling upon" is not a prayer. The latter is directed in Paul exclusively to God. To the "Lord" he directs the cultic invocation, and also possibly personal requests (2 Cor 12:8); Bultmann, *Theology* 1:126–128 [128–130].

39 Ulrich Wickert, "Einheit und Eintracht der Kirche im Präskript des ersten Korintherbriefes," *ZNW* 50 (1959): 73–82, thinks he can dispose of the difficulty of v 2 by referring $\sigma \acute{\upsilon} \nu$, "with," not only to the Corinthians, but also to Paul and those about him.

Paul, he argues, is not extending the peace greeting to the rest of Christendom, but is telling the Corinthians that they have a share in the salvation which has been secured for all by Christ. This exposition ignores the wording. The difficulty remains.

40 On the basis of two synagogue inscriptions: Samuel Klein, *Jüdisch–palästinisches Corpus Inscriptionum* (Vienna: Löwit; 1920), 77f, no. 6 (= *CIJ* 2:159, no. 973): יהי שלום על המקום הזה ועל כל מקומות עמו ישראל, "May peace be in this place and in all the places of his people Israel" [Trans.] (from Alma, north of Safed). Klein, 78f, no. 8 (= *CIJ* 2:159f, no. 974): [יהי שלום ב]מקום הזה ובכל מקומות ישראל, "May peace be in this place and in all the places of Israel" [Trans.]. The fact that $\tau \acute{o} \pi o s$, "place," in Jewish usage can mean the house of worship is of no significance here. But we do have to note that the phrase $\grave{\epsilon} \nu \pi \alpha \nu \tau \grave{\iota} \tau \acute{o} \pi \omega$, "in every place," is more or less a set phrase, cf. 2 Cor 2:14; 1 Thess 1:8; 1 Tim 2:8; *Did.* 14:3 (quotation from Mal 1:11); Hans–Werner Bartsch, *Die Anfänge urchristlicher Rechtsbildung: Studien zu den Pastoralbriefen*, Theologische Forschung, 34 (Hamburg: Reich, 1965), 47–49. The phrase gives expression to an idea of the church that is governed by world mission. The linguistic difficulty of the passage cannot be denied, but there is no difficulty of content if the wording is not pressed.

41 Yet the absence of the article cannot, as Lohmeyer thinks, be taken to be a mark of liturgical style; see Friedrich, "Lohmeyers These," and cf. 16:23.

40)[42] to which Paul regularly adds his "grace" wish.[43] This gives the greeting a specifically Christian sense, since χάρις, "grace," is naturally meant to be understood on the analogy of the common, clearly defined Pauline sense of this word; indeed it is taken up again at once in the very next verse.[44] χάρις and εἰρήνη, "grace and peace," together describe the state of salvation as such, firstly as an eschatological state (Rom 5:1ff), and secondly as a pure gift. God and the "Lord" are not merely the once–for–all authors of this state, but continually remain the givers of it. This indeed is already implied in the way the blessing is constantly repeated anew. "Father" is a widespread title for God.[45] Christianity of course takes it over from the Old Testament and Judaism:[46] God is the Creator and Preserver, the Protector of his people ("Son"). The Father and the Lord Jesus stand side by side as the bestowers of salvation. We should not translate "From God, our Father and the Father of the Lord Jesus Christ," but "From God, our Father, and from the Lord Jesus Christ" (cf. 1 Thess 1:1; 3:11). Certainly, Paul can also describe God as the Father of Jesus Christ (2 Cor 1:3). This juxtaposition reflects his Christology; it is a case of "theoretical" subordination and "practical" cooperation. Since the Lord is nothing other than the one who accomplishes the saving work of the Father, the two are a unity from the standpoint of salvation and faith; hence they can be coordinated by the simple word "and" (cf. also 8:6).[47]

---

42 שָׁלוֹם is primarily *well–being*, in the first instance material well–being, whereas in Greek εἰρήνη primarily means rest. In the NT the idea of peace is related, following the Jewish example, to the relationship between God and man (or the world). This means the preservation of the original note, that peace is thought of objectively, i.e., not as "inward" peace of the soul, but as the *state* of peace declared by God (Lk 2:14); it is only from this standpoint that it is then also related to the inner life (Rom 15:13); cf. the expression, "the peace of God," Phil 4:7; God is the God of peace, Rom 15:33; 16:20; 2 Cor 13:11; Phil 4:9; 1 Thess 5:23. εἰρήνη can sum up the whole content of the "gospel": Rom 5:1; Eph 2:17. On the Hebrew peace greeting, see Irene Lande, *Formelhafte Wendungen der Umgangssprache im Alten Testament* (Leiden: Brill, 1949), 3–9.

43 Since χάρις, "grace," is a word that is characteristic of the language of Paul, we can assume that it was he who introduced it into the formula of greeting, perhaps as a substitute for ἔλεος, "mercy" (see above, n. 6) and with an outward ring of the Greek χαίρειν, "greet."

44 χάρις is favor, bestowed as a *gift*, radiated as *charm*, and on the other hand, the *favor* received, the *gift* that is reciprocated in the form of *gratitude*. The LXX uses χάρις, etc. to render the word group חנן (not חסד: "ἔλεος"). Paul takes his bearings not on attributes of God, but on the saving work of Christ. Thus God's χάρις is not his gracious disposition, but the act of grace shown in Christ (Rom 3:24). Gillis Petersson Wetter, *Charis: Ein Beitrag zur Geschichte des ältesten Christentums*, UNT, 5 (Leipzig: Hinrichs, 1913); James Moffatt, *Grace in the New Testament* (London: Hodder & Stoughton, 1931); Joseph Wobbe, *Der Charis–Gedanke bei Paulus*, NtlAbh, 13, 3 (Münster: Aschendorff, 1932); Bultmann, *Theology* 1:288–292 [287–292].

45 Zeus is the "father of men and gods"; Jup–piter.

46 Gottlob Schrenk, *TDNT* 5:1006–1010.

47 The fact that "our" stands only with God is of little significance from the point of view of content; acoustic reasons were probably decisive; cf. 1 Thess 3:11.

1   The Proemium (Thanksgiving)

4   I thank (my)[1] God always on your behalf
for the grace of God,[2] which has been
bestowed upon you in Christ Jesus,
5/ that[3] in everything you have been
made rich in him,[4] in all eloquence and
in all knowledge; 6/ for indeed[5] the
testimony of Christ[6] has been confirmed
in you,[7] 7/ so that you are lacking in
no gift of grace, while you await the
revelation of our Lord Jesus Christ,
8/ who will also confirm you to the end
(that you may be)[8] without reproach on
the day of our Lord Jesus (Christ).[9]
9/ God is faithful, by whom you were
called into fellowship[10] with his Son
Jesus Christ, our Lord.

■ **4** The "proemium" is, following the profane epistolary style, an established element at the beginning of Paul's epistles.[11] This thanksgiving already belongs (again as in profane letters) to the "context"; it can even introduce the main theme.[12] Although it is adapted to the receiver and the peculiar content of the letter, it has fairly constant structure.[13] And its style is not that of simple communication, but of solemnly formulated prayer of a Jewish type. The latter is already evidenced in the use of the catchword εὐχαριστεῖν, "to thank."[14] The "individual" element lies in the way the tone consciously mounts to the climax at the end, vv 8f.

---

1   μου om. B ℵ*. For μου cf. Rom 1:8; Phil 1:3; Phlm 4.

2   εὐχαριστεῖν is constructed with περί, 1 Thess 1:2; Philo (person and thing in one) *Spec. leg.* 1.211; with ἐπί and dative (of the thing) Philo. *Spec. leg.* 1.67; Jos., *Ant.* 1.193; inscriptions; papyri; Paul, Phil 1:3, 5; Preisigke, *Sammelbuch*, no. 7172, line 25: εὐχαριστῶν τοῖς θεοῖς ἐπὶ τῷ συντελέσαι αὐτοὺς ἃ ἐπηγγείλαντο αὐτῷ, "giving thanks to the gods for their fulfillment of the things which were promised to him"; with ὑπέρ, 2 Cor 1:11.

3   ὅτι gives the explanation, not the reason (against Héring): "for the fact that," see Bauer *s.v.*; Rom 1:8, cf. Ps.–Callisth., *Hist. Alex. Magn.* 2.22.11, and see note 13 below.

4   Cf. 2 Cor 9:11. A significant wordplay with πᾶς.

5   Cf. 5:7; Bauer, *s.v.*; Blass–Debrunner §453(2).

6   One should not read θεοῦ, "of God" (as in B* G), see Zuntz, *Text*, 101f; see on 2:1.

7   That is, "in your midst."

8   Brevity of speech, cf. 1 Thess 3:12; 5:23; Phil 3:21; Winer, *Grammatik*, 579f; Winer–M.[3], 778f.

9   Χριστοῦ om. p[46] B.

10   Or: "participation in . . . ."

11   The sole exception—for which there is a reason—is Gal. The connection with the ancient epistolary custom is shown by Wendland, *Literaturformen*, 213f.

12   Paul Schubert, *Form and Function of the Pauline Thanks-*

givings, BZNW, 20 (Berlin: Töpelmann, 1939), shows that the proemium in Paul represents an independent part of the information contained in the letter, particularly marked in 1 Thess, where it merges with the body of the letter.

13   *Ibid.* Types are: (*a*) εὐχαριστῶ, then one or more participles, a final clause or final infinitive; 1 Thess 1:22ff; Phil 1:2ff; Phlm 4ff; (*b*) (as here) εὐχαριστῶ . . . ὅτι and a consecutive clause; 2 Thess 1:3f. Cf. the celebrated letter of Apion (*BGU* 2:423); Deissmann, *Light*, 179–183 [145–150]; Hans Lietzmann, *Griechische Papyri*, KIT, 14 (Bonn: Marcus & Weber, ²1910, 4f, no. 1): Ἀπίων Ἐπιμάχῳ τῶι πατρὶ καὶ / κυρίῳ πλεῖστα χαίρειν. Πρὸ μὲν πάν / των εὔχομαί σε ὑγιαίνειν καὶ διὰ παντὸς / ἐρωμένον εὐτυχεῖν μετὰ τῆς ἀδελφῆς / μου καὶ τῆς θυγατρὸς αὐτῆς καὶ τοῦ ἀδελφοῦ / μου. Εὐχαριστῶ τῷ κυρίῳ Σεράπιδι, ὅτι μου κινδυνεύσαντος εἰς θαλάσσαν / ἔσωσε εὐθέως, "Apion to Epimachus his father and lord many greetings. Before all things I pray that thou art in health, and that thou dost prosper and fare well continually together with my sister and her daughter and my brother. I thank the lord Serapis that, when I was in peril in the sea, he saved me immediately" (Deissmann, *Light*, 180).

14   Or εὐλογητός (thus 2 Cor 1:3; Eph 1:3; 1 Pet 1:3). On the forms of the "eucharistia" or "eulogy" (with an oversharp distinction between them), see Nils A.

The object for which thanks is given is introduced by the word $\pi\epsilon\rho\acute{\iota}$[15] and explained by $\ddot{o}\tau\iota$.[16] $\dot{\epsilon}\pi\acute{\iota}$ indicates the reason.

The assurance that he gives thanks incessantly ($\pi\acute{\alpha}\nu\tau o\tau\epsilon$), is typical of proemia.[17] The receiver of the prayer is God, not the "Lord."[18] This phraseology, which in itself gives the impression of being a mere form, is used by Paul to construct a living bond between the Apostle and the community.

The character of $\chi\acute{\alpha}\rho\iota\varsigma$, "grace," as a free gift is underlined by adding the passive of $\delta\iota\delta\acute{o}\nu\alpha\iota$, "to bestow." Paul is fond of doing this, both when he is speaking of what is given to the community (2 Cor 8:1; Rom 12:6), and also when he is speaking of "his own" special grace, his apostolic office (3:10; Gal 2:9; Rom 12:3; 15:15). $\dot{\epsilon}\nu$ $X\rho\iota\sigma\tau\hat{\omega}$ $^{\prime}I\eta\sigma o\hat{\upsilon}$, "in Christ Jesus," has to be taken with $\delta o\theta\epsilon\hat{\iota}\sigma\alpha\nu$, "bestowed":[19] God has instituted and at the same time transmitted his grace "in Christ Jesus."[20] The idea becomes understandable when we

hold to the nonmystical sense of the phraseology: it is the Christ *extra nos* who is meant. This is confirmed by v 5.

■ 5 This verse describes the significance of grace. Paul's concern is not to give an exhaustive definition of the concept, but as the following verses show, to illustrate it by means of the concrete gifts of grace which are manifest in the community. He gives a first pointer here to the nature and intensity of community life in Corinth;[21] and this pointer is a clue to the tone and content of the whole letter: $\dot{\epsilon}\pi\lambda o\upsilon\tau\acute{\iota}\sigma\theta\eta\tau\epsilon$, "you have been made rich."[22] The addition of $\dot{\epsilon}\nu$ $\alpha\dot{\upsilon}\tau\hat{\omega}$, "in him," has the critical intention of warding off any self–contemplation in the mirror of their own riches.[23] $\dot{\epsilon}\nu$ $\pi\alpha\nu\tau\acute{\iota}$, "in everything," naturally must not be pressed; the practice of speaking in general terms of this sort is widespread.[24] The concrete content of such a $\pi\hat{\alpha}\varsigma$, "everything," is provided by the context, in this case by the reference to the $\chi\alpha\rho\acute{\iota}\sigma\mu\alpha\tau\alpha$, "gifts of grace" (Phil 4:6, 12; 1 Thess 5:18). Illustrative material is provided above all by chaps.

Dahl, "Adresse und Proömium des Epheserbriefes," *ThZ* 7 (1951): 241–264. The meaning, "give thanks," for $\epsilon\dot{\upsilon}\chi\alpha\rho\iota\sigma\tau\epsilon\hat{\iota}\nu$ is Hellenistic (since Polybius; for evidence, see Bauer and *TDNT*, *s.v.*; Epict., *Diss.* 1.4.22, 10.3; 2.23.5 [$\dot{\upsilon}\pi\acute{\epsilon}\rho$]; LXX: Jdt 8:25; *2 Macc.* 1:11; *3 Macc.* 7:16). The style of the thanksgiving is that of Jewish liturgy. Schubert has to be modified accordingly. He rightly declares the proemium to be a Hellenistic, non–Jewish stylistic form. But the execution in Paul follows the Jewish style of prayer. See Elias Bickerman, "Bénédiction et prière," *RB* 69 (1962): 524–532; James M. Robinson, "Die Hodajot–Formel in Gebet und Hymnus des Urchristentums," in *Apophoreta: Festschrift Ernst Haenchen*, ed. Walter Eltester and F. H. Kettler, BZNW, 30 (Berlin: Töpelmann, 1964), 194–235; here evidence is given for the Jewish liturgical use of $\epsilon\dot{\upsilon}\chi\alpha\rho\iota\sigma\tau\epsilon\hat{\iota}\nu$ (see also on 14:16): *Const. Ap.* 7.30.1: $\epsilon\dot{\upsilon}\chi\alpha\rho\iota\sigma\tau o\hat{\upsilon}\nu\tau\epsilon\varsigma$ $\tau\hat{\omega}$ $\theta\epsilon\hat{\omega}$ $\kappa\alpha\grave{\iota}$ $\dot{\epsilon}\xi o\mu o\lambda o\gamma o\acute{\upsilon}\mu\epsilon\nu o\iota$ $\dot{\epsilon}\phi^{\prime}$ $o\hat{\iota}\varsigma$ $\epsilon\dot{\upsilon}\eta\rho\gamma\acute{\epsilon}\tau\eta\sigma\epsilon\nu$ $\dot{\eta}\mu\hat{\alpha}\varsigma$ $\dot{o}$ $\theta\epsilon\acute{o}\varsigma$, "giving thanks to God, and praising Him for those mercies God has bestowed upon [us]" (ANF 7:741). *Ibid.* 7.38.4: $\pi\epsilon\rho\grave{\iota}$ $\pi\acute{\alpha}\nu\tau\omega\nu$ $\sigma o\iota$ $\delta\iota\grave{\alpha}$ $X\rho\iota\sigma\tau o\hat{\upsilon}$ $\epsilon\dot{\upsilon}\chi\alpha\rho\iota\sigma\tau o\hat{\upsilon}\mu\epsilon\nu$, $\dot{o}$ $\kappa\alpha\grave{\iota}$ $\phi\omega\nu\grave{\eta}\nu$ $\acute{\epsilon}\nu\alpha\rho\theta\rho o\nu$ $\epsilon\dot{\iota}\varsigma$ $\dot{\epsilon}\xi o\mu o\lambda\acute{o}\gamma\eta\sigma\iota\nu$ $\delta\omega\rho\eta\sigma\acute{\alpha}\mu\epsilon\nu o\varsigma$, "For all which things we give thee thanks through Christ, who has given us an articulate voice to confess withal" (ANF 7:745).

15 See above, n. 2.

16 Rom 1:8, cf. Ps.–Callisth., *Hist. Alex. Magn.* 2.22.11.

17 Cf. typical clichés in proemia such as $\dot{\epsilon}\nu$ $\pi\alpha\nu\tau\grave{\iota}$ $\kappa\alpha\iota\rho\hat{\omega}$, $\dot{\alpha}\delta\iota\alpha\lambda\epsilon\acute{\iota}\pi\tau\omega\varsigma$, $\delta\iota\grave{\alpha}$ $\pi\alpha\nu\tau\acute{o}\varsigma$, "at all times, incessantly, always"; 1 Thess 1:2f; Rom 1:9; Phil

1:3f; Col 1:3; Evald Lövestam, *Spiritual Wakefulness in the New Testament*, Lunds Universitets Årsskrift, n.s. 1, 55, 3 (Lund: Gleerup, 1963), 72.

18 See above, 37, n. 38.

19 Not with $\dot{\upsilon}\mu\hat{\iota}\nu$ ("to you, insofar as you are in Christ").

20 For $\dot{\epsilon}\nu$ cf. 15:22; 2 Cor 1:18ff.

21 We may speak of the community's *experience*, yet we must maintain in so doing that experience is no criterion for the evaluation of spiritual gifts, but is subject to the criterion "in Christ"; cf. comment on 12:3. The passive form of expression also points in the same direction: $\dot{\epsilon}\pi\lambda o\upsilon\tau\acute{\iota}\sigma\theta\eta\tau\epsilon$, "you have been made rich." Paul does not invite them to observe themselves, but to render thanks to the Giver; see the criticism of the Corinthians' "riches" in 4:8.

22 There is a specifically religious use of the word group $\pi\lambda o\upsilon\tau$-: God is rich and bestows of his riches, Rom 2:4; 11:33; Phil 4:19; see on 4:8.

23 By way of commentary, cf. 2 Cor 8:9.

24 3:21: "All things are yours." 2 Cor 7:11, 16; 8:7; 9:8, 11; Mt 11:27; Acts 17:23ff: God, who has made all things, gives all things to us all. The motif is of course transformable according to the particular context. For a philosophical use of it, see on 3:21. It is developed pantheistically in *Corp. Herm.* 5.10.

12—14. From the abundance of χαρίσματα (12:4ff), two that are especially significant for the spiritual condition of the Corinthians and are later to be discussed in critical terms (e.g., 8:1ff) are here singled out: λόγος, "eloquence," and γνῶσις, "knowledge" (cf. 12:8; 13:1f, 8f; 2 Cor 8:7; 11:6; in a different sense 4:19f).[25] The question is of supernatural gifts, not the superelevation of natural ones.[26]

■ 6 καθώς, "for indeed":[27] Paul continues to indicate criteria for the evaluation of pneumatic phenomena and these, moreover, not psychological, but objective: the gospel by which the community is grounded. Its content is indicated by the objective genitive τοῦ Χριστοῦ, "of Christ."[28] The content will be more precisely described later, 2:1ff. ἐβεβαιώθη, "has been confirmed," is a Hellenistic form of expression[29] that has an eye to the founding and development of the community, again in a way that brings out the objectivity of the factors comprising its life; ἐν ὑμῖν does not mean "in your

hearts," but "in your midst" (cf. Phil 1:6). This kind of retrospect belongs to the established motifs of the proemia (1 Thess 1:2ff; Phil 1:3ff).

■ 7 Verse 7 repeats v 5 in a negative form. ὥστε κτλ., "so that, etc.,"[30] expresses the result of "grace" (i.e., the actual condition of the community); the conjunction must not be referred in a restrictive sense to v 5 or to v 6. ὑστερεῖσθαι means either "to suffer lack" or (in a comparative sense) "to come behind." In the former sense we should expect a genitive. The word ἐν also favors the second meaning, for which cf. 2 Cor 11:9; Phil 4:12.[31] Nevertheless, the first interpretation is to be preferred. For the intention is not to make comparison with other communities, but to point out the riches of the

25   Barth, *Resurrection*, 13f [2f], recognizes the critical sense: ". . . utterance [λόγος] and knowledge [γνῶσις] and spiritual gifts [χαρίσματα] are to him [sc. Paul] manifestly no ends in themselves, religious vitality itself no guarantee for Christian severity that, blameless [ἀνέγκλητος], awaits the end (i. 7–8)." The criticism is for the moment only hinted at by ἐν αὐτῷ, "in him," by the reference to the parousia (see above), and by the use of the passive.

26   Thus Philipp Bachmann, *Der erste Brief des Paulus an die Korinther*, with additions by Ethelbert Stauffer, KNT (Zahn), 7 (Leipzig and Erlangen: Deichert, ⁴1936), ad loc.: "In this [sc. Greek] variety of nature the Spirit of God set his seeds." There is no trace of irony (against Allo): what is criticized is not the gifts, but the Corinthians' management of them. Lietzmann places the accent wrongly when he says that Paul mentions "only" intellectual and charismatic (sic!) excellences, and that he expects moral perfection only from the future. Perfection ("irreproachableness") is a gift, not the result of their achievement. It is bestowed upon them already; but it comes to light only in the future: 4:5; Phil 1:10f. The content of λόγος and γνῶσις must for the moment be left in the indefiniteness which here surrounds the two words as being so far only hints; see later on 8:1ff; 12:8.

27   Cf. 5:7; Bauer, s.v.; Blass–Debrunner §453(2); the word must not (following Rom 12:6) be taken in the narrow sense: "To the extent that. . . ." Weiss says: "as indeed," and believes Paul is appealing to the experience that their testimony is confirmed by the

     conferring of λόγος and γνῶσις. Normal usage and the tenor of the passage are against this; see Bachmann, who rightly points to the aorist tense.

28   τοῦ θεοῦ B* G is secondary; see on 2:1.

29   *Inschr. Priene*, no. 123, line 9: ἐβεβαίωσεν τὴν ἐπαγγελίαν, "he fulfilled the promise"; Philo, *Conf. ling.* 197. Heinrich Schlier, *TDNT* 1:602f, would understand the word in the widespread juridical sense of the term: the gospel has been validly declared. But the wording does not invite this narrow view. βεβαιοῦν can be linked with juridical and soteriological terms: 2 Cor 1:21, see Hans Windisch, *Der zweite Korintherbrief*, KEK, 6 (Göttingen: Vandenhoeck & Ruprecht, ⁹1924), ad loc.; Erich Dinkler, "Die Taufterminologie in 2 Kor. 1 21f," in *Neotestamentica et Patristica: Eine Freundesgabe Herrn Professor Dr. Oscar Cullmann zu seinem 60. Geburtstag überreicht*, SNT, 6 (Leiden: Brill, 1962), 173–191, here esp. 177–180, now in his *Signum Crucis: Aufsätze zum Neuen Testament und zur christlichen Archäologie* (Tübingen: J. C. B. Mohr [Paul Siebeck], 1967), 99–117, here esp. 102–105; cf. Rom 15:8; Phil 1:7; Heb 2:3; 6:16; 9:17.

30   On the ὥστε clauses in proemia, see above, n. 13 (P. Schubert). ὥστε is not final (against Allo, who reads irony into the preceding remark and must now shift the statement in v 7 into the future).

31   Schlatter, ad loc., with reference to 2 Cor 11:5. Plato, *Resp.* 484d: μηδ' ἐν ἄλλῳ μηδενὶ μέρει ἀρετῆς ὑστεροῦντας, "[those who] are not second to them in any part of virtue" (Loeb 2:5).

Corinthian community; it has been given "everything," it lacks nothing, i.e., no χάρισμα, "gift of grace."[32]

With seeming abruptness Paul now passes over to an eschatological outlook.[33] But this, too, is proemium style (Philippians). It gives expression to his idea of the church: the present working of the Spirit in the community is a foretoken of the future. At the same time the reference to the latter points to a limit; the possession of χαρίσματα is not yet the realization of the eschaton, but an earnest of what *will be*. The age of the Spirit is still the age of expectation—to be sure accompanied by positive signs of the working of divine powers. The word ἀποκάλυψις, "revelation," is not used elsewhere by Paul of the parousia of Jesus.[34] On the other hand, he does link the title Kyrios with it.[35] In view of the indications provided by χάρις/χαρίσματα/πλοῦτος, we look forward to it not in neutral "waiting," but in positive hope.[36]

■ **8** The end of v 7 is repeated at the end of v 8, to which

Weiss takes exception. ὅς κτλ., "who, etc.": the βε-βαιῶν, "confirmer," is God (cf. 2 Cor 1:21 and v 9).[37] καί following the relative is not to be translated.[38] Paul is expressing not a wish but a certainty, as in the proemium of Philippians (1:6).[39] The (future) destiny of the community is assessed from the standpoint of the parousia.[40] ἕως τέλους in this context must mean "to the end of the world."[41] ἐν τῇ ἡμέρᾳ, "on the day": the correct form would be εἰς . . . (Lietzmann).[42] "Day of the Lord" is an eschatological expression derived from the Old Testament ("day of Yahweh"[43] is ἡμέρα κυρίου; κύριος is reinterpreted to apply to Jesus). ἀνέγκλητος, "without reproach": the form of expression is in keeping with the forensic style of eschatology; the day of the Lord brings the judgment.[44] Their blamelessness becomes manifest to believers only in the judgment, through the verdict of the judge. It is not an object for reflection in the present.

---

32 For χάρισμα, see on 12:4ff. Weiss rightly observes that ἐν, "in," carries on the force of the ἐν παντί, "in everything," v. 5.

33 ἀπεκδέχεσθαι, "await," means the whole of their attitude to the future, and therewith the believing attitude as such. The transition of thought is in reality not so abrupt as appears at first sight; faith is understood to be eschatological through and through, and the expectation prevails that the Lord is near. ἀπεκδέχεσθαι has eschatological significance throughout the NT: Rom 8:19, 23, 25; Gal 5:5; Phil 3:20; 1 Pet 3:20.

34 So also in 2 Thess 1:7.

35 Phil 3:20; 4:5. The link is already given him in the cry "maranatha"; see on 16:22.

36 John Albert Bengel, *Gnomon of the New Testament*, tr. Charlton T. Lewis and Marvin R. Vincent (Philadelphia: Perkinpine & Higgins; New York: Sheldon, 1864), 2:167 (*Gnomon Novi Testamenti* [Stuttgart: Steinkopf, ⁸1887]): "The test of the true or false Christian is his waiting for, or dreading the revelation of Christ."

37 Not so Gerhard Friedrich, "Christus, Einheit und Norm der Christen: das Grundmotiv des 1. Korintherbriefes," *KuD* 9 (1963): 235–258, esp. 239f, who sees a Christological concentration throughout and accordingly interprets the word as referring to Christ.

38 See Ernst Haenchen, *The Acts of the Apostles*, tr. ed. Robert McL. Wilson (Oxford: Blackwell; Philadelphia: Westminster, 1971), 140, n. 8 (*Die Apostelgeschichte*, KEK, 3 [Göttingen: Vandenhoeck &

Ruprecht, ¹⁰1965], 108, n. 6).

39 Cf. 2 Cor 1:21 and στηρίζειν, "strengthen," in Rom 1:11f; on the content see also 1 Thess 3:2, 13.

40 For the prospect, see Phil 1:6, 10. There we see how Paul himself is included in the expectation: he must use his work to give an account of himself in the judgment.

41 D G: ἄχρι; p⁴⁶: τελείους; on this see Zuntz, *Text*, 20: from a (substantially correct) gloss τελείως? ἕως τέλους: Dan 6:27 Θ; cf. 2 Cor 1:3, where Bauer (*s.v.*) and Windisch (*Der zweite Korintherbrief, ad loc.*) take it eschatologically, whereas Lietzmann renders it "perfect"; here, on the other hand, Lietzmann likewise supports the eschatological view.

42 In Phil 1:10, on the other hand, ἐν would be more appropriate.

43 Amos 5:18ff; Joel 3:4 = Acts 2:20; see on 3:13; 4:5.

44 Paul can speak of the βῆμα, "judgment seat," both of Christ (2 Cor 5:10) and also of God (Rom 14:10; variant reading Χριστοῦ); for the content see Rom 2:5. The style is again typical of the proemium, cf. ἀπρόσκοποι, "blameless," Phil 1:10, also 1 Thess 3:13; 5:23; Col 1:22.

■ **9** Is the play on ἐκλήθητε, "you were called," and ἀνεγκλήτους, "without reproach," intentional? For πιστὸς ὁ θεός, "God is faithful," cf. 10:13; 1 Thess 5:24; Ps 144:13a.[45] διά, "by (whom)," here of course denotes not the mediator but the author (cf. v 1).[46] The passive form (in the aorist) is still maintained. The understanding of our fellowship with Christ is also determined by the idea of calling. It is not understood as an experience of mystical communion, but in terms of belonging to the Lord until his parousia.[47] The reason why the title "Son" is employed at this point can be seen from 1 Thess 1:10; Gal 4:1ff; Rom 8:29.[48]

45 Jack T. Sanders, "The Transition from Opening Epistolary Thanksgiving to Body in the Letters of the Pauline Corpus," *JBL* 81 (1962): 348–362, esp. 358f, sees in the phrase a rendering of the Jewish berakah (elsewhere εὐλογητός, 2 Cor 1:3). Willem C. van Unnik, "Reisepläne und Amen–Sagen, Zusammenhang und Gedankenfolge in 2. Korinther 1:15–24," in *Studia Paulina in honorem Johannis de Zwaan septuagenarii* (Haarlem: Bohn, 1953), 215–234, esp. 221, points to the benediction, האל הנאמן האמר ועושה, "O faithful God, who say and do." Cf. 1 Thess 5:24.

46 For this reason διά is partly replaced in the MSS by ὑπό (D * G). For evidence see Bauer, *s.v.* διά, A III 2 b β; cf. 2 Cor 1:1; 8:5; Gal 1:4; 4:7. God as the one who calls: 7:15ff; Gal 5:8; Phil 3:14; 1 Thess 2:12; 4:7; 5:24; Rom 8:30; 9:12, 24; 11:29.

47 Sacramental participation in the Lord (see 10:16) is not thought of in this passage.

48 On the link between the proemium and the letter, cf. Sanders, "Transition"; Terence Y. Mullins, "Disclosure: A Literary Form in the New Testament," *NovTest* 7 (1964–65): 44–50

This part of the letter is not a unity, neither in style nor in content. But a compact piece of theology does emerge from behind the manifold individual topics.

The correspondence begins with 1:10. Now of course the whole letter is concerned with topical subjects which had arisen in Corinth or been put to Paul in the form of inquiries. Compared to these, however, this first part again forms an exception, because Paul must first of all make the Corinthians aware of pertinent questions that are posed by their party system. A preliminary survey is provided by the section 1:10–17. Here the tone is set by the opening word παρακαλῶ, "I beseech," with its contrast to the thanksgiving. Afterwards Paul goes far beyond the concrete occasion (from v 18 onward): he interprets the nature of the community in fundamental expositions of the content and form of the gospel. This is presented as the wisdom of God, which in the world appears as a paradox, in the form of what (according to worldly standards) is foolishness. With 2:6 the exposition passes over into the mystery style. From 3:1 onward Paul again addresses himself directly to the community. Again, even from the stylistic standpoint, high points are attained which go far beyond the occasion of the moment: 3:21–23; 4:8–13. In the end Paul returns to the paraenetic style, and thus rounds off this part of the epistle (4:14–21).

1

The Groups in the Community

10 But I beseech you, brothers, by the name
of our Lord Jesus Christ, all to be in
agreement with each other[1] and not to
have any divisions among you, but to
be perfectly united[2] in the same (single)
mind and in the same conviction. 11 / For
I have been told, (my)[3] brothers, by
Chloe's people, that there are quarrels
among you. 12 / What I mean is that each
of you says: I belong to Paul, I to
Apollos, I to Cephas, I to Christ.[4] 13 / Is
Christ divided? Was it Paul by any
chance who was crucified for you? Or
were you baptized in the name of Paul?
14 / I am thankful[5] that I baptized none
of you except Crispus and Gaius, 15 / so
that no one can say you were baptized
in my name. 16 / O yes, I did baptize
also the household of Stephanas. Apart
from that I cannot think of anyone else
that I baptized.[6] 17 / For Christ did not
send me to baptize, but to preach, and
not with wisdom of words, lest the
cross of Christ should be emptied of
meaning.[7]

■ **10** The emphatically "paraenetic" opening of the correspondence[8] does not conflict with its being addressed
to "brothers"; exhortation is a constitutive part of

---

1 On the use of ἵνα with the infinitive, see Blass–Debrunner §§389–395; with verbs of wishing, §392(1);
cf. 16:15f; 2 Cor 12:8. For τὸ αὐτὸ λέγειν, see Thuc.,
Hist. 5.31.6: Βοιωτοὶ δὲ καὶ Μεγαρῆς τὸ αὐτὸ λέγοντες ἡσύχαζον, "But the Boeotians and Mega-
rians, though holding the same views, kept quiet"
(Loeb 3:61); also the scholion thereto: τὴν αὐτὴν
γνώμην ἔχοντες, "having the same mind." *IG*
12.1.50, no. 149 (grave inscription): ταῦτα λέγοντες, ταὐτὰ φρονοῦντες ἤλθομεν τὰν ἀμέτρητον
ὁδὸν εἰς Ἀΐδαν, "Holding the same views and being
of the same mind, we have set out on the measure-
less way to Hades" [Trans.].

2 See Bauer, *s.v.* καταρτίζω. It is mistaken to render
σχίσμα as "breach" and καταρτίζω as "repair."

3 Om. p[46] C*.

4 The construction μέν ... δέ ... δέ shows that Paul
is writing from the standpoint of the reporter.

5 + τῷ θεῷ, "to God," C D G ℜ.

6 Bauer, *s.v.* οἶδα, 5, holds that the word takes on the
meaning, "I do not remember that . . ."; cf. Lucian,
Dial. Meretr. 1.1: οἶσθα αὐτὸν ἢ ἐπιλέλησαι τὸν
ἄνθρωπον;, "Do you know him, or have you forgotten the fellow?" (Loeb 7:357). Christoph Burchard, "Εἰ nach einem Ausdruck des Wissens oder
Nichtwissens Joh 9:25, Act 19:2, 1 Cor 1:16, 7:16,"
ZNW 52 (1961): 73–82, esp. 81f, renders: "For the

rest, I wouldn't be knowing that. . . ." For εἰ =
"that," see on 7:16.

7 τοῦ Χριστοῦ, "of Christ," is not to be taken as a
title, despite the article. The use of the article is occasioned by ὁ σταυρός, "the cross"; cf. also the use of
the article with Ἰησοῦς, "Jesus," in 2 Cor 4:10f.
For the use of Χριστός, see on 15:3ff.

8 For παρακαλῶ, "I beseech," as a key-word of paraenesis, cf. Rom 12:1. On παρακαλεῖν in letters,
see T. Y. Mullins, "Petition as a Literary Form,"
NovTest 5 (1962): 46–54; "Disclosure," *NovTest* 7
(1964–65): 44–50; Carl J. Bjerkelund, *Parakalô:
Form, Funktion und Sinn der parakalô–Sätze in den paulinischen Briefen*, Bibliotheca theologica Norvegica, 1
(Oslo: Universitetsforlaget, 1967). παρακαλῶ,
ἐρωτῶ, καλῶς ἂν ποιήσαις, "I beseech, I request,
please . . .," belong to private style; δέομαι, ἀξιῶ,
"I beg, I pray," to official style (letters to authorities), *ibid.*, 43. παρακαλεῖν in letters of recommendation, *P. Oxy.* 292, 5–7: διὸ παρακαλῶ σε μετὰ
πάσης δυνάμεως ἔχειν αὐτὸν συνεσταμένον,
"Wherefore I entreat you with all my power to take
him under your protection" (Loeb 1:297). When a
Hellenistic ruler uses the word, he is being distinctly
polite: he refrains from "commanding" (Bjerkelund, *Parakalô*, 59–63; *Milet* 1.3:300–307, no. 139;
Ditt., *Or.* 1:353 [no. 223, line 31]). [Bjerkelund cites

brotherly relationships.[9] The summons is strengthened by the reference to the name of the Lord.[10] The name represents the person. The use of ἵνα became very much more extensive in the Koine as compared with classical usage.[11] τὸ αὐτὸ λέγειν, "to be in agreement," is a common phrase.[12] Paul uses it as a paraenetic slogan for which no concrete occasion is necessary; for the content cf. Phil 1:27—2:5. In the case of the Corinthians, to be sure, there is occasion for it. The word σχίσματα, "divisions,"[13] implies in itself merely a neutral statement of the existence of divisions. It does not mean the existence of different systems of doctrine. Paul indeed hopes that unity will be restored as a result of his exhortation. The split into groups has not yet led to the dissolution of the community; they celebrate the Lord's Supper together (11:17ff), and Paul can address his letter to the whole community.

Verse 10b is a variation on the thought of 10a. Between νοῦς, "mind," and γνώμη, "conviction," there is here no difference of meaning.[14]

■ **11** Establishing who "Chloe's people" are[15] (children, members of her household?) is not possible. Nor can we be sure whether Chloe lives in Corinth (which after all is the more likely assumption) or possibly in Ephesus. In the latter case her people would have returned from a visit to Corinth. The difficulty of the passage lies in the fact that Paul says nothing of the representatives of the Corinthian community who according to 16:17 are at present with him; in the latter passage he ignores Chloe's people. The silence is all the more striking for the fact that in the immediate sequel he mentions one of the visitors from Corinth, but not as being present and not as the bringer of news.[16] The content of the information[17] is in the first instance more or less neutrally expressed: δηλοῦν—ἔριδες, "he told—quarrels."

■ **12** This verse explains the nature of the disputes: these are not cases of personal quarrels but of differences in

---

the Miletus inscription also from C. Bradford Welles, *Royal Correspondence in the Hellenistic Period* (New Haven: Yale University Press, 1934), 71–77, which gives an English translation and commentary as well as the Greek text—Trans.].

9   Cf., at the same point, Phil 1:12; for the form of address, cf. also Rom 12:1; 1 Cor 16:15f.

10   For διά = "with appeal to," cf. 2 Cor 10:1; Rom 12:1; 15:30. Adolph Schettler, *Die paulinische Formel "Durch Christus"* (Tübingen, J. C. B. Mohr [Paul Siebeck], 1907), 50–56, takes διά in a causal sense: in virtue of the authority of Christ. He argues that the formula has nothing to do with calling upon his name. To be sure, he must concede (p. 51) that ἐν ὀνόματι, "in the name," is the equivalent of διὰ τοῦ ὀνόματος, "by the name," but denies that the same is true of διὰ Χριστοῦ, "through Christ."

11   See above, n. 1.

12   See above, n. 1.

13   *P. Lond.* 2710 (= Preisigke, *Sammelbuch*, no. 7835), 13: μηδὲ σχίματα (sic!) συνίστασ[θαι], "[It shall not be permissible for any one of them . . .] to make factions," namely, in the σύνοδος τοῦ Διὸς Ὑψίστου, "gild of Zeus Hypsistos." [Text, translation and commentary in Colin Roberts, Theodore C. Skeat, and Arthur Darby Nock, "The Gild of Zeus Hypsistos," *HTR* 29 (1936): 39–88.] Nock (*ibid.*, 51) advocates the correction σχίσματα (not σχήματα). Cf. the parallel concept αἵρεσις, "faction," 11:19. Max Meinertz, "Σχίσμα und αἵρεσις im Neuen Testament," *BZ*, n.s. 1 (1957): 114–118, thinks that αἵρεσις implies an intensification. But αἵρεσις,

too, is in the first instance neutral and acquires only secondarily the derogatory sense of "sect," "heresy."

14   With Bultmann, γνώμη, *TDNT* 1:717f. In itself νοῦς is more the power of observation, while γνώμη includes more strongly the note of judging. Yet the latter is also contained in the NT meaning of νοῦς. Paul uses neutral, anthropological designations of this kind without sharp distinction; see Bultmann, *Theology*, 1:204f [205f]. When the church fathers again make a subtler differentiation (theoretical understanding—practical disposition), then this is an overinterpretation.

15   The name Chloe is known also from Horace (*Carm.* 3.9, etc.) and Longus.

16   Because of this difficulty, Schmithals assigns the two passages to different letters. In chap. 1, he argues, Paul is better informed than in chap. 11. Chap. 11 belongs to the earlier letter A, which was delivered by Stephanas, while chaps. 1–4 belong to the later letter that was occasioned by the arrival of further news. But why should Stephanas not have informed Paul about the situation in Corinth? If Chloe's people live in Ephesus, then we can also understand why Paul quotes them for this embarrassing news, and not the delegation from Corinth.

17   The word δηλοῦν denotes a rationally intelligible communication; Josh 4:7; Jos., *Ant.* 4.105; *c. Ap.* 1.286; Bultmann, *TDNT* 2:61f.

the attitude of the individual to the community. The word ἔκαστος, "each," must not of course be pressed to the effect that every single member has associated himself with one of the groups mentioned.[18] Paul is simply pointing to the process of division and at once indicating its ground: the position of the individual in the community is a matter of his own personal decision, in which he freely chooses his own master.

ἐγὼ μέν εἰμι κτλ., "I belong, etc.":[19] the expression has nothing to do here with the celebrated revelation formula. It is a case of a simple declaration of party allegiance.[19a] There are two problematical points: (1) the nature of the groups, the relationship between the member and the head of the party; (2) the meaning of the fourth slogan and therewith the number of the groups.

The names of the heads do not tell us anything certain: Cephas,[20] Apollos,[21] Paul himself. Of Apollos we know only what can be gathered from the few references in the epistles of Paul and from one or two passages in Acts. His theology is unknown to us.[22] 1 Corinthians reflects his personal success in Corinth.

Whether the Peter group arose as the result of a personal appearance of Peter in Corinth is a moot point.[23]

Excursus:
The "Parties"

The question of the nature of the groups is bound up with the other question as to whether there was a "Christ party." The existence of such a party has long been disputed (already by Chrysostom). It is argued, (1) that Paul adds the slogan ἐγὼ δὲ Χριστοῦ, "I to Christ,"[24] in order to reduce the other three ad absurdum, or (2) that ἐγὼ δὲ Χριστοῦ is not a fourth slogan, but a declaration of Paul's own: "You confess to men; I confess to Christ." If this interpretation is adopted, then it is certainly hardly possible to find a link between v 12 and v 13. Nor is any sure criterion provided by 3:22.

Where the existence of a Christ group is maintained because of the parallelism in the phrasing—a conclusion also supported by the wording and the logic[25]—attempts are made to define this party more closely. Earlier expositors saw in these people Judaists or Jewish Christians who were opposed to Paul. Lütgert on the contrary (whose view is adopted in modified form by Schmithals) considers them to be hyper–Paulinists, Gnostics, who identify their own Self with Christ. True, there is no sign of an alternative between Jewish and Gentile Christians. Yet one thing must be maintained in face of all at-

---

18 Cf. ἔκαστος . . . ἴδιον δεῖπνον, "each . . . his own supper," 11:21. In later passages the structure of this individualism can be seen: it is not a matter of enlightened emancipation of the personality, but of religious enthusiasm. Reitzenstein, *Mysterienreligionen*, 333–396, describes the groups as θίασοι with their mystagogues.

19 See above, n. 9.

19a Blass–Debrunner §162(7).

20 As always in Paul, except in Gal 2:7; on this, see Erich Dinkler, "Die Petrus–Rom–Frage: Ein Forschungsbericht," *ThR*, n.s. 25 (1959): 189–230, esp. 213.

21 The name is frequent in papyri. It is a shortened form of Ἀπολλώνιος (Acts 18:24 D; *MAMA* 7:513, etc.), Ἀπολλωνίδης (*MAMA* 7:328), and suchlike.

22 According to Acts (18:24) he was from Alexandria and was a learned exegete. Conclusions regarding his theology (via Philo) are precarious.

23 Lietzmann, *ad loc.*; Charles K. Barrett, "Cephas and Corinth," in *Abraham unser Vater: Juden und Christen im Gespräch über die Bibel. Festschrift für Otto Michel zum 60. Geburtstag*, ed. Otto Betz, Martin Hengel, Peter Schmidt, AGSU, 5 (Leiden: Brill, 1963), 1–12: from 9:5 Barrett concludes that Peter was accompanied by his wife. In favor of a sojourn in Corinth it can be pointed out that the membership of a group

appears to have been determined by baptism. Barrett (following T. W. Manson, "The Corinthian Correspondence") seeks for further indications: in 3:1–9; 5:9–13 (an echo of the dispute in Antioch?); 6:1–6, which he argues is typically Jewish and would be well suited to the Cephas party, as is also true of the problems in chaps. 8—10. These assumptions overtax the text. It should be noted that Peter is not mentioned in chap. 3.

24 Heinrici and Weiss delete the phrase as an interpolation, Heinrici with reference to *1 Cl.* 47:3, against which Bachmann rightly observes (pp. 57f): This passage merely shows how *1 Cl.* understood the situation in Corinth.

25 Schmithals, *Gnosticism in Corinth*, 199–206 [188–194]; survey of research, 117–124 [110–117]. Wilhelm Lütgert, *Freiheitspredigt und Schwarmgeister in Korinth*, BFTh, 12, 3 (Gütersloh: Bertelsmann, 1908): tradition stands over against Spirit; the first three groups form a relative unity as against the fourth; cf. 4:7.

tempts at a precise definition: while it is certainly possible to detect clearly in the Corinthian community tendencies of a pneumatic, enthusiastic, individualistic kind, yet these are to be found in the party system as such, rather than in the peculiarity of the individual groups. Of these groups we know nothing. For example, there is no ground for the assumption that Peter's people reject Paul. It should be noted that the object of Paul's attack is not Peter and his party, but all parties. The same applies to the Apollos group, which many exegetes think to be the object of attack in 1:18ff (the representatives of wisdom). Acts 18:15; 19:3f should not be appealed to in support of this (against Heinrici and Weiss).

On the other hand, it will not do to dismiss the group question as being merely a matter of harmless squabbles.[26] The energy Paul expends upon it is too great for that.[27]

He can discuss the party system comprehensively, without entering into differences between the groups, because the community still exists as a whole and all the groups recognize the traditional creed. This of course is presupposed in 11:23ff and 15:3ff. The point at issue here is the exposition of the creed. In Corinth it is apparently understood in the sense that we have to take our bearings on the glory of the exalted Lord; the cross is annulled by the exaltation. This view of faith expresses itself in terms of a spiritual elevation of the individual to meet the Lord: the individualization and formation of groups that take place on this free "pneumatic" basis is a complex phenomenon.[28] Here must be asked (with Lütgert) how far the developments in Corinth were initiated by the theology of Paul himself. They cannot, at all events, simply be traced back in a causal sense to external "influences."

Once the background of the formation of groups is recognized—namely, the pneumatic Christology of exaltation—then there is no room for the helplessness of many exegetes in face of the Christ slogan. Heinrici, for example, thinks that this is not in itself a fault, but will be quite in order once the other groups disappear.[29] By no means! This will be in order when "Christ" is understood as the crucified. The error lies in turning the confession into a slogan.[30] It is *this* that Paul summarily demolishes when he says: "But you are Christ's" (3:22).[31]

---

26 Johannes Munck, *Paul and the Salvation of Mankind*, tr. Frank Clarke (London: SCM, 1959; Richmond: John Knox, 1960), 135–167 [127–161]. Nils A. Dahl, "Paul and the Church at Corinth according to 1 Corinthians 1:10—4:21," in *Christian History and Interpretation: Studies Presented to John Knox*, ed. William R. Farmer, Charles F. D. Moule, and Richard R. Niebuhr (Cambridge: University Press, 1967), 313–335: the disputes are bound up with the notion that Paul will not come any more (4:18), and now the point in dispute is whether they should write to Paul, or to Cephas, or whether as "Christians" they are strong enough to stand on their own feet.

27 As rightly observed by Ulrich Wilckens, *Weisheit und Torheit*, BHTh, 26 (Tübingen: J. C. B. Mohr [Paul Siebeck], 1959), 5, n. 1.

28 To this extent we may compare them (as Lietzmann does) with the Hypsisterians of the Crimea; see *IPE* 2:246–286, nos. 437–467.

29 Similarly Weiss, who disputes the existence of a Christ party by arguing that if such a party had existed, Paul could have professed allegiance to it. This is a complete misunderstanding. The point lies in the abrogation of *every* standpoint that has saving significance ascribed to it as such. The decisive points have been discerned by Barth, *Resurrection*, 13–18 [2–6], and Bultmann, *Faith und Understanding*, 1:68–

70 [40–42]. Reitzenstein *Mysterienreligionen*, 333–396, actually imagines that Paul wants to procure the success of *his* party!

30 Schlatter is right up to a point when he says that with the Christ slogan the church is severed from the apostles. It is true that behind it there stands an unhistoric doctrine of salvation. Only, this is equally true of the other groups. Common to all is the fact that their slogans become exclusive (cf. Schlatter, 31).

31 "In his view, the question as to which amongst these groups was relatively most right, and the other question as to how the disputants could be reconciled, were manifestly quite secondary in comparison with the need for making all of them realize that it was not meet that the testimony of Christ set up among them, in contrast to the phenomena of the variegated religious fair, in the midst of which the Church life of the Corinthian Christians was lived, should be made into a cause, an idea, a programme, an occasion for intellectual exuberance and spiritual heroics. . . . The main defect of Corinthian conditions, from this point of view, Paul sees to consist in the boldness, assurance, and enthusiasm, with which they believe, not in God, but in their own belief in God and in particular leaders and heroes; in the fact that they confuse belief with specific human experi-

■ **13** Here the criticism begins. μεμέρισται ὁ Χριστός, "Is Christ divided," is usually taken as a question, on the analogy of the following questions.[32] The sense is provided by the connection with the preceding ἐγὼ δὲ Χριστοῦ, "I to Christ."[33] The simplest way of understanding the expression and the argument is to presuppose the view of the church as the body of Christ.[34] The transition of thought appears abrupt.

The connecting link is the reference to baptism, that is, our being crucified with Christ (Rom 6:3ff). The second question, ἢ εἰς τὸ ὄνομα κτλ., "or . . . in the name,

etc.," is—in contrast to the first—one that Paul can exemplify by reference to himself. It may be that in Corinth this was a widely adopted view of baptism,[35] namely, that baptism is the ground of a relationship between baptizer and baptized similar to that established in the mysteries.[36] "In the name" implies the *naming* of this name, as is shown by the context.[37] Usually this is understood as committal to the ownership of Christ, subjection to his lordship and his protection.[38] Over against this, Delling[39] emphasizes that it is a case of the name of the *crucified*, and not of the exalted Christ (hence

---

ences, convictions, trends of thought and theories. . . . In Corinth the testimony of Christ is threatening to become an object of energetic human activity . . ." (Barth, *Resurrection*, 15 [3f]).

32 Weiss: the absence of a μή heightens the emphasis. On μερίζειν, "divide" (see Bauer, *s.v.*), cf. Just., *Dial.* 128.4: ὡς ἀπομεριζομένης τῆς τοῦ πατρὸς οὐσίας—μεριζόμενα καὶ τεμνόμενα, "as though the being of the Father were divided . . . divided and cut off" (A. Lukyn Williams, *Justin Martyr: The Dialogue with Trypho*, Translations of Early Christian Literature, Series I—Greek Texts [London: SPCK; New York: Macmillan, 1930], 266). On the sect of the Meristai, see Marcel Simon, *Jewish Sects at the Time of Jesus*, tr. James H. Farley (Philadelphia: Fortress, 1967), 93–96 (*Les sectes juives au temps de Jésus*, Mythes et Religions, 40 [Paris: Presses Universitaires, 1960], 81–84). Wilckens, *Weisheit und Torheit*, 12, thinks that Paul leaves the answer open for a moment, that for him himself the answer is plain, but that now the Corinthians for their part have to give an answer. Schmithals, *Gnosticism in Corinth*, 199–206 [188–194], holds that the question is directed only to the Christ group, and that the mistake of the other groups lies merely in the fact that in rejecting these Gnostics they appeal to men instead of to Christ. This is to misjudge Paul's attitude in the same way as Heinrici, etc. (see on v 12).

33 This phrase is accordingly not to be deleted as an interpolation, against Weiss, who thinks that v 13 is formulated as if ἐγὼ δὲ Χριστοῦ were not there, and that the metaphor of the body of Christ would not be appropriate if *one* party claimed the "whole Christ" for itself. Against this, the "whole Christ" is an idea of Paul's; it is not necessarily an idea of the Corinthians.

34 Weiss; Kümmel; Stig Hanson, *The Unity of the Church in the New Testament*, ASNU, 14 (Uppsala: Almqvist & Wiksell, 1946), 74f, reprinted (Lexington, Ky.: American Theological Library Association, 1963). Or is the thought simpler if we say, in analogy to

the question whether Paul has been crucified: Christ is one; he cannot be divided, and therefore his church cannot be so either? Cf. *1 Cl.* 46:7: ἱνατὶ διέλκομεν καὶ διασπῶμεν τὰ μέλη τοῦ Χριστοῦ . . .; "Why do we divide and tear asunder the members of Christ . . .?" (Loeb 1:89).

35 It can also be a case of a polemical *ad hoc* statement; but cf. the sequel.

36 This is one argument for a sojourn of Peter in Corinth (Lietzmann; not so Kümmel or Maurice Goguel, "L'apôtre Pierre a-t-il joué un rôle personnel dans les crises de Grèce et de Galatie?" *RHPhR* 14 [1934]: 461–500); Oscar Cullmann, *Peter*, tr. Floyd V. Filson (London: SCM; Philadelphia: Westminster, ²1962), 55–57 (*Petrus* [Zurich and Stuttgart: Zwingli, ²1960], 60–62), leaves the question open.

37 For this reason there is no use in referring to the Jewish expression לְשֵׁם The latter says nothing of a real name; it has hardened into a mere prepositional phrase; see Gerhard Delling, *Die Zueignung des Heils in der Taufe* (Berlin: Evangelische Verlagsanstalt, 1961), 36–42. Herodian, *Hist.* 2.13.2: ὁμόσαι ἐς τὸ Σεβήρου ὄνομα. "They were to swear their allegiance to (the name of) Severus" [Trans.]. Totally different is the technical expression of the business world: εἰς τὸ ὄνομα = to the account of someone. The single-membered formula of baptism is presupposed.

38 Wilhelm Heitmüller, *"Im Namen Jesu": Eine sprach- und religionsgeschichtliche Untersuchung zum Neuen Testament, speziell zur altchristlichen Taufe*, FRLANT, 2 (Göttingen: Vandenhoeck & Ruprecht, 1903). Heitmüller distinguishes between ἐν (Acts 10:48) or ἐπί with the dative (Acts 2:38), "under naming of the name," and εἰς, "into possession of." This is an oversubtle view.

39 See above, n. 37; on Paul, see Delling, *Zueignung*, 68–83.

$X\rho\iota\sigma\tau\acute{o}s$, not $\kappa\acute{\nu}\rho\iota\sigma s$). According to him, what is meant is therefore not incorporation in the body of Christ, but the transmission of the cross event to the person baptized. The same sense, he holds, attaches also to the simple expression $\epsilon\acute{\iota}s\ X\rho\iota\sigma\tau\acute{o}\nu$, "into Christ."[40] This view is too narrow. According to the context, the effect of baptism "in the name of Christ" is that we "belong to Christ"; such baptism is therefore commission into his hands.[41]

■ **14** $\epsilon\grave{\nu}\chi\alpha\rho\iota\sigma\tau\hat{\omega}$, "I am thankful," is used as a rhetorical phrase: "Thank God!" (cf. 14:18). In order to spotlight the absurdity of what was going on in Corinth, Paul has indicated the possibility (i.e., impossibility) of his having adopted the role of $\sigma\omega\tau\acute{\eta}\rho$, "Savior." He now makes it correspondingly clear that he did not set up as a mystagogue.[42] The main emphasis in his work lay not on the administration of the sacrament, but on the preaching. A spiritual paternity in the sense of the mysteries is thereby rejected; such a paternity exists only in terms of word and faith (4:15; Phlm 10). Of the people baptized by Paul we know little.[43]

■ **15** $\acute{\iota}\nu\alpha\ \mu\acute{\eta}\ \tau\iota s\ \kappa\tau\lambda.$, "so that none, etc.," refers not to Paul's intention at the time, but to the practical result which his conduct at that time has for the present situation. The variant reading $\grave{\epsilon}\beta\acute{\alpha}\pi\tau\iota\sigma\alpha$, "I baptized (you),"[44] if the precise wording is pedantically pressed, is logically better—since of course not all were baptized by Paul—but would presumably be assimilation to v 14.

■ **16** The baptism of a "household": this expression has its pattern in the Old Testament.[45] It is frequent in Acts: 11:14; 16:15, 32, 34; 18:8. In regard to the question whether in such a case children were also baptized, the term leads us nowhere.[46]

■ **17** The explanation in v 17a does not devalue baptism,[47] but defines the personal commission to which Paul is subject. Baptism can be administered by anyone. *He* has to preach the gospel to the Gentiles (Gal 1:16). To wander about as a baptizer would be a nonhistoric

---

40 He interprets Rom 6:3ff accordingly; Gal 3:27, he says, is no counterargument, since here "baptized into Christ" and "putting on Christ" do not mean the same thing (Delling, *Zueignung*, 75f).

41 In view of Rom 6 it must be said that Delling does not do justice to the Pauline "$\sigma\grave{\nu}\nu\ X\rho\iota\sigma\tau\hat{\omega}$," "with Christ." See further Georg Braumann, *Vorpaulinische christliche Taufverkündigung bei Paulus*, BWANT, 82 (Stuttgart: Kohlhammer, 1962).

42 Bachmann: v 15 also gives no indication that the Corinthians believed in a mystic bond between baptizer and baptized. Paul is speaking of an absurdity to which the situation might lead.

43 Crispus: Acts 18:8. The name Gaius is frequent; another Gaius (from Macedonia) is mentioned in Acts 19:29. Stephanas: see 16:15, 17; for names ending in −as, see Blass–Debrunner §125(1). Why does Stephanas occur to Paul only as an afterthought, although (assuming the unity of 1 Cor, cf. n. 16 above) he is there with Paul? Weiss suggests that it is perhaps for that very reason.

44 D G it $\aleph$.

45 But cf. the Hellenistic evidence in Bauer, *s.v.*: Artemid., *Oneirocr.* 2.68; Preisigke, *Sammelbuch* 7912: $\sigma\grave{\nu}\nu\ \tau\hat{\omega}\ \pi\alpha\nu\tau\grave{\iota}\ \sigma\acute{\iota}\kappa\omega$, "with the whole household."

46 Cf. 16:15: the "household of Stephanas" occupies a leading position in the community; cf. Kurt Aland, *Did the Early Church Baptize Infants?*, tr. G. R. Beasley–Murray (London: SCM; Philadelphia: Westminster, 1963), 88, n. 1 (*Die Säuglingstaufe im Neuen Testament und in der alten Kirche*, Theologische Existenz Heute, n.s. 86 [Munich: Kaiser, ²1963],

61, n. 303). On the controversy: Joachim Jeremias, *Infant Baptism in the First Four Centuries*, tr. David Cairns (London: SCM; Philadelphia: Westminster, 1960), 19–24 (*Die Kindertaufe in den ersten vier Jahrhunderten* [Göttingen: Vandenhoeck & Ruprecht, 1958], 23–28); *The Origins of Infant Baptism*, tr. Dorothea M. Barton, SHT, 1 (London: SCM, 1963) (*Nochmals: Die Anfänge der Kindertaufe*, Theologische Existenz Heute, n.s. 101 [Munich: Kaiser, 1962]). Counter–arguments: Aland; Peter Weigandt, "Zur sogenannten 'Oikosformel,'" *NovTest* 6 (1963): 49–74. On "household" see August Strobel, "Der Begriff des 'Hauses' im griechischen und römischen Privatrecht," *ZNW* 56 (1965): 91–100. On the position of a "household," cf. also Hdt., *Hist.* 3.83: the house of Otanes is the only Persian house that is free, $\kappa\alpha\grave{\iota}\ \acute{\alpha}\rho\chi\epsilon\tau\alpha\iota\ \tau\sigma\sigma\alpha\hat{\nu}\tau\alpha\ \acute{\sigma}\sigma\alpha\ \alpha\grave{\nu}\tau\grave{\eta}\ \theta\acute{\epsilon}\lambda\epsilon\iota$, $\nu\acute{o}\mu\sigma\nu s\ \sigma\grave{\nu}\kappa\ \grave{\nu}\pi\epsilon\rho\beta\alpha\acute{\iota}\nu\sigma\nu\sigma\alpha\ \tau\sigma\grave{\nu}s\ \Pi\epsilon\rho\sigma\acute{\epsilon}\omega\nu$, "and is not compelled to render any unwilling obedience, so long as it transgresses no Persian law" (Loeb 2:111).

47 This is shown by Rom 6 (against Lietzmann).

mode of existence. His task is nontransferably historic.[48] In ἀποστέλλειν, "send," we catch the sound of the title "apostle."[49] εὐαγγελίζεσθαι, "preach,"[50] describes the whole of his task. With seeming abruptness the gospel is defined within negative limits; we ask ourselves what the rejection of the σοφία λόγου, "wisdom of words," has to do with baptism.[51] The transition of thought becomes understandable in the light of the later statements in which Paul shows that the form of preaching cannot be separated from its content (the word of the cross). The developments in Corinth cannot be checked with the help of the sacrament, but only with the help of theology, and that means primarily by working out the nature of preaching, namely, the character of offense that attaches to it. By this means Paul achieves the transition to the two catchwords σοφία, "wisdom," which characterizes the state of the Corinthians and their theology, and σταυρός, "cross," which provides the criterion. It is hardly possible to define precisely

the expression οὐκ ἐν σοφίᾳ λόγου, "not with wisdom of words." What have we to relate it to, to ἀπέστειλεν, "sent," or to εὐαγγελίζεσθαι, "to preach"? The question can hardly be answered.[52] What does it mean in itself? Cf. Bauer on the word σοφία 1: "cleverness in speaking."[53] It is plain that λόγος, "word," is used in a derogatory sense as in 2:4, where 1:17 is taken up again in a different form; cf. further 2:1, 13; 4:20. What Paul means is explained by the whole context as far as 2:5. It is possible, but not certain, that with the catchword σοφία Paul is taking up a slogan from Corinth. If we assume this,[54] then we must still bear in mind the possibility that it was introduced to Corinth by Paul (and then altered in terms of the Corinthian view of wisdom). The brevity and formality of the ἵνα–clause, "lest . . .," make it likewise understandable only in the light of what follows.[55] Its phrasing does not allow us to draw any

---

48   2 Cor 10:12ff; Rom 15:16ff.

49   Even if the title cannot be derived from the verb; the latter is on the whole of no significance in Paul.

50   The content is explained in Rom 1:2f; critical delimitation: Gal 1:6–9. The terms for proclamation are early used absolutely in a technical sense: εὐαγγελίζεσθαι/εὐαγγέλιον, κηρύσσειν/κήρυγμα, λόγος, etc.; see Bultmann, *Theology* 1:87–89 [90f]; cf. 1:21; 9:27; 1 Thess 1:6, etc.

51   Lietzmann here finds an abrupt transition to a second disputed point. According to Kümmel, it is not a second point in dispute, but as in baptism, so also in preaching God's action is neglected when men and their wisdom are pushed into the foreground. This observation is right enough in itself, but does not explain the transition. Wilckens, *Weisheit und Torheit*, 14ff, would understand the latter in the light of baptism: the mention of the cross is prepared for by v 13; cross and baptism are for Paul closely bound up together; the unity of the community is grounded in the cross; "and therefore it is only by the λόγος τοῦ σταυροῦ, 'the word of the cross,' that the divided church can be 'set to rights again' " (p. 16).

52   Weiss.

53   Robertson and Plummer compare the σοφία λόγου, "wisdom of words," to the λόγος σοφίας, "word of wisdom"; but Paul does not have the latter consciously in mind here. Lietzmann interprets it as a way of speaking that sets out from human insights.

The question whether the accent falls on σοφία or on λόγος takes us nowhere. Bachmann argues that if the accent is on σοφία, then the antithesis is

something like μωρία λόγου, "foolishness of words," and λόγος has the neutral sense of the object of what is said; if the accent is on λόγος, then the antithesis is a σοφία of the *content*, and λόγος is then more or less the form of presentation. Bachmann prefers the former possibility. But the whole alternative is too subtly constructed.

54   Wilckens. Herbert Braun, "Exegetische Randglossen zum 1. Korintherbrief," *Theologia Viatorum* 1 (1948–49): 26–50, now in his *Gesammelte Studien*, 178–204, esp. 178–181: σοφία is the first of the "abolished" customary values, of the ὄντα, "things that are something" (vv 27f), cf. the sequence in v 30. This is correct. But we must bear in mind the dialectic described by Bultmann (see above): Paul, too, must pursue wisdom. The criterion ("crux") will be whether this wisdom becomes the object of faith, or whether it leads on each several occasion to an understanding of the cross.

55   κενοῦν/κενός, "empty": 5:10, 14; Gal 2:2; Phil 2:16; 1 Thess 3:5; Rom 4:14. For an explanation, cf. Gal 5:11, where we have καταργεῖν, "bring to nothing," in the same sense. Braun, *Gesammelte Studien*, 181, aptly observes (against Weiss) that Paul is not here inviting irrationality, "for the content of the λόγος τοῦ σταυροῦ, 'the word of the cross,' is no indefinite 'something.' "

conclusions in regard to specific statements in Corinthian Christology.[56]

Summary:
(The Dialectic of the Theological Standpoint)

The transformation of the understanding of faith into the support of a standpoint leads automatically to a multiplicity of standpoints, and hence to division. Over against this Paul defines his position first of all in negative terms, as a nonstandpoint. He will explain this in the next section (1:18–2:5). This negativity, which includes within it also the critical abrogation of Paulinism, has been demonstrated by Karl Barth.[57] To be sure, Bultmann points out that the ἀπὸ τοῦ θεοῦ, "from God" (4:5), or "the cross," "can in any particular case of human reality only be expressed by taking a specific stand; that is, such a party slogan can in certain circumstances be duty. . . . The solution of the problem here lies in recognizing that the *freedom* of leader and programme does not mean the proclamation of subjectivity . . . and individualism. Such freedom means freedom from one's self and at the same time from an individualism of motives and opinions based in the self. But this surrender of self is not a mere waiting, nor is it a silence (however holy) nor mysticism. It is laying hold of the Word of God."[58]

It will still have to be asked whether Paul takes his negatively defined "standpoint" and builds it up again after all into a position which as such becomes an object of theological reflection, or whether he merely asserts it as a criterion to which his own position is also subject at any given moment. How this can be done in practice is shown by the passages in which Paul describes his daily life (4:9ff; 2 Cor), as also by the dialectical definition of καυχᾶσθαι, "boasting" (see on v 31).

---

56 Docetic statements, for example. In a formal sense, the teaching of the Corinthians is orthodox, see on 15:3ff. This indeed is precisely what constitutes the difficulty in the discussion and interpretation: the point at issue is how we are to understand ourselves. When Wilckens says that the formulation shows the controversy to be a specifically Christological one, then this is correct only in the sense of Paul's Christology. It is not a question of doctrinal statements, but of the believing understanding: "Christ" is understood only when man is understood as being determined by the cross. Thus Paul is consistent in putting forward for discussion not doctrinal statements, but the nature, content and form of preaching.

57 Barth, *Resurrection*, 19–21 [6f]; cf. also n. 31 above.
58 Bultmann, *Faith and Understanding*, 1:69f [41f].

That this section must be taken as a unity is shown by its "circular" composition:[1] the section 3:18–23 leads back to the starting point. Even 3:4–17, where Paul again comes to speak of the parties, is subordinated to this comprehensive theme.

First of all, Paul discusses wisdom and foolishness in three stages: (a) 1:18–25 fundamentally; (b) 1:26–31 as exemplified by the community; (c) 2:1–5 as exemplified by himself and his preaching. He makes considerable use of the methods of rhetorical style: antithetical parallelism (v 18),[2] anaphora (the thrice repeated ποῦ,

"where," of v 20).[3] The paradoxical phenomenon of the divine wisdom is given strong linguistic expression.

From 2:6 onward the style changes. The terminology of the mysteries becomes more concentrated; 2:6–16 is a preliminary form of the "revelation schema" which has been fully worked out (and schematized) in the deutero–Pauline epistles; then follows the final discussion of the party system, introduced in 3:1–4 and worked out in 3:5–17. Here Paul again works with examples, himself and Apollos. Then he leads back again to the beginning.

---

1   The most extensive example of a "circular composition" in the Pauline epistles is Rom 5—8. Cf. N. Schmid, *Kleine ringförmige Komposition in den vier Evangelien und der Apostelgeschichte* (dissertation, Tübingen, 1961).

2   With the construction μέν . . . δέ; this construction has very much receded in the N.T., see Blass–Debrunner §447(2).

3   On the style of vv 26ff, see below.

1 Corinthians 1:18–25

1

The Word of the Cross as the Judgment of the Wisdom of the World

18 **For the word of the cross[1] is to those who are lost foolishness, but to us who are saved the power of God. 19 / For it is written: "I will destroy the wisdom of the wise and I will bring to nothing the intelligence of the intelligent." 20 / Where is a wise man? Where a scribe? Where a debater of this world? Has not God made foolish the wisdom of the world? 21 / For since in the wisdom of God the world did not recognize God by wisdom, God resolved to save, through the foolishness of preaching, those who believe. 22 / While Jews demand miracles and Greeks desire "wisdom,"[2] 23 / we[3] preach Christ as the crucified, to Jews an offense, to Gentiles foolishness, 24 / but to those who are called,[4] Jews and Greeks alike,[5] Christ the power of God and the wisdom of God.[6] 25 / For God's folly is wiser than men and God's weakness is stronger than men.[7]**

In Romans Paul expresses his doctrine of the principles of theology in terms of the concept of justification by faith. The latter provides the meaning and at the same time the regulative principle for all dogmatic statements on God, Christ, salvation history, the eschaton. In 1 Corinthians the prevailing conceptuality is that of the theology of the cross. There is agreement between the two in the fact that theology is not constructed as a system of doctrinal statements. It certainly requires doctrinal statements. But these have their criterion in the fact that they expound revelation itself—as something that happens to man—and do not propound a doctrine *about* revelation. God and world/man are not described in an objectifying way. Rather, the object of theology

---

1 The postpositive use of the genitive with article is infrequent in the NT. Blass–Debrunner §271 assumes a kind of anaphora (v 17). The article is omitted in p[46] B (for this reading, see Zuntz, *Text*, 67).

2 On καί . . . καί or τε . . . καί in the phrase "Jews and Greeks," see Blass–Debrunner §444(2); cf. v 24; 10:32. The first καί is omitted in p[46], which afterwards reads οἱ δὲ Ἕλληνες. On the absence of the article see Blass–Debrunner §254(3).

3 This rendering takes ἡμεῖς, "we," as the introduction of the second clause; in that case δέ is pleonastic, for which see Radermacher, *Grammatik*, 219; Kühner–Blass–Gerth, 2.1:275–278. Lietzmann objects that then the connective with v 21 is missing. The other possible rendering is to take ἐπειδή as "for"; then no further clause is required; see Kühner–Blass–Gerth, 2.2:461f and Blass–Debrunner §456(3). That is to say: "For the Jews demand miracles and

the Greeks desire wisdom; but we preach. . . ."

4 For the emphatic position of αὐτοῖς at the beginning, cf. 2 Cor 11:14.

5 See on v 22; τε καί without an intervening word is already classical, Blass–Debrunner §444(2).

6 p[46] Cl Alex read: Χριστὸς θεοῦ δύναμις καὶ θεοῦ σοφία. In that case v 24 is an independent sentence without a connective; see Blass–Debrunner §127(5).

7 Neuter singular of the adjective instead of the abstract noun: 2 Cor 8:8; Rom 2:4, etc.; classical and higher Koine, see Blass–Debrunner §263(2).

is the cross, the act of salvation which actualizes itself in the word: the determination of man by the arrival of the word, and the determination of the word by the cross. In all this Paul intends to do nothing else but expound the creed transmitted to him, which he quotes in 15:3ff: Christ died and rose again. Now here, at the beginning of the epistle, he does not speak explicitly of the resurrection. For on this he has no quarrel with the Corinthians. The point at issue is the relation between the exaltation and the cross. Paul does not have to assert the exaltation, but the form in which we "have" the exalted Christ, namely, as the crucified Christ. His statements on this point are fundamental. Thus he does not have to concern himself about possible doctrinal differences between the groups.[8]

■ **18** First he propounds the thesis.[9] ὁ λόγος τοῦ σταυροῦ, "the word of the cross," is, as is shown by 2:1f, an exhaustive statement of the content of the gospel.[10] The "foolishness" of the saving word is of a dialectical kind. From the formal standpoint this is evidenced by the fact that the confrontations are fluid.[11] A contrast is drawn between the lost and the saved,[12] yet not between μωρία, "foolishness," and σοφία, "wisdom," but between μωρία and δύναμις θεοῦ, "the power of God,"[13] whereby the formal antithesis is further weakened by the genitive θεοῦ, "of God."[14] This state of affairs is a warning against understanding the datives merely in the sense of a subjective attitude (so that a change in the attitude to the gospel would bring about direct insight into its wisdom character).[15] The datives certainly raise the question of how one attains to the

---

8   Verses 18ff are not directed against a specific group (according to Weiss, the Apollos party as the advocate of "wisdom"; according to Wilhelm Lütgert, *Freiheitspredigt und Schwarmgeister in Korinth*, BFTh, 12, 3 [Gütersloh: Bertelsmann, 1908], the Gnostic Christ party). Paul means all the "groups."

9   It is marked by γάρ, "for," as an explanation of v 17b. Weiss takes the whole section up to v 25 as the ground of v 17b. This is too formalistic.

10   The catchword λόγος provides the link with v 17; over against the σοφία λόγου, "wisdom of words," we now have a λόγος, "word," which presents itself as μωρία—τοῖς ἀπολλυμένοις, "foolishness—to the lost."

11   It should also be noticed that Paul is playing with a negative and a positive evaluation of σοφία, "wisdom."

12   Contrasting of the two verbs, Ceb., *Tab.* 3.4: ἐὰν δέ τις γνῷ, . . . ἡ μὲν ἀφροσύνη ἀπόλλυται, αὐτὸς δὲ σῴζεται, "But if a man know, . . . foolishness is destroyed, but he himself is saved" [Trans.]. σῴζειν, "save," is in general use as a "soteriological" term; *Corp. Herm.* 1.26; 13.19: τὸ πᾶν τὸ ἐν ἡμῖν, σῷζε ζωή, "The All which is in us, save it, O Life!" [Trans.]. In the NT the sense is eschatologically defined: for ἀπολλύναι, cf. 15:18; Rom 2:12; Lk 13:3, 5; for σῴζειν, 3:15; 5:5; 9:22; 10:33; 15:2; Rom 10:9, 26. Normally the saving is spoken of in future terms. But the substantivized present participle becomes a standard designation: Lk 13:23; 2 Cor 2:15. Thdrt., *Interp. Epist. I ad Cor.* 170A (MPG 82:236): ἀπὸ τοῦ τέλους τὰς προσηγορίας τιθείς, "naming

them according to their end" [Trans.]. Willem C. van Unnik, "L'usage de 'sauver' dans les évangiles synoptiques," in *La formation des évangiles: Problème synoptique et Formgeschichte*, RechBibl, 2 (Bruges: Desclée de Brouwer, 1957), 178–194. The present participles ought not to have mysterious hints read into them to the effect that the present tense expresses "the unfinished character of the road to σωτηρία and ἀπώλεια respectively" (so Werner Foerster, *TDNT* 7:992). οἱ σῳζόμενοι means simply "the saved," as (in profane literature) Jos., *Bell.* 5.550.

13   δύναμις θεοῦ, Rom 1:16; δύναμις alongside of σοφία. Dan 2:23 Θ. In Judaism "the power" becomes a designation of God, see Mk 14:62. Wilckens, *Weisheit und Torheit*, 24, argues that Paul avoids the word in view of the phrasing of v 17. On μωρία see Helmut O. Gibb, "*Torheit*" und "*Rätsel*" im Neuen Testament, BWANT, 80 (Stuttgart: Kohlhammer, 1941).

14   The sense of the genitive θεοῦ is modified by the fact that the term no longer designates the nature of God, but has become a predicate of the "word of the cross" = the gospel (Rom 1:16); see on v 24, and cf. the absence of the synonyms commonly used in Judaism for "power," and of their accumulation. In Col and Eph they come to the fore again: Eph 1:19.

15   The choice of δύναμις θεοῦ instead of σοφία points to the fact that faith is not a habitus which—on a higher plane—again makes possible the independent operation of a wisdom of our "own"; cf. 2 Cor 13:4. Not so Bar 3:14: μάθε ποῦ ἐστιν φρόνησις, ποῦ ἐστιν ἰσχύς, ποῦ ἐστιν σύνεσις τοῦ γνῶναι ἅμα,

41

knowledge that the word of the cross[16] is δύναμις θεοῦ, in other words, how one becomes a σῳζόμενος, "saved." But faith is not an act of the free will; it is brought about by the word itself. What Paul means can be understood in the light of the predestinarian sense of the two expressions ἀπολλύμενοι, "lost," and σῳζόμενοι, "saved":[17] the word itself creates the division between the two groups (cf. 2 Cor 4:3–5). That "we" are saved is a believing insight which is existent only in the hearing of the word. No theory is developed on the subject of the lost; it is solely a question of their objective relationship to the preaching. The two datives[18] are not equivalent, inasmuch as there is a difference of situation: the one group is aware of its destiny, the other is not. With ἡμῖν, "to us,"[19] Paul embraces all Christians regardless of their groupings: theologically speaking, they are saved and there is no more to be said.

■ **19** Next he proves the thesis by quotation[20] from the LXX text of Isa 29:14.[21] This is not only a "Scripture proof." The God of the Old Testament speaks immediately through this book today.[22] σοφία and σύνεσις, "intelligence,"[23] refer not only to theoretical knowledge, but also to the attitude, in this case *hybris*.[24] The quotation shows that the division into the two groups is God's act (not mere sufferance).

■ **20** This verse is often held to be a quotation; Paul is thought to be using a florilegium (see below). More likely we have free formulation on Paul's part in reminiscence of passages from Isaiah:[25] Isa 19:11f;[26]

"Learn where there is wisdom, where there is strength, where there is understanding, that you may at the same time discern . . ." (RSV).

16 This does not mean the cross as a symbol (see Erich Dinkler, "Kreuzzeichen und Kreuz," *JAC* 5 [1962]: 93–112, now in his *Signum Crucis*, 26–54), but the crucifixion of Christ as the event of salvation, Phil 2:8; Rom 6:3ff.

17 Robertson and Plummer dispute this. We naturally must not interpolate the predestination theory of Calvinist orthodoxy. The thought is determined by the prevenience of grace (understood as an act) and by the word–character of the event of salvation. This means the setting up of the eschatological proviso: salvation is certain, because it is not a habitual possession. Schlatter observes that if the word of the cross were "wisdom," "then it would instruct us as to how the community can help itself."

18 Wilckens, *Weisheit und Torheit*, 21–23, points emphatically to the problem of the datives. He thinks that the subjective view (the word "is held" by the one group to be wisdom, etc.) and the objective view (it brings about . . .) merge into each other. Bachmann, on the other hand, allows only the objective sense (the word *is* to them . . .). Wilckens' interpretation is in fact too subjective. To be sure, he does see that it is not merely a case of the subjective attitude. If the act of salvation appears to be μωρία, "foolishness," then that is not merely a misunderstanding, but is brought about by the phenomenon of preaching appropriate to the cross. Yet it must be more strongly emphasized that in the adopting of the particular attitude the divine election or, as the case may be, rejection takes place. The unity of subjective judging and objective being judged becomes understandable in the light of the "word."

19 Its omission, which is poorly attested, is presumably due to the desire for a parallel to ἀπολλυμένοις.

20 For the citation formula, cf. CD V, 1: כתוב, "it is written"; 1QS V, 17, etc.: כאשר כתוב, "according to that which is written"; Str.–B. 2:1; Ellis, *Paul's Use of the OT*, 22–25; Bruce M. Metzger, "The Formulas Introducing Quotations of Scripture in the New Testament and the Mishnah," *JBL* 70 (1951): 297–307, now in his *Historical and Literary Studies: Pagan, Jewish, and Christian*, NTTS, 8 (Leiden: Brill; Grand Rapids: Eerdmans, 1968), 52–63.

21 LXX: καὶ μεταθήσω αὐτοὺς καὶ ἀπολῶ . . . καὶ . . . κρύψω, "I will transform them and I will destroy . . . and . . . I will conceal." Paul puts ἀθετήσω, "I will bring to nothing," in place of κρύψω, "I will conceal"; cf. Ps 32:10. In the MT חָכְמָה, "wisdom," and בִּינָה, "intelligence," are the subject. Georg Bertram, *TDNT* 4:846: "The LXX made a general judgment out of the Mas. judgment on the wise among the people of Israel." A form that is independent of the LXX is found in Just., *Dial.* 78.11.

22 Herbert Ulonska, *Paulus und das Alte Testament* (dissertation, Münster, 1964), 94ff.

23 For the combination, cf. Aristot., *Eth. Nic.* 1103a.5. It is frequent. This is true also of the Semitic equivalents.

24 The Greek definitions are of no significance for Paul.

25 Kümmel, *ad loc.*; Munck, *Paul*, 145 [137f]; Wilckens, *Weisheit und Torheit*, 25, n. 2.

26 ποῦ εἰσιν νῦν οἱ σοφοί σου; , "where then are your wise men?"

33:18.[27] The form of the questions recalls Bar 3:16.[28] The length of the third member provides a climax to the threefold anaphora.[29] συζητητής, "debater,"[30] is found only here and in Ign. *Eph.* 18:1.[31] No subtle distinctions are to be sought between the three concepts.[32] The qualification τοῦ αἰῶνος τούτου, "of this world," stands, for rhetorical reasons, only in the third member, but applies in content to all three.[33] ὁ αἰὼν οὗτος, "this age,"[34] means the same as ὁ κόσμος οὗτος, "this world,"[35] and likewise the simple ὁ κόσμος, "the world."[36] The expression "this aeon" derives from apocalyptic; it has its counterpart in the expectation of the "coming aeon."[37] It should be noticed that the second expression is missing in Paul. His eschatology is not constructed on the basis of the apocalyptic outlook.[38] In the judgment on "this world" two elements meet: (a) it is creation and as such transient;[39] (b) it is *fallen* creation and hostile to God.[40]

The three personal expressions are summed up in the phrase, ἡ σοφία τοῦ κόσμου, "the wisdom of the world."[41] As the sequel shows, τοῦ κόσμου, "of the world," is here no longer a qualitative genitive, but a subjective genitive: the cosmos appears as collective subject, the bearer of "its" wisdom. The judgment on the latter is passed, in the form of a question, not by reasoning, but by asserting an act of God.[42] Paul does not say, "God shows that the world is foolish," but "God makes its wisdom foolish."[43] The judgment of "foolishness" is strictly related to revelation; it shows itself in the attitude to the gospel. The use of the aorist tense sets forth that here is revealed what the world long was and did, and how God reacted to this.[44] "Wisdom" is not primarily a

---

27   ποῦ εἰσιν οἱ γραμματικοί;, "where are the scribes?" Aquila has γραμματεῖς; see Michel, *Paulus und seine Bibel*, 65.

28   For the interrogative as a form of argument, cf. also Bar 3:15f, 29f (Bar 3:14 is a different case). A totally different style of question with ποῦ is found in Plut., *Cons. ad Apoll.* 110d: *Ubi sunt, qui ante nos . . .?* "Where are those who before us . . .?"

29   Chrys., Ambst.: to the Scripture exposition Paul here adds the reality that confirms it.

30   The accent does not lie on the idea of searching out. Is this an echo of popular criticism of the philosophers?

31   But συζητεῖν and συζήτησις are frequent, cf. also Bar 3:23: καὶ οἱ ἐκζητηταὶ τῆς συνέσεως ὁδὸν σοφίας οὐκ ἔγνωσαν, "and the seekers for understanding have not learned the way to wisdom" (RSV).

32   The church fathers (Cl. Alex., Thdt.) are too subtle in distinguishing σοφοί the Greeks, γραμματεῖς the Jews, συζητηταί general. Schlatter finds here the official Jewish terminology: σοφός = חכם, γραμματεύς = סופר, συζητητής = דורש.

33   It is wrong to take the genitive as an objective genitive: *causarum naturalium scrutatores* (Jerome), "investigators of natural causes."

34   οὗτος following the noun is a semitism, Blass–Debrunner §292A.

35   Concepts of time and space merge into each other, cf. 2:6; 3:19; Gal 1:4; Bultmann, *Theology*, 1:256, n. † [256, n. 2].

36   Cf. 3:19; 5:10; 7:31 (with variant reading!) with 1:27f; 2:12 (variant reading); 7:33f, etc.

37   העולם הזה—הבא, see Str.–B. 4.2:799–976; Hermann Sasse, *TDNT* 1:197–209; the latter points to the inherent contradiction of "trying to think in the category of time what really stands in antithesis to time." The scheme of aeons: *4 Ezra*; *S. Bar.*; *Eth. En.* 71.15; *Sl. En.* 65; then in the rabbis.

38   The statement so often heard, that for Paul the new aeon has already dawned, is a misunderstanding of his eschatology.

39   *S. Bar.* 44.9; Sasse, *TDNT* 3:891.

40   Cf. 2:6, 8; 2 Cor 4:4; Jn 12:31, etc.; *4 Ezra* 4.29; *Eth. En.* 48.7.

41   τούτου, "this," would presumably be a secondary addition, following the customary phrase.

42   Paul does not discuss doctrines of worldly wisdom, nor does he contrast such doctrines with the statements of a "Christian" wisdom. He executes wisdom as a destruction of worldly wisdom.

43   μωραίνω, "make foolish," is intransitive in classical Greek. The sense is illumined by v 18; for the content, see Isa 44:25. The Pauline epigram has nothing to do with oxymora such as Luc., *Alex.* 40, μωρόσοφοι, and Horat., *Carm.* 1.34.2, *insaniens sapientia*.

44   Günther Bornkamm, "Faith and Reason in Paul," in his *Early Christian Experience*, tr. Paul L. Hammer (London: SCM; New York: Harper & Row, 1969), 29–46, here esp. 30 (*Studien zur Antike und Urchristentum. Gesammelte Aufsätze II*, BEvTh, 28 [Munich: Kaiser, ²1963], 119–137, here esp. 120): "The 'wisdom of the world' is a very definite way of thinking, qualified by its content. It has always run aground on *God's* wisdom." Charles Masson, "L'évangile

piece of knowledge, but an attitude. It cannot be abstracted from its bearer.[45]

For what follows we have constantly to keep in view the analogous exposition in Rom 1:18ff, which can provide a commentary on the briefer hints of 1 Corinthians.

Excursus I

Reference was made above to reminiscences of Bar 3. H. St.J. Thackeray[45a] and E. Peterson[45b] consider Bar 3:9—4:4 to be a homily on Jer 8:13—9:24, the lesson for the Fastday Ninth Ab.[46] They believe that here Paul is likewise expounding this fastday text (v 31). Of this it can be said only that here Paul in fact does operate with the concepts and style of Jewish wisdom theology (see below).

Excursus II

Does Paul in 1 Cor 1:18ff make use of a collection of "testimonies"?

Those who accept the suggestion that Paul is quoting in v 20 (and not merely freely alluding to Scripture passages) have to explain the deviations from the wording of the Bible. J. R. Harris in particular upheld the thesis that the early church made use of collections of chosen proof passages for its theologoumena.[47] O. Michel rejected this thesis; L. Cerfaux defended it again.[48] An intermediate position is adopted by C. H. Dodd, who believes the early Christians did not work with written collections, but with an orally transmitted, more or less fixed body of Scripture passages together with a tradition of their exposition.[49] Since the discovery of florilegia in Qumran the question has again become pertinent.[50]

■ **21** The proof[51] is an anticipatory form of Rom 1:18ff. A double antithesis is indicated: (a) σοφία τοῦ θεοῦ—

et la sagesse selon l'apôtre Paul," *RThPh*, 3rd series, 7 (1957): 95–110.

45 Cf. Rom 1:22ff, where it is said what constitutes the foolishness of the world: the confusing of God with an image of God, that is to say, of God and world.

45a Henry St. John Thackeray, *The Septuagint and Jewish Worship*, Schweich Lectures of the British Academy, 1920 (London: Oxford University Press, 1921, ²1923), 95–100.

45b Erik Peterson, "1 Korinther 1,18f. und die Thematik des jüdischen Busstages," *Biblica* 32 (1951): 97–103, now in his *Frühkirche, Judentum und Gnosis* (Rome, Freiburg, and Vienna: Herder, 1959), 43–50.

46 *Meg.* 31a; Str.-B. 4.1:80. On the whole section see Str.-B. 4.1:79–114; George Foot Moore, *Judaism in the First Three Centuries of the Christian Era* (Cambridge, Mass.: Harvard University Press, 1927–30), 2:65–67; Johannes Behm, *TDNT* 4:930f. On Thackeray see O. H. Steck, *Israel und das gewaltsame Schicksal der Propheten*, WMANT, 23 (Neukirchen–Vluyn: Neukirchener Verlag, 1967), 132f.

47 J. Rendel Harris, *Testimonies* (Cambridge: University Press, 1916–20), 2 vols.; see already Hans Vollmer, *Die alttestamentlichen Citate bei Paulus* (Freiburg and Leipzig: J. C. B. Mohr [Paul Siebeck], 1895).

48 Michel, *Paulus und seine Bibel*, 37–54. Cerfaux, "Vestiges d'un florilège dans I Cor., I,18—III,24?" *RHE* 27 (1931): 521–534, now in his *Recueil*, 2:319–332. According to Cerfaux, Paul begins with Isa 29:14; there follow allusions to Isa 19:11f; 33:18; 40:13; 44:25, then passages from the Hagiographa: Job 5:12f; Ps 33:10; 94:11; Jer 9:22f; there is a keyword connection between the texts; Paul quotes them not according to the LXX, but according to a more vulgar tradition. This artificial thesis cancels itself out. The fact that would have to be proved—namely that Paul is quoting—is presupposed.

49 C. H. Dodd, *According to the Scriptures* (London: Nisbet, 1952); the book is directed above all against the assumption of written collections. See now Lindars, *NT Apologetic*. For Dodd it is an important point that on each occasion the context of the OT passage is included in the application. This is untenable. For criticism of Dodd, see Albert C. Sundberg, Jr., "On Testimonies," *NovTest* 3 (1959): 268–281, who holds that in the NT there is no unified exegetical tradition or method, and that the OT context has no significance.

50 4QTest is a series of biblical passages, presumably intended to be proof-texts for the messianic expectations of the Qumran community. John Marco Allegro, "Further Messianic References in Qumran Literature," *JBL* 75 (1956): 174–187, here esp. 182–185. For text and translation see *Die Texte aus Qumran*, ed. and tr. Eduard Lohse (Darmstadt: Wissenschaftliche Buchgesellschaft, 1964), 249–253 (4QTest), 255–259 (4QFlor). 4QFlor is a collection with commentary. Allegro, "Fragments of a Qumran Scroll of Eschatological Midrāšîm," *JBL* 77 (1958): 350–354.

51 ἐπειδή, "since," in the NT has come to be almost only causal, Blass–Debrunner §455(1). Wilckens, *Weisheit und Torheit*, 29, is too specific in arguing that v 22 explains v 21a and vv 23f explain v 21b. The

τοῦ κόσμου, "wisdom of God—of the world"; [52] (b) σοφία—μωρία, "wisdom—foolishness." [53] The attitude
of God, as stated in v 20, is now explained: it is a reaction
to the attitude of the world. [54] The nonrecognition of
God is not a merely negative fact; it is the active refusal
of recognition (Rom 1:18ff) and the attempt on the
world's part to provide "its own" wisdom.

The meaning of ἐν τῇ σοφίᾳ τοῦ θεοῦ, "in the wisdom of God," is disputed. It seems simplest to relate
ἐν to γινώσκειν, "recognize by . . ."; that is to say the
world did not recognize God by (in the light of) his
wisdom as it has shown itself in the creation. [55] Yet this
usage would not be usual. [56] Others take ἐν in a temporal
sense: during the epoch of wisdom, i.e., when God still
manifested his wisdom directly; that is to say, before
the Fall. But Paul elsewhere does not have any knowledge
of an epoch in history without sin. [57] This fact is taken
into account in a further suggestion, [58] namely, to interpret ἐν in spatial terms; in the midst of wisdom. The
latter would then be the sphere of existence and at the
same time (διά) the means of knowledge. Here it is
rightly perceived that a distinction between different
epochs in salvation history is of no significance, and that

Paul is working with motifs of the Jewish wisdom teaching. [59] For this very reason we must hold to the fact
that he *sets out* from the temporal sense; Jewish wisdom
can expound biblical narratives in a way that dehistorizes
them. This is particularly true of the creation story, but
also of the history of Israel. [60] For this type of thinking,
wisdom's existence in the world "once upon a time"
no longer requires that it be realistically conceived, as an
epoch in history. It is merely its present pastness at any
given moment. [61] Paul here eliminates the original time
factor in much the same way as in Rom 7:7ff, where
he expounds the history of paradise and the fall as the
history of the ego. [62] In 1 Corinthians he takes his bearings not on Adam and the Fall, but on the fate of wisdom,
and transforms the mythic narratives of Judaism in a
characteristic way. He borrows from one specific variety
of wisdom speculation, on the vanished wisdom, which
appeared in the world, was rejected, withdrew to heaven,
appeared again from there, but now only to the small

play on the catchwords (μωραίνω/μωρία) already
tells against this narrow relationship.

52 Cf. the antithesis in 2:12; 2 Cor 7:10. On the genitive τοῦ θεοῦ, "of God," cf. vv 18, 24; Eph 3:10. For
the predication of God as "wise," see Sir 1:8, etc.;
in the Hellenistic world (applied to Zarathustra),
Eus., *Praep. Ev.* 1.10.43; in the NT, Rom 16:27 (not
Pauline).

53 μωρία τοῦ κηρύγματος, "the foolishness of preaching," means in content: the word of the cross. κήρυγμα is one of the words which early became
technical terms of the "proclamation"; cf. also the
verb: Rom 10:14f; 1 Cor 9:27; Mk 3:14; see on v 17.

54 κόσμος, "world," embraces Jews and pagans together; cf. v 22.

55 Kümmel, *ad loc.*

56 Wilckens, *Weisheit und Torheit*, 32, is of the contrary
opinion, arguing that γινώσκειν ἐν elsewhere means
to recognize a thing by a sign or something of the
sort, cf. Lk 24:35. This does not suit here. Schlatter
understands ἐν in the instrumental sense, i.e., as
synonymous with διά. A rhetorical change of preposition of this sort is in itself good Pauline style; but
then the genitive τοῦ θεοῦ, "of God," becomes difficult.

57 In Rom 1:18ff he knows only an epoch of *wrath*, in
Rom 3:26 one of forbearance (in the latter case

following a prescribed pattern).

58 Heinrich Schlier, "Kerygma und Sophia. Zur neutestamentlichen Grundlegung des Dogmas," *EvTh*
10 (1950–51): 481–507, here esp. 484f, now in his
Die Zeit der Kirche (Freiburg: Herder, 1956), 206–
232, here esp. 209f; Bornkamm, *Early Christian Experience*, 30 (*Studien*, 120f); Wilckens, *Weisheit und
Torheit*, 33f.

59 Wilckens, *Weisheit und Torheit*, 29f rightly observes
that Paul is interested not in the temporal sequence
of the epochs but in the antithesis between them.
All the same, Wilckens does allow the word "epochs"
to slip out.

60 Sir 24:1ff; Wis 7:22ff.

61 If the appearing of wisdom does not require to be
"historically" verified, yet this is all the more necessary in the case of its absence, the age of foolishness
—in the conceptuality of justification, the age of
wrath. The Jewish model is Bar 3.

62 In Rom 1:18ff, too, the connection with the Jewish
wisdom tradition is palpable; Bornkamm, "The
Revelation of God's Wrath (Romans 1—3)," *Early
Christian Experience*, 44–70 (*Das Ende des Gesetzes.
Gesammelte Aufsätze I*, BEvTh, 16 [Munich: Kaiser,
⁵1966], 9–33).

circle of the chosen, i.e., the wise.[63] Paul does not say that wisdom withdrew, but that it was exterminated by God as a possibility open to the world.[64] The question whether wisdom is an attribute of God or, alternatively, a capacity of man, must not be raised.[65] Here, too, Paul is true to the tradition: wisdom is εἰκών, "image" (Wis 7:22ff), that is, the revealing power of God, the transmitter of God's wisdom to men (Sir 1:9f). This also makes the relation between ἐν and διά understandable: God is the wise one (see n. 52). Wisdom is "his."[66] That is to say, wisdom comes to man only from God (cf. ἀπὸ τοῦ θεοῦ, 4:5): Wis 9:1ff. For this very reason it really does come to him (3 Ezra 4:59f). The possibility of knowing God does not belong essentially to man (as a "property"); it is bestowed on him by revelation. The psychological capacity for knowledge does not concern Paul in the least (it is the same in Rom 1:18ff). He does not say that it was possible by means of reason to attain to doctrinal statements about God from observation of the world, but that it was possible to adopt a relation to God as God in the sense of nonworld, as the Creator, to honor him as God. To know him is as such to give him recognition. Likewise, on the other hand, Paul does not first of all speak in general terms of "foolishness" (of which the foolishness of preaching would then constitute a special case). The expression μωρία τοῦ κηρύγματος, "foolishness of preaching," is inseparable. Along with the

preaching there immediately goes also the thought of its content, the cross. Preaching is not merely *considered* to be foolish; it *is* foolish,[67] by God's resolve.[68] The expression has been carefully chosen: there is a correspondence between σοφία τοῦ θεοῦ and μωρία τοῦ κηρύγματος. Only from this standpoint does the expression τὸ μωρὸν τοῦ θεοῦ, "God's folly," in v 25 become understandable. It denotes not an "attribute," but God's free dealings with the world. Revelation is not formal communication of new knowledge about God,[69] but an act of salvation,[70] intended, to be sure, for the *world* (2 Cor 5:19), but accorded exclusively to faith.[71] This condition is explained by Rom 1:16f and 3:27ff. The very universality both of the event of salvation and also of the offer of salvation (2 Cor 5:18ff) constitutes the presupposition for this restriction to believers. τοὺς πιστεύοντας, "those who believe," sets aside every human barrier to salvation.

■ **22** The classifying of mankind from the standpoint of salvation history as Jews and Greeks[72] is a Jewish equivalent for the Greek classification "Greeks and barbarians."[73] Paul, however, is not concerned here in the first instance with the distinctive characteristics of the two groups from the standpoint of salvation history[74] (law, covenant, promise, etc.; cf. Rom 3:1ff; 9:1ff), but with their psychological attitude.[75] The context shows that his reproach is not meant in a moralizing sense. He does

---

63 *Eth. En.* 42; Jn 1:1ff. Other variants are *hidden* wisdom (see on 2:6ff) and *nearby* wisdom (Rom 10:6ff). For the motif cf. also Hes., *Op.* 197–201; Ovid., *Met.* 1.129.

64 From Rom 1:22f we can add: it thereby became perverse; hence the behavior here described in the next verse.

65 Karlheinz Müller, "I Kor 1,18–25. Die eschatologisch–kritische Funktion der Verkündigung des Kreuzes," *BZ*, n.s. 10 (1966): 246–272, would understand διὰ τῆς σοφίας, "by wisdom," in a modal sense—on the way to wisdom (Blass–Debrunner §223[3])—and points to wisdom as a guide, Wis 9:17ff, etc.

66 The doxological style of such passages is significant: Job 12:13; Dan 2:20; Wis 9:9.

67 Calvin, Bengel, Bachmann. It is naturally also *considered* to be foolish, but because it *is* so; see on v 18 (on the datives).

68 εὐδοκεῖν, "resolve": Gal 1:15; Col 1:9.

69 In that case it would be subject to man's free decision for or against it.

70 The sense of σῴζειν, "save," is as comprehensive as in the term οἱ σῳζόμενοι, "the saved"; cf. εἰς σωτηρίαν, "for salvation," Rom 1:16.

71 Cf. the alternation between "world" and "we" in 2 Cor 5:18f.

72 Hans Windisch, *TDNT* 2:504–516.

73 Julius Jüthner, *Hellenen und Barbaren*, Das Erbe der Alten, 2, 8 (Leipzig: Dieterichsche Verlaghaus, 1923). Cf. Rom 1:16 with 1:14.

74 They are indicated later when instead of Ἕλληνες, "Greeks," we have ἔθνη, "Gentiles."

75 αἰτεῖν, "demand": λόγον, "account," 1 Pet 3:15. ζητεῖν is a term for philosophical investigation, but here means simply "desire"; cf. Luc., *Hermot.* 66 τὴν εὐδαιμονίαν, "(desire) happiness." On the characteristic of the Jews cf. Mk 8:11; Mt 12:38f; Lk 11:16; Jn 6:30. Miracles are granted. To *demand* them is to prove one's wickedness. For the Greeks: Ἕλληνας πάντας ἀσχόλους εἶναι ἐς πᾶσαν σοφίαν πλὴν Λακεδαιμονίων (Hdt., *Hist.* 4.77), "All Greeks were zealous for every kind of learning, save only the Lacedaemonians" (Loeb 2:277).

not mean conscious malevolence. For indeed their attitude is provoked by God through the preaching. It is solely a question of how they react to the latter. This brings their foolishness to light, a foolishness for which they have but themselves to blame. Common to both parties is the demand for a *proof* of the divine truth. In this way they set themselves up as an authority that can pass judgment upon God.[76] This is what makes their attitude "worldly." They expect God to submit himself to their criteria. This, however, would mean that revelation would have to present itself as a factor belonging to the world—which is of course perverse. The failure of the attempt to pass judgment on God means that revelation shows itself to be divine.[77]

■ **23** Over against Jews and Greeks (later called "pagans"[78]) stand "we," i.e., the σῳζόμενοι, "saved" (v 18). The choice of the first person makes the style that of confession, of adopting the standpoint of faith, which in turn causes the opponents also to take a stand. There is a correspondence between σημεῖα/σκάνδαλον, "miracles/offense,"[79] and σοφία/μωρία, "wisdom/foolishness." Looking back to v 21, we see that the "proclamation of the crucified" has this effect because

it *is* "offense" and "foolishness." It is not the propagating of a *Weltanschauung*, but the destruction of every attempt to regard a *Weltanschauung* as the way of salvation.

With the datives the situation is the same here as in v 18: they indicate both the standpoint of the groups and also the fact that this standpoint is determined by the encounter with the preaching. The subjective view of the Greeks is illustrated by the ridicule of Lucian and the polemic of Celsus, that of the Jews by Justin, *Dial.* 32.

■ **24** The construction is loose. Χριστὸν . . . follows the preceding objects of κηρύσσειν, "preach"; yet it is presumably no longer felt to belong to the object, but to be an independent statement, "Christ is. . . ."[80] The contrast between the "called"[81] and the rest is now expressed in the third person; the subjective perspective of v 23 is supplemented by the objective perspective. Here, too, the dative indicates the unity of attitude and being (on this cf. v 30).[82] The previous classification (Jews and Greeks) now becomes fluid inasmuch as both groups are taken up into the third. This shows them their opportunity. The tenor of the statement is that the power and wisdom of God is *Christ*.[83] This is a typical Pauline transformation of the Jewish way of praising the

---

76 Bachmann says of the attitude of the Jews: "Not that they await a single specific sign, but that they found their religious behavior in general upon the desire for signs, was the typical thing about them."

77 This thought is thematically worked out in the Fourth Gospel. It should be noticed (*a*) that Paul never mentions the miracles of Jesus; this is in harmony with his Christology; (*b*) that miracles take place in the community (12:9f) and that Paul himself possesses the gift of working miracles (2 Cor 12:12). These gifts are χαρίσματα, "gifts of grace"; they have an immediate effect, and are not recounted for propaganda purposes. Lessing's rationalist criticism of the possibility of a "proof by means of miracle" may be recalled here.

78 τὰ ἔθνη is the Greeks' designation for foreigners. The LXX uses it to render גּוֹיִם.

79 The word σκάνδαλον occurs only in the LXX, the NT and Christian writings; σκανδάληθρον, "trap," corresponds to the Hebrew מכשול (Qumran). Gustav Stählin, *Skandalon: Untersuchungen zur Geschichte eines biblischen Begriffs*, BFTh, 2, 24 (Gütersloh: Bertelsmann, 1930); on v 23, 201–210. Karlheinz Müller, *Der paulinische Skandalonbegriff* (dissertation, Würzburg, 1965); "I Kor 1,18–25," where in analyzing the present verse it is argued that to κηρύσσομεν, "we preach," there belongs "immediately"

also "the whole series of definitions that follows."

80 With Lietzmann, against Heinrici; cf. p⁴⁶. Weiss observes that the sense is obscured by the rhetoric, namely, by the repetition of Χριστόν, which leads the reader to repeat κηρύσσομεν, "we preach," contrary to Paul's intention.

81 See on v 2. Note the ringing of the changes on σῳζόμενοι, πιστεύοντες, κλητοί, "the saved, the believing, the called."

82 Bachmann denies that a subjective judgment is thought of at all. Paul, he argues, is speaking only of the objective effect on the called. But of course, the effect comes about through faith, and faith judges; cf. the verbs of judging: κρίνειν, "resolve" (2:2; 2 Cor 5:14), λογίζεσθαι, "hold" (Rom 3:28). The point is precisely the unity of judging and being. This unity is possible because Christ signifies *a priori* that the saving act has reference to man and because faith is nothing else save the acceptance of the proclaimed word.

83 In the same vein as "*L'état c'est moi*."

power and wisdom of God.[84] It goes without saying that God is strong and wise, but the point is to make clear *how* he is so, namely, in revealing his power and wisdom "in Christ." We can say that Christ is God's "nature." This way of transforming statements about God's nature into definitions of revelation is the same as we find in the case of the concept of the "righteousness of God" (cf. v 30). By the Christological setting of his concepts Paul makes clear that wisdom is not a new attitude of mind in which man after all can gain direct insight into the divine wisdom (so that the insight of the pious would become an object of the doctrine of revelation). Believers are wise in the sense of 3:18f. They do not advance beyond the situation of hearing and believing (2 Cor 5:7).[85]

The conjunction of δύναμις, "power," and σοφία, "wisdom,"[86] shows that here "wisdom" is not a hypostasis[87] but a conceptual term. This is confirmed by the variant v 30 (ἡμῖν—ἀπὸ θεοῦ, "our—by God").[88] The (seemingly personifying) mode of expression is stylistically typical.[89]

■ **25** This verse is thrown into relief by its style, parallelism,[90] and also by the chiastic relation to v 24: τὸ μωρόν, "folly," answers to σοφία, "wisdom." τὸ ἀσθενές, "weakness," answers to δύναμις, "power." The sentence must be read in the first instance as a maxim on its own. In itself it is formulated without regard to the fact that God's appearing in foolishness represents only his reaction to the attitude of the world. It expresses in epigrammatic form a timeless rule of the relation between divine and human power.[91] The context, to be sure, raises it to the level of Pauline reflection. It becomes a definition of the historic relationship which God establishes through the cross.

84   The wisdom of God, see v 21; his δύναμις, "power," see v 18 and cf. Wis 7:25; Hab 3:19: God is my δύναμις.

85   Wilckens, *Weisheit und Torheit*, 39: wisdom is proclaimed only as the wisdom of God. Cf. Rom 1:16: the righteousness of God becomes manifest in the *gospel*.

86   Job 12:13, cf. 1QS 4.3 (חכמת גבורה, "almighty wisdom"). L. A. Rood, "Le Christ comme ΔΥΝΑΜΙΣ ΘΕΟΥ," in *Littérature et théologie pauliniennes*, RechBibl, 5 (Bruges: Desclée de Brouwer, 1960), 93–108. *PGM* 1:210f (in a Jewish prayer by Adam for rescue from ἀνάγκη, "distress"): Adam (the primordial man) is saved by his (!) σοφία and δύναμις; see Peterson, *Frühkirche*, 117.

87   In *PGM*[1] 1:210f the situation is that Adam has become an aeon, not that σοφία is hypostatized. This must be maintained also in Paul's case despite all links with wisdom speculation, against H. Windisch, "Die göttliche Weisheit der Juden und die paulinische Christologie," in *Neutestamentliche Studien: Georg Heinrici zu seinem 70. Geburtstag*, UNT, 6 (Leipzig: Hinrichs, 1914), 220–234 (see on 10:1ff). Wilckens assumes that the Corinthians use σοφία as a concept of hypostasis. But Paul does not frame his argument polemically against a Corinthian thesis. It is not possible to draw conclusions from v 24 regarding the Corinthian position. See K. Niederwimmer, "Erkennen und Lieben: Gedanken zum Verhältnis von Gnosis und Agape im ersten Korintherbrief," *KuD* 11 (1965): 75–102, here esp. 78, n. 11.

88   In 6:11 the same thing can be expressed in verbal form.

89   Eph 2:14: "He is our (!) peace." Suet., *Vitell.* 15.4: *ipsum esse concordiam*, "he himself was Concord" (Loeb 2:273). See William Chase Greene, "Personifications," *OCD*[1], 669–671.

90   See Blass–Debrunner §490, where, however, the reading of D G is preferred: σοφώτερόν ἐστιν τῶν ἀνθρώπων. But this is surely a secondary smoothing.

91   Lietzmann observes: "A pregnant way of expressing the reversal of values in the new aeon." But (*a*) the statement is in itself timeless; it speaks not of a revaluation, but of the real, timeless relationship between God and man; (*b*) the context then turns it into the statement of a reversal—not, however, in the new aeon, but in the hearing of the preaching. Not so Weiss: "The neuter adjectives do not require, as for example in 2 Cor 4:17; 8:8; Phil 4:5 . . . . to stand for the abstract substantive (foolishness, weakness); on the contrary, the very definite (hence the article) single act of God is highlighted, namely, the death of Christ on the cross, which is held by men to be a sign of foolishness and weakness." Against this stands the fact that while Paul is naturally thinking of the cross, yet he now derives from it a general rule in the style of a maxim concerning recognized fact. The view of Weiss is adopted also by Wilckens, *Weisheit und Torheit*, 37 (the appeal to Blass–Debrunner §263[2] is misleading), and by K. Müller, "I Kor 1,18–25."

1   The Shape of the Community

26   Look at your calling, then, brothers:[1]
there are not many who are wise according to the flesh, not many powerful,
not many highly born. 27 / But God has
chosen the foolish things of the world
to shame the wise, and God has chosen
the weak things of the world to shame
the strong, 28 / and God has chosen
the low and contemptible things of the
world, things that are nothing, to bring
to nothing things that are something,
29 / so that no flesh should boast before
God. 30 / By his act you are in Christ
Jesus, who has been made our wisdom
by God, our righteousness, sanctification and redemption,[2] 31 / in order that,
as it is written, "he who boasts, let
him boast in the Lord."

Stylistically speaking, the section vv 26–29 is a unity. The parallelism (cf. already v 25) "is carried out in the entire passage as exactly as the thought permits without sacrificing the clarity of thought to the form."[3] For reasons of content the parallelism is broken, inasmuch as Paul begins with the masculine ($\sigma o \phi o i / \epsilon \dot{v} \gamma \epsilon \nu \epsilon \hat{\iota} s$, "wise/highly born") and then passes over into the neuter. The previous catchwords are in part continued: from $\delta \acute{v}$-$\nu \alpha \mu \iota s / \sigma o \phi i \alpha$, "power/wisdom" (v 24) via $\sigma o \phi \acute{o} s /$ $\dot{\iota} \sigma \chi \nu \rho \acute{o} s$, "wise/strong" (v 25) to $\sigma o \phi \acute{o} s / \delta \nu \nu \alpha \tau \acute{o} s$, "wise/powerful" (v 26, with the addition of a third member). The expansion in the final member is in accordance with a demand of rhetoric (cf. v 20). The language shows traces of the Old Testament ($\kappa \alpha \tau$-$\alpha \iota \sigma \chi \acute{v} \nu \epsilon \iota \nu$, $\pi \hat{\alpha} \sigma \alpha \sigma \acute{\alpha} \rho \xi$, $\dot{\epsilon} \nu \acute{\omega} \pi \iota o \nu$, "shame, all flesh,

before"). The statements presuppose that the content of the preaching determines also the form of the community; both are "scandalous."

■ **26** Paul introduces a dialogical element; this is diatribe style.[4] The summons to observe themselves is paradoxical: they are to look where "nothing" is to be seen. The condition of the community demonstrates the freedom of God's electing grace.[5] $\kappa \lambda \hat{\eta} \sigma \iota s$ is here the act of calling[6] rather than the state of being called.[7] As the verb of the $\ddot{o} \tau \iota$–clause we can supply simply $\epsilon \dot{\iota} \sigma \acute{\iota} \nu$, "there are. . . ."[8] Since $\sigma o \phi \acute{o} s$, "wise" (unlike $\delta \nu \nu \alpha \tau \acute{o} s$, "powerful," and $\epsilon \dot{v} \gamma \epsilon \nu \acute{\eta} s$, "highly born"), is equivocal in this context, a qualification is added: instead of $\tau o \hat{v} \kappa \acute{o} \sigma \mu o \nu$, "of the world," as with the substantive (v 20), we have here in the case of the sub-

---

1   $\gamma \acute{\alpha} \rho$ with the imperative: Bauer, *s.v.* $\gamma \acute{\alpha} \rho$, 3; Diog. L., *Vit.* 6.47: $\pi \alpha \hat{v} \sigma \alpha \iota \gamma \acute{\alpha} \rho$, "cease then!"

2   $\tau \epsilon \ldots \kappa \alpha \iota \ldots \kappa \alpha \iota \ldots$: Blass–Debrunner §444(4): $\tau \epsilon$ is here simply a connective, not correlative to $\kappa \alpha \iota$; Heb 6:2.

3   Blass–Debrunner §490, where, to be sure, in v 28 the shorter reading is preferred (without $\dot{\epsilon} \xi \epsilon \lambda \acute{\epsilon} \xi \alpha \tau o$ $\dot{o}$ $\theta \epsilon \acute{o} s$, "God has chosen," following $\dot{\epsilon} \xi o \nu \theta \epsilon \nu \eta \mu \acute{\epsilon} \nu \alpha$, "contemptible things"), which is vouched for in this form only by Chrysostom; see Lietzmann. Weiss observes that the three members of the negative statement in v 26 provide the pattern for the three statements of the positive presentation. On the construction of the sentence Blass averred (see Blass–Debrunner §490): "From any Greek orator the artistry of this passage . . . would have called forth the utmost admiration. . . ." To this Eduard Norden, *Agnostos Theos: Untersuchungen zur Formengeschichte*

religiöser Rede (Leipzig and Berlin: Teubner, 1913; Darmstadt: Wissenschaftliche Buchgesellschaft, ⁵1971), 356, retorts: "This 'period' would have been described by any Greek orator and teacher of rhetoric as the 'utmost' monstrosity."

4   Bultmann, *Stil*, 32, 86 (imperative).

5   For this reason there can be no aesthetic play with "poverty" and "foolishness." Even the fact of "being nothing" is not a factor in salvation.

6   Weiss; Bauer, *s.v.* $\kappa \lambda \hat{\eta} \sigma \iota s$: "i.e., what happened when it occurred."

7   Karl Ludwig Schmidt, *TDNT* 3:491f; cf. 1 Cor 7:20.

8   Weiss would insert $\dot{\epsilon} \kappa \lambda \acute{\eta} \theta \eta \sigma \alpha \nu$, "are called." This accords with his understanding of $\kappa \lambda \hat{\eta} \sigma \iota s$, "calling" (explained by $\ddot{o} \tau \iota$, "that" [i.e., "look at your calling —that not many wise, etc., are called"]).

stantival adjective the synonym κατὰ σάρκα, "according to the flesh."[9] δυνατός emphasizes rather the political aspect, εὐγενής the social; the group comprises the educated, the influential, the people of distinguished family.[10] The fact that Paul is not upholding an ideal of poverty here is shown at once by the form of expression "not many." The rich are not excluded as such.[11]

■ **27–29** The three catchwords of v 26 are taken up:

οὐ πολλοὶ σοφοί: τὰ μωρά, τοὺς σοφούς

"not many wise": "the foolish things, the wise";

δυνατοί: τὰ ἀσθενῆ, τὰ ἰσχυρά

"powerful"[12]: "the weak things,[13] the strong";

εὐγενεῖς: τὰ ἀγενῆ

"highly born": "the low."[14]

Then comes a considerable expansion: τὰ ἐξουθενη-μένα, τὰ μὴ ὄντα, τὰ ὄντα, "contemptible things, things that are nothing, things that are something."[15] The style sharply underlines the σκάνδαλον, "offense," of free election. This is a Pauline way of taking up and working out Christologically the Jewish[16] idea of the overthrow of the lofty and the exalting of the lowly by God.[17] This time, appropriately enough and to emphasize the contrast, the qualification τοῦ κόσμου, "of the world," is added to all three groups of those who "are something."[18] ἐκλέγεσθαι, "choose," can denote the prehistoric decree of God, which takes concrete form in the historic "calling." Paul, however, does not attach any importance, in the sense of a theory of predestination, to the conceptual differentiation of individual acts that together make up election.[19] The sovereignty of God, which is envisaged in the concept of election, is brought out by the ἵνα–clauses, "to . . ."; they show the (realized) purpose of God, though not, to be sure, his ultimate aim. The latter appears in the ὅπως–clause, "so that . . ." (on the content cf. 3:19, 21). We notice again the conscious choice of words: καταισχύνειν, "shame," paves the way for the warning against καυχᾶσθαι, "boast";[20] it is replaced in the third member

---

9 Cf. σοφία σαρκική, "earthly wisdom," 2 Cor 1:12. The phrase κατὰ σάρκα with the substantive means "worldly"; with the verb, on the other hand, it designates in antithesis to πνεῦμα the behavior that is qualifiedly hostile to God; κατὰ σάρκα περιπατεῖν, "walk according to the flesh"; see Bultmann, *Theology* 1:237–239 [238f]. Lietzmann (translation) has "to men's way of thinking." Agreed, if we do not understand this in purely psychological terms, but as a characteristic in the sense of τοῦ αἰῶνος τούτου, "of this aeon (world)."

10 Cf. the series in 4:10; Orig., *Cels.* 2.79. Josef Bohatec, "Inhalt und Reihenfolge der 'Schlagworte der Erlösungsreligion,' I Kor. 1:26–31," *ThZ* 4 (1948): 252–271. On religion and social standing, see Franz Bömer, *Untersuchungen über die Religion der Sklaven in Griechenland und Rom*, AAM, 1957, 7; 1960, 1; 1961, 4; 1963, 10 (Wiesbaden: Steiner, 1957–63), *passim*; *ibid.* 3:152: the dividing line is ultimately between rich and poor, not between bond and free.

11 On the abrogation of worldly differences, see 12:13. Social differences come to light at the end of chap. 11 (cf. also Rom 16:23, Erastus).

12 Thuc., *Hist.* 2.65.2.

13 Plato, *Resp.* 364a: ἀσθενεῖς τε καὶ πένητες, "weak and poor."

14 ἀγενής in the sense of *ignobilis* (= ἀγεννής, Epict., *Diss.* 4.1.10): Jos., *Bell.* 4.148.

15 The use of the neuter for persons emphasizes the attribute, Blass-Debrunner §138(1), §263(4) (with genitive).

16 And moreover common to the whole ancient world.

Eur. *Tro.* 612f; Horat. *Carm.* 1.34.

17 Jos., *Ant.* 1.227; Philo, *Somn.* 1.155; 2 Cor 10:4–6; Lk 1:51ff (here the link between primitive Christianity and the OT and Judaism is especially clear). As an eschatological principle, "The first will be last," Mk 10:31 etc.

18 κόσμος in itself is neutral in value. The creation becomes "world" in the negative sense when it emancipates itself from the Creator and depends on its own power and wisdom.

19 This is not the intention in the articulated statement of Rom 8:28f either (τοῖς κατὰ πρόθεσιν κλητοῖς, "those who are called according to his purpose"); cf. Rom 9:11f: ἡ κατ᾿ ἐκλογὴν πρόθεσις—ἐκ τοῦ καλοῦντος, "the purpose of election—because of his call."

20 καταισχύνω, "shame": 11:4f, 22; Rom 5:5; 9:33; 10:11; 1 Pet 2:6; 3:16. Already in the OT with God as subject: Ps 43:10 (with the variant reading ἐξουδενέω, "bring to nothing"). The word designates primarily not the mental condition of shame, but the situation of ignomy in which the person concerned is placed; the antithesis is ἀγαλλιᾶσθαι, "exult," εὐφραίνεσθαι, "rejoice," also δοξάζεσθαι, "be honored," καυχᾶσθαι, "boast," Isa 45:24f; Ps 96:7ff.

by καταργεῖν, "bring to nothing," which is appropriate to "things that are something,"[21] as also to the rising climax in the last member.[22] The election of "that which is not"[23] is a religious rule in the devout Jewish practice of poverty, whereas in Paul it means the abrogation of the rule through the act of salvation, the cross. This puts an end to every (Paul is emphatic: πᾶσα σάρξ, "all flesh"[24]) possibility of human self–glorification.

καυχᾶσθαι/καύχησις, "to boast/boasting," is in Paul the basic human attitude toward God, that which man pursues by means of σοφία, "wisdom." The proclamation of the cross does not by any means replace unchristian self–glorification with self–glorification of a Christian kind, but with the renunciation of our own glory. For to glory "in the Lord" lays a one–sided emphasis on the "alienness" of this new possibility; *this* glory means glorying in the cross (Gal 6:14). Paul demonstrates it in his own person in the "foolish" self–glorying of 2 Cor 11:16—12:10

Paul is not here singing the "praise of folly." What he puts forward is strictly an interpretation of the event of salvation. He is not cultivating the resentment of the humiliated (however much the Christian community might appear to the Greeks to be a group with the moral disposition of the social underworld; cf. Celsus). Paul does not teach that "the" lowly will be exalted, but that faith becomes the receiver of salvation regardless of its worldly standing. He teaches not resentment, but freedom.

■ **30** The expression ἐξ αὐτοῦ κτλ., "by his act, etc.," is a description of *election*. This is shown by the correspondence with v 24 and with 3:23; on the content cf. Rom 9:11f.[25] The unity of thought in the whole verse is strictly soteriological: You are, by God's act, in Christ, insofar as salvation has been transmitted to you by the proclamation. Correspondingly, v 30b is an interpretation of the being of the crucified Lord. It was said above that he *is* God's δύναμις, "power," and σοφία, "wis-

---

21 ἐξουθενεῖν would also be appropriate (see previous note). But this word is ruled out by τὰ ἐξουθενημένα, "contemptible things."

22 καταργεῖν, frequent in Paul. In the LXX only in Ezra. τὰ ἐξουθενημένα: cf. 6:4. Philo. *Vit. Mos.* 2.240f: the ἀλαζόνες, "boasters," should learn ὅτι οὕτω ταπεινοὶ καὶ ἀτυχεῖς εἶναι δοκοῦντες οὐκ ἐν ἐξουθενημένοις καὶ ἀφάνεσι τάττονται παρὰ τῷ θεῷ, "how the persons who seem thus lonely and unfortunate are not treated as nothing worth and negligible in the judgment of God" (Loeb 6:569). The intensely eschatological sense of καταργεῖν is shown by passages like 2:4; 6:13; 13:8, 10; 15:24, 26.

23 τὰ μὴ ὄντα, "things that are nothing": Eur., *Tro.* 612f; Rom 4:17; Herm., *Vis.* 1.1.6; *Mand.* 1.1. The expression is readily employed for the doctrine of creation out of nothing: 2 Macc. 7:28; *S. Bar.* 21.4f; Philo, *Spec. Leg.* 4.187; see Bauer, *s.v.* εἰμί; Martin Dibelius, *Der Hirt des Hermas*, HNT, supplementary vol. (Tübingen: J. C. B. Mohr [Paul Siebeck], 1923), 415–644, here esp. 497. In Judaism it is transferred to conversion, which is interpreted as new creation, *Jos. et As.* 8.15. There is here no allusion of this kind to the (new) creation. For indeed τὰ ὄντα, "things that are (do mean) something," belongs to the negative side. An allusion of this kind should not be sought in v 30 either (by emphasizing ἐστέ, "you are"). For the reversal cf. Sir 10:14; Mt 11:25ff; Jas 2:5.

24 Rom 3:20; cf. for the content 3:21; Ps 143:2.

25 Others take it of the creation, cf. 8:6, where the link between the creation motif and the σοφία motif is plain. In that case, to be sure, ἐστέ, "you are," must be taken as an independent predicate and ἐν Χριστῷ, "in Christ," as an adverbial definition. The context tells against this, inasmuch as τὰ μὴ ὄντα, "things that are nothing," is used in a social, not a cosmological sense. In v 28b, too, what is emphasized is not the antithesis between what is and what is not, but the action of God in choosing what is not and destroying what is. In the same way, the accent here lies on the fact that they are *of God* and *in Christ*; cf. the accentuation of τοῦ θεοῦ, ἐξ αὐτοῦ, ἀπὸ θεοῦ, "before God, by his act, by God." The expression that Christ is "our" wisdom prohibits any interpretation which would here regard him as the hypostatized creation Wisdom; cf. the parallel concepts and 2 Cor 5:18, 21.

dom." Now it is said that he was made such, by God.[26] This points to the origin and direction of the event of salvation: from God, "in Christ," to us. And it shows that here we have not to do with general definitions of the being of Christ (in the sense of a speculation on hypostases), but with the exposition of the cross. This explains our existence in the world; we possess God's wisdom "in Christ," i.e., as an "alien" wisdom.

The three soteriological concepts are not systematically arranged.[27] The starting point here is δικαιοσύνη, "righteousness."[28] The commentary is provided by

2 Cor 5:21: Christ has been made sin by God "for us." Thus we are God's righteousness "in him."[29] ἁγιασμός, "sanctification," is explained by the verbal paraphrase in 6:11.[30] ἀπολύτρωσις, "redemption," is rare in Paul.[31]

■ **31** The "Scripture passage"[32] is an allusion to Jer 9:22f.[33] The sense depends on the emphasizing of ἐν κυρίῳ (see on v 30).

26 For the style, cf. the predications of σοφία also outside Judaism. Ael. Arist., *Or.* 8.51f; see Anton Höfler, *Der Sarapishymnus des Ailios Aristeides*, Tübinger Beiträge zur Altertumswissenschaft, 27 (Stuttgart and Berlin: Kohlhammer, 1935), 46–54. Isis is φρόνησις, "understanding," or σοφία θεοῦ, "wisdom of God," Richard Reitzenstein, *Poimandres. Studien zur griechisch–ägyptischen und frühchristlichen Literatur* (Leipzig and Berlin: Teubner, 1904; Darmstadt: Wissenschaftliche Buchgesellschaft, 1966), 44. See also Eduard Norden, *Die Geburt des Kindes*, Studien der Bibliothek Warburg, 3 (Leipzig and Berlin: Teubner, 1924), 98.

27 Bohatec, "Inhalt und Reihenfolge," 259 takes them as strict antithesis to the foregoing: τὰ μωρά—σοφία, τὰ ἀσθενῆ—δικαιοσύνη, τὰ ἀγενῆ—ἁγιασμός, τὰ μὴ ὄντα—ἀπολύτρωσις, "the foolish things—wisdom, the weak things—righteousness, the low things—sanctification, the things that are nothing—redemption." This is artificial; for the free construction of a series of this kind, cf. 6:11. Heinrici takes the last three concepts as exegesis of σοφία. This accords neither with their soteriological sense nor with the use of σοφία.

28 In 6:11 the verbal equivalent stands at the end, because Paul had there chosen a different starting point (baptism). The dilemma as to whether δικαιοσύνη is the saving action of God or the fruit of salvation is an abstract one, in view of the Christological character of the statement.

29 The alienness of righteousness is maintained: ἀπὸ θεοῦ, "by (from) God." Cf. Phil 3:9.

30 The word ἁγιασμός is rare in the LXX. It stands alongside δικαιοσύνη also in Rom 6:19(22); in paraenesis, 1 Thess 4:3–7.

31 ἀπολύτρωσις is a rare word (attested from the second/first century B.C.); in the LXX only in Dan 4:34. The meaning is ransom, ransom money (cf. λύτρωσις, Lk 1:68; 2:38). Paul uses it in few passages, but emphatic ones: Rom 3:24 in his introduction to the quotation in v 25; Rom 8:23 (apocalyptic). He does not link any specific theory of redemption with this word. Deissmann, *Light*, 327–334 [278–284], sought to discover one: Paul, he argued, interprets redemption with the help of sacral emancipation of slaves. But in the NT there is no realistic thought of ransom money, cf. Rom 8:23; Eph 1:14; 4:30; Friedrich Büchsel, *TDNT* 4:351–356. And Deissmann's interpretation of the material concerning a sacral emancipation (inscriptions from Delphi) is inaccurate; see Bömer, *Untersuchungen*, vols. 1 and 2; *ibid.* 2:123–129: even as a result of the fictitious consecration to the god, the slave does not enter into his service—the very opposite! On the facts of the situation in Delphi, *ibid.*, 2:29–51. Criticism of Deissmann ("highly imaginative"), *ibid.*, 2:133–141. On ἀπολύτρωσις see Stanislas Lyonnet, *Theologia Biblica Novi Testamenti: De peccato et redemptione*, vol. 2 (Rome: Biblical Institute Press, 1960).

32 See on v 19.

33 The same passage in greater detail, *1 Cl.* 13.1, in allusion to 1 Sam 2:10, but in remarkable agreement with Paul: ἀλλ' ὁ καυχώμενος ἐν κυρίῳ καυχάσθω, "but he who boasts, let him boast in the Lord." Was this taken over from Paul?

2 The Figure of the Preacher and the Form of His Preaching

1 And when I came to you, brothers,[1] I did not come[2] in such a way[3] as to distinguish myself in eloquence or wisdom, in order[4] to proclaim[5] to you the testimony (or: mystery[6]) of God. 2 / For[7] I was resolved not to know anything[8] among you save Jesus Christ, and the crucified Jesus Christ at that.[9] 3 / And I came to you[10] in weakness and fear and great trembling, 4 / and my message and my preaching consisted not in persuasive words of wisdom, but in a demonstration of the Spirit and of power, 5 / in order that[11] your faith should rest not on the wisdom of men, but on the power of God.

Just as the attitude of the community must accord with the word of the cross, so also must the form of the preaching and the bearing of the preacher. Thus vv 1 and 2 show the unity between the form and the content of the preaching, vv 3–5 the unity between the preaching and

1 Heinrici and Allo accentuate πρὸς ὑμᾶς, "to you" (because of ὑμῖν, "[proclaim] to you," and because of ἐν ὑμῖν, "among you," in v 2). Heinrici observes: "Paul's intentionally rudimentary (!) proclamation was particularly appropriate to the circumstances of this community." This shows how the psychological interpretation reduces itself *ad absurdum*.

2 For ἐλθών . . . ἦλθον, "when I came . . . I did (not) come," cf. Rom 15:29. The phrase has nothing to do with the customary LXX rendering of the Hebrew genitive absolute. ἦλθον, "I came," is here a statement on its own account; the word is to be taken with οὐ καθ' ὑπεροχήν, "not so as to distinguish" (Weiss), not with καταγγέλλων, "to proclaim" (as in Heinrici).

3 κατά of the manner, see Bauer, *s.v.* κατά, II 5b β.

4 Despite the *present* participle. Cf. 4:14; Acts 15:27; Xenoph., *Hell.* 2.1.29 (ἀπαγγελλοῦσα); Blass-Debrunner §339(2).

5 καταγγέλλων, "to proclaim": for the construction, see n. 2. Weiss observes that grammatically speaking we have here a conjunctive participle, but stylistically speaking a loosely appended independent statement.

6 μυστήριον, "mystery," is an "Egyptian" reading: p[46] ℵ* A C. Is Pol., *ad Phil.* 7.1 an echo (ὃς ἂν μὴ ὁμολογῇ τὸ μαρτύριον τοῦ σταυροῦ, "whosoever does not confess the testimony of the Cross" [Loeb 1:293])? If so, this passage would be the oldest evidence for the reading μαρτύριον. It is impossible to decide. Probably μυστήριον has here intruded itself from v 7 (with Zuntz, *Text*, 101f). Yet μαρτύριον,

too, can have intruded itself from 1:6. μυστήριον is supported by Lietzmann (on the ground of the "Egyptian" tradition), and by Bornkamm, *TDNT* 4:819, n. 141, for reasons of content. Bornkamm holds that in content μυστήριον means κηρύσσειν Χριστὸν ἐσταυρωμένον, "preaching Christ crucified," 1:23, cf. v 2, and that the μυστήριον is explained in vv 6ff.

7 γάρ is explanatory. Not so Weiss, who holds that then the imperfect would be required. But this is asking too much. According to Weiss, γάρ indicates the material reason.

8 οὐ can be taken with ἔκρινα: "I refused." Weiss holds that because of εἰ μή, οὐ belongs to τι: "I resolved to know nothing." Thus despite the word order, οὐ "is joined to τι in accordance with a well-known Greek rule," see Kühner–Blass–Gerth 2:180. Origen has οὐδὲν ἔκρινα εἰδέναι, "I resolved to know nothing."

9 Epexegetical καί, "and . . . at that" (with οὗτος), Blass–Debrunner §442(9).

10 Bachmann takes ἐγενόμην with ἐν: "I was among you in weakness"; cf. 1 Macc 1:27 (A): ἐγένετο ἐν πένθει, "she was in mourning." But πρός, "to," is too strong, and cf. v 1: ἐλθὼν πρὸς ὑμᾶς, "when I came to you." For ἐν cf. Rom 15:32 (ἐν χάρᾳ ἐλθών, "coming with [in] joy").

11 ἵνα final, of the purpose of God; thus the objective result is indicated at the same time.

the existence of the preacher.[12] This unity will then be the theme of 2 Corinthians.[13]

■ **1** Paul achieves the transition by means of a simple κἀγώ, "and I" (cf. v 3; 3:1), which corresponds to βλέπετε . . ., "look . . .," in 1:26. ἐλθών, "when I came": Paul frequently looks back upon the beginnings of his work in a particular community, in proemia (1 Thess 1:5; Phil 1:5), but also elsewhere (1 Thess 2:5ff; Gal 4:13). The two terms from the proemium, λόγος, "eloquence," and γνῶσις, "knowledge," are taken up in the variant form of 1:17 (σοφία, "wisdom," and λόγος, "eloquence"). The interchange of γνῶσις and σοφία shows that the two expressions cannot be strictly distinguished from each other. When Paul programmatically excludes λόγος and σοφία from *his* λόγος, this is done neither for tactical reasons nor from psychological motives (his personal make-up), but is strictly determined by the matter in hand. Everything is discarded which could provide additional human support for the message. For otherwise the latter would be subjected to human criteria and would no longer be revelation (cf. v 5).

■ **2** This statement brings a positive definition of the content and shows that the corresponding statements in 1:17, 23 were intended to be exhaustive.[14] οὐ γὰρ ἔκρινα κτλ., "for I was resolved, etc.": κρίνειν here means "resolve," cf. 5:3; 2 Cor 2:1. This resolve is not arbitrary;[15] it is reached on the ground of his understanding of the message, on the ground of the cross.[16] This also determines the sense of εἰδέναι, "know": not knowledge in general, but theological knowledge.[17]

■ **3** This is essentially a variant form of v 1[18] with a shift of emphasis from the preaching to the preacher. The threefold characterization[19] is again to be taken in a strictly theological sense; the state in question is not brought about by Paul himself (e.g., by asceticism and meditation, by inward exercises of penance). Rather, he understands his state (illness?) in the light of the cross; God brings him outwardly and inwardly into conformity with his preaching.

■ **4** He continues the explicatory variant on v 1 and goes on to describe his bearing also from the positive angle. In view of the correspondence with v 1, we ought not to seek any difference of meaning between λόγος "message,"[20] and κήρυγμα, "preaching"; it is a case of rhetorical duplication. The negative description is diffi-

12 There is a formal analogy with Epictetus' instructions to the Cynics, *Diss.* 3.22; cf. also Dio Chrys., *Or.* 16 [33]; Dieter Georgi, *Die Gegner des Paulus im 2. Korintherbrief*, WMANT, 11 (Neukirchen–Vluyn: Neukirchener Verlag, 1964), 192–200. Epict., *Diss.* 1.24.1: αἱ περιστάσεις εἰσὶν αἱ τοὺς ἄνδρας δεικνύουσι, "It is difficulties that show what men are" (Loeb 1:151). But the sense stands in antithesis to that of Paul: the περιστάσεις, "difficulties," call out the philosopher's own power and prove him to be a θεῖος ἀνήρ, "divine man."

13 The question of the literary unity of 2 Cor can be left open here. Cf. especially the observations on the unity in the bestowal of καταλλαγή, of the λόγος τῆς καταλλαγῆς, and of the διακονία τῆς καταλλαγῆς, "reconciliation, message of reconciliation, ministry of reconciliation," 2 Cor 5:18f.

14 There is no preparatory connecting link and no expansion of the content. This of course raises the problem of 2:6ff. According to Bachmann, v 2 cannot define the compass of the preaching, but only its quality. This is an un–Pauline alternative. It is true that there are certain elements that are seemingly added to the doctrine of the cross—eschatology, etc. But for all of these the cross is the criterion. Only the cross can be "proclaimed."

15 Here, too, it is wrong to psychologize, e.g. in the sense that Paul, having failed in his attempt to proffer wisdom in Athens, tried it the other way round in Corinth.

16 This establishes the antithesis to the Corinthian tendency. The Corinthians have gone on from the cross to the exaltation. Paul reverses the direction of thought: from exaltation to the cross. The result of the resurrection is not that the cross is superseded, but rather that it becomes possible to speak of it (see Wilckens, *Weisheit und Torheit*).

17 This is already evidenced by the fact that the term is subsumed under the head of ἔκρινα, "I was resolved," and more precisely defined by the addition of ἐν ὑμῖν, "among you." Paul's program has nothing in common with the philosophical attitude of agnosticism (Epict., *Diss.* 2.1.36; Dio Chrys., *Or.* 11[12].5).

18 Weiss observes that κἀγώ, "and I," points again to the arrival in Corinth, ἔκρινα, "I was resolved," having referred back to an earlier decision.

19 The combination of φόβος and τρόμος, "fear and trembling," is common; LXX, Isa 19:16, etc.; 2 Cor 7:15; Phil 2:12.

20 "My" word: cf. 2 Cor 1:18; similarly, 1 Thess 1:5: "our" gospel.

cult from the standpoint of the textual critic. The most important readings are these:

1. a) ἐν πειθοῖς σοφίας λόγοις, B ℵ* D.
   b) ἐν πειθοῖς ἀνθρωπίνης σοφίας λόγοις, A C ℜ.
   c) ἐν πειθοῖς σοφίας (om. λόγοις), p46 Ggr.

The difficulty lies in the fact that there is no evidence for the word πειθός, "persuasive," elsewhere. Yet it is etymologically unexceptionable (Lietzmann).[21]

2. a) ἐν πειθοῖ σοφίας λόγων, Origen, *Comm. in Matt.* 14.14; *in Joh.* 4.1; minuscules.[22]
   b) ἐν πειθοῖ σοφίας λόγου, d.
   c) ἐν πειθοῖ ἀνθρωπίνης σοφίας, Amb.
   d) ἐν πειθοῖ σοφίας, g.[23]

Lietzmann's solution is that 1(b), 2(a), (b) can be understood as corrections of 1(a). This, however, applies also to the other variants.[24] In view of the tradition, 1(a) is to be preferred. σοφίας is a qualitative genitive.[25]

And now the corresponding positive statement: ἀλλ' ἐν ἀποδείξει πνεύματος καὶ δυνάμεως, "but in a demonstration of the Spirit and of power."[26] Many exegetes are for taking πνεύματος and δυνάμεως as objective genitives.[27] Then Paul would be adopting almost exactly the position of the Corinthians. It is easier to take them as possessive genitives. To be sure, this can also be understood in the sense of the Corinthians: by their gifts of the Spirit they prove the truth of their views. It will depend on the theological interpretation of their existence as

a whole; Paul, too, holds the ecstatic phenomena and the miracles that take place in the community to be workings of the Spirit. But in his eyes these phenomena are subject to the eschatological proviso. They are provisional/transitory (see chap. 13). They do not prove the truth of the word of the cross, but are for their own part subject to the criterion of the cross. When Paul presents himself as a pneumatic, then he points to his "weakness" (2 Cor 12:6ff).

■ 5 He indicates the point of his appearing on the scene in this form. On the antithesis σοφία ἀνθρώπων = τοῦ κόσμου/δύναμις θεοῦ, "wisdom of men = of the world/power of God," cf. 1:20ff. The genitive ἀνθρώπων, "of men," contains a barb directed against "human" party slogans (cf. 3:3f). The antithesis makes it impossible for the believer to demonstrate his faith by displaying his power.

God's wisdom is defined in 1:24 as "Christ," as a wisdom which does not subject itself to human criteria, but confounds all such criteria. The next section, 2:6–16, deals with the *hiddenness* of wisdom.

---

21 The church fathers do not object to it. Cf. the word φειδός; Blass–Debrunner §112A (where, however, a corruption of the text from πειθοῖ is assumed). Radermacher, *Grammatik*, 63, would take πειθοῖς as genitive of πειθώ: "words of persuasion." Zuntz rejects the word πειθός, arguing that the abstract possibility of this word–form counts for nothing in view of the absence of actual examples—despite the frequency of the word-group πειθ– in rhetoric. Radermacher, *Grammatik*, 63, holds that φειδός has itself the nature of a gloss and was scarcely in living use any longer, so that it hardly provides a reason for accepting πειθός.

22 On the irregular position of the genitive in this reading, see Blass–Debrunner §474(4).

23 Plat., *Resp.* 411d: πειθοῖ διὰ λόγων χρᾶσθαι, "to make use of persuasion by speech" (cf. Loeb 1:293).

24 Zuntz, *Text*, 23–35, argues that Lietzmann made a false choice between the two oldest forms. The "Egyptian" and "western" texts are opposed to each other. It is not D that has the oldest form of the latter group; this is found in F G. The original text

is: οὐκ ἐν πειθοῖ σοφίας. λόγοις is a gloss from v 13, facilitated by the doubling of the initial sigma of σοφίας.

25 Bachmann takes it as a subjective genitive; *Corp. Herm.* 1:29: τοὺς τῆς σοφίας λόγους, "the teachings of wisdom."

26 ἀπόδειξις is a technical term in rhetoric: Plat., *Tim.* 40e; *3 Macc.* 4.20; *4 Macc.* 3.19; Epict., *Diss.* 1.24.8. According to Weiss, Paul rejects the γένος ἐπιδεικτικόν, "epideictic style." But there are other forms of rhetoric to which he comes nearer, namely, the Stoic and Cynic diatribe. It is also mistaken to point to the distinction between demonstrative presentation and mystical speech, Plut., *Def. orac.* 422c.

27 Bachmann, Schlatter; not so Bauer, *s.v.* ἀπόδειξις.

2

Hidden Wisdom

6   **Yet we do speak wisdom among those who are perfect, although it is not a wisdom belonging to this world, nor to the governing powers of this world, which are being brought to nothing, 7/ but we speak God's wisdom in a mystery,[1] the hidden wisdom which God purposed before the worlds (or: ages),[2] with a view to our glory. 8/ This wisdom none of the governing powers of this world (-age)[3] has known. For if they had recognized it, they would not have crucified the Lord of glory. 9/ But as it is written, "Things that[4] no eye has seen and no ear has heard and that never entered into any man's heart, all the things[5] that God has prepared for those who love him." 10/ For to us God has revealed them through the Spirit. For the Spirit explores all things, including even the depths of God. 11 / For who among men knows what a man is but the man's own spirit within him? In the same way no one has recognized what God is but the Spirit of God. 12 / We, however, have received not the spirit of the world, but the Spirit that comes from God, so that we may know what has been bestowed upon us by God. 13 / And it is also of this that we speak, not in words taught us by human wisdom,[6] but in words taught us by the Spirit, interpreting spiritual things in spiritual terms.[7] 14/ The unspiritual ("psychical") man, however, does not receive the things of God's Spirit. For they are foolishness in his eyes and he cannot recognize them, because they are (or: must be) spiritually interpreted. 15/ The spiritual man, however, judges all things,[8] but is not himself subject to anyone's judgment. 16/ For "who has discerned the mind of the Lord, so as to instruct him?" We, however, have the Spirit of Christ.**

---

1   ἐν μυστηρίῳ, "in a mystery," can be taken either with σοφία, "wisdom," or with λαλεῖν, "speak." (*a*) With σοφία: "in the form of a mystery" (similar to classical usage; Blass–Debrunner §220[2]), or "God's mysterious wisdom" (Lietzmann). For this it can be argued that ἐν μυστηρίῳ is further explicated—namely, in connection with hidden wisdom. (*b*) The very same argument is employed by Weiss in favor of taking it with λαλεῖν. A decision is impossible.

2   The meaning of αἰών is dubious. If we would show constancy in its usage, we must render "world." The sense requires "world–ages."

3   It would be best—though not linguistically speaking —to abide by "aeon."

4   The construction of the sentence is confused. ἅ, "things that," is both object and subject. *1 Cl.* 34.8 has presumably a principal clause: ἅ is presumably not the original text in *1 Cl.*, see the editions of Funk–Bihlmeyer, Fischer, and Knopf *ad loc*. But then there arises a further confusion, see below.

5   For ὅσα p[46] ℵ D G write ἅ. *1 Cl.* (except L): ὅσα. In that case the ὅσα clause ("all the things that...") is on the one hand subject and on the other hand object of the verbs in the previous clause.

The new section has the effect of retrospectively countering the preceding one. From the standpoint of 1:18ff, 2:1–5 is a program; in the light of 2:6–16, however, it is a curtailment. In the former passage the word of the cross was the *sole* content of the preaching, but now it is its *provisional* content. What is the relationship between these two aspects? Are they mutually exclusive? How, in that case, is their juxtaposition to be explained?

The section 2:6–16 stands out from its context both in style and in content. It presents a self-contained idea, a commonplace of "wisdom." It is a contradiction of his previous statements when Paul now announces after all a positive, undialectical possibility of cultivating a wisdom of the "perfect."

The structure provisionally appears to be: (a) wisdom (vv 6–9); (b) (wisdom) among the perfect (vv 10–16).

The conceptuality changes: the place of the eschatological terms (σωζόμενοι, ἀπολλύμενοι, "saved, lost") is taken by the language of the mysteries. The question[9] is, how far this implies a material shift in the position and the argument.[10] According to the argument so far, *this* σοφία, "wisdom," cannot be a supplementary factor alongside the word of the cross, but can only be the understanding of this word, which includes in particular the understanding of its foolishness. Wisdom would then be theology as a clarification of the proclamation; the "perfect" would be believers as the receivers of the teach-

ing; "we" would be the preachers.[11]

To be sure, the statements of the new section go a great deal further than this. The section is dominated by a pneumatic enthusiasm, a distinction between two classes of believer. The pneumatics here do not comprise all Christians, but only a superior class. The offense of the cross appears to be thrust aside in favor of the direct knowledge of spirit by spirit.[12] Bultmann explains this break in the thought as being due to the polemical situation. He thinks that Paul, in his eagerness to refute the ideas of his opponents, allows himself to be carried away into linking up with these ideas for the sake of argument, and in so doing is himself drawn a certain distance within their orbit.

It is clear that "wisdom" is a Corinthian topic. To be sure, it seems that in Corinth itself it was rather gnosis that was the operative word (see 8:1ff). And the catchword "wisdom" was apparently introduced to Corinth by Paul himself.[13]

Was this section conceived primarily as polemic or primarily as a statement of Paul's position? And how, accordingly, is it to be evaluated for the reconstruction of his theology on the one hand and that of the Corinthians on the other?

---

6   The genitive (designating the author) of the non-substantivized verbal adjective is singular in the NT. It is joined with λόγοις "as if διδακτοῖς were not there," Blass–Debrunner §183.

7   συγκρίνειν, "interpret": Gen 40:8; cf. Dan 5:7, 12 LXX: σύγκριμα (of dreams, signs). πνευματικοῖς can also be taken as masculine: "interpreting spiritual gifts for spiritual men." But it is simpler to take it as neuter: it is a question of the criterion.
    Two other meanings of συγκρίνειν are also possible: "compare" (so Reitzenstein, *Mysterienreligionen*, 336): "comparing spiritual gifts (which we receive) with spiritual gifts (which we already have)"; Max. Tyr., *Dial.* 6.4a. Or "combine": "bringing spiritual contents into spiritual form." Wilckens, *Weisheit und Torheit*, 85, prefers the second or third possibility on the ground that συγκρίνειν is a term of logic. This is not conclusive.

8   p⁴⁶ A C D* omit μέν and have the article before πάντα. Zuntz, *Text*, 109f, pleads for this reading: "D F G have a strange tendency never supported by p⁴⁶, to reduce the typically Pauline expression τὰ

πάντα by omitting the article." Here, he argues, the omission is suggested by v 10. Thus he thinks it would appear difficult to regard the article as secondary. This is not convincing.

9   Raised by Bultmann, *Faith and Understanding*, 1:71f [43f].

10   Wilckens, *Weisheit und Torheit*, 52–96.

11   So Barth. The same conclusion—by way of religious–historical analysis and critique of the content—is finally reached by Bultmann. Like Barth, K. Niederwimmer, "Erkennen und Lieben," *KuD* 11 (1965): 75–102 finds in 2:6–10 only exposition of the kerygma, not any new content. On this point see the exegesis in detail.

12   To the verge of identifying divine and human spirit (according to the principle "like by like," see below).

13   Cf. the eagerness with which he safeguards himself in 2:1–5 against the misunderstanding of his teaching.

The answer is partly determined by the observation that we can detect traces of a certain theological schema, the "revelation schema":[14] the "mystery" had been decreed by God from eternal ages, but remained hidden, and *now* it is revealed. This schema is found in the deutero–Pauline epistles and their neighborhood.[15] The question is whether Paul is already acquainted with it as such and is using a free adaptation of it in 2:6–16, or whether he himself is here developing the beginnings of the schema which was then further developed by his disciples. The former thesis is upheld by Lührmann.[16] In apocalyptic, he argues, μυστήριον, "mystery," means knowledge of the law of history, while in Gnosticism it means self–knowledge as redemption. He holds that both elements are contained in the revelation schema.[17] The schema, according to him, is not a *Christological* formula. The argument is not that Christ incorporates the revelation, but that since Christ revelation as proclamation is possible. The recipient is the pneumatic, who at once becomes the mediator of revelation.

Yet in all the passages outside the influence of Paul we find not the schema, but only individual motifs belonging to it. In its established form it first occurs in the deutero–Pauline epistles and is not gnostically conceived. On the contrary, it is constructed from the motifs of Hellenistic σωτήρ–ἐπιφάνεια, "savior–epiphany," religion.[18] It must therefore be assumed that the schema evolved within the internal life of the Pauline school, and that here we can see it *in statu nascendi*. This has consequences both for Paul and for the Corinthians (as also for the development of the Pauline school).

Lührmann rightly calls attention to the esoterism put forward in this section, the only instance of its kind in Paul. He concludes that here the Gnostic way of preaching has been taken up. But what is the source of the Corinthians' esoterism? Was it developed possibly from hints they received from Paul himself? We may take it that his written statements do not cover the whole compass of oral teaching. A difference between the levels of written publication and oral teaching is in accordance with good Greek tradition (cf. Plato), but also with good Jewish tradition (apocalyptic and rabbinism).

The decisive point, of course, is not general reflection on the history of religion, but the analysis of the section itself. Lührmann begins by noticing that in vv 8–10 breaks are apparent both in the train of thought and in the style. He argues that the break does not lie between v 9 and v 10 (as is held by many exegetes, taking γάρ, "for," antithetically as "but," see below), but that v 9 provides a transition to v 10, and that the break is indicated by ἀλλά, "but," in v 9. The situation, he says, is explained by the fact that Paul is taking over the revelation schema of his opponents and now proceeding to correct it in detail. The insertion (into the schema) of vv 8 and 9 asserts the place of the cross. Verse 14 makes clear to the opponents that all Christians have the Spirit, whereas they restrict the Spirit to an esoteric circle. He deletes the νῦν, "now," which belongs to the style of the schema,[19] and therewith the separation between the times of hiddenness and revelation.[20]

This does not explain adequately the fact that the

---

14 On the "revelation schema" see Nils A. Dahl, "Formgeschichtliche Beobachtungen zur Christusverkündigung in der Gemeindepredigt," in *Neutestamentliche Studien für Rudolf Bultmann su seinem siebzigsten Geburtstag am 20. August 1954*, BZNW, 21 (Berlin: Töpelmann, ²1957), 3–9; Ceslaus Spicq, *Agapé dans le Nouveau Testament*, Études Bibliques (Paris: Gabalda, 1958–59), 3:15–17; Dieter Lührmann, *Die Offenbarungsverständnis des Paulus und in paulinischen Gemeinden*, WMANT, 16 (Neukirchen–Vluyn: Neukirchener Verlag, 1965), 113–117.

15 Col 1:26f; Eph 3:5, 9f; 2 Tim 1:9f; Tit 1:2f; 1 Pet 1:20 (see Windisch *ad loc.*); Rom 16:25f (see Ehrhard Kamlah, *Traditionsgeschichtliche Untersuchungen zur Schlussdoxologie des Römerbriefes* [dissertation, Tübingen, 1955]).

16 Lührmann, *Offenbarungsverständnis*, 113–117.

17 Evidence: Just., *Apol.* 1.13.4; Iren., *Haer.* 3.13.1;

Hipp., *Ref.* 5.8.5, 26; 6.35.1; 7.25–27; Cl. Al., *Strom.* 1.55.1, 179.1; 5.60f, 64.6, 65.5, 87.1; 6.166.3. Yet all these passages show only motifs which are found in the revelation schema, but not the schema itself.

18 See Martin Dibelius and Hans Conzelmann, *The Pastoral Epistles*, tr. Philip Buttolph and Adela Yarbro, Hermeneia (Philadelphia: Fortress, 1972), excursus on 2 Tim 1:10, 100ff; (*Die Pastoralbriefe*, HNT, 13 [Tübingen: J. C. B. Mohr (Paul Siebeck), ⁴1966]).

19 νῦν: Col 1:26; Eph 3:10; 2 Tim 1:10; Rom 16:26; modified in Tit 1:3; 1 Pet 1:20.

20 Lührmann goes on to ask whether Paul in v 10 has put ἡμῖν . . . διὰ τοῦ πνεύματος, "to us . . . through the Spirit," in place of an original (ἡμῖν) τοῖς πνευματικοῖς, "(to us) who are spiritual."

section itself is nonpolemically conceived.[21] What is polemical is precisely the totally different context. The "we" within the section are those in the know as distinct from the powers of this world and the nonpneumatics. The character of *direct* polemic against the Corinthians attaches to the "we" only through its being placed between 2:1–5 and 3:1ff.[22] Paul is obviously here presenting his own wisdom, to which he then adds polemical highlights.[23] His starting point is the combination in Hellenistic Judaism of wisdom and apocalyptic, inspiration and vision. Paul sharpens this to mean the destruction of worldly wisdom. The derivation is betrayed by the fact that the content of 2:6–16 is in substance not Christian.[24] The marks of Paul's hand can be seen in the first instance in the *reduction* of the motifs of wisdom speculation. Just as in 1:18ff he took up the motif of *vanished* wisdom and concentrated on that, so he does here with the motif of *hidden* wisdom. He has before him the understanding of wisdom teaching as μυστήριον and

unveiling of the "mystery." The prevailing schema in the wisdom school is elementary teaching—higher gnosis.[25] Here the difficulty of knowledge of the mystery can be indicated.[26] Typical, too, is the picture of food (for children—adults),[27] and also the seeming contradiction: on the one hand it is emphasized that the perfect require no further instruction, while on the other hand such instruction is offered to them after all through the λόγος τέλειος, "perfect word."[28] This contradiction is explained by the structure of wisdom teaching. The wise are autonomous and teach each other wisdom.

For Paul, perfection is not only the goal, but also the status of every believer (a status, to be sure, which is dialectically understood, Phil 3:12–15). The division between believers of a lower and a higher order arises from the fact that the addressees do not conform to the true status conferred upon them (3:1ff). In order to bring this out, he takes up the two–order schema. The modification lies not so much within the present section as in

---

21 This is confirmed by the development of the schema in the deutero–Pauline epistles.

22 Cf. the forced transition to 3:1 with a break in the train of thought.

23 Hence the breaks noted by Lührmann. They indicate not a pre–Pauline schema and Paul's assimilation of it, but studies within the Pauline school and the application of them.

24 This leads Lührmann to the assumption that the "schema" is not Christological; he holds that it is not Christ who is "revealed," but a soteriological value (grace, or the like). It is true that in the passage before us only the polemical points are Christian. These are characteristically Pauline: the reference to the cross; at the end the characterization of the Spirit as the "Spirit of the Lord."

25 Bousset, *Schulbetrieb*; Ernst Käsemann, *Das wandernde Gottesvolk*, FRLANT, 55 (Göttingen: Vandenhoeck & Ruprecht, 1938), 117–124. The twofold gradation appears already in Philo, *Cher.* 48f; *Sacr. AC* 60; Jn 3:1–36. Heb 5:1–14 is especially pertinent. Joseph Pascher, Η ΒΑΣΙΛΙΚΗ ΟΔΟΣ: *Der Königsweg zu Wiedergeburt und Vergöttung bei Philon von Alexandreia*, Studien zur Geschichte und Kultur des Altertums, 17, 3–4 (Paderborn: Schöningh, 1931; New York: Johnson, 1968), thinks he finds behind the twofold gradation in Philo a mystery with two degrees of initiation: (1) the leading of the mystes through the cosmos; here he is a learner; (2) the mystes as visionary, who no longer needs the mystagogue. Pascher's view has this much truth in it, that the underlying ideas are of a mystical kind.

26 *Corp. Herm.* 13, beginning; *Naassene Sermon* 23 (Hipp. *Ref.* 5.8.22–29); cf. also Philo, *Rer. div. her.* 133, 121; symbolically represented by the nocturnal staging of Jn 3, where the two grades are defined as ἐπίγεια and ἐπουράνια, "earthly and heavenly." Heb 5:14: those who receive must be already τέλειοι, "perfect."

27 Heb 5:11ff: (a) τὰ στοιχεῖα τῆς ἀρχῆς/γάλα, "the first principles/milk"; (b) λόγος δικαιοσύνης/τροφή, "word of righteousness/(solid) food." Here Windisch observes: the second grade corresponds to Philo's instruction in morals. This is correct as far as the content is concerned, but not in regard to the schema. In the schema the moral teaching belongs in Philo to the lower grade.

28 Philo, *Migr. Abr.* 29: τὸ αὐτομαθές, τὸ αὐτοδίδακτον, τὸ νηπίας καὶ γαλακτώδους τροφῆς ἀμέτοχον, "Its own pupil, its own teacher, that needs not to be fed on milk as children are fed" (Loeb 4:149). *Leg. all.* 1.94: τῷ μὲν οὖν τελείῳ κατ' εἰκόνα προστάττειν ἢ ἀπαγορεύειν ἢ παραινεῖν οὐχὶ δεῖ, οὐδενὸς γὰρ τούτων ὁ τέλειος δεῖτα, τῷ δὲ φαύλῳ προστάξεως καὶ ἀπαγορεύσεως χρεία, τῷ δὲ νηπίῳ παραινέσεως καὶ διδασκαλίας, "There is no need, then, to give injunctions or prohibitions or exhortations to the perfect man formed after the (Divine) image, for none of these does the perfect man require. The bad man has need of injunction and prohibition, and the child of exhortation and teaching" (Loeb 1:209). Eph 4:13f.

the context. In a similar way the seeming contradiction, too, is transformed. In the schema itself, secret discipline can be demanded, although in a strictly logical sense it is pointless; for indeed the nonpneumatic simply *cannot* understand. Thus Paul declares that as yet he has been unable to impart wisdom to the Corinthians. He does not uphold any secret discipline, however, but explains his silence as merely a matter of pedagogy.[29]

Paul, like Philo, holds that the content of knowledge is the spirit—through the spirit. It is accordingly self–knowledge, and moreover unmediated (in contrast to the mediated self–knowledge of 1:18ff).[30]

■ **6** σοφίαν δὲ λαλοῦμεν κτλ., "Yet we do speak wisdom, etc.," sounds like an emphatic antithesis. To what? The simplest suggestion is v 5, an antithesis to the σοφία

ἀνθρώπων, "wisdom of men." In that case, the accent lies on ἐν τοῖς τελείοις, "among those who are perfect."[31] Who, then, are the "perfect"? We assume at first, of course, that they are the believers/saints. But 3:1ff show that Paul is thinking only of a higher class of believer. This is in conformity with a widespread use of the word τέλειος.[32] It belongs to the sphere of the language of the mysteries.[33] In the philosophic tradition the τέλειος is the man of perfect wisdom.[34] By way of anticipation, it can also be applied to the man who is on the road to the goal.[35]

Philo[36] takes up this usage.[37] But in his case a new element is added: perfection is reached through ecstasy.[38] The dominant note is a new style of esoterism[39] appropriate to the mysteries,[40] such as is found also in *Corp.*

---

29 In this he differs also from Qumran, especially from 1QS IX.17, 22; see Herbert Braun, *Qumran und das Neue Testament* (Tübingen: J. C. B. Mohr [Paul Siebeck], 1966) 1:188f (though Braun fails to notice 1 Cor 3:1–3). On Qumran see also Béda Rigaux, "Révélation des mystères et perfection à Qumrân et dans le Nouveau Testament," *NTS* 4 (1957–58): 237–262. In Qumran there is no trace of the basic principle of Hellenistic (and Pauline) pneumatism: "Like by like."

30 Philo, *Fug.* 49–52; *Cher.* 42–50; *Quaest. in Ex.* 2.39–47. Wilckens, *TDNT* 7:501, finds the basic principle already in Wis 6—10: "In Philo, too, [*sc.* as well as in Wis 6—10] the content of knowledge and the medium of knowledge are identical." σοφία and πνεῦμα Wis 7:7; 9:17.

31 λαλεῖν ἐν = λαλεῖν with the dative, 3:1; between λαλεῖν, "speak," and κηρύσσειν, "preach," no distinction should be made. Wilckens finds a twofold point here: (*a*) wisdom, though not man's wisdom, is nonetheless the content of the proclamation; (*b*) only among the perfect. This is surely to overestimate the importance of λαλοῦμεν. The plural is epistolary style. Naturally, every pneumatic can speak thus. But Paul is here dissociating himself in the first instance from the rest.

32 P. J. du Plessis, ΤΕΛΕΙΟΣ: *The Idea of Perfection in the New Testament* (Kampen: Kok, 1959); Reitzenstein, *Mysterienreligionen*, 338f; Käsemann, *Gottesvolk*, 82–90, 117–124; Hans Jonas, *Gnosis und spätantiker Geist*, vol. 2, pt. 1 (Göttingen: Vandenhoeck & Ruprecht, ²1966), 57–65. Literature: Gerhard Delling, *TDNT* 8:67–78.

33 Weiss is opposed to the derivation from the language of the mysteries. But the evidence cannot be overlooked. His argument that according to v 6 perfection is the *presupposition*, and not the result of

initiation into the mystery, is not to the point. For perfection and the communication of the λόγος τέλειος, "perfect word," are not to be separated from each other; one is initiated and then marches on from knowledge to knowledge.

34 See Delling, *TDNT* 8:69–72; Stob. *Ecl.* 2.7, 11g: (The Stoics) πάντα δὲ τὸν καλὸν καὶ ἀγαθὸν ἄνδρα τέλειον εἶναι λέγουσι διὰ τὸ μηδεμιᾶς ἀπολείπεσθαι ἀρετῆς, "But [the Stoics] say that every noble and good man is perfect, because no excellence is lacking in him" [Trans.].

35 Sen., *Ep.* 94.50. The προκόπτων, "the man who is making progress," can already be regarded in the light of perfection, Epict., *Ench.* 51.1f; *Diss.* 1.4.18–32.

36 Emile Bréhier, *Les idées philosophiques et religieuses de Philon d'Alexandrie*, Etudes de philosophie médiévale, 8 (Paris: Vrin, ³1950), 242–249; Walther Völker, *Fortschritt und Vollendung bei Philo von Alexandrien*, TU, 49 (Leipzig: Hinrichs, 1938); Jonas, *Gnosis* 2.1:70–121.

37 The three grades of the σπουδαῖος, Philo, *Leg. all.* 3.159: ὁ ἀρχόμενος, ὁ προκόπτων, ὁ τέλειος, "the man who is just beginning his training," "the man who is making gradual progress," "the perfect man" (Loeb 1:407); cf. *Agric.* 165.

38 Philo, *Som.* 2.230–233.

39 Philo, *Cher.* 42 (cf. 48): τελετὰς δὲ ἀναδιδάσκομεν θεῖος τοὺς τελετῶν ἀξίους τῶν ἱερωτάτων μύστας, "For this is a divine mystery and its lesson is for the initiated who are worthy to receive the holiest secret" (Loeb 2:35).

40 Perfection is the receipt of holy consecration, Philo, *Leg. all.* 3.219.

Herm. 4.1[41] and in the so–called *Naassene Sermon* in Hippolytus,[42] that is to say in the milieu of Gnosticism.[43]

If the wording is not pressed, and vv 10ff are taken into account along with 3:1ff, then Paul is here hinting at additional pieces of knowledge which he has so far withheld from the Corinthians. In that case we have to ask what relation this bears to his previous statements.

The question whether the ἄρχοντες, "governing powers," are demons or political powers has long been in dispute.[44] The mythical context suggests the interpretation demons,[45] and so also does the solemn predication τῶν καταργουμένων, "which are being brought to nothing."[46] They are the minions of the "god of this aeon" (2 Cor 4:4).[47]

---

41 *Corp. Herm.* 4.4: ὅσοι μὲν οὖν συνῆκαν τοῦ κηρύγμα-τος καὶ ἐβαπτίσαντο τοῦ νοός, οὗτοι μετέσχον τῆς γνώσεως καὶ τέλειοι ἐγένοντο ἄνθρωποι, τὸν νοῦν δεξάμενοι. ὅσοι δὲ ἥμαρτον τοῦ κηρύγματος, οὗτοι μὲν οἱ λογικοί, τὸν νοῦν μὴ προσειληφότες, ἀγνο-οῦντες ἐπὶ τί γεγόνασιν καὶ ὑπὸ τίνων . . ., "Now those who gave heed to the proclamation, and who were baptized with the baptism of mind, these men got a share of *gnosis*; they have become *perfect* men, for they have received mind. But those who have failed to heed the proclamation, they are the *logikoi*, those who . . . have not acquired mind, and know neither why nor whence they were born" (cf. *Hermetica*, ed. and tr. Walter Scott [Oxford: Clarendon, 1924], 1:151, 153.

42 *Naassene Sermon* 21 (Hipp., *Ref.* 5.8.21): οὐ δύναται οὖν, φησί, σωθῆναι ὁ ⟨μὴ⟩ τέλειος ἄνθρωπος, ἐὰν μὴ ἀναγεννηθῇ διὰ ταύτης εἰσελθὼν τῆς πύλης (Gen 28:7, 17) . . ., "Therefore, he says, the perfect man will not be saved unless born again by entering in through this gate" (Francis Legge, *Philosophou-mena*, Translations of Christian Literature, ser. 1 [London: SPCK, 1921], 1:134). *Naassene Sermon* 23 (Hipp., *Ref.* 5.8.26): καὶ ταῦτα, φησίν, ἐστὶ τὰ τοῦ πνεύματος ἄρρητα μυστήρια . . ., "and these, he says, are the ineffable mysteries of the Spirit" (Legge 1:135f), which only the perfect Gnostics know. See Wilckens, *Weisheit und Torheit*, 55; Richard Reitzen-stein and Hans Heinrich Schäder, *Studien zum antiken Synkretismus aus Iran and Griechenland*, Studien der Bibliothek Warburg, 7 (Leipzig and Berlin: Teub-ner, 1926), 169f.

43 Wilhelm Bousset, *Die Hauptprobleme der Gnosis*, FRLANT, 10 (Göttingen: Vandenhoeck & Rup-recht, 1907), 238–276. Justin in Hipp., *Ref.* 5.24.2: τελειῶν τοὺς μύστας τὰ ἄλαλα μυστήρια, "per-fecting the mystae by unspoken mysteries" (Legge 1:171). *Ev. Phil.* 40 (cf. 100, 106): "Man ploughs the field by means of the beasts which are subject [to him]. . . . So it is with the perfect man [τέλειος]. Through powers [δυνάμεις] which are subject [ὑπο-τάσσειν] he ploughs. . . . The Holy Spirit tends everything and rules [ἄρχειν] all the powers . . ." (*The Gospel of Philip*, tr. Robert McL. Wilson [Lon-don: Mowbray, 1962], 36). *Od. Sal.* 35.6.

44 A review of the argument is already provided by Theodore of Mopsuestia; see Karl Staab, *Paulus-kommentare aus der griechischen Kirche aus Katenenhand-schriften*, NtlAbh, 15 (Münster: Aschendorff, 1933), 174. Theodore himself supports the demonological interpretation. The political view is upheld by Julius Schniewind, "Die Archonten dieses Äons, 1. Kor. 2,6–8," in his *Nachgelassene Reden und Aufsätze*, ed. Ernst Kähler (Berlin: Töpelmann, 1952), 104–109. He bases his argument on the fact that the word ἄρχοντες does not elsewhere in the NT denote de-mons. Feuillet is for a combination of both positions, *Le Christ Sagesse*, 25–36.

45 Hans von Campenhausen, "Zur Auslegung von Röm. 13: Die dämonische Deutung des ἐξουσία-Begriffs," in *Festschrift für Alfred Bertholet zum 80. Geburtstag*, ed. Walter Baumgartner *et al.* (Tübingen: J. C. B. Mohr [Paul Siebeck], 1950), 97–113, here esp. 100f, now in his *Aus der Frühzeit des Christentums* (Tübingen: J. C. B. Mohr [Paul Siebeck], 1963), 81–101, here esp. 84–86; Wilckens, *Weisheit und Torheit*, 61–63. Rabbinic demonology: Str.-B. 4.2, index, *s.vv.* "Dämonologie," "Engel"; *Sifre zu Numeri*, ed. Karl Georg Kuhn, Rabbinische Texte, 2. Reihe: Tan-naitische Midraschim, 3 (Stuttgart: Kohlhammer, 1959), 698–700. ἄρχοντες in this sense: Ign., *Tr.* 5.2; *Sm.* 6.1; *Act. Joh.* 114; *Act. Thom.* 10, 143; *Pist. Soph.* (see index).

46 Present participle: "transient," 2 Cor 3:11, 13; for the eschatological use, cf. 15:24, 26.

47 Against the political interpretation it may be asked: What should earthly powers have to do with super-natural wisdom? Feuillet, "Les 'chefs de ce siècle' et la sagesse divine d'après *1. Co.* II,6–8," in *Studi-orum Paulinorum Congressus Internationalis Catholicus 1961*, Analecta Biblica, 17 (Rome: Biblical Institute Press, 1963), 1:383–393, recalls Bar 3:16ff: ποῦ εἰσιν οἱ ἄρχοντες τῶν ἐθνῶν; . . . (19) ἠφανίσθησαν, "Where are the princes of the nations? . . . They have vanished." The Syriac version presupposes עולם instead of עמים (τοῦ αἰῶνος instead of τῶν ἐθνῶν, "age" instead of "nations"). But in Bar we have before us a totally different case.

■ **7** This verse describes the positive antithesis to worldly wisdom, God's wisdom ἐν μυστηρίῳ, "in a mystery."[48] The expression is to be taken as a unity. μυστήριον is not merely a fortuitous accidental, but constitutes the structure of this wisdom. μυστήριον is so widely used as a catchword, and is in the first instance so formal, that the content to be ascribed to it can be gathered only from the context at hand. Apart from the classical and Hellenistic mystery celebrations,[49] there are two types which provide material for comparison: (1) the Gnostic tradition;[50] (2) the Jewish tradition (a) of "wisdom";[51] (b) of apocalyptic.[52] The common factor is their esoterism. The latter is found in intensified form in the Qumran writings.[53] It evolves in a type of rabbinic speculation.[54] Here it should be noted that "wisdom" and apocalyptic pass over into each other.[55] Both aspects are also linked together in Paul.

A constitutive element of the "mystery" is its unveiling (by the prophet, wise man, or Gnostic, who receives it by means of vision or illumination and communicates it to the initiates/initiands).

ἣν προώρισεν, "which he purposed before":[56] The interplay between God's pretemporally conceived plan of salvation and his calling in history is the basic characteristic of the view of election (Rom 8:28ff; 9:23f). In the deutero–Pauline literature it is objectified to become a "revelation schema" (see above). In 1 Corinthians an intermediate stage can be seen. The "present" unveiling is indicated by the expression εἰς δόξαν ἡμῶν, "with a view to our glory."[57] δόξα, "glory," describes our new being as supernatural.[58] Paul is on the verge of a self–understanding in Gnostic terms of habitual disposition, but avoids it by pointing to the "*extra nos*" factor.[59] The decree of God[60] is not speculatively expounded or mythically illustrated. It is merely referred to as marking the horizon of the saving knowledge that is proclaimed by those in the know.[61]

■ **8** This verse gives an impression of indefiniteness.[62]

---

48 On the relationship of ἐν μυστηρίῳ, see n. 1.

49 H. Krümer, "Zur Wortbedeutung 'Mysteria,' " *WuD* n.s. 6 (1959): 121–125. μυστήριον denotes that the events of the feast are ineffable, Epict., *Diss.* 3.2.13–24.

50 Hipp., *Ref.* 5.7.27: κεκαλυμμένον καὶ ἀνακεκαλυμμένον, "veiled and unveiled." *Naassene Hymn* (Hipp., *Ref.* 5.10.2): μυστήρια πάντα δ' ἀνοίξω, μορφὰς δὲ θεῶν ἐπιδείξω. [καὶ] τὰ κεκρυμμένα τῆς ἁγίας ὁδοῦ, γνῶσιν καλέσας, παραδώσω, "All mysteries I will disclose; / The forms of the gods I will display; / The secrets of the holy way / Called Gnosis, I will hand down" (Legge 1:145). *Corp. Herm.* 1.16; 16.2.

51 Wis 2:22; 6:22; 14:15, 23. Raymond E. Brown, "The Semitic Background of the New Testament *Mysterion*," *Biblica* 39 (1958): 426–448; 40 (1959): 70–87, now reprinted in his *The Semitic Background of the Term "Mystery" in the New Testament*, Facet Books, Biblical Series, 21 (Philadelphia: Fortress, 1968).

52 Dan 2:18f, 27ff. The antithesis is the "keeping" of the secrets, 1Q27 (=1QMyst) I, 7, cf. 2 Thess 2:6f (?).

53 Rigaux, "Révélation des mystères et perfection," *passim.* Revelatory speech: 1QS III, 13—IV, 25, esp. IV, 6, 22. Illumination: 1QS XI, 3–6. Further: 1QH VIII, 10–36; XII, 12; XIII, 13f; 1QpHab VII, 3–5 (eschatology and understanding of Scripture).

54 In the throne–chariot speculation, see *Chag.* 2.1; cf. *b. Chag.* 11b–14b; Str.–B. 1:579; 2:302–333, esp. 307f.

55 From the side of apocalyptic, in Daniel; from the side of "wisdom," in Wis.

56 According to Weiss, a change of thought has intruded between the principal clause and the relative clause: ἣν προώρισεν is out of place, but what Paul means is something like καθ' ἣν προώρισεν ... δοξάζειν ἡμᾶς, "according to which he predetermined ... our glorification." Weiss fails to notice that σοφία is not merely a formal statement of the fact of God's being wise, but that Paul is already thinking of the content, God's plan of salvation.

57 Quite apart from whether or not we join εἰς δόξαν and προορίζειν (Bachmann, Bauer, *s.v.* προορίζειν), cf. Eph 1:5.

58 Rom 8:18, 21, 30; 9:23; 2 Cor 4:17.

59 E.g., by means of the preposition σύν, "with" (Rom 8:17), cf. σύμμορφος, "conformed," Rom 8:29; Phil 3:21. In itself, this mode of expression is mystical. But the σὺν Χριστῷ formula points at once to the *Christus extra nos*, and indeed doubly so—sacramentally and eschatologically (Rom 6; 1 Thess 5:10).

60 προορίζειν in Rom 8:29 refers to the election of the individual, here to God's plan for the world.

61 Apocalyptic could present at this point the epochs of the world's course, Gnosticism the prehistory of the Light–Self and the sending of the revealer (conversations in heaven).

62 Weiss finds here again his construction pattern a b a: vv 6, 7, 8a.

For the initiate can only hint that he knows the "Lord of glory." A divine predicate is here transferred to the "Lord" Jesus.[63] That he is hidden from the powers of the world is again a view that is common both to wisdom and to apocalyptic.[64] For in his descent through the cosmos he has disguised himself.[65] Lietzmann sees in the background the well–known motif of the deception of the devil.[66]

In Paul's case a twofold contradiction now arises. (a) Externally, the passage is in contradiction to the context; contrary to 2:1–5 Paul here points after all to a supplementary, higher wisdom teaching, namely, an insight into the cosmic background of the crucifixion. (b) When the mythical idea of the descent of the revealer is transferred to a historic process, the result is to upset the idea itself. If the ἄρχοντες, "governing powers," did not recognize Jesus, why then did they crucify him? Did they know that he was the revealer, but not that his death was to be the very means of their own annihilation?[67] The wording makes this latter interpretation hardly possible. So the contradiction remains. This is the very means of bringing out the point, the *theologia crucis*, and hence the paradoxical conjunction of Kyrios and cross.[68] This is obvious polemic against the Corinthians' exaltation Christology.

The phrasing makes it impossible to interpret wisdom as a hypostasis.[69]

■ **9** The quotation cannot be found either in the Old Testament or in extracanonical Jewish writings.[70] But there is a wide scattering of similar passages, in keeping with the widespread religious motif of hiddenness and unveiling.[71] There are reminiscences (a) of the Bible, Isa

---

63 τῆς δόξης, "of glory," is in keeping with εἰς δόξαν ἡμῶν, "with a view to our glory." For the qualitative genitive, cf. Eph 1:17; Heb 9:5; Ps 28:3; *Eth. En.* 63.2: "the Lord of glory and the Lord of wisdom" (Charles, *APOT* 2:229).

64 Wisdom: Bar 3, etc. Apocalyptic: according to *Eth. En.* 16.3 God does not disclose all his plans even to the angels.

65 This motif has a part to play in Gnosticism: *Asc. Is.* 10; Epiph., *Haer.* 21.2.4; *Pist. Soph.* 7; *Ev. Phil.* 26; Ign. *Eph.* 19; cf. also *Epist. Ap.* 13 (24); see Heinrich Schlier, *Religionsgeschichtliche Untersuchungen zu den Ignatiusbriefen*, BZNW, 8 (Giessen: Töpelmann, 1929), 5–81.

66 Basilides (Iren., *Haer.* 1.24.4); Orig., (*Comm. in Matt.* 16.8); Martin Dibelius, *Die Geisterwelt im Glauben des Paulus* (Göttingen: Vandenhoeck & Ruprecht, 1909), 92–99.

67 So Weiss; Rudolf Liechtenhan, *Die urchristliche Mission*, AThANT, 9 (Zurich: Zwingli, 1946), 71, n. 12. Against this, Kümmel argues that Paul never presupposes the possibility of knowing Christ but failing to see the meaning of the cross. We should bear in mind, however, that here it is a question of cosmic powers.

68 The κύριος title is found elsewhere in reference to the cross only in Gal 6:14. Lührmann, *Offenbarungsverständnis*, 137, observes: "The hiddenness of God's wisdom is radicalized by the paradoxical combination κύριος—cross; the cross for Paul does not mean revelation, just as little as does the 'historical Jesus.'" We naturally must not go on to ask what would

have happened if the *archontes* had not crucified Jesus. The myth functions merely as a means of interpreting the actual fact of the cross.

69 So Wilckens, who argues that the "wisdom of God" is identical with the "Lord of glory." Not at all! Wisdom is "spoken"; it is the *teaching* about this Lord.

70 According to Origen, it comes from the Elijah apocalypse (Orig., *Comm. in Matt.* 5.29, on Mt 27:9): *Et apostolus scripturas quasdam secretorum profert, sicut dicit alicubi "quod oculus non vidit nec auris audivit": in nullo enim regulari libro hoc positum invenitur nisi in secretis Eliae prophetae*, "The Apostle, too, quotes certain apocryphal writings, as when he somewhere says, 'that which eye has not seen nor ear heard': for indeed this passage is not found in any canonical book, but only in the apocryphon of Elijah the prophet" [Trans.]. Pierre Prigent, "Ce que l'oeil n'a pas vu," *ThZ* 14 (1968): 416–429; Marc Philonenko, "Quod oculus non vidit, I Cor. 2,9," *ThZ* 15 (1959): 51f; André Feuillet, "L'Énigme de *I Cor.*, II,9: Contribution à l'étude des sources de la christologie paulinienne," *RB* 70 (1963): 52–74 (rev. ed. now in *Le Christ Sagesse*, 37–57). For τοῖς ἀγαπῶσιν, "for those that love," see J. B. Bauer, ".... τοῖς ἀγαπῶσιν τὸν θεόν, Rom 8:28 (I Cor 2:9, I Cor 8:3)," *ZNW* 50 (1959): 106–112.

71 Parallel passages in secular Hellenistic literature, such as Plut., *Aud. poet.* 17e, are of no consequence.

64:3; Ps 31:20;[72] (b) of rabbinical literature;[73] (c) of apocalyptic, *Asc. Is.* 11:34 (2nd century A.D.): "For thou hast seen what no other born of flesh has seen."[74]

The quotation in 1 Corinthians does in fact have an apocalyptic ring. But here we have to bear in mind the affinity between apocalyptic and (d) wisdom.[75] (e) The Qumran texts, too, have a place in this stylistic context.[76] A saying of this kind is naturally also preeminently suited for use by (f) Gnostics.[77] But, as the material shows, it did not *arise* within Gnosticism.[78]

In view of the dual role played by ἅ, "things that," as subject and object, all attempts to rescue the construction of the sentence are to no purpose. ὅσα[79] ἡτοίμασεν, "all he has prepared": the good things of the beyond even now lie ready.[80] On τοῖς ἀγαπῶσιν αὐτόν, "for those who love him," cf. Rom 8:28.[81] Over against the eschatological interpretation of the benefits of salvation in terms of future blessedness stands a different interpretation, in terms of wisdom.[82] The conclusion vigorously emphasizes that salvation (whether it is understood in an eschatological or a present and spiritual sense) is the work of God alone. This is a Jewish idea.[83] Everything will now depend on how man understands himself as the receiver of the gift: whether he keeps the *sola gratia* continually before him, or whether the gift is swallowed up in the past, so to speak, and replaced by a habitual state of grace. The proof will lie in the question whether man as the receiver of grace is included in theology as an object, or whether theology remains strictly exposition of the event of grace.

---

72 Prigent again assumes that we have here a combination of these two passages. The combination originates, he says, in the liturgy of the synagogue; cf. the liturgical context of the quotation in Christian sources.

73 Str.–B. 3:327–329. The material context is the statement that the predictions of the prophets extend only to the messianic age, not beyond it.

74 Cf. *Asc. Is.* 8:11; Ps.–Philo, *Ant. bib.* 26.12–14; Philonenko, "Quod oculus non vidit."

75 For the overlapping of prophecy and wisdom, cf. Isa 45:3; Prov 2:3ff; Rom 10:6–8; 11:34f (Isa 40:13); cf. Wis 9:13; Sir 1:3. Feuillet, "L'Énigme," and *Le Christ Sagesse*, 37–57, rightly points to hidden wisdom in Prov 30:1–4; Sir 1:10; Job 28; Bar 3f. The content can be cosmological knowledge (Wis 7:17–19). ἐπιστήμη, "knowledge" (= σοφία) is the Mother of the All, Philo, *Ebr.* 31; cf. Aristob., Fr. 5 (Eus., *Praep. Ev.* 13.12.11a), where we have the same tradition; see Nikolaus Walter, *Der Thoraausleger Aristobulos*, TU, 86 (Berlin: Akademie–Verlag, 1964), 64f. Contemplation of God with the eyes of the *nous*: Philo, *Quaest. in Ex.* 2.39f.

76 1QS XI.5–7; 1QpHab VII.

77 *Ev. Thom.* 17: "Jesus said: I will give you what eye has not seen and what ear has not heard and what hand has not touched and (what) has not arisen in the heart of man" (*The Gospel According to Thomas*, ed. and tr. A. Guillaumont *et al.* [Leiden: Brill; New York: Harper & Row, 1959], 13). Manichaean Turfan fragment M 789 (*New Testament Apocrypha*, ed. Edgar Hennecke, rev. Wilhelm Schneemelcher, tr. and ed. Robert McL. Wilson [London: Lutterworth; Philadelphia: Westminster, 1963–65], 1:300). Mandaean liturgies: Mark Lidzbarski, *Mandäische Liturgien*, AGG, n.s. 17, 1 (Berlin: Weidmann, 1920; Hildesheim: Olms, 1962), 77, line 4; see thereon

M.–J. Lagrange, "La gnose mandéenne et la tradition évangélique," *RB* 37 (1928): 5–36, here esp. 11. Further information in Prigent, "Ce que l'oeil n'a pas vu," 423.

78 With Oepke, *TDNT* 3:989, against Wilckens, *Weisheit und Torheit*, 75, n. 1. Passages outside Gnosticism: *1 Cl.* 34.8 (last line not parallel); *2 Cl.* 11.7; *Mart. Pol.* 2.3; Cl. Al., *Prot.* 10.94.4; *Const. ap.* 7.32.5. ἐπὶ καρδίαν οὐκ ἀνέβη, "did not enter into the heart," is Jewish style, Isa 65:16; Jer 3:16; cf. Lk 24:38; Acts 7:23.

79 On the later history of the passage see Prigent, "Ce que l'oeil n'a pas vu," and Feuillet, "L'Énigme." We find (a) stich 1–3; (b) stich 3 (*2 Cl.* 14.5); (c) stich 1+2, but introduced by a phrase corresponding to stich 3 (Hipp. *In Dan.* 4.59; *2 Cl.* 11.7; *Mart. Pol.* 2.3; Cl. Al., *Prot.* 10.94.4); (d) finally even 3+1+2+3, cf. *S. Nu.* 27.12.

80 *4 Ezra* 8.52–62; *Eth. En.* 103.3.

81 1 Cor 8:3; *Ps. Sal.* 4.25; 6.6; 10.3; 14.1. *1 Cl.* 34.8: τοῖς ὑπομένουσιν αὐτόν, "them that wait for him" (Loeb 1:67). Weiss presumes that we have here an apocalyptic messianic formula which Paul in Rom 8:28 explains by the phrase τοῖς κατὰ πρόθεσιν κλητοῖς οὖσιν, "those who are called according to his purpose." J. B. Bauer, ". . . τοῖς ἀγαπῶσιν" (see n. 70).

82 Dupont, *Gnosis*, 107f, 190, n. 2; Feuillet, "L'Énigme," argues that a strictly eschatological interpretation is not in harmony with the context. The quotation, he says, provides an explanation of σοφίαν ἐν μυστηρίῳ, "wisdom in a mystery."

83 1QH I.21: "These things have I known because of Thine understanding; for Thou hast uncovered my ear to marvellous Mysteries" (André Dupont–Sommer, *The Essene Writings from Qumran*, tr. Geza Vermès [Cleveland and New York: World/Merid-

■ **10** ἡμῖν, "to us," is emphatic, strengthened by γάρ, "for."[84] It is explained (after the anticipation in v 6) by the context: the τέλειοι, "perfect," are the ἀγαπῶντες, "those who love," who are the pneumatics.[85] Paul now replaces σοφία, "wisdom," with πνεῦμα (πνευματικά), "spirit (spiritual things)."[86] Here it remains an open question to begin with whether he is speaking of God's Spirit as his power to reveal (in the sense of "all that God has prepared") or of the divine Spirit in man as that which makes possible the receiving of revelation (in the sense of "for those who love him"). In the underlying schema of the mysteries the essential idea is precisely the identity of the power to reveal and to receive. Paul does in fact go on in this sense. In so doing he is on the verge of Gnosticism—to be sure, without developing the mythical motif of descent. He speaks in a way that takes no account of the historic character of revelation, but solely of the illumination of the recipients. The object of knowledge is not the historic Christ, but the mystery, and only in a secondary sense the mythical background of the historic crucifixion.

Where does the unity between the metaphysical and anthropological senses of πνεῦμα, "spirit," originate, and with it the affinity between πνεῦμα and σοφία? It is anticipated in the Stoa, where πνεῦμα is a cosmological and anthropological factor in one.[87] The concept is taken up and transposed into the typical wisdom style of Hellenistic Judaism in the Wisdom of Solomon, where σοφία is defined as a πνεῦμα.[88] This transformation is one of the presuppositions in Paul. There is also another: knowledge is no longer rationally attained (whether in the Greek or the Jewish fashion), but by means of "illumination."[89] The transition can be observed in Philo.[90] Here the coherent world of the Stoics is rent apart. Knowledge has to do with supranatural things and itself becomes a supranatural power. The πνεῦμα banishes the human νοῦς, "mind."[91] The pneumatics are of supraworldly nature and recognize each other (*Migr. Abr.* 38f), and can communicate with each other in the language of the spirit.[92]

In itself the causal statement in v 10b can be understood in a Stoic sense. But the context requires the sense to be that of the "mysteries." The formal presupposition of this thesis is the common Greek epistemological axiom "like by like" (see v 11). πᾶς κτλ., "all things, etc.," is a characteristic expression in the context of revelation and

---

ian, 1967], 203). 1QH XII.12f.

84   Lietzmann reads δέ, arguing that the contrast with the uninitiated is emphasized. But γάρ is supported by p[46].

85   This in turn sheds light on λαλοῦμεν, "we do speak," v. 6.

86   According to Wilckens, the transition from σοφία to πνεῦμα is made because both are identical in Corinthian Gnosticism. The pneumatic knows himself one with the pneuma–revealer. Both terms denote the revealer. But σοφία and πνεῦμα are by no means identical; note the use of διά, "through."

87   Hermann Kleinknecht, *TDNT* 6:354–356; Dupont, *Gnosis*, 155–172, 458–471. Orig., *Cels.* 6.71: τῶν Στωικῶν φασκόντων ὅτι ὁ θεὸς πνεῦμά ἐστιν διὰ πάντων διεληλυθὸς καὶ πάντ᾽ ἐν ἑαυτῷ περιέχον, "the Stoics . . . who affirm that God is spirit that has permeated all things and contains all things within itself" (Origen, *Contra Celsum*, tr. with introd. and notes by Henry Chadwick [Cambridge: University Press, ²1965], 385). The identification of God and spirit is traced back to Cleanthes (fr. 533, in v. Arnim, *SVF* 1:121.6f). Sen., *Ep.* 66.12: *ratio autem nihil aliud est quam in corpus humanum pars divini spiritus mersa*, "Reason, however, is nothing else than a portion of the divine spirit set in a human body" (Loeb 2:9, 11).

88   Wis 1:6; 7:22; cf. 1:5 (Cod. Alex.); 7:7; 9:17. The connection with the Stoa is shown by 1:7; 7:22f; 12:1; here the process of transformation can be immediately perceived.

89   This is unstoic. Scipio's visionary dream (Cic., *Rep.* 6) is no proof to the contrary.

90   Hans Leisegang, *Pneuma Hagion*, Veröffentlichungen des Forschungsinstituts für vergleichende Religionsgeschichte in der Universität Leipzig, 4 (Leipzig: Hinrichs, 1922); Max Pohlenz, *Die Stoa*, vol. 1 (Göttingen: Vandenhoeck & Ruprecht, ³1964), 374–378; Jonas, *Gnosis* 2.1:99–102; Wilckens, *Weisheit und Torheit*, 157–159; Dupont, *Gnosis*, 457–459. Philo, *Leg. all.* 1.38; *Gig.* 27. Cf. *Corp. Herm. Ascl.* 6.16f.

91   Philo, *Rer. div. her.* 264f. Here the identity of σοφία and πνεῦμα is presupposed, cf. Philo, *Gig.* 47; Pascher, *Königsweg*, 180.

92   This can be ecstatic speech (glossolalia, see on 12:10), but it can also be λόγος σοφίας, "a word of wisdom," or γνώσεως, "of knowledge" (12:8), which of course only the pneumatic can comprehend.

the knowledge of revelation. "All things" does not mean everything whatsoever, but the benefits of salvation.[93]

ἐρευνᾶν, "explore," is used already in classical Greek in religious and philosophical contexts.[94] βάθος, "depths,"[95] is specially well suited for adoption by Gnosticism. Here God himself can be defined as βάθος.[96]

The positive thesis that the action radius of πνεῦμα, in accordance with its origin, is unlimited corresponds to the negative thesis contained in v 9, that without the Spirit no "vision" is possible.[97]

■ 11 This verse proves the thesis by means of the analogy between human and divine spirit. Here πνεῦμα has in the first instance a purely anthropological sense and is practically synonymous with νοῦς, "mind" (v 16).[98] Paul applies the old principle "like by like."[99] In the Stoa

this principle was related to the Logos.[100] But it runs through the whole of ancient philosophy. There are examples in Philo[101] and Neoplatonism.[102] It is eminently suitable for adoption as a Gnostic principle: light by light, spirit by spirit.[103]

For τὸ ἐν αὐτῷ, "within him," cf. Zech 12:1: רוח אדם בקרבו, "the spirit of man within him." The application of the principle in v 11b is influenced by the Jewish idea that no one has ever seen God.[104]

■ 12 Between v 11 and v 12 we have to supply the tacit assumption that "we" do in fact know the things of God. Hence the conclusion can be drawn that the Spirit of God is in us,[105] recalling v 10, and in a polemical

---

93 Rom 8:28; Mt 11:25ff. In content, πάντα, "all things" = τὰ χαρισθέντα ἡμῖν, "what has been bestowed upon us" (v 13).

94 In a religious sense already in Pindar, Sophocles. In a philosophical sense, Plat., *Leg.*, 821a; *Ap.* 23b; Philo, *Leg. all.* 3.84; *Fug.* 165. The link between Jewish wisdom and Paul may be seen in a comparison with Jdt 8:14.

95 (Plat., *Theaet.* 183e); Jdt 8:14; Dan 2:22; Rom 11:33; Rev 2:24. Not so 1QS XI.18f. (". . . and to contemplate the depth of Thy mysteries" [Dupont-Sommer, 103]); cf. *1 Cl.* 40.1; Eph 3:18 among other spatial concepts; Iren., *Haer.* 1.21.2; Hipp., *Ref.* 5.6.4: ἐπεκάλεσαν ἑαυτοὺς γνωστικούς, φάσκοντες μόνοι τὰ βάθη γινώσκειν, "they called themselves Gnostics alleging that they alone knew the depths" (Legge 1:120). The so-called *Unknown Old Gnostic Work* 2 (enumeration of the twelve βάθη), in Carl Schmidt (ed.), *Koptisch–gnostische Schriften*, vol. 1, rev. Walter Till, GCS, 45 (Berlin: Akademie–Verlag, ²1954), 336f.

96 *Act. Thom.* 143; Hipp., *Ref.* 6.30.7. Wilckens interprets Paul, too, in a Gnostic sense, holding that the βάθη are identical with the revealer "who—as the image of the protofather—sums them up in himself." But in that case Paul's way of speaking becomes incomprehensible.

97 Kümmel seeks to tone down the sense: the divine Spirit knows *all things*, the τέλειος, "perfect man," only what the Spirit discloses to him. This does violence to the wording, cf. v 12.

98 Rom 8:16. It is not a question here of the antithesis between human νοῦς and divine πνεῦμα, as in Philo, *Rer. div. her.* 265.

99 Democritus: Diels, *Fragmente* 2:176 (68B.164). Plat., *Prot.* 337c–338a; *Resp.* 508a–511e; *Tim.* 45c. Carl Werner Müller, *Gleiches zu Gleichem: Ein Prinzip früh-*

griechischen Denkens, Klassisch–philologische Studien, 31 (Wiesbaden: Harrassowitz, 1965).

100 Poseidonius and his followers. Manil., *Astronom.* 2.115f: *Quis caelum posset nisi caeli munere nosse et reperire deum, nisi qui pars ipse deorum est?* "Who could know heaven except by heaven's gift, who find God except one who is himself a portion of the gods?" [Trans.]. Sext. Emp., *Math.* 7.92f (*Log.* 1.92f); Cic., *Nat. deor.* 2.32.81–38.97; 2.61.153–67.168; *Tusc.* 1.20.46. Müller, *Gleiches zu Gleichem*, 3–7.

101 Philo, *Mut. nom.* 6: νοήσει γὰρ τὸ νοητὸν εἰκὸς μόνον καταλαμβάνεσθαι, "For what belongs to mind can be apprehended only by the mental powers" (Loeb 5:145); *Gig.* 9.

102 Plot., *Enn.* 4.5.7.23–62; 1.6.9.30–45.

103 *Corp. Herm.* 11.20: τὸ γὰρ ὅμοιον τῷ ὁμοίῳ νοητόν, "For like is known by like" (Scott 1:220). Literature: Karl Reinhardt, *Poseidonios* (Munich: Beck, 1921), 414–422; *Kosmos und Sympathie* (Munich: Beck, 1926), 92–111; Willy Theiler, *Die Vorbereitung des Neoplatonismus*, Problemata, 1 (Berlin: Weidmann, 1930), 99–109; Arthur Schneider, "Der Gedanke der Erkenntnis des Gleichen durch Gleiches in antiker und patristischer Zeit," in *Abhandlungen zur Geschichte der Philosophie des Mittelalters: Festgabe Clemens Baeumker zum 70. Geburtstag*, Beiträge zur Geschichte der Philosophie des Mittelalters, TU, Supplement 2 (Münster: Aschendorff, 1923), 65–76; Müller, *Gleiches zu Gleichem*.

104 Jn 1:18; see Rudolf Bultmann, *The Gospel of John*, tr. G. R. Beasley–Murray *et al.* (Oxford: Blackwell; Philadelphia: Westminster, 1970). ad loc, (*Das Evangelium des Johannes*, KEK, 2 [Göttingen: Vandenhoeck & Ruprecht, ¹⁸1964]).

105 Weiss understands the logic the other way round: we have received the Spirit, therefore we know.

tone:[106] οὐ τὸ πνεῦμα τοῦ κόσμου, "not the spirit of the world." Is Paul here seriously thinking of a "spirit of the world"?[107]

The object of knowledge is given as τὰ χαρισθέντα ἡμῖν, "what has been bestowed upon us." Is this a sign that the language of the mysteries is being used in a nonmystical sense? Does it mean that for Paul ultimately (even if he may not be clearly aware of it) the content of σοφία is really nothing else but the understanding of the event of salvation? The deliberate allusion to χάρις, "grace," points in this direction. On the other hand, in the Hellenistic world χάρις, too, can assume the tenor of the mysteries and denote the power within the pneumatic, thus becoming synonymous with πνεῦμα.[108] It will therefore be necessary to look for further indications.

■ **13** Verse 13 links up with v 6 (cf. vv 1, 4)[109] and makes the transition from knowing to speaking.[110] Now both can be explained. This is done in the inverse order: (a) σοφίαν οὐ . . ., "not a wisdom . . .," is equivalent to οὐκ ἐν διδακτοῖς. . . ., "not in [words] taught . . .";[111] (b) πνευματικοῖς . . ., "in spiritual terms." Here we have the practical application of the principle stated in v 11.

Apart from the uncertainty in the textual tradition,[112] we cannot be certain whether πνευματικοῖς is masculine or neuter. The context points to the neuter; Paul is stating the criterion and possibility of judgment.[113]

The polemic is plain: if the Corinthians do not understand, they show themselves to be "psychical."

■ **14** Here is the other side of the argument, with the same polemical point as v 13. The question is again: Are the "psychics" unbelievers or a lower class of Christian?

Excursus:
ψυχή, "Soul"

The striking negative sense of ψυχή, "psyche" or "soul," has been traced to Gnosticism by Reitzenstein. H. Jonas[114] has shown the underlying cause of this change of meaning, namely, the Gnostic transformation of values which leads to a trichotomous anthropology. Man as a whole, traditionally seen in the dichotomy of body and soul, is here regarded as a worldly being and contrasted with the unworldly self, the πνεῦμα. To be sure, this final stage of the development is not yet found in Paul (see 15:44ff).

Further traces in the New Testament are found in Jas 3:15; Jude 19 (cf. v 10 and 2 Pet 2:12). A trace,

---

106 Against voices which denied that Paul had the Spirit? See 2 Cor.

107 So Weiss. Paul would accordingly be thinking of demonic inspiration. 2 Cor 4:4 can hardly be claimed as support for this, rather 1 Cor 12:3. λαμβάνειν τὸ πνεῦμα, "receive the Spirit," is common parlance, Rom 8:15; Gal 3:2, etc.

108 Wetter, *Charis*. According to Heinrici and Weiss, τὰ χαρισθέντα, "the things bestowed," are identical with ἃ ἡτοίμασεν, "the things he has prepared." But this still leaves the whole question open.

109 According to Wilckens, *Weisheit und Torheit*, 88, v 13 corresponds to v 5: Paul is taking the basic Gnostic antithesis, σοφία θεοῦ—σοφία ἀνθρώπων, "wisdom of God—wisdom of men," against the Corinthians themselves. But the phraseology arises simply from vv 1 and 4, supplemented by the notion of "like by like." At this point we cannot yet speak of a clear breakthrough which abandons the wisdom style in favor of the *theologia crucis*. It depends, of course, on how τὰ χαρισθέντα is to be understood and what ἃ . . . is related to.

110 Verse 13a is said by Hipp., *Ref.* 7.26.3 to have been quoted as γραφή, "Scripture," by Basilides.

111 διδακτός, "taught," corresponds formally to πειθός, "persuasive"; ἀνθρώπινος, "human," corresponds to κατὰ σάρκα, "according to the flesh." For the

genitive, cf. 1:17, σοφία λόγου; 2:1, οὐ καθ' ὑπεροχὴν λόγου . ., "not so as to distinguish myself in eloquence . . ." The antithesis is explained from this standpoint. Heinrici holds that ἀνθρωπίνης σοφίας and πνεύματος are dependent not on λόγοις, but on διδακτοῖς; cf. Soph., *El.* 343f: τἀμὰ νουθετήματα κείνης διδακτά, "admonitions . . . learnt of her" (Loeb 2:151). Not so Blass–Debrunner §183, where the genitive is held to designate the agent, but it is said that the connection between ἀνθρωπίνης σοφίας and λόγοις is unclear, "as if διδακτοῖς were not there . . . (Soph., *El.* 343 . . . is different)."

112 B 33 read πνευματικῶς. This is assimilation to v 14.

113 With Lietzmann; after διδακτοῖς λόγοις and before πνευματικά. Because of the sequel, Weiss assumes the masculine, arguing that ψυχικὸς ἄνθρωπος, "the unspiritual man," appears to be an antithesis to πνευματικοῖς; Max. Tyr., *Dial.* 16.4c: συνετὰ συνετοῖς λέγων, "speaking wise things to the wise"; there ἄνθρωπος is expressly stated. Eur., *Iph. Taur.* 1092: εὐξύνετον ξυνέτοις βοάν, "calling on the hospitable for those in need of hospitality."

114 Jonas, *Gnosis* 1:178–214, and see index *s.v. Seele*.

but no more, can be detected in Iamblichus, *Myst.* 6.6: the ἀνθρωπίνη ψυχή, "human psyche," in antithesis to the gods and to Gnosticism.[115] There remain a few Gnostic texts: a passage in the "Mithras Liturgy"[116] and immediately after it in *PGM* 4.724f. These passages, too, belong to the rapture type, and not yet to the specifically Gnostic trichotomy. The *Naassene Sermon* 2 (Hipp., *Ref.* 5.7.7.) takes us a step further: ἵν' οὖν τελέως ᾖ κεκρατημένος ὁ μέγας ἄνθρωπος ἄνωθεν, ["ἀφ' οὗ," καθὼς λέγουσι, "πᾶσα πατριὰ ὀνομαζομένη ἐπὶ γῆς καὶ ἐν τοῖς οὐρανοῖς" συνέστηκεν],[117] ἐδόθη[118] αὐτῷ[119] καὶ ψυχή, ἵνα διὰ τῆς ψυχῆς πάσχῃ καὶ κολάζηται καταδουλούμενον τὸ πλάσμα τοῦ μεγάλου καὶ καλλίστου καὶ τελείου ἀνθρώπου, "In order then that the Great Man on high, from whom, as they say, 'every fatherhood named on earth and in the heavens' is framed, might be completely held fast,

there was given to him also a soul, so that through the soul he might suffer, and that the enslaved 'image of the great and most beautiful Perfect Man' —for thus they call him—might be punished."[119a] Then comes the Christian–Gnostic elaboration, Irenaeus, *Haer.* 1.7.1 (Valentinians);[120] 1.21.5 (Marcosians).[121]

The "psychical" man's incapability is one of principle;[122] he "does not receive. . . ."[123]

Paul's logic is specifically non–Gnostic: his thesis is not founded upon the nature of man, but upon the encounter with revelation. Nevertheless, here again we have the same shift of accent. It was said above that man regards the message as foolishness because, by the will of God, it *is* foolishness. Here, on the contrary, it is only the

---

115 *Corp. Herm.* 9.9 does not belong in this context: all things that exist are created by God, τὰ μὲν διὰ σωμάτων ἐνεργοῦντα, τὰ δὲ διὰ οὐσίας ψυχικῆς κινοῦντα, τὰ δὲ διὰ πνεύματος ζωοποιοῦντα . . ., "whether they be things that put forth activity by means of their bodies, or things that effect movement by means of soul–stuff, or things that generate life by means of vital breath . . ." (Scott 1:185). Likewise Lucan, *Bell. Civ.* 5.122–139: the divine *spiritus* banishes the *mens*. This is the same view as Philo adopts in *Rer. div. her.* 265. The passage has nothing to do with a revaluation of ψυχή in the Gnostic sense.

116 *PGM* 1:90 (no. 4, lines 524f): τῆς ἀνθρωπίνης μου ψυχικῆς δυνάμεως, "my human psychic power"; cf. *PGM* no. 4, line 510: τὸ ἱερὸν πνεῦμα, "the holy spirit."

117 For the bracketing of these words, see Reitzenstein–Schäder, *Studien*, 162, n. 1.

118 ἄνωθεν goes with ἐδόθη, [i.e. "Great Man from whom . . . was given to him from on high . . ."] Reitzenstein–Schäder, 162.

119 Carsten Colpe, *Die religionsgeschichtliche Schule*, FRLANT, 78 (Göttingen: Vandenhoeck & Ruprecht, 1961), 161, takes this to apply to the image of the little man, cf. *ibid.* (Hipp., *Ref.* 5.7.6): the *protoplast* is the εἰκών, "image," of the higher *anthropos*. The latter is included in the lower man by means of the soul.

119a Legge, 1:122f.

120 Iren., *Haer.* 1.7.1: τοὺς δὲ πνευματικοὺς ἀποδυσαμένους τὰς ψυχὰς καὶ πνεύματα νοερὰ γενομένους . . ., "The spiritual seed, again, being divested of their animal souls, and becoming intelligent spirits . . ." (ANF 1:325).

121 Iren., *Haer.* 1.21.5: αὐτὸν δὲ πορευθῆναι εἰς τὰ ἴδια ῥίψαντα τὸν δεσμὸν αὐτοῦ, τουτέστι ⟨τὴν⟩ ψυχήν, "But he goes into his own place, having thrown

[off] his chain, that is, his animal nature" (ANF 1:346f).

122 Then the "psychical" man cannot attain the knowledge necessary for salvation. Then being a Christian and being a "psychical" man are mutually exclusive. But how, then, can Paul nevertheless designate the Corinthians as "psychical"? The end of the argument comes to be (3:1ff) that he reproaches them with not being (=not giving realization to) what from God's standpoint they are. There, to be sure, he no longer says "psychical" but "fleshly."

123 δέχεσθαι: *Corp. Herm.* 4.4 τὸν νοῦν, "mind." Valentinians in Iren., *Haer.* 1.6.2: ὡς γὰρ τὸ χοϊκὸν ἀδύνατον σωτηρίας μετασχεῖν (οὐ γὰρ εἶναι δεκτικὸν αὐτῆς λέγουσιν αὐτό) . . ., "For, just as it is impossible that material substance should partake of salvation (since, indeed, they maintain that it is incapable of receiving it) . . ." (ANF 1:324). Weiss renders οὐ δέχεται "he refuses"; cf. 1 Thess 1:6; 2:13; Prov 4:10. But it is not a question of a free decision. For indeed he is completely *incapable* of "receiving."

subjective side that is in view, namely, that the "psychical" man *sees* wisdom as foolishness, ὅτι πνευματικῶς ἀνακρίνεται, "because it is spiritually discerned" (see the translation).

■ **15** This statement resumes the theme of vv 10f and applies the fundamental insight to the pneumatic *man*; the spirit in the pneumatic is the Spirit of God. πάντα, "all things," is to be interpreted in the light of the understanding of revelation, as in v 10. Knowing is not merely a matter of theoretical knowledge; it turns into "judging." Once again the person who judges is for his part subject to no authority.[124] Again we are faced by the question whether this supraworldliness is meant in the habitual sense of the mysteries, or in the sense of the "new creature's" superiority over the world, in terms

of the dialectic of 2 Cor 5:16ff.

■ **16** The concluding argument appeals to Isa 40:13 (cf. Rom 11:34). νοῦς, "mind," is here synonymous with πνεῦμα.[125] συμβιβάζειν,[126] "instruct" (Acts 19:33; Col 2:2?). ἡμεῖς δέ, "we, however," does not mean all Christians, but the group of pneumatics, as emerges from 3:1. Paul declares that the Corinthian pseudopneumatics are incapable of understanding him. They can think only within the radius of the world. The pneumatic, however, is hidden from the world's eyes (cf. Jn 3:8).

It is still an open question how his being takes concrete shape.

---

124 *Corp. Herm.* 11.20f; 13.15.
125 Χριστοῦ is the original text, κυρίου is assimilation.
126 For ὅς, "so that he," see Kühner–Blass–Gerth 2.2:438f; Blass–Debrunner §239(5) (relative after a verb of knowing).

3

Concluding Discussion of the Party System; Preacher and Community

1 And I, brothers, was not able to speak to you as[1] men of spirit, but (only) as men of flesh, as children in Christ.[2] 2 / I gave you milk to drink,[3] not solid food.[4] For you were not yet strong enough. And indeed,[5] you are not strong enough even now[6] 3 / for you are still fleshly. For since[7] jealousy and envy prevail among you, does that not mean that you are fleshly and are behaving in human ways? 4 / For when one says: I[8] belong to Paul, another: I belong to Apollos, are you then not men? 5 / What[9] then[10] is Apollos? What is Paul? Servants through whom you became believers— each, moreover, as the Lord granted to him.[11] 6 / I planted, Apollos watered, but God caused the growth. 7 / So neither the planter nor the waterer is anything, but he who causes the growth, namely, God. 8 / The planter and the waterer, however, are one. But each will receive his own reward according to his own labor. 9 / For we are God's fellow–workers.[12] You are God's field, God's building. 10 / According to the grace of God that was bestowed upon me, I, like a competent master–builder, have laid a foundation; another is building upon it. But let each take care how he builds upon it. 11 / For no one can lay any foundation other than[13] the one that has been laid, namely, Jesus Christ.[14] 12 / But if[15] anyone builds on this foundation gold, silver, fine

1   "As": cf. v 10; Bauer, *s.v.* ὡς.

2   The emphasis is of course on "children"; Lietzmann says: "adolescent (*unmündige*) Christians."

3   For the double accusative, see Bauer, *s.v.* ποτίζω.

4   Zeugma observes that ποτίζειν, "give to drink," fits only with γάλα, "milk"; Blass–Debrunner §479(2).

5   Emphatic ἀλλά: Blass–Debrunner §448(6).

6   ἔτι is omitted by p[46] B. οὐδὲ ἔτι νῦν: see Bauer, *s.v.* νῦν 1c. ἔτι νῦν, "even now," Plut. *Sept. sap. conv.* 162d; Ael. Arist., *Or.* 13.185; Jos., *Ant.* 1.92; 2.313.

7   ὅπου causal (like ἐπεί, cf. 1:21, 22), Blass–Debrunner §456(3).

8   For μὲν—[δὲ] see on 1:12.

9   p[46] C D G ℵ read τίς, "who," twice. Verse 7 requires τί, "what." τίς is grammatically easier. Lietzmann, *ad loc.*; Zuntz, *Text*, 131f. The chiasmus, Paul—Apollos (vv 4/5), is eliminated in the *Reichstext*.

10   τί οὖν: Epict., *Diss.* 1.11.5, 20, 27, etc.

11   Shortened from ἕκαστος ὡς ὁ κύριος ἔδωκεν αὐτῷ with attraction of the dative.

12   Or: "fellow–laborers in the service of God" (Bauer). See n. 54 *infra*.

13   παρά after ἄλλος: Bauer, *s.v.* παρά III.3.

14   ὅς ἐστιν to emphasize the apposition: cf. 3:17; Eph 6:17; 1 Tim 3:15.

15   Albert Debrunner, "Neutestamentliche Wortforschung: Zu themelios, 1. Kor. 3,11," *ThZ* 3 (1947): 156, takes εἰ δέ as the introduction of an indirect question: Whether anyone builds thereon, is no concern of mine; each man's work will be revealed. This is improbable (with Kümmel), because a subsequent clause has to be understood.

16   Or: jewels, see below.

17   Or: cane. The meaning of καλάμη, "straw," overlaps that of κάλαμος, "cane," see Bauer; Moulton–Milligan. For κάλαμος as a building material, cf. Diod. S., *Bibl. hist.* 5.21.5?

stones,[16] wood, hay, straw,[17] 13 / each
man's work will be made manifest. For
the day (of judgment) will disclose it,
because that day will be revealed with
fire.[18] And the fire[19] will test the quality
of each man's work.[20] 14 / If the work
which anyone has built[21] remains,
he will receive a reward. 15 / If anyone's
work burns, he will be punished (or:
will suffer loss), but he himself will be
saved, though as through fire. 16 / Do
you not know that you are the temple
of God and that the Spirit of God
dwells in you? 17 / If anyone destroys
the temple of God, God will destroy him.
For the temple of God is holy, and
that is what you are.[22]

■ 1 The transition is provided by 3:1–4, which supplies
the link between the discussion of hidden wisdom and
its application.

Paul's assertion that he commands a wisdom which is
unknown to the Corinthians, that his religious status is
accordingly superior to theirs, has been buttressed by
mythological allusions. This provokes the question why
he has kept it to himself. The answer of course is that
as nonpneumatics they were not able to understand·it.
Now he says as much outright. With this, the thought begins to shift. The fundamental assertion of their in-

capability now turns into a pedagogic verdict: "not yet."
This is already indicated by the characterization σάρκι-
νοι, "men of flesh." It describes the Corinthians neither
as fundamentally blind, nor as qualified sinners, but
as "natural" men, as ἄνθρωποι, "humans" (v 4).[23]
The language of the mysteries recedes altogether in favor
of the terminology of education: they are νήπιοι, "children."[24] The idea of παιδεία, "training," suggests
itself.[25] But it remains only a suggestion. Paul's concern

18 ἐν can be taken as instrumental (Lietzmann). It is
better to take it of the accompanying circumstances,
cf. 1 Thess 4:16. ἡμέρα, "day," is the subject.

19 αὐτό can be taken with πῦρ, (i.e. "the fire itself");
but one does not see why; there is no emphasis on
the latter. p⁴⁶ ℵ D 𝔐 omit.

20 τὸ ἔργον can be accusative or nominative. If accusative (so Heinrici), then ὁποῖον . . . is a closer definition of ἔργον. Otherwise ὁποῖον introduces an
indirect interrogative clause dependent on δοκιμάζειν.

21 Or: "has built thereon." In that case the foundation
is regarded from the start as firm.

22 Attraction of number. According to Blass–Debrunner §293(4), οἵτινες in Paul stands not for οἵ, but
for τοιοῦτοι.

23 σάρκινος: 9:11; Rom 15:27; 2 Cor 1:12; 10:4. The
variant reading σαρκικός is assimilation to v 3. σάρκινος is chosen because Paul now has his eye on the
"human" and v 3 paves the way for his proof. It
is apparent that neither in Paul nor in Corinth do
we have a fully developed Gnostic terminology.

Eduard Schweizer, TDNT 7:10f; "Die hellenistische
Komponente im neutestamentlichen σάρξ–Begriff,"
ZNW 48 (1957): 237–253, now in his Neotestamen-
tica (Zurich and Stuttgart: Zwingli, 1963), 29–48.

24 See 13:11.

25 Is the connecting association that of the way of perfection, which is suggested in the philosophical term
προκόπτειν, "make progress"? Epict., Ench. 51.1:
οὐκ ἔτι εἶ μειράκιον, ἀλλὰ ἀνὴρ ἤδη τέλειος, "You
are no longer a lad, but already a full–grown man"
(Loeb 2:535). Philo, Agric. 9: ἐπεὶ δὲ νηπίοις μὲν
ἐστι γάλα τροφή, τελείοις δὲ τὰ ἐκ πυρῶν πέμ-
ματα, "for babes milk is food, but for grown men
wheaten bread" (Loeb 3:113). Epict., Diss. 2.23.40:
διὰ λόγου καὶ τοιαύτης παραδόσεως ἐλθεῖν ἐπὶ
τὸ τέλειον δεῖ, "A man must advance to perfection
through the spoken word and such instruction as
you receive here" (Loeb 1:417).

is not with education and development, but with the antithesis of the moment.[26] νήπιοι ἐν Χριστῷ, "children in Christ," here means no more than that they are still beginners in the field of Christian knowledge. They can make progress, but they must show it. The shift is plain. A moment ago the object of discussion was the pneumatic in terms of his isolation and of what he can achieve as an individual. Now, on the contrary, he emerges in his relationship to the community. The full exposition of this is provided by chaps. 12–14.

■ 2 Paul explains νήπιοι in an expanded metaphor from the diatribe: they could—and can—stomach only infant food.[27] This is immediately understandable.[28] In the context it is meant in a critical sense: *only* baby food. All the same, it was a beginning. οὔπω, "not yet," also affords the prospect of a possible advance.

■ 3 The retrospect is followed in vv 2b–3 by a quick aside and the cutting remark ἀλλ' οὐδὲ ἔτι νῦν δύνασθε, "and indeed you are not strong enough even yet." This is again an *ad hoc* statement; it does not agree with 1:5, but it gives us an idea of the sense in which Paul will discuss the Corinthian slogan, πάντες γνῶσιν ἔχομεν, "we all have knowledge."[29] There is no difference in meaning between σαρκικός, "fleshly," and σάρκινος, "of flesh," as is shown also by the causal clause which follows: ὅπου κτλ., "for since, etc."[30] Being fleshly expresses itself as κατὰ ἄνθρωπον περιπατεῖν, "be-

have in human ways."[31] Or, as it can also be put, strife[32] is a work of the σάρξ, "flesh" (Gal 5:19f). Here Paul is thinking not so much of personal bickerings (although these are also included, cf. 6:1ff) as of the ecclesiastical ἔριδες, "quarrels," of 1:11f. This is proved by what follows.

■ 4 With v 4 he returns to the subject of the parties. For κατὰ ἄνθρωπον περιπατεῖν, "behave in human ways," we have now the variant, ἄνθρωποί ἐστε, "you are men."[33] The peculiar sharpness of the reproach arises from the fact that it is aimed at alleged pneumatics who claim to have the world already beneath them (4:8). If the antithesis (not expressed, but presupposed) is κατὰ πνεῦμα περιπατεῖν, "behave in spiritual ways," then πνεῦμα is here no longer the capacity for supranatural vision, but the power that is bestowed upon believers and enables them to live together in history.

The restriction to two-party slogans appears to be in keeping with the situation in Corinth—but how?[34]

Verses 5–17: Community and Office

The style is determined by the pictorial language: first the picture of planting, then that of building, which slips over into the picture of the building material, and finally the latter is supplanted by that of the testing of the material. The subjective, experiential aspect of the conduct of office is not mentioned. It is of no significance for

26 Paul does not expound the stages of pedagogical or psychological development. For these, see Philo, *Leg. all.* 3.159: ὁ ἀρχόμενος—προκόπτων—τέλειος, "the man who is just beginning his training—who is making gradual progress—who is perfect" (Loeb 1:407); on the content cf. *Cher.* 114; Epict., *Diss.* 1.4.18–27. For the Gnostic version of advancing from knowledge to knowledge, cf. *Naassene Sermon* 25 (Hipp., *Ref.* 5.8.38; Reitzenstein-Schäder, *Studien,* 170f, n. 6): ἀρχὴ γὰρ . . . τελειώσεως γνῶσις ἀνθρώπου, θεοῦ δὲ γνῶσις ἀπηρτισμένη τελείωσις, "For the beginning of perfection . . . is the knowledge of man; but the knowledge of God is completed perfection" (Legge 1:138).
27 γάλα, "milk": Bauer, *s.v.* βρῶμα: Heb 5:11–14. For the content, see Philo, *Congr.* 19; *Omn. prob. lib.* 160; *Agric.* 9; Epict., *Diss.* 2.16.39. Johannes Behm, *TDNT* 1:643.
28 The metaphor naturally lends itself to use in the mystery style. But in this passage there is no ulterior sense of this kind behind it.
29 See 8:1ff.

30 ὅπου indicating the reason (*4 Macc.* 14.11; Bauer, *s.v.*) presupposes at the same time the reality of the assumption.
31 Soph., *Ai.* 761: κατ' ἄνθρωπον φρονεῖν, "to think in the manner of man" (cf. Loeb 2:65).
32 ζῆλος, "jealousy" (literally, "zeal") is in itself a neutral term, here used in the bad sense. ζῆλος and ἔρις, "envy," are scarcely to be distinguished; they constitute a dual expression of a rhetorical kind; p[46] D G 𝔐 add καὶ διχοστασίαι, "and quarrels."
33 Reitzenstein overdoes the "mystery" interpretation when he argues that for Paul the pneumatic is no longer man. He does, however, speak "humanly." Paul has in mind simply the antithesis κατὰ ἄνθρωπον—κατὰ πνεῦμα, "in human ways—in spiritual ways."
34 Can it be used as an argument against a sojourn of Peter in Corinth?

the theological definition.

■ **5** Here the Pauline principle comes to light. It is a critical principle. From the stylistic point of view, elements of the diatribe emerge.[35] The sentence is truncated.[36] The envoys[37] are nothing but servants. Their whole existence, so far as it affects the Corinthians, is identical with their working: δι' ὧν ἐπιστεύσατε, "through whom you became believers."[38] The relation between preachers and believers is not that of mystagogues and mystics, but that of "servants of the word" and hearers, in the sense of the coordination of καταλλαγή, λόγος and διακονία τῆς καταλλαγῆς, "reconciliation, message and ministry of reconciliation."

The role of the mystagogue is interchangeable. The preacher, on the other hand, works as one who is historically irreplaceable.[39] We have here in a nutshell Paul's whole idea of office as he develops it in 2 Corinthians.

The definition of his commission as "service" does not mean the renunciation of authority, but it does mean the destruction of human authority (which would be an abrogation of freedom) in favor of theological authority. The latter is dialectical. Inasmuch as the preacher stands for the Lord, he can claim supreme authority. But this authority is critically directed also against himself. He has it, so long as he "does not proclaim himself" (2 Cor 4:5). It does not cover *any and every* assertion or claim.

■ **6** The point indicated by v 5 is illustrated in v 6 by the picture of cooperation[40] in planting and cultivation; everyone has his own commission. There is no such thing as service in general, but only the historic service of the individual in his particular station. This is analogous to what is later said of all believers and the gifts of the Spirit: the Lord, like the Spirit, singles out the individual, in order that in and through his isolation he may bring him into the community, to the "upbuilding" of the latter.[41]

The result of this conception of office is to break up both the Paul party and the Apollos party alike. Both lose their heads.

The metaphor of planting,[42] which is widespread in Judaism[43] and which is later supplemented by the metaphor of building, is understandable in itself.[44] It is a metaphor, not a symbol with a hidden meaning.[45]

The mention of "God" has here an eminently critical sense; it rules out any possible self–glorification on the

---

35 Chiasmus (Apollos/Paulus, cf. v 6); rhetorical objection; the chiasmus is altered by ℜ.

36 Lietzmann expands thus: καὶ ἕκαστος, ὡς ὁ κύριος αὐτῷ ἔδωκεν, οὕτως ἠργάσατο, "and each worked in the way the Lord granted him." Cf. 7:17; Rom 12:3.

37 The Cynic is διάκονος, "servant," i.e., representative of God, Epict., *Diss.* 3.22.63–109; further evidence in Georgi, *Gegner*, 32–38.

38 Bengel, *Gnomon, ad loc.*: "by whom, not in whom" (Lewis and Vincent 2:179).

39 For this, cf. 15:10. κύριος, "Lord," is referred by Heinrici, and by Robertson and Plummer, to God; see below on v 6.

40 Pairs of teachers: Jos., *Bell.* 1.648; 4.159; *Ant.* 15.3; Adolf Schlatter, *Die Theologie des Judentums nach dem Bericht des Josefus*, BFTh, 2, 26 (Gütersloh: Bertelsmann, 1932), 207.

41 Cf. the fivefold repetition of ἕκαστος, "each," vv 5–13; further 4:5; 7:17, 20, 24; 12:7, 11.

42 Lib., *Or.* 13.52: τὸ καλὸν ἐγὼ μὲν ἐφύτευσα, σὺ δὲ ἐθρέψας, αἱ δὲ πόλεις δρέπονται, "I planted this glorious seed; you nurture it; the world plucks the fruit of it" (Loeb 1:33). The community of Qumran is an "eternal planting." 1QS VIII.5f; cf. CD I.7; 1QH VIII.4–11. In addition to this, however, the metaphor is general in Judaism, see Str.–B. 1:720f

43 Harald Riesenfeld, "Le langage parabolique dan les épîtres de saint Paul," in *Littérature et théologie pauliniennes*, 47–59, here esp. 54f, now in his *The Gospel Tradition*, tr. E. Margaret Rowley and Robert A. Kraft (Philadelphia: Fortress, 1970), 187–204, here esp. 197–199; Otto Betz, "Felsenmann und Felsengemeinde (eine Parallele zu Mt 16,17–19 in den Qumranpsalmen)," *ZNW* 48 (1957): 49–77; Braun, *Qumran* 1:190f.

44 It is clear that the metaphor must not be pressed, as if Paul had only made converts and Apollos had only guided them further. The metaphor applies to the community, not to the individual.

45 On the question as to whether Paul is thinking of a field or a vineyard, see on v 9.

(on Mt 3:10). Rom 11:16–24; *Od. Sal.* 38.17–21.

part of the preacher.[46] The transition from the aorist to the imperfect should be noted.[47]

The express mention of God does not prove that κύριος in v 5 is the equivalent of God, but it accords with the relationship between the two as brought out in v 21; ontologically they are distinct, soteriologically they are a unity.

■ 7 This verse points up the radical conclusion to be drawn from the picture. Although Paul and Apollos are God's "fellow-workers" (v 9), they have no special merit. Their work is incommensurable with God's work.[48] They are not priestly mediators of salvation.

■ 8 The radical "they are nothing" is the presupposition for the positive possibility, their unity.[49] The implications of this for the nature of the groups are obvious (cf. 1:10). The remark about a reward for the fellow-workers, while it is formally speaking an aside which interrupts the train of thought,[50] points at the same time to an essentially constitutive feature: the fellow-worker

certainly does not have any merit of which he can boast, but he *can* hope for a reward, in keeping with his eschatological responsibility for his achievements. Once again the accent falls both on the distinctive character of each individual's work and on the unity in the joint work.[51]

■ 9 Is this meant to be the ground of v 8a, or of v 8b?[52] The dilemma is resolved when we perceive the unified structure which belongs to the idea of office and which results from its strict derivation from soteriology, from the definition of the relation between the event of salvation and the part of the fellow-worker.[53] The accent lies on θεοῦ, "God's." Under this heading the definitions of officebearer and community are bound up together. The metaphor of planting[54] is supplemented by the new metaphor of building. The transition from the metaphorically employed verbs to substantives brings out the symbolic content. οἰκοδομή[55] means: (a) the act of building; (b) the edifice. The metaphorical application

---

46 Cf. ἀπὸ θεοῦ, "by (from) God," 1:30; 4:5.

47 αὐξάνω is transitive in Attic; so also here and 2 Cor 9:10. Elsewhere in the NT it is intransitive, as in Hellenistic Greek.

48 εἶναί τι, "to be something": Acts 5:36 (τις); Gal 2:6. Heinrici is mistaken in arguing that ἐστίν may not be supplied to ἀλλ' ὁ αὐξάνων θεός because God is all. For the mode of expression cf. Gal 6:15.

49 The unity is not a psychological oneness of mind, but the unity of the church's task which, critically limits the individual. Lietzmann would interpret ἕν in a negative sense: "inseparable." This is correct, if the very negativity in which the Christian personality is placed is recognized to be the positive possibility of unity.

50 Lietzmann.

51 Cf. the emphasis: τὸν ἴδιον—μισθόν, κόπον, "his own reward—his own labor." Wilhelm Pesch, "Der Sonderlohn für die Verkündiger des Evangeliums," in *Neutestamentliche Aufsätze: Festschrift für Prof. Josef Schmid zum 70. Geburtstag*, ed. J. Blinzler et al. (Regensburg: Pustet, 1963), 199–206, argues that the reward is given not for the success, but for the effort. This is a false exposition of κόπος. κόπος is here a synonym of ἔργον, "work" (v 13), as Pesch himself explains: the instruction and guidance of the community. Paul at the Last Day has not to tell of his efforts, but to exhibit his communities, in other words, his success. Of the toil there is nothing to be said, 2 Cor 11:23ff.

52 According to Lietzmann, v 9 passes over the incidental remark in v 8b and provides the ground of v

8a: we are one, because we are God's fellow-workers.—If v 9 is joined to v 8b, then the thought is: we receive a reward, because we work together in God's work.

53 Lietzmann observes that the rendering, "people who work together with God," provides a sharper antithesis with the second half of the sentence. The rendering, "who work together in the service of God," would agree with v 8a (unity). 2 Cor 6:1 does not facilitate a decision. Robertson and Plummer hold that if Paul had wished to express the second idea, he would have formulated it more or less after the fashion of Rom 16:3.

54 It is disputed whether Paul is thinking of a field or a vineyard, see Riesenfeld, "Le langage parabolique," 54f (*The Gospel Tradition*, 197–199). Riesenfeld rightly remarks that the dilemma to some extent resolves itself when we consider the nature of southern vineyards. Sir 27:6. φυτεία, "planting" (see φυτεύω above): Ezek 17:7; Mt 15:13.

55 Philipp Vielhauer, *Oikodome: Das Bild vom Bau in der christlichen Literatur vom Neuen Testament bis Clemens Alexandrinus* (Karlsruhe–Durlach: Tron, 1940), 79–85 (on v 10); Josef Pfammatter, *Die Kirche als Bau*, Analecta Gregoriana, 110 (Rome: Gregorian University, 1960), 19–22 (on v 9).

has been worked out in Judaism.[56] Paul applies this metaphor in the first instance to the community, not to the individual (cf. chaps. 12–14).[57] The pattern is to be found in the Old Testament: Jer 1:9f; 12:14–16; 24:6; Ezr 17:1–8. Another strand of the tradition is to be seen in the diatribe metaphor of laying foundations and building thereon.[58] The symbol finds a wealth of applications in Gnosticism.[59]

The combination of these two metaphors is also traditional, in the Old Testament,[60] in Judaism,[61] Hellenism,[62] Gnosticism.[63]

■ **10** Paul now further develops the second metaphor, whereby it is hardly necessary to ask whether he is speaking in terms of metaphor or simile: "like" or "as" a competent master–builder,[64] $\theta\epsilon\mu\dot{\epsilon}\lambda\iota o\nu$[65] $\ddot{\epsilon}\theta\eta\kappa\alpha$,[66] "I have laid a foundation." The foundation is an understandable and widely used metaphor for the rudiments of doctrine.[67] Paul, to be sure, is using it of the community itself. By means of this assertion Paul maintains his

own authority (cf. 9:1f),[68] and at the same time upholds the criterion to which it is subject: $\kappa\alpha\tau\dot{\alpha}\ \tau\dot{\eta}\nu\ \chi\dot{\alpha}\rho\iota\nu$ $\kappa\tau\lambda.$, "according to the grace, etc." The allusion in $\ddot{\epsilon}\kappa\alpha\sigma\tau os\ \delta\dot{\epsilon}\ \kappa\tau\lambda.$, "but let each, etc.," is explained by vv 12f.

■ **11** Paul consistently refuses to allow that he himself can be regarded as the foundation. The expression is paradoxical.[69] The same thing is expressed nonmetaphorically in 2 Cor 4:5.

■ **12–13** Ignoring the paradox of v 11, these verses link up again with the metaphor of building, but do so with a new shift: from the act of building to the building material, first of all from the standpoint of its value (subsequently from that of its durability). To be sure, there is a tension between the metaphor and the thing intended. The material can be evaluated without more ado. On the other hand, the value of the "work" of the "fellow–workers" will be disclosed only in the future. By drawing attention to the judgment to which his own

---

56　E.g., Qumran: 1QS VIII,5–10; CD III,19.

57　2 Cor 10:8; 12:19; cf. also the opposite concept $\kappa\alpha$-$\theta\alpha\iota\rho\epsilon\hat{\iota}\nu$, "cast down," 2 Cor 10:4; cf. 13:10.

58　Epict., *Diss.* 2.15.8f; Philo, *Gig.* 30; *Mut. nom.* 211; *Som.* 2.8: $\tau\alpha\hat{\upsilon}\tau\alpha\ \mu\dot{\epsilon}\nu\ \delta\dot{\eta}\ \theta\epsilon\mu\epsilon\lambda\dot{\iota}\omega\nu\ \tau\rho\dot{\sigma}\pi o\nu\ \pi\rho o\kappa\alpha\tau\alpha$-$\beta\epsilon\beta\lambda\dot{\eta}\sigma\theta\omega,\ \tau\dot{\alpha}\ \delta\dot{\epsilon}\ \ddot{\alpha}\lambda\lambda\alpha\ \tau o\hat{\iota}s\ \sigma o\phi\hat{\eta}s\ \dot{\alpha}\rho\chi\iota\tau\dot{\epsilon}\kappa\tau o\nu os,$ $\dot{\alpha}\lambda\lambda\eta\gamma o\rho\dot{\iota}\alpha s\ \dot{\epsilon}\pi\dot{o}\mu\epsilon\nu o\iota\ \pi\alpha\rho\alpha\gamma\gamma\dot{\epsilon}\lambda\mu\alpha\sigma\iota\nu,\ \dot{\epsilon}\pi o\iota\kappa o\delta o$-$\mu\hat{\omega}\mu\epsilon\nu$, "So much by way of a foundation, As we go on to build the superstructure, let us follow the directions of Allegory, that wise Master–builder . . ." (Loeb 5:445, 447). Plut., *Fort. Rom.* 320b: Tyche lays the foundation of Rome, Arete completes the building.

59　Heinrich Schlier, *Christus und die Kirche im Epheserbrief*, BHTh, 6 (Tübingen: J. C. B. Mohr [Paul Siebeck], 1930), 49–60; *Religionsgeschichtliche Untersuchungen zu den Ignatiusbriefen*, 120f.

60　Jer 1:10. In the living conditions of that day, house–building and planting were the two constitutive labors, Deut 20:5f, see Anton Fridrichsen, "Exegetisches zu den Paulusbriefen," *ThStKr* 102 (1930): 291–301, here esp. 298f; "Exegetisches zu den Paulusbriefen," in *Serta Rudbergiana*, ed. H. Holst and H. Mørland, Symbolae Osloenses, supplement 4 (Oslo: Brøgger, 1931), 24–29, here esp. 25f.

61　Philo, *Cher.* 100–112; *Rer. div. her.* 116; *Exsecr.* 139.

62　Dio Chrys., *Or.* 52(69).3; 54(71).4f; Plut., *Virt. doc.* 439a.

63　Lidzbarski, *Mandäische Liturgien*, 190. It even comes to an identification, *ibid.*, 165: "In the building which life builds, fine trees are displayed."

64　$\sigma o\phi\dot{o}s$, "competent": Aristot., *Eth. Nic.* 6.7.1. $\sigma o\phi\dot{o}s$

$\dot{\alpha}\rho\chi\iota\tau\dot{\epsilon}\kappa\tau\omega\nu$: Isa 3:3; cf. Philo, *Som.* 2.8 (see n. 58 above).

65　There exist both a masculine and a neuter, see Blass–Debrunner §49(3); Bauer, *s.vv.*

66　In a literal sense, Dion. Hal., *Ant. Rom.* 3.69; Jos., *Ant.* 11.93; 15.391.

67　See n. 58 above. 1QS V, 5; 1QSa I, 12, etc.; Heb 6:1; Eph 2:20 (N.B. $\alpha\ddot{\upsilon}\xi\epsilon\iota$, "grows," in v 21; see Martin Dibelius, *An die Kolosser, Epheser; an Philemon*, rev. Heinrich Greeven, HNT, 12 [Tübingen: J. C. B. Mohr (Paul Siebeck), ³1953], *ad loc.*); cf. 2 Tim 2:19.

68　The counterpart is his principle not to labor on someone else's ground, 2 Cor 10:14f; Rom 15:20.

69　Weiss observes: "Paul is no longer thinking metaphorically, but has in mind the thing itself." Anton Fridrichsen, "Neutestamentliche Wortforschung: Themelios, 1. Kor. 3,11," *ThZ* 2 (1946): 316f, presumes in view of *IG* 12.2:8f, no. 11, that Paul is borrowing an expression from technical building language: "the foundation laid down" (not the ground—that is $\ddot{\epsilon}\delta\alpha\phi os$—but the foundation walls). In the same inscription the $\theta\epsilon\mu\dot{\epsilon}\lambda\iota\alpha$ are the four walls which together constitute the foundation. But even if Paul were using a technical term, the paradoxical mode of expression is not thereby explained.

work will be exposed, Paul sets himself on the same footing as the other workers and party heads; no work of this kind can be developed into a "position." The building materials[70] appear to suggest a fabulous building[71] with precious stones[72] as building material. Bauer rightly poses the alternative: either Paul is thinking of fantastic, possibly apocalyptic.buildings,[73] or he has not taken the applicability into account at all.[74] At all events he is not painting an apocalyptic scene. Even the fiery judgment on the "day"[75] is only touched upon, from the standpoint of the picture of a burning house. In the foreground we have not the scene of the last judgment, but the process of disclosure (4:5).[76] No less than four expressions allude to this disclosure. And it is to this, too, that the apocalyptic idea of fire refers; the fire is the instrument of testing, ἐν πυρί, "with fire,"[77] τὸ ἔργον . . . δοκιμάσει, "will test . . . the work."[78]

Schlatter takes the tested work to be the people brought into the community. Kümmel objects that it is not the individual members of the community who are tested, but the community as an edifice. If ἔργον, "work," is here taken as a building, then the transition to the temple (vv 16f) is smoother.[79] But the whole alternative is unnecessary. The meaning "achievement" is sufficient to indicate the sense.[80]

■ **14–15**[81] "Remain" means withstanding the test of fire. Verse 15 is obscure. ζημιοῦσθαι can mean (a) to be punished (see Bauer, s.v.); (b) to suffer loss,[82] i.e., to lose one's reward. Either way the question is: What is suffered by the person concerned? Obviously the picture

---

70 *Gn. R.* 1.8: "A builder requires six things: water, earth, timber, stones, canes, and iron. And even if you say, He is wealthy and does not need canes . . ." (*Midrash Rabbah,* tr. H. Freedman and Maurice Simon [London: Soncino, 1939] 1:7f). In rabbinical writings hay and straw are also used metaphorically of worthless men. Straw: Sen., *Ep.* 90.10; cane and wood: Diod. S., *Bible. hist.* 5.21.5.

71 A *domus aurea,* "house of gold," Suet., *Nero* 31; Dio Chrys., *Or.* 30(47).14; cf. 62(79).

72 Bauer, s.v. λίθος: λίθοι τίμιοι can hardly mean anything else. In addition to Suet., *Nero* 31 ("*gemmae*"), cf. Diod. S., *Bibl. hist.* 3.47.6f: the use of gold, silver, precious stones in building the houses of Saba. Luc., *Imag.* 11: (ὁ νεὼς) λίθοις τοῖς πολυτελέσιν ἠσκημένος καὶ χρυσῷ, "[The temple] built of costly stones and adorned with gold" (Loeb 4:277). As against this, Deissmann, *Paulus,* 244–247 (not in ET) and Joachim Jeremias, *TDNT* 4:269, n. 5, think of costly building material, such as marble, pointing to 1 Kgs 6:1; 7:46–48 (LXX). For precious stones see Dan 11:38; Rev 21:11, 19.

73 Isa 54:11f; Tob 13:17; Rev 21:18ff; Ps.–Callisth., *Hist. Alex. Magn.* 3.28.4: in the city of Helios on the Red Sea there are twelve πύργοι χρυσῷ καὶ σμαράγδῳ ᾠκοδομημένοι· τὸ δὲ τεῖχος ἐκ λίθου Ἰνδικοῦ, "towers built of gold and emerald and the wall was of Indian stone" [Trans.]. Ps.–Philo, *Ant. Bib.* 12.9.

74 So Weiss, rightly.

75 ἡ ἡμέρα, "the day," is an eschatological term: Bauer, s.v., Gerhard Delling, *TDNT* 2:952. For fire in an eschatological context, see Mt 3:11; Lk 12:49ff, etc; F. Lang, *TDNT* 6:936–948.

76 Bachmann understands τὸ ἔργον, "the work," as subject of ἀποκαλύπτεται, "will be revealed." Weiss avers that nothing is gained by this, save a tautology with the following sentence. The (Greek) present tense in the ὅτι–clause ("because . . .") marks it out amid the surrounding futures as a general, doctrinal statement.

77 For fire and the day of Yahweh, see Joel 2:3; 3:3; Mal 3:19; Isa 66:15f. Apocalyptic: Paul Volz, *Die Eschatologie der jüdischen Gemeinde im neutestamentlichen Zeitalter* (Tübingen: J. C. B. Mohr [Paul Siebeck], 1934; Hildesheim: Olms, 1966), 318f. *Jub.* 9.15: God judges with fire. *Or. Sib.* 3.72f; 2 Thess 1:17f.

78 On the merging of the three ideas, see Lang, *TDNT* 6:944f. The idea of the fire ordeal is ultimately Persian. Judaism: Mal 3:2f; *Or. Sib.* 2.252f, 285–347; *Gr. Bar.* 48.39. Everywhere current is the idea of fire as a means of testing, especially of gold: Ovid., *Tr.* 1.5.25. Proverbial: Prov 17:3; 27:21; 1 Pet 1:7.

79 So Erik Peterson, "ἔργον in der Bedeutung 'Bau' bei Paulus," *Biblica* 22 (1941): 439–441; Bauer *s.v.* with evidence; not so Pesch, "Sonderlohn," 200, n. 5.

80 ὁποῖόν ἐστιν . . . can be a closer definition of ἔργον, or an indirect interrogative clause dependent on δοκιμάζειν.

81 The style of vv 14f is that of an antithetical *parallelismus membrorum* with an overrunning member at the end; threefold–ήσεται. On the form κατακαήσεται, "burns," see Blass–Debrunner §76(1) (Hellenistic second future).

82 Bachmann.

must not be realistically pressed. It is only a brief hint. To interpret it of purgatory[83] is misguided.[84] Paul is obviously borrowing from a common phrase, "barely escaped from the fire."[85] Particularly striking is the notion of a punishment which nevertheless does not cancel our eternal salvation. Does Paul think of the character received by baptism (6:11) as being *indelebilis*? Other passages also point in this direction; see above all 5:5. But the notion is contradicted by passages which warn against bringing Christians into danger: 8:11; Rom 14:15. Obviously the idea has to be understood in the wider context of the doctrine of justification. The loss of faith means the loss of salvation. On the other hand, unsatisfactory works performed by the Christian *as a Christian* do not cause his damnation. This is the reverse side of the fact that works do not bring about salvation. But we remain responsible for our works before God (2 Cor 5:11); for the life of believers is service. Thus understood, v 15 rounds off the whole section.[86]

■ 16 Verse 16 addresses the reader with surprising directness with its dialogical οὐκ οἴδατε;, "do you not know?"[87] and introduces a new metaphor. The notion is no longer that of God's building, but of his dwelling.[88] Paul is alluding to the apocalyptic expectation of the temple of the last days[89] and spiritualizes it:[90] (a) to be-

---

83 Str.–B. 4.2:1043–1049: in Judaism since the second century A.D.

84 Lang, *TDNT* 6:944f; Joachim Gnilka, *Ist 1. Kor. 3,10–15 ein Schriftzeugnis für das Fegfeuer?* (Düsseldorf: Triltsch, 1955): the thought is only of a testing fire, not of a purifying fire. There are, however, two consecutive fires. The first separates those who receive a reward from those who lose their reward. The second group is subjected to a second testing. See also Johannes Michl, "Gerichtsfeuer und Purgatorium," in *Studiorum Paulinorum Congressus* 1:395–401. Liselotte Mattern, *Das Verständnis des Gerichtes bei Paulus*, AThANT, 47 (Zurich and Stuttgart: Zwingli, 1966), 109f: v 15 warns, as does 4:5, against anticipation of the judgment. The punishment at the Last Judgment relates to the *work* of the Christian, but not to his salvation. For the latter depends exclusively on the fact of his being a Christian. See 11:31.

85 Eur., *El.* 1183; Liv., *Urb. cond.* 22.53.3: *prope ambustus evaserat*, "all but burned, he had escaped." OT: "as a brand plucked out of the burning," Amos 4:11; Zech 3:2. Weiss would take διά literally: through the midst of the whole θλῖψις, "trial"; the righteous man does not notice the fire as he goes through it. This is reading things into the text from the Persian fire ordeal. In Isa 43:2; *Ps. Sal.* 15.4–15; *Or. Sib.* 2.252f the thought has a different nuance from that of Paul.

86 Mattern, *Verständnis*, 109f (on v 15), 168–179 (on vv 5–15); see on 5:5; 11:31f.

87 Epict., *Diss.* 1.4.16, etc. This frequent, pedagogical phrase from the diatribe style must not be taken to mean that Paul had never given the readers instruction on this matter.

88 With Lietzmann. For the temple as "house," cf.

CD III,19 (see on v 9). Bachmann takes vv 16f closely with the foregoing, holding that vv 12 and 17 are parallel. Paul, he argues, is setting three possibilities side by side: that of building true to style, building without style, destroying the building—and accordingly that of receiving a reward, being rescued (but only just), being destroyed. But v 17 has a different character from v 12, see below.

89 Cf. Mk 14:58. Marcel Simon, "Retour du Christ et reconstruction du Temple dans la pensée chrétienne primitive," in *Aux sources de la tradition chrétienne: Mélanges offerts à M. Maurice Goguel à l'occasion de son soixante–dixième anniversaire* (Paris: Delachaux & Niestlé, 1950), 247–257. Bertil Gärtner, *The Temple and the Community in Qumran and the New Testament*, SNTS Monograph Series, 1 (Cambridge: University Press, 1965), 57.

90 H. Wenschkewitz, "Die Spiritualisierung der Kultusbegriffe Tempel, Priester und Opfer im Neuen Testament," *Angelos* 4 (1932): 70–230. Wenschkewitz underlines the Hellenistic (p. 180: Stoic) influence. The latter is unmistakable. God dwells in man: Sen., *Ep.* 41.2; Porphyr., *Marc.* 19; Wis 3:14; 2 Macc 14:35; Philo., *Virt.* 188; *Som.* 1.149; *Sobr.* 62f; *Cher.* 106. Here the metaphor is related exclusively to the individual. The Qumran texts speak in a different sense of man as a building: 1QH I, 21f; XIII, 15. For the collective sense in Paul the link with the OT and Judaism should be noted; see next note.

come a symbol of the community of the last days (that is, of the present);[91] (b) by introducing the Spirit[92] (cf. 6:19). The appeal to the community to be its true self is in 6:19 addressed to the individual.

■ **17** This verse brings the application of the definition of the community, with the help of a proposition stated in the style of sacred law.[93] The style expresses the meaning. The coming (note the future) divine punishment[94] is announced to be valid. The formal correspondence between the offense and God's reaction to it[95] marks it as "due retribution." This is the basic idea in the Jewish

expectation of judgment.[96] In this pronouncement we have the realization of a radically eschatological understanding of the community.[97] Its verdicts are valid through the Spirit. They are passed by pneumatics, but they are not executed by the community. The judgment remains God's. It is not anticipated by means of disciplinary measures on the community's part (this holds even in view of 5:1ff). The holiness of the community is presupposed. It is given with the Spirit.

---

91 Cf. already Isa 28:16 and thereto 1QS VIII, 7f; 1QH VI, 26; VII, 9. On Qumran: Braun, *Qumran* 1:190; Betz, "Felsenmann," *passim*; Oscar Cullmann, "L'Opposition contre le temple de Jérusalem, motif commun de la théologie johannique et du monde ambiant," *NTS* 5 (1958–59): 157–173; Rudolf Schnackenburg, "Die 'Anbetung in Geist und Wahrheit' (Joh 4,23) im Lichte von Qumran-Texten," *BZ* n.s. 3 (1959): 88–94. NT: Eph 2:21f; 1 Pet 2:5; Ign., *Eph.* 9.1; *Mg.* 7.2. In Eph there is a movement within the building itself. This distinguishes it from Paul.

92 Weiss finds a contradiction: Paul appeals to the Corinthians' possession of the Spirit, which at the same time he has refused to allow. But for Paul the Spirit is not a habitual possession, but a gift, and moreover a gift to the community.

93 Ernst Käsemann, "Sentences of Holy Law in the New Testament," in his *New Testament Questions for Today*, tr. W. J. Montague (London: SCM; Philadelphia: Fortress, 1969), 66–81 [2:69–82] (originally in *NTS* 1 [1954–55]: 248–260. Characteristic is the chiasmus ($\phi\theta\epsilon\acute{\iota}\rho\epsilon\iota\nu/\phi\theta\epsilon\acute{\iota}\rho\epsilon\iota\nu$, "destroy"), further the tension between the present on man's side and the future on God's. 14:38; 16:22. The underlying idea is that of the ancient legal principle, "an eye for an eye, a tooth for a tooth"; cf. Gen 9:6; Aesch., *Choeph.* 312f; Rev 22:18f (Deut 4:2).

94 $\phi\theta\epsilon\acute{\iota}\rho\epsilon\iota\nu$, etc., with God as subject: Gen 6:13 etc.; Rev 11:18. The question whether $\phi\theta\epsilon\acute{\iota}\rho\epsilon\iota\nu$ means disgracing or destroying should not be raised here, see next note. $\phi\theta\epsilon\acute{\iota}\rho\epsilon\iota\nu$ is the opposite of $\sigma\acute{\omega}\zeta\epsilon\iota\nu$, "save." Greek examples: Plat., *Leg.* 958c: $\mathring{o}\lambda\eta\nu\ \tau\mathring{\eta}\nu$

$\pi\acute{o}\lambda\iota\nu\ \kappa\alpha\grave{\iota}\ \nu\acute{o}\mu o\upsilon\varsigma\ \phi\theta\epsilon\acute{\iota}\rho\omega\nu$, "subverting the whole state and its laws" (Loeb 2:529); Xenoph., *Mem.* 1.5.3: $\mu\grave{\eta}\ \mu\acute{o}\nu o\nu\ \tau\grave{o}\nu\ o\mathring{\iota}\kappa o\nu\ \tau\grave{o}\nu\ \mathring{\epsilon}\alpha\upsilon\tauo\mathring{\upsilon}\ \phi\theta\epsilon\acute{\iota}\rho\epsilon\iota\nu,\ \mathring{\alpha}\lambda\lambda\grave{\alpha}\ \kappa\alpha\grave{\iota}\ \tau\grave{o}\ \sigma\mathring{\omega}\mu\alpha\ \kappa\alpha\grave{\iota}\ \tau\grave{\eta}\nu\ \psi\upsilon\chi\acute{\eta}\nu$, "to ruin not one's home merely, but the body and the soul" (Loeb 65).

95 It can be objected that there is an exact correspondence only in the formal sense, since the punishment consists in the annihilation of the violator. But the violation of a temple, or a virgin, is an act of annihilation.

96 Cf. on the one hand Mk 8:38, on the other hand Rom 1:28 and Erich Klostermann's comment on it, "Die adäquate Vergeltung in Rm 1,22–31," *ZNW* 32 (1933): 1–6; Jeremias, "Zu Rm 1,22–32," *ZNW* 45 (1954): 119–121. Wis 18:4f; *Test. N.* 3.2–4; 1QpHab XI, 5, 7, 15; Acts 7:41f. To this context belongs also the divine judgment on Ananias and Sapphira, Acts 5:1ff.

97 The (Greek) relative is to be taken with $\nu\alpha\acute{o}\varsigma$ (i.e., that temple is what you are") rather than with $\mathring{\alpha}\gamma\iota o\varsigma$ (i.e., "that—namely, holy—is what you are). Peculiar is the attraction of number, Blass–Debrunner §131f: in individual statements the pronominal subject is made to agree.

3   Critique of καύχησις,
"Boasting"

18   Let no one deceive himself:[1] if anyone
imagines that as one of your circle[2] he is
wise in this world, then let him become
foolish, that he may become wise.
19 / For the wisdom of this world is foolishness with God. For it is written:
"He traps the wise in their own cunning,"
20 / and again:[3] "The Lord knows that
the reasonings of the wise are useless."
21 / So[4] let no one boast among men.[5]
For all things are yours, 22 / whether
Paul, Apollos, Cephas, world, life, death,
things present, things to come; all is
yours, 23 / but you are Christ's, and
Christ is God's.

The section brings the cycle to an end: it takes us back to 1:18ff.

■ **18**   The tone, a warning in diatribe style,[6] is determined by v 17, as is shown by the continuing form of conditional statement. Now the fundamental teaching of 1:18ff is applied to the Corinthians in the style of the judicial principle stated in v 17:[7] wisdom is acquired by renouncing wisdom in the sense of self–assertion before God, by recognizing the foolishness of preaching. The summons to become foolish is not a general principle requiring a *sacrificium intellectus*. It is strictly related to the object of faith, the word of the cross; faith, and nothing else, *is* the foolishness in question.

The demand naturally has also its peculiar pertinence and its polemical edge.[8] But first and foremost it is a fundamental, theological definition, as is shown by the exposition in 8:1ff.[9]

The paradox becomes sharper: ἐν τῷ αἰῶνι τούτῳ, "in this world (aeon)."[10] "This" aeon is not spiritually

---

1   Cf. ταπεινοῦν ἑαυτόν, "humble oneself," Mt 18:4; 23:12.
2   Lietzmann: "If anyone among you believes."
3   καὶ πάλιν, "and again," corresponds to וְחוּב, but is good Greek in joining together quotations, see Bauer, *s.v.* πάλιν 3. Rom 15:10–12; Heb 1:5; Diod. S., *Bibl. hist.* 37.30.2; Plut., *Is. et Os.* 361a.
4   ὥστε, "so," with imperative: 4:5 etc.; very rare except in Paul.
5   Lietzmann: "Therefore no one should boast of a man." καυχᾶσθαι ἐν of the person or thing: ἐν θεῷ, Rom 2:17; ἐν κυρίῳ, 1 Cor 1:31; 2 Cor 10:17; cf. Jer 9:22f. Blass–Debrunner §196 (ἐν denoting the ground).
6   Epict., *Diss.* 2.22.15.
7   According to Bachmann, εἴ τις, "if anyone," in v 18 is not parallel to εἴ τις in v 17, else there would be a dull repetition. In the earlier verse Paul is speaking of a possibility, here of a reality. True, yet in such a way as now to apply the principle of v 17 as a norm.
8   εἴ τις δοκεῖ κτλ., "if anyone imagines, etc.," is given a sharper edge by the Corinthian slogan, πάντες γνῶσιν ἔχομεν, "we all have knowledge" (8:1ff).

According to Weiss, ἐν ὑμῖν, "among you," is not the same as ὑμῶν, "of you," but means the circle in whose eyes someone seeks to be wise, cf. v 21. δοκεῖν is roughly the equivalent of κρίνειν, 2:2. Epict., *Ench.* 13: μηδὲν βούλου δοκεῖν ἐπίστασθαι· κἂν δόξῃς τις εἶναί τισιν, ἀπίστει σεαυτῷ, "Do not make it your wish to give the appearance of knowing anything; and if some people think you to be an important personage, distrust yourself" (Loeb 2:493).
9   Hence it is not enough to say, with Lietzmann, that Paul is characterizing "the others." Lietzmann himself has to concede that with v 21 Paul is speaking in "average" and "general" terms.
10   Weiss holds that "in this world" does not belong to the protasis, otherwise it would be a doublet of ἐν ὑμῖν, "as one of your circle." Either way the expression is stylistically inelegant. But the verdict is perhaps more sharply pointed if "in this world" is related to the protasis, see the following note.

skipped over with the help of *this* wisdom, but only mastered.[11]

■ **19** The paradox is formulated again as in 1:18ff. Whether it is also the same as in 3:18 depends on the exposition of ἐν τῷ αἰῶνι τούτῳ, "in this world (aeon)."[12] The evaluation of worldly wisdom is not in terms immanent to the world; Paul is not singing the "praise of folly," as if the latter were the way to salvation, and he is not commending the irrational as a religious value. The destruction of worldly wisdom has a point of reference, παρὰ τῷ θεῷ, "with God" (cf. Rom 2:13).

There follows a twofold Scripture proof, from Job 5:13 and Ps 93:11 LXX. The Job passage suggests the picture of a hunt or a match. Paul heightens it.[13] He adapts the Psalm passage to his subject by putting σοφῶν, "of the wise," in place of ἀνθρώπων, "of men."[14]

■ **21** This remark draws the conclusion in good Pauline terms (cf. 1:31).[15] The act, seemingly negative, of refraining from "human" boasting is, positively speaking, freedom.

■ **22–23** This is shown by employing a philosophic and, more particularly, a Stoic, maxim: "All things are yours."[16] According to the Stoic principle, "All things belong to the wise man," i.e., he is lord over all that comes to him from without.[17]

Since the principle is formal and acquires its concrete content from the particular circumstances of the moment, it cannot by itself be made the basis for a definition either of the Corinthians' position or of that of Paul.[18] For the sense ascribed to it by Paul, we have to take into account not only the exposition that follows, but also the expectation of world sovereignty for believers (6:1ff).[19] The resources of rhetoric are called upon in order to give concrete shape to πάντα, "all things." We have a sequence consisting of twice three members, two members, repetition of the thesis, reorientation.[20] For the sense of κόσμος, "world," it is significant that this word is described with the help of existential concepts

---

11 If "in this world" is related to the protasis, then Paul is already pronouncing his own verdict. The Corinthians do not imagine that they are wise "in this world," but that they are wise. Now a limit is set them by pointing out their action radius: this world. In the following verse this changes into a definition of quality.

12 If v 18 is construed with Weiss, then the thought is here repeated. Otherwise there is a nuance: (*a*) v 18, foolishness is the true world–wisdom, (*b*) v 19, world–wisdom is foolishness before God.

13 MT לֹכֵד חֲכָמִים בְּעָרְמָם, "He takes the wise in their own craftiness" (RSV). Did Paul have before him a translation differing from the LXX? Lucien Cerfaux, "Vestiges d'un florilège dans I Cor., I,18–III,24?" *RHE* 27 (1931): 521–534, now in his *Receuil* 2:319–332, finds (following Michel, *Paulus und seine Bibel*) here, too, a tendency toward the traditions of Aquila, Theodotion, Symmachus. Paul, he argues, has not independently altered the LXX, for δράσσειν, "trap," is not a Pauline word, whereas καταλαμβάνειν, "catch," is. For the antithesis σοφία—πανουργία, "wisdom—cunning," see Plat., *Menex.* 247a.

14 διαλογισμοί, "ideas," Rom 1:21. μάταιος, "useless," is a standard term in Jewish polemic against graven images.

15 ἐν ἀνθρώποις can mean (*a*) in the eyes of men (cf. ἐν ὑμῖν, v 18), or (*b*) it can be understood in the same sense as ἐν κυρίῳ, (i.e., "boast of men"). In the latter case the phrase is polemically directed against the veneration of party heads. The sequel is in keeping

with this. Cerfaux (see n. 13 above) on μὴ καυχάσθω, "let him not boast," observes that 1 Sam 2:10 (LXX) is an intermediate stage between Jer 9:23 and *1 Cl.* 13.1. But *1 Cl.* is not simply dependent on 1 Sam and dependence on Paul is unlikely; otherwise the author must have had all three instances in mind at the same time; hence we have here a separate tradition.

16 The maxim is naturally transferable, e.g. into Gnosticism, for it is formal.

17 Diog. L., *Vit.* 7.125 (cf. von Arnim, *SVF* 3:154–156, nos. 589–603); Dupont, *Gnosis*, 301–305. The wise man as king is one of Epictetus' themes. Cic., *Acad.* 2.44.136f; *Fin.* 3.22.75f; Sen., *Benef.* 7.2.5. Herbert Braun, "Exegetische Randglossen zum I. Korintherbrief," *Theologia Viatorum* 1 (1948–49):26–50, now in his *Gesammelte Studien*, 178–204 (here esp. 182–186): the Stoic superiority is limited to the *regnum sapientiae*, Sen., *Benef.* 7.10.6; cf. 7.3.3; on the attitude toward his fellow men, 7.3.2: *omne humanum genus potentissimus eius optimusque infra se videt*, (the wise man) "being the most powerful and best of mankind, sees the whole human race beneath him" (Loeb 3:465).

18 It is equally impossible to derive it unequivocally from the history of religion (see Dupont, *Gnosis*, 282–327).

19 The sovereignty of the latter–day people of God: see Daniel. 1 Cor 4:8; 6:1ff; 2 Tim 2:12; Rev 20:4–6.

20 For the enumeration, cf. Epict., *Diss.* 1.11.33; Philo, *Vit. Mos.* 2.16; Sir 40:9.

(cf. Rom 8:38). The action radius of faith reaches out beyond all worldly power, i.e., it has the prospect of surmounting fear and attaining to freedom. The presupposition is "to belong to Christ,"[21] i.e., to be his slave. Christological subordinationism emerges in the reference back to God.[22] While this subordinationism may here appear to be rhetorical and schematic, other passages show that it has also a systematic and essential character. The *crucified* Christ is the power and wisdom *of God* (1:30); and the *exalted* Christ accomplishes the work *of God*; as "the Son," he brings the powers into subjection to God (15:28). The party slogans are now replaced by an exposition of existence as taking place on the basis of the event of salvation, and the event of salvation is given concrete shape as a definition of existence in its relation to the world.

---

21 Χριστοῦ εἶναι: Gal 3:29; Rom 14:7ff, where an interesting alternation takes place between κύριος and Χριστός. It is overstraining Χριστός to find in the word an allusion to the "Christ" party.

22 Gal 1:4; Phil 2:11. For the subordination, cf. 15:28; *1 Cl.* 42.2. On the relation between Christ and God, see Wilhelm Thüsing, *Per Christum in Deum*, NtlAbh n.s., 1 (Münster/W.: Aschendorff, 1965), 10–20 (on v 23); see below on 15:28.

1 Corinthians 4:1–5

4

The Application of the Criterion

1   **Thus we are to be regarded as[1] servants of Christ and stewards of the mysteries of God. 2 / It is of course[2] required of stewards that[3] they should prove faithful. 3 / To me it is a matter of complete indifference[4] whether I am judged by you or by any other human tribunal. I do not even judge myself.[5] 4 / I am not, indeed, conscious of any fault; yet I am not justified by that. But it is the Lord who judges me. 5 / So do not pass any premature judgments, until[6] the Lord comes, who will bring to light what is hidden in darkness[7] and disclose the plans of the heart. And then each will receive (his) praise from God.**

The principle, "All is yours," cannot lead to καύχησις, "boasting." For it was safeguarded from the start by the dialectic of σοφία, "wisdom," and μωρία, "foolishness"; and then we were shown how it can be arrived at only by tracing it back to Christ and God. Now it becomes the criterion of office. Verses 6–13 then show that officebearer and community are subject to the same

determination. It is this that shapes their mutual relationship, vv 14–21.

■ **1** If a moment ago it was the "servant's" responsibility that was in the forefront, and now his authority, then it is already plain that the latter cannot become autocratic. οὕτως, "thus," sums up, holds fast the viewpoint of 3:21, and provides the transition from the community

---

1   οὕτως, "thus," sums up: it does not point forward to the following ὡς, "as." To take οὕτως with ὡς would shift the accent; and moreover, the asyndeton would be "hard to justify" (Bachmann). For οὕτως pointing backwards, cf. 8:12; Rom 11:5; "therefore," Rom 1:15; 6:11. ὡς then naturally does not point backwards, but is the equivalent of a double accusative, cf. 2 Thess 3:15; Blass–Debrunner §157(3), (5). Not so Heinrici, Weiss, Bauer, *s.v.* οὕτως ("thus . . . as"), though the last named *s.v.* λογίζεσθαι renders "consider, look upon someone as"; cf. 2 Cor 10:2.

2   For ὧδε λοιπόν, see Blass–Debrunner §451(6): "Out of the λοιπόν used with asyndeton to begin a sentence 'further, as far as the rest is concerned, now' (cf. §160) there developed an inferential 'therefore' in Hell. (MGr)": Polybius, papyri; Ign., *Eph.* 11.1; with ὧδε, Epict., *Diss.* 2.12.24. Anton Fridrichsen, "Sprachliches und Stilistisches zum Neuen Testament," in *Kungliga Humanistiska Vetenskaps–Samfundet i Uppsala, Årsbok 1943* (Uppsala: Almqvist & Wiksell; Leipzig: Harrassowitz, 1943), 24–36, here

esp. 25f: *somit also*. Lietzmann holds that the indicative is better, "for here a fact is being stated." Weiss has to give up ἐν τοῖς οἰκονόμοις for the sake of the imperative.

3   ἵνα, "that," with ζητεῖν, "require": 14:12. Increasing use of ἵνα: Blass–Debrunner §392(1).

4   Two phrases have been telescoped together: (a) ἐλάχιστόν ἐστιν; (b) εἰς ἐλάχιστον γίνεται. Both have the sense given above, see Bauer, *s.v.* εἰμί III.2. The non-Attic λογίζεσθαι εἰς (LXX) may be the cause of the blending (Blass–Debrunner §145[2]). ἵνα is here not final, but takes the place of the infinitive, Blass–Debrunner §393(6).

5   According to Weiss, the accent lies not on ἐμαυτόν, "myself" (accusative) but on a phrase that has to be supplied, (οὐδέ) ἐγὼ αὐτός, "(not even) I myself (judge myself)." This is correct.

6   ἕως ἄν for the classical πρὶν ἄν, Blass–Debrunner §383(3).

7   For the genitive, see on 2:13 (ἐν διδακτοῖς πνεύματος); 14:25; Rom 2:16; Blass–Debrunner §183.

that is addressed (ὑμεῖς, "you") to the paradigmatic officebearers (ἡμεῖς, "we"). Paul accordingly returns here to the theme of 3:5ff. He explains the sense of διάκονοι/ὑπηρέται, "servants," and συνεργοί/οἰκονόμοι, "fellow–workers/stewards," by appealing to the judgment of the readers.[8] He thus demands an *objective* judgment and the corresponding recognition.[9] The words ὑπηρέτης and οἰκονόμος are taken over from the language of administration.[10] It is only the object of administration that provides the reference to the church: μυστήριον, "mystery."[11]

■ **2** ὧδε λοιπόν (see n. 2) serves to develop the thought further. The indicative ζητεῖται, "it is required," is to be preferred to the imperative ζητεῖτε. The metaphor of the steward is made use of with a view to one specific point, his faithfulness.[12] Thus it is again a question of being called to account for what he has done, as in 3:10ff.[13] Once again a criterion is set up;[14] first of all formally, by calling for appropriate criteria that are not applied from without. To be sure, the thought is now developed in a totally different direction.

■ **3** Paul does not demonstrate his own faithfulness, but abruptly (ἐμοὶ δὲ . . ., "to me . . .") rejects any control.

The idea that provides the transition is not expressed, but has to be reconstructed.[15] Surprisingly, Paul does not hark back to 2:6ff and 3:1ff and declare, "You cannot judge me, for you are fleshly." But then, according to 3:1ff, he would also have to leave open the possibility that they could make progress and would then be able to judge him. But that is not a possibility open to men at all during this aeon. The only competent tribunal is the eschatological one (v 5). Hence Paul cannot submit himself to any "examination" (ἀνακρίνειν) by a human authority,[16] not even by himself. For this very reason his relation to the community is one of freedom.[17]

Is that not to put him beyond all human responsibility? This impression is first strengthened in v 4. Paul, however, means the opposite: he is judged by God, and God's judgment is for him no mere hypothetical factor. The Lord is near. The tenor is: above me there is a higher authority.

■ **4** This eschatological freedom is more precisely expressed. His conscience does not accuse him.[18] But this is only an intraworldly verdict. Conscience cannot pronounce the final verdict, that of justification. It is only a

---

8 According to Weiss, ἄνθρωπος stands as the antithesis of κύριος. This is to overestimate the term, which has faded to the sense of "one." There is nothing to indicate that in λογίζεσθαι, "regard," we have to see one of the slogans of the opposition.

9 Weiss proposes the alternative: (a) we are to be judged according to the standard which is applied to servants of Christ, or (b) we are to be estimated as servants of Christ. He argues that in the latter case ὡς contains a value–judgment, but that Paul does not demand this, certainly not of his opponents, and that for this reason οὕτως is presumably to be taken as pointing forward to ὡς.

10 ὑπηρέτης can denote the assistant, secretary, or manager, e.g., of a religious society, Acts 26:16; Preisigke, *Sammelbuch* 7835, 11. Epictetus uses it of the true cynic, *Diss.* 3.22.82: τοῦ Διός, "of Zeus" (Loeb 2:159). The word οἰκονόμος points in the same direction: Tit 1:7; 1 Pet 4:10; Epict., *Diss.*, 3.22.3. The fact that the word is used in religious societies does not in itself mean that it has a mystery sense. It should also be noticed that the civic "stewards" have religious duties, see John Reumann, "Stewards of God," *JBL* 77 (1958): 339–349.

11 μυστήριον: see on 2:1, 7. We must not read into the term, from 2:6ff, that Paul here means special revelations. The very plural shows that he means *the*

revelation.

12 Weiss thinks that Paul had been threatened with something like court proceedings in Corinth. This assumption is not necessary. It is sufficient that certain pneumatics had presumed to criticize him.

   Luther mistakenly renders: "Now no more is required of stewards save that . . ." (the 1956 revision merely alters to "than that"). The meaning is, however, that a lofty demand is made; Gerhard Delling, "Zur Revision der Luther–Bibel," *WZ* (Halle) 16 (1967): 1–14, here esp. 7.

13 εὑρίσκεσθαι, "be found" (="prove") is the equivalent of נִמְצָא, but there is evidence for it also in Greek: Dio C., *Hist. Rom.* 36.27.6; Jos., *Bell.* 3.114.

14 More especially when we read ζητεῖται.

15 The only thing which vv 2 and 3 have in common is the demand for an appropriate criterion.

16 ἡμέρα, court–day; cf. ἡμέραν τάσσεσθαι, etc., Acts 17:21; 28:23.

17 2 Cor 4:1ff.

18 σύνοιδα, "I am conscious," contains an allusion to the tribunal of the συνείδησις, "conscience," see 8:7ff; Job 27:6; Plat., *Ap.* 21b: ἐγὼ γὰρ δὴ οὔτε μέγα οὔτε σμικρὸν ξύνοιδα ἐμαυτῷ σοφὸς ὤν, "For I am conscious that I am not wise either much or little" (Loeb 1:81); Horat., *Ep.* 1.1.61.

"judging," not a constitutive authority.[19] It controls me in the world and keeps before me the norms of conduct. Beyond this it does not go.[20]

■ **5** The implications for the behavior of the readers are fundamental, because eschatologically determined. Since judgment belongs to the Lord, it cannot be anticipated by men.[21] The judgment as disclosure is presented in terms of the well–known symbolism of light and darkness.[22] The form of expression is so strongly apocalyptic that it may be asked whether the relative clause with its *parallelismus membrorum*[23] is a quotation.[24] $\kappa\alpha\rho\delta\acute{\iota}\alpha$, "heart," is the organ of aspiration ($\beta o\upsilon\lambda\acute{\eta}$) and thought ($\delta\iota\alpha\lambda o\gamma\iota\sigma\mu o\acute{\iota}$).[25] The old doctrine that God knows the inner depths of man[26] is here subjected to eschatological modification. $\kappa\alpha\grave{\iota}\ \tau\acute{o}\tau\epsilon\ \kappa\tau\lambda.$, "and then, etc.": the expectation is not a formal expectation of judgment, but a positive expectation of salvation: $\check{\epsilon}\pi\alpha\iota\nu os$, "praise."[27] Once again it is a question of reward, not of merit. This is shown by the final emphasis on $\mathring{\alpha}\pi\grave{o}\ \tau o\hat{\upsilon}\ \theta\epsilon o\hat{\upsilon}$, "from God" (cf. 3:23).

19 For literature on $\sigma\upsilon\nu\epsilon\acute{\iota}\delta\eta\sigma\iota s$, see Christian Maurer, *TDNT* 7:898f.

20 Mattern, *Verständnis*, 179–186, finds in vv 4f the same thought of judgment as in 3:15.

21 $\pi\rho\grave{o}\ \kappa\alpha\iota\rho o\hat{\upsilon}$: before the specific time, the parousia. Sir 30:24; 51:30; Mt 8:29.

22 Cf. 2 Cor 5:10, and Hans Windisch, *Der zweite Korintherbrief*, KEK, 6 (Göttingen: Vandenhoeck & Ruprecht, ⁹1924), *ad* 2 Cor 4:2. $\kappa\rho\upsilon\pi\tau\acute{o}s$, "hidden": 14:25; Rom 2:16; Sir 1:30; Jos., *Bell.* 5.402, 413. On the genitive $\tau o\hat{\upsilon}\ \sigma\kappa\acute{o}\tau o\upsilon s$, "in darkness," cf. again $\delta\iota\delta\alpha\kappa\tau\grave{\alpha}\ \pi\nu\epsilon\acute{\upsilon}\mu\alpha\tau os$; Blass–Debrunner §183.

23 $\kappa\alpha\acute{\iota}$—$\kappa\alpha\acute{\iota}$ does not here mean "both—and."

24 Weiss, cf. Lietzmann.

25 2 Cor 9:7; Rom 1:24. Theoretical and practical abilities are not distinguished. The heart can be illumined or darkened or hardened, 7:37; Rom 1:21. It does not denote a constituent part of man, but the Ego as willing and planning, and is in this respect akin to the NT use of $\nu o\hat{\upsilon}s$; see Bultmann, *Theology* 1:220–227 [221–226]. In the Stoa the heart becomes the central organ, as the seat of reason. "On the whole, however, this discussion does not go beyond the question of the seat of the spiritual life in the body. There is no strict transposition of the concept $\kappa\alpha\rho\delta\acute{\iota}\alpha$ into the spiritual realm" (Johannes Behm, *TDNT* 3:609. For Paul the situation in Stoicism is of no significance.

26 14:25; Jer 11:20; 1 Thess 2:4; Rom 8:27.

27 $\check{\epsilon}\pi\alpha\iota\nu os$ is used in political life: the magistrates pronounce a declaration of praise ($\check{\epsilon}\pi\alpha\iota\nu os\ \gamma\acute{\iota}\nu\epsilon\tau\alpha\acute{\iota}\ \mu o\iota$, "praise is accorded to me"; Ditt., *Syll.* 1:519 [no. 304, lines 24f]); August Strobel, "Zum Verständnis von Rm 13," *ZNW* 47 (1956): 67–92. Praise from God: Rom 2:29.

4

6   But this, brothers, I have exemplified by reference to myself and Apollos[1] (or: have referred to myself and Apollos) for your sakes, in order that from our example you may learn "not to go beyond what[2] is written," so as not to be puffed up against each other as one favors another. 7/ Who gives you preference then? What do you have that you did not receive? But if in fact[3] you have received it (sc. giftwise), why do you boast, as though you had not received it (as a gift)? 8/ You are (or: are you[4]) already satiated, already rich.(?) You have attained to sovereignty without us. If only you really had[5] attained to sovereignty, in order that we, too, might attain to sovereignty along with you! 9/ For it seems to me that God has made us apostles to be the last of all, like men condemned to death. For we have become a spectacle to the world, to angels and to men. 10/ We are fools for Christ's sake, you are wise in Christ; we are weak, you are strong; you are honored, we are despised. 11/ To this very moment we are hungry and thirsty and ill–clad and maltreated and homeless 12/ and wear ourselves out with the work of our own hands. When we are abused, we bless; when persecuted, we bear it; 13/ when we are insulted, we speak kindly. We have become like the refuse of the world, the dregs (or: scum) of everything to this day.

The principles that have been laid down are valid not only for the officebearer. The latter possesses no special quality, but is an instance of Christian existence in general.[6] This is the fundamental idea also of 2 Corinthians. Paul has now laid the basis for an attack on the general practice of passing judgment, as being eschatologically impossible. The officebearer is an example, precisely as a servant.

The mode of expression is difficult. What does $\mu\epsilon\tau\alpha$-$\sigma\chi\eta\mu\alpha\tau\acute{\iota}\zeta\epsilon\iota\nu$ mean in this passage?[7] It is often interpreted to mean saying something with the help of a figure of speech.[8] Others hold that since no figure of speech occurs in the context, the sense must be: to express something in a form other than usual.[9] Here it must be

1   'Aπολλῶν: Blass–Debrunner §55(1g) considers the accusative 'Aπολλῶ to be the correct form; cf. Acts 19:1; Tit 3:13 C D* K L P etc.

2   ἅ: variant reading ὅ D G 𝕽.

3   εἰ δὲ καί: 2 Cor 4:3; 11:6; Lk 11:18.

4   Blass–Debrunner §495(2) (figure of irony).

5   Blass–Debrunner §67(2): "Ὄφελον is not unaugmented ὤφελον . . . but a participle with which an original ἐστίν is to be supplied (§127(2))." In Hellenistic Greek it has turned into a particle (= εἴθε), §359(1).

6   Paul as an example: see on 11:1.

7   Johannes Schneider, *TDNT* 7:957f. The only other passages where Paul uses the word are 2 Cor 11:13–15 and Phil 3:21; neither passage helps us further here.

8   Philostr., *Vit. soph.* 2.17 (2.100.27); 2.25 (2.110.6); Ps.–Demetr., *Eloc.* 287; 292–294; 298: περὶ μὲν δὴ πλάσματος λόγου καὶ σχηματισμῶν ἀρκείτω ταῦτα, "With regard to moulded speech and the employment of figures, this treatment must suffice" (Loeb 483).

9   Lietzmann; see Albrecht Dihle's note to Schneider, *TDNT* 7:958, n. 10.

conceded that this use of μετασχηματίζειν ("exemplify") is catachrestic.[10] At all events it here becomes plain who are meant by the "we" in v 1.

The phrase τὸ μὴ ὑπὲρ ἃ γέγραπται is unintelligible.[11] Those who do not decide (with Baljon) to delete it as a gloss[12] do not get beyond guesswork.[13] The latter points more or less in the direction of the principle, μήτε προσθεῖναι μήτε ἀφελεῖν ("neither add nor take away").[14] The second ἵνα–clause, ("so as . . ."),[15] with its shortened form, is likewise difficult to fathom. Here the general sense is certainly plain,[16] but the expression is not.[17]

■ 7 The style is diatribelike and dialogical, with its series of three questions and the chainlike intertwining of the catchwords. The use of the second person singular means that the Christian Everyman is being addressed.[18] The absolute use of διακρίνειν, "give preference," is remarkable.[19] The first question suggests the answer "nothing"; so also does the second.[20] The third and final question links up with the second, as having admittedly received the answer "nothing"; it seeks no further answer, but cuts off the possibility of any such answer. εἰ, "if,"

10 Morna D. Hooker, " 'Beyond the Things Which Are Written': An Examination of I Cor. IV.6," *NTS* 10 (1963–64): 127–132, holds that Paul is recurring to the metaphors of planting and building: these figures I have transposed = applied.

11 O. Linton, " 'Nicht über das hinaus, was geschrieben ist' (1 Kor. 4,6)," *ThStKr* 102 (1930): 425–437; Lyder Brun, "Noch einmal die Schriftnorm I Kor. 4,6," *ThStKr* 103 (1931): 453–456. Overview: P. Wallis, "Ein neuer Auslegungsversuch der Stelle I. Kor. 4,6," *ThLZ* 75 (1950): 506–508.

12 *Novum Testamentum Graece*, ed. J. M. S. Baljon (Groningen: Wolters, 1898), taken over by Schmithals, *Gnosticism in Corinth*, 122, n. 11 [115, n. 1]: the μή of the second ἵνα clause was subsequently inserted above εἷς (= ἃ) or above the α of ἵνα, this was noted in the margin, and finally the note found its way into the text.

13 Examples: (1) Weiss: τὸ μὴ ὑπερ . . . and ἵνα μὴ εἷς ὑπὲρ . . . are doublets. "The transmitted text is not intelligible." (2) Lietzmann: the meaning must be, in order that you may learn by our example to live according to Scripture. Is there an underlying allusion which is incomprehensible to us? To some Corinthian slogan? (3) Wallis: in view of the article, γέγραπται is to be taken as referring neither to the Bible nor to what was written in the preceding section. τό points to a recognized principle. The punctuation is: τὸ μὴ ὑπέρ, ἃ γέγραπται. μὴ ὑπέρ is a slogan, cf. 2 Cor 11:23. ἃ γέγραπται means: here you have it in black and white. Hooker, " 'Beyond the Things Which Are Written,' " holds that Paul is recurring to the OT allusions in 3:19f, which in turn go back to chaps. 1f.

14 Rev 22:19; Willem C. van Unnik, "De la règle Μήτε προσθεῖναι μήτε ἀφελεῖν dans l'histoire du canon," *VigChr* 3 (1949): 1–36; Kurt Galling, "Das Rätsel der Zeit im Urteil Kohelets (Koh 3, 1–15)," *ZThK* 58 (1961): 1–15, here esp. 13.

15 According to Hooker, the second ἵνα clause depends on the first, and accordingly indicates the content of what is written.

16 For the content, cf. Rom 12:3.

17 φυσιοῦν, "puff up," for the classical φυσᾶν; Epict., *Diss.* 1.8.10: ἐπηρμένος ἡμῖν καὶ πεφυσημένος περιπατεῖ, "and strut about in our presence, all conceited and puffed up" (Loeb 1:61). 1 Cor 4:18f, etc. What is meant is not merely subjective conceit, but the speculatively grounded behavior of the Corinthians. Attempted interpretations: (1) Weiss: cf. the comment on ὑπέρ, 2 Cor 9:2. The sense is, so as not to be high and mighty toward *one* teacher in favor of another teacher; cf. the antithesis ὑπέρ/ κατά (the antithesis is *not* between εἷς and ἕτερος). (2) Lietzmann: ὑπέρ means "in favor of"—so as not to be high and mighty one toward another in favor of *one* particular teacher (brother, according to Schmiedel), cf. 2 Cor 5:20;7:7. (3) Bachmann: the remark—so near to v 6a—can refer only to one of the two there mentioned; cf. also Allo: do not be puffed up, one in favor of the other (in favor of Paul or of Apollos), one against the other. (4) Schmithals, *Gnosticism in Corinth*, 179–182 [169–171]: there is an intermingling of polemic against boasting in favor of a teacher and against boasting in general.

18 The form of the argument shows that what is censured in v 6 is not the directing of the act of φυσιοῦσθαι, "being puffed up," toward a false object, but the act of φυσιοῦσθαι as such.

19 11:29, 31 does not help. Vulgate: *Quis enim te discernit?* "For who distinguishes you?" Theodore of Mopsuestia (Staab, *Pauluskommentare*, 177): διακρίνει· διερευνᾷ καὶ ἀντεξετάζει πρὸς ἄλλον, "διακρίνει: examines and measures (you) against another."

20 Not so Weiss, according to whom Paul is not denying that they can recognize their advantage at all, but is asking: Who confers on you, by his *authoritative* recognition, the *right* to consider yourselves something special? But with the second question the answer expected is clear; from this we have to draw our conclusions as to the first one. τί ἔχεις, κτλ., "What do you have, etc.," cf. 3:5; 15:10.

presents the case in question as being really given:[21] Paul is choosing his words in view of the actual attitude of the Corinthians.[22] The thought of grace finds radical expression (cf. 2 Cor 4:8, 12; 6:3–10), as opposed to the Corinthian exaltation Christology, in which the moment of receipt is left behind, replaced by the habitual possession of the benefits of salvation.[23]

■ **8** Paul resorts to irony. This holds whether the sentences are taken as rhetorical questions[24] or as statements (thus Heinrici, Lietzmann). "Satiated":[25] this is aimed at a self–assurance similar to that which emerges in

Phil 3:12ff in the claim to be already perfect. ἐπλουτήσατε: the catchword "rich" was already touched upon earlier.[26] The climax is reached with the third question (or statement): χωρὶς ἡμῶν[27] ἐβασιλεύσατε, "you have attained to sovereignty without us." Here we have a widespread motif. For Stoics and Cynics, following Plato, the wise man is "king."[28] Naturally this way of speaking can be employed without more ado by apocalyptic[29] and Gnosticism.[30] For Paul the eschatological sense is a matter of course. That is to say, the Corinthians are convinced that they already have part in God's

---

21 εἰ δὲ καί: καί accentuates the antithesis to οὐκ ἔλαβες, cf. 7:11 (Lietzmann).

22 καυχᾶσθαι, "boast": a Hellenistic formation after the model of verbs in –μι, Radermacher, *Grammatik*, 88f; Blass–Debrunner §87.

23 Once again the consequences of the exaltation theology become visible: the situation of receiving grace gives place to the possession of it. Cf. the description of the Gnostic attitude in Iren., *Haer.* 1.6.4: "they declare . . . that they themselves have grace as their own special possession from above" (ANF 1:324). Augustine employs the statement against the Pelagians.

24 After the pattern of v 7. Here, too, we have three clauses with a change in the third. Whether the question form or the statement form is rhetorically the more effective is open to dispute.

25 κορέννυμι is used figuratively (also in Philo, Jos.; see Bauer, *s.v.*).

26 See on 1:5 (here as commendation); cf. 2 Cor 9:11. The motif of "riches" is fully explored in philosophy: "To the wise man all things belong" (see 3:21f). He shares in the riches of God, who is perfectly rich, Philo, *Leg. all.* 1.34; 3.163; *Rer. div. her.* 27; Eph 2:4, etc. For the Christological paradox, see 2 Cor 8:9. *Ev. Thom.* 81: "Let him who has become rich become king, and let him who has power (δύναμις) renounce (ἀρνεῖσθαι) (it)" (Guillaumont *et al.*, 45). See below, n. 28.

27 Either "without our aid" or, with Theodoret, *ad loc.*: ἡμῶν ἔτι ταλαιπωρουμένων . . . ὑμεῖς ἀπηλαύσατε τῆς βασιλείας, "While we were yet afflicted . . . you drove us away from the kingdom" [Trans.].

28 The wise man is king, Epict., *Diss.* 3.22.63: κοινωνὸν αὐτὸν εἶναι δεῖ τοῦ σκήπτρου καὶ τῆς βασιλείας, "He must share with him his sceptre and kingdom" (Loeb 2:153). Philo, *Abr.* 261: αἱ μὲν γὰρ ἄλλαι βασιλεῖαι πρὸς ἄνθρωπον καθίστανται . . . τὴν δὲ τοῦ σόφου βασιλείαν ὀρέγει θεός, ἣν παρακαβὼν ὁ σπουδαῖος οὐδενὶ μὲν αἴτιος γίνεται κακοῦ, "For other kingdoms are established among men . . . But the kingdom of the Sage comes by the gift of God,

and the virtuous man who receives it brings no harm to anyone" (Loeb 6:127, 129). On riches and kingship, see Plut., *Tranq. an.* 472a (on the Stoics): τὸν σοφὸν παρ' αὐτοῖς μὴ μόνον φρόνιμον καὶ δίκαιον καὶ ἀνδρεῖον, ἀλλὰ καὶ ῥήτορα καὶ ποιητὴν καὶ στρατηγὸν καὶ πλούσιον καὶ βασιλέα προσαγορευόμενον, "In their sect the wise man is termed not only prudent and just and brave, but also an orator, a poet, a general, a rich man, and a king" (Loeb 6:207, 209). *Ev. Thom.* 2 promises the Gnostic sovereignty over the universe. On the three catchwords in v 8, see Ernst Haenchen, *Die Botschaft des Thomasevangeliums* (Berlin: Töpelmann, 1961), 70f. Since in Corinth the Gnostic myth—or to be more precise, the Gnostic stage of reflection on the myth—is not yet fully developed, we must speak of proto–Gnosticism: they are directly on the threshhold of moving over to Gnosticism.

29 In the tradition of oriental "court style."

30 The Gnostic is of course already in possession of the life of the beyond, 2 Tim 2:18; Iren., *Haer.* 1.23.5. *Corp. Herm.* 10.9: ὁ γνοὺς . . . ἤδη θεῖος, "The one who knows . . . is already divine." The *Books of Jeu* 44 (in Schmidt–Till, *Koptisch–gnostische Schriften* 1:306f) say of the initiates: "And I say to you that they, since they have been on earth, have inherited the Kingdom of God already; they have a part in the treasure of light and are immortal gods." *Ev. Hebr.*, fr. 4b: οὐ παύσεται ὁ ζητῶν, ἕως ἂν εὕρῃ, εὑρὼν δὲ θαμβηθήσεται, θαμβηθεὶς δὲ βασιλεύσει, βασιλεύσας δὲ ἀναπαύσεται, "He that seeks will not rest until he finds; and he that has found shall marvel; and he that has marvelled shall reign; and he that has reigned shall rest" (Hennecke–Schneemelcher–Wilson 1:164, from Cl. Al., *Strom.* 5.14.96). Otfried Hofius, "Das koptische Thomasevangelium und die Oxyrhynchus–Papyri Nr. 1, 645 und 655," *EvTh* 20 (1960): 21–42, here esp. 27–29, supposes that the passage from Clement is erroneously ascribed to *Ev. Hebr.* The same logion is found in *P. Oxy.* 654, 6–9 (Hennecke–Schneemelcher–Wilson

sovereignty (this is the meaning of συμβασιλεύειν, cf. 2 Tim 2:12) in having part in the exalted Christ, i.e., in having the Spirit. Against this Paul maintains the eschatological proviso, as in Phil 3:12ff. The Corinthians misjudge the situation: between the present and the "goal" there intervenes the parousia and the judgment, which they in their spiritual self–assurance believe they have behind them.[31]

The wish[32] paves the way for v 9.[33]

■ **9** This verse begins pointedly: δοκῶ κτλ., "it seems to me, etc." (cf. 7:40; 11:16). The Apostle[34] presents himself as an example in a paradoxical sense: as a sufferer.[35] The *theologia crucis* interprets the existence of the confessor in terms of exposing himself to death. 2 Cor 4:7ff; 6:4ff can serve as commentary. The Stoic picture of the philosopher's struggle as a spectacle for the world[36] is taken over by Paul into his world–picture (cosmos and angels) and reshaped in terms of his eschatology;[37] "spectacle" has for him a derogatory sense. He is thinking not of the warrior who is admired by God for his hero-

---

1:297) = *Ev. Thom.* 2. For the catchword "satiate," cf. *Ev. Thom.* 60; for "rich," 3, 29, 85. Thus it is plain that we have here a set combination of language and motifs which expresses the self–consciousness of the Gnostic; see Haenchen, *Botschaft*, 70f.

31 Thus they no longer need God. This means that they have no longer a future before them either.

32 ὄφελον with indicative: LXX, Epict., etc.

33 Weiss offers a psychological interpretation: Paul, he says, is repelled by the Corinthians' exuberance. This is to mistake the fundamental character of his statement. For that reason it must not be asked whether all apostles found themselves in the situation described in what follows. The analysis is valid even when, biographically and psychologically speaking, all is well with them. For it does not present their inward or outward experience (however much this may also be included), but explains existence in the light of the cross—in other words, it is self–understanding on the basis of faith.

34 "Apostle" here manifestly refers to a restricted circle. Who belongs to it, does not emerge here; see chap. 9; 15:3ff. Weiss thinks that Apollos cannot be included, and that in that case there remain only Timothy and Silvanus. But Paul does not allow these the title of apostle. For the title, cf. Rom 16:7; 2 Cor 8:23; 11f; Phil 2:25; Kümmel, *Kirchenbegriff*, 6; Klein, *Die zwölf Apostel*, 41f, 56f.

35 Suffering has a vicarious effect, 2 Cor 4:12. No exposition is given in this passage of the idea of the apostle's sufferings as "sufferings of Christ" (2 Cor). For this, see Erhardt Güttgemanns, *Der leidende Apostel und sein Herr*, FRLANT, 90 (Göttingen: Vandenhoeck & Ruprecht, 1966).

36 The figure of the theatre (Gerhard Kittel, *TDNT* 3:42f) is used also outside philosophy. Sallust., *Jug.* 14.23: *At ego infelix, in tanta mala praecipitatus ex patrio regno, rerum humanarum spectaculum praebeo*, "While I, poor wretch, hurled from my father's throne into this sea of troubles, present a tragedy of human vicissitude" (Loeb 165). Plin., *Panegyr.* 33.3: *nemo ex spectatore spectaculum factus*, "No spectator found him-self turned spectacle" (Loeb 2:395). For the Stoic, adverse fate is the contest in which he can prove himself, Sen., *Ep.* 64.4–6; *Prov.* 2.9; God rejoices in it, *Prov.* 2.11. Wendland, *Literaturformen*, 357, n. 1; Adolf Bonhöffer, *Epiktet und das Neue Testament*, RVV, 10 (Giessen: Töpelmann, 1911), 170; Johannes Leipoldt, "Das Bild vom Kriege in der griechischen Welt," in *Gott und die Götter: Festgabe für Erich Fascher zum 60. Geburtstag* (Berlin: Evangelische Verlagsanstalt, 1958), 16–30; Braun, *Gesammelte Studien*, 186–191.

37 Apparently he has in mind the eschatological idea of the reversal of first and last; in terms of Paul's anticipatory eschatology this idea now serves the interpretation of present existence in the world. ἔσχατος: Diod. S., *Bibl. hist.* 8.18.2: οἱ ἔσχατοι, "the lowest of men" (Loeb 3:411), those who live in utmost misery.

ism,[38] but of the scenes in the Roman theatre with those condemned to death.[39] This destiny is not "necessary" in the sense of fate. It is ordained by God for a specific purpose, which lies beyond the people concerned.[40]

■ **10** The style is heightened; three antitheses follow each other. The third exchanges "we" and "you" in chiastic form and thereby provides a smooth connection with v 11 ("we"). The representation of the opponents' position is essentially accurate; what makes it ironical is the criterion, the *theologia crucis*. Paul repeats earlier catchwords: μωρός, ἰσχυρός, ἀσθενής, "foolish, strong, weak." This makes the verdict plain (1:25ff; 3:18f).[41] The fact that this time he uses not σοφός but φρόνιμος for the antithesis of μωρός is merely a rhetorical variation without inherent meaning.[42] The motif

of ἄτιμοι/ἔνδοξοι, "despised/honored," is also inherently contained in 1:26ff.

■ **11–13** These verses constitute a brief catalogue of adverse circumstances, which in v 12b passes over into antitheses.[43] The verb κολαφίζεσθαι, "to beat with the fist," "to maltreat," is very rare.[44] There follow three antitheses.[45] λοιδορούμενοι εὐλογοῦμεν, "when abused, we bless," is a general requirement of all primitive Christianity, arising from the nature of faith itself (Mt 5:44; Rom 12:14, 20). διωκόμενοι, "when persecuted" (Mt 5:11) ἀνεχόμεθα: "hold out."[46] δυσφημούμενοι is replaced in B D 𝔖 by the more usual βλασφη-

---

38 See above, n. 36. Braun, *Gesammelte Studien*, 181–191 observes that Seneca's God looks on in wonder, whereas Paul's God rescues from death and leaves the looking on (but without wonder) to men and angels. The Stoa is not aware of any genuine transcendence at all. "God" is there merely a cipher for the brave man's evaluation of himself. Paul is not aware of any necessity of suffering. And it is not the behavior of the sufferer that interests him. His eyes are not on his own proving, but on his brother: vv 12f.

39 ἐπιθανάτιος: cf. 15:31; 2 Cor 4:10f; Rom 8:36. The meaning is: "condemned to death," Dion. Hal., *Ant. Rom.* 8.18.2: ὅθεν αὐτοῖς ἔθος βάλλειν τοὺς ἐπιθανατίους, "from which they used to hurl those who were condemned to death" (Loeb 4:245); Bel 31. For the motif, cf. also Heb 10:33. The Stoic analogy is the idea of *cotidie mori*—which, however, again expresses heroic self-assertion; Bultmann, *TDNT* 3:11.

40 There is no thought of a Christian asceticism.

41 διὰ Χριστόν, "for Christ's sake," and ἐν Χριστῷ, "in Christ," point to the place and conditions of the verdict: it is valid according to the criterion of the cross, not of worldly reason.

42 φρόνιμος: Prov 3:7, μὴ ἴσθι φρόνιμος παρὰ σεαυτῷ· φοβοῦ δὲ τὸν θεόν, "Be not wise in your own eyes; fear the Lord"; 2 Cor 11:19.

43 Cf. 2 Cor 6:9f; for the content, 2 Cor 4:7–10; 11:23ff. For catalogues of adverse circumstances, see Bultmann, *Stil*, 19. Preservation amid περιστάσεις, "adverse circumstances," proves the presence of divine power in the missionary, Epict., *Diss.* 1.24; Georgi, *Gegner*, 194f. Bultmann, *Theology* 1:350[351]: "In such acceptance of sufferings, the believer, as one 'who is made like him [Christ] in his death,' concretely experiences the 'fellowship of his suffer-

ings' (Phil. 3:10) . . . for 'fellowship' with Christ is also 'fellowship' with all who belong to his *soma* (1 Cor. 12:25f.)." Lucien Cerfaux, "L'antinomie paulinienne de la vie apostolique," *RechSR* 39 (1951): 221–235, now in his *Receuil* 2:455–467.

44 Karl Ludwig Schmidt, *TDNT* 3:818–821. 2 Cor 12:7.

45 Weiss again discovers the schema a b a (εὐλογοῦμεν/ παρακαλοῦμεν); for the schema cf. 13:8; Rom 12:8.

46 Used ironically in 2 Cor 11:20.

μούμενοι (cf. Rom 3:8).[47] The sense of the metaphor[48] περικάθαρμα and περίψημα is disputed: Have we here a metaphor at all, or is it nonfigurative speech?[49]

The final note ἕως ἄρτι, "to this day," corresponds to the beginning of v 11: ἄχρι τῆς ἄρτι ὥρας, "to this very moment."

---

47 Theodore of Mopsuestia (Staab, *Pauluskommentare*, 177) distinguishes εὐλογοῦμεν (ἀντὶ τοῦ εὐχόμεθα ὑπὲρ τῶν ὑβριζόντων, "over against which we pray for those who commit these outrages") from παρακαλοῦμεν (ἀντὶ τοῦ ἠπίως τοῖς διαβάλλουσι διαλεγόμεθα παρακαλοῦντες μὴ καταψεύδεσθαι ἡμῶν, "over against which we discuss gently with the slanderers, appealing to them not to lie about us" [Trans.]).

48 Weiss: "For indeed we must . . . appear to be. . . ."

49 The two words are practically synonymous. περικάθαρμα (Friedrich Hauck, *TDNT* 3:430f) is that which is removed in the cleaning, dirt. περίψημα, (Gustav Stählin, *TDNT* 6:84–93), from περιψάω, is that which is wiped away. περικάθαρμα: Prov 21:18 for כֹּפֶר; κάθαρμα: Aesch., *Choeph.* 98; Eur., *Herc. fur.* 225; *Iph. Taur.* 1316; περίψημα: Tob 5:19; Ign., *Eph.* 8.1; 18.1; *Barn.* 4.9; 6.5; see Edgar Hennecke, *Handbuch zu den neutestamentlichen Apokryphen* (Tübingen: J. C. B. Mohr [Paul Siebeck], 1904), 218. Both terms are found in a twofold sense. περικάθαρμα (Epict., *Diss.* 3.22.78, usually κάθαρμα: Jos., *Bell.* 4.241; Philo) becomes a term of abuse, "scum": Luc., *Hermot.* 81; cf. Philo, *Virt.* 174 (κάθαρμα), Poll., *Onom.* 5.163. The other sense, "expiatory sacrifice," is first found in Suidas (s.v. κάθαρμα) and Photius. Much the same is true also of περί-

ψημα, though it is certainly weaker; it appears as a modest self–designation (Eus., *Hist. eccl.* 7.22.7). The second meaning provides the basis for one specific exposition of this passage: in certain expiatory rites someone—e.g., a criminal condemned to death —is vicariously sacrificed for the purity of the city; Nilsson, *Geschichte* 1:103f, 109f; Erwin Rohde, *Psyche*, tr. W. B. Hillis (London: Kegan Paul; New York: Harcourt, Brace, 1925; Harper & Row, 1966), 296 (*Psyche* [Tübingen: J. C. B. Mohr (Paul Siebeck), ⁶1910], 2:78f). To be sure, we should not here speak of an expiatory sacrifice. In the light of this rite, the explanation is then given: "I have been made into an expiatory sacrifice." In favor of this the following points are adduced: (*a*) πάντων: the περικάθαρμα goes to his death for a whole community; (*b*) ἐγενήθημεν is said to allude to a ritual phrase, περίψημα ἡμῶν γενοῦ; (*c*) the catchword ἐπιθανάτιος; (*d*) the three pairs of antitheses give expression to the blessing which accrues from the accursed one. But point (*d*) cancels itself out, the word ἐπιθανάτιος tells *against* this interpretation, and the rite in question is a long way out of the picture. The two words had long since become popular terms.

4   Apostle and Community—
Conclusion; Correspondence

14   It is not to shame you that I write this, but
to admonish you as my beloved chil-
dren.[1] 15 / For even if[2] you were to have
ten thousand "schoolmasters" in Christ
(or: ten thousand Christian "schoolmasters"), yet (you have) not many
fathers. For in Christ Jesus I became
your father through the gospel. 16 / So I
exhort you: become my imitators! 17 / It
is for this (very)[3] reason that I sent
Timothy to you, who is my beloved and
faithful child in the Lord. He will remind
you of my ways in Jesus Christ, of how
I teach everywhere in every church.
18 / Some have become arrogant,
imagining that I am not coming to you
at all.[4] But I shall come to you quickly, if
the Lord will, and shall find out not the
word, but the power of these arrogant
people. 20 / For it is not on word(s) that
the kingdom of God rests (or: not in
word[s] that it consists), but on (or: in)
power. 21 / What is your mind? Am I
to come to you with a stick or with love
and a spirit of gentleness?

■ **14** The tone changes;[5] Paul now speaks in conciliatory
fashion, characterizing his observations as νουθετεῖν,
"admonish,"[6] and contrasting them with ἐντρέπειν,
"shame,"[7] and going on to explain νουθετεῖν: ὡς[8]
τέκνα[9] κτλ., "as my children, etc."

■ **15** On the other hand, ἐντρέπειν is here the work of
the "pedagogue,"[10] which is again contrasted with the
behavior of a father. The phrasing shows that fatherhood
is no mere metaphor;[11] it is real, "spiritual" fatherhood.[12] "In Christ" denotes the objective sphere which
is constitutive for the relationship of father and children.
"Gospel" is one of the concepts which early became

1   Present participle in a final sense. The future participle has become rare and is frequently supplanted
by the present, Blass–Debrunner §339(2c). Weiss
prefers νουθετῶ (p⁴⁶ B D G 𝔐) as being the *lectio
difficilior*.

2   ἐάν expresses "indefinite relation to a present reality"
(Blass–Debrunner §372[1a]). Classical Greek would
have a potential or unreal condition.

3   αὐτό is omitted by p⁴⁶ B C D G; Zuntz, *Text*, 63.

4   ὡς with participle, "imagining that," Blass–Debrunner §425(3).

5   Weiss speaks of polite accommodation as in 2 Cor
7:3; 1 Thess 4:1; 4:9f; Rom 15:14f; Lietzmann of a
change of mood. Such a change explains nothing:
Why does Paul then allow to stand what he had
written in a different mood?

6   νουθετεῖν, Wis 11:10: of children; Jos., *Bell.* 1.481:
Herod "threatens" his sons as king and admonishes
(νουθετεῖν) them as father; Plat., *Leg.* 845b: as a
measure against the free man as distinct from πλη-
γαῖς κολάζειν, "punish with blows," for the slave;
Philo, *Decal.* 87: ὡς δικαστής, "as judge."

7   The antithesis between ἐντρέπειν and νουθετεῖν is
not immediately given in the meaning of the word;
ἐντρέπειν can also be the work of a father, νουθετεῖν
that of a judge (see Philo in previous note).

8   ὡς here does not mean "like" but "as": Paul is not
speaking figuratively, but in the proper sense; cf. v15.

9   τέκνον, 2 Cor 6:13; Phlm 10.

10   The "pedagogue" does not impart instruction; he is
distinguished from the διδάσκαλος (evidence in
Bauer; *P. Oxy.* 930 in Moulton–Milligan); he is usually a slave, Plat., *Lys.* 208c; cf. Epict., *Diss.* 1.11.22;
3.22.17. Albrecht Oepke, *Der Brief des Paulus an die
Galater*, ThHK, 9 (Berlin: Evangelische Verlagsanstalt, ²1957), 86–91; E. Schuppe, Pauly–W.
18:2375–2385. For the rhetorical exaggeration μύ-
ριοι, cf. 14:19; Philo, *Leg. Gaj.* 54; Epict., *Diss.*
4.13.21.

11   Metaphorical in 1 Thess 2:11.

12   ἐγέννησα, "I became [your] father": Phlm 10.
Spiritual fatherhood: cf. Epict., *Diss.* 3.33.81 (upbringing); Philo, *Leg. Gaj.* 58. In the mysteries the
mystagogue is the "father" of the initiands. Reitzen-

technical terms for the proclamation, like κήρυγμα, etc.[13]

■ 16 The summons to "imitate" him is a paraenetic topos in Paul (11:1 etc.).[14] "Imitate" is not identical with "follow."[15] The word group μιμεῖσθαι, "imitate," is used of the pupil's relation to his teacher.[16] If the question is asked to what extent Paul is to be taken as an example, then the preceding observations must be borne in mind; he does not present himself as a Christian personality. This summons is always bound up with the paradox that he is an example inasmuch as he is nothing and as he suffers (cf. 1 Thess 1:6; 2:14; Phil 3:17; 1 Cor 10:33—11:1). This is in keeping with the Christological argument for his summons in 11:1: he for his part imitates Christ (cf. 1 Thess 1:6),[17] namely, the preexistent Christ

(2 Cor 8:9). The argument is accordingly soteriological.[18] The summons cannot be separated from Paul's missionary work.

■ 17 This is shown by the further elucidation in v 17: Timothy[19] is to remind them of Paul's "ways." The question of course is how strictly we have to take the logical connection between v 16 and v 17. διὰ τοῦτο (αὐτό), "for this [very] reason," sounds as if it were particularly closely connected with the summons to imitation.[20] Paul's "ways"[21] are here more especially his *teaching*, as is shown by the explanatory καθώς clause ("of

stein, *Mysterienreligionen*, 40f; Gottlob Schrenk, *TDNT* 5:958f.

13   The technical use is Christian. The word is not a technical term in emperor worship.

14   Did Paul not thereby suggest a Paul slogan after all? At all events he seems to have been understood in this sense. For παρακαλεῖν, "exhort," see on 1:10.

15   Edvin Larsson, *Christus als Vorbild*, tr. Beatrice Steiner, ASNU, 23 (Uppsala: Almqvist & Wiksell; Lund: Gleerup; Copenhagen: Munksgaard, 1962); Willis Peter de Boer, *The Imitation of Paul* (Kampen: Kok, 1962); Anselm Schultz, *Nachfolgen und Nachahmen*, SANT, 6 (Munich: Kösel, 1962), here esp. 309f; Wilhelm Michaelis, *TDNT* 4:659–674; David M. Stanley, " 'Become imitators of me': The Pauline Conception of Apostolic Tradition," *Biblica* 40 (1959): 859–877; Hans Dieter Betz, *Nachfolge und Nachahmung Jesu Christi im Neuen Testament*, BHTh, 37 (Tübingen: J. C. B. Mohr [Paul Siebeck], 1967), here esp. 153–169.

16   Xenoph., *Mem.* 1.2.3; 1.6.3. In a general sense: Plut., *Alex.* 332ab (Alexander): Ἡρακλέα μιμοῦμαι καὶ Περσέα ζηλῶ καὶ τὰ Διονύσου μετιὼν ἴχνη, "I imitate Heracles, and emulate Perseus, and follow in the footsteps of Dionysus" (Loeb 4:413). Philosophy: Plat., *Theaet.* 176b; *Resp.* 613a; *Leg.* 715f. In the Stoa the idea of man's kinship with God is naturally definitive; Sen., *Ep.* 95.50; Muson. (*C. Musonii Rufi reliquiae*, ed. O. Hense [Leipzig: Teubner, 1905], 90). The expression is taken over by Hellenistic Judaism: *Ep. Ar.* 188, 210, 281; Wis 4:2; *4 Macc.* 9.23; Jos., *Bell.* 4.562; *Ant.* 1.109, etc.; Philo, *Op. Mund.* 79; *Virt.* 66. Adalhard Heitmann, *Imitatio Dei. Die ethische Nachahmung Gottes nach der Väterlehre der zwei ersten Jahrhunderte*, Studia Anselmiana, 10 (Rome: Herder, 1940); Schulz, *Nachfolgen*, 209f.

17   In itself the series can be traced back from Christ to

God after the pattern of 3:21f. But the *imitatio Dei* is not found until Eph 4:32; 5:1 (cf. Col 3:13); 1 Pet 1:15f.

18   This is rightly emphasized by Michaelis. Yet the thought of the exemplariness of Paul must not be eliminated.

19   τέκνον, "child": that is to say, he was converted by Paul. Acts (16:1f) does not say so explicitly. Timothy is not the bearer of the letter. ἔπεμψα, "I sent," is not an epistolary aorist. In 16:10 he has already departed (and is not mentioned among the senders). He came early to Corinth along with Silas, 1 Thess 3:2, and was accordingly known to the community from the start. For the style and content of his recommendation of Timothy, cf. 1 Thess 3:2f; Robert W. Funk, "The Apostolic *Parousia*: Form and Significance," in *Christian History and Interpretation: Studies Presented to John Knox*, ed. William R. Farmer, Charles F. D. Moule, and Richard E. Niebuhr (Cambridge: University Press, 1967), 249–268.

20   Not so Schulz, *Nachfolge*, 309f, who argues that διὰ τοῦτο does not have any necessary relation to the imperative and can point forward to the relative clause (in a final sense). This is correct; but there remains the context, "Become my imitators!" and "Let yourselves be reminded of my ways!"

21   The significant history of the concept in Greek (since the days of Parmenides) is of no relevance for our understanding of Paul. He uses his terms on the lines of the OT. As regards way and teaching: the sentence, "In the wilderness prepare the way," is explained in 1QS VIII, 15 by the observation: "This is the study of the Law" (Dupont–Sommer, 92). Friedrich Nötscher, *Gotteswege und Menschenwege in der Bibel und in Qumran*, BBB, 15 (Bonn: Hanstein, 1958); S. Vernon McCasland, "The Way," *JBL* 77 (1958): 222–230.

how . . .").[22] The latter's "ecumenical" style recalls the proemia.[23] διδάσκειν, "teach" (and διδαχή, "teaching"), likewise belong to the technical terminology of proclamation.

■ **18** The expression is obscure. Paul apparently means that some are giving themselves airs, as if he would not come.[24] Another possible interpretation is that they are giving themselves airs inasmuch as they declare that he will not come.[25]

Their false opinion can be further strengthened by the sending of Timothy. τινες, "some," already contains a value judgment.

■ **19** Against this, Paul emphatically announces his early[26] coming and the manner of his appearance; he will confront the arrogant enthusiasts with power, as one who puts them to the test. On the distinction between λόγος, "word," and δύναμις, "power," cf. 1 Thess 1:5.[27] The plans for his journey are stated more precisely in chap. 16. The proviso to which he subjects his plans is not a loophole, since personal arbitrariness is the one thing it particularly rules out.[28]

■ **20** He grounds the (proposed) measures in the nature of the kingdom of God. The phrasing is aphoristic (cf.

Rom 14:17). Its intention is not to provide an exhaustive definition, but to bring out an essential feature which is important at the moment. But it goes beyond the immediate context.[29]

One might feel that the dialectic is missing here. Is Paul setting himself up after all as a spiritual strong man? However, he has not forgotten that δύναμις appears in weakness. The power in virtue of which he will put them to the test is no other than the power indicated in 2:1ff.

■ **21** The alternative has an ironical ring, which suggests the δύναμις of Paul, but at the same time also indicates that his coming with a stick[30] would be an *opus alienum*. πνεῦμα is here not the Holy Spirit, but is used, as is good Jewish practice, in a formal sense.[31] πραΰτης is here not humility as an attitude, but as a mode of behavior.[32]

The discussion of the σχίσματα, "divisions," has reached its conclusion. There follows a loosely connected string of topics arising from community life in Corinth. Theologically speaking, they are held together by the eschatological view of the church in an eschatologically circumscribed world.

---

22 *Eth. En.* 104.13: μαθεῖν . . . πάσας τὰς ὁδοὺς τῆς ἀληθείας, "to learn . . . all the paths of uprightness" (Charles, *APOT* 2:277). Mt 21:32.

23 For the content, cf. 7:17; 14:33. For the rhetorical alliteration with π, cf. the beginning of Hebrews. Weiss doubts the genuineness of the passage (as also of the other "ecumenical" passages; see on 1:3). But we have here a good Pauline principle: 11:16.

24 2 Cor 10:14. Soph., *Ai.* 904: ὡς ὧδε τοῦδ' ἔχοντος αἰάζειν πάρα, "Thus lies he overthrown; 'tis ours to wail" (Loeb 2:77). According to Kühner–Blass–Gerth 2.2:90–96, the ground is designated subjective.

25 So apparently Lietzmann.

26 ταχέως, "quickly," is given a closer definition by 16:1ff. On the situation in the letter, see the Introduction.

27 2:1ff. Diog. L., *Vit.* 1.108: ἔφασκε δή, μὴ ἐκ τῶν λόγων τὰ πράγματα, ἀλλ' ἐκ τῶν πραγμάτων τοὺς λόγους ζητεῖν, "He used to say we should not investigate facts by the light of arguments, but arguments by the light of facts" (Loeb 1:113).

28 This "Jacobean clause" is a fundamentally pagan phrase, see Martin Dibelius, *Der Brief des Jakobus*, rev. Heinrich Greeven, KEK, 15 (Göttingen: Vandenhoeck & Ruprecht, [11]1964), *ad* Jas 4:15; Acts 18:21; 1 Cor 16:7 etc. Bauer, *s.v.* θέλω 2.

29 οὐκ ἐν, "not on [in]": 1 Macc 3:19, "The victory . . . standeth not in . . ."; Epict., *Diss.* 2.1.4, etc. (Definitions: "The thing does not consist in . . ."). According to Weiss, neither rendering suits here. ἐν . . . is the accompanying circumstance which serves as a distinctive mark. Cf. 2:4.

The eschatological character of the "kingdom of God" is not abrogated by the fact that it provides a criterion in the present; 6:9f; 15:50; Rom 14:17; Gal 5:21; 1 Thess 2:12 (2 Thess 1:5).

30 Luc., *Dial. mort.* 28(23).3(428): καθικόμενος ἐν ῥάβδῳ, "touching with his wand" (cf. Loeb 7:167). LXX: Gen. 32:10(f); 1 Sam 17:43. ῥάβδος, "stick": of the pedagogue or the teacher, Plat., *Leg.* 700c.

31 Dan 3:39, πνεῦμα ταπεινώμωνον; 1QS III, 8; IV, 3, רוח ענוה, "spirit of humility" (Dupont–Sommer, 77–79), here at the head of a list.

32 Ceslaus Spicq, "Réminiscence de Job XXXVII,13 dans I Cor. IV,21?" *RB* 60 (1953): 509–512, finds a reminiscence of Job 37:13; Paul, he holds, is presenting himself as God's representative.

1 Corinthians 5

5

πορνεία, "Sexual Immorality"

1 In general[1] there are reports of sexual immorality among you,[2] and indeed[3]
immorality of a kind that is unheard of
even among pagans—that a man[4] has his
father's wife. 2 / And you are arrogant[5]
instead of having been sorrowful so
that the man who has done[6] this deed
might be removed from your midst?[7] 3 / I
for my part,[8] absent in person but
present in the spirit, have now—as
though present in person—already resolved[9] to consign the man who has
done this, 4 / in the name of the Lord
Jesus,[10] when you are assembled and I
with you in spirit with the power of
our Lord Jesus—5 / to consign this man
to Satan for the destruction of his
flesh, that his spirit may be saved on the
day of the Lord. 6 / Your boast[11] is not
a good thing. Do you not know that
(even) a little leaven leavens all the
dough? 7 / Cleanse out[12] the old leaven,
that you may be new dough, as indeed
you are (in fact) "unleavened." For
indeed[13] our paschal lamb has been
sacrificed—Christ. 8 / So let us keep our
festival not with old leaven and not
with the leaven of vice and wickedness,
but with the unleavened bread of
sincerity and truth. 9 / I wrote you in my

1   ὅλως in this sense is not found elsewhere at the be-
     ginning of a sentence, although the synonymous
     expression τὸ ὅλον is.

2   The meaning is: "that there is immorality among
     you." ἐν ὑμῖν is not to be taken with ἀκούεται, "there
     are reports" (so Henrici); the word order is loose.

3   Schmiedel observes that καί does not mean "to be
     precise," but that there are general reports, and
     among them such a case.

4   The position of τινα emphasizes both γυναῖκα and
     πατρός, Blass–Debrunner §473(1).

5   The sentence can be taken as a statement or a ques-
     tion; the latter is more effective.

6   ποιήσας is preferred by Zuntz, Text, 130f.

7   The expression (cf. Col 2:14) corresponds to the
     Latin de medio tollere, but need not be a Latinism,
     Blass–Debrunner §5(3b). ἵνα here is not final, but
     "almost consecutive" (Weiss).

8   μέν underlines the subject (1 Thess 2:18). γάρ con-
     tinues, approaching the sense of δέ; Bauer, s.v. γάρ 4.

9   Not "have passed judgment"; otherwise the infini-
     tive remains hanging in the air.

10   +ἡμῶν before Ἰησοῦ p⁴⁶ B D G 𝔐 lat syᵖ; +Χρι-
     στοῦ p⁴⁶ ℵ G 𝔐 lat syᵖ.

11   Either: the thing of which you are proud, cf. 9:15f;
     2 Cor 1:14; Rom 4:2; Phil 2:16; or: your behavior,
     the fact that you boast, cf. φυσιοῦσθαι, v 2.

12   ἐκκαθαίρω with accusative (of the thing removed):
     Plat., Euthyphr. 3a; Philo, Vit. Mos. 1.303. If the
     expression is derived from the rabbinical בָּעֵר חָמֵץ,
     "remove the leaven" (Friedrich Hauck, TDNT
     3:430), then the ἐκ– is not explained.

13   καὶ γάρ: Blass–Debrunner §452(3) insists that καὶ
     γάρ is not merely to be understood as simple "for,"
     but as "for also."

letter that you should not associate
with sexually immoral people, 10 / not
meaning in general[14] the immoral
people of this world or avaricious people
and robbers or idolaters; for then you
would have to[15] depart from the world.
11 / In actual fact I wrote you[16] not
to have such associations when a
so-called brother is immoral or avaricious or an idolater or slanderer or
drunkard or robber—not even to eat
with such a man. 12 / For what business
is it of mine to judge outsiders?[17] Do
you not judge those within? 13 / The outsiders God will judge. "Drive out the
wicked person from your midst!"

■ 1   The transition to the new subject is apparently unmediated. Paul does indeed indicate an external ground,
oral reports from Corinth.[18] The people vouching for
this information are not named, and cannot be inferred
from other passages.[19] Despite the absence of a connecting link it must be asked whether the themes of
"Logos" in chaps. 1–4 and "Bios" in chaps. 5 and 6 do
not supply evidence of a uniform attitude in Corinth,
which Paul counters with a single comprehensive theological refutation—the more so as there emerge at least
hints that the conversation between the apostle and
the community has a wider context. According to vv 9f
the subject of πορνεία has already been discussed in
an earlier letter, manifestly in an apodictic form. Now
Paul has not only to apply his injunction to the mastering
of a real situation but must also safeguard it against
being transformed into an ascetic principle.

Barth rightly stresses that the accusation is not directed
in a moralizing sense against the sins of the world, nor
yet in a moralizing sense against particular individuals,
but "it is directed against the Church, as such, and runs:
It—the Church—is not what it yet *is* in Christ!"[19a]
Paul's warning is not "This sort of thing could happen to
any of you—the way you look at things," but "By your
behavior—as a community—you betray yourselves."

πορνεία is one of the most important key words of
primitive Christian paraenesis (cf. 5:9f, and see on 6:9f,
12f). This is in line with the tradition of Jewish sexual
ethics.[20] Naturally, our picture of pagan ethics must not
be drawn according to Jewish polemic.[21] It is the picture

14   οὐ πάντως: Blass–Debrunner §433(2).

15   ὠφείλετε, Blass–Debrunner §358: "The imperfect
(without ἄν) in expressions of necessity, obligation,
duty, possibility, etc. denotes in classical something
which is or was actually necessary, etc., but which
does not or did not take place (cf. Latin). In this
case German uses the unreal subjunctive, which corresponds to 'should, could,' or 'should have, could
have' in English." 1 Cor 5:10, "you would have
in that case to go . . .' (but do not go) is somewhat
different, where class. *might* have inserted ἄν."

16   Lietzmann takes νῦν as temporal and ἔγραψα as
epistolary aorist: "But now I am writing to you."

17   τί γάρ μοι: "For what business is it of *mine* . . .?"
Epict., *Diss.* 2.7.14: καὶ τί μοι νῦν; "And yet what
need is there for me now to . . .?" (Loeb 1:341).

18   Cf. 11:18.

19   Schmiedel observes that ὅλως ἀκούεται, "in general there are reports," is an effective asyndeton, as
a result of which 5:1ff becomes the justification of
4:21.

19a   Barth, *Resurrection*, 30 [13].

20   Wis 14:12ff, 24ff; Rom 1:18ff. Sexual immorality is
in the Jew's eyes *the* sin of the Gentiles, *Jub.* 25.1.
The connection between the Jewish and the Christian views is clear also in the "apostolic decree,"
Acts 15:20, etc.

21   Musonius, Plutarch, Epictetus; see 7:1ff. The average Greek verdict is mildly defensive; see Friedrich
Hauck and Siegfried Schulz, *TDNT* 6:582f.

of the "pagan trademark." When Paul points to the pagan world with the remark ἥτις οὐδὲ ἐν τοῖς ἔθνεσιν, "of a kind unheard of even among pagans," then this does not contain a relative acknowledgment of the fact that they, too, have a certain moral standard.[22] The pagans serve only as a foil for the sharpness of his judgment concerning the case in the community.[23] The latter is merely indicated, since of course it is known to both sides. He has his father's wife:[24] What does this mean? The simplest explanation is that after the death of his father he has married the latter's widow, his stepmother.[25] The present of ἔχειν, "have," points to a lasting state, marriage or concubinate (cf. 7:2, 29; Jn 4:18). Also conceivable is the fact that his father has secured a divorce and is still alive. We can rule out[26] a marriage with his own mother, which is forbidden in Lev 18:7. Such a marriage is inconceivable even in Greece and Rome.[27] Less likely also (in view of ἔχειν) is an adulterous relationship with his stepmother.[28] Marriage between stepmother and stepson is forbidden both by Jewish and by Roman law.[29] What the community thought of the case cannot be ascertained. At all events it took no measures against it.[30]

Paul does not explicitly state the ground of his judgment, because the ground is self–evident: the community is the temple of God (6:19). A specific link between this case and the Corinthian slogan of freedom, that is to say a speculative ground for the incestuous man's behavior, is not suggested. But Paul certainly does have to assert the nature of the community, both in face of this "free" libertinism and also in face of libertinism of a speculative kind. It is against the community that his criticism is directed.

■ **2** "Proud of yourselves" repeats an earlier judgment and gives concrete proof of it. What is meant is again the total attitude. "Sorrow"[31] is not primarily a feeling, but likewise a judgment—a judgment on sin, on the profanation of the sanctuary. ἵνα is explicatory. The

---

22 Elsewhere Paul can take up this point—and that, too, without limitations of a moralizing kind: Rom 2.

23 Wolfgang Schrage, *Die konkreten Einzelgebote in der paulinischen Paränese* (Gütersloh: Mohn, 1961), 190f.

24 Paul's lack of concern for the general moral aspects of the case is shown by the fact that he pronounces no judgment on the woman. She seems not to have belonged to the community.

25 אֵשֶׁת אָב (LXX: γυνὴ πατρός, "father's wife") is an OT and rabbinical designation for a stepmother: Lev 18:8, etc., Str.–B. 3:343–358. A parallel: Mart., *Epigr.* 4.16.

26 Ernst von Dobschütz, *Christian Life in the Primitive Church,* tr. George Bremner, ed. W. D. Morrison (London: Williams and Norgate; New York: Putnam, 1904), 387f (*Die urchristliche Gemeinden* [Leipzig: Hinrichs, 1902], 269f).

27 Iambl., *Vit. Pyth.* 31.210; Ael., *Nat. an.* 3.47. Ancient folklore marks marriage or sexual intercourse with one's mother as a Persian practice: Quint. Curt. Ruf., *Hist. Alex.* 8.2.19; Philo, *Spec. leg.* 3.13; Tat., *Or. Graec.* 28.

28 Judaism's warning illustration is Reuben, Gen 35:22; 49:4; *Test. R.* According to Jewish law, the man who lies with his father's wife is to be stoned, *Sanh.* 7.4. According to *b. Sanh.* 54a, this holds even after the father's death; Str.–B. 3:349f.

29 In Roman law, relatedness by adoption rules out marriage between adoptive parents and children, even after cancellation of the adoptive relationship, and also between steprelatives in direct line; Wolfgang Kunkel, "Matrimonium," Pauly–W. 14:2259–

2286, here esp. 2267. Caius, *Inst.* 1.63: *item eam (sc. uxorem ducere) non licet, quae mihi quondam socrus aut nurus aut privigna aut noverca fuit. ideo autem diximus "quondam," quia, si adhuc constant eae nuptiae, per quas talis adfinitas quaesita est, alia ratione mihi nupta esse non potest, quia neque eadem duobus nupta esse potest neque duas uxores habere,* "Neither can I marry her who has aforetime been my mother–in–law or step–mother, or daughter–in–law or step–daughter. I say 'aforetime'; for if the marriage which has created the affinity still subsist, I cannot take her to wife for this other reason,—that neither can the same woman have two husbands, nor can the same man have two wives" (*The Institutes of Gaius and Rules of Ulpian,* ed. and tr. James Muirhead [Edinburgh: Clark, 1880], 24f. Cic. *Cluent.* 6(15), of marriage with a son–in–law: *O mulieris scelus incredibile et praeter hanc unam in omni vita inauditum,* "Oh! to think of the woman's sin, unbelievable, unheard of in all experience save for this single instance!" (Loeb 237.)

For Judaism, see preceding note. Philo, *Spec. leg.* 3.12–21. Jos., *Ant.* 3.274. Ps.–Phocylides, *Poema admon.* 179ff. The opinions of the rabbis are divided as to whether Gentiles are allowed marriage with a stepmother, Str.–B. 3:358.

30 Hurd, *Origin,* 278 ventures the risky suggestion that perhaps they were conducting a spiritual marriage.

31 Aorist, as immediate reaction. "Sorrow" for the sins of others: 1 Esd 8:69; 9:2; 2 Esd 10:6; for one's own: *Test. R.* 1.10.

96

measure is aimed in the first instance at the purification of the *community* (cf. 3:16f).

■ **3–5** Possible constructions are these:

1. ἐν τῷ ὀνόματι belongs to συναχθέντων ὑμῶν, σὺν τῇ δυνάμει belongs to παραδοῦναι (Heinrici: "when you are assembled in the name," "consign him by the power").

2. Both belong to συναχθέντων ὑμῶν (Weiss, Lietzmann: "when you are assembled in the name [and] by the power").

3. Both belong to παραδοῦναι ("to consign him in the name [and] by the power").

4. Both belong to both (Bachmann).

5. ἐν τῷ ὀνόματι belongs to παραδοῦναι, σὺν τῇ δυνάμει to the participial clause (Robertson and Plummer, Allo: "to consign him in the name, when you are assembled in the power").

6. ἐν τῷ ὀνόματι belongs to κέκρικα, σὺν τῇ δυνάμει to συναχθέντων ὑμῶν (Schlatter: "I have resolved in the name . . . when you are assembled in the power").[32]

What is plain is that Paul is resolved upon a judicial act of a sacral and pneumatic kind against the culprit.[33]

The community merely constitutes the forum; it does not share in the action.

What is the effect and purpose of consigning the man to Satan, the Destroyer? It is clear that the δύναμις, "power," of the Lord is made effectual by calling upon his name. πνεῦμα, "spirit," is now, in contrast to v 3, the power which represents the Lord himself.[34] The destruction of the flesh can hardly mean anything else but death (cf. 11:30).[35] The shocking idea[36] is to be understood in the first instance within the context of contemporary history: the view of curse and ban as entertained by the whole ancient and Jewish world.[37] Here it is not a case of mere exclusion from the church,[38] but of a dynamistic ceremony. The holiness of the church is conceived in metaphysical categories. Yet the point does not lie in the physical aspect of the working of a supernatural power, but in the fact that the accursed man is thrust out of the body of Christ into the realm

---

32 Bachmann prefers in v 4a the longer text form, which is supported also by p⁴⁶. Weiss, on the contrary, maintains that the formula is given its full form where it constitutes the closing chord: Rom 1:4; 5:1, 11, 21, but that in the course of speaking it is short: 11:23; Rom 14:14.

33 Gustav Karlsson, "Formelhaftes in Paulusbriefen?" *Eranos* 54 (1956): 138–141, suspects that ἀπὼν τῷ σώματι, παρὼν δὲ τῷ πνεύματι, "absent in person but present in the spirit," is a formula of Greek epistolary style; cf. Col 2:5: On the "presence" of the apostle, see Robert W. Funk, "The Apostolic *Parousia*: Form and Significance," in *Christian History and Interpretation: Studies Presented to John Knox*, ed. William R. Farmer, Charles F. D. Moule, and Richard R. Niebuhr (Cambridge: University Press, 1967), 249–268.

34 Then in v 5 the person; Bultmann, *Theology* 1:208 [209].

35 This is in accordance with the terminology of 15:39ff. σάρξ, "flesh," is synonymous in both passages with σῶμα, "body"; Alexander Sand, *Der Begriff "Fleisch" in den paulinischen Hauptbriefen*, Biblische Untersuchung, 2 (Regensburg: Pustet, 1967), 129, 144f; see n. 40 *infra*. σάρξ and sexuality: Eduard Schweizer, *TDNT* 7:104f.

36 Schmiedel, the liberal, is offended by this. Allo, the Catholic, defends it, arguing that the idea is not inhuman, since the salvation of the soul is at stake. This is the well-known argument for the Inquisition! *O benedictae flammae!*

37 Lyder Brun, *Segen und Fluch im Urchristentum*, Norske Videnskaps–akademi i Oslo, historisk–filosofisk klasse, Skrifter 1932, 1. Bd. (1933), no. 1 (Oslo: Dybwad, 1932), 106ff. The expression παραδοῦναι recalls rites of devotion (to the nether gods), Deissmann, *Light*, 302 [257]. *PGM* 4.1247f: παραδίδωμί σε εἰς τὸ μέλαν χάος ἐν ταῖς ἀπωλείαις, "I give you over to black chaos in utter destruction" (Moulton and Milligan, *s.v.* ἀπώλεια). Synagogue ban: Str.–B. 4.1:293–333.

38 Maurice Goguel, *The Primitive Church*, tr. H. C. Snape (London: Allen & Unwin; New York: Macmillan, 1964), 233–235 (*L'église primitive*, part 3 of his *Jésus et les origines du Christianisme* [Paris: Payot, 1947], 242–245). Not so von Campenhausen, *Ecclesiastical Authority*, 134 [147, n. 1], who argues that Paul means exclusion.

of wrath.[39] This is plain from the purpose of the ceremony, the saving of the πνεῦμα. This is an enigmatic statement. Does the baptized man possess a *character indelebilis*?[40] Or is the intention precisely that the Spirit should be taken from him?[41]

With vv 6–13 the special case issues in general reflections on the purity of the community and its attitude toward the world.[42]

■ **6** Verse 6a confirms v 1 (ὅλως ἀκούεται, "in general there are reports"). καύχημα, "boast," presumably means active self-glorification (corresponding to πεφυσιωμένοι ἐστέ, "you are arrogant," v 2). With the familiar οὐκ οἴδατε, "do you not know" (see on 3:16), Paul points to a known fact, a proverb about leaven.[43] He is thinking in the first instance not of leaven as a

(traditionally Jewish) symbol of impurity, but rather of its effects.[44]

■ **7** To be sure, v 7 then introduces the Jewish association of leaven and Passover; the leaven becomes the symbol of that which is unclean and indeed actively polluting: ἐκκαθάρατε, "cleanse out."[45] Hence the important thing is to remove the "old"[46] leaven from the house and so make the latter fit for the cult.[47] Then the metaphor changes again; the thought is no longer that of the house, but the people themselves are the unleavened bread.[48] The imperative is grounded on the indicative; holiness is not the goal of conduct, but its presupposition. The reason (καὶ γάρ, "for indeed") introduces another change, because Paul here takes up a stock tradition con-

39 Ernst Käsemann, "Sentences of Holy Law in the New Testament," *NT Questions*, 66–81 [2:69–82], originally in *NTS* 1 (1954–55): 248–260. Cf. Acts 5:1–11; *Act. Pt. Verc.* 2; *Act. Thom.* 6.

40 There is no thought of an opportunity for repentance (say, in the Beyond)—just as little as in Acts 5:1–11 (against Lietzmann, Brun)—nor yet of an expiatory effect of the man's death (against Gillis P. Wetter, *Der Vergeltungsgedanke bei Paulus* [Göttingen: Vandenhoeck & Ruprecht, 1912], 145–148). Mattern, *Verständnis*, 103–108, interprets as follows in the light of 3:15; 11:31f. The ("spirit" of the) man seized by God will be saved by the annihilating of the "flesh" sold to sin. His immediate physical death preserves him from eternal death. The deeds of the flesh (Rom 8:13) are thereby radically destroyed; similarly Eduard Schweizer, *TDNT* 6:435f.

41 So Günther Bornkamm; see von Campenhausen, *Ecclesiastical Authority*, 134, n. 50 [147, n. 1]: the Spirit is taken from the perpetrator, in order that the perfectness of the body of Christ may appear at the Last Day. Against this, Eduard Schweizer, *TDNT* 6:435f, maintains that in view of 1 Pet 4:6 and the reference to the day of judgment, this explanation is impossible.

42 On vv 6–8 see Joachim Jeremias, *The Eucharistic Words of Jesus*, tr. Norman Perrin (London: SCM; New York: Scribner, 1966), 59f (*Die Abendmahlsworte Jesu* [Göttingen: Vandenhoeck & Ruprecht, ⁴1967], 53f). Klein, *Die zwölf Apostel*, 198f. (Just., *Dial.* 14.2f is not dependent upon Paul.

43 Proverb: Gal 5:9. Lietzmann goes too far in expanding the word μικρός, "little," to mean that Paul adds this as a warning pointer because the Corinthians may object that this is only a single instance. He also points out that the variant reading δολοῖ, "spoils," is out of place, since of course the leaven

does not *destroy* the dough. But cf. Plut., *Quaest. Rom.* 289f (§109): leaven destroys and defiles.

44 Not, however, its infectious effects (with Schlatter), but the *single* case has the result of defiling the whole community. Small causes/great effects: Lk 13:21 par. Mt 13:33; Jas 3:2–5; Hans Windisch, *Die katholischen Briefe*, rev. Herbert Preisker, HNT, 15 (Tübingen: J. C. B. Mohr [Paul Siebeck], ³1951), *ad loc.*

45 Philo, *Spec. leg.* 1.193; *Quaest. in Ex.* 1.15: ζύμη, "leaven," is a symbol of pride, the ἄζυμα, "unleavened," are a symbol of humility. Hans Windisch, *TDNT* 2:902–906.

46 παλαιός: leaven is in actual fact old dough. But the catchword παλαιός is hardly derived from the figure itself. What is in mind is rather the schema once/now = old/new, the antithesis of the old and new man, Rom 6:6; 7:6; Col 3:9; Eph 4:22, etc.

47 Ex 12:15, 19; 13:7; Deut 16:3f (thereto Philo, *Congr.* 161f); Ign., *Mg.* 10.2; Just., *Dial.* 14.2f. Lietzmann observes that the metaphor is not applied consistently. For indeed, he says, it is the leaven that first makes the dough usable. Paul, he argues, brings in the application of the figure too quickly. Against Lietzmann, see n. 43 above. And the objection disappears at once when we think of the Passover bread; so, rightly, Windisch.

48 It is presupposed that the Corinthians are familiar with Jewish Passover usage. For the regulations, see Str.-B. 3:359f. On the primitive community and the Passover, see Joachim Jeremias, *TDNT* 5:901–904; Bernhard Lohse, *Das Passafest der Quartadecimaner*, BFTh, 54 (Gütersloh: Bertelsmann, 1953), 101–112.

cerning "Christ" as the Passover Lamb.[49] The metaphor is not to be pressed beyond the ideas of sacrifice and covenant.[50] The tradition emerges in such passages as 1 Pet 1:19; Jn 1:29, 36; 19:36; Rev 5:6, 9, 12; 12:11.[51]

The Jewish cultic categories (the death of Jesus as expiatory sacrifice, covenant sacrifice, Passover sacrifice) are adequate categories of interpretation insofar as they represent the character of reconciliation as an act (cf. the background that has to be reconstructed as the basis of Rom 3:24–26). Their limitation lies in the fact that they apply in the first instance only to the collective body of the community, as the new people of the covenant, not to the individual as such. For this reason Paul himself goes on to expand the interpretation by introducing in Rom 3:24ff the ideas and concepts of the doctrine of justification: grace, faith, the view of the act of salvation as taking place in the present. In addition to this, the Jewish categories must be made intelligible to non–Jews. For this reason Paul supplements them

by means of the notion of participation taken over from the mysteries.[51a]

■ **8** This verse points the conclusion in terms of the schema indicative–imperative, retaining to begin with the metaphor of the Passover: when the lamb has been slain, the festival is celebrated. ζύμη, "leaven,"[52] is now interpreted in moral terms by means of κακία, πονηρία, "vice, wickedness,"[53] and their corresponding opposites, εἰλικρίνεια, "sincerity" (cf. 2 Cor 1:12; 2:17) and ἀλήθεια, "truth" (here "sincerity").[54]

■ **9–13** These verses expand the theme of πορνεία: Paul recalls an earlier letter,[55] in which he had obviously laid down the principle, "no association with πόρνοι!"[56] Apparently the Corinthians had replied to

---

49   τὸ πάσχα ἡμῶν can be taken as a predicative definition: "as our paschal lamb"; in that case Paul would be apprising the readers of something about which they do not yet know. But he uses the statement to ground his argument and presupposes that it is known. τὸ πάσχα ἡμῶν is accordingly the subject: our passover lamb has indeed already been slaughtered, namely, Christ. θύνειν τὸ πάσχα: שָׁחַט הַפֶּסַח, "to kill the Passover (lamb)," Ex 12:21. Naturally, despite 1 Cor 16:8, the statement cannot be used for the dating of the epistle. ἐτύθη, "has been sacrificed," refers to Golgotha, not to a Christian memorial feast (Lietzmann).

50   There is, e.g., no hint of a typology of Egypt and the wilderness. Such a typology underlies chap. 10; but despite the proximity of the observations on the Lord's Supper no reference is made to the Passover. Here, vice versa, no lines are drawn to the Lord's Supper. This is highly significant not only for Paul's view of the Lord's Supper, but also for the reconstruction of the primitive Christian view in general. The construing of Jesus' Last Supper as a Passover meal is a secondary piece of interpretation.

51   On the role of the word "Christ" in the interpretation of the death of Jesus, see on 15:3ff.

51a   See on 10:14ff; Bultmann, *Theology* 1:298–300 [297–300].

52   ἐν ζύμῃ: "afflicted with. . . ."

53   The two words are synonymous (already in the LXX): the duplication is rhetorical. The variant reading πορνεία arose from v 1; cf. the situation in Rom 1:29; πονηρία and πορνεία are found side

by side in the catalogue in Mk 7:21f.

54   It was said above that Christians are ἄζυμοι, "unleavened." Here they are those with a supply of ἄζυμα "unleavened bread." Jeremias, *TDNT* 5:901, supposes that the Christians of Paul's day already celebrated the Passover as a Christian festival. This, however, cannot be deduced from the present passage. It can at most be concluded that the Passover was *not* celebrated in Corinth. Otherwise Paul would have had to take up the point in chaps. 10 and 11 (Lord's Supper).

55   That is to say, a *first* epistle to the Corinthians. ἔγραψα, "I wrote," cannot be an epistolary aorist (and thus refer to the present epistle); this is clear from the content. On the question as to whether this earlier letter has been preserved, see the Introduction. Conclusions in regard to the development of the discussion between Paul and Corinth are given by Hurd, *Origin*, 77f.

56   συναναμίγνυσθαι, "associate with": *Ep. Ar.* 142. A. Wilhelm, "Σύμμειξις," *AnzAW* 74 (1937): 39–57 points to Aristot. *Ath. resp.* 3.5 (re γάμος, "wedding"). "Of sexual union, μείγνυσθαι and μεῖξις are used, but not συμμείγνυναι and σύμμειξις" (48). Cf. Plat., *Leg.* 839a (against Liddell–Scott) (cf. 836c); Dion. Hal., *Art. rhet.* 1.2.3; Plut., *Num.* 4 (against Liddell–Scott); Hdt., *Hist.* 2.64; 4.114; Dio C., *Hist. Rom.* 61.8.6; Ditt., *Or.* 1:378 (no. 231, line 9); 2:492 (no. 751, line 3); 2:505 (no. 763, line 3). But cf. Plat., *Leg.* 930d.

this in their letter (see on 7:1) by asking how this is
to be carried out in practice. Paul now explains (and
thereby sets the theme of πορνεία in a general light) in
v 10.

■ **10** The demand did not refer to outward dealings
with non–Christians, but to the question of order in the
community: its intention is not to shut Christians off
from the world,[57] but to clarify their standing in the
world.[58] The community practices not an ascetic ideal,
but that freedom which includes freedom to separate
itself from vice. It is of the very essence of the community
to manifest its freedom from sin *in* the world, not alongside of it. We do not have to depart from the world
in order to be able to believe. On the contrary, the world
is the place of faith, because it belongs to God and, as
his creation, is not abandoned. To put it the other way
round, outward separation from the world would not be a
radical overcoming of the world. The "world" would
draw us with it into exile, into the "wilderness."[59]

Excursus:
The Catalogues of
Virtues and Vices

This is a form which has no model in the Old Testament.[60] Where it emerges in Judaism, Greek
influence is at hand. It is worked out, following earlier patterns,[61] in the Stoa as a table of cardinal
virtues and vices.[62] It is taken up, understandably
enough, into popular philosophy. In the process,
the rigid schema dissolves.[63] The lists can be de-
tached from their specific speculative framework and
introduced into a different one (Jewish, Gnostic) or
presented as universal moral values. Thus we find
ethical lists in the form of "trademarks" of rulership,
or vocational ethics.[64] They are employed in astrology.[65]

In Hellenistic Judaism they are taken over both
for purposes of ethical instruction, and also for apologetic ends (catalogues of vice as "pagan trademarks"). The virtues are here understood as commandments of God; the traditional commandments

57 After the fashion of, say, the Qumran sect or the
Therapeutae. ἐπεὶ γάρ, "otherwise indeed."

58 πόρνοι is not used in a figurative sense (from idol
worship), but literally, as the catalogue shows.

59 Windisch, *TDNT* 2:902–906, considers the passage
to be a short Passover address which supplies an
illustration of the transfer of cultic ideas to the ethical
realm. Formulas of priestly exhortation from the
cult (ἐκκαθάρατε τὴν ... ζύμην ..., καὶ γὰρ τὸ
πάσχα ... ἐτύθη ... ὥστε ἑορτάζωμεν μὴ ἐν ζύμῃ
..., ἀλλ᾽ ἐν ἀζύμοις, "Cleanse out the ... leaven ...
for indeed the paschal lamb ... has been sacrificed
... so let us keep our festival, not with leaven ...
but with unleavened bread") are given a moral
sense by the addition of παλαιός/νέος, κακίας καὶ
πονηρίας, εἰλικρινείας, ἀληθείας, "old/new, of vice
and wickedness, of sincerity, of truth." The linguistic material for this is taken from the exhortation
to repentance (old/new: Rom 7:6; Col 3:9) and
from the realm of allegory (the community as dough).

60 The decalogue is not a comparable form.

61 Plat., *Gorg.* 525a.

62 Anton Vögtle, *Die Tugend– und Lasterkataloge im Neuen
Testament*, NtlAbh, 16, 4–5 (Münster/W.: Aschendorff, 1936), 58–62. The schema of the four cardinal virtues (Plut., *Stoic. Rep.* 1034c; von Arnim,
SVF 1:49, no. 200) is older than the Stoa. But the
Stoa works it out systematically and builds it into
the context of its world picture. Here already we
find the form of asyndetic stringing together. Von
Arnim, *SVF* 3:99, no. 412 (Diog. L., *Vit.* 7.110–114);
cf. nos. 377–490 (*de affectibus*) in *SVF* 3.

63 Vögtle, *Tugend– und Lasterkataloge*, 62–73. Dio.
Chrys., *Or.* 45(62).2, 6; 49(66).1; 52(69).1; 56(73).1;
Ceb., *Tab.* 19.5; Cic., *Tusc.* 4.3.5; 4.6.11—4.14.33;
Muson. (ed. Hense, 87, lines 2–7); Plut., *Ser. num.
pun.* 556b; *Tranq. an.* 468b; Epic., *Diss.* 2.16.11–17,
45; 3.2.3, 14.

64 Vögtle, *Tugend– und Lasterkataloge*, 73ff, 78–81.

65 *Ibid.*, 84–88. The stars determine the behavior of
man.

66 Dependence on the Decalogue is possible, Philo,
Rer. div. her. 168–173, to a lesser degree Ps.–Phocylides, *Poema admon.* 3–77; 1 Tim 1:19f. Jewish catalogues: Wis 14:25f—Philo, virtues: *Sacr. AC* 27
(between vices in 22f and 32); *Det. pos. ins.* 34 (with
vices); *Poster C.* 181; *Mut. nom.* 197 (with vices);
Vit. Mos. 1.154; *Virt.* 182; *Exsecr.* 160; *Omn. prob. lib.*
83f; vices: *Cher.* 71, 92; *Sacr. AC* 15, 22f, 32; *Det. pos.
ins.* 34; *Poster C.* 52; *Deus imm.* 162–165; *Agric.* 83;
Ebr. 15–18, 21–23; *Conf. ling.* 21, 47f, 117; *Migr. Abr.*
60; *Rer. div. her.* 109, 173; *Mut. nom.* 150, 197; *Som.*
2.40, 168; *Spec. leg.* 4.84, 87; *Virt.* 180—Test. XII: R.
3.2–8; L. 14.5–8; Jud. 16.1; G. 5.1f; A. 2.5; 5.1; B.
6.4—Ass. Mos. 7; Gr. Bar. 4.17; 8.5; 13.4; Eth. En.
91.6f; Jub. 21.21; 23.14; Ps.–Phocylides, *Poema
admon.* 3.77; Or. Sib. 2.254–283; 3.36–45—Lucian:
see Hans Dieter Betz, *Lukian von Samosata und das
Neue Testament*, TU, 76 (Berlin: Akademie–Verlag,
1961), 206–211. A surprise was caused by the double
catalogue in 1QS IV. It is adapted to the speculative, dualistic framework: the two catalogues represent the respective "ways" under the sovereignty
of the two Spirits.

are expounded with the help of the notions of popular philosophy. Outstanding examples are provided by the Wisdom of Solomon and Philo.[66]

Gnosticism, too, appropriates the catalogues and transforms their sense according to its view of man and the world; the virtues become δυνάμεις, "powers," of man, the vices become τιμωρίαι,[67] "punishments."

The New Testament, with significant exceptions,[68] is permeated by catalogues.[69] They are applied in manifold ways. They serve to illumine the past,[70] and are naturally used above all for positive instruction. Christianity does not take them over directly from Greek philosophy, but from Judaism; the same loose, unsystematic compilation prevails.[71]

The recognition of the fact that we have here a traditional form forbids an assessment in terms of the contemporary scene, as if, for example, we had

to do with a realistic description of conditions in Corinth.[72] The table is intended to operate as such, as a typification. The contents are essentially Jewish. Naturally, a specifically Christian intrusion can be seen here and there (e.g., in the inclusion of ἀγάπη, "love.")

The fact that Christianity takes over the Jewish ethic must be theologically understood. Christianity regards itself not as a new system of ethics, but as a practical exercise of the will of the long–known God.[73] The new aspect is the eschatological (not apocalyptic) foundation (cf. chap. 7). Its morality is homely, because its faith is eschatological.[74]

---

67   *Corp. Herm.* 13.7–13: cf. *Corpus Hermeticum*, ed. Arthur Darby Nock and tr. André–Jean Festugière (Paris: Les Belles Lettres, 1938–54, vols. 1–2: ²1960), 2:212, n. 36. The δυνάμεις and τιμωρίαι are not "attributes" in the sense of Greek anthropology, but are immediately constitutive of existence. The latter is constructed of good or evil deeds as the case may be. The standard of value is specifically Gnostic, not generally ethical. Cf. *Corp. Herm.* 1.22f, 25 (laying aside of vices in our ascent); *Pist. Soph.* 102ff.

68   John, for example.

69   The form is purely asyndetic, partly polysyndetic; Blass–Debrunner §460(2); cf. 444(4). Catalogues: (*a*) Vices: Mk 7:21f par. Mt 15:19; Rom 1:29–31; 13:13; 1 Cor 5:10f; 6:9f; 2 Cor 12:20f; Gal 5:19–21 and correspondingly 5:22f; Eph 5:3–5; Col 3:5 and correspondingly 3:8; 1 Tim 1:9f; 2 Tim 3:2–5; Tit 3:3; 1 Pet 2:1; 4:3, 15; Rev 21:8; 22:15. (*b*) Virtues: 2 Cor 6:6f; Eph 4:2f, 32; 5:9; Phil 4:8 (allusively); Col 3:12; 1 Tim 4:12; 6:11; 2 Tim 2:22; 3:10; 1 Pet 3:8; 2 Pet 1:5–7. Post–NT: *Did.* 2.6; *Barn.* 19; Pol., *Phil.* 2.2; 4.3; Herm., *Mand.* 5.2.4; 6.2.2–5; 8.3–5; etc.

70   Specially plain is the connection with the schema "once/now" in 1 Cor 6:9f and Col 3:5, 8. The confrontation knows only good and evil, no degrees, no psychological nuances. The ethic of the catalogue is not a mental ethic. In this respect it has completely separated itself from its Greek origin.

71   There is no plan of construction, but only on occasion a certain rhetorical order: Rom 1:29–31. In each of the two antithetical catalogues in Col 3:5, 8 there are five vices. Here the Iranian pentad presumably plays a role: the five virtues or vices are the "members" which constitute being.

72   Vögtle, *Tugend– und Lasterkataloge*, 31f, concedes too much in this respect. The vices listed are not indi-

vidual (Corinthian), but typical. This is evident from the standard catchwords: πορνεία, "sexual immorality," appears 11 times (μοιχεία, "adultery," 3 times), ἀκαθαρσία, "uncleanness," 5 times, ἀσέλγεια, "licentiousness," 6 times, πλεονεξία, "avarice," 6 times, etc.; see the tables in Siegfried Wibbing, *Die Tugend– und Lasterkataloge im Neuen Testament und ihre Traditionsgeschichte unter besonderer Berücksichtigung der Qumran–Texte*, BZNW, 25 (Berlin: Töpelmann, 1959), 82, 87f.

73   The commandment of love is consciously quoted as an OT commandment (Rom 13:9).

74   Literature: Vögtle, *Tugend– und Lasterkataloge*; Wibbing, *Tugend– und Lasterkataloge*; Ehrhard Kamlah, *Die Form der katalogischen Paränese im Neuen Testament*, WUNT, 7 (Tübingen: J. C. B. Mohr [Paul Siebeck], 1964). Wibbing would trace the catalogue form to Qumran, Kamlah to Iran (the two contentions are not necessarily mutually exclusive; the double catalogue in 1QS stands at the point at which Iranian influence can be proved with certainty). Both theses are wrong from the methodological standpoint because they confuse form and content. The basic Greek form underwent manifold changes in Hellenistic syncretism. But this does not compel us to seek another derivation for the form. The latter is adapted to the momentary world picture and the momentary view of salvation. Cf. e.g., Philo, *Virt.* 180, 187; and thereon Kamlah, *Form*, 104–115. It goes without saying that the catalogues are respectively combined with a promise of salvation and a threat of disaster. In this very way they serve to give instruction concerning the way of salvation, whether the latter be understood in Stoic, traditional Jewish, syncretistic Jewish, or Gnostic terms. It is mistaken to speak of a "dualistic structure" of the catalogues. What is dualistic is not the catalogue, but the *contrasting* of

■ 10–11 The similarity between vv 10f and 6:9f can be explained harmlessly as repetition.[75] If it were possible to assign the two passages to two different letters, then it would have to be assumed that Paul had (written?) catalogues ready–to–hand among his working materials. As for the individual concepts, in the forefront are the πόρνοι, "sexually immoral," as in 6:9f; this is in harmony with the context. πλεονέκτης, "avaricious man," is likewise one of the main words of paraenesis.[76] ἅρπαγες, "robbers," requires no special explanation.[77] εἰδωλολατρία, "idolatry," is a specifically Jewish sin.[78] The succeeding vices are again general: λοίδορος, "slanderer,"[79] μέθυσος, "drunkard."[80] The demand for the suspension of table fellowship is general. It is not to be restricted to community meals (with Kümmel).

νῦν, v 11, is logical (against Lietzmann): Paul is explaining what he really wrote, i.e., meant.[81]

■ 12–13 These verses provide the reason. To be sure, the train of thought can be followed only with difficulty because the mode of expression is highly compressed. Verse 12b gives the impression of an intrusion between 12a and 13. If the wording were to be pressed, we could read out of it: *I* do not judge at all. For the members of the community are judged by you. The outsiders will be judged by God. But this provides us with false alternatives and places the accents wrongly. Paul is not excluding his own person altogether from the function of judging, but is explaining that he and those who belong to the community are not competent where "the outsiders" are concerned.[82] He takes himself, in keeping with the train of thought so far, as the starting point: I wrote, that is, I meant . . . that is, dealings with *Christians;* for what have non–Christians to do with me? This he now exemplifies in the case of the addressees: *you* in fact judge those who belong to the community. That is the way it is, and that is the way it ought to be. The accent lies on ὑμεῖς (note the word order).[83] Two lines of thought intersect: the delimitation ("not outsiders") and the admonition to keep due order within. Then the delimitation is underlined: for the others, God is the competent authority.[84] Finally, Paul uses a biblical formula from the realm of sacred law[85] to corroborate the *second* thought.

---

catalogues within the framework of a dualistic, eschatological view of salvation. For the rest, the proximity of the catalogue in vv 10f to Qumran is negligible and provides no help toward its interpretation.

75 This is suggested also by the affinity between Gal 5:19ff and 2 Cor 12:20. When divisions are made in terms of literary criticism, then 6:1–11 must be assigned to the first letter. In that case ἔγραψα, "I wrote," would refer to 6:9f. Bornkamm, *Vorgeschichte*, 34, n. 131, suggests this for consideration, without personally adopting the thesis.

76 Cf. *Test. L.* 14.5–8; *Test. G.* 5.1; etc.; *1 Cl.* 35.5; *Barn.* 20.1; *Did.* 5.1. πορνεία and πλεονεξία are the two cardinal points of the paraenesis in 1 Thess 4:1ff. Highly remarkable is the interpretation of πλεονεξία as εἰδωλολατρία in Col 3:5; Eph 5:5.

77 Cf. κλοπή, "theft," and similar terms. One naturally thinks here of the seventh (eighth) commandment of the decalogue; Mk 7:21f/Mt 15:19; 1 Pet 4:15; μοῖχος, "adulterer," alongside of κλέπτης, "thief": Philo, *Conf. ling.* 117; *Test. R.* 3.2–8; *Test. A.* 2.5; *Or. Sib.* 4.31f; cf. Epict., *Diss.* 1.18.3, 12; 3.3.12; etc.; Wis 14:22–31; Philo, *Decal.* 168–174; *Rer. div. her.* 173; *Spec. leg.* 4.84.

78 *Or. Sib.* 2.254–283 (among others): κλέπται, κλεψιγάμοι, εἰδωλολάτραι, "thieves, seekers after illicit love, idolaters." *Test. Jud.* 19.1; Gal 5:20; Col 3:5; Eph 5:5; Pol., *Phil.* 11.2.

79 *Test. B.* 5.4; 6.4.

80 *Test. Jud.* 14.1. Cf. the significance of "soberness" in the figurative sense. It is an outstanding catchword in eschatological paraenesis.

81 It is unlikely that ἔγραψα, "I wrote," should have changed its sense between v 9 (true aorist) and v 11.

82 Despite 6:2. There it is not a case of *present* judgment. The passage also shows that we must not pose the alternative: Christians judge Christians, God judges the rest. At the Last Day believers judge the world.

83 Not on τοὺς ἔσω, "those within." Weiss observes: "Far from limiting its competence, the church's rights and duties are, on the contrary, strongly emphasized."

84 The future is the correct reading, cf. 8:2.

85 Deut 17:7 etc.: καὶ ἐξαρεῖς τὸν πονηρὸν ἐξ ὑμῶν αὐτῶν, "So you shall purge the evil from the midst of you" (RSV). With the transition to the imperative plural (ἐξάρατε) comes a change in the usage of αὐτός, Blass–Debrunner §288(1).

6   Church and World

1   When one of you has a case against another,[1] does he dare[2] to go to law[3]
before the unrighteous instead of before
the saints? 2 / Or do you not know that
the saints will judge the world? And
if the world is brought to judgment before you,[4] then are you not competent
to deal with the pettiest cases? 3 / Do
you not know that we shall judge
angels?—to say nothing of everyday
matters! 4 / So when you have everyday
disputes, do you then appoint as judges
those of all people who count for
nothing in the church?[5] 5 / I say this to
shame you. Is there not a single competent man among you, then, who can
judge between his brothers?[6] 6 / But one
brother goes to law with another—and
that, too, before unbelievers? 7 / Why,[7]
it is already a fault[8] that you have
lawsuits with each other at all. Why not
rather let yourselves be wronged? Why
not rather let yourselves be robbed?
8 / But you actually do wrong to others
and rob others, and brothers at that.
9 / Or do you not know that unjust men
will not inherit the kingdom of God?
Make no mistake! Neither the sexually
immoral, nor idolaters, nor adulterers,
nor perverts, nor homosexuals, 10 / nor
thieves, nor the avaricious, no drunkards
or slanderers or robbers will inherit
the kingdom of God. 11 / And that is
what some of you were. But you have
been washed, but you have been sanctified, but you have been justified through
the name of the Lord Jesus Christ and
through the Spirit of our God.

---

1   πρᾶγνα ἔχειν, "have a lawsuit"; *P. Oxy.* 743.19;
further instances in Moulton and Milligan *s.v.*
πρᾶγμα.

2   *3 Macc.* 3.21; Philo, *Somn.* 1.54; Jos., *Ap.* 1.318;
Bauer, *s.v.* τολμάω.

3   κρίνεσθαι does not have to be rendered "let oneself
be judged," see Bauer, *s.v.* κρίνω 4aβ; the middle
and passive can mean "to have a dispute before
a court"; Thuc., *Hist.* 4.122.4; LXX.

4   Forensic ἐν: Ditt., *Syll.* 1:195, lines 57–59 (no. 147,
45): κρινέσθω ἐν Ἀθηναίοις καὶ τοῖς συμμάχοις ὡς
διαλύων τὴν συμμαχίαν, "Let him be judged by
the Athenians and their allies as one who destroys
the alliance." Not so Ps.–Callisthenes, *Hist. Alex.
Magn.* 2.21.21: βούλομαι δὲ μὴ ἐν ἑαυτοῖς κρίνειν,
ὅσον τις ὑμῶν ἔχει πρὸς ἕτερον, οὐδὲ ἐφ' οὗ βούλε-
σθε, "I do not want you to have lawsuits with each
other, whatever any of you may have against an-

other, not even before anyone you wish" (following
Conzelmann's German). ἐν is not to be compared
with Acts 17:31.

5   καθίζω, "appoint as": Plat., *Leg.* 873e, δικαστήν,
"judge"; Jos., *Ant.* 20.200, συνέδριον κριτῶν, "an
assembly of judges." The sentence is more simply
taken as a question than as an ironical summons.

6   The expression is short for ἀνὰ μέσον ἀδελφοῦ καὶ
(ἀνὰ μέσον) τοῦ ἀδελφοῦ αὐτοῦ, "between a brother
and his brother."

7   Om. p⁴⁶ ℵ* D* 33.

8   See Hans Lietzmann, *An die Römer*, HNT, 8 (Tübingen: J. C. B. Mohr [Paul Siebeck], ⁴1933), *ad*
Rom 11:12, with a reference to Lib., *Or.* 11.167; εἰς
ἐλάττωμα κέκριται, "It is reckoned as a defect."
Bauer (*s.v.* μέν 2a) abides by "defeat": "indeed it is
already a defeat for you"; cf. Epict., *Diss.* 2.18.6.

For literary criticism see on 5:10f.[9]

The Christians' relationship to their world is illustrated in one particular case, that of proceedings between Christians before worldly courts. Paul speaks in loose diatribe style: "Do you not know . . .?" The criterion is supplied by eschatology. The apocalyptic idea of the role of the "saints" in the last judgment is reinterpreted in terms of the present, *not* in the sense that the church anticipates the judgment in moralistic ways, but in the indirect sense that it practices its eschatological sovereignty in the world.

This section is highly significant from the standpoint both of ecclesiastical and of secular history. It shows us the first hints of an internal jurisdiction on the church's part which ever since Constantine's day has been a regular part of the legal setup and has belonged as such to the system of church and state. To put it the other way round, the church sees itself constrained to develop organizational forms of a worldly kind, and thereby to mark itself off in visible/organizational ways from the "world."

This raises the question of how far the church will come to be molded by these forms, which of course are "worldly," whether the church will itself become a part of the world; in other words, whether its openness toward the world in the sense of 5:10 is understood positively in terms of the church and its eschatology or whether the result is a compromise on the part of a religious society with the external conditions of its life.[10] Paul can maintain the eschatological interpretation, because for him eschatology leads not to the negation of the present, but to a critique of it. For this very reason he has likewise no need to abandon it in favor of a Christian world–program. The forms of the world's life are subjected to eschatological neutralization and can there-

fore be taken over.

■ **1** The opening verse states the theme and, by doing so in the form of a question,[11] already contains the verdict. πρὸς τὸν ἕτερον, "against another," clearly means a fellow Christian. "The outsiders" (5:13) are now called ἄδικοι, "unrighteous." This provides a pointed indication of the absurdity of the position which Christians adopt when they not only recognize such people as judges, but even claim their services as such.[12] The contemporary presupposition of Paul's ordinance is the Jewish court of arbitration.[13] The latter is a result of Jewish exclusiveness. Paul reinterprets it in terms of a Christian eschatological relationship to the world by bracketing together two facts: (a) God will judge outsiders (5:12f), and (b) the saints will have part in the judgment of the world— and the pagan judges are "world." The criterion of conduct is accordingly found in the nature of the community, and vice versa the conduct in question can demonstrate the nature of eschatological existence. This is the concrete working out of the statement, "All things are yours."

■ **2** The loose diatribe phrase (ἢ) οὐκ οἴδατε . . .; "[or] do you not know . . .?" (cf. vv 3, 9, 15f, 19; 3:16; 5:6; 9:13, 24) does not require to be pressed as if it always implied the giving of previous instruction. It can also simply characterize an idea as self–evident. In the present instance, however, Paul in fact is referring back to one of the teachings of the primitive Christian catechism.[14] The idea is described in 1 Thess 4:13ff: at the "arrival" of the Lord, believers will be snatched up to him in the air; and thus they provide the forum for the judgment, which is the execution of the ὀργή, "wrath." The conceptual material, which stems from Jewish

9 In the face of the critical operations it will have to be said that the section is well fitted into the context, e.g. by the catchword κρίνειν, "judge," which vacillates between its eschatological and its legal use. The theme remains constant: πορνεία and πλεονεξία, "sexual immorality" and "avarice."

10 Verses 7f show that for Paul arbitration procedure is not yet a part of the church's legal order, but the mark of an emergency. Erich Dinkler, "Zum Problem der Ethik bei Paulus: Rechtsnahme und Rechtsverzicht (1 Kor 6,1–11)," *ZThK* 49 (1952): 167–200, now in his *Signum Crucis*, 204–240.

11 Weiss: protasis with a conditional sense, swinging loosely between question and statement; cf. 7:21.

12 ἄδικος, "unrighteous," is not a *moral* judgment, as if the Corinthian courts were corrupt; cf. the way it is interchanged with ἄπιστος, "unbelieving."

13 Jews must not go to law before non–Jews, Str.–B. 3:362f; Emil Schürer, *A History of the Jewish People in the Time of Jesus Christ*, vol. 2, part 2, tr. Sophia Taylor and Peter Christie (Edinburgh: Clark, 1885), 265f, 303f (*Geschichte des jüdischen Volkes im Zeitalter Jesu Christi*, vol. 3 [Leipzig: Hinrichs, ³1898], 74, 114); Jean Juster, *Les Juifs dans l'empire romain* (Paris: Geuthner, 1914), 2:110f.

14 Assuming 1 Thess 5:1ff to be an established part of

apocalyptic,[15] is subjected to Christian modification. The judging of the world[16] is reserved in Judaism to God.[17] In Christianity the office of judge is transferred also to Christ. And thus those who are "in Christ" also have part in it.[18] ἀνάξιοι, "not competent," is not meant merely in a subjective sense, in each other's eyes. They are in actual fact what they consider themselves to be; they behave as ἀνάξιοι. κριτήριον can denote the tribunal.[19] The meaning "lawsuits" is more suitable here.[20] The verdict that they are "petty" comes of applying the eschatological standard of the future role of Christians,[21] whereby the eschatological proviso has always to be observed: the future judgment cannot be anticipated by Christians within the world.

■ **3** This verse is couched in parallel terms and expands the idea to include even the angels. The argument rests on an unexpressed deduction *a maiore*: μήτι γε . . ., "to say nothing of. . . ."[22]

■ **4–5** τοὺς ἐξουθενημένους, "those who are [count for] nothing": the world's standard (1:28) is reversed. Paul is attacking not the law and its norms in general, but the recognition of the world as an authority in matters concerning the community.[23] πρὸς ἐντροπήν, "to shame you": here Paul speaks in different terms from 4:14. The question in v 5b reminds us of 1:5, and has an ironical sound in view of the Corinthians' conceit of themselves (incidentally, it stands in contrast to 1:26).[24]

■ **6** Standing as it does between vv 5 and 7, this should be taken as a question.

■ **7** This verse shows that a Christian court of arbitration is only a concession.[25] "The right thing" would be to renounce the asserting of one's rights. The setting up of a court is possible, however, because the renunciation of our rights is not a principle. κρίμα here can only mean the point at issue in a lawsuit; there is no evidence elsewhere for this meaning. The word ἄδικος, "unrighteous," which was applied in v 1 to outsiders, is now turned against the Christians.[26] What we have here

---

elementary teaching. 1QPHab V, 4f: "But God will judge all the nations by the hand of His elect. And it is by the chastisement which the elect will dispense that all the wicked of His people will atone" (Dupont–Sommer, 261).

15 Str.–B. 3:363. Dan 7:22; *Eth. En.* 1.9 (cf. Jude 14f), 94–105; Wis 3:8; Mt 19:28; Rev 20:4; Volz, *Eschatologie*, 275.

16 κόσμος, "world," does not mean nature, but the totality of personal beings, men and angels.

17 Rom 3:3; Jn 3:17; cf. 12:47.

18 The Greek equivalent is the wise man's share in the divine government of the universe, Epict., *Ench.* 15. Sallust. Neoplat., *Deor. et mund.* 21 (Sallustius, *Concerning the Gods and the Universe*, ed. Arthur Darby Nock [Cambridge: University Press, 1926], 36, lines 13f): τὸν ὅλον κόσμον συνδιοικοῦσιν ἐκείνοις—the pious "share with them [i.e. the gods] the government of the whole universe" (Nock, p. 37).

19 Jas 2:6. Bauer, *s.v.* κριτήριον 1 considers the rendering: "Are you unfit to form even the most insignificant courts?"

20 Diod. S., *Bibl. hist.* 1.72.4 (cited by Friedrich Büchsel, *TDNT* 3:943, n. 5).

21 Rom 8:18 likewise applies this standard for purposes of evaluation, though admittedly from a different point of view.

22 The fallen angels. Jude 6, 2 Pet 2:4; *Eth. En.* 91.15 (cf. 18.11—19.3); Bousset–Gressmann, *Die Religion des Judentums*, 251f. βιωτικά are general concerns of everyday life, disputes which, according to Philostr., *Vit. Soph.* 1.25.2, should be settled at home, more

especially matters concerning capital (Preisigke, *Wörterbuch* 1:270).

23 Dinkler, "Zum Problem der Ethik bei Paulus," rightly observes that Paul does not have any program for the abolishing of the legal system as an institution, the establishing of a new world order without a legal system. His criticism is more radical than that of fanatics: his verdict on the world is eschatological. The world order is not impugned, because within it we can believe. Albert Stein, "Wo trugen die korinthischen Christen ihre Rechtshändel aus?" *ZNW* 59 (1968): 86–90, takes καθίζειν in a juristic sense: to appoint to a judicial function which the person in question did not have before. In that case, however, the word cannot apply to the *iudex* of Roman civil suits (for he is instituted by the praetor); but neither can it apply to the provincial investigation process, where the state official examines and decides. So the meaning is: the Christians had recourse to *Jewish* judges and submitted themselves to the jurisdiction of the synagogue. This view is misguided.

24 Zuntz, *Text*, 15 (cf. Blass–Debrunner §139A) assumes that the text has not been negligently formulated, but corrupted by *homoioteleuton*.

25 No precise logic can be found in expressions like ἤδη μὲν οὖν ὅλως; something like "now actually already" (Bauer, *s.v.* ὅλως; cf. *s.v.* μέν 2a: "indeed it is already a defeat").

26 ἀδικεῖν, "do wrong," and ἀποστερεῖν, "rob": cf. Lev 19:13 (ἀδικεῖν and ἁρπάζειν, "seize").

is a Christian principle,[27] but also one that is already Greek.[28] As compared with the Greek slogan, "Better to suffer wrong than to do wrong," there is a change of sense inasmuch as what was a general principle has here become a concrete rule for the ordering of a specific community.

■ 8 The expression is aggressive. ἀδικεῖτε καὶ ἀποστερεῖτε, "you do wrong and rob," does not mean that they have become criminals in the legal sense. The conditions in question are already fulfilled, in the light of the standard indicated in v 7, by the very act of going to law.[29]

■ 9–10 The catalogue (see on 5:10f) is propounded this time as a list of (negative) conditions of entry into the kingdom of God. It is plainly drawing on set tradition.[30] The terms of expression (kingdom of God, inherit) are common Christian parlance, not specifically Pauline. The original apocalyptic sense of the concept "kingdom of God" is maintained.[31] The opening sentence makes

ἄδικος the keynote of the sequence. For the rest, the list is broadly the same as the former one. The style is more strongly emphatic.[32] The sins of sexual immorality[33] are made specific by the introduction of both passive (μαλακός, "pervert [effeminate]")[34] and active homosexuality. The Jewish verdict on the latter is unequivocal:[35] Pseudo–Phocylides, *Poema admon.* 3–5: μήτε γαμοκλοπέειν, μήτ᾽ ἄρσενα κύπριν ὀρίνειν, μήτε δόλους ῥάπτειν, μήθ᾽ αἵματι χεῖρα μιαίνειν· μὴ πλουτεῖν ἀδίκως κτλ., "Do not have illicit intercourse, or stir up a passion for another male, or lay plots, or stain your hand with blood. Do not enrich yourself unrighteously, etc."[36] The Greek verdict cannot be unified. Despite the classical role played by erotic relationships with boys, such relationships do not attain by any means to moral recognition.[37] Yet the verdict of the Romans is far sharper than that of the Greeks.[38]

■ 11 Verse 11a contains an echo of the "once—but now" schema which naturally lends itself to this form of presen-

27 Mt 5:29f; 1 Pet 2:23.

28 Plat., *Gorg.* 509c; Epict., *Diss.* 4.5.10; M. Aur. Ant., *Medit.* 2.1.

29 καὶ τοῦτο ἀδελφούς naturally does not mean that such behavior was practiced only toward Christians, but emphasizes that it is impossible among brothers. The phrase is accordingly not a limitation, but a concretization.

30 Cf. also the double intimation, first as an editorial introduction, and then with a "regular" eye to the catalogue. μὴ πλανᾶσθε, "make no mistake!" underlines in the style of the diatribe, see Herbert Braun, *TDNT* 6:244f; Epict., *Diss.* 4.6.23; cf. 2.20.7.

31 Paul did not spiritualize the concept. The catalogue presupposes a judgment according to works, cf. Rom 2. The mode of expression ("inherit") is that of the OT, where it is used in the first instance of the occupation and possession of the land of Israel, then in a wider sense: Ps 24:13, etc.; *1 Macc.* 2:57; 1 Cor 15:50; Gal 5:21; Ign., *Eph.* 16.1; *Phld.* 3.3; Pol., *Phil.* 5.3. In these concepts the objective element is maintained, as in the word "peace," see on 1:3. The relation between the sanctifying and reconciling that has taken place and the as yet future life (in the "kingdom of God") is the same as in Rom 6: we *have died* with Christ—we *shall be* raised with him; in the present the new "life" is bestowed upon us—in the form of περιπατεῖν, "walking." On vv 9–11 see Eduard Schweizer, "Dying and Rising with Christ," *NTS* 14 (1967–68): 1–14.

32 Cf. the strengthening by means of synonyms. Philostr., *Vit. Ap.* 4.22: μοιχοὶ καὶ πόρνοι καὶ τοιχωρύχοι καὶ βαλαντιοτόμοι καὶ ἀνδραποδισταὶ καὶ τὰ τοιαῦτα ἔθνη, "adulterers and fornicators and burglars and cutpurses and kidnappers and such–like rabble" (Loeb 1:397).

33 Impressive is Ditt. *Syll.* 3:117, lines 26–31 (no. 985, 19f) in a long list of conditions for admission to the sanctuary: [ἄνδρα παρὰ / τὴν] ἑαυτοῦ γυναῖκα ἀλλοτρίαν ἢ [ἐλευθέραν ἢ] / δούλην ἄνδρα ἔχουσαν μὴ φθερε[ῖν μηδὲ παῖδα μη/δὲ] παρθένον, etc., "a man, in addition to having a wife of his own, is not to seduce another man's wife, whether she be free or a slave with a husband, nor a boy nor a virgin, etc."

34 Instances in Bauer *s.v.* μαλακός; Dion. Hal., *Ant. Rom.* 7.2.4. Hans Herter, "Effeminatus," *RAC* 4:620–650. Wilhelm Kroll, "Kinaidos," Pauly–W. 1:459–462.

35 Str.–B. 3:70–74. Homosexual intercourse is punished by stoning. For the Jew it is one of the most abhorrent vices of the Gentiles.

36 Cf. further *Or. Sib.* 2.73: μὴ ἀρσενοκοιτεῖν, μὴ συκοφαντεῖν, μή τε φονεύειν, "Do not be a sodomite or an extortioner or a murderer." Instances in Johannes Geffcken (ed.), *Die Oracula Sibyllina*, GCS, 8 (Leipzig: Hinrichs, 1902), 30; *Ep. Ar.* 152; *Test. L.* 7.11; Philo, *Spec. Leg.* 3.39; etc.

37 Dio Chrys., *Or.* 49(66).25; Luc., *Cyn.* 10, etc.; see Betz, *Lukian*, 199–201. Hans Licht, *Die Homoerotik in der griechischen Literatur*, Abhandlungen aus dem Gebiet der Sexualforschung, 3, 3 (Bonn: Marcus & Weber, 1921); Joseph Vogt, *Von der Gleichwertigkeit der Geschlechter in der bürgerlichen Gesellschaft der Griechen*, AAM, 1960, 2 (Mainz: Akademie der Wissen-

tation (cf. Col 3:5, 8). A certain measure of realism in the construing of the list is shown by the qualification "some."[39] Verse 11b states the presupposition of the "now," i.e., of the new life of the new man: baptism as the bath of purification.[40] Its effect is described in triadic form.[41] The interpretation of baptism as "purification" is traditional.[42] ἀπελούσασθε, despite its form, is not to be construed as middle,[43] but as passive on the analogy of the succeeding passives.[44] The connecting of baptism with the receipt of holiness likewise belongs to the average church view. δικαιοῦν, "be justified," has the full sense of the Pauline concept of justification.[45] The effect depends on the name (see on 1:13). How and why are explained by καὶ ἐν τῷ πνεύματι τοῦ θεοῦ ἡμῶν, "and through the Spirit of our God." Once again the

prevailing schema is that of tracing everything back to God.[46]

When the sacramental ground of the exhortation is here set alongside the eschatological one, then the presupposition is again the relation between indicative and imperative, holiness and active sanctification (cf. 1 Thess 4:1ff). This safeguards the view of the Sacrament against magical interpretations.

The question will now be whether the two grounds are recognizably related to each other, and how; whether their interconnection points to a systematic center.

---

schaften und der Literatur; Wiesbaden: Steiner, 1960), 220.

38 Examples in Herter, "Effeminatus," *RAC* 4:620–650.

39 I.e. as an actualization of the "pagan trademark."

40 Tit 3:5: λουτρὸν παλιγγενεσίας, "bath of regeneration"; cf. the continuation.

41 Thrice repeated ἀλλά, "but": cf. 2 Cor 7:11; Xenoph., *An.* 5.8.4.

42 This follows from the rite itself and from the Jewish tradition. Gerhard Delling, *Die Zueignung des Heils in der Taufe* (Berlin: Evangelische Verlagsanstalt, 1961), 56; 1QSᵇ IV, 22.

43 Bachmann renders: "You have had yourselves washed"; Robertson and Plummer: "You have washed your sins from off you."

44 Lietzmann. Joseph Ysebaert, *Greek Baptismal Terminology* (Nijmegen: Dekker & Van de Vegt, 1962), 63, points out the rareness of the passive in general usage and rightly observes that here we have already the technical language of baptism. This despite Isa 1:16: λούσασθε, καθαροὶ γένεσθε, ἀφέλετε τὰς πονηρίας ἀπὸ τῶν ψυχῶν ὑμῶν . . ., "Wash yourselves; make yourselves clean; remove the evils from

your souls."

45 With Dinkler, "Zum Problem der Ethik bei Paulus," 189, n. 3 (*Signum Crucis*, 227, n. 44) against Bultmann, *Theology* 1:136 [139], who finds that justification has here only the negative sense, remission of sins. Eduard Lohse, "Taufe und Rechtfertigung bei Paulus," *KuD* 11 (1965): 308–324, here esp. 321f, considers v 11 to be "a statement from the primitive Christian baptismal instruction"; in that case, justification has still the pre–Pauline sense (as in the pre–Pauline formula contained in Rom 3:25f). So likewise Karl Kertelge, "*Rechtfertigung*" *bei Paulus*, NtlAbh, n.s., 3 (Münster: Aschendorff, 1967), 242–246.

46 The Spirit is here not given in baptism, but the efficacy of the sacrament is the efficacy of the Spirit. Dinkler, "Zum Problem der Ethik bei Paulus," 189 (*Signum Crucis*, 227), argues that baptism is here described as an act of creation. Now Paul does use the terminology of the (new) creation in 2 Cor 4:6. Here, however, the conceptuality springs from the soteriological language already formed by the community. This determines our exposition of it.

6 Freedom and Sexuality

12   I am free to do anything, but not everything is for the best. I am free to do
anything, but I will not let myself be
dominated by anything. 13/ Food is for
the belly, and the belly for food. God
will put an end to both alike. Yet the
body is not for immorality, but for the
Lord, and the Lord for the body. 14/ God
raised the Lord, and he will raise[1] us,
too, by his power. 15/ Do you not know
that your bodies are members of Christ?
Am I then to take[2] the members of
Christ and make them members of a
prostitute? Never! 16/ Or do you not
know that the man who clings to a
prostitute is one body (with her)? For
"the two," it is said, "shall be one
flesh." 17/ But the man who clings to
Christ is one spirit (with him). 18/ Shun
fornication! Every sin that a man
commits is outside his body. But the
fornicator sins against his own body.
19/ Or do you not know that your body
is the temple of the Holy Spirit within
you, (the Spirit) which you have from
God, and that you do not belong to
yourselves? 20/ For you have been
bought and paid for. So glorify God with
your body.

For literary criticism see the Introduction. According to
Schmithals, 6:12 belongs to letter A, 10:23 (where
the same slogan is repeated) to letter B. The diatribe
style with its οὐκ οἴδατε; "do you not know?" remains,
but the tone changes: it assumes more firmly the form
of argument. Hurd finds[2a] that the style characteristically
lies halfway between that of Paul's reactions to the oral
information and that of his discussion of the written
inquiries from Corinth. He thinks Paul uses it to form a
transition from the one (up to 6:11) to the other (from
7:1 onward). Lietzmann concludes from the twofold
theme of πορνεία, "sexual immorality," and εἰδωλόθυτα, "meat sacrificed to idols" (chaps. 8—10), that
Paul is alluding to the "apostolic decree." In that case it
would be all the more striking that he does not mention it.
But he has no knowledge of it. The section takes us
beyond what has been said so far, for Paul now discusses
the old topic of πορνεία on the basis of a general principle, which he himself recognizes but which he expounds

in terms of the *theologia crucis*.

■ **12** πάντα μοι ἔξεστιν, "I am free to do anything":
the way in which he introduces this statement leads us
to the assumption that it was known and used in Corinth;
cf. the repetition of it in 10:23.[3] Thus πορνεία in Corinth is not merely a remnant of pagan custom. It is provided with an active/speculative justification on the
ground of this basic principle.

The statement, like others of its kind, is so formal as to
be suited for use in various speculative frameworks,
e.g., Cynic, Stoic, Gnostic.[4] We must therefore distinguish between its historic source and the Corinthian
understanding of it, and we must go on to ask how far
Paul himself had an influence on the latter.

The language points to a previous history in Stoicism.
Only the Stoics and Cynics provide material for comparison.[5] The same origin is indicated by the catchword
συμφέρειν, "be for the best."[6]

---

1   p[11] p[46]* A D G: ἐξεγείρει. p[46c2] B 1739 (Origen):
     ἐξήγειρειν; this is an interpretation which applies
     it to baptism.

2   A pleonastic phrase. Vulgar speech.

2a   J. C. Hurd, *The Origin of I Corinthians*, 86ff.

3   Lietzmann asks whether the statement is an anti–
     Judaistic slogan of Paul's own (3:21f).

4   For the Stoa, see on 3:21f; Dupont, *Gnosis*, 301–308.

Of the two meanings [7] of ἔξεστιν, "it is possible" and "it is permitted," only the latter can be considered here. [8] The Corinthians apparently derive it from Paul's doctrine of freedom. The spheres of application show that the freedom of the Stoics merely provides the terminological starting point, but does not determine the way in which freedom is understood. It is not a question of capability, as in the Stoa, but of (enthusiastic) "knowledge" (8:1ff). And the "permission" does not apply to anything and everything. It is related to the "flesh." So it is demonstrated in the form of sexual freedom and in the form of freedom to participate in pagan meals (see on v 13). Thus this slogan spans the whole content of chaps. 6–10. [9]

Paul's attitude appears in the first instance to be ambiguous. He recognizes the slogan, but his twofold limitation seems to abrogate it as far as its content is concerned. What he is really doing is to give it concrete shape and show that in Corinth the slogan is used abstractly and does not open the way to freedom. The first definition is formulated in Stoic terms (see above): the main thing is the question of the συμφέρον, "what is for the best." What this means concretely for Paul is shown by the parallel in 10:23ff: he does not mean another new principle, but the edification of the community, and this results in the destruction of individualism as a factor in salvation. This point opens the way for the argument of vv 13ff. The second restriction also follows earlier philosophic patterns; [10] freedom cannot cancel itself by making me unfree. [11] My freedom does not

---

5 Dupont, *ibid.*, 282–290, observes that when Paul is speaking freely he says ἐλευθερία, "freedom"; ἐξουσία, "power," he uses outside of Corinthians only in Rom 9:21 in a harmless sense (and in a political sense in Rom 13:1); ἐξόν, "permissible," only in 2 Cor 12:4. ἐλευθερία is originally a political term, becomes a speculative one in the Stoa, see Heinrich Schlier, *TDNT* 2:493–496. Definition Epict., *Diss.* 4.1.1: ἐλεύθερός ἐστιν ὁ ζῶν ὡς βούλεται, "He is free who lives as he wills" (Loeb 2:245). This, too, is characteristic enough a formal definition. ἐξουσία also is a Stoic term. Epictetus distinguishes between outward things, over which others have power, and the inward bearing, over which *we* have power. Diog. L., *Vit.* 7.121: εἶναι γὰρ τὴν ἐλευθερίαν ἐξουσίαν αὐτοπραγίας, "freedom being power of independent action" (Loeb 2:227). Epict., *Diss.* 3.24.70: τίς οὖν ἔτι ἔχει μου ἐξουσίαν; "Who, then, has authority [power] over me?" (Loeb 2:207). The acceptance of the term in Gnosticism is illustrated by the closing words of Poimandres in *Corp. Herm.* 1:32: εὐλογητὸς εἶ, πάτερ· ὁ σὸς ἄνθρωπος συναγιάζειν σοι βούλεται, καθὼς παρέδωκας αὐτῷ τὴν πᾶσαν ἐξουσίαν, "Blessed art thou, Father; thy Man seeks to share thy holiness, even as thou hast given him all authority" (Scott 1:133). This is preceded by the dual terms γνῶσις—ἄγνοια, "knowledge—ignorance." On the question of "freedom," see Ceslaus Spicq, "La liberté selon le Nouveau Testament," *ScEccl* 12 (1960): 229–240; Kurt Niederwimmer, *Der Begriff der Freiheit im Neuen Testament* (Berlin: Töpelmann, 1966), esp. 54–68 on gnosis; Dieter Nestle, *Eleutheria*, vol. 1 (Tübingen: J. C. B. Mohr [Paul Siebeck], 1967), on the Greeks.

6 This is not part of the slogan, but is introduced by Paul. Dupont observes that συμφέρει, "it is for the best, it is expedient," is suggested to him by ἔξεστιν,

"I am free to" (literally "it is permitted"). The underlying philosophic idea is τὸ ἀγαθὸν συμφέρον ἐστιν, "The good is expedient." Epict., *Ench.* 31.4: ὅπου γὰρ τὸ συμφέρον, ἐκεῖ καὶ τὸ εὐσεβές, "For where a man's interest lies, there is also his piety" (Loeb 2:513).

7 Corresponding to the meaning of ἐξουσία: the *ability* or the *right* to do something.

8 So rightly Schmithals, *Gnosticism in Corinth*, 230f [217f]. But to hold that the Corinthians consider their ἐξουσία to derive from ἐξουσία over the demons, is to read things into the text. There is no trace here of a Corinthian demonology (though such a thing no doubt existed). It is Paul who brings it into the discussion: 8:1ff; 10:18ff. Naturally, submerged relics of the enlightened preachings of popular philosophy have also a role to play in the syncretistic potpourri. Iren., *Haer.* 2.32.3, says of the Gnostics: *qui quidem Epicuri philosophiam et Cynicorum indifferentiam aemulantes, Jesum magistrum gloriantur . . .*, "These men, while they boast of Jesus as being their Master, do in fact emulate the philosophy of Epicurus and the indifference of the Cynics" (ANF 1:408).

9 This applies to the topics discussed. The statement in itself is made without prejudice to the question of literary unity.

10 The passive of ἐξουσάζειν, "dominate," appears to be a pointed *ad hoc* construction on Paul's part.

11 Sen., *Ep.* 14.1; Xenoph., *Mem.* 4.5. Porphyr., *Abst.* 1.42 conducts a polemic against the Cynics. He advocates abstention from meat and from wine. They, on the other hand, declare that food cannot defile where there is βαθὸς ἐξουσίας, "depth of authority"; κυριεύομεν γὰρ βρωτῶν ἁπάντων . . . δεῖ δὲ πάνθ' ἡμῖν ὑποτετάχθαι, "For we have dominion over all eatables. . . . But it is requisite that all things

derive from things.[12] It has its place, namely, the church. This the Corinthians will also say. So now it all depends on the concrete exposition of church and conduct. What Paul here presents is nothing else but the πάντα ὑμῶν—ὑμεῖς δὲ Χριστοῦ, "all things are yours—but you are Christ's," of 3:21ff.[13] This provides the distinction from the freedom of the Stoics. The starting point is the freedom which we acquire over against the world in the service of Christ; that is to say, it is not an "inner" freedom acquired by withdrawing from the world and then externally demonstrated.[14]

■ 13 Paul applies the basic principle to two realms: (a) only in passing, to that of food (κοιλία, "belly"); and (b) to πορνεία (σῶμα, "body").

a) To food:[15] he proclaims an undisputed freedom in clichélike terms, apparently again taking up a Corinthian slogan, τὰ βρώματα τῇ κοιλία, "food is for the belly."[16] Basing the argument on the fact of transience means that food is worldly, i.e., free to be used.[17] The transience of the world implies the neutrality of things and at the same time also cancellation of the neutrality of the use of things, that is to say, desacralization of the world and radicalization of the attitude toward it.[18] This means that Paul's position differs fundamentally from the Stoic view of the ἀδιάφορα, "matters of indifference."

b) πορνεία/σῶμα: here we have a very different case, despite the parallel phrasing. This is already manifested by the change from κοιλία, "belly," to σῶμα, "body": I am σῶμα inasmuch as I am not a "thing" but enter a relationship. The relationship to the prostitute is not one of a neutral, thinglike kind. It can never be an ἀδιάφορον, "matter of indifference." For the prostitute likewise, the man who has intercourse with her is not a thing. The relationship is a specifically human one. To this extent it involves the Lord to whom I belong. Paul naturally does not mean that any reciprocity prevails between "body" and "Lord." The relationship of sovereignty is a one-sided one. The result is both to establish

should be obedient to us" (*Select Works of Porphyry*, tr. Thomas Taylor [London: Thomas Rodd, 1823], 31). Epict., *Diss.* 4.7.17: no one has ἐξουσία over me, ἠλευθέρωμαι ὑπὸ τοῦ θεοῦ, ἔγνωκα αὐτοῦ τὰς ἐντολάς, "I have been set free by God, I know His commands" (Loeb 2:367).

12 That is, by "practice," in the sense of "independent action."

13 Bultmann, *Theology* 1:342f [343f] explains that Paul is showing the ambiguity of the formula. The world around me turns into that which is μὴ συμφέρον, "not for my good," when I lose my freedom to something in which the surrounding world encounters me. In this explanation there lurks a relic of Stoicism. The end of freedom appears where it is made into a principle. The point is the relation of freedom to the communal life of the community; this gives it historic character.

14 For the thought context see Christian Maurer, "Ehe und Unzucht nach 1. Korinther 6,12–7,7," *WuD* n.s. 6 (1959): 159–169 (on 7:1ff) 168: "With οὐκ ἐγὼ ἐξουσιασθήσομαι ὑπό τινος ('I will not let myself be dominated by any thing') he has already implicitly in view the sexual partner's power of disposal as grounded in the surrender of the body."

15 Schmithals, *Gnosticism in Corinth*, 231f [219f]: the argument becomes intelligible, if Paul has heard that the Corinthians appeal to the principle "Everything is allowed," as a ground for abandoning restrictions on food (with the additional ground that the belly is transient). But he has not heard that this applies in particular to sacrificial meat. This he does not learn till just before the composition of letter B.

This assumption can be dismissed in view of the fact—which Schmithals disallows—that in chaps. 8—10 *two* topics are discussed in regard to eating: the act of eating and the food eaten. It is true that these chapters are concerned with removing restrictions from sacrificial meat in particular. But for one thing, Paul can speak in abbreviated terms by way of anticipation. And secondly, Rom 14f show that the question of permitted and non-permitted food was in the air in general.

16 Mk 7:19. Does the reasoning, that the belly is transient, also come from Corinth? See the foregoing note. According to Schmithals, *Gnosticism in Corinth*, 230–237 [217–225], Paul accepts the thesis in regard to food, and rejects it in regard to the κοιλία, "belly." For κοιλία, cf. Sir 23:6 (Sense? Organ of digestion, or—probably—of sex).

17 According to Schmithals, *ibid.*, this basis of the argument is non-Pauline; it would be Pauline to base it on freedom; this does not happen till v 15. In actual fact, v 13 accords very well with Paul's understanding of the world. He does not operate with a general concept of the world and with a relation to the world that is regulated by speculative principles, but points forward to an eschatological intervention on God's part. Flesh and blood will not inherit the kingdom of God, but the body will be raised.

18 The neutrality ceases when the act of eating is related to the communal life. Foods are indirectly described as things that are neutral in themselves,

and to limit my freedom. This is expounded in vv 14, 17, 19. The rhetorical expression must not be pressed.

■ **14** The "body" differs from the "belly" in being destined for resurrection. The commentary is provided by chap. 15.[19] Eschatology assumes the transparent form of immediate rules for the conduct of life. The place of "body" is taken by ἡμεῖς, "us"; this interchangeability illumines the meaning of the word.[20] The future raising of the body as providing a standard for our relationship to the body is set over against the Corinthians' enthusiastic anticipation of the resurrection and the conclusion to which this leads them, namely, their demonstration of the devaluation of the body into an earthly thing. What they are really doing here is not to attain to freedom in their dealings with each other, but to dehumanize the realm of sexuality.

■ **15** The eschatological hope is actualized; it results in our *now* belonging to Christ. The underlying thought is that of the body of Christ.[21] A realistic conception of this idea is the presupposition for the conclusiveness of the argument:[22] ἄρας[23] . . . ποιήσω κτλ., "shall I take . . . and make, etc." μὴ γένοιτο, "never!" is grounded on what follows.

■ **16** This assertion is founded upon the citing of an obvious fact, and then of Scripture. To have extramarital sexual intercourse[24] is to repudiate the relationship of belonging to the body of Christ.[25] The Scripture passage marked by the quotation-word φησί[26] is Gen 2:24.[27] Paul presupposes that σάρξ, "flesh," is the equivalent of σῶμα, "body."[28]

---

since they are related not to "me," but to the "belly." The κοιλία is here only the organ of digestion, not of sexual life as well.

19 There it is also necessary to go into the question how Jesus' resurrection and our own are related to each other. Here Paul does not explicitly make a causal connection; but the latter is for him a matter of course. The phrasing is the result of dependence on the traditional creed, which is at once made good use of. Traditional, too, is the designation of God as the raiser, 15:15; cf. 15:20; Rom 8:11; 2 Cor 4:14; Gal 1:1. δύναμις: 2 Cor 13:4; Mk 12:24. In Rom 8:11 its place is taken by πνεῦμα. Ingo Hermann, *Kyrios und Pneuma*, SANT, 2 (Münich: Kösel, 1961), 21.

20 The interchange of σῶμα and ἡμεῖς is objected to by Lietzmann.

21 μέλη, "members," is not merely a figure, but signifies real connection; see on 12:12ff.

22 There exists a certain reciprocity, inasmuch as by sinning against the Lord I affect also myself, and by sinning against myself I affect also the Lord. But it is one-sidedly constituted by the Lord.

23 The reading ἄρας is to be preferred (with Lietzmann, Kümmel). αἴρω is in Epictetus (*Diss.* 2.1.31) —in antithesis to τιθέναι—sometimes a logical judgment, sometimes a moral one, also the result of such a judgment.

24 κολλᾶσθαι, "to cling to": Mt 19:5 (Gen 2:24); Sir 19:2; for v 17 cf. Deut 10:20; Ps 72:28.

25 We can add: it is to lose one's freedom. The meaning of σῶμα vacillates here: the body and at the same time the person; the person is for Paul indivisible. Bultmann, *Theology* 1:194f [196].

26 "It is said"; *1 Cl.* 30.2 etc.

27 Cf. Mt 19:5. οἱ δύο is an addition on the part of the LXX, cf. *Tg. J. I* (Adalbert Merx, *Das Evangelium Matthaeus nach der Syrischen im Sinaikloster gefundenen Palimpsesthandschrift*, Die vier kanonischen Evangelien nach ihren ältesten bekannten Texten, 2, 1 [Berlin, Reimer, 1902], 273 [on Mt 19:1ff]): תרויהון; Eph 5:31. εἶναι εἰς has a Semitic color, Blass–Debrunner §145(1). For Gen 2:24 in the halakha, see Str.–B. 1:802f.

28 σάρξ changes its meaning: here in an anthropological sense, not so in v 17; Eph 5:29. As against Gerhard Delling, *Paulus' Stellung zu Frau und Ehe*, BWANT, 56 (Stuttgart, Kohlhammer, 1931), 62–66, it has to be said that for Paul sexual intercourse in itself is not sinful. Nor indeed is σάρξ in itself a factor opposed to God. Here the sense is anthropological and neutral. Maurer, "Ehe und Unzucht," 166f observes: "The εἷς κύριος, 'one Lord' (8:6) . . . contains within it the μία σάρξ εἶναι, 'being one flesh,' which means a marriage that is exclusive and at the same time fully affirmed in its corporeality." Against this, D. J. Doughty, *Heiligkeit und Freiheit* (dissertation, Göttingen 1965), 173, contends that in Paul there is—as distinct from Eph—no reversal of the relation between Christ and the community according to 2 Cor 11:2ff. The relation of the community to Christ is seen in analogy to marriage, but not marriage in analogy to the relation to Christ. μία σάρξ, "one flesh," applies also to the union with a prostitute. "The μία σάρξ is accordingly for Paul not an essential mark of Christian marriage, but simply describes sexual union in general. 1 Cor 7:2–5 is not to be understood simply as an interpretation of Gen 2:24."

■ 17 Verse 17 is expressed in terms parallel to v 16. The significance of the Scripture is further heightened by means of the antithesis $\sigma\acute{a}\rho\xi/\pi\nu\epsilon\hat{v}\mu\alpha$. We naturally expect ὁ κολλώμενος, "he who clings" . . . is *one body with the Lord* (following v 15).[29] This thought is, as a matter of fact, the inherent presupposition. ἓν πνεῦμα, "one spirit," now explains what is the nature of this one body.[30]

■ 18[31] φεύγειν, "shun," is a characteristic catchword in paraenesis. The new life is first and foremost a discarding of the "old,"[32] a delimitation over against the world[33]—to be precise, the external world—just because of the eschatological indirectness of our new relationship to it. The demand as such is characteristic of Christianity in general.[34] The thesis on which it is founded, that fornication is the only offense against one's own body, is of course formulated *ad hoc*.[35] Paul at the moment has only this one instance, fornication, in view. Whether there may also be other offenses against the body is not here considered. Nor does Paul show any concern for the body of the prostitute and the abusing of it. He is plainly taking his cue from a Jewish saying which describes fornication as the direst of sins (Prv 6:25ff). Thus by "surrendering"[36] myself, I harm my own self. I cannot do as I please with myself. I am responsible also for myself, for my conduct toward myself.

■ 19 What was said in 3:16 of the community, that it is the temple of God, that the Spirit of God dwells in it, is here transferred to the individual.[37] The pneumatological grounding of the paraenesis links up with v 17,[38] but in so doing strongly modifies the thought. In v 17 it is a question of the pneumatic body of Christ; in v 19 it is a case of the earthly body as the dwelling place of the Spirit.[39] The point, as in 3:16, is holiness,[40] which includes also sexual purity.

The nonmystical sense of the idea of the Spirit is plain. The Spirit does not lead us away from the body, but defines existence in the body as existence before God. As

---

29 Alternation of σῶμα, μέλη and personal pronoun: Rom 6:12f, 16, 19.

30 There is no thought of mystical identity. This is obvious at once from the counterpart, union with a prostitute. Hermann, *Kyrios und Pneuma*, 63f contends that the idea of 2 Cor 3:17, the identity of κύριος and πνεῦμα, is presupposed. This is too schematic and vague; cf. on the contrary 2 Cor 3:17b: the Spirit is "the Spirit of the Lord."

31 Verse 18 gives the impression of an intrusion: a rational argument inserted into the pneumatological argument of vv 17 and 19.

32 For this reason the catalogues of *vices* predominate. φεύγειν: 10:14; 1 Tim 6:11, etc.; Epict., *Diss.* 1.7.25; Ditt. *Syll.* 3:395 (no. 1268, lines 1, 3); *4 Macc.* 8.19; *Test. R.* 5.5; Sir 21:2. Cf. also ἀπέχεσθαι, 1 Thess 4:3; 5:22; 1 Pet 2:11; ἀποτίθεσθαι, Rom 13:12; Col 3:8; Eph 4:22. The antithesis is διώκειν, "pursue."

33 Rom 12:1f; Phil 3:20. The moment the Pauline dialectic is no longer taken strictly, the demand soon changes into direct tactics of desecularization—by means of asceticism or libertinism. Once again it can be seen how in Corinth impulses emanating from Paul himself are at work, but changed into a direct, tensionless relation of the religious man to himself and therewith to the world.

34 In philosophy: Musonius, Plutarch, see on v 9.

35 Cf. Sir 23:16.

36 Muson., *Reliq.* (ed. Hense, 65f) distinguishes between ἁμαρτάνειν and ἀδικεῖν; sinning through sexual immorality is also a form of wrongdoing, since the person concerned debases himself. ἀδικεῖν is the comprehensive term. Here the idea of personality is normative. Paul knows nothing of this idea.

37 On the metaphor, see Cerfaux, *Church*, 148 [127]: "But this theme of the individual and inner temple (which comes first for Philo with his Greek taste for what is individualistic) is secondary for Paul." Thus the application in 3:16 is primary as compared with 6:19. In this statement the facts are not adequately grasped. We must ask how this transfer from the collective body to the individual is rendered possible by the understanding of faith and the idea of the church (the relation of the church to the individual).

38 Passing over v 18. According to Lietzmann, v 18 argues from the very concept of an ἴδιον σῶμα, "body of one's own," which is rejected in v 19, cf. v 13; 2 Cor 6:16. Lietzmann fails to realize that the idea of the body of Christ does not abrogate individuality. Each has his own gift, his own measure of faith and remains in his individual position. It is precisely as an individual that he is addressed and is responsible.

39 Rom 8:11. God in us: Epict., *Diss.* 1.14.14; 2.8.12. Sen., *passim*. The soul as the house of God: Philo, *Somn.* 1.149: σπούδαζε οὖν, ὦ ψυχή, θεοῦ οἶκος γενέσθαι, "Be zealous, therefore, O soul, to become a house of God" (Loeb 5:377). See on 3:16f.

40 Cf. the emphatic position of ἁγίου (B transposes).

one who has bodily existence, I belong to God; or to put it otherwise, the body is the place of divine service.[41] οὐκ ἐστὲ ἑαυτῶν, "you do not belong to yourselves,"[42] is the presupposition of the πάντα ἔξεστιν, "I am free to do anything." It amounts to a crystallization of the basic principle in v 3.[43]

■ **20** This is the basis of the statement that we are not our own: we have been bought by God. The interpretation of redemption in the sense of ransom is presumably traditional; it is found again in 7:23 (cf. Gal 3:13; 4:5). The metaphor is not developed. The point is merely that you belong to a new master. Beyond this the metaphor should not be pressed. There is, for example, no reflection as to who received the payment, despite the word τιμῆς, "for cash."[44]

Excursus: The Ransoming of Slaves

Deissmann[44a] points to the use of τιμῆς in the case of ransoming a slave, and would accordingly interpret Paul as working with a formula of emancipation from the realm of sacred law: the God buys the slave; by this means the latter becomes a free man. The form is found in inscriptions from Delphi and its neighborhood.[45] There is a set pattern: "N.N. sold to the Pythian Apollo a male slave named X.Y. at the price of . . . minae, for freedom (or, on condition that he shall be free)."[46] According to Deissmann, Paul is adapting himself to an idea that was common in the neighborhood of Corinth. His hypothesis is contradicted by F. Bömer:[47] Deissmann takes *donations* as proof texts for ransom. For the rest, see on 7:23. The word ἀγοράζειν does not fit in with the texts from Delphi. It does not mean "to ransom," but "to buy in the market"; this applies also to the passage in Ditt. *Or.* 1:536 (no. 338, line 23) which Deissmann cites in his support; the latter, moreover, has nothing to do with sacral ransoming.[47a]

The body is the place and the means of glorifying God.[48] This statement is a general one. It is not to be restricted to the specific context, the avoidance of fornication.

---

41 Paul says "God," not "Christ." The point ἀπὸ θεοῦ, "from God," is maintained.

42 Rom 14:7.

43 Apul., *Met.* 11.15.5: . . . *teque iam nunc obsequio religionis nostrae dedica et ministerii iugum subi voluntarium. nam cum coeperis deae servire, tunc magis senties fructum tuae libertatis*, ". . . dedicate thy mind to the obeying of our religion, and take upon thee a voluntary yoke of ministry: for when thou beginnest to serve and honour the goddess, then shalt thou feel the more the fruit of thy liberty" (Loeb 565). A thoroughly non–Greek idea.

44 Acts 7:16. On the price, see Eph 1:7. The Vulgate is false to the content in rendering: *pretio magno*, "with a great price." τιμῆς absolutely, without the statement of a sum: *P. Tebt.* 5.185, 194. ἐξαγοράζειν: Stanislaus Lyonnet, "De notione emptionis seu acquisitionis," *VD* 36 (1958): 257–269.

44a *Light*, 319–330 [271–281].

45 On the expression "and its neighborhood," see Bömer, *Untersuchungen* 2:133, n. 4.

46 Delphic inscription (Deissmann, *Light*, 323 [274f]; Ditt., *Syll.* ²845 [not in 3rd ed.]): ἐπρίατο ὁ Ἀπόλλων / ὁ Πύθιος παρὰ Σωσιβίου / Ἀμφισσέος ἐπ' ἐλευθερίαι / σῶμ[α] γυναικεῖον, ἀι ὄνομα / Νίκαια, τὸ γένος Ῥομαίαν, τιμᾶς / ἀργυρίου μνᾶν τριῶν καὶ / ἡμιμναίου . . ., "Apollo the Pythian *bought* from Sosibius of Amphissa, *for freedom*, a female slave, whose name is Nicaea, by race a Roman, *with a price* of three minae of silver and a half–mina . . ." . . . *seller according to the law* . . . τὰν τιμὰν / ἀπέχει. τὰν δὲ ὠνὰν / ἐπίστευσε Νικαια τῶι / Ἀπόλλωνι ἐπ' ἐλευθερίαι, "The price he hath received. The purchase, however, Nicaea hath committed unto Apollo, *for freedom*" (italics Deissmann's).

47 Bömer, *Untersuchungen* 2:133–141. Against Deissmann (and Lietzmann), see also Werner Elert, "Redemptio ab hostibus," *ThLZ* 72 (1947): 265–270: (*a*) (against Lietzmann): in 7:23 the thought is not that of a sale, but a *manumissio*; (*b*) (against Deissmann): in the sacral legal proceedings the purchase by the deity is merely a fiction. See also Friedrich Büchsel, *TDNT* 1:125f; Th. Thalheim, "Freigelassene," Pauly–W. 7:95–100; E. Weiss, "Manumissio," Pauly–W. 14:1366–1377.

47a Bömer, *Untersuchungen* 2:135, n. 9.

48 δοξάζω, "glorify": Lev 10:3; Ps 49:23.

1 Corinthians 7:1–7

7

General Observations

1 Now concerning the questions you wrote
about: It is well for a man not to touch a
woman. 2/ But because of the sins of
sexual immorality let each man have his
own wife and each woman her own
husband. 3/ Let the husband give the
wife what is due to her, and let the wife
likewise also give her husband his
due. 4/ The wife's body is not at her own
disposal, but at the husband's. Likewise
the husband's body, too, is not at his
own disposal, but at the wife's. 5/ Do
not deny yourselves to each other—save
perhaps[1] for a time by mutual consent,
so that[2] you may devote yourselves
to prayer and then come together again
—lest Satan should lead you astray
because of your incontinence (so
Lietzmann; or: as a result of your un-
restrained desire; so Bauer). 6/ I say this,
however, by way of concession, not of
command. 7/ To be sure, I should like all
men to be as I am; but each has his
own particular gift from God, one in one
direction, the other in another.[3]

Following the general observations in vv 1–7, Paul speaks
of various groups and their situations: the unmarried
vv 8f, the married vv 10f, mixed marriages between
Christians and pagans vv 12–16. Then comes the question
of principle in vv 17–24, which works out the eschatological norm for the whole area of concern.[4] Verses
25–38 make three approaches to the question of virginity: (a) vv 25–28; (b) vv 29–35; (c) vv 36–38. In an
appendix, vv 39f, Paul also comes to speak of widows.

In Judaism marriage is a command of duty. Its purpose
is the procreation of children.[5] The Essenes are reported
to have renounced marriage.[6] The situation of the
group represented by 1QS is disputed.[7]

For the Greeks, marriage is the normal thing. But there

---

1   On ἄν see Blass–Debrunner §376: "a hypothetical
    modification of εἰ μή τι which was felt to be a unit
    . . . after the analogy of ὅστις ἄν, etc." ἄν om. p⁴⁶
    B.
2   ἵνα is final, but begins to vacillate because ἦτε is
    also dependent on it.
3   p⁴⁶ and others read ὅς twice. Blass–Debrunner §250
    observes that in the NT the forms with the relative
    (ὃς μέν—ὃς δέ) are more frequent than those with
    the article (ὁ μέν—ὁ δέ). Zuntz, *Text*, 52, prefers
    this reading, arguing that the article in B, etc. is an
    Atticist correction.
4   E. Neuhäusler, "Ruf Gottes und Stand des Christen:

Bemerkungen zu 1 Kor 7," *BZ* n.s. 3 (1959): 43–60,
observes that in chaps. 6 and 7 we find two series
of motifs which belong together—a presentative one
and a futuristic one. But the presentative/futuristic
pattern of popular eschatology does not help us to
grasp either the Pauline eschatology or the motivation of these two particular chapters.
5   Str.–B. 2:372f; Philo, *Spec. leg.* 3.1–82; Jos., *Ap.*
    2.199f.
6   Jos., *Bell.* 2.120; *Ant.* 18.21.
7   Cf. also 1QSᵃ I, 9–12.

are also ascetic tendencies for which various reasons are given.[8]

■ 1 From 5:9 it appeared that, subsequent to his earlier letter, Paul had received news from Corinth; he is aware of a misunderstanding of his attitude toward dealings with πόρνοι, "sexually immoral persons." It could not there be said with certainty whether it was a case of oral or written news. From 7:1 onward we can be certain for a time; Paul is giving a direct answer to written questions. These apparently constitute the thread running through the part of the letter that begins here. The answer is introduced on each occasion by the phrase περὶ κτλ., "now concerning, etc.": vv 25; 8:1; 12:1; cf. also 16:1, 12.[9] The question of the Corinthians must have been: Is sexual intercourse allowed (at all)?[10]

It reflects the discussion between the libertinist and ascetic persuasions within the community. Paul's letter had apparently had a stimulating effect on the latter.[11]

Paul's statement is not a prescription, but in the first instance a general thesis: καλόν, "it is better."[12]

There follows a summary of the individual cases. Paul's view has an ascetic stamp; he does not give reasons for it.[13] The manner in which he then applies it in the concrete instances is, to be sure, specifically theological, in the sense of his doctrine of the freedom of the Christian.[14]

■ 2 Coming after the principle stated in v 1, this is a

---

8   An entirely different matter is the abstinence required by the cult—e.g., that of the Roman Vestal virgins. For the Cynics, celibacy represents a higher degree, Epict., *Diss.* 3.22.77. Stob., *Ecl.* 4.22.28: ὅτι οὐκ ἀγαθὸν τὸ γαμεῖν, "It is not good to marry." Philostr., *Vit. Ap.* 1.13. On the asceticism of the Neoplatonists, see Herbert Preisker, *Christentum und Ehe in den ersten drei Jahrhunderten*, Neue Studien zur Geschichte der Theologie und der Kirche, 23 (Berlin: Trowitzsch, 1927), 32ff.
Literature: Albrecht Oepke, *TDNT* 1:776–789; "Ehe 1 (Institution)," *RAC* 4:650–666; Gerhard Delling, "Ehebruch," *RAC* 4:666–677; "Ehegesetze," *RAC* 4:677–680; "Ehehinderniss," *RAC* 4:680–691; "Eheleben," *RAC*, 4:691–707; "Ehescheidung," *RAC* 4:707–719; "Eheschliessung," *RAC* 4:719–731; Walter Erdmann, *Die Ehe im alten Griechenland*, Münchener Beiträge zur Papyrusforschung und antiken Rechtsgeschichte, 20 (Munich: Beck, 1934); see further on 7:10f.

9   Schmithals, *Gnosticism in Corinth*, 95 [89], holds that 7:1—9:23 and the other sections beginning with περί, "concerning," belong to letter B.

10 It will also be due to the formulation of their question that v 1 speaks only of the conduct of the man. This is the prevailing approach in the ancient world. Paul replies on the basis of equal rights, vv 2ff. That this equality of rights is not abstractly understood is shown by chap. 11.
Philippe-H. Menoud, "Mariage et célibat selon saint Paul," *RThPh*, ser. 3, 1 (1951): 21–34, here esp. 26, ascribes the formulation of the principle καλὸν, κτλ., "It is good . . .," also to the Corinthians. So also Joachim Jeremias, "Zur Gedankenführung in den paulinischen Briefen," in *Studia Paulina*, 146–154, now in his *Abba*, 269–276, here esp. 273. Verses 8, 26 tell against this: καλὸν, κτλ. is Pauline style.

11 Schmithals, *Gnosticism in Corinth*, 234f [222], contends that no ascetic persuasion in Corinth can be inferred from 7:1. What is wanted in Corinth is simply clarity concerning marriage, seeing that Paul had declared πορνεία to be impossible. But this is to attribute to the community a high degree of ignorance of language and morals—even to the point of stupidity. After all, πορνεία had a definite meaning even in these days. And that there was asceticism in Corinth is clearly shown by vv 25ff.
Christian Maurer, "Ehe und Unzucht nach 1. Korinther 6,12—7,7," *WuD*, n.s. 6 (1959): 159–169, here esp. 160, argues that Paul in 7:1–7 is not attacking ascetic denial of sexuality. Else he would have to point out the complete validity of the body (?). He is contesting the proclamation of free sexual intercourse. The accent lies on ἑαυτοῦ, ἴδιον, "his, own,"—that is, on exclusivity. Over against promiscuity he sets the exclusivity of marriage; over against licentiousness the order, "no abstinence!"

12 Cf. vv 8, 26; 9:15; Rom 14:21.

13 Xavier Léon-Dufour, "Mariage et continence selon s. Paul," in *A la rencontre de Dieu: Mémorial Albert Gelin*, ed. André Barucq, Bibliothèque de la Faculté Catholique de Théologie de Lyon, 8 (Le Puy: Mappus, 1961), 319–329, contends that the superiority of the position of abstinence is not of a subjective kind, but "the state of virginity is objectively 'superior,' for it expresses the figure of the eschatological world."

14 Weiss observes that here for the first time in Christianity there emerges the idea of a higher perfection. But the slant of Paul's thought is different: he finds himself presented with the notion of the superiority of asceticism, and reduces it with the help of theology.
Schlatter holds that celibacy is considered in Corinth to be just as much an exercise of Christian power

115

concession,[15] though certainly one which, according to the criteria of Paul's theology, is not only possible, but also consistent: "He may have her; she may have him."[16] A positive ground for marriage is not given,[17] but only its negative aim, the avoidance of πορνεία.[18] It can be asked whether Paul has in mind a possible entry into matrimony or the proper conduct within existing marriages.[19] But Paul is not yet thinking of this alternative here. His observations are in the first instance of a general kind.[20]

With this concession Paul makes plain that sexual asceticism, the direct exercise of the negation of the flesh, is certainly not a way of salvation. Here he gives a practical illustration of what he had earlier demanded where

---

as, on the other side, the allowability of πορνεία. Celibacy is regarded as an achievement. The road to the prostitute is regarded as a way out of the difficulty. This is an impossible combination. Rather, two different demonstrations of Christian existence are presented in Corinth.

According to Bachmann, Paul does not say that celibacy is good and marriage bad, but that celibacy is good and not bad. This brings Paul on to the lines of Lutheranism with its mildly favorable attitude to culture. Lietzmann (rightly) fails to discover in Paul the higher evaluation of marriage, such as is found, e.g., in Musonius; Paul has nothing to say of earthly love. True marriage and sexual life are in Paul's eyes not "values." According to Kümmel, Paul depreciates marriage, not because he sees in sexual intercourse something that is evil in itself, but in view of the near approach of the end and because he himself has the gift of abstinence. This is not so. The nearness of the end he relates not to sexual intercourse, but to marriage, and the principle of v 1 has specifically *not* an eschatological ground. A special nuance would attach to Paul's recommendation if he were a widower, as is suggested by Joachim Jeremias, "War Paulus Witwer?" *ZNW* 25 (1926): 310–312; "Nochmals: War Paulus Witwer?" *ZNW* 28 (1929): 321–323; against this, Erich Fascher, "Zur Witwerschaft des Paulus und der Auslegung von I Cor 7," *ZNW* 28 (1929): 62–69; Albrecht Oepke, "Probleme der vorchristlichen Zeit des Paulus," *ThStKr* 105 (1933): 387–424, here esp. 406ff.

15 Christian Maurer sees the argument as follows: vv 2ff form an exposition of Gen 2:24 (see above, 6:16), on the lines of Jesus, not of Jewish tradition. This determines all the instructions in the chapter: μία σάρξ, "one flesh," and εἷς κύριος, "one Lord," both expressions in an intensive and extensive sense: the Lord is the sole Lord and exists entirely for the community.

16 Imperative as concession, Blass–Debrunner §387. ἑαυτοῦ, "his," of the man: Eph 5:28, 33; ἴδιος, "own," of the woman: 14:35; Eph 5:22; Tit 2:5; 1 Pet 3:1, 5. Diog. L., *Vit.* 8.43: πρὸς τὸν ἴδιον ἄνδρα πορεύεσθαι, "going in to her own husband" (Loeb 1:359). But cf. the unemphatic ἴδιος in v 4.

17 To the distress of modern theology. Lietzmann, see above. Weiss, too, holds up the mirror of Muson. (ed. Hense, 67f): Βίου καὶ γενέσεως παίδων κοινωνίαν κεφάλαιον εἶναι γάμου. Τὸν γὰρ γαμοῦντα, ἔφη, καὶ τὴν γαμουμένην ἐπὶ τούτῳ συνιέναι χρὴ ἑκάτερον θατέρῳ ὥσθ' ἅμα μὲν ἀλλήλοις βιοῦν, ἅμα δὲ ⟨παιδο⟩ποιεῖσθαι, καὶ κοινὰ δὲ ἡγεῖσθαι πάντα καὶ μηδὲν ἴδιον, μηδ' αὐτὸ τὸ σῶμα ... δεῖ δὲ ἐν γάμῳ πάντως συμβίωσίν τε εἶναι καὶ κηδεμονίαν ἀνδρὸς καὶ γυναικὸς περὶ ἀλλήλους, "That the primary end of marriage is community of life with a view to the procreation of children. The husband and wife, he used to say, should come together for the purpose of making a life in common and of procreating children, and furthermore of regarding all things in common between them, and nothing peculiar or private to one or the other, not even their own bodies ... But in marriage there must be above all perfect companionship and mutual love of husband and wife" (*Musonius Rufus "the Roman Socrates,"* tr. Cora E. Lutz [New Haven: Yale University Press; London: Oxford University Press, 1947], 89). Hierocles in Stob., *Ecl.* 4.22.24: συμφωνούντων μὲν ἀλλήλοις καὶ πάντα κοινὰ πεποιημένων μέχρι καὶ τῶν σωμάτων, μᾶλλον δὲ καὶ αὐτῶν τῶν ψυχῶν, "being in mutual harmony and holding all things in common, even to their bodies—to their very lives" [Trans.].

18 Plural of πορνεία: Mk 7:21; Mt 15:19. Paul differs from the Stoa in suggesting no spiritual training for the control of passion. The fact of the case— whether a man has the χάρισμα, "gift," of continence or not—is simply accepted.

The Jewish argument for sexual intercourse (procreation of children) does not appear. For because of the nearness of the end it is better not to have children.

This definition of the aim of marriage is unfashionable, but realistic.

19 According to Bachmann, διὰ τὰς πορνείας, "because of the sins of sexual immorality," shows that Paul is not speaking of the continuance of existing marriages. According to von Campenhausen, *Begründung*, 21, n. 38, vv 2–6 are concerned only with conduct within marriage; ἀνήρ, or ἄνθρωπος, means the husband; ἔχειν is not the equivalent of γαμεῖν.

the parties are concerned: the critical refusal to regard even one's own standpoint as a factor in salvation. This repudiation leads to freedom, which in the present instance means the equality of the marriage partners. And indeed the latter is now explicitly stated in the form of equal rights and, in v 3, equal obligations.[21]

■ **3** According to the particular way in which we understand ἔχειν[22] γυναῖκα, "to have a wife," in v 2, v 3 either supplements or explains v 2.[23]

■ **4** Paul takes the schema of equality a step further: the equality results from the limitation of freedom which is given with the presence of the partner.[24]

■ **5** The demand μὴ ἀποστερεῖτε, "do not deny yourselves (to each other)," results from v 4. This precept, too, is naturally not to be taken legalistically; it is valid for those who do not have the charisma of abstinence. It is a prohibition against turning abstinence into a matter of principle. The free nature of the exhortation is made plain by the concession: "in order to devote yourselves to prayer."[25] But why is abstinence necessary for this? Apparently Paul is thinking of continuous prayer carried out with the persistence of a rabbi's study of the Torah.[26]

The question of entry into marriage by unmarried people and widows is discussed only from v 8 onward. This disposes of the contradiction that Paul in v 2 seemingly recommends marriage to all and sets restrictions to it in vv 8ff. According to Robertson and Plummer, (a) ἄνθρωπος (v 1) is not the equivalent of ἀνήρ: (b) ἔχειν means "have," not "retain," cf. vv 12f. The imperative is not merely permissive.

20 It is true that the wording seems better suited to married people. But the tone of vv 1 and 2 and the argument in vv 2 and 6 show that the observations are of a general, and already at this point concessive, character. There is no contradiction with v 8.

21 Weiss thinks the exhortation to the wife is "a shade more emphatically accentuated" by δὲ καί. Considering the sequence of thought and the word order (chiastic interchange), we shall hardly reach this verdict. Moreover, δὲ καί is found in v 4 also in reference to the husband.

For the ancient background, see Joseph Vogt, *Von der Gleichwertigkeit der Geschlechter in der bürgerlichen Gesellschaft der Griechen*, AAM, 1960, 2 (Mainz: Akademie der Wissenschaften und der Literatur; Wiesbaden: Steiner, 1960). Muson. (*supra*, n. 17): married people should regard "all things in common between them, and nothing peculiar or private to one or the other, not even their own bodies" (Lutz, 89). Weiss admires Plut., *Praec. coniug.* (*Mor.*) 140c, as "the more noble Greek view": Λάκαινα παιδίσκη, πυνθανομένου τινὸς εἰ ἤδη ἀνδρὶ προσελήλυθεν, "οὐκ ἔνωγ'" εἶπεν "ἀλλ' ἐμοὶ ἐκεῖνος." οὗτος ὁ τρόπος, οἶμαι, τῆς οἰκοδεσποίνης μήτε φεύγειν μήτε δυσχεραίνειν τὰ τοιαῦτα τοῦ ἀνδρὸς ἀρχομένου μήτ' αὐτὴν κατάρχεσθαι, "A young Spartan woman, in answer to an inquiry as to whether she had already made advances to her husband, said, 'No, but he has made them to me.' This behaviour, I take it, is characteristic of the true mistress of the household, on the one hand not to avoid or feel annoyed at such actions on the part of her husband if he begin them, and on the other not to take the initiative herself" (Loeb 2:311). This is typical "bourgeois" male ethics, romantically misinterpreted by Weiss.

22 See above, n. 19.

23 D. J. Doughty, *Heiligkeit und Freiheit* (dissertation, Göttingen, 1965), 173, points out that in v 3 the exhortation is not based upon a reference to the danger of immorality, but on a statement of the mutual equality of husband and wife. The question would now arise, whether in Paul's eyes the two motivations belong together. The answer is given by 6:16.

24 Weiss thinks the ἐξουσία τοῦ σώματος, "power over the body," is really suited only to the husband. In that case the parallelism would be more of a formal kind. But it is surely simply a question of the case in which the wife demands intercourse and the husband refuses it. Against this it is maintained that the wife has a claim on the body of her husband. This is to state the reciprocality of the relationship; cf. the way in which both are addressed together in v 5.

25 In σχολάζειν it is not necessary to emphasize the note of *rest* (the Zwingli Bible renders: "so as to have leisure for prayer"); the word means simply "to devote oneself to something." ἐπὶ τὸ αὐτό, see Bauer, *s.v.* ἐπί III 1aζ.

26 For vows by which a man withholds himself from cohabitation for a time, see Str.–B. 3:371f. The aim is the study of the Torah, or prayer. The wife is not consulted. Günther Harder, *Paulus und das Gebet*, Neutestamentliche Forschungen, 1, 10 (Gütersloh: Bertelsmann, 1936), 20–24. Lietzmann thinks that in the background there lies the idea that sexual intercourse causes cultic uncleanness (Eugen Fehrle, *Die kultische Keuschheit im Altertum*, RVV 6 [Giessen: Töpelmann, 1910], 25–42], cf. Exod 19:15; Lev 15:18, etc.; Ovid, *Fast.* 2.329f; *Am.* 3.101f; Ditt., *Syll.* 3:109–112 (no. 982). But the text contains no reference to this motivation. It is simply a case of the influence of Jewish custom (with Kümmel); *Test. N.* 8.8.

Once again there follows a limitation, which takes us back to the beginning: διὰ τὴν ἀκρασίαν.[27] Lietzmann's translation, "because of your incontinence," meets the point.[28]

■ **6** Verse 6 agrees in content with the attitude of vv 1–5. This provides an answer to the question whether it refers only to v 5 or to the whole context: it refers to the whole (cf. v 12).[29] The imperatives must not be pressed. They do not all have the same force. In v 2 the sense is that of a concession; v 3 is a command. Now, without any imperative, we have another concession: κατὰ συγγνώμην,[30] since abstinence of course is not forbidden in itself.[31]

■ **7** θέλω, "I should like," corresponds to οὐ κατ' ἐπιταγήν, "not by way of command," in v 6 and καλόν, "it is a good thing," in vv 1 and 8. ὡς καὶ ἐμαυτόν, "even as I am":[32] that is, unmarried, abstinent. Once again the wish is not made into a principle. The reason adduced is in keeping with Paul's view of faith and grace. He differs both from the Gnostics and also from the legalists in holding not that everyone's gifts are the same, but that each has his own, peculiar gift, cf. 12:11; Rom 12:3.[33] Hence there is no such thing as "the" Christian way of behaving, but only each man's particular way in his particular place. I cannot do my own particular duty by binding myself to a rule and thereby evading responsibility.

It is not, of course, that marriage is here described as a charisma. This is evident at once from the sequel:[34] ὁ μὲν οὕτως, ὁ δὲ οὕτως, "one in one direction, the other in another."

---

27 The phrasing is such that we cannot excuse ourselves by appealing to Satan, the Seducer; for of course it is man who first gives him a hold.

28 For *incontinentia* is of course of the nature of married people; otherwise they would have remained unmarried. Muson. (ed. Hense, pp. 66f): ὅτι δ' ἀκρασίας ἔργον καὶ οὐδενὸς ἄλλου ἐστὶ τὸ δεσπότην δούλῃ πλησιάζειν, "It is an act of licentiousness [incontinence] and nothing less for a master to have relations with a slave" (Lutz, 89).

29 In favor of this Lietzmann points also to v 7. Not so Weiss, because the demands μὴ ἀποστερεῖτε, "do not deny yourselves to each other," and ἀποδιδότω, "give what is due," are unconditional. This logic is not conclusive.

30 "By way of concession," not, "as my own personal opinion"; not so vv 25f; cf. vv 10, 12, 40.

31 Note that in Judaism marriage is a command of duty.

32 ἐμαυτόν is attracted to πάντας.

33 Bultmann, *Theology* 1:325 [326]: "For as 'faith' is individualized in various concrete ways of acting, so divine 'grace' is also individualized in various concrete 'gifts of grace.'"

34 Against Allo. Continence as a gift of God: Wis 8:21; *1 Cl.* 38.2. ἐγκράτεια, "continence," is one of the δυνάμεις which constitute the being of the Gnostic in the catalogue in *Corp. Herm.* 13.9. The opposite concept is ἀκρασία. Preisker, *Christentum und Ehe*, 34ff.

7

Concerning the Unmarried,
the Widowed, and Those
Living in Mixed Marriages

8   To the unmarried and to widows, however,
       I say that it is well for them if they
       remain as I am.[1] 9/ But if they cannot[2]
       live continently, let them marry.[3] For it
       is better to marry[4] than to burn. 10/ For
       the married, however, it is not my
       command, but the Lord's, that a wife is
       not to separate[5] from her husband—
       11/ but if she has nevertheless[6] done so,
       then let her remain unmarried or be
       reconciled with her husband—and that
       a husband is not to put away his wife.
       12/ To the rest I say—not the Lord—
       that if a brother has an unbelieving wife,
       and she agrees to live with him, then he
       is not to put her away. 13/ And a
       woman who[7] has an unbelieving hus-
       band, and he agrees to live with her, is
       not to put away her husband. 14/ For
       the unbelieving husband is sanctified
       through his wife, and the unbeliev-
       ing wife is sanctified through the
       brother. For otherwise[8] your children
       would be unclean; but as it is they are
       holy. 15/ But if the unbelieving partner
       is for separating, then let him separate.
       In such cases the brother or the sister
       is not bound. God has called you in
       (or: to) peace. 16/ For how do you know,
       wife, whether you will (not)[9] save your
       husband? And how do you know,
       husband, whether you will (not) save
       your wife?

■ **8–9** The principles of vv 1–7 are now applied to individual groups belonging to the community, first of all to those who (at the moment) are not married. So now the question is whether marriages may be *contracted*.[10] Paul's decision remains true to the style of the foregoing: καλόν, "it is well." The comparative sense ("it is pref-

---

1   κάτω: for καί cf. v 7; καί in comparisons: Blass–Debrunner §453(1).

2   The negative οὐ in the conditional clause is the rule with real conditions in the NT, Blass–Debrunner §428(1).

3   ἐγάμησα is a Hellenistic aorist.

4   p⁴⁶ B D G ℵ: γαμῆσαι; ℵ A C: γαμεῖν. Moulton–Howard–Turner, *Grammar* 3:79, says (without consideration of the textual tradition): "to be in a married state," not "to marry." This is wrong. A difference of meaning between present indicative and aorist does not exist in this case; cf. 1 Tim 5:14: βούλομαι οὖν νεωτέρας γαμεῖν, "I desire therefore that the younger widows marry," also the tenses in v 10: μὴ χωρισθῆναι, but in A D G(!): χωρίζεσθαι.

5   "*Have* herself divorced" is not in keeping with ancient marriage law, according to which divorce is not carried out by a court.

6   ἐὰν δὲ καί: see Bauer, *s.v.* ἐάν I 3a; v 28; 2 Tim 2:5.

7   The variant reading εἴ τις, p⁴⁶ ℵ D * G, is an assimilation to v 12. ἥτις is to be preferred also because of the word order. On the anacolouthon which results in this case, see Blass–Debrunner §469: "Another clause in which the relative cannot take the same form is sometimes joined to a relative clause by a coordinating particle (καί, etc.)" (Classical, Kühner–Blass–Gerth 2:431–434).

8   ἐπεὶ ἄρα: without ἄρα in the same sense 5:10; Rom 3:6, etc. It makes little difference whether the unreal form (Weiss) or the real form is adopted in translation. The meaning is: otherwise—assuming the contrary—they are unclean, see Winer–Moulton, *Grammar*, 283.

9   See the commentary.

10 See on v 2 (von Campenhausen, *Begründung*, 21, n. 38). Widows: cf. vv 39f. Xavier Léon-Dufour, "Ma-

erable") can be seen from a comparison with v 9 ($\kappa\rho\epsilon\hat{\iota}\tau$-$\tau o\nu$, "it is better"). $\epsilon\hat{\iota}$ $\delta\grave{\epsilon}$ $\kappa\tau\lambda$, "but if, etc.,"[11] is to be understood in the light of the foregoing: if they do not have the gift of $\dot{\epsilon}\gamma\kappa\rho\acute{\alpha}\tau\epsilon\iota\alpha$, "continence." No reproach to the noncontinent may be read into this, as is shown by v 7. Since $\dot{\epsilon}\gamma\kappa\rho\acute{\alpha}\tau\epsilon\iota\alpha$ is a charisma, it is not practiced as a virtue.[12] It is not a standard that has to be achieved and is measured by criteria of a general kind, but it is an individual gift which cannot be acquired by imitation. This is why it is possible both to make the concession $\gamma\alpha\mu\eta\sigma\acute{\alpha}\tau\omega\sigma\alpha\nu$, "let them marry," and to pass the considered judgment, $\kappa\alpha\lambda\acute{o}\nu$, "it is well," or $\kappa\rho\epsilon\hat{\iota}\tau$-$\tau o\nu$, "it is better."[13]

■ **10–11** In the new instance, divorce, the regulation is absolute; for it comes from the Lord himself—one of the words of Jesus so very rarely found in Paul.[14] To $\dot{o}$ $\kappa\acute{v}\rho\iota o\varsigma$, "the Lord," we have of course to supply the present: $\pi\alpha\rho\alpha\gamma\gamma\acute{\epsilon}\lambda\lambda\epsilon\iota$, "commands." The regulation given by the historical Jesus is also that of the exalted Lord; it is a supratemporal command. The historic character of the command is not thereby canceled; it is not turned into a casuistical rule, as the following applications show.

$\dot{\epsilon}\grave{\alpha}\nu$ $\delta\grave{\epsilon}$ $\kappa\alpha\grave{\iota}$ $\kappa\tau\lambda$. does not mean the conceding of exceptions ("if she separates herself after all"), but refers to an already existing situation: "if she has separated herself"—despite the linguistic difficulty of $\dot{\epsilon}\acute{\alpha}\nu$ with the aorist subjunctive referring to the past.[15]

One wonders if it was possible that this rudimentary principle, which is alien to ancient society but was recognized by the whole of primitive Christianity,[16] should have remained unknown in Corinth. At all events it is expressed in such a way that it sounds as if Paul was making it known for the first time.

He appears in the first instance to make a correct distinction between the "separation" of the wife from her husband and the putting away of the wife by the husband.[17] But later he interchanges the verbs: vv 13, 15, an indication of the equality of the sexes.[18] This is reflected also in the change of order: the wife is mentioned before the husband, but on the question of mixed marriages after him. This change has no bearing on principle; it is purely a matter of choice.

In the Jewish law of divorce, the rights of the wife are limited in the extreme.[19] In Greek law, divorce is possible at the instigation of the husband, by common agreement (see n. 18), or at the instigation of the wife.[20] The authentication of the divorce by an official authority is not necessary, only its registration.[21] In Rome, too, divorce is freely allowed.[22]

---

riage et continence selon s. Paul," in *A la rencontre de Dieu: Mémorial Albert Gelin*, ed. André Barucq, Bibliothèque de la Faculté Catholique de Théologie de Lyon, 8 (Le Puy: Mappus, 1961), 319–329, observes: $\ddot{\alpha}\gamma\alpha\mu o\iota$ alongside of $\chi\hat{\eta}\rho\alpha\iota$ does not mean "not yet married," but "no longer married"; cf. v 34. This is too narrow.

11 See above, n. 2.

12 $\dot{\epsilon}\gamma\kappa\rho\acute{\alpha}\tau\epsilon\iota\alpha$ is generally recognized as a virtue: Philo, *Spec. leg.* 2.195; *Test. N.* 8.8. Essenes: Jos., *Bell.* 2.120. On *Corp. Herm.* 13.9, see above p. 118, n. 34. Gal 5:23; 2 Pet 1:6; Acts 24:25; *1 Cl.* 38.2.

13 $\pi\upsilon\rho o\hat{v}\sigma\theta\alpha\iota$, "burn," as a figure of (sexual) passion: Friedrich Lang, *TDNT* 6:948–951.

14 9:14; 1 Thess 4:15; 11:23ff is a different case. On this topic see von Campenhausen, *Begründung*, 21f.

15 Blass–Debrunner §373.

16 This holds despite all the variations in the transmission of the saying, which severally reflected differences of standpoint and legal situation; cf. Mk 10:1ff with Lk 16:18 (Q). Only Mt introduces the regulation of an exceptional case, 5:32 (Q) and 19:9 (Mk). The sense of the prohibition's validity is not restricted, but given concrete expression, by the fact that $\pi o\rho\nu\epsilon\acute{\iota}\alpha$ is "impossible."

17 $\dot{\alpha}\phi\iota\acute{\epsilon}\nu\alpha\iota$ $\gamma\upsilon\nu\alpha\hat{\iota}\kappa\alpha$, "put away a wife," already in Hdt., *Hist.* 5.39.

18 *PSI* 166.11f: $\dot{\alpha}\pi'$ $\dot{\alpha}\lambda\lambda\acute{\eta}\lambda\omega\nu$ $\chi\omega\rho\iota\sigma\theta\hat{\eta}\nu\alpha\iota$, "separate from one another." *P. Ryl.* 2:154.24f (A.D. 66): $\dot{\epsilon}\grave{\alpha}\nu$ $\delta\grave{\epsilon}$ $\delta\iota\alpha\phi o\rho\hat{\alpha}\varsigma$ $\alpha\dot{v}\tauo\hat{\iota}\varsigma$ $\gamma\epsilon\nu\alpha\mu\acute{\epsilon}\nu\eta\varsigma$ $[\chi]\omega\rho\acute{\iota}\zeta o\nu\tau\alpha\iota$ $\dot{\alpha}\pi'$ $\dot{\alpha}\lambda\lambda\acute{\eta}\lambda\omega\nu$, "If on a difference arising between them they separate from each other" (Loeb 1:15). *BGU* 1103: the erstwhile married couple Zois (named first) and Antipater inform the authorities: $\sigma\upsilon[\nu\chi\omega]$-$\rho o\hat{v}\sigma\iota\nu$ $Z\omega\grave{\iota}\varsigma$ $\kappa\alpha\grave{\iota}$ $'A\nu\tau\acute{\iota}\pi\alpha\tau\rho o\varsigma$ $\kappa\epsilon\chi\omega\rho\acute{\iota}\sigma[\theta]\alpha\iota$ $\dot{\alpha}\pi'$ $\dot{\alpha}\lambda\lambda\acute{\eta}\lambda\omega\nu$ $\tau\hat{\eta}\varsigma$ $\sigma\upsilon\sigma\tau\acute{\alpha}\sigma\eta\varsigma$ $\alpha\dot{v}\tauo\hat{\iota}[\varsigma$ $\sigma\upsilon\mu]\beta\iota\acute{\omega}\sigma\epsilon\omega\varsigma$ $\kappa\alpha\tau\grave{\alpha}$ $\sigma\upsilon\gamma\chi\acute{\omega}\rho\eta\sigma\iota\nu$ . . ., "Zois and Antipater agree that they have separated from each other, severing the union which they had formed . . ." (Loeb 1:23).

19 Example of a Jewish bill of divorce: Murabba'at no. 19 (*DJD* 2:104–109). See Str.–B. 1:303–312, 318; 2:23f; Albrecht Oepke, *TDNT* 1:783.

20 *BGU* 1105.

21 Theodor Thalheim, "Ehescheidung," Pauly-W. 5:2011–2013: the $\dot{\alpha}\pi o\pi\acute{\epsilon}\mu\pi\epsilon\iota\nu$, "sending away," of the wife by the husband takes place before witnesses.

■ **12–13** οἱ λοιποί, "the rest," is not intended in an exhaustive sense, but, as emerges only later, it means those Christians who are living in a Christian/pagan mixed marriage. Paul can express himself in such general terms because the principle is generally valid, even for every possible future case. This section is instructive in regard to the relation of law and freedom. There are two questions: (a) May Christians and pagans live together in marriage at all?[23] (b) What rule, in view of the prohibition of divorce, is to be recognized by the Christian partner when the pagan partner secures a divorce? Does the marriage still continue to be valid for him, so that he cannot marry again? In that case the pagan partner prescribes the law of the Christian partner's behavior.

For the answer to both questions the common presupposition is the absolute prohibition of divorce. This provides the first answer. The equality of rights appears again in the parallel between v 12 and v 13.

The application of the rule is not by any means mechanical and legalistic. The ground adduced in v 14 must be borne in mind from the start. Freedom is maintained: his worldly status cannot impose any constraint upon the Christian; it is of a worldly, not of a negatively sacral kind.

The second question arises from the fact that the prohibition is valid only for the Christian partner.[24] Paul distinguishes between the absolutely valid command of the Lord and his own exposition of it.[25] Once again he expounds it in such a way that it is not a formal prescription, but means the practicing of our freedom to be worldly.

■ **14** In accordance with the principle of equality, this verse is also expressed in double form.[26] Its interpretation is very difficult. To what extent is the pagan partner "sanctified in" the Christian partner?[27] To what extent are the children holy? What is the relation between vv 14a and 14b?

It looks as if holiness is crassly regarded as a thing; it is transferable, without faith (and even baptism) being necessary.[28] There can in fact be no denying the massively thinglike character of the idea.[29] We must not seek

---

The wife must indicate the divorce to the archon. A declaration on the latter's part is apparently not necessary. Mitteis–Wilcken 2.1:213–217.

22 R. Leonhard, "Divortium," Pauly-W. 5:1241–1245: "Divorces in Rome depended in principle on the free choice of the marriage partners and were rendered difficult only by the fact they were partly bound up with certain forms and partly subject to penalties."

Literature: Stawros G. Huwardas, *Beiträge zum griechischen und gräkoägyptischen Eherecht der Ptolemäer- und frühen Kaiserzeit*, Leipziger rechtswissenschaftliche Studien, 64 (Leipzig: Weicher, 1931); Gerhard Delling, "Ehescheidung," *RAC* 4:707–719; Heinrich Greeven, "Zu den Aussagen des Neuen Testaments über die Ehe," *Zeitschrift für Evangelische Ethik* 1 (1957): 109–125; Hans Julius Wolff, "Die Grundlagen des griechischen Eherechts," in *Zur griechischen Rechtsgeschichte*, ed. Erich Berneker, Wege der Forschung, 45 (Darmstadt: Wissenschaftliche Buchgesellschaft, 1968), 620ff.

23 The question is only as to the agreement of the pagan partner. This emerges simply from the exhortation addressed to the Christian. If such agreement does not exist, the pagan will arrange a divorce in any case.

24 Paul's view of marriage is diametrically opposed to that of the Roman Catholic Church. He does not seek to get hold of the non–Christian partner, but gives instructions to the Christian one.

25 Yet it is not enough to say that Paul is here presenting only his own personal opinion. It is theologically speaking no accident that the application is not "commanded." The command is *a priori* not legalistically framed. It is for this very reason that it requires exposition. So Paul's application of it is in agreement with the sense of the command, and is to this extent authoritative.

26 If also with a slight incongruence: ἐν τῇ γυναικί— ἐν τῷ ἀδελφῷ, "through his *wife*—through the brother."

27 We must not make too sharp a distinction as to whether ἐν, "through," has here a causal sense (Heb 10:10) or expresses the relation in a general way.

28 For the Jewish idea of *unholiness* as an infectious force, see Friedrich Hauck, *TDNT* 3:428f; cf. the interplay of ἅγιος, "holy," and ἀκάθαρτος, "unclean." Joachim Jeremias, *Infant Baptism in the First Four Centuries*, tr. David Cairns (London: SCM; Philadelphia: Westminster, 1960), 44–48 (*Die Kindertaufe in den ersten vier Jahrhunderten* [Göttingen: Vandenhoeck & Ruprecht, 1958], 52–57), holds that Paul is using Jewish ritual language.

29 With Kümmel; Braun, *Gesammelte Studien*, 191–195.

to evade this verdict by weakening the sense.[30] In saying this, however, we certainly have not yet arrived at an interpretation of the content. The question is: Is this kind of thinking a foreign body in the theology of Paul? Here it will have to be noticed that in the last anaylsis the whole conceptual material is already given, and is thus in a certain sense a collection of foreign bodies: motifs, forms of thought. We must therefore go on to ask: Is it possible to detect a way in which the motif is related, perhaps remodeled, to the interpretation of faith?[31]

The explanations that have so far been suggested are almost without exception unsatisfactory.[32] The force of the passage is certainly not to be taken as that of a stated proposition on holiness. The conception of holiness is already prescribed for Paul by his Jewish upbringing. Now he applies it and gives it a critical point: the "world" is denied any power of its own; in concrete terms, this means any such power over believers. The world is desacralized. By this means freedom is brought to light.

Through the believing partner, the marriage between a pagan and a Christian is withdrawn from the control of the powers of the world.[33] In living together with the world, the "saints" are the stronger party. The decisive idea lies not in an ontological definition of the state of the non–Christian members of the family, but in the assertion that no alien power plays any part in the Christian's dealings with them.[34]

The critical position here adopted by Paul in between the two extremes would be thrown into specially sharp relief if in Corinth the ascetic demand had in fact been made: to annul mixed marriages in order to avoid the world and the powers of the world. Intrinsically speaking, at any rate, Paul here, too, refuses to allow the direct demonstration of desecularization by means of a rule of abstinence. This would again be a way of salvation by achievement (cf. 5:9f).

The understanding of holiness (and uncleanness) in v 14b is the same as in v 14a. But what is the connection

---

Cf. the apocryphon in *1 Cl*. 46.2: κολλᾶσθε τοῖς ἁγίοις, ὅτι οἱ κολλώμενοι αὐτοῖς ἁγιασθήσονται, "Cleave to the holy, for they who cleave to them shall be made holy" (Loeb 1:87).

30 By reducing holiness to something like "destined for salvation."

31 On this question, see Braun, *Gesammelte Studien*, 193: "According to his terminology elsewhere, Paul is not aware of any comprehensive, objective state of being unholy or unclean, but he does know an objective state of being a sinner"—which is *not* abrogated in a thinglike, objective way.

32 Overview: Gerhard Delling, "Nun aber sind sie heilig," in *Gott und die Götter: Festgabe für Erich Fascher zum 60. Geburtstag* (Berlin: Evangelische Verlagsanstalt, 1958), 84–93, now in his *Studien zum Neuen Testament und zum hellenistischen Judentum. Gesammelte Aufsätze 1950–1968*, ed. Ferdinand Hahn *et al*. (Göttingen: Vandenhoeck & Ruprecht, 1970), 257–269. Oscar Cullmann, *Baptism in the New Testament*, tr. J. K. S. Reid, SBT, first series, 1 (London: SCM, 1950), 43–45 (*Die Tauflehre des Neuen Testament* AThANT, 12 [Zurich: Zwingli, 1948], 38f), holds that the non–Christian members of the family are also taken up into the body of Christ. Against this, Johannes Schneider, *Die Taufe im Neuen Testament* (Stuttgart: Kohlhammer, 1952), 55f, contends that then the body of Christ would have unbelieving members. The fullness of grace is conferred only by baptism. The latter is not rendered superfluous by v 14, but actually demanded by it.

33 The interpretation which moves most clearly in this

direction is that of Delling, "Nun aber sind sie heilig," 87f: Paul takes over from Corinth the concept of uncleanness in the sense of infection, but surmounts and corrects it: "But as it is . . ." Pages 92f: "If the uncleanness which the Corinthians feared was understood in a purely material sense, then this at any rate is not true of the 'holiness' asserted by Paul. Paul surmounts the idea of transmission both in regard to the view of uncleanness and also of holiness, and corrects it by means of the idea of ascription.

34 *Ibid*., 89: in relation to the Christian member of the family the non–Christian one is clean in the sense that the Christian one can live together with him. This, to be sure, is less than what we find in Paul. Paul outstrips the question of being *able* to live together.

35 According to Lietzmann, the connecting link is perhaps the notion that just as children are clean in virtue of their Christian parentage, so the pagan partner is clean in virtue of sexual intercourse with the Christian partner. A misguided idea. Nor is it proved in any way by the Jewish rule in *b. Yeb*. 78a (Str.–B. 1:112): "If a pregnant Gentile woman was converted, there is no need for her son to perform ritual immersion" (Epstein 2:530). According to this rule, Jeremias, *Infant Baptism*, 44–48 (*Kindertaufe*, 52–57), arrives at the interpretation: the cleanness in question applies to children born after the conversion of the—now—Christian parent. From this it can be concluded that such children were not baptized. But the analogy with proselyte baptism

of thought between the two sentences? Is Paul now simply appealing to actual views and to facts, that is, that the Christians do not as a matter of fact regard their children born of mixed marriages as unclean? Not even the unbaptized?[35]

The expression ἐπεὶ ἄρα,[36] to be sure, cannot prove this. It is hotly disputed to which children this statement, that they are holy, refers:[37] (a) to children of mixed marriages (this is in keeping with the context);[38] (b) to children born of Christian marriages;[39] (c) to both.[40] Delling would find an answer in the light of the question why these children are not baptized, and explains that this is manifestly because they themselves have rejected baptism. Thus it is a case of the dealings of Christian parents with their pagan children. The parents are not

afraid of thereby becoming unclean. From this Paul draws the conclusion for dealings with a non–Christian spouse. This interpretation is artificial.[41] The most natural interpretation is the application to children born of mixed marriages.

■ **15** Here the second case is introduced: the pagan partner desires a divorce, and that means, of course, he can secure it. Once again the "law of freedom" prevails: the Christian is not subjected to any constraint because of the pagan's behavior.[42] He can marry again.

The reason ἐν δὲ εἰρήνῃ κτλ., (note the word order) "in peace, etc.,"[43] is obscure for us.[44] In the context it can relate only to the declaration of freedom.[45] Incidentally, Paul does not think of the possibility of the divorced parties' being reconciled again (see v 17).

---

is not conclusive. The text gives no indication that Paul recognizes the cleanness only of some of the children of these parents. This is rightly pointed out by Kümmel, likewise by Kurt Aland, *Did the Early Church Baptize Infants?*, tr. G. R. Beasley–Murray (London: SCM, 1963), 80–86 (*Die Säuglingstaufe im Neuen Testament und in der alten Kirche*, Theologische Existenz heute, n.s. 86 [Munich: Kaiser, ²1963], 53–59)—answered again by Jeremias, *The Origins of Infant Baptism*, tr. Dorothea M. Barton, SHT, 1 (London: SCM, 1963), 36–38 (*Nochmals: Die Anfänge der Kindertaufe*, Theologische Existenz heute, n.s. 101 [Munich: Kaiser, 1962], 30–32); Delling, "Nun aber sind sie heilig," 89f.

36 "Otherwise"; abbreviation of an unreal case. Present indicative in the principal clause of an unreal condition is very rare. For the brachylogy, cf. Rom 11:18; Blass–Debrunner §483; Josef Blinzler, "Zur Auslegung von I Kor 7,14," in *Neutestamentliche Aufsätze: Festschrift für Professor Josef Schmid*, ed. Josef Blinzler, Otto Kuss, and Franz Mussner (Regensburg: Pustet, 1963), 23–41, here esp. 26, n. 13.

37 There is no thought of a state of innocence on the part of the child. This idea is found in *Ep. Ar.* 15.11 Athenag., *Res. mort.* 14; Aland, *Did the Early Church Baptize Infants?*, 103–111 (*Säuglingstaufe*, 75–82).

38 Kümmel; Albrecht Oepke, "Urchristentum und Kindertaufe," *ZNW* 29 (1930): 81–111, here esp. 83–89; von Campenhausen, *Begründung*, 22.

39 Ragnar Asting, *Die Heiligkeit im Urchristentum*, FRLANT, 46 (Göttingen: Vandenhoeck & Ruprecht, 1930), 209, n.1: unbaptized children of Christian marriages; "otherwise the children could not be used as an argument."

40 Heinrici; Allo; Hans Windisch, "Zum Problem der Kindertaufe im Urchristentum," *ZNW* 28 (1929): 118–142, here esp. 121. Schlatter (on the ground

that ὑμεῖς, "you," in Paul is always addressed to the community as a whole; this is not the case, see Blinzler, "Zur Auslegung von 1 Kor 7,14," 27; cf. 6:7f; 7:5, 28, etc.).

41 Blinzler, 23ff: Paul makes no distinction between baptized and unbaptized children. τέκνον, "child," refers not to age, but to parentage. Trouble can arise only concerning *baptized* children of mixed marriages. We have to make the following distinction: the unbelieving partner has become holy, the children *are* holy. When thus interpreted as referring to baptized children, the whole problem becomes unintelligible.

42 According to Lietzmann, οὐ δεδούλωται, "is not bound (literally enslaved)," is not to be taken strictly; the sense is: "is not slavishly bound to the other partner—or, to the marrige." No, rather "in principle."

43 καλεῖν ἐν: call in order to be in peace, Gal 1:6; 1 Thess 4:7; Eph 4:4.

44 Lorenz Nieder, *Die Motive der religiös–sittlichen Paränese in den paulinischen Gemeindebriefen*, Münchener Theologische Studien, Historische Abteilung, 12 (Munich: Zink, 1956), 52–54, argues that here we have not an added reason, but δέ breaks off the argument and points to the thought of peace as the higher standpoint. Meaning?

45 Joachim Jeremias, "Die missionarische Aufgabe in der Mischehe (1. Kor. 7,16)," in *Neutestamentliche Studien für Rudolf Bultmann*, BZNW, 21 (Berlin, Töpelmann, ²1957), 255–260, now in his *Abba*, 292–298, would explain as follows on the basis of v 16 (see *ad loc.*): v 15 is a concession, which is at once restricted again: "But God has called us to peace. For perhaps you can save your partner." In that case v 15 is in parenthesis; δέ has its full adversative sense.

■ 16 If the sense of v 15b is unclear, that of v 16 is controversial. The exposition depends on the interpretation of τί γὰρ οἶδας εἰ . . ., "how do you know whether . . .?" Since the Church Fathers[46] it has been maintained that εἰ is to be understood in the sense of εἰ μή: "whether you will not (after all) save your husband."[47] But according to the context εἰ means simply "whether."[48]

Paul is not thinking of remarriage (after reconciliation); the peace in question is valid independently of the behavior of the pagan partner.

---

46 Blinzler, "Zur Auslegung von 1 Kor 7,14," 32, n. 46.

47 Cf. the discussion of this thesis by Heinrici, Weiss, Robertson and Plummer. It has been renewed by Jeremias, "Die missionarische Aufgabe"; Christian Burchard, "Εἰ nach einem Ausdruck des Wissens oder Nichtwissens Joh 9,25; Act 19,2; I Cor 1,16; 7,16," *ZNW* 52 (1961): 73–82. For εἰ = εἰ μή, "if" = "if not," see 2 Sam 12:22; Joel 2:14; Jon 3:9; *Jos. et As.* 11: τίς γὰρ οἶδεν εἰ ὄψεται (*sc.* God) τὴν ταπείνωσίν μου . . . καὶ οἰκτειρήσει με, "For who knows if he will see my humiliation . . . and pity me" [Trans.]. Ps.–Philo, *Ant. bib.* 9.6: *Et quis scit si pro hoc zelabitur deus, ut liberet nos de humiliatione nostra?* "And who knoweth if thereby God will be provoked, to deliver us from our humiliation?" (*The Biblical Antiquities of Philo*, tr. Montague R. James, Translations of Early Documents, Series 1, Palestinian Jewish Texts [pre–Rabbinic], 13 [London: SPCK, 1917; New York: Ktav, 1971], 101). Epict., *Diss.* 2.20.30: πόθεν οὖν οἶδας, εἰ αἱ αἰσθήσεις ἡμᾶς ψεύδονται; , "Well, how do you know, if the senses deceive us?" (Loeb 1:381; meaning: "if they do not deceive us"). On this question see Kühner–Blass–Gerth 2:533: εἰ and ἐάν in indirect questions "have in themselves neither affirmative (if not) nor negative (if) significance." This emerges only from the context.

48 According to Heinrici, "if not" does not suit, because in the context the point is οὐ δεδούλωται, "is not bound." So also Robertson and Plummer, referring to εἰ μή in v 17. Jeremias, "Die missionarische Aufgabe," 259, n. 14, invalidates this latter point: εἰ μή (= πλήν) is used in view of the exceptions in vv 5, 11a, 15ab, if it is not indeed to be taken as Harder explains it (see on v 17). Weiss observes that if εἰ were the equivalent of εἰ μή, then vv 14, 15a would be in parentheis. It would only be with ἐν δὲ εἰρήνῃ, "[God has called you] in peace," that Paul returns to exhortation; this exposition is "the mockery of all that is natural." Weiss, to be sure, has to concede a certain contradiction between v 14 and v 15.

G. Ringshausen (in a seminar paper) argues that if we render "perhaps," then v 17 becomes unclear. Paul says: "How do you know if. . . ." It depends only on what the Lord has allotted to you. . . . On εἰ, see Eduard Schwyzer, *Griechische Grammatik*, vol. 2: *Syntax und syntaktische Stilistik*, ed. Albert Debrunner, Handbuch zur Altertumswissenschaft, 2, 1, 2 (Munich: Beck, 1950), 687: "Through closer association with particular verbs the conditional clause can become a dependent question."

7

17   But (or: Only; or: Nevertheless)[1] each
      should live according to the gift the
      Lord has apportioned to him and the
      state in which God has called him. And
      this is how I order (things) in all the
      churches. 18/ If a man was circumcised
      before he was called, then he should
      not have himself covered (with a fore-
      skin). If a man was uncircumcised when
      he was called, he should not have
      himself circumcised. 19/ Circumcision
      is nothing and uncircumcision is noth-
      ing, but what counts is keeping the
      commandments of God. 20/ Each should
      remain in the call(ing) in which he
      was called. 21/ If you were a slave when
      you were called, do not let that trouble
      you. But even if you can become free,
      remain the more readily as you are.[2]
      22/ For the slave who has been called in the
      Lord is the Lord's freedman. Likewise,
      the free man who has been called is the
      slave of Christ. 23/ You have been
      bought and paid for. Do not become
      slaves of men! 24/ Each of you, broth-
      ers, should remain before God in the
      condition in which he was called.

■ **17** Arguing whether v 17 sums up the foregoing[3] or
represents a new beginning (Robertson and Plummer) is
an idle matter. εἰ μή can be taken either way.[4] A link
with the foregoing is provided by the allusion to v 7 and
the taking up of the catchword καλεῖν, "call," from
v 15b. The thought of v 7 is now formulated in general
terms: as the gift is individual and does not schematize
man, so, too, it comes to him in his individual place,
and not in a situation that is defined on the ground of
abstract criteria, such as a general theory of sinfulness or
of the conditions of salvation. Not only the gift in itself
but its coming, too, is historic. Each receives *his* gift,
his "portion."[5] The question whether they are "spiritual"
or "natural" gifts should not be raised. Paul is not providing an analysis of man in himself and of the capa-
bilities of the "spiritual" man, but is giving an admonition to the Christian just as he is, with his particular
gifts. Here the distinction between holy and profane

---

1   See the commentary.
2   See Bauer, *s.vv.* μᾶλλον and χράομαι.
3   According to Weiss, v 17 is a transition, summing
     up vv 1–16.
4   According to Lietzmann, εἰ μή shows that v 16 does
     not belong to vv 13f as supplying a further argument
     ("whether you will not perhaps . . ."). If there is
     any connection of thought, then v 17 confirms οὐ
     δεδούλωται in particular, "is not bound." Accord-
     ing to Günther Harder, "Miszelle zu 1. Kor. 7,17,"
     ThLZ 79 (1954): 367–372, we have here a genuine
     introduction to a conditional clause, cf. 2 Kgs 5:17;
     ob 33:33; Sir 12:2; *3 Macc.* 5.32. The two ὡς clauses

5   are not parallel. ὡς κέκληκεν, "according as (God)
     has called," states the rule. ὡς μεμέρικεν, "accord-
     ing as (the Lord) has apportioned," contains a limi-
     tation of the rule: "If not according to the gifts the
     Lord has given to each . . ." This is linguistically
     artificial and inherently false. It is a misunderstand-
     ing of the individual note in Paul's view of faith.
     Weiss prefers the reading ἐμέρισεν, arguing that the
     perfect is an assimilation to κέκληκεν. μερίζειν: Sir
     45:20; *4 Macc.* 13.19; Rom 12:3; 2 Cor 10:13. Weiss
     observes that if the natural station is meant, then
     we have here a Stoic principle, cf. Ovid, *Fast.* 2.674:
     qua fueris positus in statione, mane, "abide in that sta-

becomes irrelevant.[6] Thus Paul can use the verbs με-ρίζειν, "apportion," and καλεῖν, "call," as synonyms, and can at one moment name the Lord as the giver, at another moment God. The two ὡς–clauses are synonymous.[7]

Grace creates freedom. The call comes to me just as I am; I do not first have to create by some achievement the presupposition for my attaining to salvation. That is the concretization of the *sola gratia*, "by grace alone." And grace embraces the world and holds me fast in my worldliness. No change of status brought about by myself can further my salvation. The summons to "remain" is dialectical; even this "remaining" is not a method of creating salvation, but in fact goes to show that no way of salvation by achievement is to be adopted. The sense of this remaining becomes understandable from the standpoint of eschatology (see below) and of the idea of the Church: in the Church worldly differences are already abrogated, yet not directly, for example, through the realization of a social program, but eschatologically. Every injunction in the following chapters can be understood as an application of this dialectic. Verse 17b corroborates the general validity of this "principle."[8] The observation does not necessarily presuppose that a position deliberately counter to this was advocated in Corinth (cf. 11:16). Paul is not advocating a principle of unity in church order. He is indeed attacking precisely the kind of schematization which postulates a specific mode of κλῆσις, "calling."

■ **18** Here Paul shows that the point of the general rule is precisely the liberating of the individual. This comes to expression already in the diatribe style of direct address.[9] The ὡς κέκληκεν of v 17, "as [God] has called [him]," is taken up and illustrated by the example of circumcision, which is immediately understandable in a mixed congregation of Jews and Gentiles.[10] The Jew has not to alter[11] the "standing" in which God encounters him, in order to do justice to grace as grace, and the same applies to the Gentile.[12] In the church our natural standing no longer counts; it is abrogated "in Christ."[13] It has no further influence on salvation, neither positive nor negative. Hence it is free, but not a matter of personal discretion: to change it would be to ascribe such an influence to it.[14] This would be a misunderstanding of grace and would mean the loss of freedom.

■ **19** The form of expression (ἀλλὰ κτλ. . . . , "but, etc. . . .") is compressed, but understandable.[15] οὐδέν ἐστιν, "is nothing," is related strictly to salvation. It is not a question of an abstract idea of equality. This very οὐδέν ἐστιν means, of course, that the Jew continues to remain a Jew.[16] What matters, and what is possible, is the obedience of each individual in the particular place allotted to him, that is, in the world.

---

tion in which thou hast been placed" (Loeb 107). Then, however, κύριος, "Lord," is not in place as subject, but θεός, "God"; hence the interchange in 𝔖.

6   Typical is E. Neuhäusler, "Ruf Gottes und Stand des Christen: Bemerkungen zu 1 Kor 7," *BZ*, n.s. 3 (1959): 43–60: κλῆσις, "calling," is not profane; the earthly station is embraced by the higher.

7   Against Harder, "Miszelle."

8   Weiss considers this "ecumenical" statement, too, to be an interpolation; see on 1:2.

9   Cf. vv 18–20 with vv 21–24. Both sections end on the same note. The protases swing between question and condition; parallel construction, but with variations (Weiss).

10 It is not necessary to assume that actual cases of circumcision or stretching of the foreskin had taken place in Corinth. There is—in contrast to Gal—no sign of Judaizing demands, for example.

11 On the operation cf. *1 Macc.* 1:15; *Ass. Mos.* 8.3; Str.–B. 4.1:31–57; Lietzmann, *ad loc.*

12 This is for Paul the theological foundation for the agreement at the apostles' meeting; it is not a compromise, but is theologically consistent.

13 12:13; Gal 3:28; the example of man and woman is one Paul cannot use here.

14 For this reason the change is *not* open to us. D. J. Doughty, *Heiligkeit und Freiheit* (dissertation, Göttingen, 1965), 197, says: man's worldly situation is "not simply a state . . . in which he 'remains,' but rather a 'situation of responsibility' in which he acts." True, but in this case the remaining is a mode of conduct. In contrast to the Stoa, Paul does not distinguish between outward and inward and does not make freedom the result of taking ourselves in hand.

15 ἀκροβυστία, "foreskin," has probably developed from ἀκροποσθία, "tip of foreskin," Blass–Debrunner §120(4). Literally: Acts 11:3. Figuratively: the pagan world, Rom 2:15ff; Gal 5:6; 6:15. Abstract for concrete, "the uncircumcised," Rom 3:30, etc. περιτομή: circumcision as a rite Gal 5:11 and as a state Rom 2:25. Figurative Rom 2:29. Abstract for concrete: Rom 3:30, etc.

■ **20** The transition to v 20 is smooth (cf. v 17). It is doubtful whether κλῆσις here, as in v 17,[17] means calling as an act[18] or "calling" as a status.[19] Remaining in one's own particular status is, like remaining in the world, not a concession to the facts, but a logical consequence of genuine theology.

■ **21** Verses 21–24 constitute a self–contained section. Verse 21 explains the principle of v 20 by reference to the example of the slave.[20] The form of direct address is appropriate; the eschatological equality of slave and master is, of course, not of a psychological kind. The slave requires to be comforted. This is not done by consoling him with hopes of a better future in the Beyond, but by taking him further on than the situation in which such a need of comfort is felt, by means of the, at first sight, surprising demand to make no use of the possibility of becoming free:[21] ἀλλ' εἰ καὶ κτλ.[22] . . . μᾶλλον χρῆσαι:[23] what has to be supplied here? Two opposing possibilities are feasible: (a) τῇ δουλείᾳ, "slavery";[24]

(b) τῇ ἐλευθερίᾳ, "freedom":[25] if you can become free, have yourself freed. In that case the two possibilities confronting a slave are set side by side in vv 21a and 21b.[26] Since it is a question of comfort, we must in spite of the aorist supply τῇ δουλείᾳ, i.e., "be [remain] a slave." Paul is not calling for Stoic indifference, nor is he cultivating the resentment of the oppressed. This is understandable from his eschatology. As a result of the latter, civil freedom is seen to be merely a civil affair. In the church it is of no value.[27]

■ **22** In the reason adduced, the notions of freedom and service are developed in both directions. The variation in the parallelism (in the slave's case, ἐν κυρίῳ, "in the Lord!") indicates the incongruity of the content. This is obscured at first sight by the choice of words, but emerges all the more clearly on closer inspection: the statement that the slave who is called in the Lord[28] is the

16   Weiss considers the statement to be a quotation, cf. Gal 5:6; 6:15; according to Euthalius it comes from an apocryphon of Moses. Paul speaks "as one would speak among enlightened diaspora Jews and proselytes"; cf. Rom 2:12f, 25, 28f; Jos., *Ant.* 20.41. This is true. But it has now to be asked in what way the situation here is disclosed. Against Weiss' view of indifference, see Bultmann, *Faith and Understanding* 1:74f [46].

17   And 1:26? see *ad loc.*

18   Karl Ludwig Schmidt, *TDNT* 3:491–493; Kümmel *ad loc.*

19   Lietzmann. It is not possible to reach a decision on the basis of the meaning of the word, see Bauer, *s.v.* καλέω. ᾗ ἐκλήθη is also ambiguous: (*a*) (the act) by which he was called, (*b*) (the state) in which he was called.

20   For the social standing of the community cf. 1:26ff.

21   On the social question and in particular the question of slavery, see Joseph Vogt, *Sklaverei und Humanität im klassischen Griechentum*, AAM, 1953, 4 (Mainz: Akademie der Wissenschaften und der Literatur; Wiesbaden: Steiner, 1953), 159–183; William Linn Westermann, *The Slave System of Greek and Roman Antiquity*, Memoirs of the American Philosophical Society, 40 (Philadelphia: American Philosophical Society, 1955); Max Pohlenz, *Der hellenische Mensch* (Göttingen: Vandenhoeck & Ruprecht, 1947), 387–396; Heinrich Greeven, *Das Hauptproblem der Sozialethik in der neueren Stoa und im Urchristentum*, Neutestamentliche Forschungen, 3, 4 (Gütersloh: Bertelsmann, 1935).

22   Weiss renders: even if you have the wherewithal to buy your freedom. Slaves buy their freedom: Bömer, *Untersuchungen*, 2:121f. According to Robertson and Plummer, καί, "even," is to be taken not with εἰ, "if," but with δύνασαι, "can."

23   χρᾶσθαι without a dative of the object, Epict., *Diss.* 2.21.20; 2.23.17; etc. Bauer, *s.v.* χράομαι.

24   According to Lietzmann only this interpretation is suitable, since indeed the slave is being *comforted*: he loses nothing by not having his civil freedom. So also Schmiedel who, to be sure, admits that in that case the aorist χρῆσαι is strange.

25   So Robertson and Plummer, Schlatter, pointing to the aorist and the combination of καί with δύνασαι.

26   This would be an application of the principle of neutrality—a neutrality understood, to be sure, in a Stoic, not in a Pauline sense. Epict., *Diss.* 2.6.18: τί σοι μέλει, ποίᾳ ὁδῷ καταβῆς εἰς ᾍδου; ἴσαι πᾶσαί εἰσιν, "What concern is it to you by what road you descend to the House of Hades? They are all equal" (Loeb 1:251). Cf. the formalization in Ign., *Pol.* 4.3.

27   It would of course be absurd to point out the problematical character of many emancipations: the slave often does not wish to be freed, because he thereby loses his material protection. Paul presupposes that freedom is a human value. Bömer, *Untersuchungen* 2:16.

28   ἐν is not to be taken in the instrumental sense, but in terms of the formula ἐν κυρίῳ, "in the Lord": the man who was called as a slave, so that he is now in the Lord. In this passage it is clear that the κύριος

Lord's freedman does not really fit.[29] If he were a freed-man, then without detriment to any obligations of clientage and piety he would in fact be free. The meaning is rather that if he is in the Lord, if he belongs to him, then he is free in the eschatological sense, free from sin.[30] He is ἀπελεύθερος, "a freedman," not in relation to the Lord, but in relation to his erstwhile status as a slave.[31] Both statements belong together: the free man is really free as a slave of Christ. In this servitude lies the common factor: the freedom of the slave and of the civilly free man.

The demand to become the δοῦλος, "slave," of a god is radically non–Greek.[32]

■ **23** This verse further develops the motif of emancipa-tion: you have been bought for money (see on 6:20).

Deissmann would again explain the idea in the light of the sacral emancipation of slaves as practiced in Delphi: the slave is liberated by being feignedly sold to Apollo.[32a] But apart from the fact that for Paul the method of re-demption is of no significance (he does not say from whom we have been bought, and we certainly must not ask to whom the price is paid), Deissmann's interpre-tation of the inscription material is false.[33] Apart from the motif of redemption, the Stoic parallels lie nearer to hand (Weiss). Yet they remain formal because the dialectic of freedom in servitude is alien to them.[34] The summons which rounds off the section, μὴ γίνεσθε κτλ., "do not become, etc.," points both to the possi-bility of freedom and also to the demand for a concrete realization of it.

---

29 title cannot have its place taken by "Christ."

29 Does ἀπελεύθερος κυρίου, "the Lord's freedman," emphasize the freedom (Lietzmann) or the duty of service (Kümmel)? In the contrast between v 22a and b, plainly his freedom is emphasized.

30 Rom 6:18; 8:2; Gal 5:1; Karl Heinrich Rengstorf, *TDNT* 2:273–277; Heinrich Schlier, *TDNT* 2:496–502.

31 Lietzmann observes: the meaning is not, "discharged from the slavery of the Lord," but, "freed from slav-ery by him."

32 Bömer, *Untersuchungen* 2:136, observes: simultane-ousness of freedom and bondage is for the Greek un-thinkable. This finds expression also in the oxymoron (*ibid.*, n. 1) that the free man is voluntarily sub-ject to the law like a slave. We have only a pseudo–parallel in Ditt., *Or.* 1:602f (no. 383, lines 171–189), Commagenean inscription of Antiochus I on Nem-rud–Dagh: Antiochus has established "musicians" for the cult and orders that no one is to "enslave the 'hierodules' to himself, nor deliver them to any-one else in any way whatever," μήτε αὐτῷ κατα-δουλώσασθαι μήτε εἰς ἕτερον ἀπαλλοτριῶσαι τρόπῳ μηδενί.

32a Deissmann, *Light*, 322–330 [274–281].

33 Bömer closes with a discussion of this point, *Unter-suchungen* 2:134–137: there do in fact exist numerous echoes of the vocabulary. But the Delphic practice, while certainly widely recognized, was yet restricted to the locality; for its own part it apparently arose under oriental influence. Cf. the Jewish material from the northern coast of the Black Sea (*ibid.*, 2:101–106): in Delphi the slave belongs to the god only in a formal sense. He is not bound to him in any way.

34 Stob., *Eccl.* 3.2.38 (Bion): οἱ ἀγαθοὶ οἰκέται ἐλεύ-θεροι, οἱ δὲ πονηροὶ ἐλεύθεροι δοῦλοι πολλῶν ἐπι-θυμιῶν, "virtuous servants are free, but evil free men

are slaves to many desires" [Trans.]. Epict., *Diss.* 1.19.9: "ἐγώ σοι δείξω ὅτι κύριός εἰμι." "πόθεν σύ; ἐμὲ ὁ Ζεὺς ἐλεύθερον ἀφῆκεν. ἢ δοκεῖς ὅτι ἔμελλεν τὸν ἴδιον υἱὸν ἐὰν καταδουλοῦσθαι; τοῦ νεκροῦ δέ μου κύριος εἶ. λάβε αὐτόν," " 'I will show you that I am master.' 'How can *you* be my master? Zeus has set me free. Or do you really think that he was likely to let his own son be made a slave? You are, how-ever, master of my dead body; take it' " (Loeb 1:131). Epict., *Diss.* 4.7.16f: εἰς ἐμὲ οὐδεὶς ἐξουσίαν ἔχει. ἠλευθέρωμαι ὑπὸ τοῦ θεοῦ, ἔγνωκα αὐτοῦ τὰς ἐντολάς, οὐκέτι οὐδεὶς δουλαγωγῆσαί με δύναται, "No one has authority over me. I have been set free by God, I know his commands, no one has power any longer to make a slave of me" (Loeb 2:367).

35 Deissmann, *Light*, 326 [277]. The term παραμονή occurs in about a quarter of the documents; see Bömer, *Untersuchungen* 2:38–49. It means the freed-man's obligation to continue for a time in the service of his emancipator, usually till the latter's death, and "thus in practice to continue to be a slave." Deissmann explains that Delphi requires continu-ance under the old master, Paul under a new one. Bömer says this is wrong. According to Paul each is to remain where he is. And in the Jewish inscriptions from Pantikapaion (Kertsch) there is nothing cor-responding to μένειν, "remain." Deissmann, *Light*, 321 [273], refers to *IPE* 52 and 53: the freedman is to remain faithful to the synagogue. Bömer observes that in that case a *normal* παραμονή would here be required, "the very kind, that is, which Deissmann does *not* want." For the inscriptions from Pantika-paion see further Bömer, *Untersuchungen* 2:103–106: the freedman is first of all to go to the synagogue, there to pray and to remain for a specific time. This is what is meant by προσκαρτέρησις, "persever-ance." This is not the usual παραμονή. What is

■ **24** Verse 24 is a repetition of v 17. But what does
παρὰ θεῷ, "before God," mean? It is probably an (unclearly expressed) allusion to the thought of v 22. Deissmann suggests a special interpretation of μένειν, "remain"; he links it with παρὰ θεῷ and sees in this an allusion to the παραμονή, "faithfulness," which plays a role in sacral emancipation.[35] This interpretation is

voided by what we have said above, as also by Pauline
usage, in which παρά is the equivalent of ἐνώπιον,
"before the face of."

meant is not a constant remaining in or at προσευχή,
"prayer." Note that in *IPE* 53 the παραμονή is
also explicitly stipulated. For religious obligations
which the freedman takes upon him, see Bömer, *Un-*

tersuchungen 2:64f; cf. *Supp. Epigr.* 14 (1957): 109f
(no. 529); A. Cameron, "Inscriptions Relating to
Sacral Manumission and Confession," *HTR* 32
(1939): 143–179.

7

Concerning Virgins
(and the Unmarried)

25 Now concerning virgins, I have no command from the Lord. But I give my opinion as one on whom the Lord has conferred the mercy of being trustworthy. 26 / It is my opinion, then, that in view of the impending (or: present) distress this is a good thing, that it is good for a man to be as he is.[1] 27 / Are you bound to a wife? Do not seek a separation! Are you free of a wife? Do not seek a wife! 28 / But if you do marry, then you have not sinned,[2] and if a virgin marries, then she has not sinned. Certainly, such people will have trouble for the flesh. 29 / But I am for sparing you. What I mean is, brothers, that the time is short, and further that (or: and that for the future[3]) those who have wives should be as though they had none, 30 / and those who weep as though they did not weep, and those who rejoice as though they did not rejoice, and those who buy as though they were not to keep their purchases, 31 / and those who utilize the world as though they were making no use of it. For the shape of this world is passing away. 32 / But I should like you to be free from care. The unmarried man cares for the Lord's business, how to please the Lord. 33 / The married man cares for the world's business, how to please his wife, 34 / and has thus a divided mind.[4] And the unmarried woman and the virgin care for the Lord's business,

---

1 Nominative of the substantivized infinitive: Blass–Debrunner §399. Lietzmann resolves the sentence as follows: (a) νομίζω τοῦτο καλὸν ὑπάρχειν, ὅτι ὁ ἄνθρωπος οὕτως ἐστίν, "I think it is good that a man is thus"; (b) νομίζω ὅτι καλὸν ἀνθρώπῳ τὸ οὕτως εἶναι, "I think it is good for a man to be thus."

2 The meaning is: you do not sin. Futuristic aorist after a future condition: Blass–Debrunner §333(2).

3 ἵνα for the imperative (vernacular): Blass–Debrunner §387(3). ⟨τὸ⟩ λοιπόν can be construed (a) as a loose transitional phrase: "further"; (b) as inferential "therefore" (Hellenistic), Blass–Debrunner §451(6); (c) temporally, Anders Cavallin, "⟨τὸ⟩ λοιπόν. Eine bedeutungsgeschichtliche Untersuchung," Eranos 39 (1941): 121–144. Blass–Debrunner §451(6): "Out of the λοιπόν used with asyndeton to begin a sentence . . . there developed an inferential 'therefore' in Hell."; Polyb.; Epict.; Ign., Eph. 11.1; Mayser, Grammatik 2.3:146, lines 5–9. Polyb., Hist. 1.15.11: λοιπὸν ἀνάγκη συγχωρεῖν τὰς ἀρχὰς καὶ τὰς ὑποθέσεις εἶναι ψευδεῖς, "we must therefore concede that Philinus's initial statements and hy-

potheses are false" (cf. Loeb 1:39). Epict., Diss. 1.22.15; 2.5.16; etc. Cavallin, "⟨τὸ⟩ λοιπόν," observes that in Polybius λοιπόν has ousted τὸ λοιπόν. The temporal significance is primary; it is not supplanted. Epict., Diss. 1.10.5; 2.15.8. Logical λοιπόν: Polyb., Hist. 9.26a.2; Epict., Diss. 2.10.19. As an interjection: Phil 3:1; 1 Cl. 64—presumably also developed from the temporal significance. Not "for the rest" (Cavallin, "⟨τὸ⟩ λοιπόν ," 143). Anton Fridrichsen, "Sprachliches und Stilistisches zum Neuen Testament," in Kungliga Humanistika Vetenskaps–Samfundet i Uppsala, Årsbok 1943 (Uppsala: Almqvist & Wiksell; Leipzig: Harrassowitz, 1943), 24–36 says: in 1:16, "otherwise," but here in a logical sense; Epict., Diss. 2.12.24. ἵνα, "that," draws the logical consequence which is marked by λοιπόν.

4 Variant readings: (1) καὶ μεμέρισται· καὶ ἡ γυνὴ ἡ ἄγαμος καὶ ἡ παρθένος μεριμνᾷ . . ., p15 B sa, "he has a divided mind; and the unmarried woman and the virgin care . . ." (2a) καὶ μεμέρισται ἡ γυνὴ καὶ ἡ παρθένος· ἡ ἄγαμος μεριμνᾷ . . ., D, "and there is a difference between the wife and the virgin;

in order to be holy in body and spirit;[5] but the married woman cares for the world's business, how to please her husband. 35 / I say this for your own good, not to ensnare you, but to promote undistracted propriety and devotion before (or: toward) God. 36 / But if anyone thinks he is not behaving properly toward his virgin, if he (or: she) is more than mature and it has to be so, let him do as he wishes. He is not committing a sin; let them marry.[6] 37 / But if a man is steadfast in his heart and is not in any distress, but has command of his own will and has resolved in his heart to preserve his virgin (as such), he will do well. 38 / So the man who marries his virgin does well, and the man who does not marry her will do better. 39 / A wife is bound to her husband as long as he lives. But if the husband dies, she is free to marry whom she will, only in the Lord. 40 / But in my opinion she is happier if she remains as she is. And I think that I, too, have the Spirit of God.

The section 7:25–40 is obviously once more a direct answer to an enquiry.

■ **25** What is meant by the term παρθένοι is—super-fluously enough—hotly disputed: it means virgins,[7]

---

the unmarried woman cares. . . ." (2b) μεμέρισται καὶ ἡ γυνὴ καὶ ἡ παρθένος· ἡ ἄγαμος μεριμνᾷ . . ., G Tert. Ambr. Ambst., "there is also a difference between the wife and the virgin; the unmarried woman cares. . . ." (3) καὶ μεμέρισται καὶ ἡ γυνὴ ἡ ἄγαμος καὶ ἡ παρθένος· ἡ ἄγαμος μεριμνᾷ . . ., p⁴⁶ ℵ A, "and there is also a difference between the unmarried woman and the virgin; the unmarried woman cares. . . ." Reading 1 is to be preferred (with Lietzmann), 2 is an emendation in the interests of smoothness, 3 is a combination of 1 and 2.

5 Variant readings: (1) τῷ σώματι καὶ τῷ πνεύματι, p⁴⁶ A P 33 69, "in (the) body and (the) Spirit." (2) καὶ σώματι καὶ πνεύματι, p¹⁵ G ℜ, "both in body and in spirit." (3) καὶ τῷ σώματι καὶ τῷ πνεύματι, ℵ B, "both in (the) body and in (the) spirit." (4) σώματι καὶ πνεύματι, D, "in body and spirit." Zuntz, *Text*, 199f (for no. 1).

6 The present imperative indicates the quality of action, Blass–Debrunner §336(2).

7 So Allo, pointing to Rev 14:4: unmarried men and women. Kümmel argues against this that it would be an unusual linguistic usage; and in v 28 the meaning is plain. Hence it is useless to point to the fact that παρθένος can be used in the wider sense, e.g., Ign. *Sm.* 13.1: ἀσπάζομαι τοὺς οἴκους τῶν ἀδελφῶν μου σὺν γυναιξὶ καὶ τέκνοις καὶ τὰς παρθένους τὰς λεγομένας χήρας, "I salute the families of my brethren with their wives and children, and the maidens who are called widows" (Loeb 1:267). Harry J. Leon, *The Jews of Ancient Rome* (Philadelphia: Jewish Publication Society of America, 1960), points out that in the Jewish inscriptions in Rome maidens of 15–22 years of age are five times designated παρθενική. He presumes in view of their age that they were married, cf. the mention of a "virgin" wife (*CIJ* 81; 319; 242; all reprinted, with English translations, in Leon's appendix). Josephine Massingberd Ford, "Levirate Marriage in St Paul (I Cor. vii)," *NTS* 10 (1963–64): 361–365, offers the misguided interpretation: young widows and widowers who had been married only *once*, πιστός in v 25 meaning "faithful to one wife." For παρθένος see Gerhard Delling, *TDNT* 5:826–837.

not, say, *virgines subintroductae.*[8] For the form of the advice cf. v 10.[9] ὡς[10] ἐλεημένος, "as one who has received mercy": a similar asseveration rounds off v 40. πιστός, according to 1 Thess 2:4, means "trustworthy person."[11]

■ **26** This statement at last explicitly affords the long–awaited eschatological grounding. The mode of expression makes known the basic mood of the eschatological outlook, which is fear. The latter acts as a foil to the hope which is given by the fact that the judge is Christ, "in" whom believers exist. Once again Paul gives his own opinion, not a command. The expression is not clear. Does τοῦτο, "this," point backwards or forwards, *scil.* to the conjunction ὅτι, "that . . ."? The latter is presumably the case. The unclarity exists also in the ὅτι–clause. Does οὕτως εἶναι mean "remain as one is" or "remain as I am, or as the virgins are"?[12] ἀνάγκη, "distress," is an apocalyptic term.[13] The alternative as to whether ἐνεστώς means "present" or "impending" should be resolved by saying "imminent" distress (*imminet*).[14]

■ **27** For the style, see Blass–Debrunner, §§ 464, 494 (resolution of a period into disconnected members; antistrophe and anastrophe: λύσιν—λέλυσαι).

Our understanding of the train of thought depends on our view of οὕτως in v 26 (see above). But why does Paul suddenly pass over to the man?[15] Manifestly by way of illustration. In this way he can set out from the principle "each in his own calling," and now, via the unmarried man, apply this principle to the virgins (v 28). μὴ ζήτει λύσιν, "do not seek a separation," following vv 10f is in itself superfluous, but is here repeated because of the reference to the ἀνάγκη, "distress," which could be adduced as a ground for separating.[16]

■ **28** Paul explains[17] the sense in which he is not *commanding* but *advising*: to adopt a different mode of conduct is not a sin. He is giving his advice in view of the outward[18] menace of these "last evil times"; θλῖψις, "trouble," is synonymous with ἀνάγκη.[19] The use of γαμεῖν/γαμεῖσθαι, "marry," is no longer subject to

---

8 So Weiss, Lietzmann. According to Weiss, v 28, οὐχ ἥμαρτες, "you have not sinned," presupposes the breaking of a vow. παρθένοι are men and women who have vowed virginity.

9 Weiss thinks γνώμη, "opinion," is stronger than συγγνώμη, "concession"; hardly. For διδόναι, "give," cf. Diod S., *Bibl. hist.* 20.16.1.

10 ὡς: Blass–Debrunner §425(3): "as one who . . .," "with the conviction that I. . . ."

11 πιστός is actually used as a title in Syrian inscriptions, see Bauer, *s.v.*; Erik Peterson, Εἷς θεός: *Epigraphische, formgeschichtliche und religionsgeschichtliche Untersuchungen*, FRLANT, 24 (Göttingen: Vandenhoeck & Ruprecht, 1926), 32ff, 309. Achill. Tat., *Clit. et Leuc.* 8.15.1: πίστις, "position of trust." Bachmann here finds an ironical reaction to a remark in the Corinthians' letter. But the analogy in v 40 points in a different direction.

12 That is, in the context: unmarried. Lietzmann observes that if οὕτως is understood in the sense of "as one is" (vv 20, 24), then we have a smoother transition to v 27 but a foreign idea: Paul designates only the unmarried state as a positive good; the emphasis lies on v 27b. These reflections are too subtle.

13 And an established motif of apocalyptic expectation. *4 Ezra* 5.1–13; 6.18–24; 9.1–12; *Jub.* 23.11–31; etc. The same is true of θλῖψις, "trouble": cf. Mk 13:19 with Lk 21:23; Zeph 1:15. For marriage in apocalyptic see *S. Bar.* 10.13.

14 "Present": Xenoph., *Hell.* (=*Hist. Graec.*) 2.1.6: τὰ ἐνεστηκότα πράγματα, "the existing situation" (Loeb 1:91). *3 Macc.* 1.16: βοηθεῖν τοῖς ἐνεστῶσιν,

"to aid them in that which had come upon them" (Charles, *APOT* 2:164); recension q: τῇ ἐνεστώσῃ ἀνάγκῃ, "in the distress which had come upon them." "Immediately impending": *1 Macc.* 8:24; 12:44; for 8:24 cf. Jos., *Ant.* 12.418; *3 Macc.* 3.24. Even if in some passages in Paul the meaning "present" is certain (3:22; Rom 8:38; Gal 1:4), yet each particular instance must be interpreted according to the context, and the note of "imminence" must be borne in mind; 2 Thess 2:2. "Impending" (if ἐνεστώσης is the correct reading): *P. Lond.* 904.20.

15 This can be adduced as an argument for the fact that παρθένοι is used in the wider sense of ἄγαμοι, "unmarried."

16 According to Weiss, λύσις does not mean separation, but liberation from an obligation, from the spiritual betrothal. Paul has *two* persons in view and *specific* virgins, cf. v 28: ἡ παρθένος, "virgin"; Xenoph. *Cyrop.* 1.1.4: λελύσθαι ἀπ᾽ ἀλλήλων, "independent of one another" (Loeb 1:7). Teles (ed. Hense, 10f): γέρων γέγονας· μὴ ζήτει τὰ τοῦ νέου. ἀσθενὴς πάλιν· μὴ ζήτει τὰ τοῦ ἰσχυροῦ. . . . ἄπορος πάλιν γέγονας· μὴ ζήτει τὴν τοῦ εὐπόρου δίαιταν, "You have grown old: seek not the things of a youth. You have become weak: seek not the things of a strong man . . . You have become poor: seek not a rich man's way of life."

17 τοῦτο δέ φημι, "what I mean is," cf. 15:50.

18 "Outward" here in the sense of σάρξ, "flesh"; for the dative see Blass–Debrunner §190(3); 2 Cor 12:7.

19 Here the eschatological sense is made perfectly clear by the future tense and the added statement in v 29a.

the classical rules.[20] The article before παρθένος, "virgin," is generic.[21]

■ **29–31** These verses bring a broad eschatological interpretation of conduct in the world, in which the sequence of thought is plain. Paul sets out from the eschatological picture he has already indicated in vv 26 and 28: in v 29a and again to round off the passage at the close of v 31. Within this bracket, eschatology is an immediate exposition of existence. The picture is that the time (*scil.* of the world) is short.[22] The understanding of the content depends on ὡς μή, "as though . . . not."[23] This appears at first sight to be the passage most strongly subject to Stoic influence in all the Pauline epistles, and to commend the ideal of that ataraxy which is secured by dissociating oneself inwardly from one's outward

fate.[24] Even the eschatological grounding is not in itself an objection to this interpretation. Paul could simply have changed the world picture, and yet have taken over in his attitude toward the world the aloofness of the Stoics. The non-Stoic character of the relationship to the world emerges only in the wider context. Paul's advice is not to withdraw into the safe and unrestricted realms of the inner life, but to maintain freedom in the midst of involvement.[25] Eschatology really determines the conduct of life, whereas in the Stoa metaphysics is merely an expression of the attitude to the world.[26] The reference in v 29 to the approaching end of the world is taken up again by way of conclusion: παράγει κτλ., "is

---

20 Bauer, *s.v.* γαμέω; Blass–Debrunner §101 *s.v.* (on the Attic γήμη alongside the Hellenistic γαμήσης).

21 See above, n. 16 (Weiss). Contrary to Weiss, we must take the article generically (Robertson and Plummer). Lietzmann, too, finds that Paul is here speaking of virgins in general, not of the spiritually betrothed.

22 It is sufficient to interpret this, in the light of v 31, as meaning that there is now little time left. It is not necessary to think of the special motif of the sufferings being shortened by God for the sake of the righteous sufferers (Mk 13:20). Paul does not mean this statement to give apocalyptic comfort.

23 The use of the accusative with χρᾶσθαι, "utilize," which is so unusual in this period (Blass–Debrunner §152[4]) is apparently due to καταχρᾶσθαι (Lietzmann). For καταχρᾶσθαι, "use, make use of," see Bauer, *s.v.* For the content cf. Epict., *Diss.* 2.16.8: τὰ ἴδια τηρεῖν, τῶν ἀλλοτρίων μὴ ἀντιποιεῖσθαι, ἀλλὰ διδομένοις μὲν χρῆσθαι, μὴ διδόμενα δὲ μὴ ποθεῖν, "To guard what is his own, not to lay claim to what is not his own, but to make use of what is given him, and not to yearn for what has not been given" (Loeb 1:329).

24 Epict., *Diss.* 3.22.67–76; 4.7.5: ἐν μηδενὶ ποιεῖσθαι τὸ ἔχειν ταῦτα ἢ μὴ ἔχειν, "He cares not one whit about having, or not having, these things" (Loeb 2:361). Simpl., *Comm. in Epict. Ench.* 5 (ed. Dübner, 29, lines 29f): τὸ τοῖς μὴ ἐφ' ἡμῖν ὡς ἐφ' ἡμῖν οὖσι κεχρῆσθαι, "to use that which is not in our power as if it were in our power" (Bauer, *s.v.* χράομαι 1b).

25 Typical is the transformation in *Act. Paul. et Thecl.* 5: μακάριοι οἱ ἔχοντες γυναῖκας ὡς μὴ ἔχοντες, ὅτι αὐτοὶ κληρονομήσουσιν τὸν θεόν, "Blessed are they who have wives as if . . . they had them not, for they shall inherit God" (Hennecke–Schneemelcher–Wilson 2:354). Herbert Braun, "Die Indifferenz ge-

genüber der Welt bei Paulus und bei Epiktet," in his *Gesammelte Studien,* 159–167, observes: In both cases our outward life is held to be void of security, but for Epictetus obedience is possible for man, whereas Paul considers it possible only in the knowledge of one's own disobedience.

26 Wolfgang Schrage, "Die Stellung zur Welt bei Paulus, Epiktet und in der Apokalyptik" *ZThK* 61 (1964): 125–154 (in debate with Nils A. Dahl, "Christ, Creation and the Church," in *The Background of the New Testament and Its Eschatology: Studies in Honour of C. H. Dodd,* ed. W. D. Davies and David Daube [Cambridge: University Press, 1956], 422–443) denies the influence of Stoicism and asserts that of apocalyptic, cf. *6 Esdr.* 16.40–45: . . . *sic non morabuntur mala ad prodeundum super terram, et saeculum gemet, et dolores circumtenebunt illud. Audite verbum, plebs mea, parate vos in pugnam et in malis sic estote quasi advenae terrae. Qui vendit, quasi qui fugiat, et qui emit, quasi qui perditurus. Qui mercatur, quasi qui fructum non capiat; et qui aedificat, quasi non habitaturus. Qui seminat, quasi qui non metet. Sic et qui vineam putat, quasi non vendemiaturus. Qui nubunt, sic quasi filios non facturi; et qui non nubunt, sic quasi vidui,* ". . . So shall the evil not tarry to come upon the earth. And the world will suffer misery and sorrows will encompass it. Hear the word, O ye my people! Prepare yourselves for the struggle, and in the evils behave yourselves as strangers on the earth. He that selleth, let him be as one in flight; he that buyeth as he who is about to lose; he that dealeth as he who has no more profit; he that builds as he who will not inhabit; he that soweth as he that will not reap; likewise he that prunes (his vines) as he that will not gather the harvest; they that marry as those who will not beget children; and they that marry not as those who are widowed" [Hennecke–Schneemelcher–Wilson

133

passing away, etc."[27] σχῆμα, "shape," here means not the form, but the essence, that is, the world itself.[28]

■ **32–33** Weiss would take v 32a closely with 31b and regards vv 32b–35 as the second part of the "insertion." He does this more because of the style (twice two antithetical stichs) than because of the content. Intrinsically speaking, the link provided by the catchword μεριμνᾶν, "to care," is definitive. Paul is speaking with pastoral concern in view of the approaching hardships; his aim is to bring his readers even now to freedom from care.[29] The mode of expression is here purely ascetic, to "please"[30] the Lord *or* the world, as the representative of which the marriage partner functions. It will of course be asked how far the phrasing is oversharpened *ad hoc*. For it stands under the heading of advice; the renunciation of the world is not regulated by law. On the other hand we catch a glimpse of an understanding of holiness according to which the latter is practiced in order to reach a higher stage in the relation to God.

■ **34** The beginning of v 34, καὶ μεμέρισται, "and he has a divided mind," has to be taken with v 33. That is to say, the married man has worldly cares and is thereby divided.[31] The ascetic tendency is plain. But here, too, it is not elevated into a principle.[32]

■ **35** Verse 35 maintains the standpoint of v 32.[33] Paul is taking over bourgeois moral concepts which denote not absolute, but conventional values.[34] They fit into the total picture of early Christian morality.[35] The thought of "undivided" devotion is recalled by the term ἀπερισπάστως, "undistracted."[36]

■ **36–38** Here a special case is discussed. But the nature of the case is a matter of dispute. Is παρθένος the man's

2:701; for the text, see *Libri Apocryphi Veteris Testamenti Graece*, ed. Otto F. Fritzsche (Leipzig: Brockhaus, 1871)]. The analogies are clear. But why should Stoic influence be excluded by this late text?

27 Cf. *4 Ezra* 4.26: *quoniam festinans festinat saeculum pertransire*, "because the age is hastening swiftly to its end" (Charles *APOT*, 2:566); Ps 143:4.

28 Philostr., *Vit. Ap.* 8.7: καὶ τί τὸ σχῆμα τοῦ κόσμου τούτου; "and what is the shape of this world?" *PGM* 4.1139: σχῆμα κόσμου, "shape of the world."

29 For care as a mode of fallenness, see Rudolf Bultmann, *TDNT* 4:589–593. The word is lacking in the Stoa, in Philo and Josephus; in its place we have φροντίζειν, "be concerned about."

30 "To please": 1 Thess 2:15; 4:1; Rom 8:8; 2 Cor 5:9.

31 If we translate (with the Zwingli Bible [and AV, RV, NEB footnote]): "And there is a difference between the wife and the virgin," then this gives no reasonable sense. It must be presumed with Lietzmann that the reading of p[15] B sa b g is the original text. "This was found offensive both because καὶ μεμέρισται ['and is divided'] disturbs the parallel construction and because of ἄγαμος ['unmarried'] with γυνή ['woman/wife']." This is corrected in various ways—e.g., by transposing ἄγαμος and repunctuating (D[gr] G etc.). A mixed text is given by p[46] ℵ A bo. The ἄγαμος can be a widow or a divorcee.

32 σῶμα, "body," and πνεῦμα, "spirit," are not dualistic concepts. They designate together the whole man.

33 For τὸ σύμφορον ("benefit, advantage"; the plural τὰ σύμφορα and the present participle neuter plural τὰ συμφέροντα are more frequent, Bauer, *s.vv.* σύμφορος and συμφέρω) cf. 6:12. Lietzmann asks whether this strong asseveration is the reaction to an accusation. He also observes that the harsh form of v 35b (in Greek) arises from assimilation to 35a: πρὸς τὸ ὑμῶν αὐτῶν σύμφορον. The meaning is βρόχος: "lasso." What is the *tertium comparationis*, deprivation of freedom, or causing to fall? περιβάλλειν, "cast around": Philo, *Vit. Mos.*, 2.252; Jos., *Bell.* 7.250.

34 τὸ εὔσχημον, "propriety": Epict., *Diss.* 4.1.163; memorial inscriptions. εὐπάρεδρος, "devotion." The word is not found before Paul. Eur., *Med.* 843: τῇ σοφίᾳ πάρεδροι, "(loves) that are associates of wisdom"; Jos., *Bell.* 1.78, παρεδρεύειν, "constantly attend," of disciples.

35 1 Thess 4:12; Rom 13:13; Phil 4:8; 1 Cor 14:40.

36 Wis 16:11; Sir 41:2; Lk 10:38ff; Epict., *Diss.* 3.2.69: in view of the present situation the following rule holds: μὴ ποτ' ἀπερίσπαστον εἶναι δεῖ τὸν Κυνικόν, ὅλον πρὸς τῇ διακονίᾳ τοῦ θεοῦ, ἐπιφοιτᾶν ἀνθρώποις δυνάμενον, οὐ προσδεδεμένον καθήκουσιν ἰδιωτικοῖς οὐδ' ἐμπεπλεγμένον σχέσεσιν, ἃς παραβαίνων οὐκέτι σώσει τὸ τοῦ καλοῦ καὶ ἀγαθοῦ πρόσωπον, τηρῶν δ' ἀπολεῖ τὸν ἄγγελον καὶ κατάσκοπον καὶ κήρυκα τῶν θεῶν, "It is a question, perhaps, if the Cynic ought to be free from distraction, wholly devoted to the service of God, free to go about among men, not tied down by the private duties of men, nor involved in relationships which

daughter or his fiancée?[37] The traditional exposition adopts the interpretation father and daughter.[38] It takes its cue from v 38 ($\gamma\alpha\mu\acute{\iota}\zeta\epsilon\iota\nu$, "give in marriage"). In that case the meaning is that if anyone thinks he is behaving improperly[39] toward his daughter[40], if *she* is beyond maturity,[41] then he is free in his decision. $\dot{\epsilon}\xi o\upsilon\sigma\acute{\iota}\alpha$, "command," is in this case the *patria potestas*. The father, of course, has according to ancient law the power of free disposal.[42] To be sure, with this interpretation there are linguistic difficulties. $\theta\acute{\epsilon}\lambda\eta\mu\alpha$, "will," is used elsewhere by Paul only of God's will. In profane writings the

word is often used of the sexual desire of the man. This leads to the interpretation (with Kümmel) that he is free to follow his own urge. The expression $\kappa\acute{\epsilon}\kappa\rho\iota\kappa\epsilon\nu$ $\kappa\tau\lambda.$, "has resolved, etc.," is in keeping with this. In that case, what is meant is not the father, but the fiancé[43] and it is a question of real betrothals.[44]

The linguistic difficulties disappear if we adopt the interpretation of spiritual betrothals, and thus find here the earliest evidence for the phenomenon of the $\sigma\upsilon\nu\epsilon\acute{\iota}\sigma\alpha\kappa\tau\alpha$ or *subintroducta*.[45] Then there is no change of subject; the subject of $\mathring{\mathring{\eta}}$, "is [more than mature]," is the

---

he cannot violate and still maintain his role as a good and excellent man, whereas, on the other hand, if he observes them, he will destroy the messenger, the scout, the herald of the gods, that he is" (Loeb 2:155).

37 In the latter case, $\gamma\alpha\mu\acute{\iota}\zeta\epsilon\iota\nu$ in v 38 would have the meaning of $\gamma\alpha\mu\epsilon\hat{\iota}\nu$, "marry," which is possible, see below. Overview: Werner Georg Kümmel, "Verlobung und Heirat bei Paulus (I. Cor 7,36–38)," in *Neutestamentliche Studien für Rudolf Bultmann*, BZNW, 21 (Berlin: Töpelmann, 1957), 275–295, now in his *Heilsgeschehen und Geschichte. Gesammelte Aufsätze 1933–1964* (Marburg: Elwert, 1965), 310–327.

38 Theodore of Mopsuestia in Staab, *Pauluskommentare*, 183. Chrysostom, Theodoret, Augustine, Ambrosiaster; Schmiedel, Heinrici, Robertson and Plummer, Allo.

39 $\dot{\alpha}\sigma\chi\eta\mu o\nu\epsilon\hat{\iota}\nu$, "behave improperly," denotes immoral behavior and is less suitable for the relationship of father and daughter.

40 $\pi\alpha\rho\theta\acute{\epsilon}\nu o\varsigma$ = daughter: Soph., *Oed. Tyr.* 1463, etc. Beloved: see Kümmel, "Verlobung und Heirat," 291, n. 60; *Heilsgeschehen und Geschichte*, 323, n. 60. The difficulty is, however, that the meaning "daughter" does not lie in the word itself, but in the context. In chap. 7 nothing so far has pointed in this direction.

41 The subject of $\mathring{\mathring{\eta}}$, "is," must in this case be the daughter. $\dot{\upsilon}\pi\acute{\epsilon}\rho\alpha\kappa\mu o\varsigma$ = "beyond maturity." With this interpretation, this clause has to show the cause of the $\dot{\alpha}\sigma\chi\eta\mu o\nu\epsilon\hat{\iota}\nu$, "improper behavior." The difficulty is that there is nothing to indicate a change of subject. And what is then the meaning of $\kappa\alpha\grave{\iota}$ $o\ddot{\upsilon}\tau\omega\varsigma$ $\dot{o}\phi\epsilon\acute{\iota}\lambda\epsilon\iota$ $\gamma\acute{\iota}\nu\epsilon\sigma\theta\alpha\iota$, "and it has to be so"?

42 On the legal situation see above, p. 115, n. 8 and the literature cited there. Jérome Carcopino, *Daily Life in Ancient Rome*, ed. Henry T. Rowell, tr. E. O. Lorimer (New Haven: Yale University Press, 1940, 1959), 95–100 (*La vie quotidienne à Rome à l'apogée de l'empire* [Paris: Hachette, 1939], 118–124). The marriage is legally valid "through the $\dot{\epsilon}\gamma\gamma\acute{\upsilon}\eta[\sigma\iota\varsigma]$,

i.e., the binding pledge on the part of the bride's father [or whoever is the bride's $\kappa\acute{\upsilon}\rho\iota o\varsigma$, 'lord'] to the bridegroom and the latter's acceptance" (Gerhard Delling, "Eheschliessung," *RAC* 4:724).

43 Just so the lover says in Achill. Tat., *Clit. et Leuc.* 8.18.2: $\pi\alpha\rho\theta\acute{\epsilon}\nu o\nu$ $\gamma\grave{\alpha}\rho$ $\tau\grave{\eta}\nu$ $\kappa\acute{o}\rho\eta\nu$ $\mu\acute{\epsilon}\chi\rho\iota$ $\tau o\acute{\upsilon}\tau o\upsilon$ $\tau\epsilon\tau\acute{\eta}\rho\eta\kappa\alpha$, "Up to this very moment I have kept the girl a virgin" (cf. Loeb 451).

44 Against the interpretation in terms of betrothal it is objected that betrothal is a Jewish (Str.–B. 2:393–398) and Roman custom, but not a Greek one. It is true that the $\dot{\epsilon}\gamma\gamma\acute{\upsilon}\eta\sigma\iota\varsigma$ is not the betrothal, but the marriage contract; Hesych., *s.v.* $\dot{\epsilon}\gamma\gamma\acute{\upsilon}\alpha$: $\gamma\acute{\alpha}\mu o\upsilon$ $\dot{\alpha}\pi o\gamma\rho\alpha\phi\acute{\eta}$, "certificate or pledge of marriage"; Preisigke, *Wört, s.v.* $\dot{\epsilon}\gamma\gamma\acute{\upsilon}\eta\sigma\iota\varsigma$. It can take place immediately before the marriage, but also earlier: Demosthenes' father, before his death, $\dot{\epsilon}\gamma\gamma\upsilon\hat{\alpha}$, "pledges," his wife to Aphobos and his daughter, who will be marriageable only in ten years' time, to Demophon (Demosth., *Or.* 28.15f; 29.43f). Nor does the word $\nu\acute{\upsilon}\mu\phi\eta$ prove the custom of betrothal, for the $\nu\acute{\upsilon}\mu\phi\eta$ is primarily the maiden who is preparing for marriage. Nevertheless, there can be no doubt of the custom of promising and being promised. Antigone is the $\mu\epsilon\lambda\lambda\acute{o}\nu\upsilon\mu\phi o\varsigma$, "future bride" (cf. $\mu\epsilon\lambda\lambda\acute{o}\gamma\alpha\mu o\varsigma$, "future wife," codd. 628) of Haimon, Soph., *Ant.* 633; cf. also $\dot{\alpha}\rho\mu\acute{o}\zeta\omega$, "betroth," in Hdt., *Hist.* 5.47; 9.108. Examples from later period: Werner Peek, *Griechische Versinschriften*, vol. 1 (Berlin: Akademie–Verlag, 1955), nos. 658, 683, 1989, the same as his *Griechische Grabgedichte*, Schriften und Quellen der alten Welt, 7 (Berlin: Akademie–Verlag, 1960), nos. 276, 279, 460. Moreover, in the Roman colony of Corinth we can reckon with Roman influence, and in the case of Paul the Jew and the mixed congregation of Jewish and Gentile Christians we can reckon with Jewish influence. Josephus presupposes for $\kappa\alpha\tau\epsilon\gamma\gamma\upsilon\hat{\alpha}\nu$ the meaning, "to betroth."

45 See the report in Kümmel. The certain evidence is late, the early evidence uncertain. Herm., *Sim.* 9.10.6f is no proof of spiritual betrothals, but only of

spiritual bridegroom.[46] Difficulties are caused, however, by γαμίζειν, "to give in marriage" in v 38; but they are not insurmountable.[47] This interpretation is therefore linguistically possible, but it must be rejected on inherent grounds.[48] When applied to real betrothals, everything is explained without difficulty as far as the content is concerned.[49] γαμίζειν is then the equivalent of γαμεῖν, "to marry."

■ **39–40** This passage concerns widows. In the foreground stands the principle (formulated in Jewish terms) which agrees with v 10.[50] For the personal closing remark cf. v 25. Is it a subtle thrust at the pneumatics in Corinth? An adequate explanation is to assume that Paul is appealing to the idea of office (v 25) and Spirit. It is not necessary to adopt the special assumption (derived from 2 Corinthians) that his possession of the Spirit had been denied in Corinth already at the time of the composition of 1 Corinthians.

high regard for nonsexual intercourse between Christians of different sexes. The interpretation of *Did.* 11.11 as applying to spiritual marriages on the part of prophets (Rudolf Knopf, *Die Lehre der Zwölf Apostel; Die zwei Clemensbriefe*, HNT, Ergänzungsband 1 [Tübingen: J. C. B. Mohr (Paul Siebeck), 1920], *ad loc.*) is entirely uncertain.

46 Kümmel, "Verlobung und Heirat," 287; *Heilsgeschehen und Geschichte*, 320, observes: "In v 36, τίς ['anyone'] remains the subject as far as γαμείτωσαν ['let them marry'], where the παρθένος ['virgin'] can easily be associated in our minds with the plural. And we can assume without more ado that in all this the παρθένος is assumed to be in agreement with the decision of the male partner as he gives in to his urges or withstands them." On καὶ οὕτως ὀφείλει γίνεσθαι, "and it has to be so," see Henry Chadwick, " 'All Things to All Men' (I Cor. ix.22)," *NTS* 1 (1954–55): 261–275, here esp. 267, where it is argued that the expression points rather to pressure from without, by social custom, and accordingly does not suit spiritual betrothals.

47 See Lietzmann. The grammarian Apollonius Dyscolus (second century A.D.) distinguished the causative γαμίζειν, "give in marriage," from γαμεῖν, "marry": Apollon. Dyscol., *Constr.* 3.153 (ed. Gustav Uhlig, Grammatici Graeci, 2, 2 [Leipzig: Teubner, 1890], 400). But the rule is not kept, see Moulton and Milligan, *s.v.* γαμίζω.

48 Against the interpretation in terms of *subintroductae*, see Albrecht Oepke, "Irrwege in der neueren Paulusforschung," *ThLZ* 77 (1952): 449–458; Juan Leal, "Super virgine sua (I Cor 7.37)," *VD* 35 (1957): 97–102.

49 In καὶ οὕτως κτλ., "and it has to be so," Weiss sees a euphemism. Kümmel says Paul, as a Jew, is drawing attention to the fact that there is an *obligation* on the betrothed parties to contract marriage when the situation demands it.

50 It is therefore not necessary to psychologize (thus Weiss: women living under acute pressure in mixed marriages). Rather, Paul is paving the way for the announcement that a widow may marry again. κοιμᾶσθαι, "sleep," is a familiar euphemism for "die."

The new theme[1] prevails up to 11:1. The second half of chap. 11, too, is still linked with this section, through the observations on the Lord's Supper; cf. 10:14ff with 11:23ff. Despite the unified topic announced by Paul, considerable breaks and tensions are found within this section which provoke operations of literary criticism.[2] This will be clear even from an overview of the train of thought: chap. 8: on εἰδωλόθυτα, "meat sacrificed to idols"; chap. 9: on the ἐξουσία, "rights," of the Apostle (whereby differing opinions can be entertained as to the inherent connection with 9:24–27; see below); chap. 10:1–22: Scripture proof and sacrament as arguments against εἰδωλολατρία, "idol worship." Then 10:23—11:1 links up again with the topic of chap. 8. Chap. 9 creates the impression of an interruption. But chaps. 8 and 10, too, present a double face. Two questions seem to be interwoven: the question of εἰδωλόθυτα, that is, of the (unholy) substance of the meat, and the question of εἰδωλολατρία, of the eating as an act of establishing fellowship with the idol.[3] Paul's argument appears to vacillate.[4] In chaps. 8 and 10:23—11:1 he adopts in principle the standpoint of the "strong": sacrificial meat is not dangerous and can accordingly be eaten. The restriction on freedom is imposed not by the meat, but by the conscience, by the bond with the "weak" brother. The *strong* are *admonished*. In 10:1–22, on the other hand, Paul appears to vote in favor of the weak. Eating is dangerous. *All* are *warned*. In the former passages Paul argues with the idea of freedom, which has its place in the community and is thereby binding in the community; in the second passage he operates with

the idea of the sacrament, which institutes a fellowship that is exclusive. In the latter case, raising the question of conscience is not necessary at all.[5]

Now both forms of argumentation are Pauline in content. The question is, however, whether Paul can argue both ways in the same breath. A further point is the harshness of the transitions from 8 to 9:1, from 9 to 10:1, from 10:22 to 10:23. Verse 23 can be joined either to chap. 8 or to 9:27.

All the same, the very fact that there are such manifold possibilities of establishing connections is a warning against making schematic divisions.

A substantial point in *favor* of the literary unity is the parallel with Rom 14:1—15:13.[6] This passage in Romans was composed of course not long after the epistles to the Corinthians and obviously represents a revision and further development of 1 Cor 8—10. What was formulated in 1 Corinthians in the course of a topical discussion is here (in the epistle to the Roman church with which he was not personally acquainted) couched in more general terms.

Apart from questions of literary criticism the following can be said.

1) The practice adopted in Corinth is not accidental, e.g., a result of indifference, but programmatic; it is the result of enthusiasm; it is the practical application

---

1   For περί, "concerning," cf. 7:1, 25; 12:1.

2   Weiss, Schmithals; for the discussion see von Soden, "Sakrament und Ethik."

3   Schmithals, *Gnosticism in Corinth*, 92f [86f], would assign the two topics to two letters: letter A, to which 10:1–22 or 14–22 belongs, deals with εἰδωλολατρία (together with sexual immorality, 6:12–20), lack of discipline at the Lord's Supper (11:2–34), resurrection (15); letter B deals with εἰδωλόθυτα.

4   Weiss, 212f; von Soden, "Sakrament und Ethik," 17f.

5   According to Schmithals, *Gnosticism in Corinth*, 227 [215], the verdict of letter A (the "sacramental" verdict) was anti-Gnostic. The community had accepted it. But this raised the new problem as to whether it is permissible to eat meat sacrificed to idols.

Weiss holds that the prevailing lukewarmness has

apparently been brought to Paul's attention by the weak. They demand a break with paganism; but they are given the answer, (*a*) that this is impossible (5:10), and (*b*) that knowledge makes eating possible (just as πορνεία, "sexual immorality," is permitted by the principle πάντα ἔξεστιν, "I am free to do anything").

Hurd, *Origin*, 65, argues that the section belongs to the calm passages in which Paul takes up statements from the Corinthians' letter, yet not in order to operate with them, but to argue against them. In his earlier letter he had made the categorical demand: no meat sacrificed to idols (pp. 216, 226)! The Corinthians had replied that they saw no wrong in eating it.

6   Von Soden, "Sakrament und Ethik," 21, divides the passage as follows: (1) exposition, 1 Cor 8 par. Rom

of "knowledge" and of the freedom derived therefrom.[7]

2) Paul, whether operating with the idea of freedom and conscience or with that of sacrament and church, argues in terms of his dialectical theology.

There are two problems in regard to the content. One concerns the nature of the group of the "weak": Is their position, too, speculatively conditioned, e.g., by Jewish Christian influence, or are they simply weak?[8] Secondly, Paul says nothing of the "apostolic decree" (Acts 15:20f, 29; 21:25), which surely regulates the eating, or rather avoiding, of $\epsilon i\delta\omega\lambda\delta\theta\nu\tau a$, "meat sacrificed to idols." Why not? Because he is unaware of it, since it had not yet been issued at the time of 1 Corinthians? Or does he ignore it purposely? If so, why?[9]

There is no trace of a rejection or circumvention of the apostolic decree on Paul's part. Neither he himself nor the community in Corinth has any knowledge of it.[10] Once again we have to note the parallel in Romans. If the decree had been known, Paul could not there have passed over it in silence.

Paul opens his argument[11] in 8:1–6 with a piece of fundamental theological teaching on the function of love in the knowledge of God. He takes the "knowledge" to which the Corinthians appeal and probes its foundations. He does not find it sufficient to examine its content. The latter is in itself correct. Paul, however, declares that the relationship to God, or to idols as the case may be, is not a *consequence* of knowledge, but that this knowledge itself is already a relation. He asks what is the relationship to God in which I have already placed myself when I make him the object of my knowledge and then turn this knowledge into a principle of which I can make autonomous use. Thus Paul's inquiry is concerned not only with the knowledge of his opponents, but with their existence.

14; (2) Scripture proof and (3) resolution, 1 Cor 10 par. Rom 15.

7 Weiss thinks that to begin with it was simply a case of naive uninhibitedness. Later, he says, it was given a speculative ground. This is neither psychologically probable, nor does it accord with the tenor of Paul's argument. At all events, the discussion is now taking place at the speculative level. Schmithals, *Gnosticism in Corinth*, 226 [214], considers the Corinthians' attitude to be "typically Gnostic." It *may* be so; Just., *Dial.* 35.1 (Trypho); $\kappa a\dot i\ \mu\dot\eta\nu\ \pi o\lambda\lambda o\dot u\varsigma\ \tau\hat\omega\nu\ \tau\dot o\nu$ $'I\eta\sigma o\hat u\nu\ \lambda\epsilon\gamma\delta\nu\tau\omega\nu\ \delta\mu o\lambda o\gamma\epsilon\hat\iota\nu\ \kappa a\dot i\ \lambda\epsilon\gamma o\mu\dot\epsilon\nu\omega\nu\ X\rho\iota$ $\sigma\tau\iota a\nu\hat\omega\nu\ \pi\nu\nu\theta\dot a\nu o\mu a\iota\ \dot\epsilon\sigma\theta\dot\iota\epsilon\iota\nu\ \tau\dot a\ \epsilon i\delta\omega\lambda\delta\theta\nu\tau a\ \kappa a\dot i$ $\mu\eta\delta\dot\epsilon\nu\ \dot\epsilon\kappa\ \tau o\dot u\tau o\nu\ \beta\lambda\dot a\pi\tau\epsilon\sigma\theta a\iota\ \lambda\dot\epsilon\gamma\epsilon\iota\nu$, "Yet I learn that many of those who say they acknowledge Jesus and are called Christians eat the things offered to idols, and say they receive no harm by doing so" (Williams, 69). Justin asserts that we have here to do with Gnostics. Cf. further Iren., *Haer.* 1.6.3 (Valentinians); 1.24.5 (Basilides); 1.26.3 (Nicolaitans; Rev 2:6; cf. 2:15, 20, 24). Yet "gnosis" in the technical sense is not necessary in order to provide a ground for the Corinthians' attitude. The hints in 8:1–6 point in a different direction.

8 Dupont, *Gnosis*, 282–327, holds that the weak are Jewish Christians. Countered by Rudolf Bultmann, "Gnosis," *JThSt*, n.s. 3 (1952): 10–26, here esp. 20–22, pointing to 8:7.

9 According to Thomas Walter Manson, "The Corinthian Correspondence (I)," in his *Studies in the Gospels and Epistles*, ed. Matthew Black (Manchester: Manchester University Press, 1962), 190–209, here

esp. 200, the whole question was thrown up by the Cephas party. Paul says nothing of the Apostolic Decree, because to his mind it is not valid for purely Gentile–Christian communities. This is not convincing; if it had been brought into the debate, he could not have ignored it. Charles K. Barrett, "Things Sacrificed to Idols," *NTS* 11 (1964–65): 138–153, also reckons with a Petrine reaction against Paul. Paul's free approach brings him into contrast with the Cephas group; this calls his apostolic authority in question. And it brings him into undesirable propinquity to the Corinthian "Gnostics." In the light of this dual front, the topics of chap. 9 and the position of this chapter become intelligible.

At all events, it is mistaken to link the Petrine party with the Apostolic Decree. We do not know the origin of the latter. It was not known to any of the groups in Corinth.

10 It is ignored not only here, but already in the discussion of the problem of $\pi o\rho\nu\epsilon i a$.

11 Weiss divides as follows: (*a*) 1–3; (*b*) 4–6; (*c*) = (*a*), i.e., application of 1–3: 7–13. On the content see Kurt Niederwimmer, "Erkennen und Lieben: Gedanken zum Verhältnis von Gnosis und Agape im ersten Korintherbrief," *KuD* 11 (1965): 75–102.

8 The Criterion of Conduct:
Love and Knowledge

1 Now concerning meat sacrificed to idols,[1]
we are aware that we all have knowledge. Knowledge puffs up, but love
builds up. 2 / If anyone imagines that he
knows something,[2] then he does not
yet know in the proper sense. 3 / But if a
man loves God, then he is known by
God.[3] 4 / Well then, as far as eating meat
sacrificed to idols is concerned, we
are aware that no idol exists in the
world and that no god exists in the world
but one. 5 / For even if so—called gods
exist, be it in heaven or on earth, as (in
actual fact) many gods and many lords
do exist, 6 / yet for us there exists only
one God, the Father,[4] from whom all
things come, and toward whom we
move,[5] and one Lord, Jesus Christ,
through whom all things exist, and
through whom we live.

■ 1 εἰδωλόθυτον, "meat sacrificed to idols," is a Jewish term, constructed with a polemical edge against
the Greek ἱερόθυτον (10:28).[6]

For his answer Paul can rely upon the statement which
he had already quoted in 6:12 and whose validity he
had recognized: πάντα ἔξεστιν, "I am free to do any-

1 περί, "concerning," cannot be dependent on γνῶσις, "knowledge." This is clear (1) from the analogy with the other sections introduced by περί;
(2) from the word order; (3) from v 4; (4) from the
absolute use in v 7; (5) the matter is completely
clear when there is a quotation (see the commentary).
2 See next note.
3 Om. τι in v 2: p⁴⁶ Tert., Orig.; om. τὸν θεόν: p⁴⁶
Clem. Al.; om. ὑπ᾽ αὐτοῦ: p⁴⁶ Clem. Al., ℵ* 33. The
abbreviations produce a very pregnant text, though
admittedly one that is testified as a whole only by
p⁴⁶. Zuntz, *Text*, 31f, considers it to be the original,
but intermingles textual criticism, exegesis and psychology: only the abbreviated text, he holds, fits
logically into the train of thought; the other is the
result of an addition. This, however, does not explain the remarkable state of the textual tradition.
It is plain that the short text presupposes the (Alexandrian) development of the concept γνῶσις (and
ἀγάπη). The erasures in v 3 were facilitated by
v 2, whether τι originally stood there or not. In what
follows, too, there is a noticeable agreement between
p⁴⁶ and Clement (with a pervading tendency toward abbreviation).
4 ὁ πατήρ, "the Father," is in apposition. This har-
monizes with v 4 from the linguistic standpoint and

is in keeping with the content of the context. Lietzmann is apparently of a different mind, for in his
translation he takes ὁ πατήρ as predicate: ". . . yet
for us only the *one* God is Father." This destroys
the parallel between the statements on God and on
the Lord.
5 For the construction see Blass–Debrunner §297 (cf.
§469): not a semitizing, pleonastic use of the personal pronoun, but "the linking of a clause logically
parallel to a relative clause by means of καί . . .
αὐτοῦ," also unobjectionable in classical Greek; see
Kühner–Blass–Gerth 2:432f; cf. 2 Pet 2:3.
6 *4 Macc.* 5.2; Acts 15:29 (not v 20); 21:25; Rev 2:14,
20. The rabbinic equivalent is בְּשַׂר זִבְחֵי מֵתִים,
"flesh of an offering to the dead = to idols"; cf. *AZ*
2.3 (Akiba): "Flesh that is entering in unto an idol is
permitted, but what comes forth is forbidden, for
it is as *the sacrifices of the dead*" (Danby, 438f); Str.–B.
3:377. The passage has no bearing on the Corinthian
case. It is a matter of pure theory, since of course
the Jew is only allowed to partake of animals that
have been ritually slaughtered.

thing."[7] In 8:1, too, it is plain that he is directly taking up a Corinthian slogan and recognizing it in principle, by using the word οἴδαμεν, "we are aware," to include himself and his readers[8]—the slogan: πάντες γνῶσιν ἔχομεν, "we all have knowledge." Whether πάντες, "all," belongs to the quoted slogan or is an addition on Paul's part may be asked. In favor of the latter assumption is the fact that in Corinth there are of course "weak" people who do not have this knowledge. Paul would then be using the addition of "all" to make clear to the strong that they have to recognize the "weak" as being of equal standing; for indeed even *they* have not yet attained to insight in the proper sense. Yet on this assumption understanding the argument is difficult, especially the declaration: ἡ γνῶσις φυσιοῖ, "knowledge puffs up." Accordingly, πάντες will have to be reckoned as part of the Corinthian slogan. The strong can speak thus; they ignore the others. This is indicated also by v 7, where Paul qualifies their assertion: *I* tell you that *not* all have knowledge.[9]

That there is a specific slogan in the background emerges also from the actual content of the knowledge in question. It is not merely a formal capacity that can concern itself with manifold objects (knowledge of the laws of nature, for example, or of moral laws). It has a specific content: εἷς θεός, "[there is] one God," along with the conclusion: accordingly the gods are non-

existent. This provides the theoretical foundation for the practice of freedom.[10]

The specific understanding of the nature of the liberating gnosis is so far still an open question: it can be understood as enlightenment on the nature of the gods in the sense of popular philosophy, or as illumination of the pneumatic, or as a specifically Gnostic insight into the depths of the world and of being.[11] Here we must take account of the fact that these possibilities cannot always be strictly separated.

The Corinthians still employ their knowledge in a naive way, not yet at the Gnostic level of the knower's reflection on himself. They are aware of possessing pneumatic powers, but do not yet appear to have developed any Gnostic theory on the relation between the knower and the thing known in the process of knowing itself. In this respect Paul is ahead of them, and is to that extent "more Gnostic" than they. It is a striking thing that, although γνῶσις, "knowledge," is a χάρισμα, "gift," both for Paul and for the Corinthians, 8:1–6 is concerned with objective knowledge which, while it does have consequences for the knower, nevertheless does not for that reason alone bring about a change.[12] And indeed it is with the doctrinal teachings that Paul's criticism begins. First of all he sets over against the Corinthian position the sharp thesis purposely formulated in general terms: ἡ γνῶσις φυσιοῖ, "knowledge puffs

---

7   If 6:12 is assigned to letter A and 8:1ff to letter B, this makes no essential difference to the situation of the discussion. In that case, the remarks in the former passages were known in Corinth somewhat earlier. 10:23 contains the same principle; this latter passage belongs undisputedly to the same letter as 8:1.

8   The plural is better taken as communicative than as epistolary style. The suggestion that we read οἶδα μέν, "I know," is an emergency expedient.

  Weiss, 214, observes: "The repetition of the 'we' in the principle and the subordinate clause is tolerable—alternatively, οἴδαμεν ὅτι before the communicative ἔχομεν is not unduly overladen—only when the words πάντες ἔχομεν γνῶσιν (sic!) are a quotation."

9   We must, of course, take account of the possibility that Paul is here using his own words: I am setting out from the fact that we all have rudimentary knowledge of God. But in that case he cannot well object (v 7): οὐκ ἐν πᾶσιν ἡ γνῶσις, "This knowledge is not (present) in everyone." For *this* knowledge the weak also have. For the train of thought (on

the presupposition that Paul is quoting) see Jeremias, *Abba*, 273f.

10   But to say that γνῶσις is "the essence of the Corinthian proclamation or the central spiritual gift (Schmithals, *Gnosticism in Corinth*, 143f [135], is vastly exaggerated. The people who know are certainly pneumatics, and they claim that knowledge is characteristic of them. But γνῶσις does not in itself describe the whole of religious existence. Cf. n. 12 below.

11   On the topic of further education in the sense of gnosis proper, cf. *Ev. Phil.* 110: "He who has the knowledge (γνῶσις) of the truth is a free man, but the free man does not sin. . . . The knowledge of the truth lifts up the hearts, which means it makes them free. . . . But love buildeth up" (Wilson, 53). Here φυσιοῦν is interpreted positively as "to lift up the heart"; cf. Cl. Al., *Strom.* 7.104.5—105.4 (GCS 3:73, 29—74, 21).

12   Dupont consistently distinguishes in his book between the γνῶσις which everyone possesses and γνῶσις as a χάρισμα.

140

up." At the outset he takes no account at all of the fact that there is also such a thing as proper knowledge, but states his own verdict on what is pursued as such in Corinth. The sense of γνῶσις is clear from the contrast with ἀγάπη, "love." The Corinthian γνῶσις makes itself master of its object,[13] and therewith of our "brother." Love, on the other hand, means renouncing the exercise of spiritual violence. The commentary on ἀγάπη is supplied by chap. 13, that on οἰκοδομεῖ, "builds up," by chaps. 12 and 14 (cf. especially 10:23), where the antithesis emerges between freedom slogans (as understood by the Corinthians) and "upbuilding."[14] οἰκοδομεῖν in Paul does not refer primarily to the "edification" of the individual (secondarily used in this sense in 14:4), but to the building up of the community (see again 14:4).[15]

■ **2** The second verse explains the cutting remark about γνῶσις by distinguishing between knowledge in the proper sense and the improper. Knowledge is of no value

in itself. It is mistaken when it forms a conception of its "object"[16] and imagines it has thereby acquired the correct attitude towards this object.

οὔπω κτλ., "not yet, etc.": the allegedly perfect must still make further progress if they are to attain to a proper[17] attitude toward their "object." Their illusion of having reached the goal is destroyed, as in 4:8, but with new arguments.[18]

■ **3** The criterion is supplied by v 3: love for God.[19] We expect: "The man who loves God, knows him rightly." But the thought is deliberately given a different turn. Here Paul takes his stand upon a widespread religious motif, the correspondence between knowing and being known in the relation of man and God.[20] Paul differs here from Gnosticism[21] in that he is thinking not of a mutual

---

13 In fact, even if not in the mind of the "Gnostic," God becomes the means toward the emancipation of the individual; knowledge becomes self–edification at the expense of the others.

14 Weiss observes that οἰκοδομεῖν is presupposed as a recognized term, and asks: Did the Gnostics declare that the weak must be "built up"? (similarly Lietzmann on v 10).

15 Paul employs the figure of building and thing built, see on 3:10ff. Where he makes a terminological use of οἰκοδομεῖν and οἰκοδομή, the process of building is no longer in view; see Philipp Vielhauer, *Oikodome. Das Bild vom Bau im der christlichen Literatur vom Neuen Testament bis Clemens Alexandrinus* (Karlsruhe–Durlach: Tron, 1939); Otto Michel, *TDNT* 5:136–148.

16 Paul is not developing a general epistemological theory. He has *this* "object," God, in view from the start. τι, "something," has the pregnant meaning of something worthwhile (cf. 3:7; Gal 6:3). This, too, is already said with an eye to the specific content about to be indicated.

17 καθὼς δεῖ: "in the proper sense": cf. Rom 8:26. Xenoph., *Mem.* 4.6.4: the gods are to be worshiped ὡς δεῖ, sc. νομίμως, "as is proper, *sc.* lawfully."

18 The problem of the appropriateness of our knowledge of God is stated in manifold ways as one of the main themes of philosophy. The latter is at pains to distinguish between real and seeming knowledge (Epict., *Ench.* 13). Human ignorance is set over against divine wisdom (Plat., *Ap.* 23a; *Phaedr.* 278d). The possibility of knowledge must be epistemologically investigated. Here guidance is found in

such principles as: like by like (see on 2:6ff); knowledge of the master from his works; the definition of the possibilities of νοῦς, "mind," as distinct from sense–perception. Examples from Philo: *Cher.* 125–128; *Fug.* 164f; *Praem. poen.* 43–46. It is a general rule that all the reflections are pursued on objectifying lines. Literature: Weiss, 223, n. 3; Norden, *Agnostos Theos*, 347f; Dupont, *Gnosis*, 513–519; Jonas, *Gnosis*, 2.1:85f.

19 Not: for one's brother. How far the love of the brethren is neglected as a result of the Corinthians' individualism will be made plain later. To begin with, however, it is a question of the individual's immediate relationship with God.

20 The correspondence is not formally expounded here; but cf. the parallels in 13:12 and Gal 4:9. Incidentally, the formula can be turned into a harmless wordplay, Philo, *Cher.* 115: ἀλλὰ νῦν ὅτε ζῶμεν κρατούμεθα μᾶλλον ἢ ἄρχομεν καὶ γνωριζόμεθα μᾶλλον ἢ γνωρίζομεν, "Even now in this life, we are the ruled rather than the rulers, known rather than knowing" (Loeb 2:77).

21 Statements in this style are, of course, eminently suited to express the Gnostic (ontologically understood) correspondence between redeemer and redeemed. *Corp. Herm.* 10.15: οὐ γὰρ ἀγνοεῖ τὸν ἄνθρωπον ὁ θεός, ἀλλὰ καὶ πάνυ γνωρίζει καὶ θέλει γνωρίζεσθαι, "For God does not ignore man, but knows him fully, and wills to be known by him" (cf. Scott 1:197); see next note. *Ev. Thom.* 3 (a passage mutilated in *P. Oxy.* 654.16–19): "When you know yourselves, then shall you be known, and you

relationship of a mystical kind,[22] but of the concrete act of election. There is an established piece of Jewish tradition in the background.[23] ἔγνωσται, "he is known," contains the idea: he is recognized by God, i.e., elected by him.[24]

■ 4 Can more precise information about the Corinthians' question be deduced from v 4? Had they inquired not only about εἰδωλόθυτα in general, but more especially about the *eating* of sacrificial meat? At all events the basis of their argument is recognizable. They assert their freedom with the help of the content of their knowledge: οἴδαμεν κτλ., "we are aware, etc." Paul takes up their thesis just as in v 1, and discusses it in the same way.[25] The foundation of the Corinthians' argument is the basic statement of the confession of faith: εἷς θεός, "[there is] one God." This the Christians had taken over from Judaism as the self–evident presupposition of their faith.[26] The Corinthians argue after the fashion of Greek enlightenment philosophy, which seeks to

liberate man from fear through knowledge *de natura deorum*, "concerning the nature of the gods," or *de rerum natura*, "concerning the nature of things," as the case may be.[27] Hellenistic Judaism had already learned to use these arguments for polemical purposes against polytheism and image worship. For the Corinthians, εἷς θεός, "[there is] one God," is a speculative thesis, which we have up our sleeve and can make use of, and by which the problem of religion is solved: if there are no gods (or "idols"), then there is no εἰδωλόθυτον, "food sacrificed to idols," either, and there are no scruples about either of them.[28] In face of this Paul maintains that this pseudo–objectivizing fails to grasp the problem. It must be asked in what relation the (allegedly) knowing subject stands to its object. Faith consists not in the thesis that there are no gods, but in the confession of the true God—a confession whose result is not to deny the "so–called" gods, but to overthrow them.[29]

■ 5 This verse forms the introduction to Paul's criticism.

shall know that you are sons of the living Father" (Hennecke–Schneemelcher–Wilson 1:511; cf. 1:101 for *P. Oxy.* 654.16–19). *Ev. Ver.* 19.32: "They knew, they were known" (*The Gospel of Truth*, tr. Kendrick Grobel [New York and Nashville: Abingdon, 1960], 58; cf. Hennecke–Schneemelcher–Wilson 1:524). Literature: Norden, *Agnostos Theos*, 287f; Reitzenstein, *Mysterienreligionen*, 285–291; Rudolf Bultmann, *TDNT* 1:694, n. 18; Dupont, *Gnosis*, 51–88; André–Jean Festugière, *La révélation d'Hermès Trismégiste*, vol. 4 "Etudes Bibliques" (Paris: Gabalda, 1954), 56–59.

22   Bultmann, *TDNT* 1:710, n. 77, rightly asserts that *Corp. Herm.* 10.15 is not parallel in content.

23   As with knowledge, so also love is not a mystical relationship with God. One senses an echo of the Jewish phrase which Paul quoted in 2:9, see *ad loc.*

24   2 Tim 2:19: "The Lord knows those who are his" (Num 16:5).

25   Bachmann reads (as in v 1): οἶδα μέν, "I am aware." This is totally unsuitable here.

26   The formula εἷς θεός is widespread both in the Jewish and in the Gentile world. M. Aur. Ant., *Medit.*, 7.9: κόσμος τε γὰρ εἷς ἐξ ἁπάντων καὶ θεὸς εἷς δι' ἁπάντων καὶ οὐσία μία καὶ νόμος εἷς, "For there is both one Universe, made up of all things, and one God, immanent in all things, and one Substance and one Law" (Loeb, 169). Peterson, *Εἷς θεός*. The development in Judaism takes its start from the Shema (Deut 6:4). The latter originally does not yet contain the idea of theoretical monotheism. In Hellenistic Judaism the formula is then set in polemical

antithesis to polytheism and thus acquires a monotheistic sense. Cf. Aristobulus (in Eus., *Praep. ev.* 13.12.1f); Ps.–Orpheus (*ibid.* 13.12.5); Ps.–Sophocles (*ibid.* 13.13.40); Philo, *Op. mund.* 170–172; Jos., *Ant.* 3.91. For the development in Judaism see Günther Bornkamm, "Das Doppelgebot der Liebe," in *Neutestamentliche Studien für Rudolf Bultmann zu seinem siebzigsten Geburtstag*, BZNW, 21 (Berlin: Töpelmann, ²1957), 85–93, here esp. 87f, now in his *Geschichte und Glaube* 1:37–45, here esp. 39–42. For Paul cf. Rom 3:30; for the deutero–Paulines Eph 4:6; for the later period Herm., *Mand.* 1.1; Ign., *Mg.* 8.2; *Kg. Pt.* 2; Hennecke–Schneemelcher–Wilson, 2:99–101. Compare also the μόνος θεός formula.

27   Consider Epicureanism's passion for freedom; see Lucretius.

28   οὐδὲν εἴδωλον is subject. The rendering "that an εἴδωλον is a nonentity" (Luther) is "linguistically untenable" (Weiss). In the LXX εἴδωλον (literally "image") is used not only of images. The word serves also to translate designations of pagan gods, בַּעַל, אֱלִיל, אֵל (Baal, El, Elil), etc.; see Friedrich Büchsel, *TDNT* 2:377f. By this means the latter are declared to be unreal. And conversely, it is said of the images with polemic intent that they are dead, vain. For polemic against images, cf. Isa 44:6–20; 46:1–7; Wis 13–14; Bel; Let Jer; Jos., *Ant.* 10.50.

29   Von Soden, "Sakrament und Ethik," 8: "The important thing is not to have no fear of the gods, but to fear God." Page 3: "As objective knowledge, gnosis does in fact consist in knowing that there are

In the light of the exposition he has already given on the nature of knowledge, the seeming contradiction is resolved. In v 4 he acknowledged the rightness of the Corinthians' thesis that the gods do not exist; he merely stated it to be inadequate. Here, on the other hand, he qualifies his concession: there "are" "gods" and "lords."[30] This view is not so "enlightened" as that of the Corinthians, and it appears to make polemic against paganism more difficult.[31] The fact of the matter is that his view of the existential character of knowledge has here come into play: the Corinthians' knowledge is not sufficient even in the realm of objective statement. The formal knowledge of the fact that there is *one* God is not yet insight into the truth about the powers of the world. Paul indicates *his* criticism, not only of pagan be-

lief in the gods, but of the gods themselves, first of all by using the word λεγόμενοι, "so–called."[32] They may very well be existent in the sense of being "there" in the world and having a certain power—and Paul himself is convinced that they do exist. But they are not gods. The explanation is provided by Gal 4:8.[33]

The criticism now becomes sharper: they exist in heaven and on earth, i.e., in the cosmos, in the creation, and are therefore themselves creatures, if also perverted creatures.[34] The distinction between θεοί, "gods," and κύριοι, "lords," must not be taken too strictly.[35] Their conjunction is due simply to the Christian confession which is to be quoted immediately afterwards. All the same, the passage is important as evidence for the use of κύριος as a pagan predicate of God.[36]

no such things as gods in the world and that there is only one God (8:4). To this extent . . . there is no such thing as meat sacrificed to gods either, and consequently no problem in regard to our relationship to it. But with this all too simple objective statement we are not by any means at the end of the matter . . . The statement whose truth is conceded—that there are no such things as gods in the world and that there is only one God—undergoes a certain qualification, or rather a more precise definition (8:5f), when we consider not the objects but the subjects: it is valid for us Christians, those known by God, who have only the Father (so to speak, the name of the Jewish Christian God) as God and who (without the detriment to the unity of God) have only Jesus Christ as Lord; for others there are many gods and lords, who properly speaking are not rightly called such . . ., but who are in fact such inasmuch as they are such to these others (Paul is thinking of the demons, as is clear from 10:20)."

30 Thus he is not operating with Hellenistic Judaism's philosophy of religion. Nor does he here enter into the question of the veneration of images (unlike Luke in the "Areopagus speech," Acts 17:22–31). For Paul's demonology, which is an established part of his world picture, cf. 1 Cor 10:19ff. Images: 1 Cor 12:1–3.

31 For καὶ γὰρ εἴπερ, "for even if," see Bauer, *s.v.* εἰ VI.11; Blass–Debrunner §454(2) says that here, as in classical Greek, it means "however much." The reality of the assumption is presupposed. For the content cf. Cic., *Nat. deor.* 2.31: *atqui necesse est, cum sint dei, si modo sunt, ut profecto sunt, animantes esse,* "and yet from the fact of the gods' existence (assuming that they exist, as they certainly do) it necessarily follows that they are animate beings" (Loeb, 199); Ernst von Dobschütz, "Zum Corpus hellenisticum,"

ZNW 24 (1925): 43–51, here esp. 50.

32 Cf. Eph 2:11. *Corp. Herm.* 2.14: λεγόμενοι θεοί, "so–called gods," as opposed to μόνος ὁ θεός, "the only God."

33 Chrys., *Hom. in Epist. I ad Cor.* 20.2 (171d; MPG 61:163): ἔστιν μέν, ἀλλ᾽ οὐκ ἔχει τινὰ ἰσχύν· οὐδὲ θεοί εἰσιν, ἀλλὰ λίθοι καὶ δαίμονες, "Indeed there are [idols], but they have no power; neither are they gods, but stones and demons" (NPNF 1.12: 113).

34 "Heaven and earth" is a description of the cosmos commonly used by both Jews and Greeks; Ps.–Aristot., *Mund.* 2 (391b, line 9); Gen 1:1; Acts 17: 24.

35 Werner Foerster, *TDNT* 3:1090f, holds that in speaking of gods "in the world" Paul is thinking of the fact that rulers, too, are designated as "gods." But the worship of rulers is not in view here. Rather, Paul is designating the alleged gods as cosmic beings (and thus transient beings, cf. 2:6). Weiss would draw a distinction, to the effect that θεοί, "gods," are the Olympian gods, while κύριοι, "lords," are deified men.

36 Not so Foerster, *TDNT* 3:1090f. According to him, κύριος has only formal significance: that on which man is dependent. Foerster's statement that κύριος is a relational concept is correct. This means that the essential validity of Paul's observations is not bound to his world picture. Practically speaking, the gods and lords are the powers to which man is exposed and over against which he can assert his freedom as a believer.

■ **6** Here[37] the basis of the argument emerges, a formula of confession.[38] The basic situation is plain: the Jewish confession εἷς θεός, "[there is] one God," is developed further into the twofold statement: εἷς θεός—εἷς κύριος, "one God—one Lord." The parallel between the two is given by the fact that the revelation of the *one* God in the "Lord" Jesus is exclusive. On the other hand, there now emerges a *difference* between the first and second halves of the formula, when the concepts "God" and "Lord" are explained.

The concept "God" is explained in terms of *content*: as "the Father."[39] We have here a formula for pagans, to whom the nature of the "one" God has to be made known.[40] On the other hand, the meaning of κύριος, "Lord," is assumed to be known; it is accordingly not explained, but defined by naming the sole bearer of this rank.[41]

"Father" describes God not as the Father of Jesus Christ, but as the Creator. This is clear from the *two* explanatory relative clauses. These say implicitly that the creation is good.[42] They are deliberately constructed in parallel terms, thus giving expression to the correspondence between creation and redemption.[43] The formula makes use of a Hellenistic type of religious language which had been developed in Stoic pantheism.[44] The original, pantheistic sense of the phrase is clear: τὰ πάντα is the All.[45] The prepositions ἐκ, "from," and εἰς "toward," define God as its origin and goal, that is, its sum total.[46] Here of course it must be noticed that such formulas were taken up into Hellenistic Judaism and there understood in terms of Jewish faith in the Creator. This reinterpretation is presupposed when they are taken over by the Christians.[47]

The interpretation of κύριος, "Lord"—despite the formal parallelism—is deliberately set in contrast to that of the concept θεός, "God": (a) by choosing the preposition διά, "through"; (b) by using the same preposition twice.[48] Jesus, as the "Lord," is the Mediator of the

---

37 The close link with what precedes by means of ἀλλά, "yet," is loosened in p[46] and B.

38 The phrasing has not been chosen by Paul *ad hoc*. The content is not "Pauline"; and it reaches far beyond the context. This formula then became the basis for the working out of the developed creed: it serves as a formal framework into which the detailed, in itself independent, Christological exposition was inserted. This development is to be detected in the second article of the Old Roman/Apostles' Creed; Hans Lietzmann, "Symbolstudien," *ZNW* 22 (1923): 257–279, here esp. 272f.

39 According to Bachmann, "the Father" stands here "in the manner of a proper name." In that case, "God" would be explained in the same way as "Lord": by stating his name. But over against pagans the very thing which particularly matters where "God" is concerned is to explain the *content*. Weiss takes ὁ πατήρ, "the Father," as subject and εἷς θεός, "one God," as predicate. When he appeals in favor of this to the analogy with v 5, that is a misunderstanding. For in v 5 εἶναι, "exist," is not an auxiliary verb, and θεοί, "gods," is accordingly not the predicate.

40 For "Father" as a predicate of God, see 1:3.

41 For κύριος see 1:3. For the relation between θεός and κύριος see D. E. H. Whiteley, *The Theology of St. Paul* (Oxford: Blackwell; Philadelphia: Fortress, 1964), 104. For Paul's argument the difference between the Greek and oriental use of κύριος for gods is of no consequence. Foerster, *TDNT* 3:1047, rightly says that the Greek gods "are not here described

as the κύριοι of their spheres." But we find ourselves here in an age of syncretism. Corinth is the center of the cult of the "lady" Isis, and Paul is an oriental.

42 Rom 14:14, 20. The extensive correspondence between 1 Cor 8—10 and Rom 14f should be noticed also here. Cf. further 1 Tim 4:3f; Tit 1:15.

43 And the world is the place of redemption.

44 The pantheistic structure appears most clearly in the threefold formulas: Rom 11:36 (see Lietzmann *ad loc.*); M. Aur. Ant., *Medit.* 4.23 (of Nature): ἐκ σοῦ πάντα, ἐν σοὶ πάντα, εἰς σὲ πάντα, "All things come from thee, subsist in thee, go back to thee" (Loeb, 81). Series of prepositions: Philo, *Cher.* 125f (following Posidonius?). Sen., *Ep.* 65.8f. For the process of gnosticizing cf. *Corp. Herm.* 13.19. Literature: Willy Theiler, *Die Vorbereitung des Neuplatonismus*, Problemata: Forschungen zur klassischen Philologie, 1 (Berlin: Weidmann, 1930), 23–25; Norden, *Agnostos Theos*, 347f; Dupont, *Gnosis*, 330–335; Hildebracht Hommel, *Schöpfer und Erhalter* (Berlin: Lattner, 1956), 100ff.

45 Philo, *Spec. leg.* 1.208 and frequently.

46 Note 44 above (M. Aur. Ant.). An illustration of the monotheistic transformation is provided by Ps.–Aristot., *Mund.* 6 (397b, lines 14f), where the pantheistic starting point is still discernible in the context): ἐκ θεοῦ πάντα καὶ διὰ θεοῦ ἡμῖν συνέστηκεν, "all things are from God and are constituted for us by God" (Loeb, 385). Plut., *Quaest. Plat.* 1001c: ἡ δὲ ψυχὴ . . . οὐδ' ὑπ' αὐτοῦ ἀλλ' ἀπ' αὐτοῦ καὶ ἐξ αὐτοῦ γέγονεν, "But the soul . . . not only came to be by him but also from him and out of him"

creation. His preexistence is accordingly presupposed. The formula teaches the type of λόγος/εἰκών/σοφία Christology ("word/image/wisdom").[49]

If the revealer is the mediator of creation, then a foregone conclusion is that revelation is not exhausted in its historic manifestation, and indeed that it is prior to the creation.[50] The soteriological significance is not contained in a direct statement, but is expressed indirectly by the confessional style[51] and the hint that revelation is new creation.[52]

We have now to make a distinction between the sense of the formula and the use Paul makes of it. In itself it is eminently suited to the Corinthian Christology. For this very reason Paul can also use it as a common basis on which to develop his thought. By means of v 5 he has

ensured that it cannot be taken as a mere monotheistic theory. In the same sense he introduces the quotation: ἀλλ' ἡμῖν, "yet for us,"[53] shows that it is here a question of judging and adopting an attitude, but not at our own subjective discretion. The dative has the same sense as the datives in 1:23f. Here, too, Paul makes clear that it is not a question of metaphysical or ontological judgments, but of anthropological judgments which as such include the adopting of an attitude: the gods *become* gods by being believed in, and faith in the *one* God and the *one* Lord creates freedom no longer to recognize these powers.

[Trans.]. For εἰς αὐτόν cf. 15:28.

47 Cf. the reshaping of Stoic pantheism (Arat., *Phaenomena*) in Aristobulus, fr. 4 (Eus., *Praep. ev.* 13.11.3ff); the Areopagus speech, Acts 17:22–31.

48 With the genitive, against B. ὅν is a scholarly alteration: in the Stoa the accusative prevails (yet cf. Ael. Arist., *Or.* 8.51: πάντα γὰρ πανταχοῦ δι' σοῦ τε καὶ διὰ σέ ἡμῖν γίνεται, "For all things come to be for us everywhere through thee and for thy sake" [Trans.]; Ps.–Aristot., *Mund.* 6 [n. 46 above]). But Paul, and already the pre–Pauline formula, have the OT in mind: Heb 2:10. Incidentally, the preposition διά, "through," can be applied also in the NT to God: Rom 11:36; Col 1:16. On διά see: Adolph Schettler, *Die paulinische Formel "Durch Christus"* (Tübingen: J. C. B. Mohr [Paul Siebeck], 1907); Albrecht Oepke, *TDNT* 2:65–70 [64–69]; Wilhelm Thüsing, *Per Christum in Deum*, NtlAbh, n.s. 1 (Münster: Aschendorff, 1965), 165–237 (*ad loc.* 225–233). For the relation of Christ to God see 3:23.

49 Cf. Jn 1:1ff; Col 1:15ff. That the preexistence of Christology had been developed already before Paul is shown also by Phil 2:6ff—where, however, the κύριος title applies only to the dignity of the exalted Lord. The presuppositions in the history of religion are to be found partly in Jewish speculations on σοφία and the λόγος: Pr 8:22–31; Wis 7:22–30 (σοφία/εἰκών, "wisdom/image"); on Wis 18:15 see Alfred Adam, *Die Psalmen des Thomas und das Perlenlied als Zeugnisse vorchristlicher Gnosis*, BZNW, 24 (Berlin: Töpelmann, 1959), 31–33 (though indeed the religious–historical ascription of *Sapientia* to early Gnosticism is untenable); Bar 3:9—4:1; *Eth. En.* 42; Sir 24:3–34; Philo, *Leg. all.* 2.49f (αἴσθησις, "feeling, experience" [=σοφία]); cf. *Det. pos. ins.* 54; *Ebr.* 30f; *Fug.* 109; *Virt.* 62; *Tg. J. II* to Gen 1:1: God created and perfected the world בחכמת, "in Wis-

dom." Literature: Hans Windisch, "Die göttliche Weisheit der Juden und die paulinische Christologie," in *Neutestamentliche Studien: Georg Heinrici zu seinem 70. Geburtstag*, UNT, 6 (Leipzig: Hinrichs, 1914), 220–234; Rudolf Bultmann, "Der religionsgeschichtliche Hintergrund des Prologs zum Johannes–Evangelium," in ΕΥΧΑΡΙΣΤΗΡΙΟΝ. *Studien zur Religion und Literatur des Alten und Neuen Testaments, Hermann Gunkel zum 60. Geburtstag*, ed. Hans Schmidt, FRLANT, n.s. 19 (Göttingen: Vandenhoeck & Ruprecht, 1923) 2:3–26, here esp. 12f, now in his *Exegetica. Aufsätze zur Erforschung des Neuen Testaments*, ed. Erich Dinkler (Tübingen: J. C. B. Mohr [Paul Siebeck], 1967), 10–35, here esp. 19–21; F. W. Eltester, *Eikon im Neuen Testament*, BZNW, 23 (Berlin: Töpelmann, 1958), 130–166; Wilckens, *Weisheit und Torheit*, 197–205; Eduard Schweizer, "Zur Herkunft der Präexistenzvorstellung bei Paulus," *EvTh* 19 (1959): 65–70, now in his *Neotestamentica*, 105–109; Harald Hegermann, *Die Vorstellung vom Schöpfungsmittler im hellenistischen Judentum und Urchristentum*, TU, 82 (Berlin: Akademie–Verlag, 1961), 110–123, 133–137. See 10:4 (combination of wisdom motif and preexistence).

50 This sheds light on 1:18ff.

51 Note the first person plural. It is the "we" of confession; cf. Jn 1:14.

52 This idea is rightly found in the text by Heinrici.

53 ἀλλά, "yet," again illuminates the concessive significance of εἴπερ, "even if" (Bachmann).

8

The Criterion: Our Brother

7 But this knowledge is not (present) in everyone. On the contrary,[1] some, having till now been accustomed[2] to idols, eat (the meat) as meat sacrificed to idols, and because their conscience is weak, it is defiled. **8** / Food will not bring us into God's presence. We have neither a disadvantage if we do not eat, nor an advantage if we do eat.[3] **9** / But take care that this freedom of yours does not somehow become a hindrance to the weak! **10** / For if someone sees you,[4] who have knowledge, sitting (at table) in an idol's temple, will not his conscience, since of course he is weak, then be "encouraged" to eat meat sacrificed to idols? **11** / Then to be sure[5] the weak person is ruined by your knowledge, the brother for whose sake Christ died. **12** / But when you thus sin against your brothers and wound their weak consciences, you are sinning against Christ. **13** / Therefore, if food[6] causes an obstacle to my brother, then I will eat no meat to all eternity, so as not to cause an obstacle to my brother.

■ **7** Verse 7 looks back to v 1 and corrects the concession made there to the Corinthian thesis. The formal contradiction which thereby arises is not one of content: Paul still grants even now that his opponents have objective knowledge, but not that they have understanding in the proper sense.[7]

Once the thesis of the "strong" has been corrected, he can proceed to positive instruction. The argument for his qualification begins not by criticizing the content, but by pointing to the concrete common life, that is to say, the historic character of existence, which is disturbed by the theoretical principles of the strong: "some" still regard sacrificial meat as they once regarded it, not because it has a negative quality in itself, but because they

---

1   Weiss observes that δέ following a negative statement stands for ἀλλά, cf. 7:37.

2   συνηθείᾳ, "from being accustomed," dative of cause, cf. Rom 11:20. For the objective genitive with συνήθεια, cf. Ditt., *Syll.* 2:609 (n. 888, line 154): διὰ τὴν συνήθειαν τῆς τοιαύτης ἐνοχλήσεως, "through being accustomed to such annoyance." The variant reading συνειδήσει ("conscious of," literally "with conscience of") is an assimilation to what follows. It is not good linguistically: ἕως ἄρτι, "till now," does not fit in with it.

3   ℵ D G 𝔎 reverse the order. Their reading is preferred by Zuntz, *Text,* 161f, on the ground that the reading of p[46] B A* is poorly testified and intrinsically inferior. But the variant reading of ℵ D G 𝔎 can be explained as an assimilation to v 8a.

4   σέ, "you," is omitted by p[46] B G, see n. 37 below.

5   For γάρ cf. 9:10. It can also be taken in a logical

sense: "namely."

6   As compared with v 8 in the sense of βρῶμα, "food," is modified in the direction of "eating."

7   Bultmann, *Faith and Understanding* 1:75f [47]. Lietzmann minimizes the contradiction as amounting merely to a temperamental mode of expression. All the same, it must surely be asked what kind of knowledge is at issue between Paul and the Corinthians, if he can express himself both in the one way *and* in the other. According to Jeremias, *Abba,* 273f, Paul is correcting two Corinthian slogans: that of v 1 in 1b–3, that of v 4 in 7.

8   Or (see above, n. 2): "on grounds of conscience." On συνηθείᾳ, Chrysippus writes κατὰ τῆς συνηθείας, "according to habit," later περὶ τῆς συνηθείας, "on account of habit," meaning "the habitual outlook" (von Arnim, *SVF* 2:8); Max Pohlenz, *Die Stoa,* vol. 2 (Göttingen: Vandenhoeck & Ruprecht,

still classify it, e.g., avoid it, as such, from habit.[8]

Opportunities of eating sacrificial meat were frequent,[9] e.g., at club parties.[10] Friends were sent a piece of the sacrifice.[11] At public festivals sacrificial meat was distributed to the citizens and resident aliens.[12]

Paul does not here enter into the question of the holiness or unholiness of the substance at all, but discusses eating as a mode of conduct that possibly affects our brother—to be precise, his conscience.[13] Hence the decision in regard to sacrificial meat is not a subjective matter of personal discretion. The "weakness"[14] of some people's consciences creates a situation which neither the strong nor the weak can ignore. The latter is inevitably bound to the decision of his own conscience,[15] by its presence as such.[16] Notice that Paul gives no advice either to the strong or to the weak on the question of how the weak consciences could be strengthened.[17] He puts into practice here the insight of faith that each is called and able to believe in the position in which he finds himself.[18] Cf. the fact that for συνείδησις, "conscience," he says in Rom 14f πίστις, "faith."

The "weak" are neither Jewish Christians[19] nor any closed group at all. They do not represent a position. They are simply weak.[20]

■ **8** The neutrality of food in itself is laid down in a thesis

[3]1964), 17.

9   For the situation in the market, see the excursus on 10:25; Charles K. Barrett, "Things Sacrificed to Idols," *NTS* 11 (1964–65): 138–153, here esp. 144.

10 Franz Poland, *Geschichte des griechischen Vereinswesens* (Leipzig: Teubner, 1909), 248–270, shows that a sacrifice formed the center of every club party. A special case is that of memorial feasts for the dead, Paul Stengel, *Die griechischen Kultusaltertümer*, Handbuch der klassischen Altertumswissenschaft, 5, 3 (Munich: Beck, [3]1920), 144–147; Ludwig Friedländer, *Roman Life and Manners under the Early Empire*, tr. Leonard A. Magnus (London: Routledge; New York: Dutton, n.d.), 150–152 (*Darstellungen aus der Sittengeschichte Roms in der Zeit von August bis zum Ausgang der Antonine*, rev. Georg Wissowa, vol. 1 [Leipzig: Hirzel, [9]1919], 166–169).

11 Stengel, *Die griechischen Kultusaltertümer*, 106.

12 *Ibid.*, 115.

13 On the concept of conscience see 4:3ff.

14 Inner "weakness" is a topic of the Stoics. Sen., *Const.* 17.1: *tanta animorum imbecillitas est, ubi ratio discessit*, "such is the weakness of the mind when reason flees" (Loeb 1:97). Epict., *Diss.* 2.15.20.

15 Von Soden, "Sakrament und Ethik," 4, n. 1, observes: through his συνείδησις, "conscience," he knows that he is not what he would like to be; "in it he has one who shares the knowledge of his secret idolatry; and everything depends on what he thus is and does in his own self."

16 *Ibid.*: Conscience exercises its control not by reference to norms of moral obligation, but by reference to facts of actual existence.

The verdict of the weak conscience, and even of the erring conscience, is also valid. For in the Pauline view conscience does not present me with an ideal norm, but sees me as the man I am and confronts me with the situation; Bultmann, *Theology* 1:217–220 [217–221].

As far as the content is concerned, it is a matter of indifference whether Paul in using the word "weak" is taking over a slogan of the strong party in Corinth (Weiss) or whether συνείδησις, "conscience," is such a slogan (Dupont, *Gnosis*, 279f, observes that the latter term is not found in Paul prior to 1 Cor, and that it is missing in the parallel passage in Rom 14f).

17 There is no pedagogical passion. This is an example of the Christian humanity which allows our brother to stand as the man he is, not as the man he ought to be according to some ideal standard. This makes it possible for Paul to examine situations in their individual particularity and to define conduct likewise in terms of individual history as the exercise of the particular freedom of the moment, without relativizing the norm.

18 Adolf Schlatter, *Paulus der Bote Jesu* (Stuttgart: Calwer, [2]1956), 260, substitutes a modernizing, subjective interpretation: "The conscience is powerless when it is unable to prevent [!] behavior which it condemns as reprehensible or at least [!] dangerous." In Paul's sense the very opposite is the case: they prove themselves to be weak because they consider freedom dangerous; but they are right to follow the verdict of their conscience; cf. von Soden, "Sakrament und Ethik."

19 This is shown precisely by v 7, see Heinrici: ἕως ἄρτι, "till now," shows that they are not Jewish Christians. Against Dupont, *Gnosis*, 282–327.

20 They are not a "group," but "some." Weiss thinks the weak hold the same principles as the strong, but draw the opposite conclusions from them. Against this Bultmann, *TDNT* 1:705f, maintains that γνῶσις, "knowledge," has to do precisely with the practical application, and is thus lacking to the

formulated in fundamental terms.[21] Heinrici considers this sentence to be a thesis propounded by the Corinthians (noting the change of person). Paul, he says, grants the premises but draws different conclusions.[22] But we have here a positive declaration on Paul's part.[23] He repudiates the *direct* demonstration of freedom. No work, not even freedom practiced as a work, makes us acceptable before God. The neutrality of food does *not* mean neutrality of *conduct*.[24] The thought is conclusive in itself,[25] and is in conformity with v 13.[26] This makes a concrete exposition of freedom necessary in v 9.

■ **9** Conduct has its specific place in the common life of the brethren. This definition of freedom in historic terms distinguishes Paul both from Greek philosophical ethics and from Gnosticism. In the eating of sacrificial meat conscience is involved because the weak man can argue from the freedom of the strong to a general, nonhistoric freedom understood—or rather, misunderstood—as a matter of principle, and thereby falsify his own exist-

ence. It is in harmony with Paul's view of freedom that he does not proffer any general definition of a *concept* of freedom. His remarks have a definite aim; they are meant for the strong. This finds stylistic expression in the form of direct address.[27] The ἐξουσία, "freedom," of the strong is recognized and given concrete shape. The sense of "the weak" is plain from v 7: their *conscience* is weak. In πρόσκομμα, "offense," "hindrance,"[28] the figurative element is hardly felt any more.

■ **10** The use of a possible instance by way of illustration has also a specific aim and is naturally again meant for the strong. In harmony with v 8, Paul chooses the instance of eating, not of food.[29] There were not only ample opportunities to take part in meals in temples, but it was also a matter of family and social duty.[30] Paul avoids legalistic regulations. He does not forbid the visiting of temple restaurants,[31] which could be visits of a purely social kind.[32] Paul declares: your conduct does not affect *you*; your inner freedom to go to these places is no

weak. Further literature: Leendert Batelaan, *De sterken en zwakken en de kerk van Korinthe* (Wageningen: Zomer en Keuning, 1942); Max Rauer, *Die "Schwachen" in Korinth und Rom nach den Paulusbriefen*, Biblische Studien, 21, 2–3 (Freiburg: Herder, 1923).

21 παρατήσει, "bring into the presence of": *sc.* in court. The word means: (*a*) introduce; (*b*) as a technical legal term, bring before the judge, cf. 2 Cor 4:14; so Weiss understands it here; (*c*) bring near; so syᴾ; Bauer, *s.vv.* παρίστημι and παριστάνω 1e (following Richard Reitzenstein, "Religionsgeschichte und Eschatologie," *ZNW* 13 [1912]: 1–28, here esp. 19f). Lietzmann objects to the legal significance that then the verbs would have to be interchanged. He himself compares the mystical significance of συνιστάναι in Philostr., *Vit. Ap.* 1.12. The most suitable meaning in this passage is "bring near." The meaning as a technical term of sacrificial language is out of the question here.
22 Similarly Jeremias, *Abba*, 273f.
23 With Lietzmann.
24 For the neutrality of food is determined not by the fact of its being in itself, but by the fact of its being created, cf. 10:26. Hence the neutrality cannot be played off against the work of God.
25 Schmithals, *Gnosticism in Corinth*, 227, n. 151 [215, n. 1], denies that Paul now passes over to the topic "eating," and argues that he is merely choosing an extreme example for his topic "food." Against this, cf. von Soden, "Sakrament und Ethik," 6; Lietzmann.
26 In v 13 βρῶμα means "eating."

27 For βλέπετε, "take care," cf. 1:26; 10:18; as a catchword in a paraenesis (against false teachers) Mk 13:5 par.; Gal 5:15, etc. Epict., *Diss.* 2.11.22; 3.20.16. μή: Blass–Debrunner §364(3).
28 The word corresponds in content to מִכְשׁוֹל (a favorite in Qumran) which, to be sure, is usually rendered by σκάνδαλον in the LXX. Paul can use both terms promiscuously, cf. Rom 14:13. In the LXX it corresponds to מוֹקֵשׁ, Ex 23:33. Gustav Stählin, *TDNT* 6:745–758.
29 Cf. the direct address (σέ, "you," is omitted in p⁴⁶ B G). Lietzmann holds that the omission of σέ makes the example more theoretic. Weiss thinks the expression (σέ τὸν ἔχοντα γνῶσιν, αὐτοῦ ἀσθενοῦς ὄντος, οἰκοδομεῖσθαι, "you who have knowledge, since he is weak, be encouraged") is "repeated with ironical solemnity from the Corinthians' letter." But we are surely more likely to see here Pauline diatribe style (dialogue and illustration by means of examples).
30 Marriage (Poland, *Geschichte des griechischen Vereinswesens*, 274), concern for the dead (*ibid.*, 503–513); Kurt Latte, *Römische Religionsgeschichte*, Handbuch der Altertumswissenschaft, 5, 4 (Munich: Beck, 1960), 263.
31 Robertson and Plummer are wrong in saying that "this was per se idolatrous," and arguing that Paul is merely reserving censure. Against this, cf. Schlatter, 263.
32 We know of invitation cards to the table of the "lord" Sarapis; *P. Oxy.* 110: δειπνῆσαι εἰς κλείνην τοῦ κυρίου Σαράπιδος ἐν τῷ Σαραπείῳ, "to dine at the

problem. The problem is the demonstration you give
to your brother, not purposely, but in an objective sense
—in other words, the way in which he understands
your conduct.[33]

With grim irony Paul points to the possible perversion:
you encourage him—a technical term for the edification
of the church—to idol worship.[34] How and in what
sense the misled weakling practices idol worship emerges
from v 7: in his eyes the gods are still powers and by
his compliance he honors them as such.[35] The strong man
for his part has exercised his freedom in such a way, as
thereby to destroy the freedom of his brother.[36]

■ 11 $\gamma\acute{\alpha}\rho$[37] introduces the explanation of the ironical
question. The gnosis has a perverse effect because it is
employed "freely" by the isolated subject, instead of

bringing the free individual face to face with the God
from whom his freedom comes. Thus it brings about the
opposite of $o\grave{\iota}\kappa o\delta o\mu\acute{\eta}$, "upbuilding," namely, destruction.[38] In the previous section Paul defined the situation
by binding knowledge to love. Here it becomes plain
that by love he does not understand a subjective feeling.
Love is determined by the saving work of Christ. As a
result of this work the other is brought into my field
of vision as my brother.[39]

■ 12 And this, too, happens in such a way that my
brother represents to me the Lord himself: my conduct
toward my brother affects Christ himself.[40]

■ 13 Verse 13 draws the conclusion from what precedes

table of the lord Sarapis in the Serapeum." $\epsilon\grave{\iota}\delta\omega$-
$\lambda\epsilon\hat{\iota}ov$, "an idol's temple": cf. $\mu\nu\sigma\epsilon\hat{\iota}ov$, "a temple of
the Muses," $\Sigma\alpha\rho\alpha\pi\epsilon\hat{\iota}ov$, "serapeum, temple of
Sarapis," etc.; Blass–Debrunner §111(5); neverthe-
less Blass–Debrunner (cf. also §13) prefer the form
$\epsilon\grave{\iota}\delta\acute{\omega}\lambda\iotaov$, with ℵ A B etc. LXX: 1 Esd 2:7; Bel 10;
1 Macc. 1:47; 10:83.

33 Von Soden, "Sakrament und Ethik," 3–6. Weiss
understands the logic as follows: $o\grave{\upsilon}\chi\grave{\iota} \ldots o\grave{\iota}\kappa o\delta o\mu\eta$-
$\theta\acute{\eta}\sigma\epsilon\tau\alpha\iota$, "will not . . . be encouraged," is a protasis.
The conclusion Paul draws from it is given in the
following verse. But then we must read: $\kappa\alpha\grave{\iota} \, \grave{\alpha}\pi\acute{o}\lambda$-
$\lambda\upsilon\tau\alpha\iota$, "and he is ruined." $\gamma\acute{\alpha}\rho$, "for," crept in because the ironical sense of $o\grave{\iota}\kappa o\delta o\mu\eta\theta\acute{\eta}\sigma\epsilon\tau\alpha\iota$ was no
longer understood and $o\grave{\upsilon}\chi\grave{\iota} \, \kappa\tau\lambda.$ was taken as a
negative statement. Against Weiss: $\gamma\acute{\alpha}\rho$ is entirely
appropriate; see n. 37 below.
34 It is not necessary to assume a Corinthian slogan as
the basis (so Weiss), e.g., that the strong maintain
that in this way the weak are helped to stand on
their own feet. It is sufficient to assume that the
strong made use of their freedom without any consideration for the weak. Paul sees through the speculative, individualistic principle underlying this
attitude.
35 To express it in terms of Rom 14f: he does not act
from faith, and therefore he sins. Primasius, ad loc.
(MPL 68:526A): *Non omnes sciunt quod propter con-
temptum hoc faciatis; sed putant vos propter venerationem
illud facere*, "Not all know that you do this out of
contempt; but they think you do it out of veneration" [Trans.]. This does not meet the point Paul
has in mind. Rather, the thing is that the strong
think this is allowed "in itself." They put a rule in
the place of a decision, and thereby destroy freedom.
36 Schlatter, 263, observes: the man who has knowledge
must not turn his conviction into a law that is valid

for all.
37 $\gamma\acute{\alpha}\rho$ is wrongly objected to by Weiss (see n. 33
above). The variants $\kappa\alpha\acute{\iota}$ and $o\grave{\upsilon}\nu$, "and" and "therefore," were attempts to make things easier, when
Paul's question was no longer understood because
his concept of conscience was no longer understood.
Lietzmann holds that $\gamma\acute{\alpha}\rho$ does not supply the reason, but is continuative in the sense of $o\grave{\upsilon}\nu$, as in
9:10: "in that case," "consequently," cf. 4:9. It is
better to render with Blass–Debrunner §452(2):
"to be sure, just so" (classical, see Kühner–Blass–
Gerth 2:330f); 1 Thess 2:20.
38 $\grave{\alpha}\pi\acute{o}\lambda\lambda\upsilon\mu\iota$, "ruin, destroy": Rom 14:15. Used of the
destruction of one's own humanity, Epict., *Diss.*
2.9.3: $\acute{o}\rho\alpha \, o\grave{\upsilon}\nu \, \mu\acute{\eta} \, \tau\acute{\iota} \, \pi\omega\varsigma \, \grave{\omega}\varsigma \, \theta\eta\rho\acute{\iota}ov \, \pi o\iota\acute{\eta}\sigma\eta\varsigma\cdot \, \epsilon\grave{\iota} \, \delta\grave{\epsilon} \, \mu\acute{\eta}$,
$\grave{\alpha}\pi\acute{\omega}\lambda\epsilon\sigma\alpha\varsigma \, \tau\grave{o}\nu \, \acute{\alpha}\nu\theta\rho\omega\pi ov$, "See to it, then, that you
never act like a wild beast; if you do, you will have
destroyed the man in you" (Loeb 1:267); cf. the
sequel. In Paul, however, $\grave{\alpha}\pi o\lambda\lambda\acute{\upsilon}\nu\alpha\iota$ must not be
taken in a weakened sense as moral ruin; here as else-
where it means eternal damnation (so also in Rom
14:15). It is true that Paul is addressing himself to
the strong in terms of warning and is speaking of
a possibility; but in so doing he of course presupposes
the idea that the Christian, too, can lose his salvation; see 3:15; Mattern, *Verständnis*, 115–118. It is
not clear whether, in the phrase $\epsilon\nu \, \tau\hat{\eta} \, \sigma\hat{\eta} \, \gamma\nu\acute{\omega}\sigma\epsilon\iota$,
"by your knowledge," $\epsilon\nu$ has an instrumental signifi-
cance or means "by reason of" your knowledge (so
Lietzmann).
39 Christ died for him: this is not said of man in general,
but of the man who has been baptized.
40 Cf. Mk 9:37; Mt 10:40. We naturally must not raise
the theoretical question whether God suffers his
plan of salvation to be thwarted by the failure or the
wickedness of a man. Paul is speaking to the strong
man. The latter has to give account of himself. He

(cf. Rom 14:21).[41] Freedom is not merely still maintained in principle. Rather, it is the presupposition for the ordering of the situation. From the standpoint of the object: the neutrality of food, the fact of desacralization, makes it possible to make decisions in which freedom is realized.[42] The strong man's renunciation, too, is an act of freedom, since it recognizes his brother to be

one freed by Christ.[43]

---

can destroy his existence as a believer through his conduct toward his brother. We have not to ask how God will deal with the brother we have wronged, but we are being told what we are and do if we ignore the cross. Cf. again Rom 14:13ff. For the expression "wound the conscience" cf. the corresponding expression in Hom., *Il.* 19.125; Hdt., *Hist.* 3.64: Καμβυσέα . . . ἔτυψε ἡ ἀληθηΐη τῶν λόγων, "Cambyses was smitten to the heart by the truth of the words" (Loeb 2:81). 1 Sam 1:8; Prov 26:22.

41   Paul is speaking the language of the church, cf. Mk 9:42 (along with 37).

42   A difficulty is caused by κρέας, "meat," instead of εἰδωλόθυτον, "thing offered to an idol": does κρέας, too, simply mean sacrificial meat, or is Paul seeking to express the extreme conclusion, abstinence from meat altogether? There is nothing so far to suggest this idea; but it plays a role in Rome. Generally, the explanation is sought in this direction, e.g. by Lietzmann: better too much caution than too little. Bachmann argues that in fact one was never certain whether it was not sacrificial meat. Against which it has to be said that it was possible to buy

from a Jewish butcher and for the Christians to do their own butchering. It is no question at all here of meat bought in the market, but of meat that is certainly sacrificial meat. Either Paul is here replying to an objection from Corinth to the effect that if sacrificial meat were dangerous, then it would not be permissible to eat any meat at all (cf. 5:9–11). Paul accepts the conclusion (so von Soden). To be sure, the train of thought and the example chosen do not fit in very well with this. Or else Paul is simply choosing this hard remark in order to underline the absoluteness of our obligation toward our brother.

43   When the freedom remains true to itself, then it finds no need to demonstrate itself to those outside. It is a totally different matter when abstinence is proclaimed as a law—which is the case in Col and the Pastorals.

9

The Freedom of the Apostle

1 Am I not free? Am I not an apostle? Have I not seen[1] our Lord Jesus? 2 / Are you not my work in the Lord? If for others I am not an apostle, for you at least I surely am.[2] For you are the seal of my apostleship in the Lord. 3 / This is my defense against my critics: 4 / Have we not the right to eat and drink? 5 / Have we not the right to have a sister with us as a wife, as the other apostles also have and the brothers of the Lord and Cephas? 6 / Or are Barnabas and I the only ones who have no right not to work?[3] 7 / Who ever serves in the army at his own expense? Who plants a vineyard and does not enjoy the fruit of it? Or who tends a flock and does not enjoy any of the milk of the flock? 8 / Am I saying this only in a human way, or does the Law not say the same?[4] 9 / For it is written in the Law of Moses: "You shall not muzzle the threshing ox." Do you suppose God's concern is with oxen? 10 / Or is it not everywhere (or: in all circumstances) of us that he speaks? Most assuredly! For our sakes it is written that the ploughman should plough in hope and the thresher thresh in hope of having a share of the crop. 11 / If we have sown spiritual seed for you, is it then a great thing if we reap your earthly goods? 12 / If others share in rights (of disposal) over you, do not we still more? Yet we have not made use of these rights, but put up with anything so as on no account to cause an impediment to the gospel of Christ.

Chap. 9 surprisingly introduces a new theme: the apostleship of Paul. Is the present context secondary from the literary standpoint, especially as there appear to be breaks also at the end of the chapter?[5] While it is certainly possible to see a comprehensive theme in the topic of freedom, yet this is not enough to explain the state of the text. For in chap. 9 the freedom that is discussed is not the same as in chap. 8. Its sense cannot be discovered from the connection with chap. 8, but in the first instance only from chap. 9 itself. This will depend on whether—over and above the literary breaks—we also can detect interconnections that are plainly from the hand of Paul.

■ **1–2** The initial verses form the general introduction

---

1   For the forms ἑόρακα (p[46] A B[3]) or ἑώρακα (ℵ B*) see Blass–Debrunner §68.
2   ἀλλά in the apodosis, "then at least": Blass–Debrunner §§ 439(2), 448(5); classical.
3   Lietzmann's rendering, "to refrain from working," perhaps introduces a nuance that is not entirely correct.
4   Weiss takes οὐ, "not," not as an interrogative particle, but as a negation: or is it perchance the case that the law does *not* say? Paul, he argues, is anticipating an objection on the part of his opponents. But this is surely too bombastic a rendering of the word.
5   Weiss observes that the only part of chap. 9 which is comparable with chap. 8 is the section consisting of vv 19–23; and this in turn stands out from the rest of chap. 9. Schmithals, *Gnosticism in Corinth*, 93 [86f],

and announce the theme: the apostle from the standpoint of freedom (which is purposely set in the forefront). The style—a series of questions in the first person—shows that Paul is now making his own person the subject of discussion. He does not speak about the freedom of Christians in general, but about his own particular freedom; nor yet about apostleship in general, but about his own particular apostleship. This is plain from the context of the third and fourth questions. The form of the questions[6] anticipates the answer. But in v 1 it is not yet apparent what Paul is after. In the first instance he compels the reader, by means of this form, to accept the basis on which he is arguing.

How does he come to this apologia? In itself it does not require any particular reason. The freedom of the missionary was a standard theme of the wandering Cynic preachers.[7] But in the present instance there later emerges a concrete controversy. Because of this, Paul brings the apostle title into play. For as an apostle he has rights which are not denied to an apostle even in Corinth. But is he himself one?

In v 1b his claim to this standing is based on his vision of Christ (cf. Gal 1:12ff; 1 Cor 15:6ff). This is a con-clusive argument, inasmuch as the receiving of a commission from the risen Lord is constitutive for the concept of apostleship—and yet again it is not conclusive, since it is obvious that not every vision confers this dignity. For this reason an argument *ad hominem* is added—one, however, which is not by any means subjective, since the relationship between apostle and community is not an arbitrary one: the community in Corinth is his work. If it denies *his* standing, then it abrogates its own.[8] The comprehensive commentary to this is contained in 2 Corinthians.

■ 2 In v 2 we catch at least a hint of the reason for his self–defense: apparently his apostleship is in fact contested. εἰ, "if," can in itself be taken in a purely conditional sense. But the reality of the supposition is presumably included: "if, as is in fact the case." Who the ἄλλοι, "others," are,[9] it is not necessary to state; the readers understand. With ἀλλὰ γὰρ κτλ., "even if, etc.," Paul is certainly not renouncing his title for the areas outside the territory of his own mission, but is securing the basis for his argument: *here* I am indisputably an apostle, hence I am an apostle.[10] Your own existence is proof of it.[11]

---

holds that vv 24–27 belong together with 10:1–22, that is, to letter A. 8:1–13; 9:1–23; 10:23—11:1 form a closed sequence of thought (letter B). According to Héring, 9:1 is the beginning of letter B (9:1—10:22; 11—15; 16:5–9, 15ff). Lietzmann, who holds to the literary unity, describes 9:1–18 as an excursus. He thinks it is occasioned by the fact that the Cephas group have cast doubts on the apostolic rank of Paul. But Cephas is mentioned only in passing. Von Soden, "Sakrament und Ethik," 17–21, also argues in favor of unity, but says the awkward joins cannot be explained. The same is true of Christian Maurer, "Grund und Grenze apostolischer Freiheit," in *Antwort: Karl Barth zum siebzigsten Geburtstag* (Zollikon–Zurich: Evangelischer Verlag, 1956), 630–641. He sees in chap. 9 "the decisive word on the question of idol sacrifices" (630). This may be true from the systematic standpoint, though even then there are doubts to be mentioned. The discrepancy between chap. 9 and its context is not really explained even by Maurer. As far as the literary questions are concerned, we shall have to be content with a *non liquet* and give preference to the conservative view. For the proposals to excise vv 1–18 on the one hand and vv 19–27 on the other, see Jeremias, *Abba*, 289f.

6   οὐ (affirmative answer expected): Blass–Debrunner

§427(2).

7   Epict., *Diss.* 3.2.48, and the whole picture of the Cynic in 3.22, esp. 3.22.32–37, 45–49. Kurt Niederwimmer, *Der Begriff der Freiheit im Neuen Testament* (Berlin: Töpelmann, 1966); Dieter Nestle, *Eleutheria*, vol. 1 (Tübingen: J. C. B. Mohr [Paul Siebeck], 1967), for the Greeks.

8   Cf. 2 Cor 3:2f. ἔργον—ἐν κυρίῳ, "work—in the Lord": 15:10.

9   Have they already found their way into the community? See v 3.

10   The distinctions in competence as between Paul and Peter in Gal 2:7ff do not, of course, mean a territorial limitation of their standing as apostles; such a limitation is entirely out of the question.

11   The "seal" means the legally valid attestation. It is better to take μου, "my," with ἀποστολή, "apostleship" (Weiss, Lietzmann) than with σφραγίς, "seal."

12   "Apology": a juristic term; Plato (Socrates); Acts 22:1, etc. For the dative cf. 2 Cor 12:19.

13   With Weiss. Others take v 3 as still belonging to vv 1 and 2. The use of οὗτος, "this," does not answer the question: see on the one hand 2 Cor 1:12 and on the other Acts 26:26. Yet the solemn form, perhaps also the word order (pronoun at the end), suggest rather an opening than an ending.

■ **3** In v 3 the fact that we have to do with real attacks becomes still more clear.[12] In solemn tones Paul begins the statement of his rights.[13] The form of expression leads us to conclude that the ἀνακρίνοντες, "critics," are (as yet) outside the Corinthian community.

■ **4** Paul continues to operate with rhetorical questions:[14] his freedom (v 1) is more precisely defined as a *right*—in the first instance, the right to eat and drink. This seems to continue the theme of chap. 8. But it is only seeming! For here is neither a case of εἰδωλόθυτα, "meat sacrificed to idols," nor one of εἰδωλολατρία, "worship of idols," but a question of specific foods as such. The problem is accordingly stated in much the same way as that of Rom 14f.[15]

Here Paul does in fact introduce an—or better, his—apologia.[16] For it transpires that his conduct, his renunciation of apostolic rights, had been misinterpreted and used as an argument against him. He now goes back to the theological principles at the root of his case: his renunciation is not a matter of personal choice; for this reason it is not an achievement either, to which he could appeal in his favor. The renunciation has its basis in the nature of *his* office and is therefore a positive presentation of it, that is to say, an argument *for* Paul.[17]

■ **5** This verse provides a brief insight into the wealth of missionary activity in the early church.[18] Once again it must be asked whether to ἀδελφὴν γυναῖκα περιάγειν, "to have a sister with us as a wife,"[19] we have to add from v 6, "at the expense of the community."[20] Or is Paul simply pointing to the fact of his not being married as something which is not a self–evident matter of course (but a personal charisma, 7:7)?[21] Also a question is who "the other apostles" are: an essentially *closed* circle (15:7 is in favor of this) or an *open* one, that is to say, missionaries in general.[22] In the latter case the mode of expression is naturally not to be pressed: not *all* missionaries were necessarily married. A further question: what is the relation between the brothers of Jesus (Mk 6:3),[23] who here appear as missionaries, and the apostles?[24] And what relation does Cephas bear to them?[25]

---

14 μὴ οὐ, too, expects an affirmative answer, Blass–Debrunner §427(2).

15 In the light of 8:13 we are at first inclined to adopt an interpretation in terms of the question of abstaining from particular foods. On the other hand, vv 6ff lead us to supply "at the cost of the community" after "eat and drink." Against this interpretation Johannes B. Bauer, "Uxores circumducere (1 Kor 9,5)," BZ. n.s. 3 (1959): 94–102, argues that vv 7–23 are to be taken only with v 6, then vv 24–27 with vv 4f. But this is too schematic. On the other hand, it is true that to supply "at the cost of the community" would be a narrowing down of Paul's thought. It is in the first instance simply a question of his freedom in general.

16 With Allo and others against many commentators. See n. 13 above.

17 See Maurer, "Grund und Grenze," 631f, who emphasizes that the tactical situation is at best a secondary motif. The fact that the glory of apostleship appears as humiliation is the theme of 2 Cor: 4:7ff; 11:7ff.

18 Which was more varied than is shown by our sources, focussed as they are one–sidedly upon Paul.

19 ἀδελφή, "sister" (i.e. "Christian"): 7:15; Rom 16:1; Phlm 2. Bauer, "Uxores circumducere." Zuntz, *Text*, 138, declares ἀδελφήν (–ας) without valid ground to be an interpolation.

20 Thus, e.g., Lietzmann, who argues that in v 6 the accent lies on the subject, and that the predicate is in content the same as in vv 4f.

21 According to Bauer, "Uxores circumducere," 101, περιάγειν (literally "lead around") does not accentuate the thought of accompaniment on journeys, but means "to have with one continually," that is, to be married.

22 Thus Eduard Lohse, "Ursprung und Prägung des christlichen Apostolates," *ThZ* 9 (1953): 259–275, here esp. 267. Klein, *Die zwölf Apostel*, 56, objects that in that case Paul would at once characterize himself as a mere "authorized wandering preacher," and an "apostle of Jesus Christ" in the qualified sense. The explanation is too subtle.

23 Josef Blinzler, *Die Brüder und Schwestern Jesu*, Stuttgarter Bibelstudien, 21 (Stuttgart: Katholisches Bibelwerk, 1967), marshalls a wealth of resources in order to turn them into cousins—to no purpose, as always.

24 Naturally it must not be presupposed that there were definite orders of precedence. For this very reason the brothers of Jesus will not be reckoned among the apostles (against Lietzmann).

25 Paul writes "Peter" only in Gal 2:7f, otherwise "Cephas." The fact that his person played a certain

■ **6** May we conclude from v 6 that Paul's conduct was influenced by Barnabas?[26]

Now this is unequivocally a question of the right of missionaries to be supported by the communities.[27] Paul maintains this right. Indeed he has to make clear that his renunciation of it, while certainly in accord with his peculiar calling, is nevertheless in regard to the communities, in a subjective though not an arbitrary sense, freely exercised. Apparently it has been cast in his teeth that his renunciation shows he has after all a bad conscience in claiming to be an apostle.[28] No, he is simply free.[29]

■ **7** The presentation is again enlivened by the use of illustrations. The question form is employed to present them as being immediately obvious: (a) military service at one's own expense;[30] (b) the farmer;[31] (c) the shepherd.[32] A similar combination of examples is found in 2 Tim 2:3–6, apparently a copy of the present passage.

■ **8–10** To the "rational" argument κατὰ ἄνθρωπον, "only in a human way,"[33] there is added the Scripture proof.[34] The quotation—Deut 25:4[35]—is, contrary to Paul's exegesis, essentially a rule for the protection of

---

role in Corinth was already apparent from 1:12 (see *ad loc.*). The question why he is named last should give us as little cause to rack our brains as the other question whether the title of apostle is allowed to him. The answer to the question raised above is: *non liquet.*

26 Paul is writing long after his separation from Barnabas. Of their relations after this separation (Gal 2:13) we know as little as we do of the relations with Peter. It is presupposed that Barnabas, too, is known to the Corinthians by name. But there is no sign of an influence on the community.

27 If maintenance by the community is in mind already in vv 4f, then the unified sweep of the defense is clear. Otherwise the sequence of thought is: (*a*) a general assertion of his freedom; (*b*) freedom as ἐξουσία, "authority, rights"; (*c*) the special case of this ἐξουσία: the right to maintenance.

28 Weiss says: the renunciation was cast in Paul's teeth rather than the claim. Perhaps. But the accusations must have gone further; cf. also 2 Cor 10—13: doubts are cast on his standing altogether; 2 Cor 11:7ff. Missionary activity is frequently designated as "work": 3:13–15; Mt 9:37; Jn 4:35–38; 1 Tim 5:18; 2 Tim 2:15f; *Did.* 13.2. On ἐργάζεσθαι, "to work," see Moulton and Milligan *s.v.* On manual labor: Xenoph., *Cyrop.* 1.6.11; 2 Thess 3:8; Acts 18:3. Adolf von Harnack, "κόπος (κοπιᾶν, οἱ κοπιῶντες) im frühchristlichen Sprachgebrauch," *ZNW* 27 (1928): 1–10.

29 2 Cor 11:7ff; Phil 4:10ff show that Paul accepts maintenance in other cases. He does not make a principle of his renunciation, but behaves on each occasion as the case requires. This has to be borne in mind later when we come to the fundamental argument of vv 16–18.

30 *Inschr. Priene* 109.93f (cf. 121.34) shows a στρατηγός, "general," who attended to his duty ἄτερ ὀψωνίου καὶ ἐλαίου, "without wages, even in olive oil." H. W. Heidland, *TDNT* 5:592. The comparison with the soldier is so brief in this passage that it must not be expanded with the help of the notion of the

believer's warfare. For this latter see the commentaries on Eph 6:10ff; 1 Tim 1:18.

31 The planter and the enjoyment of the fruit: Deut 20:6; Pr 27:18. What Str.–B. 3:379–381 here adduce (the laborer at the harvest is permitted to eat of the fruits) suits not v 7 but v 9.

32 The preposition ἐκ, "of," with ἐσθίειν ("nourish oneself, enjoy") has no other sense than the accusative; it should not be pressed (as by Robertson and Plummer) to mean that the slave gets only a part of the produce. The thought is the same as in 2 Tim 2:6.

33 Weiss finds the reading ταῦτα λαλῶ, "I am saying this," unbearably harsh, and argues that if λαλῶ is to be read, then ταῦτα must be deleted. But λαλεῖν is used transitively by Paul just as λέγειν; nor is there any difference in content between the two words.

34 Von Campenhausen, *Begründung*, 25, finds that v 8 becomes most readily understandable if Paul is meeting a possible objection on the part of the hyper–spiritual Corinthians to the effect that such arguments of a human kind have no place in the church. To counter this, Paul now adduces (1) the Law, (2) an apocryphal quotation, (3) a word of the Lord.

35 The nonliterary word κημοῦν, "muzzle" (B* D* G) is to be preferred to φιμοῦν (Deut 25:4 LXX; p⁴⁶ ℵ A C), which is a secondary assimilation to the LXX. A different case is found in 1 Tim 5:18.

36 Ex 20:10; Prov 11:10; Jos., *Ant.* 4.233. See Gustaf Dalman, *Arbeit und Sitte in Palästina*, BFTh, 2, 29 (Gütersloh: Bertelsmann, 1933), vol. 3, plate 15. Greek evidence: Nilsson, 34.

37 Philo, *Spec. leg.* 1.260 (with regard to the regulations concerning sacrificial animals): οὐ γὰρ ὑπὲρ τῶν ἀλλόγων ὁ νόμος, ἀλλ' ὑπὲρ τῶν νοῦν καὶ λόγον ἐχόντων, "For the law does not prescribe for unreasoning creatures, but for those who have mind and reason" (Loeb 7:251). *Ep. Ar.* 144.

animals.[36] Paul, however, expounds the statement according to the Hellenistic Jewish principle that God's concern is with higher things,[37] that accordingly the detailed prescriptions of the law are to be allegorically expounded.[38]

■ **10** This is the alternative: δι' ἡμᾶς πάντως, "everywhere of us." Is the sentence to be taken as a question? In that case, after v 8 (μὴ . . . ἢ . . . οὐ) we are struck by the absence of an οὐ, "not." On the other hand, following v 8, we can hardly read the sentence as a statement.[39] According to the hermeneutic principle (see above) "we" designates men in general.[40] ἐγράφη, "it is written," presumably introduces a quotation from an apocryphon (Weiss); ὅτι, "that," is recitative; the form is *parallelismus membrorum*.[41]

■ **11** Verse 11 states the conclusion for the case in question.[42]

In this passage we are a long way from the theological topic of law and justification by faith. The Old Testament supplies authoritative examples (cf. 10:1ff). A casuistic ruling is not derived from it, not even from the words of the Lord (see above, 7:10ff). Paul turns the quotation into a metaphor: "sowing" now means the work of mission.[43] The contrast between τὰ πνευματικά, "spiritual benefits," and τὰ σαρκικά, "things of the flesh—earthly goods," is naturally not meant here in the sense of the theological antithesis between πνεῦμα and σάρξ; τὰ σαρκικά are the natural blessings, the βιωτικά, "necessities of life."[44]

■ **12** This verse continues in the conditional style, with a side glance at ἄλλοι, "others." Who are meant? The answer is bound up with our understanding of the genitive ὑμῶν "over you."[45] Objective genitive (see the translation)? It will be best not to specify the ἄλλοι, "others," too closely.[46]

An impressive contrast to their behavior is formed by the declaration of free renunciation, strengthened by ἵνα κτλ., "so as, etc." Cf. 1 Thess 2:9; 2 Cor 12:13. The sense emerges from the sequel.[47]

38 "The literal sense has to be abandoned when it expresses something that is not worthy of God" (Carl Siegfried, *Philo von Alexandria als Ausleger des Alten Testaments* [Jena: Dufft, 1875], 305). This exegetical principle is stoically determined; Isaak Heinemann, *Philons griechische und jüdische Bildung* (Breslau: Marcus, 1932; reprinted Hildesheim: Olms, 1962), 463–470. Not so the view of the rabbis (Str.–B. 3:388–399): the literal text remains valid (Str.–B. 3:392); cf. *b. BM* 88b (Str.–B. 3:385), where the passage is employed by a conclusion *a minore:* what is true of oxen is all the more true of men. Adolf von Harnack, "Das Alte Testament in den paulinischen Briefen und in den paulinischen Gemeinden," in *SAB* (1928), 124–141.

39 Weiss seeks to help matters by assuming a dash after ἤ: "or—it is altogether of us that he speaks." This is no real help. One could sooner read ἦ (Bauer, *s.v.* ἦ: "truly"). πάντως is ambiguous: "everywhere" (cf. v 22); Bauer, *s.v.* renders, "by all means" (with examples); Heinrici says, "assuredly" (cf. 5:10; Rom 3:9).

40 Not only Christians; so Chrys., Thdt.; Heinrici.

41 To be sure, the statement can also be understood as an exposition of the OT quotation: ". . . . sc. that the Christian teacher . . . ὀφείδει ('should') . . . ." Thus Schmiedel, pointing to γάρ.

42 εἰ propounds the case as real. The expression (μέγα εἰ) is abbreviated. Gen 45:28; 2 Cor 11:25.

43 Jn 4:35–38 is a typical Johannine alteration. Harald Riesenfeld, "Parabolic Language in the Pauline Epistles," in his *The Gospel Tradition*, 187–204, here esp. 190–199 (originally in *Littérature et théologie pauliniennes*, 47–59, here esp. 49–55).

44 Rom 15:27.

45 Epict., *Diss.* 3.24.70: τίς οὖν ἔτι ἔχει μου ἐξουσίαν; "Who, then, has authority over me?" (Loeb 2:207). Many take ἐξουσία as "property" (Plat., *Leg.* 828d; Thuc., *Hist.* 1.38); Weiss argues that μετέχειν is better suited to a real commodity than to a formal right [i.e. "share your wealth" rather than "share rights over you," Trans.]. But in the NT ἐξουσία never has this meaning elsewhere.

46 With Allo. Weiss is too narrow in saying that they are most likely the Judaistic intruders. He presupposes the situation of 2 Cor.

47 For the renunciation cf. Str.–B. 3:400 (Moses).

13 Do you not know that those who perform the temple service[1] eat of the proceeds of the temple service?[2] That those who attend the altar[3] have a share with the altar (in the sacrifices)? 14/ So, too, the Lord has ordained for the preachers of the gospel, that they should live from the gospel. 15/ I, however, have never made use of that. Nor am I writing[4] this in order that I should (now) be treated in this way.[5] For I would rather die than – no one shall make my boast an empty one.[6] 16/ For if[7] I preach the gospel, that is nothing for me to boast of. For I am under constraint. It is a misery to me[8] if I do not preach the gospel. 17/ For if[9] I do it willingly, I have my reward, but if I do it unwillingly, I have a charge of stewardship laid upon me.[10] 18/ What, then, is my reward? That[11] as a preacher of the gospel I present the gospel free of charge,[12] so as not to take advantage of my rightful claims on the gospel.[13]

---

1 τὸ ἱερόν (and plural): "the sacrifice," since Homer; Jos., *Ant.* 2.275. The plural means also holy things and acts, the "cult" in general, Hdt., *Hist.* 1.172, and frequently; *3 Macc.* 3.21; Jos., *Ant.* 14.237; 14.240; ἱερὰ Ἰουδαϊκὰ ποιεῖν, "to observe Jewish rites" (Loeb 7:577). For ἐργάζεσθαι cf. Num 8:15: ἐργάζεσθαι τὰ ἔτγα τῆς σκηνῆς, "to do sacrifice at the tent of meeting" (RSV). Gottlob Schrenk, *TDNT* 3:232 [231], rightly takes τὰ ἱερά here in a wider sense than merely "sacrifice"; the word denotes the whole of the priestly service.

2 Or is ἱερόν here the temple (Schrenk, *TDNT* 3:232)? In that case we have a wordplay. Lietzmann understands τὰ ἱερά as "sacrifices," here as the sacrificial elements. The expression would be simpler if τά were to be deleted with p⁴⁶ A C 𝕽. Yet the deletion is presumably a subsequent correction of the unevenness. ἐσθίειν ἐκ τοῦ ἱεροῦ, "eat of the proceeds of the temple service," is expressed in parallel form to ἐκ τοῦ εὐαγγελίου ζῆν, "live from the gospel."

3 παρεδρεύειν, "attend," is found in a sacral context: Diod. S., *Bibl. Hist.* 4.3.3: τῷ θεῷ, "to accompany the god" (cf. Loeb 2:347); Ditt., *Syll.* 2:180 (no. 633, line 20): τοῦ ταμίου τοῦ πα[ρεδ]ρεύοντος ἐν τῷ ἱερῷ θυσίας ποιήσασθαι, "of the priest who attends in the temple to offer sacrifices" [Trans.]; Jos., *Ap.* 1.30: προσεδρεύεσθαι τῇ θεραπείᾳ τοῦ θεοῦ, "to be devoted to the service of God" (Loeb 1:175).

4 As distinct from 5:9, we have here an epistolary aorist.

5 γίνεσθαι ἐν (ἐμοί), "be done to (me)": ἐν for the dative (Gen 40:14), Bauer, *s.v.* ἐν IV 4.

6 The harshness of the anacolouthon is softened in the MSS with varying success. οὐδεὶς κενώσει p⁴⁶ ℵ* B D* 33 ("no one shall make empty") is to be regarded as original. Attempted improvements: (1) οὐδεὶς μή A ("let no one make empty!"), (2) τίς G ("who shall make empty?"), (3) ἵνα τις κενώσει ℵᶜᵒʳʳ C Dᶜᵒʳʳ or κενώσῃ 𝕽 and others ("than that anyone should make empty"). Another possibility is to accentuate ἦ, "truly," instead of ἤ, "than" (Bachmann; Bauer, *s.v.* ἦ, "truly," as in v 10).

7 ἐάν! Vulg. *evangelizavero* presupposes the reading εὐαγγελίζωμαι (D G). At the end of the verse the aorist subjunctive is supported also by B C, as opposed to p⁴⁶ ℵ A K (cf. also L P: -ίζομαι). In this second passage the aorist subjunctive is better from the point of view of content, since it is here a case of an exclusively future possibility. Zuntz, *Text*, 110.

8 The rendering, "Alas for me!" would be too weak, cf. Hos 9:12.

9 Now we have a real case.

10 Another suggestion (Bachmann): εἰ δὲ ἄκων οἰκονομίαν πεπίστευμαι, τίς οὖν κτλ., "But if I have a charge of stewardship laid upon me against my will, what is then my reward?" Again advanced by Wilhelm Pesch, "Der Sonderlohn für die Verkündiger des Evangeliums," in *Neutestamentliche Aufsätze: Festschrift für Prof. Josef Schmid zum 70. Geburtstag*, ed. Josef Blinzler, Otto Kuss, and Franz Mussner (Regensburg: Pustet, 1963), 199–206, here esp. 202–204, on the ground that otherwise v 17b would be a tautology. But Weiss already rightly objected that then we should have to expect ἄρα instead of οὖν in the

■ **13** Paul is multiplying arguments. Now he brings a rule from the laws of worship; in v 14 he uses οὕτως, "so," to link it with a word of the Lord. The rule is valid, incidentally, not only for the Jews;[14] it belongs to the basic stock of cultic regulations in general. οὐκ οἴδατε, "do you not know," introduces it as known and recognized. It is not plainly discernible whether or not 13a and 13b are synonymous, that is, whether the service of the sanctuary and the service of the altar are identical, or whether or not the former is understood in a wider sense. However, this question is of no consequence for the argument. θυσιαστήριον is used in the LXX in the narrower sense to mean the altar of burnt offerings. παρεδρεύειν: "be zealously engaged." συμμερίζονται: "they have a share with the altar," *scil.* in the gifts offered.[15]

■ **14** οὕτως, "in the same way." There is no deeper reason for introducing the saying of the Lord at the end and apparently incidentally.[16] Paul is collecting arguments, without worrying about a systematic order. For the basing of a rule on a saying of Jesus, see 7:10. For the content cf. Lk 6:6; Gal 6:6; 1 Tim 5:18. Paul is playing upon the meanings of the word "gospel":[17] the

message and the proclamation of it.

In Luke the proverb that the worker (ἐργάτης; see v 6) is worthy of his hire provides the ground of the preacher's right to remuneration. In Matthew (10:8, 10) we find the twofold motif, that the gospel should be freely offered because it has been freely received, but that the preacher should be free of care, for he is worthy of his hire.[18]

■ **15** And once again[19] Paul declares his renunciation, this time expressly also for the future.[20] His tone rises.[21] The construction of the sentence breaks down.[22] The fact that Paul here lays claim to a "boast" is no contradiction of his self–understanding in terms of the theology of the cross: his boast lies precisely in his renunciation; cf. the sequel, where the sense is plain.

■ **16** Paul draws a contrast between his own personal determination and the general rule. He has not chosen his calling. He was called and accordingly stands under constraint. His behavior is here systematically grounded in theology.[23] ἀνάγκη, "constraint,"[24] here denotes not only an inner compulsion, but the apostle's destiny.[25] Yet this is not a fate which works with causal necessity. Otherwise it would be impossible to conceive of Paul's

---

apodosis; cf. Gal 2:21.

11 ἵνα for the epexegetical infinitive: Blass–Brunner §394. Future indicative after ἵνα Blass–Brunner §369(2).

12 Or: do not allow the gospel to cause any expense.

13 Or: so as not to take advantage of the rights that accrue to me in the preaching of the gospel.

14 OT: Num 18:8, 31; *Nu. r.* 18 (183d), cited in Str.–B. 3:400 f: "Normally if a man works for the sanctuary, he receives his wages from the sanctuary" (*Midrash Rabbah* 6.2:720). But Moses, to be sure, renounced this. See next note.

15 Illustrative material is provided by every ancient account of sacrifice. The adoption of cultic terminology to describe the "service" of the church (cf. Rom 12:1f) does not yet lead to the establishing of an independent language of this kind and to a phenomenology of a Christian cult with priesthood and sacrifice.

16 According to Weiss, Paul gives only a rough indication of the content, which means he assumes that the saying is known in Corinth. This is possible, but not conclusive. What matters is not an exact quotation, but the statement of the content, and the latter is sufficiently plain.

17 For the technical use of the word εὐαγγέλιον see on 4:15.

18 According to Str.–B. 1:561–564, the study of the Law is free of charge to the scribal disciple. And according to 3:401, on the other hand, the man who occupies himself with the Law earns his living by it.

19 Ernst Käsemann, "A Pauline Version of the 'Amor Fati,' " in his *NT Questions of Today*, 217–235 (originally in *ZThK* 56 [1959]: 138–154 and in his *EVB* 2:223–239), finds that the section consisting of vv 14–18 (15–18 would be better) appears superfluous in the chapter as a whole. It is quite true that it is marked out by its high feeling. But there is no break in content.

20 ἵνα οὕτως γένηται, "that I should be treated in this way," is explained by what precedes.

21 καλὸν κτλ.: infinitive after impersonal constructions: Blass–Brunner §393(2).

22 Unless we read ἤ, "truly," see n. 6 above.

23 Christian Maurer, "Grund und Grenze apostolischer Freiheit," in *Antwort: Karl Barth zum siebzigsten Geburtstag* (Zollikon–Zurich: Evangelischer Verlag, 1956), 630–641, here esp. 638–641.

24 ἀνάγκη ἐπίκειται, "constraint is laid upon me": Hom., *Il.* 6.458: κρατερὴ δ' ἐπικείσετ' ἀνάγκη, "and strong necessity shall be laid upon thee" (Loeb 1:295).

25 Käsemann, "A Pauline Version of the 'Amor Fati.' "

resisting the constraint.[26]

The question raised by Roman Catholic exegetes, as to whether here the notion of *opera supererogatoria*, "works of supererogation," emerges, is answered by the following sentences.

■ **17** The interest lies not in the theoretic structure of the ἀνάγκη, "constraint," but in the practical consequence: only voluntary labor deserves and gains a reward.[27] It is misguided to remove this rule from the framework of the argument, to regard it on its own, and then to discover a Jewish relic of thinking in terms of works and deserts. The statement has its obvious auxiliary function in between vv 16 and 18. "If willingly" is simply a foil for the real case of Paul, for the fact that he "unwillingly" has a charge of stewardship laid upon him.

■ **18** The mode of expression with its paradox[28] is appropriate.[29] Since Paul defines his reward exhaustively in the ἵνα–clause, "that, etc.," we cannot go on to ask again where, apart from this self–contained statement, he finds his reward.[30]

By explaining the matter thus and tracing his behavior back to "his" ἀνάγκη, Paul has shown that his behavior is not a matter of free decision. Yet it is precisely in acting in accordance with this constraint that he exercises his freedom in his dealings with the community. This indeed is shown elsewhere by the fact that his standpoint can lead him to behave in the opposite way.

The development of his thought from v 18 to v 19 is completely logical.

19	**For[1] although I am free of all men,[2] I have made myself the slave of all, in order to win the majority.[3] 20 / And to the[4] Jews I became (like)[5] a Jew in order to win Jews ; to those under the Law I became like (one) under the Law,[6] although I am not myself under the Law, in order to win those under the Law ; 21 / to those outside the Law I became**

26 The constraint is bound up with his calling, and indeed with his election before birth, Gal 1:12ff; 1 Cor 15:8ff. There is no question of any theoretical reflection on determination. Rather, Paul understands himself in the same way as the prophet Jeremiah (Gal 1:15; Jer 1:5).

27 Weiss excises v 17 as a gloss, arguing that it speaks in purely logical and theoretical terms, which does not suit the temperamental context. But hypotheses on the relation between understanding and temperament in Paul are questionable arguments. And v 18 presupposes v 17—against Weiss, see next note.

28 Wettstein, *ad loc.*, observes: "To put it tersely, my reward is to receive no reward."

29 Weiss (see previous note) contends that this question can only relate back to v 16, and that it is pointless as a conclusion from v 17. This explanation overlooks the fact that Paul does not conceive of the constraint in psychological terms, as an inward compulsion, but sees it strictly in the context of his call to office.

30 E.g., in interior joyousness (Weiss). Schlatter, 275–278, says his glory is in the work of his hands. Paul is laying bare to the Corinthians his "inmost heart." Käsemann, too, falls a victim to psychologizing: he seeks to make the distinction that μισθός in v 17 means God's reward at the last judgment, whereas in v 18 μισθός is a paradoxical expression for the

"committed love" whose delight is in action. This is not Paul, but Hölderlin. Pesch (n. 10) rightly observes that we cannot ascribe different meanings to the word μισθός in vv 17 and 18. Only, unlike Pesch, we must not see in v 17 an independent thesis, but only an *ad hoc* argument.

1 According to Weiss, γάρ, "for," is out of place here, but fits well after 11:1. But γάρ can be taken (with Lietzmann) simply in a continuative sense.

2 ἐλεύθερος ἐκ: like ἀπό in Rom 7:3, "independent of"; Kühner–Blass–Gerth 1:402. Opinions differ as to whether the participle has the significance of the present ("although I *am* free") or of the past ("although I *was* free"). If present, then Paul is explaining the continual dialectic of freedom and the renunciation of it. If past, then he is saying that he has given up his freedom. ἐμαυτὸν ἐδούλωσα, "I (have) made myself the slave," seems to accord better with the interpretation in terms of the past. But the sense of the context as a whole requires the present; with the participle Paul is taking up the εἰμί, "I am," of v 1.

3 Or: "more"; Blass–Debrunner §244(3).

4 Before Ἰουδαῖοι stands the article used individually: the Jews "with whom I had to deal on each occasion," Blass–Debrunner §262(1).

like one outside the Law, although
I am not outside the law of God[7] but
within the law of Christ,[8] in order to win
those outside the Law. 22 / To the weak
I became weak,[9] in order to win the
weak. I have become all things to all
men, in order to save at least[10] some.[11]
23 / But I do it all for the sake of the
gospel, in order to become a sharer in
it.[12] Do you not know that, while all the
runners in the stadium certainly run,
yet only one receives the prize? So[13] run
that you may win it. 25 / But every competitor practices all kinds of abstinence
—they in order to secure a perishable
wreath, but we an imperishable one.
26 / I for my part run with no uncertain
goal; I box as one who does not beat the
air. 27 / But I strike my own body and
subdue it, so as not to preach to others
and then myself be good for nothing.

■ **19** Lietzmann, bracketing out the "excursus" in
vv 1–18, is for linking v 19 to 8:13.[14] Others characterize
vv 14–18 as an insertion (see above; Käsemann). But
the link with 8:13 or 9:13 is no better than with v 18.[15]
The expression ἐλεύθερος γὰρ ὤν, "for though I am
free," points back to v 1 and thereby confirms the starting
point.[16] At the same time Paul recapitulates what he

has said since then, now expressed in generalizing terms:
the freedom which he claims for himself takes the concrete form of service. His statement of the aim of his
conduct has an opportunistic sound, as if it were determined by tactical considerations,[17] especially when it is
read along with vv 20–22 (see on v 22). No doubt Paul
is partly under the psychological influence of Jewish

---

5 ὡς vacillates in the context between "as" and "like."
   Here ὡς is superfluous (as also in v 22, see below),
   but not in the other instances in vv 20 and 21. Although superfluous, it is nevertheless to be regarded
   as original. γίνομαι ὡς, "I show myself as," 4:13;
   Bauer, *s.v.* γίνομαι II 1.

6 ὑπὸ νόμον, "under the Law," stands here almost as a
   substantival adjective, cf. ἄνομαι, "those outside
   the Law."

7 The Koine interchanges God and Christ—a misunderstanding as regards content.

8 For the genitive see Blass–Debrunner §182(3): it
   seems to depend on νόμος; cf. Soph., *Ant.* 369; Eur.,
   Med. 737.

9 ὡς, "as," stands before ἀσθενής, "weak," in C D G;
   see below.

10 See Bauer, *s.v.* πάντως 4.

11 Instead of πάντως τινάς, "at least some," D G have
   πάντας, "all."

12 Einar Molland, *Das paulinische Evangelion*, Avhand-
   linger utgitt av det Norske Videnskapsakademi i
   Oslo, Historisk–filosofiske Klasse, 1934, 3 (Oslo:

Dybwad, 1934), 53f: "co-worker in the gospel." But
   συγκοινωνός does not denote an active participator.

13 οὕτως points forward to ἵνα.

14 Lietzmann observes: in 8:13 he introduced himself
   as a model, with 9:1 he intended to go on using himself as an example, and now he again takes up the
   catchword ἐλεύθερος "free."

15 We can hardly do without vv 15–18. If we could,
   then we could sooner link v 19 with v 12. This shows
   the questionableness of all conclusions based on a
   schematic view of the structure and the sequence of
   thought. Heinrici points out that πᾶσιν ἐμαυτὸν
   ἐδούλωσα, "I have made myself the slave of all," has
   no direct bearing on the special problems of chap. 8.

16 Meantime, Paul had spoken of ἐξουσία, "power,
   authority, right." It is plain that ἐξουσία is the Corinthian slogan. It accords better with enthusiasm
   than does ἐλευθερία, "freedom." Dupont, *Gnosis*,
   282–327; cf. 6:12.

17 It must not be asked pedantically of whom Paul is
   thinking when he here speaks of the πλείονες, the
   "majority" or the "rest" (Bachmann holds that it

ideas of self–humiliation and accommodation.[18] And there exists also a Christian variety of these notions (Mt 10:43ff; Lk 22:25ff). The sense in which Paul now takes over and modifies these ideas must be seen in terms of his self–understanding as a whole: ἐδούλωσα ἐμαυτόν, "I have made myself a slave," is in harmony with the fact that his office is determined by the cross. A commentary is provided by 2:1–5.[19]

■ **20–22** These verses, together with v 23 which rounds them off, form a unity both in style and in content.[20] The accommodation which Paul practices is illustrated by reference to the two classes into which mankind is to be divided from the Jewish standpoint (cf. 1:18ff). He begins with the Jews as a matter of course (cf. Rom 1:16 πρῶτον, "first"). This is in keeping with the situation both from the psychological standpoint and from that of salvation history.

The statement that Paul has accommodated himself to the Jews[21] in order to win them is doubly surprising— first because of the decision on competence at the Apostolic Council (Gal 2:9): Peter is the man for the Jews, Paul for the Gentiles. Yet this agreement cannot have meant that Paul was forbidden to receive Jews into his communities, especially as his most important co–workers were Jewish Christians.[22] The second difficulty arises from his doctrine of the Law. Can he compromise here, in view of his observations in Galatians? (See Gal 2:5.) He surely declares explicitly that to be a Jew is to be under the Law.[23]

Paul himself explains, by means of ὡς, "like," and μὴ ὢν αὐτὸς ὑπὸ νόμον, "although I am not myself under the law." He is able as a Jew to practice Jewish customs, without teaching that the Law is a way of salvation. And he does not have to deliver the Jews from their practice of the Law, but from their "confidence" in the Law as a way of salvation (Phil 3:2ff). His behavior is consistent, precisely from the standpoint of his doctrine of Law, faith, and freedom: every man is addressed by God as the man he is, in his κλῆσις, "calling." Accordingly the agreement in Gal 2, that Jewish Christians are to continue to keep the Law, is not a compromise, but a direct application of the *sola fide*.

The rhetorical parallelism can obscure the fact that Paul's behavior toward Jews and toward Gentiles, while it is certainly a practical expression of the same freedom and the same understanding of faith, is nevertheless

---

refers to the number Paul could win if he did not make himself a slave). κερδαίνειν, "to win for the faith" (1 Pet 3:1) is explained by Daube, *NT and Rabbinic Judaism*, 355–361, as a rabbinic missionary term: נשכר/השתכר. To be sure, there is evidence only for the meaning "to win back." Note the interchange with σῴζειν, "save," in v 22.

18   Rom 12:16, etc.; Daube, *NT and Rabbinic Judaism*, 346–350.

19   Weiss observes: in the protasis Paul feels himself like a Stoic sage who knows himself independent of the world. This is not so. The protasis is already spoken from consciousness of the necessity of renunciation, just as 9:1, following 8:13, includes the thought of being determined by the death of Christ.

20   Weiss observes that *formally* there is a chiastic correspondence, b (c c) b, but in content a *parallelismus membrorum*, bc bc. On style and content see Günther Bornkamm, "The Missionary Stance of Paul in I Corinthians 9 and in Acts," in *Studies in Luke–Acts: Essays Presented in Honor of Paul Schubert*, ed. Leander E. Keck and J. Louis Martyn (New York and Nashville: Abingdon, 1966), 194–207.

21   To Hillel is ascribed the principle: "When you enter a city, follow its customs" (*Gn. r.* 48; Daube, *NT and Rabbinic Judaism*, 336–341). This throws no light on Paul.

22   Ernst Haenchen, *The Acts of the Apostles. A Commentary*, tr. ed. Robert McL. Wilson (Oxford: Blackwell; Philadelphia: Westminster, 1971), 466f (*Die Apostelgeschichte*, KEK, 3 [Göttingen: Vandenhoeck & Ruprecht, [10]1965], 409), aptly observes that Gal 2:9 is not an official minute of the proceedings. Is the delimitation of the missionary spheres meant in a geographical or ethnographical sense? A geographical interpretation is excluded by the missionary journeys of Peter and is indeed also inherently inconceivable. To be sure, questions of this sort are asking too much of Gal 2:9. Paul is simply stating that he was recognized as a missionary to the Gentiles.
        It would be mistaken to explain that before the Council Paul had also carried out mission work among the Jews, but afterwards did so no longer, and that accordingly he is speaking of an earlier practice. Incidentally, even then we should have to raise the question of the relation between the Law and the freedom of faith.

23   The parallelism is of a synonymous kind. There is nothing to indicate that "those under the Law" are a particular group of Jews, namely, proselytes (so Heinrici). For the expression ὑπὸ νόμον, "under the Law," cf. Rom 6:14; for the absence of the article see Blass–Debrunner §§255, 258(2). For ὑπό with

different in structure. He *is* a Jew. To the Gentiles he must *become* a Gentile. The problem is not how he can live in Jewish fashion, but how he can live in Gentile fashion. Once again this lies not in his own arbitrary choice, but in his commission. He is free not in an abstract sense, but as an apostle. The fact that the statement on his behavior toward the Jews is repeated by explaining its content ("to those under the Law—one under the Law") provides a foil for his observation that in all this he remains free,[24] and at the same time paves the way for the statement on his behavior toward those "outside the Law."

■ **21** Why does Paul not say, "to the Greeks"?[25] At all events, οἱ ἄνομοι, "those outside the Law," is an essential characterization which is important here not only for the sake of rhetoric. In the case of the Jews he had to register his abiding freedom. Here, in turn, he has to declare that his freedom from the Law is not "lawlessness."[26] For this reason he again says ὡς, "like," and μὴ ὢν κτλ., "though I am not, etc.," but this time supplies a more detailed exposition. This leads to a difficult form of expression: he is not ἄνομος θεοῦ, "outside the law of God," but ἔννομος Χριστοῦ, "within the law of Christ." Here his intention is not to suggest the idea of a "new" law. The word νόμος, "law," is used here in an improper sense (cf. Rom 8:2): Christ is the norm.[27]

■ **22** Verse 22 returns from the general observations and is aimed again at the special conditions in Corinth; cf. 8:13, but also 1:26ff.[28] The summary, τοῖς πᾶσιν γέγονα πάντα, "I have become all things to all men," takes us back to v 18.[29]

■ **23** This has a utilitarian sound: by behaving thus, Paul secures his own personal salvation. The impression that the dominating thought here is that of an extreme religious individualism is strengthened by the following section. Is it possible, then, that at bottom Paul has nothing with which to reproach his adversaries? Has he nothing more to set over against their enthusiasm than his own rigorousness and a few tactical maneuvers?

Here again the statement must not be separated from his general understanding of salvation and the saving event, of election and calling. The summons to strive after salvation, which he directs to his readers here and in the following verses, presupposes election *sola gratia*; cf. Phil 2:12ff; 3:12ff. And at the Last Judgment he will have to render account of his work; there he will point to his communities as his legitimation. Verse 23, too, has the community and his own commission in view. For the content cf. 2 Cor 1:14; 3:1–3; 5:10; 1 Thess 2:19; Phil 2:16, where the link is expressed between his self–consciousness and the task committed to him.

■ **24–27** The section consisting of vv 24–27 is unified in style and content and stands out from its context.[30] Yet it cannot be separated from its context on grounds of

---

24 Incidentally, this passage cannot serve as an argument for the historicity of the circumcision of Timothy by Paul (Acts 16:3). Paul is speaking of his behavior toward non–Christians. According to Acts 16:3 he would have been bringing a baptized Christian back under the Law (and the whole Law at that!—according to the rule in Gal 5:3).

25 Schlatter replies: because to Greek life there belong things from which Paul stands aloof. And what about "lawlessness"?

26 Cf. the rejection of antinomianism in Rom, especially Rom 7:7ff.

27 With Kümmel, who observes: the expression is due to the parallelism and means only "obliged to be obedient to Christ." Paul is using a phrase appropriate to the context in order to indicate the viewpoint of Χριστοῦ εἶναι, "being Christ's" (see 3:23). Not so C. H. Dodd, "Ἔννομος Χριστοῦ," in *Studia Paulina*, 96–110, now in his *More New Testament Studies* (Manchester: Manchester University Press;

the accusative answering the question "where?" see Blass–Debrunner §232(1).

Grand Rapids: Eerdmans, 1968), 134–148: Paul acknowledges a "law of the Spirit" (Rom 8:3) and a "law of Christ." The former expresses the indicative: πνεύματι ζῶμεν, "we live in the Spirit," while the latter expresses the imperative: πνεύματι στοιχῶμεν, "let us walk in the Spirit" (cf. Gal 5:25). In content, the law of Christ comprises the tradition of the teaching of Jesus, which indeed is cited as an authority in the same chapter. This interpretation is at variance with the whole Pauline use of νόμος.

28 It is appropriate that there is no ὡς, "as," before ἀσθενής, "weak." One is introduced secondarily in C D G 𝔐 (on the analogy of vv 20–21) in order to remove the offense of the suggestion that Paul should be said to have been weak.

29 Henry Chadwick, " 'All Things to All Men' (I Cor. ix.22)," *NTS* 1 (1954–55): 261–275.

30 Weiss says the section "has very good relations with 10:1–23 and 6:1–20, very bad relations with 9:19–22, tolerable relations with 9:1–18." But this section in particular once again sheds light on the forego-

literary criticism. It is bound up with this context by means of v 27, which corresponds to v 23. In regard to content, the coherence of the thought is thoroughly Pauline: Paul's mode of behavior, which he has not freely chosen, is an example for believers. In the background stands the paraenetic motif, μιμηταί μου γίνεσθε, "become imitators of me" (11:1).

Paul moves over from self–representation to address in diatribe style: οὐκ οἴδατε, "do you not know" (v 13, etc.). In harmony with this, he also uses metaphors (see v 7) and more especially sport metaphors.[31] The comparison with a race[32] requires in itself no explanation. But the moral which Paul derives from it—namely, that only one wins the prize[33]—appears out of place. For surely all believers should not only strive after this prize,

but also receive it. However, apparently this remark is only an auxiliary notion,[34] to help strengthen the point: τρέχετε, "run!" In harmony with this, he goes on to the call for training.[35] The wreath as a prize is familiar to everyone.[36] But wreaths and suchlike have also become the symbol for the goal of the (religious) "race" of life.[37]

■ 26 We are not altogether prepared for the transition to the person of Paul, the return to self–representation, but it is understandable in the light of the underlying idea of example (see above). The new note is that of

---

ing. H. von Soden, "Sakrament und Ethik," 7: the behavior there portrayed, the renunciation, has no value in itself. It is a case of "the asceticism of the competitor who is out to win, the behavior of the man who does not roam the vast field of what is permitted, but presses forward on the narrow path of what is beneficial. Once again the problems attaching to behavior of this sort are, *in statu confessionis*, not envisaged at all."

31 Diatribe: see the index to *Epicteti Dissertationes ab Arriano digestae . . .*, ed. Heinrich Schenkl (Leipzig: Teubner, 1916), s.v. ἀθλητής, παλαιστής, etc. Philo, *Leg. all.* 2.108; Sen., *Ep.* 78.16. On ancient sport: Julius Jüthner, "Gymnastik," Pauly–W. 7:2030–85. Athletic clubs: Franz Poland, *Geschichte des griechischen Vereinswesens*, 147–152. Paul: Phil 3:14.

Since the metaphor is widespread, and since sport is an everyday feature in the life of every Greek city, there is no need to think particularly of the isthmic games at Corinth and the pine–wreath as prize (Luc., *Anach.* 9). For the figurative language see Arnold Ehrhardt, "An unknown Orphic writing in the Demosthenes scholia and St. Paul," *ZNW* 48 (1957): 101–110; Victor C. Pfitzner, *Paul and the Agon Motif*, SNT, 16 (Leiden: Brill, 1967), *ad loc.*, 82–98.

32 τρέχειν, "run": Gal 2:2; 5:7; Phil 2:16; Rom 9:16; 2 Thess 3:1.

33 βραβεῖν: Bauer, *s.v.*

34 Is Paul taking his cue from a proverbial phrase? Luc., *Anach.* 13: ἀτὰρ εἰπέ μοι, πάντες αὐτὰ (sc. τὰ ἆθλα) λαμβάνουσιν οἱ ἀγωνισταί; οὐδαμῶς, ἀλλὰ εἷς ἐξ ἁπάντων ὁ κρατήσας αὐτῶν, Anacharsis: "But tell me, do all the contestants get them [i.e., prizes]?" Solon: "Not by any means; only one among them all, the victor" (Loeb 4:15).

35 ἐγκράτεια: Gal 5:23; *1 Cl.* 35.2; 62.2; 64. The figure is not applied strictly, see Lietzmann: no notice is taken of the fact that the ἐγκράτεια precedes the contest in time. The ideal of continence is of course also good Stoic doctrine. For ancient training see Plat., *Leg.* 840a (Olympic oath that the contestants have trained for ten months). Paul Stengel, *Die griechischen Kultusaltertümer*, 190–258. Pfitzner, *Paul and the Agon Motif*, 88f, thinks that if οὕτως τρέχετε is taken as imperative ("so run!"), then v 24 is given an independent significance which in fact it does not have: it serves merely to pave the way for v 25. The difficulty, he argues, is avoided if τρέχετε is taken as indicative ("you are running"). But the context demands an imperative; it, too, can be understood in the sense Pfitzner seeks, see the commentary above.

36 Prize: Jos., *Ant.* 4.182; 12.304; 8.208. Adolf Schlatter, *Die Theologie des Judentums nach dem Bericht des Josefus*, BFTh, 2, 26 (Gütersloh: Bertelsmann, 1932), 153. Exaltation of the ἀγὼν στεφανίτης, "contest for a crown," over against the χρηματίτης, "contest for a money prize," *IG* 12.8:63 (no. 190, lines 41–43); Lyc., *Leocr.* 12 (51). Wreath: Ludwig Deubner, "Die Bedeutung des Kranzes im klassischen Altertum," *ARW* 30 (1933): 70–104; K. Baus, *Der Kranz in Antike und Christentum*, Theophaneia, 2 (Bonn: Hanstein, 1940, repr. 1965).

37 Wis 5:15f; Philo, *Leg. all.* 2.108; 2 Tim 4:8; 1 Pet 5:4; Jas 1:12; Rev 2:10. ἄφθαρτος, "imperishable": cf. 15:42.

38 Epict., *Diss.* 2.15.20: ἀσθενὴς ψυχή, ὅπου μὲν κλίνει,

running unerringly.[38] The figure changes from running to boxing. ἀέρα δείρειν, "beat the air,"[39] is used of unpracticed fighters.[40]

■ **27** Taking up the metaphors, Paul presents himself as an athlete; but he goes on from the metaphor to its application: his battle is with himself.[41] The choice of the word κηρύσσειν, "preach," could in itself still be

influenced by the idea of a contest in the stadium; the word is intelligible also without it. Nor indeed is it meant metaphorically, but literally,[42] in the sense of the terminology generally prevailing in the early church (1:17, 18, 21, etc.).

ἄδηλον ἔχει, "the sick mind is uncertain which way it is inclined" (Loeb 1:321). The opposite of ἀδήλως, "uncertainly," is κατὰ σκοπόν, "toward the goal," Phil 3:14. Heinrici holds that ἀδήλως is presumably to be taken in an objective sense (one can see where he is going) rather than a subjective one (so Bengel, *Gnomon, ad loc.*: "I know what to aim at, and how" [Lewis and Vincent 2:214]).

39 ὡς again vacillates: from the point of view of the figure it means "like," from that of the application to Paul in v 27 "as."

40 Bauer, *s.vv.* ἀήρ, δείρω. Cf. Hom., *Il.* 20.466; Virgil, *Aen.* 5.377, etc.; Theophil., *Autol.* 3.2: τρόπῳ γάρ τινι οἱ τὰ ἄδηλα συγγράφοντες ἀέρα δέρουσιν, "for they who write of things unascertained beat the air" (ANF 2:111). Eustath. Thessal., *Comm. in Il.* 7.39f (p. 663, line 16): ὁ μόνος ὡς ἐν σκιαμαχίᾳ μαχόμενος καὶ ὅ φασιν ἀέρα δείρειν, "he who fights

alone, as in shadowboxing and that which they call 'beating the air' " [Trans.]. In the light of this Bachmann adopts the interpretation "pseudo-struggle"; too subjective.

41 *Test. Job* 4 (*Apocrypha Anecdota*, ed. Montague R. James, second series Texts and Studies, 5, 1 [Cambridge: University Press, 1899], 106): ὡς ἀθλητὴς πυκτεύων καὶ καρτερῶν πόνους καὶ ἐκδεχόμενος τὸν στέφανον, "like an athlete sparring and enduring his labors and receiving the crown" [Trans.]. Bachmann argues that it is not the body as such that is the opponent; Paul is thinking of misusage (4:11), deprivations. This brings about an inner connection between vv 23–27 and 1–22. Against Bachmann: Paul here lays the emphasis precisely on his own action, not on what comes upon him from without.

42 The same is true of ἀδόκιμος, "good for nothing." Ign., *Tr.* 12.3.

10

The Warning Example of the Wilderness Generation

1 For I would not have you ignorant, brothers, of the fact that our ancestors were all under the cloud and all passed through the sea, 2 / and were all baptized[1] into Moses in the cloud and in the sea, 3 / and all ate the same spiritual food and all drank the same spiritual drink.[2] 4 / That is, they drank[3] from a spiritual rock which followed them. The rock, however, was Christ. 5 / But with most of them God[4] was not well pleased;[5] for "they were laid low in the wilderness." 6 / But these things have become[6] examples for us, in order that we should not have a craving for evil as they craved it. 7 / Do not become idolaters either, as some of them were; as it is written, "The people sat down to eat and drink,[7] and rose up to play (or: dance)." 8 / Neither let us practice sexual immorality, as some of them did; and twenty–three thousand fell in one day. 9 / Neither let us tempt Christ,[8] as some of them did; and they were destroyed[9] by serpents. 10 / Do not grumble either, as some of them did; and they perished at the hand of the Destroyer. 11 / But these things happened to them by way of example; and they were written down to be a warning to us, upon whom the end of the ages has come. 12 / Therefore let the man who thinks he stands beware lest he fall! 13 / You have (so far) been overtaken by no temptation save only what is human. But God is faithful. He will not allow you to be tempted beyond your powers, but along with the temptation he will also provide a way out, so that you can bear it.

---

1 $\mathfrak{p}^{46}$ originally had $\dot{\epsilon}\beta\alpha\pi\tau\dot{\iota}\zeta o\nu\tau o$, but corrected it to $\dot{\epsilon}\beta\alpha\pi\tau\dot{\iota}\sigma\alpha\nu\tau o$. Zuntz, *Text*, 234, holds that the road from middle to passive is easier than the reverse.

Caution is called for in assessing the middle, since the use of the language has lost its precision and the sense is determined not so much by the formal rules of grammar as by the actual process of baptism. All the same, it may well be that we here catch a glimpse of the paraenetic purpose. They had themselves baptized, and afterwards changed their minds again. Take warning!

2 The aorist indicates a fact.

3 The imperfect indicates the manner.

4 Om. Marcion, see below.

5 Notice the tone that is imparted by putting the negative at the beginning [in the Greek text]. $\epsilon\dot{\upsilon}\delta o\kappa\epsilon\hat{\iota}\nu$ $\dot{\epsilon}\nu$, "be well pleased with": רצה ב.

6 Number [of the Greek verb] in accordance with the noun in the predicate: also classical, Kühner–Blass–Gerth 1:75f. The aorist denotes the result, Blass–Debrunner §327.

7 $\pi\epsilon\hat{\iota}\nu$ is the Hellenistic, contracted infinitive of $\pi\dot{\iota}\nu\omega$, Blass–Debrunner §31(2).

8 $X\rho\iota\sigma\tau\dot{o}\varsigma$ is the reading of $\mathfrak{p}^{46}$ D G Marcion, Clem Al, Orig, $\mathfrak{M}$ latt, $\kappa\dot{\upsilon}\rho\iota o\varsigma$ ℵ B C $\mathfrak{p}^{33}$ syr^{hmg}. Zuntz, *Text*, 126f is emphatically in favor of $X\rho\iota\sigma\tau\dot{o}\varsigma$.

9 $\dot{\alpha}\pi\dot{\omega}\lambda\lambda o\nu\tau o$ ℵ B; $\dot{\alpha}\pi\dot{\omega}\lambda o\nu\tau o$ C D G $\mathfrak{M}$.

10 His exegetical method has earlier patterns in Hellenistic Judaism. The content is in part also drawn from there. The most important material for comparison is provided by Philo. Perhaps we have a glimpse of differences between Jewish schools of exegesis, see on 11:2ff. On Philo see Edmund Stein, *Die allegorische Exegese des Philo aus Alexandrien*, BZAW, 51 (Giessen: Töpelmann, 1929). On typology in general: Leonhard Goppelt, *Typos. Die typolo-*

Verses 1–10 constitute a self–contained, scribal discourse on passages from the biblical exodus narrative: the cloud (Ex 13:21), the sea (Ex 14:21f), the manna (Ex 16:4, 14–18), the spring (Ex 17:6; Num 20:7–13), the apostasy (Ex 32:6). The style of Paul's "typological" exposition shows that the biblical material is assumed to be known:[10] "the" cloud, etc. The new element which Paul has to offer is the *interpretation* introduced by οὐ θέλω ὑμᾶς ἀγνοεῖν "I would not have you ignorant."

At first sight this section appears to be totally foreign to its context. Its significance in the context of this epistle[11] only gradually becomes plain when Paul comes to the topic of εἰδωλολατρία "idolatry" (v 7), and then in the concluding warning against *securitas*, "cocksureness" (vv 11–13).[12] Once again we have apparently a piece of teaching that was already established before the composing of the epistle.[13]

■ **1** οἱ πατέρες ἡμῶν, "our ancestors": Paul is speaking as a Jew, but includes also his Gentile–Christian readers. The church is the true Israel.[14] The result is that, as compared with Jewish typology, both method and content of the exposition are transformed in accordance with the church's historic self–understanding. The

biblical story of "the cloud" requires only to be alluded to because it is known. The accent lies on πάντες, "all"; cf. the repetition in vv 2, 3, 4. The interpretation is focused in the first instance entirely upon the collective people of God: sin consists somewhat in failure on the part of the whole people, but somewhat also in lapsing from this people.

That they were "under" the cloud is in keeping with the LXX of Ps 104:39 (cf. Wis 10:17; 19:7), whereas in Ex 13:21 the cloud goes before them. Paul uses the former version because of the analogy to διελθεῖν, passing through the sea (Ex 14:21ff), that is, because of the parallel interpretation of cloud and sea in terms of baptism. In so doing he can claim the support of conceptions of Jewish exegesis.[15]

■ **2** Verse 2 brings the typological interpretation in terms of baptism.[16] How far is it possible for Paul here, too, to operate with motifs from Jewish and pre–Pauline Christian exposition?[17] And how strictly does he regard the correspondence? Does he think that the process recounted by the Old Testament was really a sacrament? That is to say, is the baptism "into Moses" meant real-

---

gische Deutung des Alten Testaments im Neuen, BFTh, 2, 43 (Gütersloh: Bertelsmann, 1939); *ThWNT* 8:246–260 (bibliography); Rudolf Bultmann, "Ursprung und Sinn der Typologie als hermeneutischer Methode," in *Pro Regno, pro Sanctuario: een bundel studies en bijdragen . . . bij de zestigste verjaardag van Prof. Dr. G. van der Leeuw*, ed. Willem Jan Kooiman and J. M. van Veen (Nijkerk: Callenbach, 1950), 89–100, also published in *ThLZ* 75 (1950): 205–212, and now in his *Exegetica*, 369–380. On 1 Cor 10:1–13 see Gustave Martelet, "Sacrements, figures et exhortation en 1 Cor X,1–11," *RechSR* 44 (1956): 323–359, 515–559; Ulonska, *Paulus und das Alte Testament*, 110ff; Klaus Galley, *Altes und neues Heilsgeschehen bei Paulus*, Arbeiten zur Theologie, 1, 22 (Stuttgart: Calwer, 1965), 12–17; Feuillet, *Le Christ Sagesse*, 87–111. Ulonska denies that we have "typology" here. τύπος, he argues, denotes not a method of exegesis, but the paraenetic aim. But this is not a sound objection. The fact remains that the OT narrative points beyond itself, and moreover to the church. Ulonska is, however, right in maintaining that Paul does not offer an argument in terms of "salvation history" in favor of the validity of Christian baptism.

11 Or of a part of this epistle.

12 Weiss argues that Paul does not here adopt the standpoint of the "free" and that the section is better

assigned to the earlier letter.

13 Ulrich Luz, *Das Geschichtsverständnis des Paulus*, BEvTh, 49 (Munich: Kaiser, 1968), 117–123.

14 Gal 6:16; Phil 3:3.

15 See Str.–B. 3:405f. In the Midrash we find the idea: (*a*) that the people were enveloped in the cloud, *M. Ex.* 13:21 [30a], cited in Str.–B., *Tg. J.* I to Ex 13:20–22: "And they journeyed from Succoth, the place where they had been covered with the clouds of glory. . . . And the glory of the Shekinah of the Lord went before them by day in the column of the Cloud . . . and at night the column of the Cloud removed behind them . . . to be a column of fire to enlighten them before" (John Wesley Etheridge, *The Targums of Onkelos and Jonathan ben Uzziel of the Pentateuch with Fragments of the Jerusalem Targum from the Chaldee* [London: Longmans, 1862; New York: KTAV, 1968] 1:484f); (*b*) that the sea became a tunnel, so that the people "passed through" the sea: *M. Ex.* 14:16 (36a): "Ten miracles were performed for Israel at the sea. The sea was broken through and made like a vault" (Lauterbach 1:223).

16 For baptismal typology cf. also 1 Pet 3:20f.

17 According to Gerhard Friedrich, *TDNT* 6:837, the linking together of baptism and the wilderness period must be pre–Pauline because Paul himself avoids the linking together of Moses and Christ.

istically?[18] In what sense? Or is the expression "into Moses" merely formed on analogy to "into Christ," and thus merely an *ad hoc* construction in the service of the exegesis? But this alternative is hardly one of which Paul was conscious in this form. It should be noted that his thought moves back to the Old Testament from the present datum, baptism, and certainly does not vice versa derive and interpret baptism from the Old Testament. Paul does not seek a point–for–point correspondence; he is satisfied with the exemplary character of the history of Israel in one specific respect:[19] apparently the cloud is the sign of the divine presence, and to this the Spirit in baptism corresponds.[20]

■ **3–4** The presentation of the second sacrament[21] (according to Ex 17:6; Num 20:7–11) is twofold in accordance with the two acts of the celebration of the Lord's Supper (in the same sequence as the latter, see on vv 16f). The distribution of the accent between πάντες, "all," and τὸ αὐτό, "the same," corresponds to the thought of sacramental κοινωνία, "communion," which is developed later. Here, too, Paul is thinking not of a real, Old Testament sacrament, but of a prefiguration. The form of expression, "spiritual food" and "spiritual drink," is apparently assumed to be familiar.[22] It expresses a realistic concept of the sacrament.[23] This is maintained by Paul, though admittedly also further developed insofar as his historic intention later becomes visible.

Verse 4b brings to light the systematic presupposition of this exegesis:[24] the concept of the preexistence of

---

Joachim Jeremias, "Der Ursprung der Johannestaufe," *ZNW* 28 (1929): 312–320, says the underlying motif is a rabbinical Scripture proof which is meant to justify the practice of proselyte baptism. In criticism of this Maurice Goguel, *The Primitive Church*, tr. H. C. Snape (London: Allen & Unwin, 1964), 291f (*Jésus et les origines du christianisme*, vol. 3 [Paris: Payot, 1947], 304–306), points out that Paul also speaks of the Eucharist, and that there no Jewish model can be postulated; so that we have presumably an original train of thought developed by Paul. And Kümmel observes that the rabbinical tradition is in fact at a loss to find a Scripture proof for proselyte baptism; Paul has worked out his exegesis himself on the basis of the Midrash.

18 So Lietzmann: because of course the rock was Christ. "When one follows out the Apostle's typological exposition, it is easy to understand how salvation was bound up with Moses for the Israelites in much the same way as for Christians it is bound up with Christ." Against Lietzmann: his expression "for the Israelites" is not covered by the text. Weiss is similarly subjective: they delivered themselves into the possession of Moses; they were *materially* bound up with him. Paul Neuenzeit, *Das Herrenmahl*, SANT, 1 (Munich: Kösel, 1960), 47, holds that the comparison is not in the first instance between the OT marks of salvation and the sacraments, but between libertinism then and now, and that we accordingly must not jump to the conclusion that Paul ascribes sacramental character to these marks of salvation. But why, in that case, does Paul take up this typology at all? We must draw a different conclusion: it is the very structure of the typology itself that tells against the direct equation of sacrament then and sacrament now.

19 With Per Ivar Lundberg, *La typologie baptismale dans l'ancienne église*, ASNU, 10 (Uppsala: Lundequist; Leipzig: Lorentz, 1942), 135–145.

20 See Kümmel; he rightly lays down that the passage through the sea must not be interpreted as a representation of the baptism "of death." There exists no evidence that the Red Sea was regarded as a death element.

21 The combining of baptism and the Lord's Supper shows that Paul has a comprehensive concept of "sacraments," even if he has not yet a word for it. The question as to whether the number of the sacraments can be multiplied is misguided.

22 *Did.* 10.3.

23 It will not do to reduce the sense of πνευματικός, "spiritual," to "supernatural." Certainly the manna is supernatural, heavenly food (Ps 77:24 LXX), and the Spirit comes from heaven. But the idea of the Spirit contains a substantial component. The latter is not to be denied by pointing out that the Spirit cannot be strictly bound to the element in practice, and arguing that accordingly πνευματικός means simply imparting the Spirit (Käsemann, *Essays on New Testament Themes*, tr. W. J. Montague, SBT, 1, 41 [London: SCM, 1964], 113 [15]), not "containing the Spirit." Against Eduard Schweizer, *TDNT* 6:436f.

24 Without prejudice to the link with the Jewish method; the latter is theologically refashioned.

25 In it the rock becomes peripatetic, see *T. Sukka* 3.11 (196): "So the well, which was with Israel in the wilderness . . . travelling with them up the mountains and going down with them in the valleys" (*Sukkah, Mishna and Tosefta*, tr. A. W. Greenup, Translations of Early Documents, Series III: Rabbinic Texts [London: SPCK, 1925], 76). Ps.–Philo, *Ant. bib.* 10.7. Oscar Cullmann, *TDNT* 6:97; Str.–B. 3:406–408.

Christ. Once again Paul sets out from a Jewish haggadic tradition.[25] The "was" of the typological statement, of the interpretation of the rock as being Christ, means real preexistence, not merely symbolic significance.[26] This is plain from the dependence upon Jewish tradition, which interprets the rock as referring to preexistent Wisdom:[27] Philo, *Leg. all.* 2.86: "For the flinty rock [ἀκρότομος πέτρα] is (!) the Wisdom of God, which He marked off highest and chiefest from His powers, and from which He satisfies the thirsty souls that love God" (Loeb 1:279). The common tradition is all the plainer for the fact that the interpretations of Philo and Paul are different.[28]

■ **5** Following the repeated πάντες, "all," we have a strong contrast: ἀλλ' οὐκ ἐν τοῖς πλείοσιν κτλ., "but with most of them . . . not. . . ."[29] εὐδοκεῖν, "to be well pleased," is not an emotion on God's part, but means his election, or, to put it otherwise, negates his rejection. That is to say, the presence of Christ does not work in the manner of a natural charm. This means for the Christian that partaking of the sacrament does not confer a *character indelebilis*. The application to the "strong" and to their combination of pneumatism and sacramentalism

is obvious.[30] The statement is proved by an allusion to Num 14:16, 30. γάρ, "for." designates the criterion.

■ **6** τύπος, "example," means the prototype or pattern, and the copy. Both meanings provide possibilities for developing the word into a hermeneutic concept (see on v 1). *Here*, to be sure, we have not yet to do with the technical, hermeneutical use of the term, but with its moral sense; the latter is determined by v 5 and by the imperative in v 7.[31] The warning against ἐπιθυμία, "craving" (note the choice of the first person: τύποι ἡμῶν, "examples for us"), is comprehensive;[32] it is then made specific in terms of the two topics already discussed before: εἰδωλολατρία, "idolatry," and πορνεία, "sexual immorality."

Paul does not say that the sacrament becomes effectual only through obedience, but on the contrary that the effectual sacrament is partaken of to our judgment if we misuse it through disobedience.

■ **7** Cf. the LXX of Ex 32:6. The connection between "eating" and idolatry is understandable to the reader from chap. 8, while the combination of eating and drinking has been prepared for by vv 3f. παίζειν, "play," can mean "dance," *scil.* in the cult, idolatry.[33]

---

26 Neuenzeit, *Herrenmahl*, 52, is of a different mind: the statement is no proof of the personal presence of Christ, against Johannes Behm, *TDNT* 3:738f. But the presence of Christ is the presupposition of this exegesis. It is this that also lends significance to the choice of the imperfect instead of a purely exegetical present. For the present see *CD* 6.4: "The well is the Law" (Dupont–Sommer, 131); 1QS VIII,7 "It is the tried wall" (*ibid.*, 91); *CD* 20.3 (9.31 B): "He is the man who is melted in the midst of the furnace" (cf. *ibid.*, 139); cf. Acts 4:11: οὗτός ἐστιν ὁ λίθος κτλ., "this is the stone, etc."

27 For preexistence Christology and Wisdom, see on 8:6.

28 Philo allegorically equates the three elements rock, water and manna (cf. *Det. pos. ins.* 118). Paul breaks through the analogy on the basis of his Christology. For the stone–water typology see Just., *Dial.* 114.4. Cf. also Ps.-Cl., *Recog.* 1.35. Klein, *Die zwölf Apostel*, 197, asks whether 1 Cor 10:4c is a gloss. It is not.

29 Cf. Ps 77:31 LXX (B S).

30 Cf. the popular idea of the power of the mysteries and the philosophical criticism of it. Plut., *Aud. poet.* 21F: Diogenes objects that, if the mysteries are effectual, morality will be destroyed, for κρείττονα μοῖραν ἕξει Παταικίων ὁ κλέπτης ἀποθανὼν ἢ Ἐπαμεινώνδας ὅτι μεμύηται, "Pataecion, the rob-

ber, will have a better portion after death than Epaminondas, just because he is initiate" (Loeb 1:113). On the effect of the mysteries see Rohde, *Psyche*, 228f, 238–240, 294–297 [1:298–300, 307–314; 2:69–80]; Nilsson, *Geschichte*, 2:657–672. The Gnostics know themselves to be immunized and behave accordingly, Iren., *Haer.* 1.6.3, on the Valentinians: καὶ γὰρ εἰδωλόθυτα ἀδιαφόρως ἐσθίουσιν, "For instance, they make no scruple about eating meats offered in sacrifice to idols" (ANF 1:324).

31 Lietzmann finds here the starting point of the technical development. For the latter cf. Rom 5:14; then *Barn.* 7.3, 7, 10f, etc. On the whole topic see Goppelt, *Typos*.

32 Rom 7:7ff sums up the whole Law in the prohibiting of ἐπιθυμεῖν; cf. here the general term κακῶν, "evil things."

33 Hebrew לְצַחֵק. Rabbinical exegesis interprets צַחֵק as referring to idolatry, and finds support for this in Ex 32:6; see Str.-B. 3:410. In itself it is tempting to interpret the parallelism as follows: they sit down to the meal =εἰδωλολατρία, and rise up to παίζειν =πορνεία—the more so as in the OT and Judaism the association εἰδωλολατρία/πορνεία is already traditional. But in the warning against πορνεία Paul alludes to a different passage.

■ **8–10** These verses recall Num 25:1ff, and a commentary on their content is provided by 5:1ff.[34] The number in Num 25:9 is 24,000. Has Paul been led astray by a recollection of Num 26:62 (and Ex 32:28?)? The tone is intensified by the change from the imperative of v 7 to the first person plural.

■ **9** Cf. Num 21:5f. While we may here think of the spiritual pride of the Corinthians, yet the warning is purposely couched in general terms.[35]

■ **10** Between πειράζειν, "tempting," and "grumbling" (Num 14:2, 27, 36f; 17:6ff) no clear–cut distinction is to be made.[36]

■ **11** Here the paraenetic sense of τύπος (see on v 6) is explicitly affirmed.[37] A further element of the exegesis now emerges, the eschatological aspect. The typology is not arbitrary. The Old Testament narrative has an eye to the last age.[38] Weiss understands: "we in whom the ends of the aeons meet." But the starting point is not called τέλος; rather, the plural τέλη is to be understood in a singular sense of the end of a unity.[39] The plural αἰῶνες, "aeons," likewise does not have to be taken as referring to a number of world–epochs.[40] The plural designates simply the world–age, from the point of view of its limitation.[41] Paul does not develop the apocalyptic picture beyond the statement that the end is immediately imminent (cf. 7:26, 29).

■ **12** Verse 12 issues in the form of a maxim a warning to the strong: the sacrament is spiritual food, yet the latter is not effectual *qua* substance, but by bringing us into the body of Christ and to newness of life. The formulation in general terms shows that the criticism is directed not merely at individual improprieties, but at the Corinthian position as a whole, the unity of sacramental and pneumatic *securitas*, "cocksureness."[42] The important thing is not so much the censure for the past as the warning for the future.[43]

■ **13** The truth underlying the maxim of v 12—that the man who stands can fall—is *manifested* in the fact of

---

34 On the affinity between εἰδωλολατρία and πορνεία, cf. Wis 14:12; *Test. R.* 4.6; Philo, *Vit. Mos.* 1.302.

35 The content of πειράζειν is explained by Ps 77:18: καὶ ἐξεπείρασαν τὸν θεὸν ἐν ταῖς καρδίαις αὐτῶν τοῦ αἰτῆσαι βρώματα ταῖς ψυχαῖς αὐτῶν, "And they tested God in their hearts by demanding food for their selfish desires" (literally "for their souls").

36 Does the return to direct address (imperative) imply an intentional dig at the bravado of the strong? Heinrici holds that Paul is presumably alluding not to Num 14 (where a violent death is not in place) but to the LXX of Num 16:6, 21, 32, 41, 46, 49. Cf. ὁ ὀλεθρεύων, "the destroyer," in Ex 12:23 for הַמַּשְׁחִית On the orthography: usually ὀλεθρευτής. In Judaism מַשְׁחִית had become the proper name of an angel, Str.–B. 3:412f; see Johannes Schneider, *TDNT* 5:169f. Variant reading ὀλεθρεύων as in Ex 12:23; Wis 18:25; cf. Heb 11:28.

37 Zuntz, *Text*, 233, would delete as a gloss both τυπικῶς and also the variant, τύπος, which according to Adamantius is to be postulated for Marcion; cf. *ibid.*, 166, n. 5.

38 The time factor in the typology can have nothing corresponding to it in Philo.

39 Bauer, *s.v.* αἰών 2 b.

40 So Robertson and Plummer. Completely mistaken is the notion that each epoch has the quintessence of the preceding one transmitted to it. Allo changes the idea into its opposite when he explains that the final epoch can last a long time.

In itself the division of the course of the world into several epochs is good apocalyptic practice: *4 Ezra* 6:7–10; the apocalypse of (ten) weeks, *Eth. En.* 93+ 91.12–17; the genealogy of Jesus in Mt 1:1ff. In Qumran the near expectation is combined with the ordering of the ages, 1QpHab VII,1f: "and God told Habakkuk to write down the things which will come to pass in the last generation, but the consummation of time He made not known to him" (Dupont–Sommer, 262). There follows an eschatological paraenesis. Then VII, 12f: "for all the ages of God come in their order" (cf. *ibid.*, 263).

Paul makes no play with divisions of this kind. Where he contrasts periods in salvation history with each other (Adam – Moses – Christ, Rom 5; Abraham – Moses – Christ, Gal 3), he neither develops the period schema as such, nor does he designate the epochs as αἰῶνες.

41 *Test. L.* 14.1: ἐπὶ τὰ τέλη τῶν αἰώνων, "at the end of the ages" (Charles, *APOT* 2:312); Heb 9:26 (συντέλεια, "consummation").

42 For a variant in the Qumran style, see 1QS III,4: the obdurate "shall not be absolved by atonement, nor purified by lustral waters" (Dupont–Sommer, 76).

43 "Stand" in the sense of having oneself under control; cf. 7:37; 2 Cor 1:24; Rom 11:20. The warning is addressed not only to the strong, but to the whole community, see on v 22. The statement provokes the question as to the possibility of assurance of salvation. This is not denied here by Paul. For assurance is gained not by self–observation, but by applying oneself to the proffered salvation: it is appropriated by word and sacrament.

πειρασμός, "temptation," which does not merely have to be reckoned with as a possibility, but is rather already a reality in Corinth. We cannot say what kind of events are in mind.[44] Paul is concerned only to indicate the sense. That the temptation is "human" does not mean that it proceeds from men, but presumably simply that it is still relatively bearable.[45] Verse 13a is of course comfort, not warning.[46]

Temptation brings to light how unrealistic the knowledge of the strong people is. For indeed they adopt a position as if nothing could happen; they put an unhistoric world picture in the place of existence. When temptation comes, then in Corinth there are no longer strong people and weak people, but people in need of comfort. This comfort is derived from the knowledge of the nature of God: πιστὸς ὁ θεός, "God is faithful" (see on 1:9).[47]

ὑπὲρ ὁ δύνασθε, "beyond your powers": the measure of the bearable cannot be theoretically determined. It shows itself on each occasion in the measure God appoints.

ἀλλὰ ποιήσει κτλ., "but he will provide, etc.": this in itself can be a mere cliché. But in its Pauline context we have here a reference to the eschatological manifestation and liberation. Paul does not say that God helps again and again, He is speaking of the *one* eschatological act of salvation.

Here God appears to be described as the author of πειρασμός, "temptation": οὐκ ἐάσει . . . ἀλλὰ ποιήσει κτλ., "he will not suffer . . . but will provide, etc." But ἐάσει cannot be reduced to a mere tolerance of temptation on God's part, and Paul has just as little interest in a theory of its origin. He derives his statement from the awaited eschatological salvation, not from a theoretical consideration of the course of the world.[48]

ἔκβασις is (from the perspective of the present situation) either the way out (Lietzmann) or the issue, the end (Weiss).[49] According to the interpretation adopted, the infinitive ("so that you can") is to be taken as final or explicative respectively.

---

44 The question should not be raised whether πειρα-σμός here means "temptation" or "trial" as alternatives. It depends of course on what we understand by the one thing and by the other. Both can tacitly be taken in a Stoic sense. Paul gives no guidance as to how one can become "steadfast" through training. Of the readers' attitude he says nothing at all—or if so, then in warning (v 12).

45 So Joachim Jeremias, *TDNT* 1:366f; cf. Poll., *Onom.* 3.131: ὃ οὐκ ἄν τις ὑπομένειεν, ὃ οὐκ ἄν τις ἐνέγκοι, . . . τὸ δ' ἐναντίον κοῦφον, εὔφορον . . . ἀνθρώπινον, "that which one need not submit to, need not bear, . . . but that which on the contrary is light, easily borne . . . human" [Trans.]. Epict., *Diss.* 1.9.30; *Ench.* 26; Num 5:6. Others understand "human" as opposed to the apocalyptic trial (Schlatter).

46 Von Soden, "Sakrament und Ethik," 11f. Bachmann holds that v 13a is not yet comfort, but a strengthening of the warning: Paul is telling them that they have not yet had to endure severe testing. Heinrich Seesemann, *TDNT* 6:28f, argues that the word of comfort does not really fit into the context.

Both explanations fail to understand the text. Temptation is not being theoretically discussed, but Paul is relating the objective situation of the Corinthians to their subjective attitude and revealing the contradiction, to their genuine comfort.

47 This comfort is genuine only when "God" does not remain a cipher, but is known through the *demonstration* of his faithfulness.

48 σὺν τῷ πειρασμῷ, "with the temptation," can be taken temporally, Karl Georg Kuhn, "New Light on Temptation, Sin, and Flesh in the New Testament," in *The Scrolls and the New Testament*, ed. Krister Stendahl (New York: Harper, 1957), 94–113, here esp. 108f (originally in *ZThK* 49 [1952]: esp. 217f). We can also assume that it is governed at the same time by ποιήσει, "he will provide" (Weiss; von Soden, "Sakrament und Ethik," 11, n. 1), cf. Rom 8:32; 1 Cor 11:32; 2 Cor 1:21; 4:14; Gal 3:9; 5:24; Col 2:13; 3:4, 9; 1 Thess 4:14, 17 (passages in which σύν, "with," links up with the object).

49 According to Weiss, if the meaning were "the way out," the words τοῦ δύνασθαι ὑπενεγκεῖν, "so that you can bear it," would be superfluous.

10

The Lord's Supper as Criterion

14 Therefore, my dear friends, shun idolatry! 15 / I speak to you as intelligent people. Judge for yourselves what I say! 16 / The cup of blessing which we bless, is it not participation in the blood of Christ?[1] The bread[2] which we break, is it not participation in the body of Christ? 17 / For we are one body, one bread, many as we are; for we all partake of the one bread.[3] 18 / Look at the earthly Israel: are not those who eat of the sacrifices partners in the altar? What do I mean then? 19 / That meat sacrificed to an idol is anything? or that the idol is anything?[4] 20 / No, rather that what they sacrifice, they sacrifice "to demons and not to God." But I do not want you to become partners of demons. 21 / You cannot drink the cup of the Lord and the cup of demons. You cannot partake of the Lord's table and the table of demons.[5] Or would we seek to provoke the Lord to jealousy? Are we by any chance stronger than he?

The train of thought in this section is self–contained. It stands out plainly from vv 23ff.

■ **14–15** The catchword $\epsilon\dot{\iota}\delta\omega\lambda o\lambda a\tau\rho\dot{\iota}a$, "idolatry," is prepared for by v 7. But it is hardly possible to discern a strict connection of thought with the preceding section, in spite of $\delta\iota\dot{o}\pi\epsilon\rho$, "therefore."[6] Formally speaking, the movement of thought is loose. It is only gradually that the intrinsic coherence emerges; the assertion in the preceding section, that not even the sacrament works as a charm, now becomes the criterion of conduct. But what is the problem involved here? Is the topic the same as in chap. 8, that is, $\epsilon\dot{\iota}\delta\omega\lambda\dot{o}\theta v\tau a$, "meat sacrificed to idols"?[7] A connection does exist, but we have also to notice a shift. In the former passage it was a question of eating, here it is a question of the food.[8] There the rule was freedom (together with the limitation of it by our brother). For the matter of eating was to begin with an open question. Where the worship of idols is concerned, on the other hand, there is no question at all. Here the rule is the apodictic $\phi\epsilon\dot{v}\gamma\epsilon\tau\epsilon$, "shun!"[9] There the criterion was the conscience, which has to decide. Here the emphasis is on the sacrament, which creates ex-

---

1 Note the use of Christ again with the article.

2 Note the accusative. $\tau\dot{o}v\ \dot{a}\rho\tau ov$ is attracted to $\ddot{o}v$ by inverse attraction: Blass–Debrunner §295.

3 "Because *one* bread, we, many as we are, are *one* body." So Bachmann, arguing that $\epsilon\dot{\iota}s\ \ddot{a}\rho\tau os$ cannot be taken with $\dot{\epsilon}\sigma\mu\dot{\epsilon}v$ as predicate, and that consequently $\ddot{o}\tau\iota$ introduces a causal protasis. But see Weiss: if the $\ddot{o}\tau\iota$ clause is an elliptical protasis, then in the ensuing asyndeton "the sudden transition of thought is doubly disconcerting."

4 This clause is omitted by p[46] ℵ* A C*. Is it a result of homoioteleuton?

5 For the omission of the article see Blass–Debrunner §259(3): It occurs when the emphasis is on the characteristic quality: a table of the Lord—a table of demons.

6 According to Lietzmann, Paul now returns to the main topic, which was abandoned in chap. 9 and only briefly touched upon in 10:6f. But have we here the same topic as in chap. 8? See below. Weiss points to 8:13 for $\delta\iota\dot{o}\pi\epsilon\rho$; v 14 can be taken as a conclusion or as a transition to what follows.

7 Von Soden, "Sakrament und Ethik," 20, observes (on the link between chap. 8 and 10:14ff): "The question introduced in 10:19 can hardly be understood otherwise than as a resumption of 8:4; for indeed the concession in 8:4 appears to be abandoned in 10:14ff. 8:5 indicates that the question of the reality of idols has not yet been brought to a conclusion in 8:4; how far idols nevertheless do have a reality, though not the reality they are conceived to have, namely, that in effect they are demons— in other words, how far it is true that although there exist no idols, yet there does exist idol worship—is shown by 10:20."

8 Naturally, the other factor is also in view in either

clusiveness.[10]

Once again Paul appeals to the power of discernment.[11] The formal contradiction to 3:1ff is of no great importance.[12]

■ 16 In introducing the Lord's Supper as criterion, Paul resorts to the traditional terminology and the recognized significance of the Lord's Supper as a communal act. The formal parallelism is presumably also inspired by the tradition. If we have now to inquire into the relationship between the tradition and Paul's shaping of it, then the first problem is the sequence of the two sacramental acts, the distribution of the bread and of the cup. When Paul mentions the cup first, is he then linking up with a form of celebration of the Lord's Supper in which the cup was distributed first? Or has he himself reversed the order for particular reasons?

His dependence on the tradition appears in the expression "cup of blessing." It derives from the practice at Jewish meals, as is already indicated by the non–Greek form of expression (the use of the genitive, the meaning of εὐλογία, "blessing"; see on 14:16).[13] There follows the interpretation: this cup "is" the κοινωνία τοῦ αἵματος τοῦ Χριστοῦ, "participation in the blood of Christ." The traditional element is in the first instance the presupposed identification of the wine distributed and drunk with the blood of Christ; see on 11:25. The basic idea is that of the atoning power of the blood.[14] Does κοινωνία,[15] then, mean "communion" or "participation"? For the answer, we have to take account of the word "is,"[16] and then of the commentary which Paul himself provides in v 17. It becomes plain that the proposed alternative is not a real one. The starting point is certainly the meaning "participation":[17] the partaking of the meal confers a share in the blood,[18] and that means in terms of content, communion with the death of Christ.[19] The thought is understandable from the idea that a sacral meal establishes communion with the god of the cult (see below).[20]

9　φεύγετε is a standard term of paraenesis, cf. 6:18; with ἀπό, Mt 3:7. The use with the accusative and with ἀπό is identical in meaning.

10　An excellent description of the situation is provided by von Soden.

11　Cf. 11:13; 14:20. It is not necessary to lay emphatic stress on ὑμεῖς.

12　φρόνιμος, "intelligent," is not ironical; cf. the proemium.

13　After the meal the prayer of thanksgiving is spoken over the "cup of blessing" (כּוֹס שֶׁל בְּרָכָה), see b. Ber. 51a; Str.–B. 4:630f; Leonhard Goppelt, TDNT 6:153–158. At the Passover meal it is the third cup, see Str.–B. 4:72. Since the cup of blessing does not belong only to the Passover meal, the term tells us nothing as to whether the Lord's Supper was understood as a Passover meal (see on 11:23ff). ὃ εὐλογοῦμεν, "which we bless," is declared by Lietzmann to be a pleonasm. Goppelt sees in the expression an attempt to distinguish the Christian from the Jewish cup of blessing. But no anti–Jewish polemic is in view in this passage. It is a question of ceremonious style.

14　It is indicated by ὑπέρ. According to Goppelt, TDNT 6:143, n. 70, "blood" does not mean the blood as a substance, "but the death of Christ as a saving event" (cf. Johannes Behm, TDNT 1:174) in which we acquire a part only through his self–oblation.

15　Friedrich Hauck, TDNT 3:797–809.

16　This, according to Lietzmann, is a pregnant form of expression. The meaning is: "is a means to the acquiring of communion." Heinrich Seesemann, Der Begriff κοινωνία im Neuen Testament, BZNW, 14 (Giessen: Töpelmann, 1933), 34–56, holds that the believer enjoys in the wine and bread the blood and body of the Lord. Against this, Kümmel argues that it is rather that the eating of the one bread creates participation in the body of the Lord, cf. 11:26–29. 10:20 does not speak of eating the demons, but of participation in them. Christ is not the object of the drink, but the giver of it. Their joint partaking of it confirms the Christians to be members of the body. The constitutive factor is the participation in the meal, not the partaking of the elements; see von Soden, "Sakrament und Ethik," 26–30.

17　Note μετέχομεν. Johannes Betz, Die Eucharistie in der Zeit der griechischen Väter, vol. 2, part 1 (Freiburg: Herder, 1961), 110–114. Neuenzeit, Herrenmahl, 178–183.

18　Objective genitive, cf. Plat., Soph. 250b: ἡ τῆς οὐσίας κοινωνία, "participation in existence" (cf. Loeb, 2:389).

19　The elements certainly must not be eliminated. But Betz goes too far when he speaks of a "physical" link with the person of Jesus, Eucharistie 2.1:113.

20　Material: Hauck, TDNT 3:798–800 (on κοινων– in sacral language). Demosth., Or. 19.280: κρατήρων κοινωνοὺς πεποίησθε (sc̄. τοὺς ἥρωας), "you have given [the heroes] shares of the drink–offerings" (cf. Loeb, 431). Plat., Symp. 188b: ἔτι τοίνυν καὶ αἱ θυσίαι πᾶσαι καὶ οἷς μαντικὴ ἐπιστατεῖ— ταῦτα δ᾽ ἐστὶν ἡ περὶ θεούς τε καὶ ἀνθρώπους πρὸς

There follows an analogous interpretation of the breaking of bread.[21] The formal parallel must not cause us to overlook the fact that at the Pauline level of interpretation the parallel is modified: for Paul, "body" is not simply the correlate of "blood." He is thinking already of the "body of Christ," the church. This explains also the reversal of bread and cup: Paul is aiming at an interpretation of the community by means of the Lord's Supper; cf. the step from v 16 to v 17. This link between the Lord's Supper and the concept of the church is the new element which he introduces into the understanding of the sacrament.[22] Thus we have not to deduce from v 16 a peculiar form of the liturgy of the Lord's Supper, in which the cup was distributed before the bread.[23]

■ **17** Verse 17a[24] gives us light on the sequence in v 16: Paul takes up the notion of ἄρτος/σῶμα, "bread/body," because he has the thought of the body of Christ in mind. "Body" as a designation of the church is not meant figuratively, but in the proper sense: the church is not "like" a body, but *is* "the" body of Christ; see on 12:13. The sacramental participation in Christ's body makes us into the body of Christ.[25] The emphasis lies on the unity.[26] In correspondence with this the church is collectively divorced from the demons.

If ὅτι, "for," in v 17b is taken in a causal sense,[27] then this is a more precise explanation of the reason why the bread can have this effect. That would be an artificial notion. Otherwise the passage explains the thesis as a whole: unity, for . . . μετέχειν ἐκ, "partake of," explains the meaning of κοινωνία. In view of the situation in Corinth this means that partaking of the Lord's Supper does not first and foremost serve the edification of the individual, but unites the individuals to form the body of Christ. Otherwise the nature of the bread as *one* bread would be left out of account.[28]

■ **18** This verse brings a "historical" proof (but one extending into Paul's own day) by citing the practice of Israel,[29] which is unquestioningly recognized as valid. The scriptural foundation is Lev 7:6, 15; Deut 18:1–4. The sacrifice institutes a communal meal, and this means communion with the god to whom the sacrifice is made and to whom the altar belongs.[30] The Old Testament regulation refers in the first instance to the cult personnel, but also the the people; cf. Deut 12:11f.[31]

■ **19–20** The thoughts tumble over each other. Paul begins by assuming the reader already knows, as indeed

---

ἀλλήλους κοινωνία, "So further, all sacrifices and ceremonies controlled by divination, namely, all means of communion between gods and men" (Loeb 5:131). Ael. Arist., *Or.* 27: καὶ τοίνυν καὶ θυσιῶν μόνῳ τούτῳ θεῷ διαφερόντως κοινωνοῦσιν ἄνθρωποι τὴν ἀκριβῆ κοινωνίαν, καλοῦντές τε ἐφ᾽ ἑστίαν καὶ προϊστάμενοι δαιτυμόνα αὐτὸν καὶ ἑστιάτορα . . ., "And furthermore, in sacrificing to this one god men severally share genuine communion, both calling him to the altar as their guest and deferring to him as their host . . ." [Trans.].

21 See on 11:24 below. Against an ecclesiological interpretation of σῶμα already in v 16, see Betz, *Eucharistie* 2.1:113f.

22 See references to Käsemann and Bornkamm in the notes on 11:23ff below.

23 Nor is Lk 22:17ff evidence for such a form of celebration. The sequence there—cup, bread, cup—has arisen from a combination of sources. It does not represent the actual course of the Supper.

24 Weiss declares v 17 to be a digression. But it is a well-aimed interpretation.

25 The absence of a reference to death does not prove that here we have a glimpse of an old view of the Lord's Supper which did not take its bearings on the death of Christ (Weiss). Rather, Paul is here working out the implications of *one* point in the tradition

we have before us in v 16. On the notion of the body of Christ, see Käsemann, *Essays on NT Themes*, 109–112 [12–15]. Neuenzeit, *Herrenmahl*, 211 (cf. 218), here finds a combination of the eucharistic and ecclesiological ideas of σῶμα, "body." According to Cerfaux, *Church*, 265 [203], σῶμα in v 17 has still to be taken in a eucharistic sense. Paul sets out from the unity of bread and body. ἐν σῶμα: "the body of Christ, his real and individual body, become present in the Eucharist." Here no regard is paid to the intention of Paul, who takes the traditional "This is my body" and places upon it the interpretation: "This is participation in my body."

26 οἱ πολλοί, "all," cf. Rom 5:15. Cf. the further ecclesiological development in Eph 4:4f.

27 Bachmann, Allo.

28 According to Schmithals, *Gnosticism in Corinth*, 246, n. 173 [233, n. 3], vv 16f have their roots in Gnostic tradition. In vv 16b–17 Paul takes over a formula which he links to his own word about the cup. In this formula σῶμα, "body," originally meant the church, which does not suit the present context. But Paul is not aware of the original mythological meaning. With this last statement Schmithals abrogates the presupposition of his assertion.

29 Of Israel κατὰ σάρκα, "after the flesh, earthly," that is to say, the historical Israel; on κατὰ σάρκα

he now wishes to prove,[32] that the κοινωνία τοῦ θυ-σιαστηρίου, "partnership in the altar," of the "one" God rules out communion with demons, that is, partaking of their "table." Before expounding this, Paul rules out a possible objection (the same one as emerges in 8:4). In so doing he seemingly involves himself in a certain self–contradiction. The reason lies in the argumentation of his opponents, and in the tradition in which Paul himself stands: for the polemic literature of Hellenistic Judaism, the "gods" are nonexistent.[33] Paul, on the contrary, regards them as real beings (see on 8:5), namely, demons. To be sure, he denies "that they are anything," but this is not to say that they do not exist at all.[34] The expression is not meant in a metaphysical sense, but anthropologically: "by nature" they are not gods (8:5; Gal 4:8). The thing is to behave accordingly, that is, not to participate in their cult, since otherwise we make them "something"; and that is perverse.[35]

The presupposition of vv 19–20 is the same as of 8:5: behind the gods there lurk demons. Paul bases this view on Deut 32:17.[36] This makes his demand clear. Sacrifices would make the demons into gods, powers, and bring the participants into bondage to them.[37]

■ **21** Verse 21 expresses with fundamental sharpness the

---

30   κοινωνός: companion at a sacrificial meal; Hauck, *TDNT* 3:797–809. κοινωνεῖν for partaking of sacrificial meat: Jos., *Ant.* 4.75; inscriptions. Ditt., *Syll.* 3:260 (no. 1106, line 6): τ[οὶ τῶ]ν ἱερῶν κοινω-νεῦντες, "temple colleagues" (of a hereditary college of priests); cf. κοινωνός, Philo, *Spec. leg.* 1.131.

31   Philo, *Spec. leg.* 1.221: God, εὐεργέτης καὶ φιλό-δωρος ὢν κοινωνὸν ἀπέφηνε τοῦ βωμοῦ καὶ ὁμοτρά-πεζον τὸ συμπόσιον τῶν τὴν θυσίαν ἐπιτελούντων, "the benefactor, the bountiful, who has made the convivial company of those who carry out the sacrifice partners of the altar whose board they share" (Loeb 7:229). Cf. also κοινωνεῖν τραπέζης, "to have table–fellowship," Ps.–Cl., *Hom.* 8.20.1; cf. 9.15.1 (μεταλαμβάνειν, "to have a share"); ὁμοτράπεζος, "sharing the same table," in 7.3.3, alongside of ὁμοδίαιτος, "sharing the same life or food," in 7.3.2.

32   Weiss says of v 19: "The conclusion drawn by the opponents is reflected in the οὖν, 'then,' of the question."

33   From Deutero–Isaiah onward; Bel et Draco. Of course, the other view, from which Paul sets out, also exists, see below.

34   τι is pregnant: a real sacrifice, a real god. For the expression cf. Gal 6:3. Should the second clause be accentuated τί ἔστιν, "can there be such a thing"? Or is it to be deleted with p⁴⁶ ℵ* A C*? The linking of v 20 to v 19a would be subtler: θύου-σιν—εἰδωλόθυτον. For the shorter text, see Küm-mel, *ad loc.*; Kenneth W. Clark, "Textual Criticism and Doctrine," in *Studia Paulina*, 52–65, here esp. 59f. It can of course also be held that the ommission is erroneous, a result of homoioteleuton. Weiss observes: "If the words are genuine, then they are a striking proof of our ascription of this section to an earlier letter than chap. 8." To be sure: "If, how-

ever, they are not genuine, our hypothesis is no less convincing." The difficulty is in fact that εἰδω-λόθυτον recalls chap. 8, whereas the problem is a different one.

35   Paul's reflections far transcend the views of the world around him, the usual demonology and more particularly the Jewish view that the divine worship of the pagan world is in fact addressed to demons, cf. Deut 32:17; Ps 95:5; 105:37; *Jub.* 1.11; *AZ* 2.3: pagan offerings are "offerings to the dead"; cf. *Jub.* 22.17; Str.–B. 3:51f, 54; Bousset–Gressmann, *Die Religion des Judentums*, 305f. Hellenism: Orig., *Cels.* 3.29 (of pagans): οἱ μὲν ἐπὶ γῆς δαίμονες, παρὰ τοῖς μὴ παιδευθεῖσι περὶ δαιμόνων νομιζόμενοι εἶ-ναι θεοί, "the daemons on earth, who are thought to be gods by people who have not been educated in the matter of daemons" (Chadwick, 147); Porphyr., *Abst.* 2.40: the demons would be gods. Christianity: Just., *Apol.* 1.5, 9, etc.; Athenag., *Suppl.* 26f; demonology: Johannes Weiss, *RE*³ 4:408–410.

36   There the antithesis is between God and θεοῖς οὓς οὐκ ᾔδεισαν, "gods they had never known" (RSV). Von Soden, "Sakrament und Ethik," 10, n. 1, asks: Does Paul mean that they sacrifice to demons and not to a god, or does οὐ θεῷ mean non–god (Leitz-mann)? The sense of the original passage could also be maintained, if the verse is referred to Israel. But the latter expedient is out of the question in the context. We have to adopt the interpretation: they sacrifice to demons, see v 21 and 8:5.

37   κοινωνός, see on v 16 above; Diod. S., *Bibl. hist.* 4.74.2: μετασχὼν κοινῆς τραπέζης, "being admitted to the common table" (Loeb 3:53). Porphyry in Eus., *Praep. ev.* 4.23 treats of the entry of the deity into the celebrant in the eating. Thus we cannot here raise the alternative: Is it a question of the food (as substance) or of the act of eating? Both coincide

cf. Rom 9:5 (of Christ).

impossibility of participating in the pagan cult,[38] and does so with special reference to participation in meals, drinking and eating. The allusion to competition between pagan meals and the Christian[39] Lord's Supper is unmistakable: the order (drinking/eating) is the same as in v 16; μετέχειν, "to partake," (v 17) corresponds to κοινωνία, "participation"; cf. v 20.[40] On the question of opportunity for participation in sacral meals, see on 8:10; 10:27. These had widely become social occasions in the temple restaurant. To the ritual there belongs the drink offering[41] with, of course, the drinking that follows.[42] τράπεζα κυρίου, "the table of the Lord," is presupposed as an established designation.[43] But the expression is also in accordance with general pagan usage: one sits at the "table" of the god,[44] entertains the

god,[45] partakes of him.[46] Paul is accordingly aware of the analogy between the Christian meal and the pagan festivals.[47]

■ 22 The train of thought is explained by the constitutive significance of the εἷς θεός—εἷς κύριος confession, "one God—one Lord." It is exclusively valid; God watches jealously over his honor (Deut 32:21).[48] Is ἰσχυρότεροι, "stronger," an ironical allusion to the "strong"? No![49] The rhetorical question must be related to the Corinthian mentality as a whole (see 4:8); cf. v 12.

here. Hugo Gressmann, "ἡ κοινωνία τῶν δαιμονίων," ZNW 20 (1921): 224–230; Fritz Bammel, *Das heilige Mahl im Glauben der Völker* (Gütersloh: Bertelsmann, 1950).

38 This is expressed also in the rhetorical style: parallelism, anaphora, antistrophe. The underlying principle is that of the impossibility of a κοινωνία ἀνομοίων, a "communion of unlikes"; see Hans Windisch, *Der zweite Brief an die Korinther*, KEK, 6 (Göttingen: Vandenhoeck & Ruprecht, ⁹1924), 213.

39 κύριος contrary to the original sense of the quotation, is in this context Christ.

40 Goppelt, *TDNT* 6:156–158, declares that the distinction from the pagan cult can be shown only in terms of the cup, not of the breaking of bread which is there unknown. But Paul is arguing simply in terms of the sacral meal as a whole, in terms of the "table."

41 Englebert Huber, *Das Trankopfer im Kulte der Völker* (Hanover–Kirchrode: Oppermann, 1929); Franz J. Dölger, "Der Kelch der Dämonen," *Antike und Christentum* 4 (1934): 266–270; Theodor Klauser and S. Grün, "Becher," *RAC* 2:37–62; Stengel, *Die griechischen Kultusaltertümer*, 103f; Krister Hanell, "Trankopfer," Pauly–W. 6A:2131–37; K. Schneider, "Mahlzeiten," Paul–W. 14:524. Literature: Goppelt *TDNT* 6:158, n. 89.

42 There is naturally no thought of a transsubstantiation, but as a result of consecration the wine becomes the property of the god.

43 OT: Mal 1:7, 12 (cf. Isa 41:22; 44:16). τράπεζα κυρίου is the table of the shewbread, or bread of the Presence. For τράπεζα δαιμονίων cf. Isa 65:11;

Ps.–Cl., *Hom.* 7.4.2; 7.8.1.

44 τράπεζα θεοῦ: the sacrificial table, Ditt., *Syll.* 3:264 (no. 1106, line 99), etc., H. Mischkowski, *Die heiligen Tische im Götterkultus der Griechen und Römer* (dissertation, Königsberg, 1912). *P. Oxy.* 1.110 (see on v 27); cf. *P. Oxy.* 3.523. Ael. Arist., *Or.* 27, see n. 20 above for the text.

45 Rohde, *Psyche*, 109, n. 26 (to p. 96) [2:129, n. 3]; Hugo Hepding, *Attis: Seine Mythen und sein Kult*, RVV, 1, 1 (Giessen: Töpelmann, 1903; Berlin: Töpelmann, 1967), 137.

46 See the Dionysus cult. See Franz Cumont, *The Oriental Religions in Roman Paganism* (Chicago: Open Court, 1911; New York: Dover, 1956), 68–71 [108–113].

47 Lietzmann. Not so Goppelt, for whom Paul's argument is based not on pagan but on OT ideas. This cannot be upheld in view of vv 19–21. For the distinction from the meals of the mysteries, cf. Just., *Ap.* 1.66; Tert., *Praescr. haer.* 40; Firm. Mat., *Err. prof. rel.* 18.2.

48 For the phrase, "Are we stronger?" cf. Job 9:32; Isa 45:9, etc. For the form παραζηλοῦμεν see Blass–Debrunner §91 (subjunctive of verbs in –οῦν: ου rather than ω).

49 For Paul uses this word not to describe a group, but as characteristic of the Corinthian attitude in general; 4:10.

10		**Idol Sacrifices and Conscience (Freedom)**

23   One is free to do anything, but not everything is for the best. One is free to do
anything, but not everything builds up.
24 / Let no one seek his own interests,
but rather those of his neighbor.[1]
25 / You may eat anything sold in the
market, without raising questions of
conscience. **26 /** For "the earth is the
Lord's and all it contains." **27 /** If[2] one of
the unbelieving invites you and you are
willing to go, you may eat whatever
is put before you, without raising questions of conscience. **28 /** But should
someone say to you, "This is sacrificial
meat,"[3] then do not eat, for the sake
of the man who gave you the information and for conscience' sake. **29 /** I do
not mean your own conscience though,
but the other man's. For why should my
freedom be subject to the judgment of
another man's conscience? **30 /** If I
partake with thankfulness, why should I
be denounced for that which I give
thanks? **31 /** So whether you eat or
drink or whatever else[4] you do, do
everything to the glory of God. **32 /** Give
no offense, neither to Jews nor to
Greeks nor to the church of God,
33 / even as I, too, am obliging to everyone in all things, and do not seek my
own advantage, but that of the many, in
order that they may be saved. **11 :1 /** Follow my example, as I follow Christ's.[5]

The thought of this section is self–contained. It links up
with 8:13, taking over the slogan of 6:12. Once again
the subject is eating. The criterion, which is to be understood as an inherent unity, is conscience and the bond
with our brother.[6] There is no connection with the
preceding section.[7]

---

1   For the brachylogy cf. 11:1; Blass–Debrunner
§479(1).
2   Compare $\epsilon\iota$ here (real condition) with $\dot{\epsilon}\dot{\alpha}\nu$ in the
following verse.
3   C D G $\aleph$ read $\epsilon\iota\delta\omega\lambda\dot{o}\theta\upsilon\tau o\nu$—an unsuccessful attempt
at improvement.
4   For the ellipsis of $\ddot{\alpha}\lambda\lambda o$ see Blass–Debrunner §480(1).
5   Cf. 10:24 (brachylogy).
6   Unlike the previous section, Paul now adopts once
more in principle the standpoint of the strong—
except for the fact that, as in chap. 8, he calls for renunciation for the sake of our brother. Von Soden
finds the whole exposition in chaps. 8—10 to be a
unified composition: (1) exposition, chaps. 8, 9;
(2) Scripture proof, 10:1–22; (3) resolution, 10:23–
33. The same pattern, he argues, is found in Rom
14f, which is a literary unity. But there we have no
such dislocations as in 1 Cor. Nevertheless the signs

of linkages are considerable: 8:12 indicates the
theme of 10:1–12; 10:19 takes up 8:4; 10:23—11:1
can, according to von Soden, be fully understood
only as a link between 8—9 and 10:1–22. Important,
too, is the question as to how the two aspects of
chaps. 8—10 are related to each other within Paul's
theology as a whole. His view of the sacrament appears in terms of history, and his view of freedom and
conscience has its presupposition in the receiving
of salvation, i.e. in the sacrament.
7   For this reason Weiss and others resort to operations
of literary criticism, see on 8:1. According to Weiss,
v 24 is better taken as a conclusion of chap. 8, and
is not so good as an introduction to what follows.

■ 23 The principle of 6:12 is here quoted in a shorter, and thus sharper form, without μοί, "to me."[8] The actual content is not thereby altered in any way. The limitation of the freedom, too, is in content the same: οὐ πάντα συμφέρει, "not everything is for the best"; cf. v 33, where that which is "for the best" is governed by the notion of community. In keeping with this, we have here a reference to the church: οὐ πάντα οἰκοδομεῖ, "not everything builds up." οἰκοδομεῖν denotes first and foremost the upbuilding of the community, not the edification of the individual. This becomes clear from its usage in chaps. 12 and 14.[9]

■ 24 This verse, taken in itself, is a maxim in the style of Wisdom literature (cf. 13:5). In v 33 Paul illustrates it by reference to himself.[10] It acquires its concrete mean-ing by being applied in each particular instance to the specific situation.

■ 25–26 The first instance Paul discusses has to do with meat. It is frequently maintained that in Paul's day practically all meat offered in the market came from animals that had been sacrificed, since a minimum of ritual custom was observed in slaughtering them.[11] Yet this cannot be maintained in such general terms.[12] In any case, Paul's observations are independent of this question, or rather, they render it superfluous. He sets out simply from the everyday practice of buying in the market.[13] Whether only sacrificial meat or also "pro-fane" meat is offered is a matter of indifference, since the principle of freedom is upheld.[14] The conscience is not involved at all. This is how the expression διὰ τὴν

---

8   This is no argument for ascribing the two passages to different letters.

9   The connection between οἰκοδομή and ἀγάπη should be noticed (cf. also the observations on γνῶ-σις and ἀγάπη in 8:1ff). According to von Soden, "Sakrament und Ethik," 25, God himself marks the bounds of the otherwise unbounded ἐξουσία. We can add: that was already said in 6:12. Now it is shown where this God is to be found.

10   Cf. Rom 14:19; 15:2f; Phil 2:4ff. We can see the many-sided possibilities of its application.

11   In that case Christians could have bought only from a Jewish or Christian butcher.
     The literature gives no clear information. Eustath. Thessal., *Comm. in Od.* 2.56 (p. 1434, line 15): ἱερεύ-ειν means not only θύειν, "to kill for sacrifice," ἀλλὰ καὶ τὸ ἁπλῶς σφάζειν, "but also simply to slaugh-ter." Stengel, *Die griechischen Kultusaltertümer*, 105, says: "We have no sure information as to whether they [the butchers] in slaughtering the animals prac-ticed the customs usual at sacrifice, but it may be assumed that every animal at the point of slaughter was also regarded and treated as a sacrificial ani-mal." Cf. Artemid., *Oneirocr.* 5.2 (ed. Hercher, 254); 3.56 (ed. Hercher, 190); also the expressions κατα-θύειν for "slaughter" (Hdt., *Hist.* 8.19), θυσία for "festal meal." Similarly Heinrich Nissen, *Pompeiani-sche Studien zur Städtekunde des Altertums* (Leipzig: Breitkopf & Härtel, 1877), 276. This is not conclu-sive. Incidentally, it should be noted that the con-sumption of meat played a much smaller role in everyday life than it does today.

12   Rightly Henry Joel Cadbury, "The Macellum of Corinth," *JBL* 53 (1934): 134–141, here esp. 141; Charles K. Barrett, "Things Sacrificed to Idols," *NTS* 11 (1964–65): 138–153; cf. Plut., *Quaest. conv.* 729c, concerning the Pythagoreans: ὡς μάλιστα

μὲν ἐγεύοντο τῶν ἱεροθύτων ἀπαρξάμενοι τοῖς θεοῖς, "if they tasted flesh it was most often that of sacrificial animals" (Loeb 9:179). This presumably means that they ate meat only when it was the flesh of sacrificial animals; hence the presupposition is that other meat was also available.

13   μακέλλον, Latin *macellum* (but not originally a Latin word taken into Greek, for it is evidenced in Greek as early as *ca.* 400 B.C.; see Bauer, *s.v.*); also in rab-binic literature as a loan word. Illustrative material is provided by the *macellum* of Pompeii, see Nissen, *Pompeianische Studien*, 275–286; for illustrations, August Mau, *Pompeii: Its Life and Art*, tr. Francis W. Kelsey (London and New York: Macmillan, 1907), 94–101 (*Pompeii in Leben und Kunst* [Leipzig: Engel-mann, ²1908], 90–97); Building inscriptions of the *macellum* have been found in Corinth; see Fowler, *Corinth*, 8.2:124f; Cadbury, "The Macellum at Co-rinth." The agora at Corinth: Robert Scranton, "Two Temples of Commodus at Corinth," *Hesperia* 13 (1944): 315–348; Oscar Broneer, "Investigations at Corinth, 1946–1947," *Hesperia* 16 (1947): 233–247; Saul S. Weinberg, "Investigations at Corinth, 1947–1948," *Hesperia* 18 (1949): 148–157; Broneer, "Investigations at Corinth, 1950," *Hesperia* 20 (1951): 291–300; Ernst Kirsten and Wilhelm Krai-ker, *Griechenlandkunde* (Heidelberg: Winter, ⁴1962), 319f; Johannes Schneider, *TDNT* 4:370–372; K. Schneider, Pauly-W. 14:129–133.

14   The Jewish practice can serve as a comparison (Str.-B. 3:420–422). A Jew when buying meat must ascertain whether the animal was slaughtered by a Jew, and whether it had any connection with a pagan cult. According to *AZ* 2.3, "Flesh that is en-tering in unto an idol is permitted, but what comes forth is forbidden, for it is as the sacrifice of the dead" (Danby, 438f). *T. Chul.* 2.20; *b. Chul.* 94b.

συνείδησιν, literally "for conscience' sake," is to be understood (von Soden): it should not be imagined that conscience calls for further inquiries.[15] The reason offered (v 26) is in keeping with this. It is taken from Ps 24:1.[16]

■ **27** Verse 27 brings a second case, an invitation to a meal, whether in a private house,[17] or in a temple.[18] For the latter we can refer to 8:10. Paul's ruling can be understood from the same presupposition as that on which Christians do not leave the world. The decision is the same as in the preceding case; it is also formulated in parallel terms: διὰ τὴν συνείδησιν—the conscience is

not involved here either.[19] But what is the relation of this to vv 20f? Apparently Paul is thinking there of direct cultic proceedings, here of social occasions which can acquire a cultic tendency, but do not have to do so.[20]

■ **28** A hypothetical case which is subsumed under the case of v 27. Who is the μηνύσας, "informant"? It is usually supposed that he is a pagan; this is said to be shown by the word ἱερόθυτον, which is the correct term for "sacrificial meat" from the pagan standpoint (Lietzmann).[21] Or is he one of the "weak"? τοῦτο ἱερόθυτόν ἐστιν, "this is sacrificial meat," makes the meal—

A Jew does not have to make enquiries in the case of objects which can be neutral. He must not, for example, use implements of a pagan cult, but he may well employ objects which *can* be used in the pagan cult. He does not have to ask whether such a use is intended, say, for the candles he buys.

15 Von Soden, "Sakrament und Ethik," 15: "The Jewish ruling indicates how a religious man can protect himself against pollution without economic disadvantages; Paul's ruling shows how we grasp and fulfil the will of God. In the former case conscience is abrogated, resolved into the rule, in the latter case conscience is most firmly bound in all its freedom. In the former case we have legal casuistry, in the latter the resolving of law into love."

If διὰ τὴν συνείδησιν is taken to mean "so as to give conscience no cause for complaint," then we have precisely the Jewish, legalistically oriented attitude. For the expression cf. Polyb., *Hist.* 4.86.5: διὰ τὸ συνειδέναι; Sextus, *Sent.* 52 (*The Sentences of Sextus*, ed. Henry Chadwick, Texts and Studies, 5 [Cambridge: University Press, 1959], 88): διὰ τὸ συνειδός; Philo, *Flacc.* 145: ἕνεκα τοῦ συνειδότος; Diod. S., *Bibl. hist.* 4.65.7: διὰ τὴν συνείδησιν.

16 Paul is manifestly unaware of any words of the Lord on the question of clean and unclean. This is particularly noticeable in Rom 14:14: πέπεισμαι ἐν κυρίῳ, "I am persuaded in the Lord." For the content cf. Rom 14:14, 20, a further development of the statements of 1 Cor. Both epistles here provide a paradigm for the significance which belief in the Creator has for our attitude to the world, as a ground of our freedom in it. *T. Ber.* 4.1: Let no one eat anything before he has spoken a benediction; "for thus is it said: Ps 24:1"; cf. *b. Shab.* 119a; *b. Ber.* 35a Bar.; Eduard Lohse, "Zu 1 Cor 10,26.31," *ZNW* 47, (1956): 277–280. The latter explains γάρ, "for," as a sign that we have here a quotation: "for it is said."

17 Where a certain measure of religious ceremony is practiced. It is of no consequence how far the latter has weakened to mere habit. It *is* reverence for the gods and can at any moment be taken seriously by a

religious man in its original sense and thereby be made binding for others. Then freedom is gone. For a festal meal in a private house see *P. Oxy.* 3:523; for the religious solemnifying of family festivals *P. Oxy.* 12:1484.

18 καλεῖν, "invite": Xenoph., *Mem.* 2.9.4: ὁπότε θύοι ἐκάλει, "when he sacrificed, he invited him" (Loeb, 161). *P. Oxy.* 1:110 (second cent. A.D.): ἐρωτᾷ σε Χαιρήμων δειπνῆσαι εἰς κλείνην τοῦ κυρίου Σαράπιδος ἐν τῷ Σαραπείῳ αὔριον, "Chaeremon requests your company at dinner at the table of the lord Sarapis in the Serapeum tomorrow." For the furnishing of a temple of Sarapis for meals see Otto Weinreich, *Neue Urkunden zur Sarapisreligion*, SGV, 86 (Tübingen: J. C. B. Mohr [Paul Siebeck], 1919), 31–33. Illustration: Johannes Leipoldt, *Die Religionen in der Umwelt des Urchristentums*, Bilderatlas zur Religionsgeschichte, ed. Hans Haas, 9–11 (Leipzig: Deichert, 1926), plate 16. καλεῖν, "invite": Lk 14:9, etc.

19 Weiss asks in view of the stereotype repetition whether Paul is here quoting one of the weak party's phrases from the Corinthians' letter. Yet it is surely he himself who introduces the catchword συνείδησις. In the phrase, "if you are willing to go," Weiss sees a certain limitation of Paul's assent. But considering the voices in Corinth which forbid the acceptance of the invitation, the very point of this passage is to make way for freedom.

20 On the social intercourse of the Jews see Str.–B. 3:421f.

21 In contrast to the Jewish and Christian term εἰδωλόθυτον. Lietzmann observes that if a weak fellow–Christian sitting at the table were meant, then one would expect καὶ τὴν συνείδησιν αὐτοῦ, "and for the sake of his conscience," and adds: "and Paul would not have required the long–winded explanation in v 29a." Now eating is no longer ἀδιάφορον, "a matter of indifference"; now the rejection of idolatry has to be demonstrated and the Christian "must not give any offense to his weaker brother, who of course is not present, but will hear of it."

in itself harmless—into a sacrificial meal. Participation in it is now participation in the cult, and thus an act both of confessing to the gods and also of establishing communion with them in the sense of vv 14–22.

Of the purpose for which the man gives his information,[22] the text says nothing, and in this respect it must not be pressed; for it regards this point precisely as a matter of indifference, and the same is true of the question whether the informant is the host or a guest.[23] For this reason it will be best not to inquire too closely about the τις, "someone."[24] We have here of course a hypothetical instance of church law in the casuistic style. The sense of διὰ τὴν συνείδησιν, "for conscience' sake," has now changed. This is explained by v 29a.

■ **29** Paul's concept of conscience must be distinguished from modern subjectivistic conceptions.[25] Paul does not ask whether our conscience is free: he presupposes that it *is* free, but for this very reason open toward our neighbor and bound by him. Once again the question is: Who is this neighbor? The μηνύσας, "informant," or another—now perhaps a weak brother? The form of expression in v 28 most readily suggests that the conscience of the *pagan* μηνύσας is meant.[26] The latter

would not only be strengthened in his conviction, but the Christian would objectify the power of the gods, and thereby "preach" faith in them.[27]

If we take it thus, then v 29b, too, provides an understandable reason.[28] Any other view produces difficulties which are reflected in the literature. Lietzmann explains vv 29b–30 as an exclamation on the part of one of the strong whom Paul here (in the style of the diatribe) introduces as speaker: he objects to the rule in v 28. Against this, Bultmann takes v 29 as explanation of v 28:[29] I should desist for the sake of the other—the weak man (!). If I were to imagine that I must desist for the sake of my own conscience, then I should have surrendered my freedom, which I do not do, even when I desist. Strictly speaking, I can eat anything that I can enjoy with thankfulness.

With this explanation, to be sure, the conscience is again understood subjectivistically after all and the renunciation is seen as a withdrawal into the realm of inward freedom.[30]

■ **30** This verse provides a further argument in favor of v 28 by pointing to the practice of saying grace.[31] In content, it again takes up v 26. The idea can be under-

22 Is he trying to put the Christian to the test? But why, in that case, must the latter not eat? Or does he in fact mean well? So Max Rauer, *Die "Schwachen" in Korinth und Rom nach den Paulusbriefen*, Biblische Studien, 21, 2–3 (Freiburg: Herder, 1923), 44, n. 3. Von Soden, "Sakrament und Ethik," 13f, is undecided.

23 Weiss holds him to be a guest; for this τίς, "someone," cannot, he argues, be identical with the one in v 27.

24 Heinrici, Allo.

25 The modern Christian solution would be more or less: if your conscience does not oppose you, then you are free. This would either be the autonomy of the absolute subject, for which the epithet "Christian" would now be no more than a traditional designation, but would not be constitutive for the self–understanding—or else it would be the pseudo-freedom of a subjective Christianity of experience, which in actual fact is secretly tied up in legalistic norms.

26 The form of expression (tacked on by means of καί, "and," and without αὐτοῦ, "his") is explained by the fact that Paul is already using διὰ τὴν συνείδησιν, "for conscience' sake," as a set phrase (cf. also Rom 13:5) and at once digresses into an explanation. Others hold that the μηνύσας is a pagan, but

not identical with the ἕτερος, "other man" (von Soden, "Sakrament und Ethik," 14); or the μηνύσας is a weak Christian, the ἕτερος identical with him (Schmiedel)—or: a weak Christian, not identical (Heinrici).

27 This emphasizes the validity of von Soden's insight ("Sakrament und Ethik," 14) that claims on conscience are made not by things, but by people. "It is not eating as such that constitutes a case of conscience, but only eating as an act of proclamation and confession before others; and what matters is how this act is understood or misunderstood, not how it is intended."

The interpretation in terms of the weaker brother is an interpolation from 8:10.

28 Namely, the other's conscience binds me, though my own does not.

29 Bultmann, *Theology* 1:219 [220]. Allo, too, is against Lietzmann: we have no dialogue here; cf. Rom 14:16. Weiss observes that if this were an exclamation on the part of one of the strong, then we should expect δέ or ἀλλά rather than γάρ. Weiss, however (following Hitzig), asks whether we have here a marginal note by a hyper–Paulinist.

30 Much the same as with Weiss. Not so von Soden, "Sakrament und Ethik," 16, n. 1, who rightly rejects also the interpretation as a gloss (see previous note).

stood by placing the emphasis on v 29a: I do *not* mean your own conscience, nor your *inner* freedom either. Paul means that the subjective conscience is not called upon at all, but the *status confessionis*, the "situation of confession," has arisen.

This makes the next step in the progress of thought also understandable.

■ **31–32** In a style characteristic of Paul,[32] freedom is declared: the criterion lies outside of myself. It is an objective and at the same time also a historic criterion: the glory of God.[33] οὖν, "so," indicates the conclusion to be drawn from the now established possibility of freedom of action.[34] The statement πάντα κτλ., "do all, etc.," taken in itself, can be a cliché.[35] But its content is determined in the whether–or clause, and is given concrete shape in v 32 with regard to conduct toward "outsiders" on the one hand, and brothers on the other. In the context it is a *critical* statement.[36] The rule in v 32 also becomes understandable and fulfillable in the community,[37] namely, in the exercise of freedom.[38]

■ **33** καθώς, "even as": Paul presents himself as an example. Yet he does not point to his moral behavior in general, but to his church work. The idea of "Paul as an example" has also to be interpreted essentially in the context of his self–understanding as a whole, his understanding of his office. πάντα πᾶσιν ἀρέσκω, "I am obliging to everyone in all things," has the same sort of opportunistic sound as 9:20–22, and has to be understood in the light of that passage. This statement, too, must not be isolated from Paul's self–understanding as a whole.[39] And the participial clause (lit. "not seeking my own advantage, etc."), ensures that it is not a case of opportunism, but of devotion and service in terms of his apostleship.[40] The content of what is "advantageous" is defined by the ἵνα–clause: salvation.

With the return to v 24 the section is rounded off in itself. Verse 1 of chap. 11 is merely a further comment on καθώς, "even as."

■ **11:1** A summons to the imitation of Paul,[41] grounded in his imitation of Christ. Paul does not make his own person the content of his preaching. His exemplariness consists in the fact that—in himself, objectively, on the basis of his calling—he is nothing. In all the passages on the *imitatio Pauli* the paradox of this exemplariness appears. And v 2 then emphasizes that what is essential and exemplary is the *teaching* which he has transmitted

---

31 Rom 14:6; 1 Tim 4:3f.

32 εἴτε . . . εἴτε, "whether . . . or": 2 Cor 5:9 (Phil 1:20); 1 Thess 5:10; Blass–Debrunner §454(3).

33 See on v 26; *T. Ber.* 4.1: "One must use one's face, one's hands and feet only to the Creator's glory"; Lohse, "Zu 1 Cor 10,26.31."

34 Weiss argues that if vv 29f are genuine, then οὖν is dubious, because it could be taken to mean approval for the opinion of the strong (v 30). But v 30 gives the opinion not of the strong, but of Paul. εἴτε . . . εἴτε states the conclusion from εἰ, ἐάν in vv 27, 28.

35 To the effect, for example, that the Christians' whole life must be divine service. Barth's argument against this trite rendering is to the point, *Resurrection*, 56 [28].

36 In view of v 31 one wonders whether the Corinthians had not also raised the question of food (meat) and drink (wine) being forbidden as such. Yet this is merely an impression suggested by Rom 14f.

On ancient rules of abstinence (Orphics, Pythagoreans) see Muson., *Reliq.* (ed. Hense, 9.94); Strabo, *Geog.* 7.296; *Corp. Herm. Ascl.* 41; Philostr., *Vit. Ap.* 1.8; Rohde, *Psyche*, 360, n. 78 (to p. 346) [2:133, n. 1]; Rauer, *Die "Schwachen,"* 139–147.

37 ἀπρόσκοπος, "giving no offence": Phil 1:10; Sir 32:21 (likewise transitive).

38 Rom 14:13ff; 1 Thess 4:12; "church of God," see on

1:2.

39 ἀρέσκειν, "seek to please, be obliging," 1 Thess 2:4; but cf. Gal 1:10.

40 τὸ σύμφορον, "advantage," explains (οὐ) συμφέρει, "it is (not) for the best." Aristot., *Eth. Nic.* 8.10.2 (p. 1160 b 2): ὁ μὲν γὰρ τύραννος τὸ αὑτῷ συμφέρον σκοπεῖ, ὁ δὲ βασιλεὺς τὸ τῶν ἀρχομένων, "a tyrant studies his own advantage, a king that of his subjects" (Loeb, 489, 491).

41 (a) Phil 4:8f; 1 Cor 4:16; Phil 3:17; 1 Thess 1:6. (b) 1 Thess 2:14; Phil 2:1ff; Rom 15:1–3; Eph 5:1. E. J. Tinsley, *The Imitation of God in Christ* (London: SCM; Philadelphia: Westminster, 1960). See on 4:16; D. M. Stanley, " 'Become Imitators of Me': The Pauline Conception of Apostolic Tradition," *Biblica* 40 (1959): 859–877; W. P. de Boer, *The Imitation of Paul* (Kampen: Kok, 1962), 154–169, (cf. 139–154 on 4:16); Hans Dieter Betz, *Nachfolge und Nachahmung Jesu Christi im Neuen Testament*, BHTh, 37 (Tübingen: J. C. B. Mohr [Paul Siebeck], 1967), 153–169.

to the Corinthians.[42] The imitation *of Christ* takes its bearings not on the person of the historical Jesus, not on his way of life,[43] but—in the sense of Phil 2:6ff—on his saving work.[44]

42 For this reason Wilhelm Michaelis, *TDNT* 4:668f, denies that Paul speaks of himself as a model at all. He argues that Paul means: "I have commanded you, and Christ has commanded me." That is less than stands in the text. Against Michaelis see de Boer, *Imitation*, 130–139, 154–169.

43 According to Robertson and Plummer, the question is not "What would Jesus do?" but "Lord, what wilt Thou have me to do?"

44 The primary factor is Christ as *sacramentum*, not as *exemplum*. Anselm Schulz, *Nachfolgen und Nachahmen*, SANT, 6 (Munich: Kösel, 1962), 285–289.

11   Women in Divine Worship

2   I commend you for being mindful of me in all respects and maintaining the traditions as I passed them on to you. 3 / I would have you know, however, that every man's head is Christ,[1] but a woman's head is the man, and Christ's head is God. 4 / But any man who prays or prophesies with something on his head[2] dishonors his head. 5 / Any woman, however, who prays or prophesies with her head unveiled[3] dishonors her head. For she is just the same as if she were shaven. 6 / For if a woman is not veiled, she might just as well have herself shorn. But if it is a disgrace for a woman to have herself shorn or shaven,[4] then she should be veiled. 7 / For a man must not veil his head, since he is the image and reflection of God. 8 / But a woman is the reflection of man. For man did not originate from woman, but woman from man. 9 / Neither was man created for woman's sake, but woman for man's. 10 / For this reason a woman must have a power on her head, because of the angels. 11 / Of course, in the Lord there is neither woman without man nor man without woman.[5] 12 / For just as woman originated from man, so, too, man exists through woman.[6] But everything comes from God. 13 / Judge for yourselves: Is it proper for a woman pray to God with head unveiled? 14 / And does not nature itself teach you that it is a disgrace for a man to have long hair, 15 / but that it is a woman's glory to have long hair? For her hair was given her[7] for[8] a covering. 16 / But if anyone thinks he should be contentious (about this): we have no such custom, nor do the churches of God.

---

1   Again with the article; not so B * D * G—which, however, likewise have the article in the second case.

2   κατά with the genitive: cf. Plut., *Apophth.* 200f; ἐβάδιζε κατὰ τῆς κεφαλῆς ἔχων τὸ ἱμάτιον, "he was walking with his toga covering his head" (Loeb 3:191).

3   For the word order (predicate position of the participle) see Blass–Debrunner §270(1).

4   The word can be accented ξυρᾶσθαι (present infinitive middle of ξυράω) or ξύρασθαι (aorist infinitive middle of ξύρω). The forms ξυρέω, ξυράω and ξύρω are found. The aorist κείρασθαι suggests the corresponding aorist ξύρασθαι; v 5 ἐξυρημένος as in Attic; Blass–Debrunner §101. On the meaning of

κείρω and ξυρ– see Bauer, *s.v.* Dio C., *Hist. Rom.* 57.10.5 (Tiberius): κείρεσθαί μου τὰ πρόβατα, ἀλλ' οὐκ ἀποξύρεσθαι βούλομαι, "I want my sheep shorn, not shaven" (Loeb 7:137).

5   Carl Weizsäcker, *Das Neue Testament* (Tübingen: J. C. B. Mohr [Paul Siebeck], [11]1927), 320, translates: "Only, in the Lord the principle holds: just as woman does not exist without man, no more does man without woman. . . ."

6   With the genitive after διά compare the accusative in v 9.

7   Om. p[46] D G 𝔑; see the commentary.

8   ἀντί,, "as, for": see Liddell–Scott, *s.v.* ἀντί A III 2;

181

There is a certain tension between the outward and inward plan of chaps. 11–14. A new topic is introduced only in 12:1, once again with περί, "concerning," and thus apparently once again on the basis of an inquiry from Corinth. But chap. 11 already deals with conduct at divine worship; the new topic is introduced entirely out of the blue. Is this unevenness to be regarded as calling for literary criticism (see below)?

Both parts of the service of worship, proclamation and celebration of the Supper, give Paul reason to intervene.[9] Here again the unified background of the situation in Corinth is discernible: enthusiasm.

The first section, 11:2–16, regulates the conduct of women in the service of worship,[10] namely, the question of their clothing, more especially of their headgear. Paul bases his ruling on cosmological and anthropological observations of a fundamental kind. In these we can again discern a measure of his esoteric wisdom teaching, and therewith also a measure of his Hellenistic Jewish presuppositions, of his speculative material.[11] On the one hand the section stands out as a block from its context, while on the other hand the arguments within it are somewhat confused. We have in fact the impression that it reflects the to and fro of a school discussion. It is probably a piece that was first talked over and sketched out in the schoolroom, if indeed it was not entirely composed there.

■ 2 Verse 2 serves to incorporate the "block" into the epistle[12] by means of a *captatio benevolentiae*.[13] The content of the commendation explains the surprising course, at first sight, of the thought from v 1 to v 2;[14] even if the commendation already points forward to things which Paul *cannot* commend,[15] yet the primary connection is with the thought of 10:33–11:1:[16] the summons to imitation of Paul implied an allusion to the conduct of his office as a whole, and thus also to his teaching.[17] And the latter is anchored in the tradition.[18] By this means Paul has secured a foundation for what he himself feels to be the difficult problem of a ruling on women's dress.

■ 3 What Paul now propounds from v 3 on is, to be sure, not the doctrinal tradition of the Christian creed (see on 15:3ff), but a speculative school tradition founded on a Hellenistic–Jewish basis and aimed at providing a *fundamental* ground on which to argue the special problem. The disproportion between the problem and the effort expended on it shows, for one thing, the degree of

---

Bauer, *s.v.* ἀντί 2.

9   Bornkamm, *Early Christian Experience*, 176, n. 2 (to p. 161) (*Das Ende des Gesetzes*, 113, n. 2) finds in the plan of chaps. 11—14 the division of divine worship into service of the word and celebration of the Supper: following the references to the Supper already in the argument of 10: 14–22, 11:2–16 deals with the service of the word, 11:23–34 with the Supper, 12—14 with spiritual gifts, i.e. questions of the service of the word (cf. esp. 14:25–27).

Even if Bornkamm may well be right in holding that the service of the word and the celebration of the Supper were separated in Corinth (see on 11:25; 16:19ff), yet the plan of the argument here cannot be used as proof of this. For it must be assumed that there was prayer, prophecy and speaking with tongues also at the Supper. The sections concerned accordingly cannot be restricted to the "service of the word."

10 Not so Bachmann. The service of worship, he holds, is discussed only from v 17 on, as a new topic, cf. v 18: *here* it is a question of family worship in the home. The advantage of this explanation is that it removes the contradiction with 14:33–36. But it is impossible.

11 The heart of the argument is obviously formed by the peculiar εἰκών, "image," speculation, which at the same time is clearly anchored in Hellenistic Jewish thinking, see below.

12 Schmithals, *Gnosticism in Corinth*, 90f [84f] (following Weiss, see below), holds that vv 18f form a *first* reference to controversies in the congregation, at a time when Paul was not so well informed as in 1:11. Hence 11:2–34 belongs to letter A. But the alleged contradiction between 1:11 and 11:18f is no greater than between 11:2 (ἐπαινῶ, "I commend") and 11:17 (οὐκ ἐπαινῶ, "I do not commend").

13 Lietzmann asks whether the commendation was occasioned by a remark in the Corinthians' letter. But there is no need to seek a specific ground for it. A commendation of this kind is epistolary style. ἐπαινεῖν is used as a formula in imperial letters, see August Strobel, "Zum Verständnis von Rm 13," *ZNW* 47 (1956): 67–93, here esp. 80–90.

14 Weiss holds that v 2 can possibly be taken as a semi-retraction of the exhortation in v 1, but would be well suited to the *beginning* of a correspondence.

15 Robertson and Plummer.

16 Allo.

17 See on v 1 (Michaelis). πάντα, "in all respects"; cf. 10:33; Blass–Debrunner §154.

18 παράδοσις, "tradition" (see on v 23), is already a technical term. It has a previous history in Judaism; see the commentaries on Gal 1:14; 2 Thess 2:15;

resistance with which Paul reckons. It is plain that he has to break with an existing custom. And secondly, the style and range of his argument show that it is not simply formulated *ad hoc*, but that Paul is delving deeply into the treasury of his knowledge: "I am offering you a new insight"—θέλω δὲ ὑμᾶς εἰδέναι, "I would have you know" (cf. 10:1; Col 2:1).

Hellenistic Judaism had developed various series of "image"/"reflection" patterns (see on v 7), taken over from Greek philosophy (Platonism and the Stoa): God is the archetype of the cosmos and of man. This idea Paul now presses into the service of Christology.[19] The kinship with the school tradition of Alexandria (Wisdom of Solomon, Philo) is plain. A peculiarity of the school from which Paul comes appears to emerge in the fact that here

in place of the usual εἰκών, "image," concept, with which Paul is *also* familiar (v 7), the word κεφαλή, "head," is used.[20] Neither Old Testament usage[21] nor that of classical Greek[22] is sufficient to explain this.[23] We have here a postclassical development, for which an analogy is provided more especially in the history of the concept εἰκών.[24] The words denote at this late level of their development a connection in terms of essence. The constitutive element is not the form (that is, the similarity), but the substantiality.[25] The statement that God is the head of Christ contains the ideas: (a) subordination of Christ;[26] (b) preexistence of Christ. The meaning of this idea is expressed in 8:6.[27] It is not developed by Paul beyond this point;[28] in fact it is broken off. Paul does not draw the conclusion of extending the

---

3:6. But there is also a corresponding Hellenistic use, in the sense of school tradition; Epict., *Diss.* 2.23.40. Beyond this, it means esoteric teaching in general, see Norden, *Agnostos Theos*, 290f; Hans von Campenhausen, "Lehrereihen und Bischoffsreihen im 2. Jahrhundert," in *In Memoriam Ernst Lohmeyer*, ed. W. Schmauch (Stuttgart: Evangelisches Verlagswerk, 1951), 240–249. παράδοσις then plays an important role in Gnosticism; Ptol., *Ep. ad Flor.* 2.10 (in Epiph., *Haer.* 33.7.9; *Brief an die Flora*, ed. Adolf von Harnack, KIT, 9 [Bonn: Marcus & Weber, ²1912]). For the Jewish material see Birger Gerhardsson, *Memory and Manuscript*, tr. E. J. Sharpe, ASNU, 22 (Lund: Gleerup; Copenhagen: Munksgaard, 1961). For Paul see Klaus Wegenast, *Das Verständnis der Tradition bei Paulus und in den Deutero-paulinen*, WMANT, 8 (Neukirchen–Vluyn: Neukirchener Verlag, 1962), *passim*.

19 It is presupposed that the idea of the preexistence of Christ already exists. It cannot, vice versa, simply be deduced from this primarily anthropological and cosmological speculation; see on 8:6.

20 It is noteworthy that in Paul there is no trace of the term λόγος, so significant in Alexandria. Weiss again presumes that there is a Corinthian slogan in the background. But it rather looks as if the concept has been introduced into Christology by Paul himself; cf. the situation in the rest of the NT and in the Apostolic Fathers. It is taken up in the deutero–Pauline epistles (Col, Eph), but in modified form, for it is there combined with the concept of the σῶμα Χριστοῦ, the "body of Christ." This combination must not be read into 1 Cor 11. Where the real "body of Christ" appears in 1 Cor (see on 12:13), there is no trace of κεφαλή. Heinrich Schlier, *TDNT* 3:673–682; Stephen Bedale, "The Meaning of κεφαλή in the Pauline Epistles," *JThSt*, n.s. 5

(1954): 211–215.

21 "Head" does not there denote the sovereignty of one person over another, but over a community.

22 In secular Greek, κεφαλή does not denote the "head" of a community. The word has this meaning in the LXX of Jdg 11:11; cf. the Latin *corpus*.

23 That we have here an extra–Christian development, emerges from the negative circumstances that the church is omitted from the series—although the idea of Christ as head would have suggested itself particularly readily to the church, especially as the concept of the "body" of Christ is already existent.

24 For the cosmological speculation see Schlier, *TDNT* 3:673–682 (literature, 676, n. 4); Ernst Käsemann, *Leib und Leib Christi*, BHTh, 9 (Tübingen: J. C. B. Mohr [Paul Siebeck], 1933).

25 Cf. the comprehensive change in the significance of Greek concepts of form which takes place in Hellenism and Gnosticism (see below, excursus on εἰκών). This change is not restricted to Gnosticism.

26 The subordination is also expressed, in terms of a totally different complex of ideas, in the "Father" title for God and the "Lord" title for Jesus; see on 8:6.

27 For the presuppositions cf. Philo, *Op. mund.* 134f; *Leg. all.* 1.31–42. The place of ideal man is taken by Christ.

28 Heinrici, 324 n., observes that Paul "never made the idea of a preexistent Christ the starting point for doctrinal definitions."

relationship between God and Christ to become a real analogy of the relationship between Christ and man.[29] Thus we have to exercise caution if we would determine the position of man in this series, and that means his nature. It is plain that Paul has altered the series *ad hoc* (as compared with the view delivered to him), by classifying the world, i.e., mankind, as male and female. What matters to him in the context is already plain from the formal reversal of the members of the series: solely the subordination of woman to man.[30] The speculative idea serves a point of purely Pauline theology. Natural differences remain. Each is encountered in his own place and held fast there. The differences are abrogated "in Christ."[31]

The male is in the cosmological system the male as such. It is true that interpreters often allude to the marriage relationship, that is, to the husband. The subordination is said to mean the status of the woman in marriage.[32] Yet it is not questions of marriage that are being discussed here, but questions of the community. It is a case of the *nature* of man and woman as such. Paul marshals a number of arguments; the argument concerning the status of the two *in marriage* is not mentioned.[33]

■ **4–6** These verses apply the principle.[34] In content the regulation is clear:[35] a man is not to have any covering on his head at divine worship (and he wears his hair short), while a woman is to have a covering (and she wears her hair long).[36] The question now is this:[37] Is Paul here simply demanding the observance of a *Greek* custom, or is he seeking to introduce into Corinth a

---

29 And he does not conceive of Christ as having cosmic dimensions. If the series is taken by itself and further developed as such, then there remains no room for the event of salvation in history. For then the relations are those of timeless metaphysic. But it may be asked whether Paul already found, in the Jewish version of his school tradition, support for relating the series to the historic person of Christ—namely, in a factor connected with salvation history in the biblical exposition, corresponding to the suggestions provided in 10:1ff. On v 3 see Wilhelm Thüsing, *Per Christum in Deum*, NtlAbh, n.s. 1 (Münster: Aschendorff, 1965), 20–29.

30 Even in this point he makes merely *ad hoc* use of the series. He does not show, for example, in what the likeness consists (say, in the possession of νοῦς, "mind"). It is identical with human nature as such.

31 See Albert Schweitzer, *The Mysticism of the Apostle Paul*, tr. William Montgomery (New York: Holt, 1931; London: Black, 1953), 9f (*Die Mystik des Apostels Paulus* [Tübingen: J. C. B. Mohr (Paul Siebeck), 1930, 1954], 9f). Schweitzer, to be sure, goes too far in saying that for Paul the natural differences are differences in nearness to God. This is true of the underlying system, but is of no significance for Paul. He does not develop a theology of the orders of creation. It should be noticed how he cuts short the inner tendencies of the series speculation.

32 Corresponding to the passages on family duties, Col 3:18, etc. In favor of this view Bachmann appeals to the absence of the article before γυναικός, "woman's." This, he argues, imparts a generalizing force to the article before ἀνήρ, "man." But the use of the article cannot prove anything as far as this question is concerned. Cf. the previous expression παντὸς ἀνδρός, "every man's." Here the meaning is woman as such, not just the married woman.

33 It appears in the interpolated passage 14:35. Lietzmann finds it unintelligible that Paul did not omit v 3 together with the strained word-play on κεφαλή, "head" (see v 4) and simply appeal to custom as in v 6. But without v 3 Paul, according to his own understanding of the matter, would have had no theological (!) foundation.

34 We must continue to bear in mind that what matters to Paul is not a theoretic development of the argument—this is only a means to his end—but carefully-aimed paraenesis addressed to specific persons. He is not discussing "the place of woman" in general. The latter topic is vastly more in keeping with the tables of household duties.

35 Strictly, Paul is speaking only of *appearance* at divine worship; this is an inspired act. The parallelism between vv 4 and 5 expresses the fundamental equality of rights, although it is only the *woman's* conduct that is at issue here. This finds expression in the formal overhang at the end of vv 5 and 6. For both, man and woman, the rule is: in speaking at divine worship they should not be otherwise dressed than in public. There is neither holy nor unholy dress, though there is certainly unseemly dress. Paul here thinks in precisely the same way as in regard to eating in chaps. 8—10.

36 The reference to hair style is only an auxiliary argument mentioned in passing. There is general agreement between Paul and his readers that a woman does not wear short hair.

37 See Gerhard Delling, *Paulus' Stellung zu Frau und Ehe*, BWANT, 56 (Stuttgart: Kohlhammer, 1931), 96–105.

38 In the latter case his ruling allows of no conclusions as to the ground of the Corinthians' behavior. The community would obviously simply have followed, till now, the general custom. Paul, on the

new custom, namely, the Jewish one?[38] The ancient material leads to no certain answer. The Jewish custom, to be sure, can be unequivocally ascertained, and corresponds to Paul's regulation: a Jewess may appear in public only with her head covered.[39] On the other hand, the Greek practice in regard to headgear and hairstyle cannot be unequivocally stated for the simple reason that the fashion varies.[40] So the question remains: Is Paul binding the Christians to a *Jewish* custom (so Kümmel) or to a *universal* one? In the latter case, tendencies toward emancipation from the tradition would have arisen in Corinth.[41] Or, a third possibility, is the alternative not to be raised so sharply at all?[42]

---

other hand, would now be declaring the Greek custom to be shameful, and would thus be separating the community visibly from the pagan world around them and making Christian women outwardly the same as Jewesses. For the veiling of women see Philo, *Spec. leg.* 3.56; Jos., *Ant.* 3.270. Adolf Schlatter, *Die Theologie des Judentums nach dem Bericht des Josefus*, BFTh, 2, 26 (Gütersloh: Bertelsmann, 1932), 169.

39 Cutting her hair is out of the question in any case, see below. *Gn. r.* 17.8(12a), in Str.–B. 3:423f: R. Joshua (*ca.* 90) was asked: "Why does a man go out bareheaded while a woman goes out with her head covered?'" (*Midrash Rabbah* 1:139); *b. Ned.* 30b: "Men sometimes cover their heads and sometimes not; but women's hair is always covered, and children are always bareheaded" (Epstein, 87). For a woman to go out with her head uncovered is a disgrace (*3 Macc.* 4.6) and a ground for divorce, *Ket.* 7.6, etc. (Str.–B. 3:427–434). On veiling see Alfred Jeremias, *Der Schleier von Sumer bis heute*, AO, 31, 1–2 (Leipzig: Hinrichs, 1931); Roland de Vaux, "Sur le voile des femmes dans l'Orient ancien," *RB* 44 (1935): 397–412, now in his *Bible et Orient* (Paris: Cerf, 1967), 407–423.

40 Plut., *Quaest. Rom.* 267a (Roman custom; Corinth is a Roman colony): συνηθέστερον δὲ ταῖς μὲν γυναι-ξὶν ἐγκεκαλυμμέναις, τοῖς δὲ ἀνδράσιν ἀκαλύπτοις εἰς τὴν δημοσίαν προϊέναι, "it is more usual for women to go forth in public with their heads covered and men with their heads uncovered" (Loeb 4:27); *Apophth. Lac.* 232c: . . . διὰ τί τὰς μὲν κόρας ἀκαλύ-πτους, τὰς δὲ γυναῖκας ἐγκαλυμμένας εἰς τοὖμ-φανὲς ἄγουσιν, "[When someone inquired] why they took their girls into public places unveiled but their married women veiled . . ." (Loeb 3:393). The testimony of illustrations is not unequivocal; see e.g. *CAH*, plates vol. 4:167, 169, 171. It is a case of portraits. That a head covering can be missing in these proves nothing in regard to appearance in public; but the *wearing* of a head covering certainly does prove something. Tertullian (*Virg. vel.* 8.8) says the Corinthian woman is striking for the fact that she wears a veil (cf. Tert., *Cor.* 4). To be sure, the custom of wearing a veil is universal oriental practice. For Tarsus cf. Dio Chrys., *Or.* 16(33).48f. From Tarsus Paul is familiar with veiling as a *universal*

custom. Dio Chrysostomus laments its decay.

The variability not only in fashion, but also in personal taste, is impressively demonstrated by Ovid., *Ars am.* 3:135–168. For illustrations from Corinth see Fowler, *Corinth* 12, nos. 239–290, 357–415.

A special case is dress at divine worship. The mystery inscription from Andania (Ditt., *Syll.* 2:401–411 [no. 736]) seems to forbid the veil for the mysteries. For unveiled women at religious ceremonies see Johannes Leipoldt, *Die Religionen in der Umwelt des Urchristentums*, Bilderatlas zur Religionsgeschichte, ed. Hans Haas, 9–11 (Leipzig: Deichert, 1926), nos. 105, 165, 168. Apul., *Met.* 11.10 (at the Isis festival in Corinth): *illae limpido tegmine crines madidos obvolutae, hi capillum derasi funditus verticem praenitentes*, "The women had their hair anointed, and their heads covered with light linen; but the men had their crowns shaven and shining bright" (Loeb, 555). It can be assumed that respectable Greek women wore a head covering in public. Ovid is of course no proof to the contrary. For the veiling of those about to be initiated see F. Matz, ΔΙΟΝΥ-ΣΙΑΚΗ ΤΕΛΕΤΗ: *Archaeologische Untersuchungen zum Dionysoskult in hellenistischer und römischer Zeit*, AAM, 1963, 15 (Mainz: Akademie der Wissenschaften und der Literatur; Wiesbaden: Steiner, 1963), plates 20–23 and pp. 15, 21; Albrecht Oepke, *TDNT* 3:561–563; Stefan Lösch, "Christliche Frauen in Korinth (I Cor. 11,2–16)," *ThQ* 127 (1947): 216–261.

41 In this case we must presume that these tendencies are bound up with enthusiasm: the Spirit makes all alike. Female charismatics can begin by drawing conclusions from this for their appearance. Paul would then be reminding them that the equality is an equality "in Christ" and that consequently women remain women. Their personality does not disappear, as in enthusiasm.

42 Schlatter observes that Paul is resisting efforts toward emancipation, but that his starting point is Jewish custom. The question is, however, whether this custom was firmly established among the Jewesses in Corinth or whether it was introduced into the community by Paul. Weiss says it is a question of offense against both Jewish and Greek custom. Weiss, too, assumes tendencies towards emancipation. A totally

The wording[43] rather tends to suggest that Paul is pressing for the observance of a *universal* custom (cf. v 16). But the reasoning causes difficulties: How does a woman dishonor her head if she does not cover it? Weiss refrains from an explanation.[44] But one emerges simply from recognition of the custom.[45] This is also in keeping with the further observation that the woman would be the same as if she were shaven.[46]

■ **6** This verse goes on to provide a further basis[47] in the universal view.[48] Conclusion: there are no new laws that apply to Christians in the world.

■ **7** Verse 7 repeats the presupposition stated in v 3. Here the meaning of κεφαλή, "head," becomes plain as a result of the interchange with εἰκών, "image," and δόξα, "reflection." Through the choice of εἰκών, Paul secures at the same time a link with the Bible, Gen 1:27.[49] But his exegesis presupposes ideas which would not be derivable from the Bible text itself if the exegete were not already furnished with them, namely, the thought–

comples of κεφαλή, εἰκών, δόξα.

κεφαλή in v 3 was the "chief"; here it means in the first instance the (anatomical) head. But how are we to understand the relation between the rule that the head or face is not to be covered and the reason for it, that a man is the image of God? Obviously in the sense that the head, and more particularly the face, constitutes in a special way the archetype/image relationship. This idea is in fact Jewish.[50]

Two points are particularly striking: (1) In contrast to v 3, Christ is here omitted from the εἰκών series, a further indication that the latter was already given. Without the Christ link it stands nearer to the Bible passage.[51] (2) the woman is here, indirectly, excluded from being an image, or she is one only in a derivative sense. This cannot be derived from Gen 1:26f either—quite the contrary! Once again the Jewish presupposition becomes visible.[52] It is not unintentionally that Paul, in the case of the woman, speaks only of δόξα, and not also of

different view of the unsolved question is adopted by Lösch, "Christliche Frauen," 251–258. The Greek cult, he says, requires letting down the hair. This rule is having an influence on the community. Against this, he goes on, Paul declares: "If you appear thus, then the *nodus sacer*, the *vinculum matrimonii*, is declared to be dissolved, and therewith the bond with Christ and God is dissolved." This is fantastic, especially as the cultic custom in question is not universal, see above.

43 Lietzmann presumes there is a wordplay on κεφαλή: she dishonors her head = her husband; Weiss is against this.

44 "On the other hand, everything would be clear, if v 3 could be taken as a gloss on vv 4f."

45 Cf. also *Act. Thom.* 56: Only shameless women go about bareheaded (γυμνοκέφαλοι).

46 It is mistaken to regard being shaven as a mark of the courtesan; rightly Delling, *Paulus' Stellung zu Frau und Ehe*, 104. In the OT it is a sign of mourning, Deut 21:12. A sign of disgrace: Aristoph., *Thes.* 837.

47 For the style cf. Gal 5:12. Bachmann holds that vv 5b and 6 are a proof of v 5a only when "head" there means the man. This is not the case.

48 Luc., *Fug.* 27: γυναῖκα ἐν χρῷ κεκαρμένην εἰς τὸ Λακωνικόν, ἀρρενωπὴν καὶ κομιδῇ ἀνδρακήν, "a woman with her hair closely clipped in the Spartan style, boyish–looking and quite masculine" (Loeb 5:85). Luc., *Dial. mer.* 5.3: καθάπερ οἱ σφόδρα ἀθλητῶν ἀνδρώδεις ἀποκεκαρμένη, "[Megilla's head] shaved close, just like the manliest of athletes" (cf. Loeb 7:383). The general custom is presup-

posed, when a virtuous wife cuts off her hair so as to be able to follow her husband into exile in disguise, Apul., *Met.* 7.6. Duris of Samos in Jacoby, *FGH* 2A:45 (no. 76, Fr. 24), reports a remarkable thing from ancient Athens. At that time, he says, the Athenian women wore Doric dresses. It was most remarkable: the Athenians κόμας ἐφόρουν, αἱ δὲ γυναῖκες ἐκείροντο, "[the men] wore long hair, but the women were close cropped."

49 εἰκών and δόξα are synonymous, see below. Weiss asks whether μέν contains a concession to the emancipated. This is too subtle. For εἰκών see Eduard Lohse, "Imago Dei bei Paulus," in *Libertas Christiana: Friedrich Delekat zum 65. Geburtstag*, ed. E. Wolf and W. Matthias, BEvTh, 26 (Munich: Kaiser, 1957), 122–135.

50 Jervell, *Imago Dei*, 303, renders: "the face as the image of God."

51 Eltester, *Eikon*, 154, observes that if Paul had known the exegesis of Philo, he would have had no difficulty; cf. Philo, *Rer. div. her.* 231; *Leg. all.* 3.96; *Plant.* 18–22; *Op. mund.* 25 (see above). He would have the series God—Logos (= Christ)—man. Jervell, *Imago Dei*, 292–312, holds that Christ is omitted here because it is precisely the abolition of the differences that is associated with him as εἰκών. This could be true of the thought of Colossians, but is ruled out here by v 3.

52 Jervell, *Imago Dei*, 292–312, holds that Paul is combining Gen 1:27 with 2:18ff: because *Adam* is the image, the serpent approaches *Eve* (see ibid., 110–112). In that case the basis would be a Jewish mid-

εἰκών. The formal sense of δόξα, because of its correspondence with εἰκών, is "reflection."[53]

Excursus:
εἰκών, "image"

The Greek material (including Philo) is treated by Eltester, *Eikon*, the Jewish and Gnostic material by Jervell, *Imago Dei*.

1. *The classical starting point:*[54] εἰκών is an image, work of art, picture; a figure; then also a pattern; also a shadow and a reflected image,[55] an imprinted image.[56] There is also the use of "imagery" in speech.[57] In Hellenistic ruler worship, the king can be described as εἰκών ζῶσα τοῦ Διός, "the living image of Zeus."[58] An important aspect is the cosmological significance which has developed since Plato's *Timaeus:*[59] the cosmos is εἰκών τοῦ νοητοῦ θεὸς αἰσθητός, "a perceptible God made in the image of the Intelligible" (Plat., *Tim.* 92c; Loeb 7:253). Side by side there develop the motifs of κοσμοποιΐα and κοσμογονία, the "creating of the world" and the "coming to be of the world."[60]

2. *Septuagint:* εἰκών is usually the rendering of צֶלֶם, of דְּמוּת only in Gen 5:1.[61] This results in a certain shift of meaning; for εἰκών is primarily an image, צֶלֶם primarily a statue, and צֶלֶם does not mean "pattern." In Judaism, to be sure, εἰκών reacts upon צֶלֶם; the latter also acquires the meaning "model."[62] For the history of the Jewish concept of εἰκών the central notion is that of man's being the

image of God: Sir 17:1ff; Wis 2:23.[63]

3. The change in the meaning of the word and the intrusion of the aspect of substance emerges, beyond the beginnings in the LXX, in the further writings of *Hellenistic Judaism*. A connecting link is Wisdom of Solomon: Wisdom is an emanation of the "glory" of God and an "image" of his goodness, Wis 7:22ff. The analogous development in extra–Jewish Hellenism is shown by Plut., *Is. et Os.* 371b: the order in the cosmos is ἀπορροὴ καὶ εἰκὼν ἐμφαινομένη, "the efflux of Osiris and his reflected image" (Loeb 5:121). *Corp. Herm.* 11.15 (at the same time also an example of the constructing of series, see below): ἔστι τοίνυν εἰκὼν τοῦ θεοῦ ὁ αἰών, τοῦ δὲ αἰῶνος ὁ κόσμος, τοῦ δὲ κόσμου ὁ ἥλιος, τοῦ δὲ ἡλίου ὁ ἄνθρωπος, "The Aeon then is an image of God; the Kosmos is an image of the Aeon; the Sun is an image of the Kosmos; and Man is an image of the Sun" (Scott 1:217, n. 5).

4. *Philo* deserves special interest: the κόσμος αἰσθητός, "perceptible world," is the image of the κόσμος νοητός, "noetic world." Here we can discern the Platonic starting point. But now Plato is transcended: the κόσμος νοητός is the Logos, and this latter is the εἰκών of God (*Op. mund.* 25). What is true of the cosmos is true also of man. This means that an εἰκών series can be constructed. The definition εἰκών can be applied[64] to the cosmos, Wisdom, man.[65] The "normal" series is: God, Logos, man.[66]

5. The situation in Philo is fully understood only when we recognize the gradual transformation of Greek concepts of form into Hellenistic concepts

---

rash.

53 This is not classical usage. But this meaning emerges plainly from the context and is explained by the Jewish combination of image and δόξα, see the excursus. The usage in the vulgar language is a different matter; *CIJ* 135: ἡ δόξα Σωφρονίου Λουκίλλα εὐλογημένη, "[Here lies the one who was] the reflection of Sophronios, blessed Lucilla." Cf. Sextus, *Sent.* 190: σέβου σοφὸν ἄνδρα ὡς εἰκόνα θεοῦ ζῶσαν, "Revere a wise man as a living image of god."

54 For examples see the lexica.

55 Plat., *Resp.* 402b; 509e. For the connection with mirror symbolism see Dupont, *Gnosis*, 119–146.

56 Plut., *Is. et Os.* 373a.

57 Plat., *Resp.* 487e: δι' εἰκόνων λέγειν, "to speak in imagery."

58 Ditt., *Or.* 1:142 (no. 90, line 3), from the Ptolemaic period. Cf. Plut., *Them.* 27(125c): the great king is εἰκών θεοῦ τοῦ πάντα σῴζοντος, "the image of that god who is the preserver of all things" (Loeb 2:73).

59 Eltester, *Eikon*, 102–120.

60 Reflection on the distinction between "creating"

and "begetting" is found in Philo, *Leg. all.* 1.31: the οὐράνιος (κατ.' εἰκόνα) ἄνθρωπος, "heavenly man (after the [divine] image)" is γένημα, "offspring," while the γήϊνος, "earthly man," is πλάσμα, "moulded"; cf. *Op. mund.* 134f. A Gnostic variation is to be found in *Ev. Phil.* 121: "He who has received the ability to create is a creature. He who has received the ability to beget is an off–spring"; the offspring of one who creates "are not his children but [his] . . . image" (Wilson, 57).

61 ὁμοίωμα (Gen 1:26 for דְּמוּת) can here be left out of account.

62 Jervell, *Imago Dei*, 23.

63 In apocalyptic the concept of being an image is related to Adam and to glory in the coming aeon. The firm connection between εἰκών and δόξα is important for the present passage (Jervell, *Imago Dei*, 101).

64 Eltester, *Eikon*, 39–41.

65 The human νοῦς, *Virt.* 205; further, the soul, the πνεῦμα.

66 *Rer. div. her.* 231. By means of this conceptuality Philo can harmonize with each other the two creation narratives of Gen 1 and 2.

of substance, which is particularly plain in the *Corpus Hermeticum*.[67] Here, too, there arises the construction of a series: God, world, man, *Corp. Herm.* 8; 12.15f.[68]

6. *Gnosticism*:[69] A fine example of the "image" motif is provided by the "Hymn of the Pearl." The "image" is the archetype in the beyond, the Gnostic's true self.[70]

7. In *Paul* the result of εἰκών speculation appears in his Christology:[71] Christ is the εἰκών of God, 2 Cor 4:4; and then in the adoption of the "series" in the present passage, in the twofold form, (a) God, Christ, man, v 3, and (b) God, man, v 7. It should be mentioned further that in Philo, too, εἰκών can contain within it the aspect of future consummation.[72] And the synonymous character of εἰκών and δόξα is prefigured in Judaism: being the image of God consists in possessing the כָּבוֹד, the δόξα.[73]

■ **8–9** These verses hark back to a different point in the biblical creation story, Gen 2:22 and 2:18 (διά, "for the sake of").[74]

The question both in regard to vv 3–7 and also in regard to vv 8f is: How does the statement that a woman has only a mediated relationship to God tally with the

immediacy of faith's relation to him, and how does it tally with the idea of the body of Christ, in which there is no longer man or woman (Gal 3:28; cf. 1 Cor 12:13)? Barth broaches the problem, yet blunts the point of Paul's statement by arguing that Paul does not wish to assert a difference in the relation to *God*. He does! Barth, however, rightly sees that even in this speculative passage the order of nature does not become the order of salvation.[75] For indeed the statement, "Here is neither man nor woman," does *not* impugn the natural order, but teaches the *eschatological abrogation*, taking place "in Christ," in his body, of the distinctions with respect to salvation.[76]

■ **10** The conclusion is that a woman *must* cover her head. This demand is compelling, since it is not merely a question of custom, but of the order of creation.[77]

The logic is understandable only when specific ideas

---

67 *Corp. Herm.* 5.2; 1.12: participation of the Anthropos in the form of the Father and equality of substance, see on 1 Cor 15:49; 2 Cor 3:18; Rom 8:29; Phil 3:21; Heb 10:1.

68 World—man: *Corp. Herm.* 8.5; *Ascl.* 10; cf. Philo, *Op. mund.* 126. *Corp. Herm.* 11.15. On *Corp. Herm.* 8.2 see Eltester, *Eikon*, 70. In 8.5 the influence of the *Timaeus* and of the Stoa is recognizable: τὸ δὲ τρίτον ζῷον, ὁ ἄνθρωπος, κατ' εἰκόνα τοῦ κόσμου γενόμενος, νοῦν κατὰ βούλησιν τοῦ πατρὸς ἔχων ... οὐ μόνον πρὸς τὸν δεύτερον θεὸν συμπάθειαν ἔχων, ἀλλὰ καὶ ἔννοιαν τοῦ πρώτου, "The third being, man, was made in the image of the cosmos and ... possesses mind according to the Father's will; and not only is he united with the second god by means of a tie of sympathy, but also he apprehends the first god intellectually" (cf. Nock–Festugière 1:89; Scott 1:177). Cf. 12.15f; Eltester, *Eikon*, 71f.

69 Jervell, *Imago Dei*, 122–170—with limitations, to be sure, because oriented on Gen 1:26f. Käsemann, *Leib*, 81–87, 148–150.

70 For the content cf. *Ginza* L 113 (Lidz., *Ginza*, 559): "I am on the way toward my archetype and my archetype is on the way toward me." *Ev. Thom.* 84: "When you see your likeness, you rejoice; but when you see your images (εἰκών), which came into being before you—they neither die nor are made manifest

—how much will you bear?" (Hennecke–Schneemelcher–Wilson 1:519).

71 Cf. Col 1:15ff; Heb 1:3. There the religious historical background becomes visible: cosmological and soteriological ideas from Judaism, which are developed in the context of Wisdom speculation.

72 Eltester, *Eikon*, 54f, 128. Philo, *Leg. all.* 2.4: the κατ' εἰκόνα ἄνθρωπος, "man made after the (divine) image" =man as image of the Logos, strives to transcend himself and attain to the εἰκών. For Paul, see on 13:10–12.

73 Jervell, *Imago Dei*, 100–104; cf. 303. For δόξα meaning "reflection" see *ibid.*, 180.

74 Eve in Philo: *Op. mund.* 151; 165.

75 And vice versa: the order of salvation does not abrogate the order of the world.

76 Bultmann, *Faith and Understanding* 1:77 [48], observes that it cannot be said on the ground of faith: "Natural relations mean nothing to us, so let us ignore them!" This is the attitude of the Gnostic; it leads to a fantasy existence. For this very reason it succumbs to the power of nature (see the instance of πορνεία).

77 Werner Foerster, *TDNT* 2:573f, says that ὀφείλει does not mean compulsion, but moral obligation. This is not an accurate alternative. The command is unconditional. For the order of creation, see Foerster, "Zu 1 Cor 11,10," *ZNW* 30 (1931): 185f; Gün-

are already given.[78] Does the connecting thought lie in the catchword ἐξουσία, "power"? The usage in this passage is singular. Any explanation on the basis of analogies is only partially satisfactory. Most expositors follow Gerhard Kittel:[79] שלטוניה in *p. Shab.* 6, 8b, 48 means something like "headband," "veil." If the word is derived from שלט, "to exercise power," then it can be rendered by ἐξουσία. Kümmel, on the other hand, declares that this explanation is impossible. According to it, Paul would have erroneously (!) rendered an Aramaic word by means of a Greek one which cannot designate any kind of headgear; and the Greek readers would not have been able to understand him. Even if this latter remark is not a conclusive argument,[80] yet the objection as a whole is to the point. We can get no further than to presume that the head covering represents a protective power.[81] But against whom? What is the meaning of διὰ τοὺς ἀγγέλους, "because of the angels"? Several suggestions are made. The fallen angels of Gen 6:1f

are meant.[82] The demons are held to be sexually libidinous.[83] Yet the thought need not be that of their sexual desire in particular. It can also be a general allusion to the possibility of woman in her weakness being harmed by demons.[84] Others think of the order of creation, arguing that the angels are the protectors of this order.[85] But Lietzmann rightly objects that in that case ἐξουσία would have to be understood as a sign of *subordination*,[86] which does not suit the word at all. Finally, there are those who think of the presence of angels at divine worship.[87]

If the statement is understood in its context as giving a reason (διὰ τοῦτο, "for this reason," and διὰ τοὺς ἀγγέλους, "because of the angels"), then the ἐξουσία is a protection, in the sense of a compensation for the natural weakness of woman (in metaphysical terms: because she is God's image only in a derivative sense) over against cosmic power. Paul has no interest in fur-

---

ther Harder, *Paulus und das Gebet* Neutestamentliche Forschungen, 1, 10 (Gütersloh: Bertelsmann, 1936), 153f.

78   From the εἰκών—δόξα series as such we could also draw the opposite conclusion: woman is not immediately exposed to the power of the cosmos, but has man as a protection between her and the power. But the prevailing view here is simply that the weaker sex requires more protection (whether the thought is of demons or of an impersonal force).

79   Gerhard Kittel, *Rabbinica*, ARGU, 1, 3 (Leipzig: Hinrichs, 1920), 17–31; Str.–B. 3:435–437. Literature: Bauer, *s.v.* ἐξουσία.

80   There is no point whatever in references to the bride's appearing unveiled on her wedding day.

81   Jervell, *Imago Dei*, 304–309, says that Judaism links the concept of being in the divine image with man's sovereign position in the world. The demons do not venture to approach Adam as long as he possesses the divine image. ἐξουσία is a substitute for the image which woman lacks. This observation, to be sure, does nothing to explain the *term* ἐξουσία.

It should be noted that in general in the whole thought–complex of archetype–copy–image there is no idea of the fall or of a loss of being an image. This too is an indication of how isolated this block of material is in the Pauline context. And the weakness of woman is not linked to her temptation by the serpent, but exclusively to her natural created condition and position in the cosmos (and this despite 2 Cor 11:3).

82   Tert., *Virg. vel.* 7.2. These angels are held to be the

origin of the demons, *Eth. En.* 15.8–12. Bo Reicke, *The Disobedient Spirits and Christian Baptism*, ASNU, 13 (Copenhagen: Munksgaard, 1946); Lyder Brun, " 'Um der Engel willen,' 1 Kor 11,10," *ZNW* 14 (1913): 298–308.

83   *Test. R.* 5.5: the women were commanded ἵνα μὴ κοσμῶνται τὰς κεφαλὰς καὶ τὰς ὄψεις αὐτῶν, "that they adorn not their heads and faces" (Charles, *APOT* 2:299).

84   Kümmel. For magical protection by means of a head covering, see *b. Shabb.* 156b; Foerster, "Zu 1 Cor 11,10," 185f. For angels as powers behind the pagan world order, see George B. Caird, *Principalities and Powers* (Oxford: Clarendon, 1956), 15–22.

85   Heinrici, Robertson and Plummer, Bachmann; Foerster, *TDNT* 2:573f; Harder, *Paulus und das Gebet*, 153f; Caird, *Principalities and Powers*, 17f.

86   Thus indeed Lösch, "Christliche Frauen."

87   Thus, again on the basis of the Qumran texts, Henry Joel Cadbury, "A Qumran Parallel to Paul," *HTR* 51 (1958): 1f; Joseph A. Fitzmyer, "A Feature of Qumran Angelology and the New Testament," *NTS* 4 (1957–58): 48–58, now in his *Essays on the Semitic Background of the New Testament* (London: Chapman, 1971), 187–204, according to whom the physically defective are excluded from the assembly כיא מלאכי קודש [בעד]תם, "for the Angels of holiness are [in] their [Congrega]tion" (IQSa II, 8f; Dupont–Sommer, 108); cf. further 1QM VII, 4–6; 4QDb (see J. T. Milik, *Ten Years of Discovery in the Wilderness of Judaea*, tr. John Strugnell, SBT, 1, 26 [London: SCM, 1959], 114 [*Dix ans de découvertes dans le désert de*

ther, more precise definitions.[88]

■ **11–12** These verses give a specially clear impression of being the result of discussions. Here the proof that has so far been offered seems to be invalidated. For now both sexes appear to be equal after all. The transition with πλήν, "of course," already marks a note of retreat. The contradiction between v 8 and v 12 seems particularly crass.

Once again we have to bear in mind that the underlying suppositions are Jewish.[89] In Judaism this statement does not mean a general definition of the nature of woman. It can be made without prejudice to her subordination in principle.[90] This of course does not suffice to explain the peculiar thought of Paul. His starting point is a thesis taken over from cosmology. Paul transplants this thesis into the realm of Christology.[91]

■ **11** One must not read v 11 in the first instance in isolation, without the expression ἐν κυρίῳ, "in the Lord." It maintains the central Pauline idea that the cancellation of distinctions has its specific place, that they are canceled "in the Lord," not "in us." In v 12 Paul can express himself so briefly because the allusion is understandable to the reader who knows his Bible.

■ **13** The appeal to the readers' own power of discernment is used as a new argument. This, while it certainly does not abandon the grounds advanced so far, nevertheless does concede that they are not yet conclusive. The summons has a Stoic ring.[92] Paul assumes of Christians that "they" know what "is proper," as in Phil 4:8f.[93] In contrast to philosophical anthropology, however, this assumption is not made an object of theoretical investigation.

■ **14** Much the same applies to v 14, where the appeal to discernment is followed by a reference to nature. In the Stoa the two would form together a firm, systematically grounded complex of thought; in Paul they constitute an incidental argument.[94]

Once again the proof is not in itself immediately conclusive. The reference to the shortness of a man's hair and the length of a woman's could in itself also be used as an argument for the contrary: if a woman has long hair by nature, then she does not require a further covering; she has sufficient protection by nature.[95] Paul's argument, however, presupposes a different view of man's relationship to nature: nature gives *directions* for conduct.[96] In point of content he presupposes not only the

---

Juda (Paris: Cerf, 1957), 76]); for criticism see Braun, *Qumran* 1:193f. In actual fact the cases in Corinthians and Qumran are different.

88   He is of course convinced that demons exist. But when he comes to define man's relation to them, he largely parts company with the demonological view and characterizes them as existential factors; cf. Rom 8:38f with 1 Cor 3:22.

89   Cf. *Gn. r.* 22 (14d), in Str.–B. 3:440: man not without woman, woman not without man, neither of them without the Shekinah.

90   Jervell, *Imago Dei*, 309–312, holds that this statement is meant to explain the plural of Gen 1:26. Adam was created alone, i.e. he alone as the divine image. Later, man, woman and Shekinah have part in the creating of the child; thus both man and woman are the divine image.

91   This is perceived by Jervell, *Imago Dei*, 310f, but confused with existence in the new aeon. See Neugebauer, *In Christus*, 135–137: "Since man and woman both have the *one* Lord, their sexuality is certainly not abrogated, but their relationship is defined as the original, creaturely togetherness" (136f).

92   Max Pohlenz, "τὸ πρέπον: Ein Beitrag zur Geschichte des griechischen Geistes," *NGG* (1933): 53–92.

93   This appeal is systematically possible in Paul. From

the standpoint of the understanding of faith, the principles of ethics are "profane," in other words, neutral. Negatively speaking it can be seen that the world picture which emerges in vv 3–9 is not a matter of faith, but a means to understanding—and the understanding of the world at that.

94   There is no anchoring of the argument in a *concept* of nature. Nature does not as such become an object of reflection, neither as teacher nor as principle (Cic., *Off*. 1.28.100: *quam* [*sc. naturam*] *si sequimur ducem, numquam aberrabimus*, "If we follow nature as our guide, we shall never go astray" [Loeb, 103]).

95   Zuntz, *Text*, 127, deletes αὐτῇ in v 15 along with p⁴⁶ D G, arguing that then the thought becomes clear. In reality it makes no difference.

96   Lietzmann. When the philosopher wears a beard, he understands this likewise to be a pointer to nature, Epict., *Diss*. 1.16.10.

97   Hdt., *Hist*. 1.82.7f; Plut., *Quaest. Rom*. 267b (see above); Ps.–Phocylides, *Poema admon*. 212: ἄρσεσιν οὐκ ἐπέοικε κομᾶν, "It is not proper for males to have long hair." Instances in H. Herter, "Effeminatus," *RAC* 4:620–650, here esp. 629.

98   Duris (see on v 6; n. 48 above) shows how one can play with the idea of a reversal of the custom. Normally, a reversal of this kind is considered a "perversity," see Herter, "Effeminatus." θηλύνεσθαι

naturally given facts, but also the prevailing custom[97] (which is held to be in harmony with nature[98]).

■ **16** Finally, v 16 shows that Paul does not completely trust any of his grounds. Thus he ends with a laboriously gilded *sic volo, sic jubeo,* "this is my will, this my command," in favor of which he advances the custom common to all the "churches of God" (see on 1:2). He is essentially right, to the extent that he was not himself the inventor of this custom. The question remains open (see above) whether it was he who introduced it into *Corinth.* In view of v 16 it can hardly be so. He is not struggling on behalf of a *new* custom, but for the upholding of the old one. The church is a unity, and in this case so also is the custom. This is, on the one hand, an indication of how a unified Christian way of life develops even in outward things. On the other hand, it is not sufficient to speak of a merely outward unity or of legalism. For obviously the deeper ground underlying this demand for unity is a thoroughgoing rejection of enthusiasm and a summons to Christian "naturalness." At bottom the summons is a critical one: not to confuse a direct desecularization that is carried on by ourselves with the eschatological desecularization brought about by Christ, but to main-

tain the imperceptibility of this unworldliness—by dint of Christians wearing their hair normally and clothing themselves in normal ways.

If we would discover a unified movement of thought in this section, then obviously we must seek to elucidate it in the light of v 16. For it is here that Paul's real argument lies, namely, the one based upon the church, which, in an awkward and obscure process of reasoning, can be discerned already in v 11. *Here* (i.e., in Christ) there is no longer man or woman. Verses 11f and 16 have to be seen together. In the light of v 16 we can, with all due reservations, reconstruct the situation. The wearing of a covering on the head is already customary in Corinth. Whether at the birth of the community the Jewish–Christian part was the decisive influence here may be left an open question. At all events the demand is not insisted upon by Paul as one of *his,* but is treated as being obviously a matter of established custom. Now it appears to be breaking down as a result of pneumatism. In this Paul appears to see the same danger of individualistic disintegration as in the Corinthian practice of the Lord's Supper. Against this he asserts the principle of chap. 7: each in his own κλῆσις, "calling."

("becoming womanish") is contrary to nature, Diog. L., *Vit.* 6.65; cf. Sen., *Ep.* 122.7. It is questionable, though, whether Paul is alluding to long–haired μαλακοί, "effeminates."

11

The Lord's Supper

17 But in giving my instructions I cannot approve[1] of the fact that your meetings are not for the better, but for the worse. **18/** In the first place I hear that there are divisions among you when you hold your church meetings;[2] and I partly believe it. **19/** For indeed there must be factions among you, so that the sound people among you may come to light. **20/** When you assemble for a meeting,[3] it is not possible to eat the Lord's Supper. **21/** For each of you takes his own supper at the meal, and one goes hungry while another is drunk. **22/** Have you no houses, then, to eat and drink in? Or do you despise the church of God and humiliate those who have nothing? What am I to say to you? Am I to commend you?[4] On this point I must disapprove of you. **23/** For I have received from the Lord,[5] what I also passed on to you: that the Lord Jesus on the night on which he was betrayed,[6] took bread, **24/** gave thanks, broke it and said: This is my body for you. Do this in remembrance of me! **25/** Likewise also the cup after supper, with the words: This cup is the new covenant in my blood. Do this, as often as you drink it, in remembrance of me. **26/** For as often as you eat this bread and drink the cup, (you) proclaim the death of the Lord, until he comes. **27/** Thus anyone who eats the bread or drinks the cup of the Lord in an unworthy manner will be guilty of an offense against the body and blood of the Lord. **28/** Let a man examine himself, and so let him eat of the bread and drink of the cup. **29/** For the man who eats and drinks, eats and drinks judgment upon himself

---

1   Readings: 1) παραγγέλλων οὐκ ἐπαινῶ ℵ G 𝔐;
        2) παραγγέλλων οὐκ ἐπαινῶν B;
        3) παραγγέλλω οὐκ ἐπαινῶν A C*;
        4) παραγγέλλω οὐκ ἐπαινῶ D*;
     2 is a mixture of 1 and 3, so also is 4. Lietzmann observes that 1 is appropriate, "for in the ὅτι clause something is censured (οὐκ ἐπαινῶ, cf. v 22), not instructed (παραγγέλλω)." Not so Anton Fridrichsen, "Non laudo: Note sur I Cor. 11,17.22," in *Mélanges d'histoire des religions et de recherches offerts à Johannes Pedersen*, Horae Soederblomianae, 1 (Stockholm: Svenska Kyrkans Diakonistyrelses Bokförlag, 1944–47), 28–32. He offers proof texts for ἐπαινεῖν in the sense of "approve" and renders: "I give the following instructions (namely, the whole of vv 17–34) in disapproval of the fact that. . . ." But this sense is brought out also by reading 1. For the official use of ἐπαινεῖν (official commendations, e.g. in

the conferring of honors) see August Strobel, "Zum Verständnis von Rm 13," *ZNW* 47 (1956): 67–93, here esp. 82–84.

2   πρῶτον μέν, "in the first place," is not followed by "in the second place" (nor δέ). ἐν ἐκκλησίᾳ: "for a church meeting," see Bauer, *s.v.* ἐκκλησία 4a and Lietzmann (referring to *Did.* 4.14) ἐν τῇ ἐκκλησίᾳ. Not so Weiss, who renders "as a community," synonymous with ἐπὶ τὸ αὐτό v 20, cf. 14:23. μέρος τι, "partly," is classical; see Bauer, *s.v.* μέρος 1d.

3   ἐπὶ τὸ αὐτό, "together, for a meeting," cf. 14:23; Acts 1:15; LXX; but also Plat., *Resp.* 329a.

4   With the same nuance as in v 17.

5   With παραλαμβάνειν, "receive," Paul normally uses παρά, "from" (so D): 1 Thess 2:13; 4:1; Gal 1:12; 2 Thess 3:6. ἀπό can hardly have a different meaning. It is overtaxing the preposition to read into it: "originally from the Lord," that is to say

if he does not distinguish[7] the body
of the Lord. 30 / This is why there are
many sick and weak among you, and
some (have fallen a–)sleep.[8] 31 / If we
entered into judgment with ourselves,
then we should not be judged. 32 / But
if we are judged by the Lord, then it
is a discipline, in order that we should
not be condemned along with the
world. 33 / Therefore, my brothers,
when you come together to eat, then
wait for each other. 34 / If anyone is
hungry, let him eat at home, so that your
coming together should not be for
judgment. The other matters I will set in
order when I come.

■ **17** This is the theme of the new section: it has to do
with a further question of the church assembly, this time
of the Supper,[9] and at the same time announces in
advance Paul's verdict on the prevailing circumstances.
The content of his censure is first formally outlined:
their meetings[10] serve not for the better,[11] but for the
worse. The sense emerges from the context.

■ **18** It is a case of the upbuilding or destroying of the
community as such, a question of the emergence of
$\sigma\chi\acute{\iota}\sigma\mu\alpha\tau\alpha$, "divisions."[12]
■ **19** This catchword is now taken up in v 19 by the

---

6   only indirectly.
    Imperfect describing the situation. The Koine form
    $\pi\alpha\rho\epsilon\delta\acute{\iota}\delta\epsilon\tau o$ is read (B ℵ A C D G), see Blass–De-
    brunner §94(1); B^c L P have the classical $\pi\alpha\rho\epsilon\delta\acute{\iota}$-
    $\delta o\tau o$.
7   Namely, "from profane food" (Lietzmann); or, "he
    does not rightly discern" (Weiss, Bauer), "honor"
    (Friedrich Büchsel, cf. *TDNT* 3:946). The render-
    ing "does not distinguish" still does not imply that
    the Corinthians treat the Lord's Supper as a profane
    meal.
8   Meaning "are dead, have died"; Vulgate *dormiunt*;
    1 Thess 4:13 $o\acute{\iota}$ $\kappa o\iota\mu\acute{\omega}\mu\epsilon\nu o\iota$.
9   $\tau o\hat{\upsilon}\tau o$ cannot be precisely defined. Weiss ascribes the
    section to the older letter, on the ground that $\dot{\alpha}\kappa o\acute{\upsilon}\omega$,
    "I hear," shows that Paul is referring to a first re-
    port about the $\sigma\chi\acute{\iota}\sigma\mu\alpha\tau\alpha$, "divisions," whereas in
    1:10ff ($\dot{\epsilon}\delta\eta\lambda\acute{\omega}\theta\eta$ $\mu o\iota$, "I have been told") he is in
    possession of further information. According to
    Weiss, 11:2–34 separates the observations $\pi\epsilon\rho\grave{\iota}$ $\tau\hat{\omega}\nu$
    $\epsilon\dot{\iota}\delta\omega\lambda o\theta\acute{\upsilon}\tau\omega\nu$ and $\pi\epsilon\rho\grave{\iota}$ $\tau\hat{\omega}\nu$ $\pi\nu\epsilon\upsilon\mu\alpha\tau\iota\kappa\hat{\omega}\nu$, "concern-
    ing meat sacrificed to idols" and "concerning spir-
    itual gifts," which both belong to the second letter.
10 $\sigma\upsilon\nu\acute{\epsilon}\rho\chi\epsilon\sigma\theta\alpha\iota$, "assemble," namely, for a meeting:
    see v 18.
11 $(\tau\grave{o})$ $\kappa\rho\epsilon\hat{\iota}\sigma\sigma o\nu$: cf. 7:9; Phil 1:23: that which is to be
    preferred on moral or religious grounds; Epictetus

    (see index to Budé edition). Weiss holds that $\epsilon\dot{\iota}s$ $\tau\grave{o}$
    $\kappa\rho\epsilon\hat{\iota}\sigma\sigma o\nu$ presumably means the same as $\epsilon\dot{\iota}s$ $\tau\grave{o}$ $\sigma\upsilon\mu$-
    $\phi\acute{\epsilon}\rho o\nu$ (cf. 7:35). Agreed.
12 Weiss holds that subsequent to the report to which
    v 18 alludes, Paul received more precise information
    which is the basis of 1:10ff. But it is not apparent
    why he should be less well informed here than in the
    latter passage. It is true that his allusions here are
    not in such precise terms. But these are unnecessary,
    if both passages belong to the same letter. For $\sigma\chi\acute{\iota}$-
    $\sigma\mu\alpha\tau\alpha$ in a religious organization cf. *P. Lond.* 2710
    (end of the Ptolemaic period, with prescriptions
    for a $\sigma\acute{\upsilon}\nu o\delta os$ of $Z\epsilon\hat{\upsilon}s$ $\H{\Upsilon}\psi\iota\sigma\tau os$; see Colin Roberts,
    Theodore C. Skeat, and Arthur Darby Nock, "The
    Gild of Zeus Hypsistos," *HTR* 29 [1936]: 39–88):
    line 13: no schismata! Lines 15–18: $\kappa\alpha\grave{\iota}$ $\mu\grave{\eta}\iota$ $\gamma[\epsilon]$-
    $\nu\epsilon\alpha\lambda o\gamma[\acute{\eta}\sigma\epsilon\iota\nu$ $\acute{\epsilon}]$ $\tau\epsilon\rho os$ $\tau\grave{o}\nu$ $\acute{\epsilon}\tau\epsilon\rho o\nu$ $\grave{\epsilon}\nu$ $\tau\hat{\omega}\iota$ $\sigma\upsilon\mu\pi o\sigma\acute{\iota}\omega\iota$
    $\mu\eta\delta\grave{\epsilon}$ $\kappa\alpha\kappa o\lambda o\gamma[\acute{\eta}\sigma\epsilon\iota\nu]$ $\acute{\epsilon}\tau\epsilon\rho os$ $[\tau\grave{o}\nu]$ $\acute{\epsilon}\tau\epsilon\rho o\nu$ $\grave{\epsilon}\nu$ $\tau\hat{\omega}\iota$
    $\sigma\upsilon\mu\pi o\sigma\acute{\iota}\omega\iota$ $\mu\eta\delta\grave{\epsilon}$ $\lambda\alpha\lambda\acute{\eta}\sigma\epsilon\iota\nu$ $\mu\eta\delta\grave{\epsilon}$ $\grave{\epsilon}\pi[\iota\kappa\alpha]\lambda\acute{\eta}\sigma\epsilon\iota\nu$
    $\kappa\alpha\grave{\iota}$ $\mu\grave{\epsilon}$ $\kappa\alpha\tau\eta\gamma o\rho\acute{\eta}[\sigma]\epsilon\iota\nu$ $[(\alpha)]$ $\tau o\hat{\upsilon}$ $\grave{\epsilon}\tau\acute{\epsilon}\rho o\upsilon$ $\mu\eta\delta\grave{\epsilon}$ $\dot{\alpha}\pi\acute{o}\rho$-
    $\rho\eta\sigma\iota\nu$ $\delta\iota\delta[\acute{o}\nu\alpha\iota]$ $\grave{\epsilon}\pi\grave{\iota}$ $\tau\grave{o}\nu$ $\grave{\epsilon}\nu\iota[\alpha\upsilon\tau]\grave{o}\nu$ $\kappa\alpha\grave{\iota}$ $\mu\eta\delta$' $\dot{\alpha}[\phi\alpha]$-
    $\nu\iota\epsilon\hat{\iota}\nu$ $\tau\grave{\alpha}s$ $\sigma\upsilon\mu\pi o\sigma\acute{\iota}\alpha s$ $\mu\eta\delta\grave{\epsilon}$ $\grave{\epsilon}\pi\epsilon\rho\gamma\epsilon\sigma$ . . ., "[it shall
    not be permissible] for men to enter into one an-
    other's pedigrees at the banquet or to abuse one an-
    other at the banquet or to chatter or to indict or
    accuse another or to resign for the course of the year
    or again to bring the drinkings to nought or . . ."

word αἱρέσεις, "factions."[13] The question is how strictly δεῖ, "must," may be taken: Does it refer to a "necessary" process, namely, one determined by an apocalyptic plan?[14] It is more natural simply to take δεῖ with the appended ἵνα–clause: the objective fruit of the divisions is the visible separation of wheat and chaff.[15]

Excursus:
The Corinthians and
the Lord's Supper[16]

Verses 17–19 show that the splitting up into individual groups has not yet led to the dissolution of the united church meeting. Yet there are already signs that it is not a question of mere cliquishness, but that a theological attitude can be discerned behind the forming of the groups, an individualistic pneumatism, which leads to rallying around party heads. Already in 1:10ff there was perhaps a reference to the idea of the body of Christ as a factor making for unity (1:13). Now the unity is specially related to coming together for the Supper: if the participants relate the Supper only to their own person, they destroy the Supper as such. How has this development arisen?

According to an older view, they despise the sacra-

ment, possibly on grounds of spiritualism, and regard it now only as a symbol; they celebrate it as an ordinary meal.[17] But this accords neither with the Corinthian pneumatism nor with the massive sacramentalism which emerges in 15:29. And why are they obviously so intensive in their celebrations?[18] Hence von Soden ("Sakrament und Ethik," 23f) explains that the Corinthians are "overheated enthusiasts for faith in the Spirit"; they think the sacraments have a magical effect. This explanation is in keeping with 10:12, with their exaltation Christology, with their view of freedom, their individualism, and their view of the Spirit: they are already "satiated" (4:8). Paul's argumentation is also in favor of it: he does not urge respect for the sacramental elements,[19] but criticizes the fact that "each" enjoys his "own supper" instead of the Lord's Supper, obviously not only to his bodily enjoyment, but to his spiritual edification.[20]

■ **20** In v 20 the censure is precisely stated. It is a question, then, of the celebration of the community meal, here described as the "Lord's Supper."[21] The Corinthians destroy its character by their conduct.

■ **21** It is not the Lord who determines the celebration, but the individual.[22] Fellowship is canceled when one

---

(p. 42). On which Nock comments (p. 53): κατηγορεῖν "means presumably . . . that no one is to hale a fellow–member into court for anything arising out of their association in the synodos." Cf. Plat., *Leg.* 915e. See on 6:1ff.

13 We can hardly make a difference of content (as Lietzmann does: the αἱρέσεις are, he says, results of the σχίσματα). Heinrich Schlier, *TDNT* 1:183, thinks that αἵρεσις is the stronger word (cf. καί, "and"). But the very word καί shows that Paul makes no distinction. Cf. the agraphon in Just., *Dial.* 35.3: ἔσονται σχίσματα καὶ αἱρέσεις, "There will be dissensions and squabbles" (Hennecke–Schneemelcher–Wilson 1:88, where parallels are listed).

14 In favor of the "sharp" view is the similarity with the eschatological logion quoted in the previous note; Walter Grundmann, *TDNT* 2:21–25. In that case the sentence is meant neither in resignation nor in irony (with Kümmel against Lietzmann). Yet this is true also of the view advocated above in the text.

15 Munck, *Paul*, 135–167 [127–161] ("The Church without Factions") disputes the existence of factions. He appeals to the agraphon cited above, and also to Gal 5:19–21; Mt 24:10f; Acts 20:30, in favor of an eschatological understanding of v 19 and argues that ἵνα οἱ δόκιμοι φανεροὶ γένωνται ἐν ὑμῖν, "so

that the sound people among you may come to light," is in the same way "probably also an eschatological statement in itself"; 1 Thess 3:3; Acts 14:22; Jas 1:12. "So it is not yet a matter of factions; they are part of the future misfortunes" (*Paul*, 137 [129]).

16 Hans–Werner Bartsch, "Der korinthische Missbrauch des Abendmahls," *Deutsches Pfarrerblatt* 49 (1949): 319f, 343f, 391f, 419f, now in his *Entmythologisierende Auslegung*, ThF, 26 (Hamburg–Bergstedt: Reich, 1962), 169–183.

17 According to Lietzmann, Paul is attacking not party views, but bad manners; Weiss, 283, speaks of "indifference toward the religious character of the meal."

18 Bornkamm, *Early Christian Experience*, 125–130 (*Studien*, 141–146), following von Soden, aptly speaks of a devaluation of the agape as a result of sacramentalism. He asks whether the outward form of the celebration is also bound up with enthusiasm: in Corinth, contrary to the provisions of v 25, the Eucharist had moved to the end of the meal.

19 So he does not presuppose the profaning of them— as indeed in 10:1ff he also assumes it to be recognized that the sacrament is regarded as spiritual food and spiritual drink.

20 Completely different is the view of Schmithals, *Gnos-*

194

suffers want and another is drunk; this holds even if the reproach of drunkenness is not taken all too strictly. It is plain that we have here not merely a sacramental proceeding, but a real meal.[23]

Lietzmann assumes that the Corinthians had passed from the Pauline type of Lord's Supper (commemoration of the death) to the older type of celebration in the primitive church, where the Lord's Supper was celebrated as a continuation of the table fellowship with Jesus. But in the first place there is no evidence for this type, and secondly the text contains no suggestions whatever in this direction.[24] That at this "private" meal Jewish ritual aspects had a role to play is not only not suggested, but ruled out of the question by the whole argumentation.[25]

■ **22** The suggestion in v 22 is not sarcastic (so Allo), but is meant in all seriousness; cf. vv 33f, surprising as it is:[26] the summons to separate satisfaction of hunger and the community Supper. It seems, indeed, that the Supper thereby loses its character of "agape." But Paul is seeking to separate the *sacrament* from satisfaction of hunger.

$\mathring{\eta} \ldots$, "or . . .," is a reproachful question.

■ **23a** Paul lays the foundation: the tradition that stems from the Lord himself.[27] $\pi\alpha\rho\alpha\lambda\alpha\mu\beta\acute{\alpha}\nu\epsilon\iota\nu$ and $\pi\alpha\rho\alpha\delta\iota\delta\acute{o}\nu\alpha\iota$, "to receive" and "to pass on," are technical terms both in the Greek and in the Jewish world. (1) In the Greek world they are used for the cultivation of the school tradition.[28] Instructive examples are their occurrence in the context of the mysteries[29] and their use

---

ticism in Corinth, 245–250 [233–246]: Paul is censuring the destruction not of community, but of the cultic element. The Gnostics, he holds, have protested against the sacrament of the body and blood of Christ. "Any sacramental piety is alien," so he says, to a true Gnostic, see Iren., *Haer.* 1.21.4, and the Corinthians cannot have been sacramentalists, because they were enthusiasts.

It is abstract speculation to think that under the compulsion of their alleged system Gnostics must have thought thus. Schmithals himself seeks to find a Gnostic tradition of the Lord's Supper in 10:16f (*ibid.*, 246, n. 173 [234, n. 3]).

21   This is the oldest title. Later $\epsilon\mathring{v}\chi\alpha\rho\iota\sigma\tau\acute{\iota}\alpha$, "Eucharist," prevails. Cf. the use of the Kyrios title in v 23. $\delta\epsilon\hat{\iota}\pi\nu o\nu$: instances of the meaning "cultic meal" in Johannes Behm, *TDNT* 2:34f.

22   $\pi\rho o\lambda\alpha\mu\beta\acute{\alpha}\nu\epsilon\iota\nu$ is not here to be understood in the sense of "take before another" (so Weiss, who argues it is to be concluded from the censure that the poorer brethren should also be provided for. This indeed is the very thing that is *not* demanded!), but of the "consuming" of food; Ditt., *Syll.* 3:328f (no. 1170, lines 7, 9, 15). Paul is not giving regulations from the standpoint of charity, nor on the basis of a principle of unity (so Musonius [ed. Hense, 101]: the reproof here is to $\acute{o}\ \mu\mathring{\eta}\ \nu\acute{e}\mu\omega\nu\ \tau\grave{\alpha}\ \mathring{\iota}\sigma\alpha\ \tau o\hat{\iota}\varsigma\ \sigma\upsilon\nu\epsilon\sigma\theta\acute{\iota}$-$o\upsilon\sigma\iota\nu$, "the one who does not distribute equal shares to those who eat with him"). For $\mathring{\iota}\delta\iota o\varsigma$, "own," cf. Eratosthenes in Jacoby, *FGH* 2B:1017 (no. 241, fr. 16, lines 2–6), on the Lagynophoria: $\tau\grave{\alpha}\ \kappa o\mu\iota\sigma\theta\acute{e}$-$\nu\tau\alpha\ \alpha\mathring{v}\tauo\hat{\iota}\varsigma\ \delta\epsilon\iota\pi\nuo\hat{\upsilon}\sigma\iota\ \kappa\alpha\tau\alpha\kappa\lambda\iota\theta\acute{e}\nu\tau\epsilon\varsigma\ \ldots,\ \kappa\alpha\grave{\iota}\ \grave{\epsilon}\xi$ $\grave{\iota}\delta\acute{\iota}\alpha\varsigma\ \mathring{\epsilon}\kappa\alpha\sigma\tauo\varsigma\ \lambda\alpha\gamma\acute{\upsilon}\nuo\upsilon\ \pi\alpha\rho'\ \alpha\mathring{v}\tau\hat{\omega}\nu\ \phi\acute{e}\rhoo\nu\tau\epsilon\varsigma\ \pi\acute{\iota}$-$\nuo\upsilon\sigma\iota\nu$, "They recline and eat the things lying before them . . ., and take and drink each from his own flagon beside him" [Trans.]. His verdict: $\sigma\upsilon\nuo\iota\kappa\acute{\iota}\alpha$ $\ldots\ \acute{\rho}\upsilon\pi\alpha\rho\acute{\alpha}\cdot\ \grave{\alpha}\nu\acute{\alpha}\gamma\kappa\eta\ \gamma\grave{\alpha}\rho\ \tau\mathring{\eta}\nu\ \sigma\acute{\upsilon}\nuo\delta o\nu\ \gamma\acute{\iota}\nu\epsilon\sigma\theta\alpha\iota$

$\pi\alpha\mu\mu\iota\gamma o\hat{\upsilon}\varsigma\ \mathring{o}\chi\lambda o\upsilon$, "a feast . . . unclean, for so it must be with the feast of a mixed crowd of all sorts" [Trans.]. For Paul's "another is drunken" cf. Plut., *Quaest. conv.* 4.6 (672a), on the Jews; Nilsson, *Geschichte* 2:638.

23   Later we see that in Corinth this meal is no longer inserted into the Eucharist but precedes it.

24   Bornkamm, *Early Christian Experience*, 125–130 (*Studien*, 141–146). For a discussion of the religious–historical parallels (continuance of the Jewish custom of sacral meals in the circle of a "guild"; meals in Qumran; meals of Greek sacral guilds and particularly commemorative meals for the dead) see Jeremias, *Eucharistic Words*, 29–36 [23–30].

25   Bornkamm, *Early Christian Experience*, 156, n. 7 (to p. 126) (*Studien*, 141, n. 7).

26   In a community of love it is expected that the rich should stand up for the poor. This can be done in a club by bringing the necessary provisions, by regulating the table service, or by subscriptions. Paul's suggestion can be understood from the circumstances: when a member has no regular time off. That is to say, rather eat something after work and then come to the meeting than shift the eating into the meeting. Then it is possible to wait for each other with the Eucharist. In this way the church celebration becomes a pure celebration of the Sacrament.

27   Cf. the procedure in 15:1ff.

28   $\pi\alpha\rho\alpha\delta\acute{\iota}\delta\omega\mu\iota$: Plat., *Phileb.* 16c; *Ep.* 12.359d ($\mu\hat{\upsilon}\theta o\nu$); Diod. S., *Bibl. hist.* 12.13.2: to coming generations $\epsilon\grave{\iota}\varsigma\ \mathring{\alpha}\pi\alpha\nu\tau\alpha\ \tau\grave{o}\nu\ \alpha\grave{\iota}\hat{\omega}\nu\alpha$, "till the end of time." $\pi\alpha\rho\alpha$-$\lambda\alpha\mu\beta\acute{\alpha}\nu\omega$: Plut., *Is. et Os.* 352c, etc.; papyri.

29   Andania: Ditt., *Syll.* 2:401–411 (no. 736); Diod S., *Bibl. hist.* 5.49.5: $\kappa\alpha\grave{\iota}\ \tau\grave{\alpha}\ \mu\grave{\epsilon}\nu\ \kappa\alpha\tau\grave{\alpha}\ \mu\acute{\epsilon}\rho o\varsigma\ \tau\mathring{\eta}\varsigma\ \tau\epsilon\lambda\epsilon\tau\mathring{\eta}\varsigma$ $\grave{\epsilon}\nu\ \tauo\hat{\iota}\varsigma\ \grave{\alpha}\pi o\rho\rho\acute{\eta}\tauo\iota\varsigma\ \tau\eta\rhoo\acute{\upsilon}\mu\epsilon\nu\alpha\ \mu\acute{o}\nuo\iota\varsigma\ \pi\alpha\rho\alpha\delta\acute{\iota}\delta o\tau\alpha\iota$ $\tauo\hat{\iota}\varsigma\ \mu\upsilon\eta\theta\epsilon\hat{\iota}\sigma\iota\nu$, "Now the details of the initiatory

in Gnosticism.[30] (2) In Judaism παραλαμβάνειν and παραδιδόναι are the equivalents of קִבֵּל מִן and מָסַר לְ.[31] The convergence of Greek and Jewish usage is seen in Hellenistic Judaism[32] and in the New Testament.[33]

Paul classifies himself as a link in a chain of tradition, as in 15:3ff, yet breaks this chain by declaring that he has received the tradition ἀπὸ τοῦ κυρίου, "from the Lord." By this means he makes himself independent of human authority.[34] He does not mean that he has received this teaching in a vision.[35] He was of course acquainted with it through the mediation of men. Yet it does not merely derive ultimately from the Lord, but also constantly maintains in being passed from hand to hand the immediacy of its origin.[36] May ἐγώ, "I," be emphasized?[37] ὃ καὶ παρέδωκα: "what indeed I also passed on," cf. 15:3.[38]

■ **23b** The quotation[39] extends to v 25.[40] An analysis confirms that we have here a piece of fixed, pre–Pauline tradition.[41] As a piece of tradition, the section has in the first instance to be interpreted on its own. In so doing we have to take account of the possibility that the wording has been changed by Paul. We have to begin with

rite are guarded among the matters not to be divulged and are communicated to the initiates alone" [Trans.]. Instances: Christian August Lobeck, *Aglaophamus* (Königsberg: Bornträger, 1829; Darmstadt: Wissenschaftliche Buchgesellschaft, 1968), 39; André–Jean Festugière, *L'idéal religieux des Grecs et l'évangile*, Études Bibliques (Paris: Gabalda, 1932), 121, n. 5; Gustav Anrich, *Das antike Mysterienwesen in seinem Einfluss auf das Christentum* (Göttingen, Vandenhoeck & Ruprecht, 1894), 54, nn. 4–5; Albrecht Dieterich, *Eine Mithrasliturgie* (Leipzig and Berlin: Teubner, 1903, [3]1923; Stuttgart: Teubner, 1966), 53f. Especially interesting is the end of the *Naassene Hymn* (Hipp., *Ref.* 5.10.2; Hennecke–Schneemelcher–Wilson 2:807f).

30   The conclusion of the *Poimandres* (*Corp. Herm.* 1.32); *Corp. Herm.* 13.15; 13.1; *PGM* 4.475; Friedrich Pfister, "Die στοιχεῖα τοῦ κόσμου in den Briefen des Apostels Paulus," *Philol* 69 (1910): 411–427, here esp. 415.

31   The *locus classicus* is *Ab.* 1 (Str.–B. 3:444): "Moses received the Torah from Sinai and transmitted it to Joshua, Joshua to the elders . . .," etc.

32   Wis 14:15; Jos., *Ap.* 1.60.

33   In the references to the traditions of the Pharisees, etc.: Mk 7:13; Gal 1:14. Literature on the idea of tradition: Norden, *Agnostos Theos*, 288f; Oscar Cullmann, *The Early Church*, ed. A. J. B. Higgins (London: SCM; Philadelphia: Westminster, 1956), 55–99 (*La Tradition*, Cahiers théologiques, 33 [Neuchâtel: Delachaux et Niestlé, 1953]); W. D. Davies, *Paul and Rabbinic Judaism* (London: SPCK, [2]1955), 248f; Josef Ranft, *Der Ursprung des katholischen Traditionsprinzips* (Würzburg: Triltsch, 1931); Gerhardsson, *Memory and Manuscript*; Wegenast, *Verständnis der Tradition*; Neuenzeit, *Herrenmahl*, 77–89.

34   For the content cf. Gal 1:12.

35   Lietzmann seeks the explanation in this direction. He resorts inevitably to the help of psychological constructions, since the text does not provide any material basis: "In his [Paul's] mind all that he had heard of Jesus before and after his conversion flows from the Damascus revelation as its single, unified source." Lietzmann, *Mass and Lord's Supper*, tr. Dorothea H. G. Reeve (Leiden: Brill, 1953–), 208 (*Messe und Herrenmahl*, Arbeiten zur Kirchengeschichte, 8 [Bonn: Marcus & Weber, 1926], 255), argues that Paul knows the story from the church tradition. "But the Lord has revealed to him the essential meaning of this story." Against this, Kümmel, *ad loc.*: Paul is thinking not of the meaning of the account, but of the tradition "which ultimately goes back to the Lord." The Lord is not merely the guarantor of the tradition, but its origin (with Bachmann, Schlatter, Allo). According to Cullmann, *Early Church*, 59–75 (*La Tradition*, 11–28), behind each act of transmission there stands immediately the Lord.

36   Inspiration or human transmission is no true alternative.

37   According to Allo, Paul is declaring in face of the Corinthians: *I* cannot ignore this tradition. But this is not the case. The accent lies on the universal validity of the tradition.

38   According to Allo, this is probably an allusion to the fact that the mode of the passing on of the tradition is the same as that of its reception. Agreed; only the mode must be determined by the facts of the tradition itself, not by psychological factors.

According to Weiss, this text is not a cultic formula to be quoted at the Lord's Supper, but is teaching on the latter. This, too, is no genuine alternative: at the Supper we receive instruction concerning it, and the teaching constitutes it. That we have here a cultic formula is shown by the situation in Mark: the "words of institution" are incorporated into the framework of the farewell Supper in such a way that the repetition of the Supper and of the words of interpretation becomes binding in the church.

39   Heinz Schürmann, *Eine quellenkritische Untersuchung des lukanischen Abendmahlsberichtes Lk 22,7–38*, NtlAbh, 19, 5, 1; 20, 4; 20, 5 (Münster: Aschendorff, 1953–

a comparison with the Lord's Supper texts in Mark and Luke.[42] A firmly established original text underlying the two strands of tradition (Synoptics, represented in the first instance by Mark, and Paul) can no longer be discovered. Both in Mark and in Paul we find older and younger elements.

Analysis

1. The historical statement of time agrees in content with the Synoptic narrative: the Supper is held immediately before the arrest. But in contrast to the Synoptics, the Supper in the Pauline version is not characterized as a Passover meal.[43] The point of this historical note is that the historic institution of the sacrament is the ground of its present validity.

The word παραδιδόναι, "betray," is an established motif of the Passion kerygma.[44]

ὁ κύριος Ἰησοῦς, "the Lord Jesus":[45] the historical Jesus acts as the exalted Lord,[46] without the historical aspect being abrogated.[47]

2. The first act: thanksgiving over the bread,[48] breaking of the bread[49] and distribution.

3. The word of interpretation: the bread is the body in

---

57) 2:50, thinks that no independent report can begin in such a way. It would have to be introduced, he argues, by the situation of the Supper. Against this, Neuenzeit, *Herrenmahl*, 103f, rightly observes that the situation is given by the celebration of the Supper itself.

40 In v 26 there is a change of person, see below.

41 The section contains theological ideas which Paul certainly takes over from the tradition, but which he does not himself introduce and develop: atonement, substitution. For the linguistic usage see Jeremias, *Eucharistic Words*, 103f [98]: here alone in Paul is παραδιδόναι used absolutely; εὐχαριστεῖν absolutely of saying grace; κλᾶν without an object; ἀνάμνησις; μετά with substantivized infinitive; δειπνεῖν, ὁσάκις, τοῦτο preceding the noun, καὶ εἶπεν; on this cf. Schürmann, *Untersuchung* 2:59f.

42 In so doing the longer form of the Lucan text is presumed to be the original text, see e.g. Bornkamm, "Lord's Supper and Church in Paul," *Early Christian Experience*, 123–160 (*Studien*, 138–176); Jeremias, *Eucharistic Words*. It is compounded of Mark and a special tradition which regards the Supper not only in setting but also intrinsically as a Passover meal, though without really representing it as such.

43 This motif must not be read into it. Paul is certainly aware of the interpretation of Jesus' death as a Passover sacrifice, 5:7. But his interpretation does not there move in the direction of the Lord's Supper—nor here, vice versa, in the direction of the Passover.

44 Mk 14:10; 9:31; 10:33; the word is already given in Isa 53. This chapter is presumably also the pattern for the combining of παραδιδόναι and ὑπὲρ ὑμῶν, "for you"; see on 15:3ff; Neuenzeit, *Herrenmahl*, 157. For παραδιδόναι see Karl Hermann Schelkle, *Die Passion Jesu in der Verkündigung des Neuen Testaments* (Heidelberg, Kerle, 1949), 70–73. Since this word denotes in the tradition the whole process of "betrayal" and "self-oblation," it must not be taken too narrowly in the present passage, i.e. merely of Judas' betrayal.

45 "Jesus" cf. 2 Cor 11:4; 1 Thess 4:14.

46 Is there an echo of the Kyrios acclamation (see on 12:3)? Maranatha has an established place in the celebration of the Lord's Supper, see on 16:23. Yet we have also to notice the use of κύριος for the historical Jesus: 7:10; 9:5, 14; see on v 26. For the linguistic usage, see Neugebauer, *In Christus*, 44–64 (on Schmithals, *Gnosticism in Corinth*, 130–132 [123f], see Neugebauer, 49, n. 23).

47 In the sense of the original narrative and of Paul. The Corinthians' view is different: for them only the exalted Lord is "present."

48 In accordance with the Jewish custom at table, see on 10:16, 30. Instead of εὐχαριστεῖν Mark has εὐλογεῖν.

49 This is a Jewish rite: in this way the head of the house marks the beginning of the meal. The expression "breaking of bread" is also Jewish; Jer 16:7; outside Judaism too, of course, bread is distributed by breaking, Diod. S., *Bibl. hist.* 17.41.7: οἱ διακλώμενοι τῶν ἄρτων, "the broken pieces of bread"; Quint. Curt. Ruf., *Hist. Alex.* 4.2.14: *panem frangere*, "to break bread." But this has no ceremonial sense of any kind. See Jeremias, *Eucharistic Words*, 119f [113]. In Luke "breaking of bread" becomes a designation of the whole Supper (Acts 2:42). There is as yet no evidence for this usage in Judaism (Jeremias against Str.–B. 4:613).

There is no symbolism of breaking of bread as representation of dying (against Weiss).

ἄρτος is used of leavened and unleavened bread (Jeremias, *Eucharistic Words*, 62–66 [56–66]). The leading position of the possessive pronoun is ascribed by Schürmann, *Untersuchung* 2:17–30, to the hand of Paul; by this means, he says, Paul secures an assimilation to Ex 24:8. Against this, Neuenzeit, *Herrenmahl*, 107 observes that *Paul* has no interest in this; the position is rather a sign of pre–Pauline existence. The sacrifice motifs were "repressed" in the course of increasing Christian self–understanding"; later they thrust themselves to the fore again *per*

the sense of sacramental identity.[50] The alternative as to whether the crucified body or the body of the exalted Lord[51] is meant, should not be raised: in the sacramental food the executed body of the—now—exalted Lord is presented. By this means the participant obtains a part in him, in the sacramental communion.[52]

To the specifically sacramental interpretation of the working of the meal, there is added a further interpretative element in wholly different terminology: the death of Christ was (!) a sacrifice "for you."[53] This can mean an atoning sacrifice or a vicarious sacrifice.[54] Either way the fruit of this sacrifice is the removal of the guilt of sin ("for our sins," 15:3). This interpretation is missing in Mark in the word on the *bread*; it is there linked with the dispensing of the cup (blood). The idea of sacrifice is accordingly not bound up with the specific "element."

4. The command for repetition: τοῦτο ποιεῖτε κτλ., "do this, etc."[55] τοῦτο, "this," refers of course to the whole administration, which is repeated in the commu-nity celebration. The meaning of the rite is interpreted by the phrase εἰς τὴν ἐμὴν ἀνάμνησιν, "in remembrance of me." ἀνάμνησις, "remembrance," is more than mere commemoration; it means a sacramental presence. Lietzmann would derive the expression and the idea from Greek memorial feasts for the dead.[56] He concludes that in the Pauline form of the celebration we have not to do with a reconstruction of the continual table fellow-ship of the disciples with Jesus, but with a repetition of the Last Supper. This is clear in any case.[57]

Against Lietzmann, Jeremias objects[57a] that there is no evidence for the expression εἰς ἀνάμνησιν in Greek memorial feasts,[58] but that it derives from the Old Testament and from Judaism.[59] He holds that we have here a formula of remembrance from the Jewish cult,[60] namely, from the Passover feast: לְזִכָּרוֹן, Ex 12:14;[61] and moreover it has its place in prayers.[62] In Palestinian Judaism it refers to *God's* remembering:[63] "that God may remember me."[64] This at any rate, Jeremias argues,

---

analogiam.

50 See 10:16. There the direction can be seen in which Paul develops the interpretation—in the direction of the "body of Christ" and κοινωνία, "communion."

51 That is to say, the historical or the sacramental body. The interpretation of σῶμα as "self" is to be avoided. The meaning of גּוּף proves nothing in this respect. The decisive thing is that the body is distinguished from the cup. And with the meaning "self," or "I myself," the addition of ὑπέρ ..., "for ...," would be impossible.

52 We can see how short the way is to the Corinthian view of the sacrament: the latter is reached the mo-ment the orientation on the exalted Lord is no longer related back to his death.

53 According to Betz, *Eucharistie* 2.1:105, and Schür-mann, *Untersuchung* 2:17–30, Paul has shortened the text (cf. the longer form of the ὑπέρ ... in Mark), and has thereby pointedly related the actual saving significance of this body more sharply to those who are present. But the phrase ὑπὲρ ὑμῶν, "for you," is a formula. It is accordingly not possible to draw critical conclusions.

54 ὑπέρ can have both meanings. For the idea of atone-ment, cf. Rom 3:24ff (not so Gottfried Fitzer, "Der Ort der Versöhnung nach Paulus: Zu der Frage des 'Sühnopfers Jesu,'" *ThZ* 22 [1966]: 161–183); substitution 2 Cor 5:21. The two are not strictly distinguished; cf. the transition between the two ideas in 2 Cor 5:14f.

55 Lietzmann says: "ποιεῖν here already borders on the cultic meaning which we find e.g. in Justin,"

Dial. 41.1: ἄρτον τῆς εὐχαριστίας ποιεῖν, "to do (i.e. offer) the bread of the Eucharist." But for Paul the normal sense of ποιεῖν is sufficient; for τοῦτο ποιεῖτε, cf. Ex 29:35; Num 15:11–13.

56 Diog. L., *Vit.* 10.18 (testament of Epicurus): εἰς τὴν ἡμῶν τε καὶ Μητροδώρου μνήμην, "to commemo-rate Metrodorus and myself"; μνήμην, to be sure, is not in the transmitted text but is a conjecture, yet it is surely guaranteed by Cicero's translation (*me-moria*); see Jeremias, *Eucharistic Words*, 238f [231]. For the founding of commemorative festivals see Bernhard Laum, *Stiftungen in der griechischen und römi-schen Antike* (Leipzig: Teubner, 1914), 2 vols.; meals, 1:74–81; further 2:141 (document no. 203, from Nicomedia): [ἐπὶ τῷ] ποιεῖν αὐτοὺς ἀνά[μ]νη[σ]ίν μου, [ἣν] ποιήσουσιν ..., "that they might celebrate my memory, which they do. ..." Laum presumes a meal is meant (ἀνάμνησις, "commemoration").

57 This, contrary to Lietzmann, is already true of the earliest form of celebration known to us.

57a Jeremias, *Eucharistic Words*, 237–255 [229–246].

58 As distinct from the Latin *in memoriam* and suchlike. Jeremias further objects that the commemorative meal mostly took place on the birthday (cf. Laum, *Stiftungen* 1:75f) and that the celebration mostly had a profane character. But cf. Ps.–Luc., *Syr. Dea* 6: The orgies are celebrated annually as μνήμη τοῦ πάθεος, "a memorial of the event"; cf. chap. 13; Betz, *Lukian*, 126.

59 εἰς ἀνάμνησιν, Lev 24:7; Ps 37:1; 69:1; Wis 16:6; Jos., *Ant.* 19.318; Just., *Dial.* 27.4; 41.1; 70.4; 117.3.

60 Erwin R. Goodenough, *Jewish Symbols in the Greco–*

is how *Paul* understood it.[64a] But this interpretation is in contradiction to the plain wording. The meaning is: "in remembrance of me."[65]

■ 25 The corresponding formula is not bread and wine, but bread and cup. Thus the interpretation attaches not to the elements as such, but to the act of administration. The cup is the "cup of blessing," 10:16. When it is given μετὰ τὸ δειπνῆσαι, "after supper," then it is plain that the agape was originally enclosed by the two sacramental acts of administering the bread and the cup.[66] In Corinth, to be sure, as the context shows, the development had gone further: the whole Eucharist had been transposed to follow the meal.[67]

The second word of interpretation is not expressed in a form analogous to the first.[68] The parallels are not body and blood,[69] but body and covenant. "Is" signifies, as above, participation. Only after this comes the addition: ἐν τῷ ἐμῷ αἵματι, "in my blood."[70] In Mark διαθήκη, "covenant," is a definition of αἷμα, "blood," in

Paul the reverse: αἷμα is a definition of διαθήκη. The mention of blood again of course contains the idea of sacrifice. If above the thought was that of atonement and/or substitution, here it is that of the covenant and the covenant sacrifice. But here too, of course, no sharp distinction is to be made.[71]

The blood of Christ plays in Paul's own soteriology only a traditional role: the term appears only where he is quoting (Rom 3:24f), and in one further passage where this tradition is echoed (Rom 5:9).[72]

διαθήκη, "covenant":[73] Paul can employ the word in the sense of "testament" (Gal 3:15). The starting point for the meaning "covenant" is the LXX, where διαθήκη is a translation of בְּרִית. There already appears the thought of the "new" covenant, Jer 38:31 LXX. On this basis Paul constructs the opposite concept παλαιὰ διαθήκη, "old covenant," 2 Cor 3:14.[74] For what *Paul*

Roman Period, Bollingen Series, 37 (New York: Pantheon, 1952–65) 1:261, 2:129.

61 On this *Tg. O.*: לְדוּכְרָנָא.

62 Cf. the variation on Prov 10:7 ("The memory of the righteous is a blessing") in funerary inscriptions, *CIJ* 1:86, 201, 370; cf. 1:496.

63 Ps 112:6 (LXX 111:6): εἰς μνημόσυνον αἰώνιον ἔσται δίκαιος. "The righteous man will be remembered for ever." On this *Tg. Ps.* 112:6: לְדוּכְרַן עֲלַם יְהֵי זַכִּי. But this instance tells us nothing.

64 Cf. the Passover prayer with the petition that God remember the messiah. According to Jeremias, *Eucharistic Words*, 252–255 [242–246], God is reminded of the still outstanding completion of the work of salvation; cf. the eucharistic prayers in the *Didache*. But the latter neither prove this meaning of ἀνάμνησις nor do they prove anything at all for the understanding of Paul.

64a Jeremias, *Eucharistic Words*, 252 [243].

65 ἐμός: the object of the remembering, cf. Mk 14:9; Wis 16:6; Sir 10:17, etc. See the inscription from Nicomedia, n. 56 above. For the discussion see Douglas Jones, "ἀνάμνησις in the LXX and the Interpretation of 1 Cor. xi.25," *JThSt*, n.s. 6 (1955): 183–191; Hans Kosmala, " 'Das tut zu meinem Gedächtnis,' " *NovTest* 4 (1960): 81–94. Kosmala compares among other passages the LXX of Lev 24:7 where, unlike here, God is mentioned. The statement, he argues, contains a unified thought and must not be split into two halves: (a) Do this! (b) in remembrance of me. He holds that Christians address to the Lord a prayer for his parousia. Against

Jeremias, he adds, is also the description of the ἀνάμνησις as κοινωνία, "communion," in 10:16.

66 The prayer over the Jewish cup of blessing is spoken *after* the main meal; Str.-B. 4:630f; Leonhard Goppelt, *TDNT* 6:154f.

67 Bornkamm. This development is reflected also in the Synoptic texts.

68 On the other hand, the word on the cup in Mark is more or less parallel to the Pauline word on the bread: τὸ ἐκχυννόμενον ὑπὲρ πολλῶν, "which is poured out for many" (Mk 14:24).

69 Paul, of course, does not say "flesh" and blood either.

70 Weiss observes that the link with διαθήκη, "covenant," would be linguistically more natural, but is not satisfying from the point of view of content, because then there is no interpretation of the *cup*.

71 The synthesis of atonement sacrifice and covenant sacrifice underlies the pre-Pauline formula which is contained in Rom 3:24f.

72 Deuteropaulines: Col 1:20; Eph 1:7. Further 1 Pet 1:2, 19; 1 Jn 1:7; 5:6, 8; Rev *passim*; Heb 9:20 (Ex 24:8); 10:29; *1 Cl.* 7.4; Ign., *Tr.* 8.1; *Phld. praef.*; *Sm.* 1.1; 6.1; 12.2; etc. In Ignatius the connection with his antidocetic Christology is very plain.

73 Covenant and blood: τὸ αἷμα τῆς διαθήκης, "the blood of the covenant," Ex 24:8 (Heb 9:20). Blood has atoning power according to the Targums. For διαθήκη see Johannes Behm, *TDNT* 2:124–134.

74 Cf. Heb 9:15 (πρώτη, "first," in terms of the typology of the epistle).

means, we have to note the specifically eschatological use of καινός, "new" (2 Cor 5:17). [75]

The command for repetition is this time given in an expanded form; here it is explicitly formulated as a "command for repetition." The form of the words [76] and the form of the celebration [77] make clear that (1) body and blood are not conceived as constitutive parts of the Lord; [78] (2) it is not the two words and acts that first constitute the whole sacrament. Each part is on its own a fully valid "communication." [79]

Excursus:
The Tradition of
the Lord's Supper

1. Can the original form of the words of institution still be reconstructed? [80] How is Paul's form related to that of Mark? It is obvious that both forms contain older and younger elements. [81] In Mark's case the word on the bread omits the passage containing the interpretative element ὑπέρ, "for." It is intro-

duced, more appropriately, into the word on the cup: τὸ αἶμα . . . τὸ ἐκχυννόμενον ὑπὲρ πολλῶν, "my blood . . . which is poured out for many." Thus in the tradition the application of the interpretation is somewhat free. Whether the short Pauline form of the ὑπέρ passage or the circumstantial Markan form is the older is a moot point. [82]

The command for repetition is missing in Mark, and is accordingly likewise not a fixed part of the tradition. [83] An obvious trace of secondary expansion is the *twofold* interpretation of the blood [84] in Mark. Even from the purely linguistic standpoint it leads to extreme harshness: [85]

a) τὸ αἶμά μου τῆς διαθήκης, "my blood of the covenant" (possessive pronoun and genitive);

b) τὸ ἐκχυννόμενον' "which is poured out."
τῆς διαθήκης, "of the covenant," is a secondary intrusion. [86] A linguistic analysis leads to the conclusion that one of the two interpretations of the sacrifice (atonement or covenant) is secondary. [87] But which? Did the words of interpretation originally speak of an atonement sacrifice? [88] Or of a covenant sacrifice? [89] Or neither? [90]

---

75 It is brought out all the more sharply by the confrontation with the "old" covenant. 2 Cor 3:1ff can be read as a commentary. R. Schreiber, *Der neue Bund im Spätjudentum und Urchristentum* (dissertation, Tübingen, 1955); abstract in *ThLZ* 81 (1956): 695–698.

76 Not "flesh," but "body" and blood.

77 The two acts originally separated by the meal.

78 *Later* they were thus understood. Then σάρξ, "flesh," logically enough took the place of σῶμα, "body," Jn 6:51bff; Ignatius.

79 See 10:16f, where the sense is developed from the standpoint of the body, and note the variable position of ὑπέρ.

80 The question is independent of that of their complete or partial authenticity.

81 Bornkamm. Caution is called for in face of the tendency to deduce the priority of Mark from alleged Semitisms in his text, see N. Turner, "The Style of St. Mark's Eucharistic Words," *JThSt*, n.s. 8 (1957): 108–111. The Marcan Semitisms in the text of the Lord's Supper are of a general Marcan kind. Nor can any argument be based on the exchange of εὐχαριστεῖν, "give thanks," and εὐλογεῖν, "bless." In itself the latter is nearer to the Hebrew equivalent ברך: בָּרוּךְ = εὐλογητός = "blessed." But in Greek-speaking Judaism εὐχαριστεῖν is found with the same meaning. NT: cf. Mk 8:6 and 7 with 6:41. The choice of term is purely arbitrary; see 14:16.

82 See on v 14. Neuenzeit, *Herrenmahl*, 111, argues that with the increasing interest of the primitive church (*sic*!) in Isa 53, the obvious allusion to the service

of worship in Mark will have supplanted the vaguer allusion in Paul. This is too schematic.

83 Intrinsically, of course, it is already given with the transmitting as such, which prescribes the repetition.

84 *Sic*! Mark, unlike Paul, sets out from the blood, not from the covenant.

85 For the linguistic harshness in Aramaic see Jeremias, *Eucharistic Words*, 193, n. 2 [186, n. 1], in debate with J. A. Emerton, "The Aramaic Underlying τὸ αἷμα μου τῆς διαθήκης in Mk. xiv.24," *JThSt*, n.s. 6 (1955): 238–240. See further Charles K. Barrett, "The Background of Mark 10:45," in *New Testament Essays: Studies in Memory of Thomas Walter Manson*, ed. A. J. B. Higgins (Manchester: Manchester University Press, 1959), 1–18; Hans Gottlieb, "τὸ αἷμά μου τῆς διαθήκης," *StudTheol* 14 (1960): 115–118; Emerton, "Mark xiv.24 and the Targum to the Psalter," *JThSt*, n.s. 15 (1964): 58f.

86 Not so Jeremias, *Eucharistic Words*, 194f [187f], who argues that the expression corresponds to the Hebrew דַּם־בְּרִיתִי or Aramaic אדם קימי, "my covenant-blood." But this does not explain the *Greek* expression (genitive and participial clause). For the participle see *Eucharistic Words*, 178f, 226f [170f, 218].

87 Not so Jeremias, *Eucharistic Words*, 194f [187f].

88 Or substitution; Jeremias.

89 Kümmel; Eduard Schweizer, "Abendmahl I. Im NT," *RGG*[3] 1:10–21.

90 Did they accordingly merely say: this is my body, this is my blood? The thought would then be that of sacramental communion. So Bultmann, *Theology* 1:146 [148].

Against this last assumption it can be objected that the formal discrepancy between the word on the bread and the word on the cup is presumably older than a smooth parallelism. And it is in harmony with an old form of the celebration, in which the two acts of distribution are separated by the meal.[91] Originally σῶμα and αἶμα, "body" and "blood," are not twin concepts. They become such only when the acts of distribution are drawn together and become one uniform act.

"The" original form can no longer be reconstructed. It is doubtful whether there was ever a uniform wording in general circulation.

2. Were there originally two types of Supper[92]—namely, the Supper of the primitive church, which was celebrated as a continuation of Jesus' table fellowship with his disciples (the "breaking of bread" in Acts 2:42), and a memorial Supper, which linked up with Jesus' *last* supper?[93]

It is in point of fact difficult to assume that already in the primitive church the sacramental idea had been worked out in the form in which we find it in the present narratives.[94] *Did.* 9f is, to begin with, aware of only one meal, without reference to the death of Jesus and without sacramental communion. Then in *Did.* 10.6 there follows the transition to the Eucharist. One has thus the impression that two types of meal have been secondarily combined. But there is no indication that the non-"sacramental" meals were celebrated as a continuance of table fellowship with Jesus. That is, there were not two types of Eucharist, but the Eucharist and the communal meal; for the latter, no historical basis was required at all. This is also in keeping with the situation as manifested by 1 Corinthians.

3. The service of the word and the Eucharist. No uniform practice can be postulated for the early church. It can neither be said that both acts of worship always went together[95] nor that they were always separate. In Corinth both belong together: Paul presupposes in 14:23ff that nonbelievers come to the meetings. But the two acts of worship are not telescoped together; they follow each other; see on 16:22ff. As for the suggestion, however, that they belonged together always, and in principle, the analogy of the synagogue service,[96] which had a strong influence on the Christian service, tells against this, and so also do analogous forms in paganism.[97]

■ **26** With v 26[98] Paul's own exposition begins. To be sure, it is not simply freely constructed; it, too, leans upon traditional terminology.[99]

Is καταγγέλλετε, "(you) proclaim," indicative or imperative? Since the sentence gives a reason (γάρ, "for"), it is more likely indicative. Does Paul mean that the Eucharistic action as such is a proclamation of the death of the Lord,[100] or is he thinking of an explicit proclamation accompanying it? Since there is no such thing as a sacrament without accompanying proclamation, we have to assume the latter.

In ἄχρι οὗ ἔλθῃ, "until he comes," the tradition

---

91 With Schweizer and Bornkamm.

92 Lietzmann, *Mass and the Lord's Supper*.

93 Modified by Ernst Lohmeyer, "Vom urchristlichen Abendmahl," *ThR*, n.s. 9 (1937): 273–312, who ascribes the two types respectively to the two primitive churches in Galilee and Jerusalem, which he regards as distinct from each other. Taken up once more by Oscar Cullmann, "The Meaning of the Lord's Supper in Primitive Christianity," in Cullmann and F. J. Leenhardt, *Essays on the Lord's Supper*, tr. J. G. Davies, Ecumenical Studies in Worship, 1 (London: Lutterworth; Richmond: John Knox, 1958), 5–23 (originally in *RHPhR* 16 [1936]: 1–22). Cullmann sees the breaking of bread in the primitive church as deriving from the table fellowship with the risen Lord. The very fact that the meal situation does not play a constitutive role in the Easter narratives tells against this.

94 Especially the thought of communion and of the consumption of pneumatic substance.

95 So Oscar Cullmann, *Early Christian Worship*, tr. A. Stewart Todd and James B. Torrance, SBT, 1, 10 (London: SCM, ²1959), 26–32 (*Urchristentum und*

Gottesdienst, AThANT, 3 [Zurich: Zwingli, ²1950], 29–34).

96 From this source come the literary forms, prayers, hymns.

97 Especially in the pagan missionary preaching of the Hellenistic world; Norden; Walter Bauer, *Der Wortgottesdienst der ältesten Christen*, SGV, 148 (Tübingen: J. C. B. Mohr [Paul Siebeck], 1930). The evaluation of the celebrated letter addressed to Trajan by the younger Pliny is disputed. It is plain that the Supper takes place in the evening. Is the assembly in the morning a service of the word, or is it a baptismal celebration that is meant? The answer is surely a preaching service, for there was not a regular assembly for baptism.

98 Lietzmann points out that v 26 in the Syrian liturgies is transposed into the first person, and is then reckoned as still belonging to the words of the Lord.

99 Bornkamm. Betz, *Eucharistie* 2.1:106–109: "The midrash, expressed in terms of real presence, on the institution narrative: 1 Cor 11:26–34."

100 Lietzmann, Weiss. Weiss observes that the action is a δρώμενον, "drama," and that a real presence of

201

once again becomes visible: to the Supper there belongs the eschatological outlook. This can be taken up into the formula of the cult itself. Paul does not have it as a part of the formula; but he is leaning upon the liturgy in which the *maranatha* has its established place; see on 16:22.[101] For the rest, Paul's view coincides with that of the tradition: the Lord's Supper is not an anticipation of the feast of the blessed,[102] but an institution for the age of the church from the resurrection of Christ to his parousia.[103]

The remembrance of the death of Christ together with the reference to the eschatological proviso, and therewith the binding of the Lord's Supper to the church and its age, are the criteria against the sacramental enthusiasm which takes its stand upon an exaltation Christology.

■ **27** Verse 27 draws the conclusion in a fundamental form, a principle of sacral law: the man who offends against the elements, offends against the Lord himself.[104] If we are to understand this, we must bear in mind that the idea of the church as the body of the Lord has a part to play.[105] The valid principle is that of fittingness: $ἀξίως/ἀναξίως$, "in a worthy/unworthy manner,"[106] i.e., it is eating unfittingly when the Supper of *the Lord*

is treated as one's "own supper." Then one becomes "guilty,"[107] inasmuch as the man who celebrates unfittingly sets himself alongside those who kill the Lord, instead of proclaiming his death.[108]

■ **27** This statement is in line with v 26: *theologia crucis* as opposed to *theologia gloriae*.

■ **28** Here Paul turns from the principle to its application to the individual, self–examination. The object of this self–examination is not one's inner state in general, but one's attitude to the sacrament, that is, the propriety of the participation, whether one "distinguishes" the body of the Lord. It is the criterion of existence in the community.[109]

■ **29** This is a variation of v 27.[110] The consequence of the guilt is shown, the guilt itself more precisely described: $μὴ διακρίνων$ . . ., "if he does not distinguish. . . ." The word $διακρίνειν$ can have several nuances.[111] There is no point in asking whether the participle is to be taken in a causal or a conditional sense.[112]

---

the body and blood is presupposed—only so is the inference in v 27 conclusive. The $κύριος$ title in the phrase "death of the Lord" is presumably chosen in dependence on the cult formula cited. Werner Foerster, *TDNT* 3:1091, says: "perhaps because $ἄχρι οὗ ἔλθη$ ['until he comes'] follows."

101 Otfried Hofius, " 'Bis dass er kommt' I. Kor. xi.26," *NTS* 14 (1967–68): 439–441, holds (with Jeremias, *Eucharistic Words*, 253 [244]) that $ἄχρι οὗ ἔλθη$ contains a note of purpose; cf. Rom 11:25; 1 Cor 15:25; Lk 21:24. In that case the expression corresponds to *maranatha*.

102 It could be that for the Corinthians.

103 That is to say, the age in which Christ exercises his sovereignty, see 15:23ff.

104 According to Lietzmann, because the body and blood of Christ are consumed. Against this interpretation is the fact that the understanding of the sacrament is oriented not to the sacramental substance, but to the act of administration and of participation in the Supper. We offend against the Lord because we offend against his body, the community.

105 The same applies, of course, to the church and the body as the temple of the Lord or of the Spirit, 3:16; 6:19.

106 See Bauer, *s.v.*

107 Jas 2:10. Vett. Val., *Anthol. lib.* 2.37 (ed. Kroll,

117, 10): $ἔνοχοι μοιχείας$, "accused of adultery."

108 Käsemann, *Essays on NT Themes*, 123f [24]. The future $ἔσται$, "will be," is intensive, Blass–Debrunner §362. $ἄξιος$, "worthy," provides in the first instance a *formal* criterion—in accordance with the norm, that is with the thing made known in the $ἱερὸς λόγος$, the "sacred word." The worthiness does not mean a state in which I must find myself *before* reception (on this point, as distinct from the mysteries, nothing is said), but it means the attitude toward the sacrament itself. Thus, in the first instance, is the unbeliever unworthy. To be sure, the situation has now arisen that the division has penetrated to within the community. This is the same situation as emerges in 12:1–3, where the confession is required no longer merely as a criterion to distinguish church and world, but as a mark by which to judge phenomena within the community.

109 The criterion is institutionalized in *Did.* 14 (confession of sins and reconciliation with one's enemies before the Eucharist).

110 The original text is the shorter form without $ἀναξίως$ and $τοῦ κυρίου$.

111 See n. 7 above.

112 Weiss says that if it is taken conditionally, then it is a clumsy addition; if it is taken causally, then $ἀναξίως$ is really indispensable. This verdict is naturally

■ **30** Instances of sickness and death[113] are consequences of offending against the sacrament. Is Paul thinking of a magical effect of the substance[114] or of material consequences of guilt, divine punishment? The context shows that he is in fact thinking of punishment of this kind. His teaching is not concerned with the elements, but with conduct and punishment.[115] The sequel is in keeping with this.

■ **31** The play upon the word group κριν–, which was introduced with v 29, is here continued. From the standpoint of its sense, διακρίνειν, "judge," points back to δοκιμάζειν, "examine": if, on the ground of our self–examination, we reach a correct verdict on ourselves, we shall not be condemned.[116] κρίνεσθαι, "be judged," does not here mean the eternal judgment, but the present

suffering of the plagues mentioned. This is shown by vv 32–34. It is a question of educative measures,[117] applied not to the dead, but to the community, with an eye to the final judgment which is here not seen as a process of separation between the accepted and the damned, but only as execution of the "wrath."[118]

■ **33–34** The final conclusion, expressed in simple terms, has a recollection of the suggestion in v 22: if they satisfy their hunger at home, they can celebrate the Supper together.[119]

For the prospect of the proposed visit, see on 4:19: 16:1ff.

---

bound up with the understanding of διακρίνειν.

113 κοιμᾶν, "sleep," is a widespread euphemism for "die," ever since Homer (see Bauer, *s.v.*). The word does not in itself already contain the idea that the sleep does not last for ever; cf. *IG* 14:929, line 13: κοιμᾶται τὸν αἰώνιον ὕπνον, "he sleeps the eternal sleep."

114 Lietzmann observes: the φάρμακον ἀθανασίας, "medicine of immortality," becomes the φάρμακον τοῦ θανάτου, "medicine of death." For criticism see n. 104 above.

115 The statement cannot be reversed. It is not an abstract principle. We cannot go on to infer that where illnesses appear, there wrong conditions prevail. What Paul here holds against the Corinthians can be said only in a unique situation. He does not accuse the individual sick people, but the community: it is sick.

116 The meaning of διακρίνειν does not have to be the

same as in v 29.

117 It should not be asked whether education or chastening is meant. In the Wisdom tradition the two are one, even if according to the particular circumstances the one element or the other can come to the fore. 2 Cor 6:9; 1 Tim 1:20; Heb 12:7; Bousset-Gressmann, *Die Religion des Judentums*, 385.

118 Mattern, *Verständnis*, 102, observes that the contrast is not between *present* and *future* judgment, but between the judgment of chastening upon the community (with a view to the averting of final destruction) and the judgment of annihilation upon the world.

119 Does this not promote further splitting up? Apparently we must make ourselves a realistic picture of the situation: a man who has worked all day comes hungry to the meeting direct from his work—and is he then to wait a couple of hours until everyone has arrived?

12

The Criterion

1　　**Now concerning spiritual gifts,[1] brothers,
I would not have you ignorant. 2 / You
know that, while you were still pagans—
how you were drawn to dumb idols
and carried away.[2] 3 / Therefore I inform
you that no one who speaks in the
Spirit of God says: "Jesus is accursed!"
and that no one can say: "Jesus is
Lord!" except in the Holy Spirit.**

■ **1** The new topic,[3] once again introduced in the style
of an answer to questions ($\pi\epsilon\rho\acute{\iota}$, "concerning"), embraces chaps. 12–14. They provide a richer insight into
community life than any other passage in the New Testament, and especially into the busy life of divine worship
in Corinth. They confirm the picture that can be gathered from other parts of the epistle, the picture of the
enthusiasm[4] prevailing there, and they provide impressive evidence, on the other hand, of the thoroughgoing
uniformity of the theological criticism of Paul, who here,
too, *practices* his eschatological proviso (see above all
on chap. 13), without yet making eschatology his explicit
theme.

The precise content of the enquiry from Corinth is un-
known to us.[5] The genitive $\pi\nu\epsilon\upsilon\mu\alpha\tau\iota\kappa\hat{\omega}\nu$, "spiritual,"
is to be taken in a neuter, not in a masculine sense ("spir-
itual gifts," not "spiritual people"); this is clear from
14:1 and from the interchange with $\chi\alpha\rho\acute{\iota}\sigma\mu\alpha\tau\alpha$.[6] Paul
is in agreement with the Corinthians on the point that

the ecstatic phenomena really are expressions of the
Spirit. The designation of them as $\pi\nu\epsilon\upsilon\mu\alpha\tau\iota\kappa\acute{\alpha}$ is not
criticized,[7] though it is certainly theologically tran-
scended and thereby corrected. The Spirit is for him, too,
a supernatural power that gives rise to "un–normal"
effects. In the *conception* of the Spirit they are at one. The
point at issue is the theological existence of believers,
their concrete determination by the Spirit. Paul raises the
discussion to the level of theology. With the acclamation
of the $\kappa\acute{\upsilon}\rho\iota\sigma\varsigma$, "Lord," the objective event of salvation
and the community are both taken into the criteria.[8]
With a powerful touch of style, in chiastically modified
parallelism, Paul sets the possibility wrought by the
Spirit, the possibility of calling upon the Lord, over
against the Spirit–less impossibility: the Spirit (who of
course is the "Spirit of the Lord," 2 Cor 3:17) cannot
contradict himself. He cannot curse Jesus. $\dot{\alpha}\nu\dot{\alpha}\theta\epsilon\mu\alpha$[9]
$\mathrm{'I}\eta\sigma\sigma\hat{\upsilon}\varsigma$, "Jesus is accursed," is an *ad hoc* construction on
Paul's part to form an antithesis to $\kappa\acute{\upsilon}\rho\iota\sigma\varsigma$ $\mathrm{'I}\eta\sigma\sigma\hat{\upsilon}\varsigma$,

---

1　In itself, the translation "spiritual people," "men of
the Spirit," is also possible, cf. 2:15; 3:1; 14:37. Yet
despite 14:37 the theme is not types of men but gifts.

2　If we read $\dot{\omega}\varsigma$ $\ddot{\alpha}\nu$ $\ddot{\eta}\gamma\epsilon\sigma\theta\epsilon$, then it is best (with Lietzmann) to take $\dot{\omega}\varsigma$, "how," as a repetition of $\ddot{\sigma}\tau\iota$,
"that" (Heinrici: "incorrect, but forceful"). The in-
terpretation of the $\dot{\omega}\varsigma$–clause as an intermediate
clause is not so good: "that, even as you were always
drawn to dumb idols, you were carried away," tak-
ing the auxiliary $\ddot{\eta}\tau\epsilon$ with $\dot{\alpha}\pi\alpha\gamma\acute{\omega}\mu\epsilon\nu\omega\iota$. $\dot{\omega}\varsigma$ $\ddot{\alpha}\nu$: aug-
mented tenses of the indicative with $\ddot{\alpha}\nu$ in an iterative
sense is Hellenistic usage; Blass–Debrunner §367.
Another possibility is to read $\dot{\omega}\varsigma$ $\dot{\alpha}\nu\acute{\eta}\gamma\epsilon\sigma\theta\epsilon$ (Weiss).

3　Literature: Bauer, *s.vv.* $\pi\nu\epsilon\upsilon\mu\alpha\tau\iota\kappa\acute{\sigma}\varsigma$, $\chi\acute{\alpha}\rho\iota\sigma\mu\alpha$.

4　This consists not in the emergence of ecstasy, but in
the way it is pursued and turned into self–edification
and freedom demonstrations.

5　Did it refer to the order of precedence among the
phenomena, more particularly between speaking
with tongues and prophecy? See on chap. 14.

6　Neuter: 9:11; 15:46.

7　On the contrary, it would have been from Paul that
the Corinthians learned this designation for the

ecstatic phenomena, as indeed it was presumably he,
too, who kindled the whole pneumatism: 14:18;
1 Thess 5:19f.

8　In keeping with this is the introduction in the sequel
of the word $\chi\acute{\alpha}\rho\iota\sigma\mu\alpha$, and of the aspect of $\sigma\iota\kappa\sigma\delta\sigma\mu\acute{\eta}$,
"upbuilding" (which in chap. 14 determines the
scale of values), as also the fact that "profane" acts
of service for the community are taken up into the
gifts of the Spirit.

9　$\dot{\alpha}\nu\acute{\alpha}\theta\epsilon\mu\alpha$ (classical $\dot{\alpha}\nu\acute{\alpha}\theta\eta\mu\alpha$), "oblation," serves in
the LXX to render חֵרֶם, that which is "delivered
up to God," consecrated or accursed. In the negative sense, Num 21:3, etc. The only extrabiblical
example for this meaning is on an imprecation tablet
from Megara (first–second century A.D.) where
the word $\dot{\alpha}\nu\alpha\theta\epsilon\mu\alpha\tau\acute{\iota}\zeta\omega$ occurs twice with the meaning "curse," in addition to the occurrence of $\dot{\alpha}\nu$-
$\acute{\epsilon}\theta\epsilon\mu\alpha$ on the reverse, at the end); Richard Wünsch,
Antike Fluchtafeln, KlT, 20 (Bonn: Marcus & Weber,
²1912), no. 1; Deissmann, *Light*, 95 [74].

10　Others assume that this curse was actually uttered:
a) One thinks of Jewish cursing of the crucified
(Schlatter, 333), which finds support in Deut 21:23

"Jesus is Lord."[10]

■ **2** The criticism is prepared for by a retrospective glance at the erstwhile participation of the addressees in the pagan cult.[11] They are here roundly treated as Gentile Christians, which is in keeping with the composition of the community. The exact sense of the allusion is disputed: the wording and the construction are unclear (see note 2 above). Is (ἀν)ήγεσθε ἀπαγόμενοι, "you were drawn and carried away," an allusion to the ecstatic character of pagan cults?[12] The significance of the words (ἀν)άγειν and ἀπάγειν allows of no certain

conclusion. The phrase certainly implies that they were not their own masters; but this can just as well mean being dominated in a general way by demons, the actors in the pagan cult (see 8:1–6; 10:20), as being swept into ecstasy.[13] *Against* the interpretation in terms of pagan ecstasy it is often said that the qualification of the idols[14]

(Gal 3:13); LXX has κεκατηραμένος, Paul ἐπικατάρατος, Hebrew קִלְלַת אֱלֹהִים, "cursed of God." The derivation from Deut 21:23 does not easily suggest itself, not even if an allusion to the passage is found in 4QpNah I, 7f (Alexander Jannaeus is accused of being the first to have men hung alive on the "tree," i.e. crucified, whereas the passage originally refers to the hanging up of the corpse of the executed criminal). Moreover, in view of the whole outlook of the epistle, a special reference to the Jews is improbable.

b) Weiss and others believe there were instances in which Jesus was actually cursed in ecstasy. But it is hard to conceive this. And the alleged pagan parallels (the Sibyl oppressed by her inspiration; Cassandra cursing Apollo under the burden of her knowledge; Allo, Spicq, see on 16:22) are no parallels. Fantastic, too, is Schmithals' suggestion, *Gnosticism in Corinth*, 124–130 [117–122], that the Corinthian Gnostics curse the σάρξ, "flesh," of the earthly Jesus. There is no evidence for the widespread contention that there were Gnostics who cursed (the earthly) Jesus. The two passages in Origen which are adduced in its favor have a different meaning:

Orig., *Cels*. 6.28, does not say that the Ophites utter curses against Jesus, but that they curse him *in fact* by equating him with the serpent. The same thing is said in the fragment from the lost Origen Commentary, Orig., *Catena fragm. 47 in 1 Cor. xii.3* (in Claude Jenkins, "Origen on I Corinthians IV," *JThSt*, o.s. 10 [1908–09]: 29–51, here esp. 30): ἔστι τις αἵρεσις, ἥτις οὐ προσίεται τὸν προσιόντα εἰ μὴ ἀναθηματίσῃ τὸν Ἰησοῦν. καὶ ἡ αἵρεσις ἐκείνη ἀξία ἐστὶ τοῦ ὀνόματος οὗ ἠγάπησεν· ἔστι γὰρ ἡ αἵρεσις τῶν καλουμένων Ὀφιανῶν, οἵτινες οὐ θεμιτὰ λέγουσιν εἰς ἐγκώμιον τοῦ ὄφεως, ὃς ἐπικατάρατός ἐστιν ἀπὸ τοῦ θεοῦ, "There is a certain sect which does not admit a convert unless he pronounces anathemas on Jesus; and that sect is worthy of the name which it has chosen; for it is the sect of the so–called Ophites, who utter blasphemous words in

praise of the serpent," *which is accursed of God* (Origen, *Contra Celsum*, tr. Chadwick, 344, n. 2). See Birger A. Pearson, "Did the Gnostics Curse Jesus?" *JBL* 86 (1967): 301–305.

The thesis in question is refuted by the fact that the Corinthians recognize without question the statement of the creed on the death and resurrection of Jesus (15:1ff). That Paul here says "Jesus," not "Christ," is due simply to the constructing of an antithesis to κύριος Ἰησοῦς. The antithesis is not between κύριος and Ἰησοῦς, but between κύριος and ἀνάθεμα. Lührmann, *Offenbarungsverständnis*, 29, rightly says: those who assume that Jesus was really cursed in Corinth leave vv 4ff out of account. Paul presupposes that they have really received the Spirit and accordingly cannot speak thus (ἀνάθεμα Ἰησοῦς).

11   This is a variation of the schema once—but now; see 6:11.

12   Illustrative material is provided by the Dionysus cult among others. Further, Ps.–Luc., *Syr. Dea*. See Nilsson, *Geschichte*, vol. 2, index, s.vv. *Ekstase, Ekstatische Strömung*, ἐνθουσιασμός, *Origen*, etc. Strabo, *Geog*. 10.3.6–16 (C466–471).

13   Athenag., *Suppl*. 26: καὶ οἱ περὶ τὰ εἴδωλα αὐτοὺς ἕλκοντες οἱ δαίμονές εἰσιν, "It is, then, these demons we have been talking about that draw men to idols" (LCC 1:329). For phenomena accompanying prophetic ecstasy see Athenag., *loc. cit.*; Luc., *Jup. trag.* 30; Liv., *Urb. cond.* 39.13.12; Tert., *Nat.* 2.7.

14   εἴδωλον: for the Greek view of the nature of images of the gods cf. Nilsson, *Geschichte* 2:502–505. In Greek these were not called εἴδωλα, but ἀγάλματα. εἴδωλον is not the image as representing the god, but as being only his image. In addition to this, εἴδωλον designates the shadowy existence of the dead (Soph., *Ai*. 126); Nilsson, *Geschichte* 1:195f; Friedrich Büchsel, *TDNT* 2:375f. When Judaism uses the word to designate images of the gods, it indicates their unreality. The LXX uses it to translate both the words for images (עֶצֶב, פֶּסֶל, צֶלֶם, etc.) and for gods (אֱלֹהִים, etc.) and also for the abominableness of

as "dumb" is not in keeping with this.[15] But the word is simply a traditional attribute in Jewish polemic against images[16] and merely points to the fact that the pagan cult is vain, and indeed surrenders its devotees to the power of the demons, but not that it is carried on quietly.[17] The decisive thing for exegesis is the fact "that here the intention is not to emphasize a distinction from paganism, but an analogy; you know of course from your own experience how a man has no will of his own when he is in the power of a $\pi\nu\epsilon\hat{\upsilon}\mu\alpha$. Thus the whole question is concerned only with ecstatics, not with men in a normal condition" (Weiss).

In view of chap. 15 we have to comment that if Paul is addressing the Corinthians as erstwhile mystes, then he believes them capable of mystery thinking even now.

This does not mean that they have a hope of life after death. The mysteries communicate vital powers for *this* life; they confer protection from sickness, from the blows of fate. A hope for the beyond, however, must not be linked with them.[18]

■ **3** It follows from v 2 that ecstasy alone is no criterion for the working of the Spirit, but itself requires such a criterion.[19] This is supplied by the $\kappa\acute{\upsilon}\rho\iota\sigma$ acclamation,[20] which is for its part an effect of the Spirit.[21] This acclamation has an established function in the cult; it is constitutive of it.[22] Thus Paul is not calling upon his own subjective experience as an ecstatic,[23] and is not discussing the phenomena as such.

image–worship (גלולים, שֶׁקֶץ, etc.). For instances of the rare Greek use of $\epsilon\check{\iota}\delta\omega\lambda\sigma\nu$ for images of the gods (in addition to Polyb., *Hist.* 30.25.13–15) see Bauer, *s.v.*

15 Dupont, *Gnosis*, 149, n. 2: $\dot{\alpha}\pi\acute{\alpha}\gamma\epsilon\sigma\theta\alpha\iota$, "be carried away," is not the same as $\dot{\alpha}\rho\pi\acute{\alpha}\zeta\epsilon\sigma\theta\alpha\iota$, "be caught up," in 2 Cor 12:2, 4. For details see Karl Maly, "1 Kor 12,1–3, eine Regel zur Unterscheidung der Geister?" *BZ*, n.s. 10 (1966): 82–95: "You know that . . . again and again you were brought to dumb idols, haled off (like prisoners)." The accent, Maly argues, lies on their being enslaved under the "dumb" idols, cf. Deut 28:36: $\dot{\alpha}\pi\alpha\gamma\acute{\alpha}\gamma\sigma\iota$ $\kappa\acute{\upsilon}\rho\iota\acute{\sigma}\varsigma$ $\sigma\epsilon$ $\kappa\alpha\grave{\iota}$ $\tau\sigma\grave{\upsilon}\varsigma$ $\dot{\alpha}\rho\chi\sigma\nu\tau\acute{\alpha}\varsigma$ $\sigma\sigma\upsilon$ . . . $\epsilon\grave{\iota}\varsigma$ $\check{\epsilon}\theta\nu\sigma\varsigma$, $\grave{\sigma}$ $\sigma\grave{\upsilon}\kappa$ $\dot{\epsilon}\pi\acute{\iota}\sigma\tau\alpha\sigma\alpha\iota$ $\sigma\grave{\upsilon}$ $\kappa\alpha\grave{\iota}$ $\sigma\grave{\iota}$ $\pi\alpha\tau\acute{\epsilon}\rho\epsilon\varsigma$ $\sigma\sigma\upsilon$, $\kappa\alpha\grave{\iota}$ $\lambda\alpha\tau\rho\epsilon\acute{\upsilon}\sigma\epsilon\iota\varsigma$ $\dot{\epsilon}\kappa\epsilon\hat{\iota}$ $\theta\epsilon\sigma\hat{\iota}\varsigma$ $\dot{\epsilon}\tau\acute{\epsilon}$-$\rho\sigma\iota\varsigma$ $\xi\upsilon\lambda\sigma\iota\varsigma$ $\kappa\alpha\grave{\iota}$ $\lambda\acute{\iota}\theta\sigma\iota\varsigma$, "The Lord will bring you and your rulers . . . into a nation which neither you nor your fathers have known, and there you will worship other gods, gods of wood and stone" [Trans.]. But this passage is not decisive for the sense of $\dot{\alpha}\pi\acute{\alpha}\gamma\epsilon\iota\nu$. Maly goes on to argue that Paul avoids a direct antithesis between $\pi\rho\grave{\sigma}\varsigma$ $\tau\grave{\alpha}$ $\epsilon\check{\iota}\delta\omega\lambda\alpha$ $\check{\alpha}\gamma\epsilon$-$\sigma\theta\alpha\iota$, "be driven to idols," and $\pi\nu\epsilon\acute{\upsilon}\mu\alpha\tau\iota$ $\check{\alpha}\gamma\epsilon\sigma\theta\alpha\iota$, "be driven by the Spirit," with an eye to Corinth, in order that $\pi\nu\epsilon\acute{\upsilon}\mu\alpha\tau\iota$ $\check{\alpha}\gamma\epsilon\sigma\theta\alpha\iota$ should not be understood as constraint. His contrast, according to Maly, is: once enslaved to dumb idols, now enabled to speak in the Spirit. $\delta\acute{\epsilon}$ in v 4, he argues, goes a step further: the activity of the Spirit is not exhausted in the spoken word. But such an exposition shifts the accents of the text. It is surely not the participants in the pagan cult who are "dumb"!

16 Hab 2:18; Ps 113:15; *3 Macc.* 4.16.

17 Lietzmann, too, finds the attribute "dumb" to be out of place here. Not at all!

18 Josef Kroll, *Gott und Hölle*. Studien der Bibliothek Warburg, 20 (Leipzig and Berlin: Teubner, 1932), 500f. Isis cult: Apul., *Met.* 11.6; Ditt., *Syll.* 3:113–119 (no. 985; for conditions of admission to the mysteries, see Otto Weinreich, *Stiftung und Kultsatzungen eines Privatheiligtums in Philadelphia in Lydien*, SAH, 1919, 16 [Heidelberg: Winter, 1919]); see also on 15:12. The silence of most of the grave inscriptions is characteristic; cf. Werner Peek, *Griechische Grabgedichte*, Schriften und Quellen der alten Welt, 7 (Berlin: Akademie–Verlag, 1960), 178 (priestess of Dionysus, from Miletus, third–second century B.C.).

19 For a history of the exegesis of v 3 see Guy de Broglie, "Le texte fondamentale de saint Paul contre la foi naturelle (*I Cor.*, XII, 3)," *RechSR* 39 (1951): 253–266.

20 The "confession" of Rom 10:9.

21 Like prayer, so also the acclamation is not a possibility proper to man. But in contradistinction to Gnosticism and normal ecstasy, the subject is not extinguished by the Spirit—a point which Paul brings out in chap. 14.

22 Christians are those "who call upon the name of the Lord," 1:2. $\kappa\acute{\upsilon}\rho\iota\sigma\varsigma$ $^{\prime}I\eta\sigma\sigma\hat{\upsilon}\varsigma$ is not constructed by analogy to $\kappa\acute{\upsilon}\rho\iota\sigma\varsigma$ $K\alpha\hat{\iota}\sigma\alpha\rho$. It is true that the Emperor was designated "Lord" already in the first century; but $\kappa\acute{\upsilon}\rho\iota\sigma\varsigma$ $K\alpha\hat{\iota}\sigma\alpha\rho$ is not a cultic acclamation (cf. its absence in the trials of Christians, Werner Foerster, *TDNT* 3:1057f), and in the milieu in which the Christian acclamation originated, emperor worship played no part.

23 Cf. 2 Cor 12:1ff.

12   The Multiplicity and Unity of Spiritual Gifts

4   There are assignments (or: varieties[1]) of (the gifts of) grace, but (it is) the same Spirit. **5 /** And there are assignments of acts of service, but the same Lord. **6 /** And there are assignments of operations, but the same God who works all in all (or: them all in all men). **7 /** But each is given the manifestation of the Spirit in order to make use of it. **8 /** For to one it is given through the Spirit to speak with wisdom, to another to speak with knowledge, according to[2] the same Spirit, **9 /** another[3] is given faith, in the same Spirit, another gifts of healing, in the one Spirit, **10 /** another the working of miracles, another prophecy, another the distinguishing of spirits, another (various) kinds of (speaking with) tongues, another the interpreting of tongues. **11 /** But all this is the work of one and the same Spirit, who assigns to each in particular whatever he pleases.

■ **4–6** These verses form a unity in style and content. Three sentences are constructed in parallel, and provided with a heavily accented conclusion. There is an underlying triadic formula: God—Lord—Spirit. Such triads are frequently found in the New Testament. The order of sequence is still free;[4] it is adapted to the context. *Here* Paul links up with the term πνευματικά, "spiritual gifts," and builds up a climax.[5] The ascription of the three concepts χαρίσματα, διακονίαι, ἐνεργήματα, "gifts of grace, acts of service, operations," to the Spirit, the Lord, and God is presumably not to be regarded as merely an arbitrary matter of rhetoric,[6] but also as being determined by the content.[7] χαρίσματα is an equivalent for πνευματικά and is ascribed as such to the Spirit. διακονίαι intentionally goes together with

κύριος, "Lord" (cf. 3:5). And finally, the linking of ἐνεργήματα and θεός, "God," is shown by the extended conclusion of the third sentence to be appropriate. We have here a formula of omnipotence, which is now related to the community (and thereby Christianized).[8]

διαίρεσις can mean "assignment" or "distinction." The second meaning is suggested by Rom 12:6 (in a parallel context). But here v 11 tells in favor of the former rendering.[9] χάρισμα, "gift of grace," takes the place of χάρις, "grace," in Paul when the differentiation is expressed, namely, the assignment in the form of in-

1   See the commentary.

2   Bauer, *s.v.* κατά II 5 a δ.

3   In vv 9 and 10 the Western text has asyndeton throughout (declared original by Zuntz, *Text*, 105–107, who says it is partly "preserved" also by the Alexandrians).

4   2 Cor 13:13; Eph 4:4–6; 1 Pet 1:2. It is not yet possible to speak of a "Trinity," not even in view of Mt 28:19. The Spirit is not a Person. Weiss observes: "The threefold character of the sentences is not the cause but the effect of the . . . triadic formula (II 13:13)."

5   For the movement of a series toward God as its goal

see 3:23.

6   Thus Lietzmann. This is not to rule out of the question that there is also a rhetorical play, here with the ending –μα so much favored in Hellenism; see Blass–Debrunner §488(3). (Weiss finds the order a b a.)

7   Heinrici; Ingo Hermann, *Kyrios und Pneuma*, SANT, 2 (Munich: Kösel, 1961), 71–76.

8   Cf. Eph 1:11. ἐν πᾶσιν is essentially neuter; it can be asked, however, whether Paul does not understand it as masculine.

9   διαιροῦν ἐκάστῳ ὡς βούλεται, "who assigns to each as he pleases." The seeming contradiction that in

dividual gifts to individual men.[10] The word is suited from the very start to be an equivalent of πνευματικά, since of course χάρις also has in Hellenistic Greek the sense of a supernatural power or force, and is thus akin to πνεῦμα.[11] Nevertheless the choice of words will be partially determined by the specifically Pauline thought of grace, and will thus include a critical component: it is through grace that the pneumatic is what he is. Not he, but the gift, is the object of theology (2:12). διακονία, "service,"[12] is essentially a profane concept.[13] The word must be allowed to keep the general character of its significance.[14] The essential point is precisely that everyday acts of service are now set on a par with the recognized, supernatural phenomena of the Spirit.[15] Thus Paul is no longer oriented to the phenomena, but to the community as the goal of the Spirit's working. He is showing the believer who has no ecstatic gifts that he is assigned "his part," and how he is assigned it. For the believer in question, grace is thereby made the key to his understanding of himself and his attitude toward his brothers.

ἐνεργήματα, "operations": cf. Gal 2:8; Phil 2:13; see on vv 9–10 (synonymous with χαρίσματα).

■ 7 Verse 7 can be regarded as summing up vv 4–6 (Robertson and Plummer) or as providing the heading for vv 8–10 (Weiss). The difference is only one of emphasis. In the former case, v 7 plainly shows that the triadic differentiation is meant as a pointer to the origin and nature of the gifts, not as a schematic division into three different sources of origin: here the Spirit is again the sole Giver of all the gifts. In the second case, a twofold standpoint is maintained: unity in differentiation.[16] The emphasis is not on ἕκαστος, "each,"[17] but on πρὸς τὸ συμφέρον, "in order to make use of it" (literally, "with a view to what is for the best"), that is, on the aspect of οἰκοδομή, "upbuilding."[18] The genitive τοῦ πνεύματος can be understood as subjective (Heinrici, despite 2 Cor 4:2: φανέρωσις τῆς ἀληθείας,

vv 4–6 the gifts are distributed in a trinitarian fashion, whereas in v 11 the *one* Spirit brings about *all* the operations, is in actual fact no contradiction. Verses 4–6, too, have in view the unity of the originator and mediator of the gifts. The Spirit is nothing other than the manifestation of the Lord, who for his part is the salvation of God. διαίρεσις, "assignment, distribution," contains an allusion both to the imparting and to the individualizing; cf. the parallel in Rom 12:6; Bultmann, *Theology* 1:325 [326]. It is presupposed that every believer has a gift, *his own* particular one. This is clear from the mention of the Lord and of God alongside the Spirit: by the Lord salvation is bestowed on all—by the God who works "all things" and bestows upon all. Once again a critical sense becomes perceptible: pneumatics are not (any longer) specially marked out individuals. The Corinthian individualism is destroyed.

10 χάρισμα can, however, also be synonymous with χάρις: the event of salvation, 2 Cor 1:11; Rom 5:15; 6:23. Here χάρισμα and φανέρωσις τοῦ πνεύματος in v 7, "manifestation of the Spirit," are essentially the same (Lührmann, *Offenbarungsverständnis*, 27f).

11 Wetter, *Charis*, 168–187.

12 See on 16:15; 2 Cor 5:18f; 11:8; 4:1; 6:3f; Rom 11:13.

13 διακονία is used first and foremost of service at table. Plato uses it in a positive sense of the civil service. In the LXX the word group is of no significance. Josephus uses it also of priestly service; but this is rare. In the NT cf. Mt 25:42–44; Lk 22:26. Paul describes the collection as διακονία, 2 Cor 8:4f.

14 It must not be taken as applying to a definite office; cf. on v 28. Eduard Schweizer, *Church Order in the New Testament*, tr. Frank Clarke, SBT, 1, 32 (London: SCM, 1961), 173–176 (*Gemeinde und Gemeindeordnung im Neuen Testament*, AThANT, 35 [Zurich: Zwingli, ²1962], 157–159).

15 J. Brosch, *Charismen und Ämter in der Urkirche* (Bonn: Hanstein, 1951), 25, argues in vain against the fact that for Paul everything done for the community is a χάρισμα.

16 Since the unity arises not from the phenomenon nor from the act of the individual, but from the gift character.

17 Although it is in fact presupposed that each Christian has his gift, cf. v 11; Rom 12:3ff.

18 See on 6:12; 10:23; we have thus to understand τῇ ἐκκλησίᾳ, "for the church"; cf. the sense of the "upbuilding" in vv 12ff and chap. 14. Weiss thinks that ἕκαστος is at least equally stressed, that we have a shortened form of expression, and that ἑκάστῳ lacks the nuance, "one thing to one, another to another." Yet the starting point is in the first instance not the process of distribution, but the act of bestowing the gift. There is no thought of the Greek motif: πάντα οὐ πᾶσιν οἱ θεοὶ διδόασιν, "the gods do not give all things to all men."

19 Blass–Debrunner §306. Robertson and Plummer are too schematic in declaring (on the basis of their view of v 7) that vv 8–10 explain ἑκάστῳ while vv 12ff explain τὸ συμφέρον.

20 Despite the personified form of expression the Spirit is not considered to be a person.

"manifestation of the truth") or as objective (Robertson and Plummer), that is to say (a) the manifestation given by the Spirit, or (b) the Spirit given by the manifestation.

■ **8–10** The enumeration in vv 8–10 is unsystematic. A certain grouping can nevertheless be discerned: (a) v 8; (b) vv 9–10a; (c) v 10b;[19] cf. the articulation by means of ἑτέρῳ—ἄλλῳ, "to one—to another."

The Spirit appears on the one hand as cause (διὰ τοῦ πνεύματος, "through the Spirit"),[20] and partly as norm (κατὰ τὸ αὐτὸ πνεῦμα, "according to the same Spirit"),[21] without it being possible to take the distinction strictly.[22] The articulation ᾧ μέν—ἄλλῳ δέ, "to one—to another," seems to suggest that a distinction is to be sought between λόγος σοφίας, "speaking with (literally, the word of) wisdom,"[23] and λόγος γνώσεως, "the word of knowledge." Yet this is in contradiction to the usage throughout the epistle.[24] Both mean the gift of speaking instructively (revealingly, 14:24f).[25] πίστις is here a special gift alongside others, and accordingly not faith, but apparently the ability to perform miracles,[26] and thus akin to the χαρίσματα[27] ἰαμάτων,[28] "gifts of healing." The change from ἐν τῷ αὐτῷ, "in the same," to ἐν τῷ ἑνί, "in the one," is merely rhetorical.

ἐνεργήματα δυνάμεων, "working of miracles," is also a related concept: δυνάμεις are miracles. Instead of χαρίσματα we have the general term ἐνεργήματα, recalling v 6; as indeed δυνάμεις, too, is more general than ἰάματα, "gifts of healing."[29] The nature of προφητεία, "prophecy," is made plain by chap. 14; διάκρισις πνευμάτων, "the distinguishing of spirits," is explained by 14:24f; speaking with tongues (and translating of tongues) is again defined by chap. 14. It is presumably no accident that this gift is mentioned last: it is the one that is most highly valued in Corinth, precisely because it is unintelligible. It is apparently regarded as having command of the language of heaven (cf. 13:1). Paul indicates his criticism by the very order of enumeration.[30]

■ **11** This takes up vv 6–7 and rounds off the section. ἕκαστος, "each," is emphatically stressed. καθὼς βούλεται, "as he pleases," underlines that the gift has the character of free grace. This denies to the pneumatic any power of his own. By placing the accent on "*one* Spirit," Paul prepares the way for the theme of the next section: "*one* body."[31] This association of ideas makes it plain that Paul's understanding of the Spirit has its roots in the bond between the Spirit and the community.

---

21 Bachmann. Lietzmann holds the two prepositions to be synonymous.

22 Bauer, *s.v. κατά* II 5 a δ: "because of, as a result of, on the basis of." κατὰ ἀποκάλυψιν, "by revelation," Gal 2:2.

23 Ben Edwin Perry, *Aesopica*, vol. 1 (Urbana: University of Illinois Press, 1952), 213, line 1: τύχη ἐχαρίσατο αὐτῷ λόγον σοφίας, "Fortune has given him a word of wisdom" [=has given him to speak with wisdom].

24 See 1:5; 1:21; 2:3; 14:6; Col 2:3. Against the assertion that γνῶσις in Paul is less than σοφία cf. 8:1ff; 13:2. Bultmann, *TDNT* 1:708, n. 73. Weiss is wrongly schematic in contending that γνῶσις denotes the content of prophecy and a λόγος γνώσεως is one like 15:23ff, 50ff, whereas σοφία points in the direction of διδαχή, "teaching": 6:5. Rather, 2:6ff is an example of speaking with wisdom.

25 The gift which they find to be wanting in Paul, according to 2 Cor 10:10 (cf. also 11:6). That is to say, they deny that he is a genuine pneumatic.

26 13:2; Bultmann, *TDNT* 6:206.

27 The evidence for the singular is poor.

28 Healing miracles in the ancient world: Epidaurus in particular is well known. Sources: Gerhard Delling, *Antike Wundertexte*. KlT, 79 (Berlin: de Gruyter, [2]1960). Albrecht Oepke, *TDNT* 3:205–213.

29 Or is Paul thinking specially of exorcisms, which of course are consciously distinguished from healings of the sick, not only in the Synoptics (indirectly also in John, where no exorcisms are recounted; nor in Epidaurus either)? ἐνέργεια/ἐνεργεῖν in the OT and NT almost always denote the working of divine (or demonic) powers; see Georg Bertram, *TDNT* 2:652–654.

30 Lietzmann speaks of "angels' tongues." The expression is an unhappy one. If the speaker with tongues speaks the language of heaven, then the angels speak "natural" language.

31 Hermann, *Kyrios und Pneuma*, 76–85, observes that the foundation is the unity of Christ and Pneuma, which is presupposed in the whole section.

12 For as the body is one, but has many members, and yet all the members of the body, although they are many, are one body, so also is Christ. 13 / For indeed in one Spirit we were all baptized into one body, whether Jews or Greeks, slaves or free men,[1] and we were all imbued with one Spirit. 14 / For indeed[2] the body is not one member but many. 15 / If the foot were to say: "Because I am not a hand, I do not belong to the body," yet it does belong to the body all the same.[3] 16 / And if the ear should say: "Because I am not an eye, I do not belong to the body," yet it does belong to the body all the same. 17 / If the whole body were an eye,[4] where would the hearing be? If it were all hearing, where would the sense of smell be? 18 / As it is, however, God has appointed the members in the body, each single one of them, as it has pleased him. 19 / If they were all one member, where would the body be? 20 / As it is, however, there are many members, but one body. 21 / The eye cannot say to the hand: "I do not need you," nor again the head to the feet: "I do not need you," 22 / but the very members of the body which are considered specially weak are all the more necessary.[5] 23 / And those parts of the body which we regard as specially dishonorable we treat with special honor, and our unseemly parts have (or: receive) special seemliness; 24 / whereas our seemly parts have no need of this. But God has fitted the body together in such a way that he has given special honor to the member that is in need,[6] 25 / in order that there should be no division in the body, but that the members should harmoniously provide for each other. 26 / And when one member suffers, all the members suffer with it; when one member is honored, all the members rejoice with it. 27 / But you are the body of Christ and individually members of it. 28 / And God has appointed some in the church to be first of all apostles, secondly prophets, thirdly teachers, then miracles, then gifts of

---

1   Such fourfold series are found in Hellenistic prose: Ditt., *Or.* 1:602f (no. 383, lines 172, 194: μήτε—μήτε); Heinrich Dörrie, *Der Königskult des Antiochos von Kommagene im Lichte neuer Inschriften-Funde*, AAG, 3, 60 (Göttingen: Vandenhoeck & Ruprecht, 1964), 152.

2   καὶ γάρ: Blass–Debrunner §452(3); καί goes with the whole sentence.

3   "That is no reason why it should not. . . ." παρὰ τοῦτο: Blass–Debrunner §236(5); εἶναι ἐκ: Bauer, *s.v.* ἐκ 4 a δ.

4   Unreal condition, cf. ἦν v 19.

5   τὰ δοκοῦντα: for the word order (preceding the subject) cf. Rom 8:18; Blass–Debrunner §474(5a).

6   Variant reading ὑστεροῦντι, "that is inferior": p⁴⁶ D G 𝔑.

**healing, acts of helping, acts of adminis-
tration, various kinds of (speaking with)
tongues. 29/ Are all apostles? All
prophets? All teachers? (Do) all (work)
miracles? 30/ Do all have gifts of
healing? Do all speak with tongues? Do
all interpret them?
But strive for the higher gifts! 31 / I will
show you a still more excellent way.**

This section is dominated by the figure of the body as an organism. This was to begin with a popular figure;[7] it was then taken over by philosophy, especially by the Stoa.[8]

To be sure, opinions are divided as to whether Paul is employing the figure purely as such, or whether he is influenced by the proper sense of the term "body of Christ" (=church). The second interpretation seems to be indicated by the break between vv 12a and 12b:[9] here the *figure* of *one* body seems to be replaced by the thing itself, *the* body of Christ.[10] On the other hand it must be asked how far the expression can be pressed: is it not simply a case of a shortened form of expression?[11]

The basis of recent discussion is provided by E. Käse-

---

7   The best known form is that of the fable of Menenius Agrippa in Liv., *Urb. cond.* 2.32, and Dion. Hal., *Ant. Rom.* 6.86. The figure is also used elsewhere of political relationships: according to Quint. Curt. Ruf., *Hist. Alex.* 10.6.8; 10.9.2, the kingdom is the body, the ruler the head, the provinces the members. Jos., *Bell.* 4.406. W. Nestle, "Die Fabel des Menenius Agrippa," *Klio* 21 (1927): 350–360.

8   Here, too, the figure is related to politics: Cic., *Off.* 3.5.22; Sen., *Ir.* 2.31.7; it is connected with the notion of συμπάθεια, "sympathy," in M. Aur. Ant., *Medit.* 5.26 (see on v 26). In a properly philosophical sense, of the unity of men and gods, Epict., *Diss.* 2.5.24f; 2.10.3f; 2.23f; Sen., *Ep.* 95.52: *omne hoc, quod vides, quo divina atque humana conclusa sunt, unum est: membra sumus corporis magni. natura nos cognatos edidit, cum ex isdem et in eadem gigneret. haec nobis amorem indidit mutuum et sociables fecit,* "All that you behold, that which comprises both God and man, is one—we are the parts of one great body. Nature produced us related to one another, since she created us from the same source and to the same end. She engendered in us mutual affection, and made us prone to friendships" (Loeb 3:91). M. Aur. Ant., *Medit.* 2.1; 7.13: οἷόν ἐστιν ἐν ἡνωμένοις τὰ μέλη τοῦ σώματος, τοῦτον ἔχει τὸν λόγον ἐν διεστῶσι τὰ λογικὰ πρὸς μίαν τινὰ συνεργίαν κατεσκευασμένα. μᾶλλον δέ σοι ἡ τούτου νόησις προσπεσεῖται, ἐὰν πρὸς ἑαυτὸν πολλάκις λέγῃς, ὅτι 'μέλος' εἰμὶ τοῦ ἐκ τῶν λογικῶν συστήματος. ἐὰν δὲ διὰ τοῦ ῥῶ στοιχείου 'μέρος' εἶναι ἑαυτὸν λέγῃς, οὔπω ἀπὸ καρδίας φιλεῖς τοὺς ἀνθρώπους, "The principle which obtains in single organisms with regard to the limbs of the body applies also in separate beings to rational things constituted to work in conjunction. But the perception of this will come home to you better, if you often say to yourself, I am a *limb* [μέλος] of the organized body of rational things. But if, using the letter ρ, you say that you are a *part* [μέρος], you do not yet love mankind from the heart" (cf. Loeb, 169). Epict., *Diss.* 2.10.3f: . . . πολίτης εἶ τοῦ κόσμου καὶ μέρος αὐτοῦ . . . . μηδὲν ἔχειν ἰδίᾳ συμφέρον, . . . ἀλλ' ὥσπερ ἄν, εἰ ἡ χεὶρ ἢ ὁ ποὺς λογισμὸν εἶχον καὶ παρηκολούθουν τῇ φυσικῇ κατασκευῇ, οὐδέποτ' ἂν ἄλλως ὥρμησαν ἢ ὠρέχθησαν ἢ ἐπανενεγκόντες ἐπὶ τὸ ὅλον, ". . . you are a citizen of the world, and a part of it. . . . To treat nothing as a matter of private profit . . . but to act like the foot or the hand, which, if they had the faculty of reason and understood the constitution of nature, would never exercise choice or desire in any other way but by reference to the whole" (Loeb 1:275). In Christian usage: *1 Cl.* 37.5.

9   Lietzmann says: "For Paul, however, this is not merely a simile, but a mystical truth. Hence the sudden transition of thought in 12bff. The mere continuation of the simile would have to be: 'So, too, the different parts of the community form a unified body'—only after this could there come the mystical statement: 'in fact, the body of Christ.' Instead of this, Paul says briefly, 'so it is also with Christ,' and then provides in the first instance an argument for the factuality of the mystic idea": v 13.

10   We must not, however, combine this passage with 11:2ff and so read into it that Christ is at once both the head and the whole of the body. It is not until Col and Eph that this idea prevails. In 1 Cor there is only the "body of Christ" = the church.

11   Weiss, and Heinrich Schlier, *Christus und die Kirche,* 40f, contend that we have here only figurative language. οὕτως καὶ ὁ Χριστός, they say, means: "So it is also, where Christ is."

mann's thesis,[11a] that the real thought of the section is that of the church as the body of Christ. The thought of an organism, he argues, is merely an auxiliary idea.

■ **13** Verse 13[12] does in fact point in the direction of the assumption that we have here not merely a figure, but a "proper" usage. This, to be sure, is not yet conclusively implied by the *expression* that we are baptized εἰς ἓν σῶμα, "into one body."[13] But the *thought* and the sequence of thought certainly do point in this direction.[14] For here Paul speaks only of the *unity* which is brought about by the abrogation of the (physical and social) differences between believers. This idea is not derivable from the figure of an organism. For the latter is designed to emphasize the belonging together of *different* elements.[15] Thus the disturbance in the sequence of thought is an indication in favor of the interpretation that the body of Christ is preexistent in relation to the "parts."[16] Incorporation into it takes place through baptism.[17] The latter brings about the eschatological[18] abrogation

of human differences:[19] in Christ they no longer exist— that is to say, in his body, in the church.[20]

■ **14** From v 14 on, to be sure, it is the *figure* of the body that dominates. From the standpoint of content, this means that now the accent again lies (as in vv 4–11) upon the notion of differentiation.[21] Lietzmann aptly remarks that the exposition of the figure is (as usually in Paul) not a happy one, because in contrast to Livy and Menenius Agrippa, there is no reason for the dissatisfaction of the parts.[22]

■ **15–16** Weiss thinks the point of vv 15f is aimed in the first instance "not against the pride of privileged members, but against the all too humble self–assessment of inferior ones." Verses 21–25, he holds, are then directed against the privileged members. Now it is plain that in Corinth there are strong people who exalt themselves over the weak, and presumably also feelings of inferiority on the part of the nonpneumatics. But the figure[23] surely suggests rather that Paul's attack is directed against

---

11a Käsemann, *Leib*, 159.

12 According to Weiss a four–line verse with the form a b b a; between a and a there is a rhymelike sound, between b and b anaphora.

13 The expression appears to mean that the body is already there when believers are taken up into it by baptism; this is in harmony with the prevailing conception of space. Not so Franz Mussner, *Christus, das All und die Kirche im Epheserbrief*, Trierer Theologische Studien, 5 (Trier: Paulinus, 1955), 125–277, who holds that the expression has not a local, but a final or consecutive sense: baptism *brings about* the fellowship. Cerfaux, *Church*, 270–277 [207–211], would understand the expression in keeping with other combinations of βαπτίζειν with εἰς: "Baptism is in one Spirit, and it consecrates us to one and the same body, the body of Christ with which it identifies us in a mystical way." Mystical!

14 According to Lietzmann, εἴτε Ἰουδαῖοι κτλ., "whether Jews, etc.," disturbingly interrupts the course of the argument. For of course, so he says, the goal of the argument is unity; he finds the passage to be in its proper place in Gal 3:27f; Col 3:11. This is to misunderstand the intention of the passage.

15 Käsemann, *Leib*, 159ff, says that after vv 4ff we expect that the body of Christ is the unity of the *charismata*, but that suddenly it is the *Christians* who constitute the body. This is surprising only when we have first raised the charismata to the dignity of hypostases.

16 That is, the church does not come into existence through the decision and association of men, but

first makes this possible.

17 Cf. 10:1ff. Is ἐποτίσθημεν, "we were imbued with" (literally "were given to drink of"), an allusion to the Lord's Supper?

18 And *not* empirical.

19 Gal 3:28; 1 Cor 7:1ff.

20 The "realistic" interpretation is confirmed by v 27 and Rom 12:4f.

21 μέλος: Johannes Horst, *TDNT* 4:555–568.

22 In Menenius Agrippa the indignation is directed against the stomach, which appears not to work, but only to enjoy. Lietzmann goes on: "And their conclusion that they 'do not belong to the body' is rather strange." Here the application does in fact intrude into the figure. But the psychological explanation given by Lietzmann can hardly be right: in Corinth, he says, it was thought that every believer must possess all the charismata, and speaking with tongues had been made the criterion of a man's being a Christian, so that people were afraid they did not belong to the church if they did not possess the gift of tongues. This is not in the text. Rather, it must be maintained that the point is all along directed against fanatical isolation, in chap. 12 as much as in chap. 11.

23 Foot and hand: Epictet., *Diss.* 2.10.4, etc. Ear and eye: "anaphora and antistrophe, and indeed even assonance [πούς—οὖς]" (Weiss).

the practice of individuals' dissociating themselves from the "body," that is, against enthusiastic individualism.[24]

■ **17** Weiss says: "Only as an appendage to the second illustration comes the reflection on how imperfect the organism would be if it all consisted of only one organ."[25] ἀκοή and ὄσφρησις can designate not only sense perception, hearing and smelling, but also the organs, ear and nose.[26]

■ **18** In v 18 the exposition of the figure is interrupted. The latter would now call for a reference to the appropriateness of the structure of the body and to the necessity of cooperation. Instead of this, Paul points to the will of God (cf. 15:38). The figure has for him no importance on its own account.

■ **19–20** Remarkable, too, are vv 19–20:[27] In v 19 the accent again lies on the differentiation; this accent is secured by interchanging μέλος, "member," and σῶμα, "body." The rhetorical question, ποῦ τὸ σῶμα; "Where would the body be?" is explained by Weiss as

meaning: "The concept of a body would be abrogated." This is correct in content, but a long way from the figure: Would that still be a body? In v 20, however, the accent then shifts once more to the notion of unity.[28]

■ **21** This continues the dialogue between the members.[29] That the eye comes before the head seems to have no particular reason.[30] Both are generally recognized to be the two most outstanding parts of the body. οὐ δύναται, "cannot," is held by Weiss to mean: "it would κατὰ φύσιν ['by nature'] be impossible." No, but simply that it would be absurd.

■ **22** Weiss thinks the expression τὰ δοκοῦντα, "which are considered," is here not so suitable as ἃ δοκοῦμεν, "which we regard," in v 23; for there is of course no doubt on the question of strength and weakness, and thus it is a case of an entirely correct opinion. In point of fact the expression is a shortened form of "the parts which, because they are weaker, are considered less valuable; but they are necessary."[31]

24 Contrary to Weiss, the polemic is not directed against the circumstance of *one* member's considering himself to be the whole and being regarded by others as such. This cannot be deduced from v 20. On παρὰ τοῦτο see Weiss: "owing to this circumstance," i.e., "this circumstance is no reason for his not belonging to the body." "The negation is doubled, because οὐκ ἔστιν (repeating οὐκ εἰμί) is an inseparable expression." Philo, *Gig.* 9: ἀλλ᾽ οὐ παρ᾽ ὅσον ἀδύνατος ἡ ὄψις ψυχῶν φαντασιωθῆναι τύπους, διὰ τοῦτ᾽ οὔκ εἰσιν ἐν ἀέρι ψυχαί, "Yet the fact that our powers of vision are incapable of any perception of the forms of these souls is no reason why we should doubt that there are souls in the air" (Loeb 2:449, 451). 2 Thess 3:9; Theophil., *Ad Autol.* 1.2: οὐ παρὰ τὸ μὴ βλέπειν τοὺς τυφλοὺς ἤδη καὶ οὐκ ἔστιν τὸ φῶς τοῦ ἡλίου φαῖνον, "Just because the blind do not see, however, the light of the sun does not fail to shine" (Grant, 3–5).

25 Lietzmann observes: "It [the figure] becomes clear only in v 17, where the butt of the attack is the pneumatics who refused to subordinate themselves to the interests of the congregation." But the figure as such is no better constructed in v 17 than in vv 15f; clearer, however, is the bias against pneumatic emancipation.

26 See Bauer, *s.vv.* Cf. the expression εἰσφέρειν εἰς τὰς ἀκοάς, "bring to the ears," in Acts 17:20; cf. Soph., *Ai.* 149; Heb 5:11; 2 Tim 4:3 (cf. v 4); Lk 7:1. ὄσφρησις occurs with ἀκοή in M. Aur. Ant., *Medit.* 10.35; Diog. L., *Vit.* 6.39: γλῶσσα, ὄσφρησις, ἀκοή.

27 For the figure cf. Cic. *Off.* 3.5.22.

28 For the working together of part and whole in the *universum*, see M. Aur. Ant., *Medit.* 2.3.

29 For the style (parallelism with antistrophe) see Weiss.

    Weiss (see on v 14) holds that vv 14–20 were addressed to the less privileged, vv 21–25 are now addressed to the more gifted who look down upon the others. He founds this interpretation on the use of the figure: up to this point, subordinate members were speaking to those of higher rank. But did Paul regard them as subordinate and introduce them *as such* into the figure? It is surely obvious that his point is the equality of rights—also in terms of the figure as he understands it, cf. v 17. Now (vv 21ff) it is true that privileged members are speaking, but once again only for the sake of the point. Cf. the change of style: *in the former passage*, the members were speaking among themselves, they were emancipating themselves.

30 And also that the eye is linked with the hand, the head with the foot. The individual members could be interchanged.

31 Weiss. But it is reading too much into the text when he assumes that Paul is here contrasting δόξα, "honor," and ἀλήθεια, "truth," after the manner of the Stoics (see the index to Schenkl's edition of Epictetus, *s.v.* ἀλήθεια). Whatever the Stoic coloring, Paul has here, as always, no interest in philosophy as such, or no familiarity with it. Verse 22 is already thinking in the direction of v 23: it is concerned with the idea of compensation as a pointer to conduct.

■ 23 In v 23 what v 22 has in view becomes visible: a kind of apologia for the weaker parts by means of a reference to the "natural" attitude toward them, namely, the compensation provided by custom.[32]

The sequence of thought is not such that Paul theoretically takes the side of the nonpneumatics for a moment. He is arguing on the presumption that *all* are charismatics.[33]

■ 24–25 That the body is "compounded together," from the elements, is a favorite expression of the Stoics among others.[34] Paul had said above that man adjusts the natural distinctions between strong and weak, etc., and that this is a model for conduct in the community. Now he says that it is *God* who adjusts them, that is, practically speaking, nature. It is not difficult to balance the two statements: nature points us toward the correct attitude, see on 11:14.

Verse 25 merely touches upon the figure ($\sigma\hat{\omega}\mu\alpha$, "body"), draws the conclusion, comes back to the starting point, the $\sigma\chi\acute{\iota}\sigma\mu\alpha\tau\alpha$, "divisions" (11:18), and shows that these are determined by enthusiasm: in the body there can be no dissension,[35] and to put it in positive terms, the body "is" the working together of the parts.[36]

■ 26 The notion of "sympathy" is Stoic (though not indeed exclusively so). The cosmos is a vast body,[37] that is shot through with sympathy. And man is part of the All which embraces men and holds them together.[38] For the counterpart, $\sigma\upsilon\gamma\chi\alpha\acute{\iota}\rho\epsilon\iota\nu$, "rejoice with," see 3:6.

■ 27 Verse 27 sums up. Here Paul comes back from the figure of an organism to the proper sense ("body of Christ," see on v 13). Now the body is no longer determined by the parts, but vice versa the parts by the whole. The *figure* may still be echoed in the expression $\acute{\epsilon}\kappa\ \mu\acute{\epsilon}$-$\rho\upsilon\varsigma$.[39] While the thought of v 27 does link up with the figure, namely, with the idea of unity which it, too, contains, yet it stands in isolation in between the figure and v 28. This shows that Paul does not *construct* his view of the church on the basis of the idea of an organism, but can use the latter merely as an illustration.

■ 28 Here Paul links up with the figure again, namely, with the thought of differentiation (and the demand for cooperation which is to be derived from the figure): in this way each man can be shown that *his* function is meaningful and necessary, that is, he can be pointed to the opportunity and norm of his work, namely, $\overset{..}{\omicron}\iota\kappa\omicron$-$\delta\omicron\mu\acute{\eta}$, "building up."

---

32 In $\dot{\alpha}\sigma\theta\epsilon\nu\acute{\eta}\varsigma$—$\dot{\alpha}\tau\iota\mu\acute{\omicron}\tau\epsilon\rho\omicron\varsigma$—$\dot{\alpha}\sigma\chi\acute{\eta}\mu\omega\nu$, "weak—dishonorable—unseemly," we have to seek neither a climax nor a definite division into categories (with Heinrici). Not so Weiss, according to whom $\dot{\alpha}\tau\iota$-$\mu\acute{\omicron}\tau\epsilon\rho\alpha$ indicates the trunk, $\dot{\alpha}\sigma\chi\acute{\eta}\mu\omega\nu\alpha$ the private parts. For $\dot{\alpha}\sigma\chi\acute{\eta}\mu\omega\nu$ in a sexual sense see Dio Chrys., *Or.* 23(40).29; Gen 34:7; Deut 24:1; Sus 63 Th; cf. the substantive Ex 20:26; Rev 16:15. $\tau\iota\mu\dot{\eta}\nu\ \pi\epsilon\rho\iota$-$\tau\iota\theta\acute{\epsilon}\nu\alpha\iota$, "treat with honor," Esth 1:20; Prov 12:9. $\acute{\epsilon}\chi\epsilon\iota$, "have," is interpreted by Weiss in terms of his stoicizing tendency: they have it already. It accords better with the train of thought (compensation) to render: they *receive* it (with Lietzmann). Phaedr., *Fab.* 4.16.5: *naturae partes veste quas celat pudor,* "those natural parts which a sense of shame causes to be hidden by our clothing" (Loeb, 327). The principle still appears in the Cynics' "shamelessness," the protest form which makes a show of life according to nature.

33 The figure must not be pressed. According to the figure, *all* the gifts would have to be together if the body is to function. Paul, however, is not thinking of a fixed number of gifts, but of all *necessary* ones. There is nothing problematical about the fact *that* the community lives.

34 Cf. Epict., *Diss.* 2.23.3f; M. Aur. Ant., *Medit.* 7.67. $\mu\hat{\iota}\xi\iota\varsigma$: Karl Reinhardt, *Kosmos und Sympathie* (Mu-

nich: Beck, 1926), 19; Käsemann, *Leib,* 40ff.

35 This is possible only in the fable, which by its very form shows the impossibility.

36 Does Paul after all have the form of Menenius Agrippa in mind, from which it would be easier to derive this utilitarian application?

37 Sext. Emp., *Math.* 9 (= *Phys.* 1 = *Dogm.* 3).78f; Epict., *Diss.* 1.14.2; Philo, *Migr. Abr.* 178, 180; M. Aur. Ant., *Medit.* 5.26; 7.9; Sen., *Ep.* 95.52 (n. 8 above). Reinhardt, *Kosmos und Sympathie,* 44–54. For sympathy between body and soul see Cleanthes in Diels, *Fragmente* 1:518. For sympathy see also Cic., *Off.* 3.5; Sext. Emp., *Astrol.* (= *Math.* 5) 44; Max. Tyr., *Diss.* 21.4f; for the expression see Diod. S., *Bibl. hist.* 18.42.4: $\sigma\upsilon\mu\pi\alpha\sigma\chi\acute{\omicron}\nu\tau\omega\nu\ \dot{\alpha}\pi\acute{\alpha}\nu\tau\omega\nu\ \tau\hat{\omega}\nu\ .\ .\ .$ $\mu\epsilon\lambda\hat{\omega}\nu$, "all its members sharing" (Loeb 9:133).

38 Not so Plut., *Solon* 18.5 (88c): $\tau\omicron\grave{\upsilon}\varsigma\ \pi\omicron\lambda\acute{\iota}\tau\alpha\varsigma\ \overset{..}{\omega}\sigma\pi\epsilon\rho$ $\acute{\epsilon}\nu\grave{\omicron}\varsigma\ \mu\acute{\epsilon}\rho\eta\ \sigma\acute{\omega}\mu\alpha\tau\omicron\varsigma\ \sigma\upsilon\nu\alpha\iota\sigma\theta\acute{\alpha}\nu\epsilon\sigma\theta\alpha\iota\ \kappa\alpha\grave{\iota}\ \sigma\upsilon\nu\alpha\lambda\gamma\epsilon\hat{\iota}\nu$ $\dot{\alpha}\lambda\lambda\acute{\eta}\lambda\omicron\iota\varsigma$, The lawgiver accustomed "the citizens, *as if* members of one body, to sympathize and suffer with each other" (cf. Loeb 1:453).

39 Weiss says: "each for his own part," not as in 13:9ff. Lietzmann renders: "taken singly," cf. 13:9, 10, 12; *Ep. Ar.* 102.

40 Notice that afterwards the construction is interrupted: $\overset{..}{\omicron}\upsilon\varsigma\ \mu\grave{\epsilon}\nu\ \kappa\tau\lambda.$, "some, etc.," is not followed up.

The chief forms of service are listed. The three outstanding ones are thrown into relief by the use of ordinal numbers.[40] These are the three offices which according to Harnack's thesis on the dual office are charismatic offices, that is, offices common to the church as a whole, whose bearers wander from community to community.[41] Against this, Kümmel objects that Paul knows nothing of a distinction between charismatic and other offices; for him all the functions in the community are charismatic. And Greeven[42] declares that the prophets and teachers are not peripatetic. They are bound to the community; cf. the picture of prophecy in chap. 14.[43]

These objections are correct in pointing out that there is no dual organization (individual community and church as a whole).[44]

Apostles[45] and prophets are also mentioned together elsewhere,[46] and so, too, are apostles and teachers.[47] The other forms of service cannot be so sharply defined; the designations indicate functions that are more of a technical kind—administrative work: ἀντιλήψεις, "acts of helping";[48] κυβερνήσεις, "acts of administration";[49] for the γένη γλωσσῶν, "various kinds of (speaking with) tongues," see on 14:1.

■ **29–30** In this list the technical forms of service, which Paul was the first to exalt to the rank of χαρίσματα, are omitted. Cf. 12:4–6.

Verse 14:1b would link up well with v 30: Paul assents to the χαρίσματα, but now establishes a new order of precedence by putting prophecy above tongues from the standpoint of οἰκοδομή, "upbuilding." But first the thought is given a surprising new turn by v 31.

■ **31** In v 31[50] the connection with δέ, "but," is not good. Verse 31a, to be sure, abides by the terminology used thus far (χαρίσματα), yet appears to bring a shift of accent with the summons ζηλοῦτε, "strive for":[51] up to this point Paul had spoken of the gifts in terms of criticism and reduction. Certainly, the shift is understandable. His criticism was directed not at the gifts, but at the Corinthians' self–understanding. Now he directs their attention to higher gifts, ones that allow of no self–development and no self–contemplation on the pneumatic's part. All the same, the summons does not go smoothly with 14:1 either.[52] And there is something remarkably antagonistic about the reference to the

---

41 Lietzmann, *ad loc.*; Adolf von Harnack, *The Mission and Expansion of Christianity in the First Three Centuries*, ed. and tr. James Moffatt, vol. 1 (London: Williams and Norgate; New York: Putnam, ²1908; reprinted New York: Harper, 1962), 319–368 (*Die Mission und Ausbreitung des Christentums in den ersten drei Jahrhunderten* [Leipzig: Hinrichs, ⁴1924] 1:332–379).

42 Heinrich Greeven, "Propheten, Lehrer, Vorsteher bei Paulus. Zur Frage der 'Ämter' im Urchristentum," *ZMW* 44 (1952–53): 1–43; von Campenhausen, *Ecclesiastical Authority*, 60–62 [65f].

43 The figure of the wandering prophet has been read into the text from the *Didache*.

44 Bultmann, *Theology* 2:103f [455f], observes that the work of the apostles and prophets does not mean a supracongregational organization, but it does manifest the church to be *one*.

45 See on 9:1ff; 15:3ff.

46 Eph 2:20; 3:5; 4:11; *Did.* 11.3.

47 2 Tim 1:11; Herm., *Sim.* 9.15.4; 9.16.5; 9.25.2; *Vis.* 3.5.1.

48 *P. Oxy.* 900.13; 2 Macc 8:19; *3 Macc.* 5.50; Sir 11:12; 51:7.

49 Literally, "piloting." The figure of the helmsman is very popular for ruling. Xenoph., *Cyrop.* 1.1.5; Plut., *Sept. sap. conv.* 162a.

50 Instead of μείζονα, "higher," D G ℵ have the reading (weak in point of content) κρείττονα or κρείσσονα, "better"; R. V. G. Tasker, "The Text of the 'Corpus Paulinum,'" *NTS* 1 (1955): 180–191, here esp. 187f. Instead of ἔτι, "still," p⁴⁶ D* read εἴ τι (defended by Albert Debrunner, "Lesarten der Chester Beatty Papyri," *CN* 11 [1947]: 33–49, here esp. 37): "and if there is anything that surpasses this, then I will show you the way." Anton Fridrichsen (in E. Lehmann and A. Fridrichsen, "1 Kor. 13. Eine christlich-stoische Diatribe," *ThStKr* 94 [1922]: 55–95, here esp. 65–70) puts forward the conjecture (see Harald Riesenfeld, "La voie de charité: Note sur I Cor. XII, 31," *StudTheol* 1 [1947–48]: 146–157): ζηλοῦτε δὲ τὰ χαρίσματα τὰ μείζονα καὶ ἔτι ⟨τι⟩ καθ' ὑπερβολήν· ὁδὸν ὑμῖν δείκνυμι, "Strive for the higher gifts and everything utterly superlative: I will show you the way."

51 ζηλοῦν: Plut., *Alex.* 5 (ἀρετή, "virtue," and δόξα, "honor"), see on 14:1.

52 Gerhard Iber, "Zum Verständnis von I Cor 12,31," *ZNW* 54 (1963): 43–52, observes that the difficulty disappears if ζηλοῦτε is taken as indicative: "you are striving for." The clause describes the attitude of the community. The μείζονα χαρίσματα, "higher gifts," are then the ecstatic phenomena. Then the place of chap. 13 is also safeguarded from the literary

"higher way" that follows. καθ᾽ ὑπερβολὴν goes attributively with ὁδόν: a still more excellent way.[53]

Excursus:
ὁδός, "Way"

The figure of the way is widespread.[54] The Old Testament speaks of the ways that God takes, on which he leads his people or the individual. The conduct of life is a "walking." Qumran dualistically contrasts the two ways that are determined by the two spirits (of light and of darkness).[55] In addition to this, the contrasting of the two ways as ethical possibilities is a paraenetic pattern that was taken over by Christianity.[56]

The symbolism of the way was employed by the Greeks from the time of Parmenides.[57] Particularly closely related to the present passage is Philo's "royal way."[58] It is the way that leads beyond the usual levels and possibilities of knowledge to the contemplation of God, whereby the divine πνεῦμα expels the human νοῦς.[59]

Paul does not promise[60] a way that leads to the πνευματικά, "spiritual gifts," but one that leads beyond them; nor is it a way that leads to love, but love *is* the way, at the same time also the goal of the διώκειν and ζηλοῦν, the "pursuing" and "striving for" (on this cf. Phil 3:12ff). The question will be whether Paul can show this higher possibility to be qualitatively different from the (other) πνευματικά.

---

standpoint; v 31a and b go together, as the Corinthian position and the Pauline counter-position. 14a is no counter-argument. For according to chap. 13 Paul can also react positively to their zeal. Moreover, he does not there speak of "greater" gifts; this expression contains criticism.

53 With Bauer, *s.v.* ὑπερβολή; Wilhelm Michaelis, *TDNT* 5:85, rightly characterizes the phrase as stereotyped. Spicq, *Agapé* 2:65, argues that καθ᾽ ὑπερβολήν corresponds not to a comparative, but to a superlative. Against this is ἔτι, "still (more)." From the standpoint of content it is pointless to argue about this; naturally, this "higher" way is the highest. It acquires a certain significance only when to the comparative contained in καθ᾽ ὑπερβολήν we supply τῶν χαρισμάτων, "than the gifts" (Richard Reitzenstein, "Die Formel 'Glaube, Liebe, Hoffnung,' bei Paulus," *NGG* [1916]: 367–416, here esp. 398, n. 2). Then faith, hope and love are not themselves χαρίσματα.

54 Michaelis, *TDNT* 5:42–96.

55 1QS III, 13–15; S. Vernon McCasland, " 'The Way,' " *JBL* 77 (1958): 222–230.

56 As happens in the two recensions of a two-way catechism in the *Didache* and *Barnabas*.

57 Parmenides, *Fr.* 1. He links up with the mysteries. The way to the light is the way to salvation. Werner Jaeger, *Theology of the Early Greek Philosophers*, tr. Edward S. Robinson (Oxford: Clarendon, 1947), 94–100 (*Die Theologie der frühen griechischen Denker* [Stuttgart: Kohlhammer, 1953], 112–118); Karl Deichgräber, *Parmenides' Auffahrt zur Göttin des Rechts*, AAM, 1958, 11 (Mainz: Akademie der Wissenschaft und der Literatur, 1958); Otfried Becker, *Das Bild des Weges und verwandte Vorstellungen im frühgriechischen Denken*, Einzelschriften zum Hermes, 4 (Berlin: Weidmann, 1937). Heraclitus, *Fr.* 135 (in Diels, *Fragmente* 1:181): συντομωτάτην ὁδὸν ἔλεγεν εἰς εὐδοξίαν τὸ γενέσθαι ἀγαθόν, "The shortest way to fame, he said, is to become good" [Trans.].

58 In connection with Num 20:17; 21:22; Pascher, *Königsweg*.

59 Philo, *Poster. C.* 101f; *Deus imm.* 159–167, 180; Ign., *Eph.* 9.1: love is ὁδὸς ἡ ἀναφέρουσα εἰς θεόν, "the way that leads up to God."

60 δείκνυμι, "I will show": Epict., *Diss.* 1.4.10–17.

13 The Higher Way

Prefatory Note to Chapter 13

This chapter is a self-contained unity. The links with what goes before (12:31) and after (14:1) are ragged. There are also difficulties in regard to the content: in the context, the higher way is the way of love. This is at variance with 13:13, according to which there are *three* highest gifts. Moreover, in the light of chap. 13 all the gifts so far mentioned are relatively degraded. This is at variance with the summons in 14:1. *

1 If I speak with the tongues of men and of angels, but have no love, then I have become a noisy gong or a clanging cymbal. 2 / And if I have the gift of prophecy, and understand all mysteries and all knowledge, and if I have all faith, so as to remove mountains, but have no love, then I am nothing. 3 / And if I distribute all my possessions as alms, and if I give up my body to be burned,[1] but have no love, then it avails me nothing.

4 Love is long-suffering, love is kind, love[2] is not jealous, not boastful, 5 / not arrogant; it is not rude,[3] it does not seek its own advantage,[4] it is not irritable, it keeps no score of wrongs, 6 / it does not rejoice over wrongdoing, but rejoices in the truth.[5] 7 / It covers everything,[6] believes everything, hopes everything, endures everything.

8 Love never fails. Gifts of prophecy—they will be destroyed. Tongues—they will cease. Knowledge—it will be destroyed. 9 / For our knowledge is fragmentary, and our prophesying is fragmentary. 10 / But when the perfect comes, the fragmentary will be destroyed. 11 / When I was a child, I spoke as a child, I thought as a child, I reasoned as a child. When I became a man, I did away with childish things. 12 / For at present we see enigmatically, in a mirror, but then face to face. At present I know in part, but then I shall know fully, even as I am also fully known.

13 But now there remain faith, hope, love, these three. But the greatest of them is love.

---

* According to Weiss, chap. 13 is here not in its original place. That Paul is recommending love as the greatest χάρισμα (Lietzmann) is not stated, and is in fact ruled out by the contrast between χαρίσματα and love and by 14:1. Chap. 13 makes the impression of an insertion; there are close links with chap. 8; both belong to the same letter (B?).

1 Variant reading καυχήσωμαι, "in order to boast of the fact," p[46] ℵ A B. Yet this reading is presumably a simplifying correction (despite its cautious acceptance by Kenneth Willis Clark, "Textual Criticism and Doctrine," *Studia Paulina*, 52–65, here esp. 61f, and against the *Greek NT*). It is hardly likely that καυχ– would be changed into κανθ– (Spicq, *Agapé*, 2:57f). Moreover, ἀγάπην δὲ μὴ ἔχω, "but have no love," is then no longer suitable (Lietzmann).

2 ἀγάπη is considered by Zuntz, *Text*, 68, to be secondary (because of the rhythm and the sentence structure); it is omitted by B 33. But see R. V. G. Tasker, "The Text of the 'Corpus Paulinum,' " *NTS* 1 (1955): 180–191, here esp. 191. p[46] has considerable variants in this section; see above, p. 1, n. 7.

The first two members can be taken as chiasmus. It is not so good to place the comma after οὐ ζηλοῖ (Nestle) or to punctuate ἡ ἀγάπη μακροθυμεῖ, χρηστεύεται, ἡ ἀγάπη οὐ ζηλοῖ, ἡ ἀγάπη οὐ περπερεύεται (Lietzmann, Robertson and Plummer).

3 Variant reading εὐσχημονεῖ, p[46]: "does not give itself airs," supported by Albert Debrunner, "Lesarten der Chester Beatty Papyri," *CN* 11 (1947): 33–49, here esp. 37–41; cf. Vulg. *non est ambitiosa*.

4 Variant reading τὸ μὴ ἑαυτῆς, p[46c] B: "what does not belong to it."

5 The meaning of the compound συγχαίρειν is here that of the simple verb, see Bauer, *s.v.*

6 Or, owing to the proximity of ὑπομένει, perhaps

Chapter 13[7] stands out from its context as a unity *sui generis*. But internally the section is made up of different stylistic forms, which also make use of correspondingly different materials. The literary critic's question, whether the passage originally stood in this context (see on 12:31; 14:1), is thereby sharpened, even to the extent of becoming a question of authenticity.[8] At all events the passage must be expounded in the first instance on its own. We must set out from the *form*.[9]

The divisions are clear: (a) vv 1–3; (b) vv 4–7; (c) vv 8–12.[10] The surprising wealth of Greek and Jewish parallels points in the first instance to the assumption of Greek motifs by Hellenistic Judaism and their transformation in the style of the Jewish Wisdom tradition.[11] The most important Greek parallels are provided by Tyrtaeus, Plato, Maximus of Tyre; the most important Jewish parallel is *3 Ezra* 4:34–40.

This last text comes particularly close, both in style and in content.[12] It is an aretalogy of $\dot{\alpha}\lambda\dot{\eta}\theta\epsilon\iota\alpha$, "truth";[13] the style bears the mark of "Wisdom."[14]

---

better: "it will bear"; see the commentary.

7 Literature: Adolf von Harnack, "Das hohe Lied des Apostels Paulus von der Liebe (I. Kor. 13) und seine religionsgeschichtliche Bedeutung," *SAB* (1911): 132–163; E. Lehmann and Anton Fridrichsen, "1 Kor. 13. Eine christlich-stoische Diatribe," *ThStKr* 94 (1922): 55–95 (not by Paul); Ernst Hoffmann, "Pauli Hymnus auf die Liebe," *Deutsche Vierteljahrsschrift für Literaturwissenschaft und Geistesgeschichte* 4 (1926): 58–73; Nils W. Lund, "The Literary Structure of Paul's Hymn to Love," *JBL* 50 (1931): 266–276; Gunnar Rudberg, *Hellas och Nya Testamentet* (Stockholm: Svenska Kyrkans Diakonistyrelses Bokförlag, 1929), 149f (this passage reprinted as "Gunnar Rudberg zu 1 Cor. 13," *CN* 3 [1938]: 32); Günther Bornkamm, "The More Excellent Way," *Early Christian Experience*, 180–193 (*Das Ende des Gesetzes*, 93–112; originally in *Jahrbuch der theologischen Schule Bethel* 8 [1937]: 132–150); E. Hoffmann, "Zu 1 Cor. 13 und Col. 3,14," *CN* 3 (1938): 28–31; Harald Riesenfeld, "La voie de charité; Note sur 1 Cor. XII, 31," *StudTheol* 1 (1947–48): 146–157; "Note bibliographique sur I Cor. XIII," *Nuntius* 6 (1952): 47f; Spicq, *Agapé* 2:53–120 (bibliography and the richest supply of material, also on all the individual issues); N. Johansson, "I Cor. xiii and I Cor. xiv," *NTS* 10 (1963–64): 383–392 (love = Christ).

8 Eric L. Titus, "Did Paul Write I Corinthians 13?" *JBR* 27 (1959): 299–302.

9 On the form, cf. above all Weiss; Bornkamm, "The More Excellent Way"; Spicq, *Agapé* 2:53–120.

10 Weiss is too schematic in contending that we have here again the division a b a, the third part returning to the charismata. The rest of his characterization is excellent. In vv 1–3 the protases follow each other with the anaphora $\dot{\epsilon}\dot{\alpha}\nu$. The climax lies in the middle; the number of syllables is 16; 25 + 18; 13 + 16. To the shortest protasis there corresponds the longest and weightiest apodosis (15—4—6 syllables). The second part is characterized by antithetical, and in part rhymelike, clauses. This part could stand on its own (see Gerhard von Rad, below, n. 51). In this part love is the subject. The third part consists of the heading v 8a, three anaphorical and antistrophic parallelisms v 8b, c, d (according to Weiss with the rhyme pattern a b a); there follows in vv 9f an antithetical parallelism, in v 11 an antithesis, in v 12 a double antithesis, in v 13 the thesis with a coda.

11 For the motifs, cf. Wisd 7:22ff, the description of $\sigma o\phi\dot{\iota}\alpha$ by means of 21 predicates, the last of which describe its effect; cf. the conclusion in verbal form.

Men's relationship to it is defined as $\sigma v\nu o\iota\kappa\epsilon\hat{\iota}\nu$, "dwelling with," through which we become beloved of God.

Totally different is Spicq's verdict on chap. 13. He holds (as also does Hoffmann) that it is not a hymn, but paraenesis and contains almost word-for-word allusions to the situation in Corinth. For the style he points to Ps 138:8f; *Ab.* 6.6. But these passages are somewhat far afield. For the rest, it is a matter of definition whether or not we would speak of a hymn. Moreover, the multiplicity of stylistic forms and the concentration of allusions to the context in particular passages has to be kept in mind. The verdict on the form also partially determines that on the religious–historical context. Classical scholars (Hoffmann, Rudberg) tend to discover the Platonic element. An oddity is the attempt to trace the chapter to the influence of Epicurus, Norman Wentworth De Witt, *St. Paul and Epicurus* (Minneapolis: University of Minnesota Press, 1954).

12 Date of origin: *ca.* 165 B.C. (after Daniel) to A.D. 90 (Josephus knows the book); see Otto Eissfeldt, *The Old Testament: An Introduction*, tr. Peter R. Ackroyd (Oxford: Blackwell; New York: Harper & Row, 1965), 574–576 (*Einleitung in das Alte Testament* [Tübingen: J. C. B. Mohr (Paul Siebeck), ³1964], 777–781); on *3 Ezra*, on the inserted story of the three pages (3:1—4:42), and on the aretalogy of truth, see Wilhelm Rudolph, *Esra und Nehemia*, HAT, 20 (Tübingen: J. C. B. Mohr [Paul Siebeck], 1949), IV–XIX.

Excursus:
The Parallels

1. Tyrtaeus, fr. 12 (=fr. 9 in Diehl's ed.):[15]

Οὔτ' ἂν μνησαίμην οὔτ' ἐν λόγωι ἄνδρα τιθείην
    οὔτε ποδῶν ἀρετῆς οὔτε παλαιμοσύνης,
οὐδ' εἰ Κυκλώπων μὲν ἔχοι μέγεθός τε βίην τε,
    νικώιη δὲ θέων Θρηΐκιον Βορέην,
οὐδ' εἰ Τιθωνοῖο φυὴν χαριέστερος εἴη,
    πλουτοίη δὲ Μίδεω καὶ Κινύρεω μάλιον,
οὐδ' εἰ Τανταλίδεω Πέλοπος βασιλεύτερος εἴη,
    γλῶσσαν δ' Ἀδρήστου μειλιχόγηρυν ἔχοι,
οὐδ' εἰ πᾶσαν ἔχοι δόξαν πλὴν θούριδος ἀλκῆς·
    οὐ γὰρ ἀνὴρ ἀγαθὸς γίγνεται ἐν πολέμωι,
εἰ μὴ τετλαίη μὲν ὁρῶν φόνον αἱματόεντα
    καὶ δῄων ὀρέγοιτ' ἐγγύθεν ἱστάμενος.
ἥδ' ἀρετή, τόδ' ἄεθλον ἐν ἀνθρώποισιν ἄριστον
    κάλλιστόν τε φέρειν γίγνεται ἀνδρὶ νέωι.

"I would neither call a man to mind nor put him in my tale for prowess in the race or the wrestling, not even had he the stature and strength of a Cyclops and surpassed in swiftness the Thracian Northwind, nor were he a comelier man than Tithonus and a richer than Midas or Cinyras, nor though he were a greater king than Pelops son of Tantalus, and had Adrastus' suasiveness of tongue, nor yet though all fame were his save of warlike strength; for a man is not good in war if he have not endured the sight of bloody slaughter and stood nigh and reached forth to strike the foe. This is prowess [literally, virtue], this is the noblest prize and the fairest for a lad to win in the world" (Loeb 1:75). The question is that of the supreme virtue, not merely in the sense that it surpasses all the other virtues, but that it first brings them to perfection.[16]

2. Plato, *Symp.* 197c–197e:[17]

Οὕτως ἐμοὶ δοκεῖ, ὦ Φαῖδρε, Ἔρως πρῶτος αὐτὸς
ὢν κάλλιστος καὶ ἄριστος μετὰ τοῦτο τοῖς ἄλλοις
ἄλλων τοιούτων αἴτιος εἶναι. ἐπέρχεται δὲ μοί
τι καὶ ἔμμετρον εἰπεῖν, ὅτι οὗτός ἐστιν ὁ ποιῶν

    εἰρήνην μὲν ἐν ἀνθρώποις, πελάγει δὲ γαλήνην
    νηνεμίαν, ἀνέμων κοίτην ὕπνον τ' ἐνὶ κήδει.

οὗτος δὲ ἡμᾶς ἀλλοτριότητος μὲν κενοῖ, οἰκειότητος
δὲ πληροῖ, τὰς τοιάσδε συνόδους μετ' ἀλλήλων
πάσας τιθεὶς συνιέναι, ἐν ἑορταῖς, ἐν χοροῖς, ἐν
θυσίαισι γιγνόμενος ἡγεμών· πραότητα μὲν πορί-
ζων, ἀγριότητα δ' ἐξορίζων· φιλόδωρος εὐμε-
νείας, ἄδωρος δυσμενείας· ἵλεως ἀγαθοῖς· θεατὸς
σοφοῖς, ἀγαστὸς θεοῖς· ζηλωτὸς ἀμοίροις, κτητὸς
εὐμοίροις· τρυφῆς, ἁβρότητος, χλιδῆς, χαρί-
των, ἱμέρου, πόθου πατήρ· ἐπιμελὴς ἀγαθῶν,
ἀμελὴς κακῶν· ἐν πόνῳ, ἐν φόβῳ, ἐν πόθῳ, ἐν λόγῳ
κυβερνήτης, ἐπιβάτης, παραστάτης τε καὶ σωτὴρ
ἄριστος, συμπάντων τε θεῶν καὶ ἀνθρώπων
κόσμος, ἡγεμὼν κάλλιστος καὶ ἄριστος, ᾧ χρὴ
ἕπεσθαι πάντα ἄνδρα ἐφυμνοῦντα καλῶς, ᾠδῆς
μετέχοντα ἣν ᾄδει θέλγων πάντων θεῶν τε καὶ
ἀνθρώπων νόημα.

" 'Thus I conceive, Phaedrus, that Love was originally of surpassing beauty and goodness, and is latterly the cause of similar excellencies in others. And now I am moved to summon the aid of verse, and tell how it is he who makes—

    Peace among men, and a windless waveless main;
    Repose for winds, and slumber in our pain.

He it is who casts alienation out, draws intimacy in; he brings us together in all such friendly gatherings as the present; at feasts and dances and oblations he makes himself our leader; politeness contriving, moroseness outdriving; kind giver of amity, giving no enmity; gracious to the good; a marvel to the wise, a delight to the gods; coveted of such as share him not, treasured of such as good share have got; father of luxury, tenderness, elegance, graces and longing and yearning; careful of the good, careless of the bad; in toil and fear, in drink and discourse, our trustiest helmsman, boatswain, champion, deliverer; ornament of all gods and men; leader fairest and best, whom every one should follow, joining tunefully in the burthen of his song, wherewith he enchants the thought of every god and man' " (Loeb 5:159, 161, slightly modified).

3. Max. Tyr., *Diss.* 20.2 (ed. Hobein; = 16.2 ed. Dübner): Love is not found among the barbarians,

---

13   The symposium motif in the surrounding narrative points to Greek (and Persian?) tradition. For the motif see, apart from Plato and Xenophon, Plut., *Sept. sap. conv.*; *Quaest. conv.*; *Ep. Ar.* 182–294. Josef Martin, *Symposion, Die Geschichte einer literarischen Form*, Studien zur Geschichte und Kultur des Altertums, 17, 1–2 (Paderborn: Schöningh, 1931).

14   Cf. the hymnic praise of σοφία, Prov 8; Sir 24; Wis 7.

15   See Werner Jaeger, "Tyrtaeus on True Arete," in his *Five Essays*, tr. Adele M. Fiske (Montreal: Casalani, 1966), 103–142 (*Scripta Minora* [Rome: Edizioni di Storia e Letteratura, 1960] 2:75–114; originally in *SAB* [1932]: 537–568); Bornkamm, "The More

Excellent Way."

16   The question is a *topos*; Xenophanes, *Fr.* 2: Wisdom is the highest virtue. Theogn., *El.* 1:699–718: the highest good is wealth; also Plat., *Leg.* 630f. For the theme τί μέγιστον;, "which is the greatest?" see Plat., *Leg.* 661a. Ulrich Schmid, *Die Priamel der Werte im Griechischen von Homer bis Paulus* (Wiesbaden: Harrassowitz, 1964) (review of the material, analysis of the form); Bruno W. Dombrowski, "Wertepriameln in hellenistisch–jüdischer und urchristlicher Literatur," *ThZ* 22 (1966): 396–402.

17   This is an ironical imitation of the style of the tragedian Agathon. Notice the transition from verbs (sub-

because there is no freedom there.

'Ο δὲ ἔρως οὐδενὶ οὕτως πολεμεῖ ὡς ἀνάγκῃ καὶ
δέει· καὶ ἐστὶν χρῆμα γαῦρον, καὶ δεινῶς ἐλεύθερον, καὶ τῆς Σπάρτης αὐτῆς ἐλευθερώτερον.
μόνον γάρ τοι τῶν ἐν ἀνθρώποις ἔρως, ἐπειδάν τῳ
καθαρῶς ξυγγένηται, οὐ πλοῦτον τέθηπεν, οὐ
τύραννον δέδιεν, οὐ βασίλεια ἐκπλήττεται, οὐ
δικαστήριον φυλάττεται, οὐ φεύγει θάνατον·
οὐ θηρίον αὐτῷ δεινόν, οὐ πῦρ, οὐ κρημνός, οὐ
θάλαττα, οὐ ξίφος, οὐ βρόχος, ἀλλὰ καὶ τὰ
ἄπορα αὐτῷ εὐπορώτατα, καὶ τὰ δεινὰ εὐμαχώ-
τατα, καὶ τὰ φοβερὰ εὐπετέστατα, καὶ τὰ χαλεπὰ
εὐκολώτατα. ποταμοὶ πάντες περάσιμοι, χειμῶνες
πλοϊμώτατοι, ὄρη εὐδρομώτατα· πανταχοῦ
θαρσεῖ, πάντων ὑπερορᾷ, πάντων κρατεῖ.

"But nothing is so hostile to love as necessity. For
it is a thing superb and free in the extreme, and even
more free than Sparta herself. For love alone of
every thing pertaining to men, when it subsists with
purity, neither admires wealth, nor dreads a tyrant,
nor is astonished by empire, nor avoids a court of
judicature, nor flies from death. It does not consider as dire either wild beasts, or fire, or a precipice,
or the sea, or a sword, or a halter; but to it things
impervious are most pervious, things dire are most
easily vanquished, things terrible are most readily
encountered, and things difficult are most speedily
accomplished. All rivers are passable, tempests most
navigable, mountains most easily run over. It is
everywhere confident, despises [or surveys] all
things, and subdues all things" (*The Dissertations of
Maximus Tyrius*, tr. Thomas Taylor [London: C.
Whittingham, 1804], 1:103).

4. *3 Ezra* 4:34–40:

καὶ ἤρξατο λαλεῖν περὶ τῆς ἀληθείας· Ἄνδρες,
οὐχὶ ἰσχυραὶ αἱ γυναῖκες; μεγάλη ἡ γῆ, καὶ
ὑψηλὸς ὁ οὐρανός, καὶ ταχὺς τῷ δρόμῳ ὁ ἥλιος,
ὅτι στρέφεται ἐν τῷ κύκλῳ τοῦ οὐρανοῦ καὶ πάλιν
ἀποτρέχει εἰς τὸν ἑαυτοῦ τόπον ἐν μιᾷ ἡμέρᾳ.
οὐχὶ μέγας ὃς ταῦτα ποεῖ; καὶ ἡ ἀλήθεια μεγάλη
καὶ ἰσχυροτέρα παρὰ πάντα. πᾶσα ἡ γῆ τὴν
ἀλήθειαν καλεῖ, καὶ ὁ οὐρανὸς αὐτὴν εὐλογεῖ,
καὶ πάντα τὰ ἔργα σείεται καὶ τρέμει, καὶ οὐκ
ἔστιν μετ' αὐτοῦ ἄδικον οὐθέν. ἄδικος ὁ οἶνος,
ἄδικος ὁ βασιλεύς, ἄδικοι αἱ γυναῖκες, ἄδικοι πάντες οἱ υἱοὶ τῶν ἀνθρώπων, καὶ ἄδικα πάντα τὰ
ἔργα αὐτῶν, πάντα τὰ τοιαῦτα· καὶ οὐκ ἔστιν ἐν

αὐτοῖς ἀλήθεια, καὶ ἐν τῇ ἀδικίᾳ αὐτῶν ἀπολοῦν-
ται. ἡ δὲ ἀλήθεια μένει καὶ ἰσχύει εἰς τὸν αἰῶνα
καὶ ζῇ καὶ κρατεῖ εἰς τὸν αἰῶνα τοῦ αἰῶνος. καὶ
οὐκ ἔστιν παρ' αὐτῇ λαμβάνειν πρόσωπα οὐδὲ
διάφορα, ἀλλὰ τὰ δίκαια ποιεῖ ἀπὸ πάντων τῶν
ἀδίκων καὶ πονηρῶν· καὶ πάντες εὐδοκοῦσι τοῖς
ἔργοις αὐτῆς, καὶ οὐκ ἔστιν ἐν τῇ κρίσει αὐτῆς
οὐθὲν ἄδικον. καὶ αὐτῇ ἡ ἰσχὺς καὶ τὸ βασίλειον
καὶ ἡ ἐξουσία καὶ ἡ μεγαλειότης τῶν πάντων
αἰώνων. εὐλογητὸς ὁ θεὸς τῆς ἀληθείας.

"And he began to speak about truth: 'Gentlemen,
are not women strong? The earth is vast, and heaven
is high, and the sun is swift in its course, for it makes
the circuit of the heavens and returns to its place
in one day. Is he not great who does these things?
But truth is greater, and stronger than all things.
The whole earth calls upon truth, and heaven blesses
her. All God's works quake and tremble, and with
him there is nothing unrighteous. Wine is unrighteous, the king is unrighteous, women are unrighteous,
all the sons of men are unrighteous, all their works
are unrighteous, and all such things. There is no
truth in them and in their unrighteousness they will
perish. But truth endures and is strong for ever, and
lives and prevails for ever and ever. With her there
is no partiality or preference, but she does what is
righteous instead of anything that is unrighteous or
wicked. All men approve her deeds, and there is
nothing unrighteous in her judgment. To her belongs the strength and the kingship and the power
and the majesty of all the ages. Blessed be the God of
truth!' " (RSV, vv 33b–40).

The comparison is particularly instructive for
the very reason that we have here a piece that is
of no significance either in style or in content; all
the plainer is a set stylistic tradition.

One negative circumstance shows how strongly the
chapter is determined by tradition: there is no trace
whatever of Christology. Apparently we have here once
more a sign of Paul's Hellenistic Jewish schooling.[18]
The Christian element is contained exclusively in the context and in the definitions of the three concepts faith,
hope, love in other passages.

■ **1** The conditional clause[19] presupposes that there are

---

18 Cf. for example, Wisd 7:25f: ἀπόρροια τῆς δόξης,
ἀπαύγασμα, ἔσοπτρον, εἰκών, "glorious emanation,
reflection, mirror, image." Wisdom, like love,
appears as abiding eternally; cf. (of truth) *3 Ezra*
4:38 (μένει καὶ ἰσχύει εἰς τὸν αἰῶνα, "endures
and is strong forever"). The comparing of these
passages shows the substantial agreement between

jeсt Eros) to nouns and adjectives.

wisdom, truth and righteousness (Sir 24); here τὰ
δίκαια ποιεῖ, "does what is righteous."
19 Ael. Arist., *Or.* 23.274: ἀλλ' οὐδ' ἄν εἰ πᾶσαν ὑπερ-
βαλοίμην τὴν ἐν ἀνθρώποις δύναμίν τε καὶ φωνὴν
..., "But not even if I should surpass every power
and tongue of men. . . ."

universally recognized values. It is then a vitally important point that Paul begins with values that are significant in the community in Corinth: speaking with tongues, prophecy,[20] etc. This is a strong link with the context. On the other hand he expresses himself in such general terms that, e.g., a Jewish reader can agree.[21] These recognized values are then relativized: they cannot make man "anything worth" without love, which accordingly qualitatively transcends these values.[22] Love is the basic attribute[23] which alone confers worth.

In Paul's sense this Wisdom teaching is *Christian* teaching, even if there is no explicit mention of Christology. For ἀγάπη, "love," is for him a given *Christian* concept (Rom 5:3ff; 8:35ff), and indeed he links up emphatically with the values of the Christian church. But at the same time he allows them to appear as universal values. He speaks, like Jewish Wisdom teaching, of love, etc., in general.[24] He is aware of the continuity in usage between the Old Testament and Judaism on the one hand and Christianity on the other.[25] This tradition, more especially the aretalogy of Wisdom, also explains the fact that the question does not arise whether it is a case of love for God or of love for men.[26]

On the individual statements and concepts, the allusion to the language of men and angels presupposes the apocalyptic world picture and is understandable in its light.[27] χαλκὸς ἠχῶν: "gong."[28] κύμβαλον is the cymbal.[29] For ἀλαλάζειν, "to clang," cf. Ps 150:5.[30] The instruments referred to are used in ecstatic cults.[31] For what Paul means, however, we have to bear in

20 Note the order. Cf. the reversal in v 8.

21 Thus he does not speak in technical terms of "tongues," but adapts the expression to the apocalyptic world picture.

22 Cf. Tyrtaeus.

23 Attribute: one "has" it, like knowledge 8:1; cf. Rev 17:9 (σοφία); Xenoph., *Mem.* 2.3.10 (σοφία). Thereby it is still an open question how the relationship between subject and attribute is understood; not, at all events, in the sense of Greek moral philosophy.

24 Cf. "the" truth, *3 Ezra* 4.

25 ἀγάπη is a LXX term. For the rare pagan instances see *Supp. Epigr.* 8:11, 6; *BKT* 2:55 (*P. Berol.* 9869); Philodem. Philos., *Lib.* (ed. Olivieri, p. 52). Especially interesting is the Isis litany in *P. Oxy.* 1380, lines 28, 109: Isis is identified with ἀγάπη, as also with ἀλήθεια, and Isis is the truth; Hans Conzelmann, "The Mother of Wisdom," in *The Future of Our Religious Past*, ed. James M. Robinson (London: SCM; New York: Harper & Row, 1971), 230–243 (*Zeit und Geschichte: Dankesgabe an Rudolf Bultmann zum 80. Geburtstag*, ed. Erich Dinkler [Tübingen: J. C. B. Mohr (Paul Siebeck), 1964], 225–234). Judaism: *Ps. Sal.* 18.3; *Ep. Ar.* 229; *Test. G.* 4.7; 5.2; *Test. B.* 8.1f; Philo, *Deus imm.* 69. Literature: Bauer, *s.v.* ἀγάπη; Spicq, *Agapé*; Harald Riesenfeld, "Étude bibliographique sur la notion biblique d'ΑΓΑΠΗ," *CN* 5 (1941): 1–32.

26 On the question see Spicq, *Agapé* 2:108–111.

27 The wording does not in itself require the equating of angels' language and speaking with tongues. Moreover the expression can also be understood as a mere hyperbole: and if I had at my command every linguistic possibility even to the language of God. Yet Paul is presumably after all thinking realistically of the language of angels, cf. 2 Cor 12:4, and further

    Asc. Is. 7.15–37; *Test. Job* 48–50: Job's daughters speak in the dialects of various classes of angels. Str.–B. 3:449f. A realistic interpretation is indicated also by the word order (γλῶσσαις and λαλῶ separated by τῶν ἀνθρώπων; καί thereby acquires an intensifying effect; Spicq, *Agapé* 2:66f). On the expression of totality by means of the contrasting of opposites, see Gustave Lambert, "Lier–délier: l'expression de la totalité par l'opposition de deux contraires," *RB* 52 (1945): 91–103; Harald Riesenfeld, "Note supplémentaire sur 1 Cor 13," *CN* 10 (1946): 1–3.

28 Hdt., *Hist.* 4.200; Plat., *Prot.* 329a.

29 Firm. Mat., *Err. prof. rel.* 18.1: ἐκ τυμπάνου βέβρωκα, ἐκ κυμβάλου πέπωκα, γέγονα μύστης Ἄττεως, "I have eaten from the tambourine, I have drunk from the cymbal, I have become an initiate of Attis" [Trans.]. Wendland, *Die hellenistisch–römische Kultur*, plate 7; Charles Victor Daremberg and Edmond Saglio, *Dictionnaire des antiquités grecques et romains d'après les textes et les monuments* (Paris: Hachette, 1873–1919) 1:1697f; Karl Ludwig Schmidt, *TDNT* 3:1037–1039. Plin., *Hist. nat. praef.* 25: Tiberius called the grammarian Apion *cymbalum mundi*. Spicq, *Agapé* 2:68f.

30 Erik Peterson, *TDNT* 1:227f.

31 See n. 29 above (Firm. Mat.). The κύμβαλον, "cymbal," belongs more especially to the cult of Cybele. According to Peterson, ἀλαλάζειν transfers the ecstatic noise of these cults to the κύμβαλον used in them. Harald Riesenfeld, "Note supplémetaire sur I Cor. XIII," *CN* 12 (1948): 50–53, holds that Paul is purposely speaking the language of the pagan cults he would disparage, cf. 12:2. Johannes Quasten, *Musik und Gesang in den Kulten der heidnischen Antike und christlichen Frühzeit*, Liturgiegeschichtliche Quellen und Forschungen, 25 (Münster: Aschen-

mind the exposition in 14:7ff.[32]

■ **2** Paul follows the Corinthian order of merit in the spiritual gifts, which he will reverse in chap. 14.[33] In doing so he emphasizes prophecy more strongly than speaking with tongues. For the arguments over prophecy are by nature more intellectually determined, and consequently hotter, because the statements of the prophet, unlike those of the speaker with tongues, can be checked.[34] Paul regards it as parallel with wisdom, the knowledge of mysteries.[35] That is, he takes a specifically Christian factor—Spirit-inspired utterance in the community—and transposes it into the universal style of Wisdom teaching. The parallel between σοφία, "wisdom," and γνῶσις, "knowledge,"[36] can be understood without more ado and was already anticipated in 12:8.[37]

πίστις, "faith" (see on 12:9), is here explicitly characterized as a miraculous force, the power "to remove mountains."[38] Compared with the overstrained protasis, the apodosis comes with cutting brevity: οὐθέν εἰμι, "I am nothing."[39]

■ **3** Thus far the question was one of attributes ("have"), now it is one of achievements. The style remains the same.[40] ψωμίζειν means (a) "give as food,"[41] (b) "divide in pieces," "split up." So the meaning in this context can be either asceticism or beneficence. The sense (b), however, can only be deduced from ψωμός, "piece," but there is no evidence for it.[42] καὶ ἐὰν παραδῶ, "and if I give up,"[43] is explained by the ἵνα–clause, "to be burned." If καυθήσομαι, "be burned," is the correct reading, Paul can be thinking of martyrdom by fire[44]

dorff, 1930); Franz Joseph Dölger, "Die gellende Klingel: 1 Kor. 13,1 in kultur- und religionsgeschichtlicher Beleuchtung," in his *Antike und Christentum*, 1, 3 (Münster, Aschendorff, 1929), 184f; "Die Glöckchen am Gewande des jüdischen Hohen priesters nach der Ausdeutung jüdischer, heidnischer und frühchristlicher Schriftsteller," *Antike und Christentum*, 4, 4 (1934), 233–244; "Echo aus Antike und Christentum, 126: Der Bacchant mit dem Schellengut," *Antike und Christentum*, 6, 1 (1940), 78: the bell as a child's plaything and an instrument of defense against disaster and demons. Dölger considers it possible that Paul is thinking of senseless manipulations of this kind. But this explanation is farfetched. It is not in accord with the instruments mentioned.

32　ἄψυχα, "inanimate things"; 14:7! Chr. Wagner, "Gotteserkenntnis im Spiegel und Gottesliebe in den beiden Korintherbriefen," *Bijdragen* 19 (1958): 370–381, here esp. 376f. For speeches as "sounds" cf. Plat., *Prot.* 329a; this becomes a commonplace: Stob., *Ecl.* 3.23.10; Diog. L., *Vit.* 6.64.

33　On the distribution of weight between protases and apodoses, see above. The alternation between καὶ ἐάν and κἄν appears to be arbitrary (in v 3 an emphatic conclusion with the full καὶ ἐάν). The text is uncertain throughout.

34　See chap. 14.

35　Cf. 2:6ff; 15:51; Rom 11:25. According to Weiss, καὶ εἰδῶ τὰ μυστήρια πάντα, "I understand all mysteries," is presumably an elucidation of ἔχω προφητείαν, "I have the gift of prophecy." The close connection between prophecy and knowledge of mysteries does in fact appear from 2 Cor 10ff; but the two must not be identified; see 14:24.

36　Heightening of the style: by means of the paranomasia πάντα—πᾶσαν. πᾶσα γνῶσις, "all knowl-

edge": Sir 21:14. πᾶς with the article: all there is; Blass–Debrunner §275(3).

37　Col 2:3.

38　A proverbial Jewish phrase: to make possible what seems impossible, Str.–B. 1:759; Mk 11:23.

39　Instances: Bauer, *s.v.* οὐδείς 2 b β; Soph., *Oed. tyr.* 56; Xenoph., *An.* 6.2.10; Epict., *Diss.* 4.8.25; 2 Cor 12:11; on 1:28 above.

40　See the antithesis and the apodosis. The ἵνα–clause corresponds to the ὥστε–clause in v 2.

41　Prov 25:21 (Rom 12:20); with accusative of the thing given: Poll., *Onom.* 6.33; Dan 4:32 LXX; with double accusative, Ps 79:6; Vulg. *si distribuero in cibos pauperum.*

42　See Lietzmann. Weiss is unnecessarily complicated in saying that the distributing of one's possessions to the poor remains without love if the ascetic achievement is in the foreground. Jewish examples: Str.–B. 1:817 (Mt 19:21).

43　Max. Tyr., *Diss.* 7 (ed. Hobein 1:9).

44　Dan 3:19f; *2 Macc.* 7:5; *4 Macc.* 6.26; 7.12; Jos., *Ant.* 17.167; *Bell.* 1.655; Dio Chrys., *Or.* 7(8).16: μαστιγούμενον ... καὶ τεμνόμενον καὶ καόμενον, "being whipped ... and cut and burned"; *1 Cl.* 45.7; Athenag., *Suppl.* 31 (Pythagoras and 300 companions).

45　Material: Karl Ludwig Schmidt, *TDNT* 4:464–467 (the burning of Jews in Alexandria—a fate which the martyrs could have evaded). Against seeking martyrdom: Tert., *Prax.* 1.

46　Cic., *Fin.* 2.27.88 (Epicurus) *ait enim se, si uratur,* "*quam hoc suave*" *dicturum,* Epicurus "tells us that if he were being burnt to death he would exclaim, 'How delightful this is!' " (Loeb, 181). Seneca in Lact., *Inst.* 6.17.28; see Dölger, "Der Feuertod ohne die Liebe. Antike Selbstverbrennung und christlicher Martyrium–Enthusiasmus. Ein Beitrag zu I Ko-

or of burning oneself to death as an ascetic act. Martyrdom, too, can be a *voluntary* act.[45] The heroic attitude in face of death by fire is a standard theme also in Greco–Roman philosophy.[46] On the other hand, the voluntary burning of oneself is so as well. It is recounted as an Indian custom,[47] but can also be taken over by Greek philosophers.[48] The brief verdict accords with the former

one: οὐδὲν ὠφελοῦμαι, "it avails me nothing."[49]

■ **4–7** With v 4 comes a change of style. Verses 4–7 constitute a form–critically independent section. The subject is now ἀγάπη, "love," in personifying style.[50] The content and style are not hymnic, but didactic. They belong to a Jewish paraenetic tradition.[51] The nearest parallel is *Test. Iss.* 4.[52] The parallels show that no spe-

---

rinther 13,3," *Antike und Christentum* 1:254–270. Spicq, *Agapé* 2:72–76.

47 The celebrated Calanus: Diod. S., *Bibl. hist.* 17.107; Philo, *Omn. prob. lib.* 96; Plut., *Alex.* 69.6–8; Erwin Preuschen, " 'Und liesse meinen Leib brennen' I Kor. 13,3," *ZNW* 16 (1915): 127–138; Richard Fick, "Der indische Weise Kalanos und sein Flammentod," *NGG* (1938): 1–32. Literature on the knowledge of India current in that time: Spicq, *Agapé* 2:75, n. 1.

48 It is in this connection that the Indian model is referred to: Luc., *Pergr. mort.* 25; Nicholas of Damascus in Strabo, *Geog.* 15.1.73 (also in Jacoby, *FGH* II A: 383, lines 6–12 [90 fr. 100]): συνῆν δέ, ὡς φησί, καὶ ὁ Ἀθήνησι κατακαύσας ἑαυτόν. ποιεῖν δὲ τοῦτο τοὺς μὲν ἐπὶ κακοπραγίᾳ ζητοῦντας ἀπαλλαγὴν τῶν παρόντων, τοὺς δ᾽ ἐπ᾽ εὐπραγίᾳ, καθάπερ τοῦτον· ἅπαντα γὰρ κατὰ γνώμην πράξαντα μέχρι νῦν ἀπιέναι δεῖν, μή τι τῶν ἀβουλήτων χρονίζοντι συμπέσοι· καὶ δὴ καὶ γελῶντα ἅλεσθαι γυμνὸν ἐπαληλιμμένον ἐν περιζώματι ἐπὶ τὴν πυράν. ἐπιγεγράφθαι δὲ τῷ τάφῳ 'Ζαρμανοχηγὰς Ἰνδὸς ἀπὸ Βαργόσης κατὰ τὰ πάντρια Ἰνδῶν ἔθη ἑαυτὸν ἀπαθανατίσας κεῖται', "And [they were accompanied also, according to him [Nicholas], by the man who burned himself up at Athens; and that whereas some commit suicide when they suffer adversity, seeking release from the ills at hand, others do so when their lot is happy, as was the case with that man; for, he adds, although that man had fared as he wished up to that time, he thought it necessary then to depart this life, lest something untoward might happen to him if he tarried here; and that therefore he leaped upon the pyre with a laugh, his naked body anointed, wearing only a loin-cloth; and that the following words were inscribed on his tomb: 'Here lies Zarmanochegas, an Indian from Bargosa, who immortalized himself in accordance with the ancestral customs of Indians' " (Loeb 7:127, 129). The prehistory of the motif leads back into classical times: Heracles. Soph., *Trach.* 1193–1202; *Phil.* 728. Further: Diod. S., *Bibl. hist.* 4.38.4; Dio Chrys., *Or.* 51(68).2; Pomp. Mel., *Chor.* 3.7; Jos., *Bell.* 7.351–356; Apollod., *Bibl.* 2.7.7; Dio C., *Hist. Rom.* 54.9.10; Coc., *Tusc.* 2.22.52; *Divin.* 123.30; Cl. Al., *Strom.* 4.4; Tert., *Apol.* 50.5f.

49 The Stoic query, τί ὠφελεῖ; "what avail is it?":

Epict., *Diss.* 2.19.10, etc. Cf. on the other hand Mk 8:36 par. The thought of reward is not un–Pauline. The thought of a reward for some achievement on man's own part is ruled out by the context. *Ev. Phil.* 45: "since if anyone does not give in love he has no profit from what he has given" (Wilson, 38). ἀγάπη, "love," and πίστις, "faith," are bound up with each other.

50 This is Wisdom style. Verse 8 takes it further, but after the closing v 7, it is a new beginning. Spicq, *Agapé* 2:77.

51 Gerhard von Rad, "The Early History of the Formcategory of *I Corinthians* xiii.4–7," in his *The Problem of the Hexateuch and Other Essays*, tr. E. W. Trueman Dicken (Edinburgh and London: Oliver and Boyd; New York: McGraw–Hill, 1966), 301–317 (*Gesammelte Studien zum Alten Testament* [Munich: Kaiser, 1958], 281–296; originally in *Geschichte und Altes Testament*, Albrecht Alt Festschrift, BHTh, 16 [Tübingen: J. C. B. Mohr (Paul Siebeck), 1853], 153–168).

52 *Test. Iss.* 4.2–6 (*Testamenta XII Patriarchum*, ed. M. de Jonge, Pseudepigrapha Veteris Testamenti Graece, 1 [Leiden: Brill, 1964], 38): ὁ ἁπλοῦς χρυσίον οὐκ ἐπιθυμεῖ, τὸν πλησίον οὐ πλεονεκτεῖ, βρωμάτων ποικίλων οὐκ ἐφίεται, ἐσθῆτα διάφορον οὐ θέλει, χρόνους μακροὺς οὐχ ὑπογράφει ζῆν, ἀλλὰ μόνον ἐκδέχεται τὸ θέλημα τοῦ θεοῦ· καίγε τὰ πνεύματα τῆς πλάνης οὐδὲν ἰσχύουσι πρὸς αὐτόν. οὐ γὰρ εἶδεν ἐπιδέξασθαι κάλλος θηλείας, ἵνα μὴ ἐν διαστροφῇ μιάνῃ τὸν νοῦν αὐτοῦ. οὐ ζῆλος ἐν διαβουλίοις αὐτοῦ ἐπελεύσεται· οὐ βασκανία ἐκτήκει ψυχὴν αὐτοῦ, οὐδὲ πορισμὸν ἐν ἀπληστείᾳ ἐννοεῖ· πορεύεται γὰρ ἐν εὐθύτητι ζωῆς, καὶ πάντα ὁρᾷ ἐν ἁπλότητι, μὴ ἐπιδεχόμενος ὀφθαλμοῖς πονηρίας ἀπὸ τῆς πλάνης τοῦ κόσμου, ἵνα μὴ ἴδῃ διεστραμμένως τι τῶν ἐντολῶν τοῦ κυρίου, "The single(–minded) man does not covet gold, does not overreach his neighbor, does not long after manifold luxuries, does not delight in varied apparel, does not desire to live a long life, but only waits for the will of God. And the spirits of deceit have no power against him, for he does not look on the beauty of women, lest he should pollute his mind with corruption. No envy enters his thoughts, no malice makes his soul pine away, he does not dwell with insatiable desire upon money-grubbing. But he walks in

cific definitions of love[53] are to be sought here either. It is a question of the ways of "love" as such (naturally, in the world). μακροθυμεῖν means (a) "to have patience,"[54] (b) "to be long–suffering."[55] The word is found also in other passages alongside the root χρηστ-.[56] χρηστεύεσθαι, "to show oneself kind," occurs only in Christian literature. ζηλοῦν, "to be zealous, jealous," has long been used in a good and a bad sense.[57] περπερεύεσθαι: πέρπερος is the braggart;[58] the word is explained by Hesychius as meaning κατεπαίρομαι, "vaunt oneself."[59] οὐ ζητεῖ τὰ ἑαυτῆς, "does not seek its own

advantage": cf. 10:24, 33; Phil 2:21. παροξύνειν is in itself neutral, "incite," but points predominantly in the direction of inciting to wrath.[60] The meaning of λογίζεσθαι here corresponds to חשב, "to set to someone's account."[61] For the antithesis of ἀλήθεια, "truth," and ἀδικία, "wrongdoing," cf. Rom 1:18; 2:8; 2 Thess 2:12.[62] Verse 7 is formally speaking a conclusion,[63] but in content a verbal description of the triad of v 13. στέγειν: (a) "draw a veil of silence over";[64] (b) "bear."[65] The second meaning is to be preferred because of the analogous ὑπομένειν, "endure."[66] πίστις, "faith," in

straightness of life, beholds all things in sincerity, shunning with his eyes the evil brought about by the world's error, lest he should see the perversion of any of the commandments of the Lord" [Trans.]. Cf. *Test. B.* 6. G. von Rad points out that the length of these series remains more or less the same (each roughly ten members). On the ground of *Test. Iss.* 4 and 1QS X,17—XI,2 he traces the form–category back to an OT and also oriental category of protestations of innocence: Deut 26:13b–14; 1 Sam 12:3. But it is not until *Test. XII Pat.* that an abstract concept appears as subject.

53 For example, such as the alternative: love for God or love for men.

54 Sir 2:4; *Test. Jos.* 2.7; 2 Cor 6:6; Rom 2:4; Gal 5:22; Plut., *Gen. Socr.* 593f.

55 Corresponding to אֶרֶךְ אַפַּיִם; Prov 19:11; Wisd 15:1 —16:14; *1 Cl.* 49.5; *Dg.* 9.2; Ex 34:6f; of men, Prov 14:29f, etc.; Wisd 5:4–8; for the relation of God's longsuffering to his wrath cf. Rom 2:4; 9:22; *1 Cl.* 13.1; Johannes Horst, *TDNT* 4:374–387. The Old Latin translates it by *magnanimitas*; see Spicq, *Agapé* 2:79.

56 See n. 54 above. In *Ab* 6.6 we find among 48 things required of pursuers of the Torah בארך אפים, "longsuffering," and בלב טוב, "generosity" (=χρηστότης).

57 Cf. the double character of *aemulatio* in Cic., *Tusc.* 4.8.17; Simpl., *Comm. in Epict. Ench.* 19.2 (ed. Dübner, p. 56, lines 29ff). In profane literature mostly "pronounce happy," "admire." For the use in the bad sense cf. also ζῆλος, 1 Cor 3:3; 2 Cor 12:20, etc. Plat., *Leg.* 679c (plural) along with ὕβρις, ἀδικία, φθόνοι.

58 Polyb., *Hist.* 32.2.5; 39.1.1–3; Epict., *Diss.* 3.2.14.

59 On verbs in –εύω (having the character of) see Schwyzer, *Grammatik* 1:732. Cl. Al., *Paed.* 3.3.1: περπερεία γὰρ ὁ καλλωπισμὸς περιττότητος καὶ ἀρχειότητος ἔχων ἔμφασιν, "For ornamentation is vainglory because it presents the appearance of extravagance and abundance" [Trans.]. The word is related in sense with ζηλοῦν, φυσιοῦσθαι (see on

8:1). The accent lies on rhetorical or literary ostentation, see Hebert Braun, *TDNT* 6:93–95. This is in harmony with the rejection of σοφία λόγου, 1:17; 2:1ff. The Stoa uses direct imperatives: Epict., *Diss.* 2.1.34: ἐμπερπερεύσῃ· ἰδοὺ πῶς διαλόγους συντίθημι, "Will you . . . boast, 'See how I write dialogues'?" (Loeb 1:223).

60 Acts 17:16; Epict., *Diss.* 2.12.14.

61 See on v 11. In Greek the word signifies on the one hand business accounting, on the other hand dispassionate, philosophical thinking. Paul's usage is determined by Jewish tradition; Zech 8:17; Qumran; see Hans Wolfgang Heidland, *TDNT* 4:284–292.

62 συγχαίρω, "rejoice (with)," as in Phil 2:17f. For the antithesis ἀλήθεια—ἀδικία cf. the combining of ἀλήθεια and δικαιοσύνη, "righteousness," in Eph 4:24; 5:9; 6:14; Tob 14:7; Philo, *Vit. Mos.* 2.237. ἀλήθεια can mean uprightness, like אֱמֶת; Jas 3:14; cf. the expression ποιεῖν τὴν ἀλήθειαν, "to do the truth," Tob 4:6; 13:6; Jn 3:21, etc.; *3 Ezra* 4:37 (ἀλήθεια—ἀδικία).

63 For the rhetorical concluding πάντα cf. Max. Tyr.; Plut., *Phoc.* 21: πάλιν οὖν ἐνεχθεὶς ἐπὶ τὸ θεραπεύειν ἐκεῖνον, αὐτὸν μὲν ὡς ἔρυμα πανταχόθεν ἀνάλωτον ὑπὸ τοῦ χρυσίου περιεδεύων ἑώρα, Χαρικλέα δὲ τὸν γαμβρὸν αὐτοῦ ποιησάμενος συνήθη καὶ φίλον ἀνέπλησε δόξης πονηρᾶς, πάντα πιστεύων καὶ πάντα χρώμενος ἐκείνῳ, "Again, therefore, he was led to pay court to Phocion, but after all his efforts to bribe him found that he was impregnable on all sides like a fortress. Of Charicles, however, Phocion's son-in-law, Harpalus made an intimate associate and friend, trusting him *in everything* and using him *in everything*, and thus covered him with infamy" (Loeb 8:193, Conzelmann's italics). Weiss observes that the rhetorical uniformity masks the dissimilarity in the thought: πάντα in the middle members is not a pure object in exactly the same way as in the first and last members; in the middle members it means almost "in all things."

64 Cf. καλύπτειν, 1 Pet 4:8; Prov 10:12; Str.–B. 3:766.

Judaism is related to "hope."[67]

■ **8** Although ἀγάπη, "love," remains the subject,[68] the style changes: vv 8–12 are no longer Wisdom teaching to the same extent as the preceding verses.[69] The polemic references become stronger.[70] οὐδέποτε πίπτει, "never fails," is an anticipation of the μένει, "remain," of v 13. The sense is determined not only by μένειν, but by καταργεῖσθαι, "be destroyed," and παύεσθαι, "cease." To be sure, the sense of μένειν itself is not unequivocal; see on v 13. πίπτειν can accordingly mean falling into decay,[71] or coming to an eschatological end.[72] Verse 8b becomes direct polemic; on the gifts referred to, see above. The argument has shifted. Above it was said: They are nothing without love; they are brought to fullness only by it. This was Wisdom's teach-ing on virtue. Now, on the other hand, love and the charismata are set in antithesis to each other, and we have the eschatological argument that the latter will cease. They are accordingly, unlike love, not the appearing of the eternal in time, but the manifesting of the Spirit in a provisional way. Thus these very gifts hold us fast in the "not yet."[73] The form of expression is purposely harsh: prophecy will "be destroyed."[74] Gnosis is mentioned because of its significance as a Corinthian slogan (cf. 8:1ff). What Paul is driving at here emerges—harshly, from the logical standpoint—in the next verse in the distinction between the transient and abiding aspects of these gifts.[75]

■ **9** The harsh confrontation in the tone of apocalyptic is followed by its implications for the understanding of the

---

Thus Spicq, *Agapé* 2:91, because of ὑπομένειν, "bear"; *Test. Jos.* 17.2.

65 Vulg. *omnia suffert*. P. Oxy. 4:1775.10; with καρτερεῖν, "bear patiently," P. Grenf. 1:1.18f.

66 ὑπομένειν, "endure," Rom 12:12. In Greek it can also mean disgraceful putting up with a thing, Hdt., *Hist.* 6.12: δουλείαν, "slavery."

67 Faith/hope: 1 Macc. 2:59, 61; Sir 2:6, 8f; Ps 77:22; Heb 11:1. πίστις and ὑπομονή: *4 Macc.* 17.2, 4 (see below); 2 Thess 1:4; cf. Rev 2:19. In the OT view of hope the element of trust is included, see Rudolf Bultmann, *TDNT* 6:197–228. ἐλπίς and ὑπομονή: 1 Thess 1:3; Rom 5:4f; in both passages we have the underlying triad faith–hope–love; Rom 8:25; 15:4.

68 For this reason Michaelis (see below) takes v 8 with the foregoing; though to be sure, the form of v 7 tells against this.

69 Hoffmann (n. 7 above), 60f, divides the third part (vv 8–12) in the light of v 8: prophecies–tongues–knowledge:
    a) prophecies: fragmentariness and perfection;
    b) tongues: child and man;
    c) knowledge: mirror and vision.
       Stylistic methods are:
    a) Interchange of positive and negative;
    b) Change of grammatical subject: I—love—the gifts; play on we and I.
    c) Intertwining of the catchwords: love—never—fragmentary, etc. "Only 'perfect' is not a catchword. To it there are only antitheses. It is stylistically and conceptually absolute" (p. 61).

70 Käsemann, *Leib*, 173, holds that from v 8 onward love appears as an aeon, as in Col 3:14 (love as the aeon that sums up all the virtues). He argues that πίπτειν, "fail," and μένειν, "remain," are aeon terminology, cf. 2 Cor 3:11 and the personifications (including Ἀγάπη) in Herm., *Vis.* 3.8.5. But even if in Herm. we have a glimpse of mythical motifs, yet they are transposed into allegory. Col 3:14 is likewise no longer mythical, 2 Cor 3:11 not at all. And this explanation fails to notice the Jewish Wisdom style.

    It must naturally be asked how man is understood when love, truth, wisdom, etc., are spoken of in *this* way. The view represented by the section could be characterized as εἰκών anthropology (see on 11:7). The prospect of perfection is one of the characteristic marks of the latter, cf. 2 Cor 3:18.

71 Lietzmann takes πίπτειν to mean "cease" (i.e. in the sense of ἐκπίπτειν, thus D R 𝔐). Cf. Lk 16:17; Ruth 3:18.

72 Objections to this interpretation are expressed by Wilhelm Michaelis, *TDNT* 6:165f: he argues that this statement must not be taken with what follows and that it has to be noted that here we have still the present tense, but in the following verses the future. μένειν, he goes on, is not synonymous with μένειν εἰς τὸν αἰῶνα. Against this, U. Schmid, *Die Priamel der Werte*, 127, n. 116: the clause cannot be taken with the foregoing. The form of the middle section tells against this. The middle section ends with πάντα. There is no connective.

    Unfortunately *3 Ezra* 4:38 does not help toward a solution (see above); see further Harald Sahlin, "I Esdras et 1 Cor 13," *CN* 5 (1941): 28f.

73 γλῶσσαι, "tongues," included. Paul is accordingly not thinking of these as the language of heaven. And γνῶσις in particular reveals the provisional character—figuratively speaking, that I am νήπιος, "a child."

74 Strictly speaking Paul would have to say: the phenomenon of prophesying.

75 ἐκ μέρους, "fragmentarily, in part." The thought

present: the character of the present is—in relation to the future wholeness—broken. But the gifts will reach their $\tau\epsilon\lambda$os, their "goal."[76] Thus the future is here not the end of the world, but its consummation. In the *former* case, according to v 8, the $\pi\nu\epsilon\nu\mu\alpha\tau\iota\kappa\dot{\alpha}$, the "spiritual gifts," pass away; in the *latter* case, however, what passes away is the "$\dot{\epsilon}\kappa\ \mu\dot{\epsilon}\rho ovs$."[77] What this means is explained by the following verses. $\dot{\epsilon}\kappa\ \mu\dot{\epsilon}\rho ovs$ means "fragmentarily," $\tau\dot{o}\ \dot{\epsilon}\kappa\ \mu\dot{\epsilon}\rho ovs$[78] means "the fragmentary."[79] In the omission of speaking with tongues we are presumably not to find any special intention.[80] The sense is determined by the following antithetical concepts.

■ **10** $\tau\dot{o}\ \tau\dot{\epsilon}\lambda\epsilon\iota ov$, "the perfect";[81] $\ddot{\epsilon}\rho\chi\epsilon\sigma\theta\alpha\iota$, "come," points to the parousia. The nature of the eschatological

state, that is, of perfection, is to be defined by the Pauline conceptions of the future world: immortality, $\delta\dot{o}\xi\alpha$, $\pi\nu\epsilon\hat{\nu}\mu\alpha$, etc.

■ **11** In v 11[82] the style is no longer traditional in the same sense as it was up to this point. With the transition to the first person, the traditional element passes over into the *content*. The antithesis between child[83] and man is a standard rhetorical theme.[84] $\phi\rho ov\epsilon\hat{\iota}v$ is not merely theoretical thinking, but includes also judging. $\lambda o\gamma\dot{\iota}\zeta\epsilon\sigma\theta\alpha\iota$ is here not the same as in v 5, but likewise means reasoning, judging (cf. Phil 4:8). The verbs cannot be sharply distinguished.[85] Once again the aspect of discontinuity prevails: knowledge will be "destroyed."

■ **12** The Figure of the Mirror:[86]

forms of eschatology and of Wisdom conflict with each other. But a uniform intention is perceptible: the future is the crisis of the present.

76 $\gamma\dot{\alpha}\rho$, "for," is not causal, but explanatory.

77 Here the same continuity is in mind as is given with the definition of the Spirit as $\dot{\alpha}\rho\rho\alpha\beta\dot{\omega}\nu$, "earnest" (2 Cor 1:22) and $\dot{\alpha}\pi\alpha\rho\chi\dot{\eta}$, "firstfruits" (Rom 8:23). This, too, contains the element of indirectness, provisionalness. Here this thought comes strongly to expression in v 11.

78 LXX; cf. $\dot{\alpha}\pi\dot{o}\ \mu\dot{\epsilon}\rho ovs$ in 2 Cor 1:14; 2:5; Rom 11:25; 15:15. Aristot., *Metaph.* 6(7).9: $\ddot{\alpha}\lambda\lambda\omega\nu\ o\dot{\nu}\kappa\ \dot{\epsilon}\chi\dot{o}\nu\tau\omega\nu$ $\tau\dot{\eta}\nu\ \tau\dot{\epsilon}\chi\nu\eta\nu\ \ddot{\eta}\ \dot{\epsilon}\kappa\ \mu\dot{\epsilon}\rho ovs$, "other things which do not possess the art, or possess it to a limited extent" [Trans.].

79 Hellenistic: Ael. Arist., *Or.* 54.148, 160; Ditt., *Syll.* 2:565 (no. 852, line 30); *P. Lond.* 1166.14; Philo, *Vit. Mos.* 2.1 and frequently.

80 Weiss considers the omission to be an argument in favor of detaching chap. 13 from its context. Bachmann says: "Their transience is self-evident." On the contrary!

81 Paul Johannes du Plessis, ΤΕΛΕΙΟΣ: *The Idea of Perfection in the New Testament* (Kampen: Kok, 1959). Hoffmann (n. 7 above), 72, observes that when Harnack holds the antithesis fragmentary–perfect to be specifically Pauline (one would expect fragmentary–whole), then we must point to Plat., *Tim.* 34b where $\ddot{o}\lambda ov$ and $\tau\dot{\epsilon}\lambda\epsilon\iota ov$ are interchangeable terms.

82 For the antistrophe cf. Epict., *Diss.* 4.9.8.

83 See on 3:1f; Georg Bertram, *TDNT* 4:912–923, here esp. 919. For childish behavior see Eur., *Iph. Aul.* 1243f; Luc., *Halc.* 3: $\dot{\alpha}\pi\epsilon\iota\rho\dot{\iota}\alpha$, "inexperience," and $\nu\eta\pi\iota\dot{o}\tau\eta s$, "childishness."

84 With the counter–term $\tau\dot{\epsilon}\lambda\epsilon\iota os$, "perfect." Xenoph., *Cyrop.* 8.7.6: $\dot{\epsilon}\gamma\dot{\omega}\ \gamma\dot{\alpha}\rho\ \pi\alpha\hat{\iota}s\ \tau\epsilon\ \ddot{\omega}\nu\ \tau\dot{\alpha}\ \dot{\epsilon}\nu\ \pi\alpha\iota\sigma\dot{\iota}\ \nu o$-

$\mu\iota\zeta\dot{o}\mu\epsilon\nu\alpha\ \kappa\alpha\lambda\dot{\alpha}\ \delta o\kappa\hat{\omega}\ \kappa\epsilon\kappa\alpha\rho\pi\hat{\omega}\sigma\theta\alpha\iota,\ \dot{\epsilon}\pi\epsilon\dot{\iota}\ \tau\epsilon\ \ddot{\eta}\beta\eta\sigma\alpha,$ $\tau\dot{\alpha}\ \dot{\epsilon}\nu\ \nu\epsilon\alpha\nu\dot{\iota}\sigma\kappa o\iota s,\ \tau\dot{\epsilon}\lambda\epsilon\iota\dot{o}s\ \tau\epsilon\ \dot{\alpha}\nu\dot{\eta}\rho\ \gamma\epsilon\nu\dot{o}\mu\epsilon\nu os\ \tau\dot{\alpha}\ \dot{\epsilon}\nu$ $\dot{\alpha}\nu\delta\rho\dot{\alpha}\sigma\iota$, "For when I was a boy, I think I plucked all the fruits that among boys count for the best; when I became a youth, I enjoyed what is accounted best among young men; and when I became a mature man, I had the best that men can have" (Loeb 2:425). Epict., *Ench.* 51.1: $o\dot{\nu}\kappa\dot{\epsilon}\tau\iota\ \epsilon\hat{\iota}\ \mu\epsilon\iota\rho\dot{\alpha}\kappa\iota ov,\ \dot{\alpha}\lambda\lambda$' $\dot{\alpha}\nu\dot{\eta}\rho\ \ddot{\eta}\delta\eta\ \tau\dot{\epsilon}\lambda\epsilon\iota os$, "You are no longer a lad, but already a full–grown man" (Loeb 2:535). Sen., *Ep.* 27.2: *Numera annos tuos, et pudebit eadem velle, quae volueras puer, eadem parare*, "Count your years, and you will be ashamed to desire and pursue the same things you desired in your boyhood days" (Loeb 1:193). Philo, *Sobr.* 8: the twenty–year–old Ishmael is $\pi\rho\dot{o}s\ \tau\dot{o}\nu\ \dot{\epsilon}\nu\ \dot{\alpha}\rho\epsilon\tau\alpha\hat{\iota}s\ \tau\dot{\epsilon}\lambda\epsilon\iota ov\ '\mathrm{I}\sigma\alpha\dot{\alpha}\kappa$, "by comparison with Isaac, who is full–grown in virtues," a $\pi\alpha\iota\delta\dot{\iota} ov$, "child" (Loeb 3:447). See on 14:20.

85 It is quite impossible to draw the analogy: $\lambda\alpha\lambda\epsilon\hat{\iota}\nu =$ speak with tongues, etc.; this is already counter to the figure and its form (first person, past tenses).

86 Richard Reitzenstein, *Historia Monachorum und Historia Lausiaca*, FRLANT, 24 (Göttingen: Vandenhoeck & Ruprecht, 1916), 242–255; Hans Achelis, "Katoptromantie bei Paulus," in *Theologische Festschrift für G. Nathanael Bonwetsch zu seinem 70. Geburtstage* (Leipzig: Deichert, 1918), 56–63; Peter Corssen, "Paulus und Porphyrios (Zur Erklärung von 2 Kor 3,18)," *ZNW* 19 (1920): 2–10; Johannes Behm, "Das Bildwort vom Spiegel I. Korinther 13,12," in *Reinhold–Seeberg–Festschrift*, ed. Wilhelm Koepp (Leipzig: Deichert, 1929) 1:315–342; Norbert Hugedé, *La métaphore du miroir dans les Épitres de saint Paul aux Corinthiens* (Neuchâtel and Paris: Delachaux & Niestlé, 1957); Dupont, *Gnosis*, 105–148; Armand Delatte, *La catoptromancie grecque et ses dérivés* (Liége: Vaillant–Carmanne; Paris, Droz, 1932).

An Old Testament model seems to be provided by Num 12:8:[87]

פֶּה אֶל־פֶּה אֲדַבֶּר־בּוֹ
וּמַרְאֶה (ותמנת on gloss a as delete)
וְלֹא בְחִידֹת
וּתְמֻנַת יְהוָה יַבִּיט

στόμα κατὰ στόμα λαλήσω αὐτῷ,
ἐν εἴδει
καὶ οὐ δι' αἰνιγμάτων,
καὶ τὴν δόξαν κυρίου εἶδεν.

"With him I speak mouth to mouth,
clearly,
and not *in dark speech* [literally, enigmatically];
and he beholds the form of the Lord" (RSV).

(Cf. Ex 33:20). מַרְאָה, "clearly," could be pointed as מַרְאָה, "mirror."[88] Yet the reference to this passage takes us no further.[89]

In Greek literature[90] the mirror symbolizes (a) clarity;[91] (b) self–knowledge[92]—and this, too, in different variations: for the Stoa the world is the mirror of the deity, while the Platonic version is to be found in Plut., *Is. et Os.* 382a: inanimate things are an αἴνιγμα τοῦ θεοῦ, "enigma of god," whereas animate things are a clear mirror of them;[93] (c) indirectness of vision.[94]

It is unlikely that Paul is thinking of catoptromancy.[95]

All three motifs are easily transposable into Gnosticism.[96] Instructive, too, is the situation in neo–Platon-

---

The fact that Corinth was famous for its mirror–making has no bearing upon our understanding of the matter; see von Netoliczka, "κάτοπτρον," *Pauly-W.* 11:29–45.

87 Gerhard Kittel, *TDNT* 1:178–180, following Harnack, "Das hohe Lied" (n. 7 above).

88 Cf. the exegesis of the rabbis: Moses saw God in a clear (!) mirror, the prophets saw him in a dark one; thereby a reference is once made to this passage.

89 In Paul the mirror belongs to the side of the enigma. See Kümmel, *ad loc.*; Dupont, *Gnosis*, 146–148; Hoffmann, "Zu 1 Cor. 13" (n. 7 above), 68–71.

90 Hugedé, *La métaphore du miroir*, 97–137.

91 Plat., *Tim.* 72c; Plut., *Is. et Os.* 384a; Apul., *Apol.* 14.

92 See Spicq, *Agapé* 2:96, n. 1.

93 αἴνιγμα and mirror are antitheses.

94 Plat., *Tim.* 71b: ἐν κατόπτρῳ δεχομένῳ τύπους καὶ κατιδεῖν εἴδωλα παρέχοντι, "in a mirror which receives impressions and provides visible images" (Loeb 7:185). Philo, *Decal.* 105: ὡς γὰρ διὰ κατόπτρου φαντασιοῦνται ὁ νοῦς θεὸν δρῶντα καὶ κοσμοποιοῦντα καὶ τῶν ὅλων ἐπιτροπεύοντα, "For in it [the number seven], as in a mirror, the mind has a vision of God as acting and creating the world and controlling all that is" (Loeb 7:61). Sen., *Quaest. nat.* 1.15.7: *non est enim in speculo quod ostenditur*, "For what is revealed does not exist in a mirror" [Trans.]. For the controversy between the philosophical schools concerning the nature of mirror images, see Sen., *Quaest. nat.*, 1.5.1. This sense is presupposed also in Philo, *Leg. all.* 3.101: Moses wishes to see God in no other mirror than in himself.

95 Thus Samson Eitrem, *Orakel und Mysterien am Ausgang der Antike*, Albae Vigiliae, n.s. 5 (Zurich: Rhein, 1947). From this standpoint, he holds, it is possible to explain the conjunction of the figures of the child and the mirror: a child usually serves as a medium.

Against this explanation: the figure is explained by the rest of the material available for comparison, and there is no trace of allusion to manticism; Spicq, *Agapé* 2:96–104; Hugedé, *La métaphore du miroir*, 75–95.

96 *Od. Sal.* 13.1f: "Behold! the Lord is our mirror: Open your eyes and see them [your eyes] in Him; and learn the manner of your face" (Harris–Mingana 2:276). The legend of the pearl, *Act. Thom.* 112: ἐξαίφνης δὲ ἰδόντος μου τὴν ἐσθῆτα ὡς ἐν ἐσόπτρῳ ὁμοιωθεῖσαν καὶ ὅλον ἐμαυτὸν ἐπ' αὐτὴν ἐθιασάμην. καὶ ἔγνων καὶ εἶδον δι' αὐτῆς ἐμαυτόν, ὅτι κατὰ μέρος διῃρήμεθα ἐκ τοῦ αὐτοῦ ὄντες. καὶ πάλιν ἕν ἐσμεν διὰ μορφῆς μιᾶς, "But suddenly when I saw the robe made like [me] as though in a mirror, I also saw myself wholly in it. And I knew and saw myself through it, that we were divided in two, though of the same origin. And again we were one through one form" [Trans.]. The robe is the Gnostic Self; vision in the mirror is self–knowledge, i.e. the coming of the Gnostic to himself. Erwin Preuschen in *Handbuch zu den neutestamentlichen Apokryphen*, ed. Edgar Hennecke (Tübingen: J. C. B. Mohr [Paul Siebeck], 1904), 591, conjectures ὡσεὶ ἐσόπτρῳ μου ὁμοιωθεῖσαν. Preuschen, *Zwei gnostische Hymnen* (Giessen: Töpelmann, 1904), 24; G. Hoffmann, "Zwei Hymnen der Thomasakten," *ZNW* 4 (1903): 273–309. Syriac (Alfred Adam, *Die Psalmen des Thomas und das Perlenlied als Zeugnisse vorchristlicher Gnosis*, BZNW, 24 [Berlin: Töpelmann, 1959], 53): "as if I encountered my reflecting image."

ism,[97] where analogies to Gnosticism are to be noticed.[98]

In the light of Porphyry, Reitzenstein would offer the interpretation that the mirror is the πνεῦμα, "Spirit."[99] This is impossible. For Paul's point is the indirectness of our seeing, the antithesis between present and future knowledge, and the latter is fullness of vision;[100] cf. 2 Cor 3:18. This emerges at once in the antithesis of now and then, in the linking of figure and riddle: "ἐν αἰνί-γματι," "enigmatically."[101] A "pure" pedigree of the figure is not to be postulated at all.[102]

In comparison to Philo: for Philo the knowledge of God by the νοῦς, "mind," is imperfect; it provides no clear picture. The full *vision* of God is attained only on the "royal way," when the human νοῦς is expelled by the divine πνεῦμα, "Spirit." Paul, unlike Philo, is thinking not in mystical, but in eschatological terms. This also indicates the sense in the present context: even the charismatic does not attain the full vision of God in this world.[103] It is future.

For the expression πρόσωπον πρὸς πρόσωπον, "face to face," cf. Gen 32:31. The temporal distance between the present and the age of vision is further indicated by ἄρτι, "at present." Verse 12b explains the figure in terms of indirectness, equivalent to imperfection, which is now expressed by ἐκ μέρους, "fragmentarily"; cf. v 9.[104] ἐκ μέρους in turn is elucidated by the antithesis: "perfect" knowledge (see v 10) is knowledge καθὼς καὶ ἐπεγνώσθην, "even as I am known."[105] The tendency is antienthusiastic:[106] the passive of (ἐπι)-γινώσκειν, "know," contains the idea of electing grace

97 Here the mirror motif becomes systematically relevant (see Eltester, *Eikon*, 88f):

a) in the sense of an emanation: the mirror image is produced *direct* from the original, without a demiurge;

b) in the sense of a correction of the emanation: it exists *only* in connection with the original.

Porphyr., *Marc.* 13: ἐφ' ὅσον τις τὸ σῶμα ποθεῖ καὶ τὰ τοῦ σώματος σύμφιλα, ἐπὶ τοσοῦτον ἀγνοεῖ τὸν θεὸν καὶ τῆς ἐκείνου ἐνοράσεως ἑαυτὸν ἀπεσκότισε, κἂν παρὰ πᾶσι τοῖς ἀνθρώποις ὡς θεὸς δοξάζηται. σοφὸς δ' ἄνθρωπος ὀλίγος γινωσκόμενος, εἰ δὲ βούλει, καὶ ὑπὸ πάντων ἀγνοούμενος, γινώσκεται ὑπὸ θεοῦ. ἑπέσθω τοίνυν ὁ μὲν νοῦς τῷ θεῷ, ἐνοπτριζόμενος τῇ ὁμοιώσει θεοῦ, "To the extent that one longs for the body and the things congenial to the body, to that extent he is ignorant of God and has blinded himself to the sight of God, even though he be thought a god by all men. But the wise man, though known as lowly, or if you will, even unknown by all, is known by God. Let the mind therefore follow God, being reflected by the likeness of God" [Trans.]. Dupont, *Gnosis*, 124, translates the last phrase: "beholding as in a mirror the likeness of God"; André–Jean Festugière, *Trois dévots paiens* (Paris: La Colombe, 1944) 2:28: "Let the mind, then, attach itself to God, of whom it is, by likeness, as it were a reflection."

Iambl., *Myst.* 2.10: αὐτὰς μὲν οἱ θεοὶ καὶ οἱ τοῖς θεοῖς ἑπόμενοι τὰς ἀληθινὰς ἑαυτῶν εἰκόνας ἀποκαλύπτουσιν, φαντάσματα δ' αὐτῶν οἷα τὰ ἐν ὕδασιν ἢ ἐν κατόπτροις μεμηχανημένα οὐδαμῶς προτείνουσιν, "The gods and their followers disclose their true images, and in no way proffer the sort of phantoms of themselves that are produced by water or mirrors" [Trans.].

98 On the relationship of Neoplatonism and Gnosticism see Jonas, *Gnosis* 2.1.

99 For criticism see Dupont, *Gnosis*, 126f; Spicq, *Agapé* 2:98; Hugedé, *La métaphore du miroir*, 49–75.

100 Dupont, *Gnosis*, 133f, 146f; Rudolf Bultmann, "Gnosis [review of Dupont]," *JThSt*, n.s. 3 (1952): 10–26, here esp. 13f.

101 Hugedé, *La métaphore du miroir*, 139–150. Athen., *Deipnosoph.* 10.452a: Καλλισθένης ἐν ταῖς Ἑλληνικαῖς φησιν ὡς Ἀρκάδων πολιορκούντων Κρῶμνον ... Ἱππόδαμος ὁ Λάκων εἷς ὢν τῶν πολιορκουμένων διεκελεύετο τῷ παρὰ Λακεδαιμονίων πρὸς αὐτοὺς ἥκοντι κήρυκι, δηλῶν ἐν αἰνιγμῷ τὴν περὶ αὐτοὺς κατάστασιν ..., "Callisthenes in his *History of Greece*: 'When the Arcadians were besieging Cromnus ... Hippodamus the Spartan, one of the men under siege, made clear by a riddle to the herald who had come to them from the Spartans the state of affairs among the besieged ...'" (Loeb 4:549). ἐν αἰνιγμῷ, ἐν αἰνίγματι is a frequent phrase: "enigmatically." For this reason there is no sense of its lack of agreement with the figure.

102 Dupont, *Gnosis*, 111f, 147f, holds that Paul changes from knowing to seeing under the influence of the OT and finds the synthesis with the help of the Hellenistic figure of the mirror. That would be a complicated process. The influence of the OT is not present in this passage. "Seeing" belongs to the figure of the mirror itself.

103 Paul is himself a visionary (2 Cor 12:2ff). One is inclined to ask whether the time component was already given in Paul's Jewish school tradition.

104 It is precisely the pneumatic gnosis that is "fragmentary." In the context there is no question of human knowledge *in general*.

105 Namely, πρόσωπον πρὸς πρόσωπον, "face to face." For the vision of god in the mysteries see Reinhold Merkelbach, *Roman und Mysterium in der Antike* (Mu-

(see on 8:3). The rhetorical correspondence between active and passive[107] is in itself admirably suited to be an expression of mysticism and Gnosticism.[108] Yet the phrasing is not *in itself* mystic or Gnostic.

■ **13** The Triad: Faith—Hope—Love[109]

Reitzenstein would derive the triad from a fourfold formula of which he finds traces in Porphyr., *Marc.* 24: τέσσαρα στοιχεῖα μάλιστα κεκρατύνθω περὶ θεοῦ· πίστις, ἀλήθεια, ἔρως, ἐλπίς, "Four principles are above all to be upheld concerning God: faith, truth, love, hope."[110] Paul, he argues, has Christianized the formula by putting ἀγάπη in the place of ἔρως, and has removed the Gnostic element. This would admirably suit the tendency of the context.[111] But there are several difficulties:

a) The formula is older than the context; it stands already in 1 Thessalonians (see below); it is not polemical, but is propounded as a thesis, and the number three is not secondary.

b) The Gnostic evidence is late and in part clearly secondary.[112]

c) Paul already found in Judaism the beginnings of triadic constructions of this kind.[113]

d) In Paul himself we find loose combinations which can be regarded as preliminary stages, namely, combinations of πίστις/ἐλπίς and πίστις/ἀγάπη, "faith/hope" and "faith/love."[114] Yet Paul may have found the formula already in the Hellenistic community. At all events he uses it as a formula from the time of 1 Thessa-

---

106 Rudolf Bultmann, *TDNT* 1:710, observes that καθὼς καὶ ἐπεγνώσθην robs the "gnosis" of its Gnostic character, although Paul speaks of it in the first instance as a pneumatic capacity.

107 Philo, *Cher.* 115: ἀλλὰ νῦν ὅτε ζῶμεν ... γνωριζόμεθα μᾶλλον ἢ γνωρίζομεν, "Even now in this life, we are ... known rather than knowing" (Loeb 2:77)·

108 Norden, *Agnostos Theos*, 287; Bousset, *Kyrios Christos*, tr. John E. Steely (New York and Nashville: Abingdon, 1970), 89f [50f]; 50f; Nock–Festugière 1:27, n. 80; *Corp. Herm.* 10.15; Porphyr., *Marc.* 13 (n. 97 above).

109 Reitzenstein, *Historia Monachorum*, 100–102, 242–255; "Die Formel 'Glaube, Liebe, Hoffnung' bei Paulus," *NGG* (1916): 367–416; "Die Formel, 'Glaube, Liebe, Hoffnung' bei Paulus: Ein Nachwort," *NGG* (1917): 130–151; "Die Entstehung der Formel 'Glaube, Liebe, Hoffnung,' " *HZ* 116 (1916): 189–208; (against Reitzenstein) Adolf von Harnack "Über den Ursprung der Formel 'Glaube, Liebe, Hoffnung,' " *PreussJahrb* 164 (1916): 1–14, reprinted in his *Aus der Kriegs– und Friedensarbeit*, Reden und Aufsätze, n.s. 3 (Giessen: Töpelmann, 1916), 1–18; Peter Corssen, "Paulus und Porphyrios," *Sokrates* 7 (1919): 18–30; A. Brieger, *Die urchristliche Trias Glaube–Liebe–Hoffnung* (dissertation, Heidelberg, 1925); Willy Theiler, *Die Vorbereitung des Neuplatonismus*, Problemata, 1, 1 (Berlin: Weidmann, 1930), 148–153; Ernst von Dobschütz, "Zwei– und dreigliedrige Formeln: Ein Beitrag zur Vorgeschichte der Trinitätsformel," *JBL* 50 (1931): 117–147 (against the assumption of an original four–part formula); Spicq, *Agapé* 2:365–378; bibliography: Riesenfeld, "Étude bibliographique" (n. 25 above). Eugen Walter, *Glaube, Hoffnung und Liebe im Neuen Testament*, Leben aus dem Wort, 1 (Freiburg: Her-

der, ²1942).

110 In the explication, ἀλήθεια, "truth," is described by γινώσκειν, "knowing."

111 Further loci:
   a) Wilhelm Kroll, *De Oraculis Chaldaicis*, Breslauer philologische Abhandlungen, 7, 1 (Breslau: Koebner, 1894; Hildesheim: Olms, 1962), 74, line 24: πίστις, ἀλήθεια, ἔρως.
   b) Cl. Al., *Strom.* 3.69.3: γνῶσις, πίστις, ἀγάπη.
   c) *Untitled Gnostic Work* 348 (GCS, 45): love, hope, faith, knowledge, peace.
   d) *Ev. Phil.* 115 has four elements: πίστις, ἐλπίς, ἀγάπη, γνῶσις. More loosely *Act. Paul. et Thecl.* 17: ἐλπίς, πίστις, φόβος θεοῦ, γνῶσις σεμνότητος, ἀγάπη ἀληθείας—"hope, faith, fear of God, knowledge of propriety, love of truth"; *Ep. Ap.* 43(54); cf. also Hans Jonas, *The Gnostic Religion* (Boston: Beacon, ³1970), 89 (on Lidz., *Joh.*, 57).

112 The four–part formula in the *Gospel of Philip* is a Gnostic further development of the triad. Clement of Alexandria *replaces* ἐλπίς by γνῶσις in terms of his theology, and is thus not a witness to γνῶσις originally having had a place in the formula. The tendency to expansion is shown by the *Acts of Paul and Thecla* and the *Untitled Gnostic Work*.

113 *4 Macc.* 17.2, 4: πίστις—ἐλπίς—ὑπομονή (see on v 7).

114 Cf. esp. Gal 5:6, πίστις δι' ἀγάπης ἐνεργουμένη, "faith working through love"; this is developed by Paul: ἡμεῖς γὰρ πνεύματι ἐκ πίστεως ἐλπίδα δικαιοσύνης ἀπεκδεχόμεθα, "For through the Spirit, by faith, we wait for the *hope* of righteousness." πίστις and ἀγάπη: 1 Thess 3:6; see on 16:13f below; Phlm 5. Catalogues: Gal 5:22. πίστις and ἐλπίς: Gal 5:5.

lonians on: 1 Thess 1:3;[115] 5:8.[116] It is contained in Rom 5:3ff,[117] where it almost disappears behind the Pauline interpretation.

The order of sequence with ἐλπίς and ἀγάπη is free.[118] That *here* ἀγάπη comes at the end is determined by the context.

Nor is their bracketing together in the context by means of τὰ τρία ταῦτα, "these three," a polemical turn of phrase, but it appeals to the presupposed knowledge of the formula by the readers.[119]

For the further history of the triad cf. 1 Tim 6:11; 2 Tim 3:10; Eph 1:3ff, 15–18; Col 1:4f; Heb 10:22–24; *Barn.* 1.6.

It is not possible to arrive at an unequivocal interpretation of the statement *concerning* the three "remaining" factors. Are (a) νυνί, "now," (b) μένει, "remain," to be taken in a logical or a temporal sense? And if νυνί has a temporal sense, to what does it refer?

There are four possible combinations: νυνί, to be sure, considering the structure of the argument, is more likely to be taken in a logical sense,[120] despite Rom 3:21, where the temporal sense emerges from the context.[121] The sense of μένει is then still open: (a) logical: they "remain"—over against the spiritual gifts mentioned, (b) they remain to eternity. In favor of the eschatological interpretation is above all *3 Ezra* 4:38.[122] It makes excellent sense in the polemical context (of the abolition of the other spiritual gifts).[123] But it is difficult, because the whole chapter is built upon the fact that love alone remains. How are we to conceive the remaining of faith and hope, which are surely consummated?[124]

We must not postulate for Paul the unity of a strictly formal logic,[125] especially as both πίστις and also ἐλπίς contain elements which make it possible to say that both remain to eternity.[126] It is accordingly possible to take μένειν in an eschatological sense. To be sure, the difficulty is less when the word is taken in a logical sense as meaning "remain valid," namely, in relation to

---

115 Genitive combinations with varying senses of the genitives.

116 The three concepts, faith, love, hope, have only two corresponding pieces of armor. This shows that the triad is already fixed.

117 Here the order faith, hope, love is presupposed.

118 *If* a fixed order were supposed to have been prescribed, it would have been that of 1 Thess, i.e. with a closer bond between faith and love. But this remains conjecture.

119 For the expression cf. Prov 30:10, 21, 24, 29; Aristoph., *Nu.* 424; Plut., *Amic. mult.* 94b: ἡ ἀληθινὴ φιλία τρία ζητεῖ μάλιστα, τὴν ἀρετὴν ὡς καλόν, καὶ τὴν συνήθειαν ὡς ἡδύ, καὶ τὴν χρείαν ὡς ἀναγκαῖον, "True friendship seeks after three things above all else: virtue as a good thing, intimacy as a pleasant thing, and usefulness as a necessary thing" (Loeb 2:53). See Spicq, *Agapé* 2:105, n. 1.

120 12:18, 20; Rom 7:17; Heb 9:26. Lietzmann, Weiss, Robertson and Plummer. Spicq, *Agapé* 2:105f, takes νυνί and μένει closely together: v 13, he argues, is not the summing up of an independent text, but provides a pure transition with the sense that we do not "remain" in heaven, which Paul has just adjured, but in Corinth, under the conditions of the Christian life.

No conclusion can be drawn from the word form (νυνί or νῦν). Paul prefers νυνί δέ: Rom 3:21; 6:22; 7:6; 7:17; 15:23, 25; 1 Cor 13:13; 15:20; 2 Cor 8:11. νῦν is testified with certainty in 1 Cor 12:20; Phil 3:18; the evidence vacillates in 1 Cor 5:11; 7:14; 12:18; 14:6; Gal 4:9. As a rule we have νυνί

after an unreal condition. But it cannot be concluded from this that where there is no unreal condition there is not a logical significance (with Weiss, against Gustav Stählin, *TDNT* 4:1109). Stählin's interpretation is not clear: " 'But there remain,' in contrast to the things of earth which are transitory and imperfect, '[now and to eternity] faith, hope, love.' "

121 And despite 2 Cor 5:7; Rom 8:24f.

122 ἡ ἀλήθεια μένει καὶ ἰσχύει εἰς τὸν αἰῶνα, "Truth endures and is strong forever" (RSV). Cf. also 2 Cor 9:9. Joachim Jeremias, "Beobachtungen zu neutestamentlichen Stellen an Hand des neugefundenen griechischen Henoch–Textes," *ZNW* 38 (1939): 115–124, here esp. 122, points to 3:14 and *Eth. En.* 97.6 and adopts the interpretation: "still remain in the presence of God." Verse 8 tells against this (Kümmel); Spicq, *Agapé* 2:105, n. 1, says this interpretation aggravates the difficulty of the mention of faith and hope in this context.

123 It is supported by v 8: οὐδέποτε πίπτει, "never fails." For the contrast between μένειν and καταργεῖσθαι, "be destroyed," cf. 2 Cor 3:11. Yet the reference to this passage does not do away with the difficulties.

124 2 Cor 5:7: faith gives way to vision. And hope is provisional in Rom 8:24f.

125 2 Cor 9:9: righteousness remains to eternity.

126 Rudolf Bultmann, *TDNT* 2:530–533 (ἐλπίς); *TDNT* 6:221 (πίστις). πίστις contains an abiding element of distance; it is not a mystic union. ἐλπίς is also the humble recognition that "remains" in the relation to God also in the beyond. This remark

the other spiritual gifts.[127] In so doing the eschatological intention is by no means lost.[128] For indeed it does not depend on the sense of the *one* word μένει, but is contained in the context, in the contrast with the gifts that are transient (and have therefore to be evaluated accordingly).

Either way, the three "remaining" gifts are ones that cannot lead to pneumatic emancipation and self–edification. For faith and love are related to their object and existent only in this relationship, or rather *qua* this relationship. Faith is faith in . . ., love does not seek its own, and hope raises against fanaticism the eschatological reservation.

The logical significance of μένει also makes it easier to understand the corrective in v 13b. The latter shows once again the tension between the members of the already established triad[129] as well as Paul's intention of assigning the preeminence to love.[130] The balance is possible for him, because the three concepts are not so abstract that a theoretical order of merit could be set up. Faith operates, indeed, through love (Gal 5:6), etc. The preeminence of love can include the validity of faith and hope. It is only in this complexity that Paul can speak also of a "way." For this term really fits only for love.

---

of Bultmann's is better than Günther Bornkamm's explanation in *Early Christian Experience*, 187 (*Das Ende des Gesetzes*, 108f) that the message we believe and the promise in which we hope are eternal. Cf. Kümmel, 189: love is an attitude, hence in the case of faith and hope he must also be thinking of an attitude. Thus Bornkamm now also says, (*ibid.*) "In the coordination of faith and hope [not as a 'value' in itself], love also remains. If faith is based on what God has done and hope directs itself to what God will do, then love—from God, to God and thus simultaneously love toward the brother [cf. 1 John 4.7ff.]—is the permanent presence of salvation, the 'bond of perfection' (Col. 3.14). As such it is the greatest."

127 Cf. Rom 9:11 etc. Plato, *Crito* 48b (Socrates): ἀλλ' ὦ θαυμάσιε, οὗτός τε ὁ λόγος ὃν διεληλύθαμεν ἔμοιγε δοκεῖ ἔτι ὅμοιος εἶναι καὶ πρότερον· καὶ τόνδε αὖ σκόπει εἰ ἔτι μένει ὑμῖν ἢ οὔ, ὅτι οὐ τὸ ζῆν περὶ πλείστου ποιητέον ἀλλὰ τὸ εὖ ζῆν. (Crito) ἀλλὰ μένει. (Socrates) τὸ δὲ εὖ καὶ καλῶς καὶ δικαίως ὅτι ταὐτόν ἐστιν, μένει ἢ οὐ μένει; (Crito) μένει, " 'But my, friend, the argument we have just finished seems to me still much the same as before; and now see whether we still hold to this, or not [literally whether it remains valid for us, or not], that it is not living, but living well which we ought to consider most important.' [Crito:] 'We do so hold to it.'

[Socrates:] 'And that living well and living rightly are the same thing, do we hold to that, or not?' [Crito:] 'We do.' " (Loeb 1:169). Willem Grossouw, "L'espérance dans le Nouveau Testament," *RB* 61 (1954): 508–532, here esp. 516–518.

128 I am indebted to my pupil David Reeves for the suggestion (alluding to Rom 9:6–13) that we should not raise the alternative, either logical or eschatological; "instead, μένειν seems to be Paul's verb for a subject which is of excellent quality and, therefore, is able to stand the test of time."

129 If it were to be taken over by Paul along with the motif of μένειν, then μένειν would presumably originally have been meant eschatologically (as *3 Ezra* 4:38) and been reinterpreted by Paul logically. Weiss holds that μένειν is meant eschatologically and really applies only to love. Paul is subject to the constraint of the triad; he must correct it by means of this addition.

130 Cf. the subordination of believing and hoping (verbs) to love in v 7.

14

Tongues and Prophecy

1 Aim at love! Strive for the spiritual gifts,
but especially that of prophesying!
2 / For the man who speaks with tongues
speaks not for men, but for God; for
no one understands him,[1] but he speaks
mysteries in the Spirit. 3 / The man
who prophesies, however, speaks for
men's edification, exhortation and
encouragement. 4 / The man who speaks
with tongues edifies himself, the man
who prophesies edifies the church.
5 / I wish you would all speak with
tongues, but still more that[2] you would
prophesy. For the man who prophesies
is greater than the man who speaks
with tongues, unless[3] he (sc. the
speaker) interprets, so that the church
may receive edification. 6 / But now,
brothers, if I come to you and speak
with tongues, what good shall I do you,
if I do not speak to you with[4] revelation
or knowledge or prophecy or teaching? 7 / For when inanimate things
produce a sound (or: So, too, with
inanimate things that produce a sound[5]),
flute or lyre, how is the tune that is
blown or played to be understood, if its
notes cannot be distinguished? 8 / And if
the bugle gives an unclear sound, who
will prepare for battle? 9 / So it is
also with you: if you do not utter plain
words with your tongue, how are people
to understand what you have said?
Then you are talking into the air.
10 / There are so many (or: who knows
how[6] many) languages[7] in the world,

---

1   Gen 42:23; Mt 13:13; Epict., *Diss.* 1.29.66; Bauer, *s.v.* ἀκούω.

2   The change from accusative+infinitive to ἵνα makes no difference to the meaning.

3   ἐκτὸς εἰ and εἰ μή have been amalgamated; Hellenistic, see Blass–Debrunner §376.

4   "Armed with" (4:21) or "in the form of."

5   ὅμως, "nevertheless," is difficult, since it is not immediately apparent where an antithesis should lie. Lietzmann explains: τὰ ἄψυχα, καίπερ φωνὴν διδόντα, ὅμως οὐ γνωσθήσεται, ἐὰν διαστολὴν μὴ δῶ, "inanimate things, though producing a sound, are nevertheless not understood unless they make a distinction" (cf. Xenoph., *Cyrop.* 5.1.26: σὺν μὲν σοὶ ὅμως καὶ ἐν τῇ πολεμίᾳ ὄντες θαρροῦμεν, "so that with you we are not afraid even in the enemy's land" [Loeb 2:17]); ὅμως, he says, has been put at the beginning as in Gal 3:15. In this way the correct antithesis does in fact appear: though sounding, nevertheless unintelligible (not: though inanimate, nevertheless sounding). There are other explanations. The old word ὁμῶς, "likewise," has brought

its influence to bear, cf. Ps.–Cl. *Hom.* 3.15.3; 19.23.1; Blass–Debrunner §450(2); Joachim Jeremias, "'Ὅμως," *ZNW* 52 (1961): 127f. Rudolf Keydell, "'Ὅμως," *ZNW* 54 (1963): 145f, refers to Agathias, *Hist.* 3.23: the general Martinus reads out a fictitious letter from the Emperor announcing reinforcements. The desired effect upon the soldiers ensues. Then (24): ἀπέβη δὲ ὁμῶς καὶ θάτερον τῶν Μαρτίνου διανοημάτων, "But Martinus' other purpose was *likewise* also realized": the Persians, too, were deceived.

6   εἰ τύχοι has become a stock phrase: "perchance," cf. 15:37; Blass–Debrunner §385(2). For the second meaning cf. Nicholas of Damascus in Jacoby, *FGH* 2A:413, line 27 (90 fr. 130): καθ' ἣν τύχοι πρόφασιν, "under who knows what sort of pretext" (Bauer, *s.v.* τυγχάνω 2b).

7   This meaning of φωνή is indeed classical. LXX: Gen 11:1; 2 Macc. 7:8 etc. *PGM* 12.188: πᾶσα γλῶσσα καὶ πᾶσα φωνή, "every tongue and every language."

and there is nothing that has no language.[8] **11 /** If, then, I do not know the meaning of the language, then I shall be a foreigner to the speaker, and the speaker will be a foreigner to me. **12 /** So it is also with you: since you are eager for spirits, then seek to be rich in them for the edification of the church! **13 /** So let the man who speaks with tongues pray that[9] he may also be able to interpret. **14 /** For if I pray in tongues, then my spirit is praying; but my understanding is barren. **15 /** What is the conclusion from this?[10] I will pray with my spirit, but I will pray also with my understanding. I will sing with my spirit, but I will sing also with my understanding. **16 /** If you utter your praises in the spirit, how is the person in a layman's position to say Amen to your prayer? For of course he does not know what you are saying. **17 /** You may indeed be saying a fine prayer; but the other is not edified. **18 /** I thank God I speak in tongues more than any of you. **19 /** But in the church I would rather speak five words with my understanding, so as to instruct others also, than ten thousand words in tongues.

However sharply outlined the *theme* of chap. 14, the *argument* is loose.

■ **1** The transition is harsh, and is not uniform in itself. ζηλοῦτε κτλ., "strive for, etc.," links up with 12:30,[11] and is not in harmony with v 1a, which links up with 13:13.[12] In the present context a unified line of thought can be discovered only with difficulty, namely, that the order of precedence which the following verses ascribe to the gifts is valid on the basis of chap. 13. Within chap. 14, however, there is no trace of this. The tenor is now different: no longer a *critique* of πνευματικά, "spiritual gifts," in general,[13] but their *classification*, in the context of the actual state of affairs in Corinth. Now it is only speaking with tongues and prophecy that are discussed as spiritual gifts. The criterion is no longer ἀγάπη, "love," but οἰκοδομή, "edification, upbuilding." From this there emerges a latent criticism, as is already indicated by the phrasing of v 1b. The presupposition is that in Corinth prophecy does not stand at the head of the list, but ranks after speaking with tongues. Thus the gifts are evaluated in Corinth according to the intensity of the ecstatic outburst; in fact, even according to the degree

---

8   καὶ οὐδέν: the expression is careless; we have to supply something like ἔθνος—"there is no nation." It is easiest to supply γένος (φωνῶν)—"there is no kind (of language)"; but this does not fit.

9   προσεύχεσθαι ἵνα: Blass–Debrunner §392(1c).

10 Cf. v 26; the classical forms are τί οὖν; (Rom 3:9; 6:15; 11:7) and τί γάρ;

11 Is 12:31 (see *ad loc.*) a secondary bracket, or is 14:1 simply a repetition of 12:31?

12 δέ is certainly harsh. Weiss observes that v 1 is a "very insipid" connection. But we should not say that διώκειν, "aim at," is a weakened metaphor for ζητεῖν, φρονεῖν, "strive after, set one's mind on"; cf.

Rom 12:13; 14:19; 9:30f. Taken in itself, v 1b is a genuine appeal; 1 Thess 5:20. Héring observes that as a result of the editorial connecting link provided by v 1a the sense of μᾶλλον is modified: originally it was comparative (cf. v 5), but now it means "especially."

13 Paul no longer says "χαρίσματα."

of unintelligibility. The latter is considered to be an indication of the working of supernatural power. Paul's evaluation is the reverse, not on the ground of rationality as such, but because the intelligibility of what is said is a condition of the internal and external upbuilding of the community.

■ **2** We learn that speaking with tongues is unintelligible to a normal man, even a Christian. On the other hand it must be meaningful, must be logical in itself. For it can be translated into normal language, which is again made possible by a special gift. The designation γλῶσσαι, "tongues," tells us nothing about the phenomenon.[14] If we would explain it, then we must set out from comparable material in the history of religion, above all from the Greek motif of the inspiring πνεῦμα, which is expressed especially in Mantic sources,[15] and is bound up more particularly with Delphi.[16] The deity speaks out of the inspired man's mouth; he himself does not know what he is saying. In Delphi the priests interpret the Pythia's babblings.[17]

A higher level of anthropological reflection is reached by Philo: the πνεῦμα, "Spirit," expels the νοῦς, "mind," and leads to the vision of God.[18]

Unlike the Greek theory, Paul's opinion is not that what is said in tongues is unintelligible to the speaker himself. But like the Greeks, he is of the opinion that it can be translated into human language. To be sure, the Pythia speaks, full of the God, to men. The speaker with tongues, on the other hand, addresses himself in the first instance to God, and it is only through mediation—his own or that of another (see below)—that he speaks to men. Paul allows the validity of speaking with tongues, but sets a lower value on it than on prophecy, because it is of service only to the inspired man himself: no one "hears," i.e., understands him.[19] λαλεῖν μυστήρια, "speak mysteries": see 2:7, where, to be sure, the sense is different, namely, Wisdom teaching, which presupposes the possession of the Spirit both by the speaker and also by the hearer.

■ **3** Verse 3 brings the decisive criterion: οἰκοδομή/ οἰκοδομεῖν, "edification/edify." The accent is plain: θεῷ—ἀνθρώποις, "for God—for men." The working ascribed to prophecy makes plain that it is not the foretelling of the future. This is later confirmed (see v 24).[20] The nature of "edification" is explained by combining it with παράκλησις and παραμυθία. παράκλησις

---

14 γλῶσσα can denote among other things (see Johannes Behm, *TDNT* 1:719f) an obsolete foreign mode of expression: Diod. S., *Bibl. hist.* 4.66.6; Plut., *Is. et Os.* 375f. But this meaning does not bring us to the phenomenon of speaking with tongues.

15 Heracl., *Fr.* 92: Σίβυλλα δὲ μαινομένῳ στόματι ... ἀγέλαστα καὶ ἀκαλλώπιστα καὶ ἀμύριστα φθεγγομένη χιλίων ἐτῶν ἐξικνεῖται τῇ φωνῇ διὰ τὸν θεόν, "The Sybil with raving mouth uttering her unlaughing, unadorned, unincensed words reaches out over a thousand years with her voice, through the (inspiration of the) god" (Freeman, *Ancilla*, 31). Divination and prophecy: Plat., *Tim.* 71f. The Gnostic hears supernatural voices of δυνάμεις in *Corp. Herm.* 1.26. Literature: excursus in Weiss and in Lietzmann; Heinrich Weinel, *Die Wirkungen des Geistes und der Geister* (Freiburg, Leipzig, and Tübingen: J. C. B. Mohr [Paul Siebeck], 1899); Eddison Mosiman, *Das Zungenreden* (Tübingen: J. C. B. Mohr [Paul Siebeck], 1911); Hans Rust, *Das Zungenreden*, Grenzfragen des Nerven– und Seelenlebens, 118 (Munich: Bergmann, 1924); Goro Mayeda, *Le langage et l'évangile* (Geneva: Labor et Fides, 1948), 87–96; Frank W. Beare, "Speaking with Tongues: A Critical Survey of the New Testament Evidence," *JBL* 83 (1964): 229–246; Rohde, *Psyche*, index, *s.v.* ἔκστασις; Nilsson, *Geschichte*, index, *s.vv. Ekstase*,

Mantik; Behm, *TDNT* 1:719–727; Hermann Kleinknecht, *TDNT* 6:345–352.

16 Plutarch. Kleinknecht, *TDNT* 6:345, believes speaking with tongues to be "a reflection of Pythian divinization"; likewise Samson Eitrem, *Orakel und Mysterien am Ausgang der Antike*, Albae Vigiliae, n.s. 5 (Zurich: Rhein, 1947), 42. Not so Gerhard Delling, *Worship in the New Testament*, tr. Percy Scott (Philadelphia: Westminster, 1962), 31–41 (*Der Gottesdienst im Neuen Testament* [Göttingen: Vandenhoeck & Ruprecht, 1952], 39–49), who makes the comparison with Dionysiac enthusiasm. But the dispute concerning the parallels is superfluous. The important point is merely the presence and wide diffusion of phenomena of this kind, which arise sporadically and spontaneously, cf. e.g. Luc., *Alex.* 13 (on this, Hans Dieter Betz, *Lukian von Samosata und das Neue Testament*, TU, 76 [Berlin: Akademie–Verlag, 1961], 140f).

17 From this Plato (*Phaedr.* 244) develops the role of the philosopher as interpreter.

18 Philo, *Rer. div. her.* 265, etc.; Jonas, *Gnosis* 2.1:99–121.

19 Accoustically speaking, as the rest of the argument emphatically shows, he is of course heard very well, as a clanging gong (13:1) when love or, as chap. 14 has it, οἰκοδομή is missing.

20 Origen (in Claude Jenkins, "Origen on I Corinthians," *JThSt*, o.s. 10 [1909]: 29–51, here esp. 36)

can mean comfort or exhortation, and it is much the same also with παραμυθία. The two terms are here practically synonymous.[21]

■ **4** This further stresses the emphasis of v 3: the antithesis "speaking to God—to men" is applied to mean "for himself—for the church." Here, too, we have to think of the Corinthians' individualism as the butt of Paul's attack.

■ **5** Here Paul applies the criterion: he allows them[22] their speaking with tongues,[23] but elucidates the evaluation he has already given. The fact that prophecy stands higher is grounded by the foregoing argument, though now, to be sure, it is again subjected to reservation. This is as it should be. For indeed Paul gives the preeminence to prophecy not because of the phenomenon itself, nor on the ground of norms imported from without, but solely because of its value toward edification. In this respect speaking with tongues *can* also be equally valuable— when it is interpreted,[24] and thus acquires the same function as prophecy.

Lietzmann finds a contradiction to 12:29f: there, he says, the gifts of speaking with tongues and of interpreting are assigned to different pneumatics, whereas here it is assumed that the speaker with tongues himself supplies the interpretation.[25] But there Paul says only that not all Christians have all gifts, not that each can have only *one* gift.[26]

■ **6** νῦν δέ, "but now," is to be taken in a logical sense,[27] not a temporal one.[28] The use of the first person is rhetorical; it serves, in diatribe style, by way of illustration.[29] Yet it may also contain a hint that Paul actually could appear on the scene as one who speaks with tongues.[30]

■ **7–11** These verses bring a series of examples (not figures) of intelligibility and unintelligibility: a melody (7), a signal (8), plus application (9); then language (understanding) (10f) plus application.[31] ἄψυχος, "inanimate," is used of musical instruments also elsewhere.[32]

---

systematizes as follows: προφητεία ἐστὶν ἡ διὰ λόγου τῶν ἀφανῶν σημαντικὴ γνῶσις ... διδαχή ἐστιν ὁ εἰς τοὺς πολλοὺς διανεμόμενος διδασκαλικὸς λόγος, "Prophecy is meaningful knowledge of unseen things through speech ... teaching is the instructive word spread abroad to many." ἀποκάλυψις and γνῶσις are thus the gifts that express themselves in prophecy and teaching.

21 Cf. 1 Thess 2:11f. For παράκλησις Bauer prefers the meaning "exhortation." The meaning "comfort" is rare in secular Greek; not so the LXX; Jer 16:7; Hos 13:14; 2 Cor 1:4ff; Epict., *Diss.* 3.23.28. παραμυθία/παραμυθέομαι denotes friendly encouragement, comfort; Ps.-Plat., *Ax.* 365a; Plat., *Phaed.* 83a; *Critias* 108c alongside παραθαρρύνειν; Aesch., *Prom.* 1063 alongside πείθειν. A certain distinction in the use of the two word groups emerges in the fact that παραμυθία is not used in the NT of God's comfort, whereas παράκλησις is (2 Cor 1:3; 1 Thess 2:11f); see Gustav Stählin, *TDNT* 5:816–823. For ancient designations of comfort see Karl Buresch, "Consolationum a Graecis Romanisque scriptarum historia critica," *Leipziger Studien zur classischen Philologie* 9 (1887): 1–170, here esp. 123–125.

22 Cf. v 18; θέλω, "I wish": 7:7.

23 He is himself a speaker with tongues, v 18.

24 12:10; there the gift of interpretation is itself a χάρισμα.

25 According to Héring, the subject of διερμενεύῃ, "he interprets," is not the speaker with tongues but a "someone." Against this translation, Heinrici.

26 See on v 13, and on vv 26–27.

27 Weiss, Lietzmann, Bachmann.

28 Robertson and Plummer; they refer it to the impending visit. Weiss finds νῦν δέ "here even more unintelligible than in 13:13; for there is no preceding unreal condition or negative clause." He asks if lines have been transposed. νῦν δέ, he says, refers back to v 5a; v 5b goes together with v 4 and finds a good continuation in v 7, while vv 5b and 6 fit in better with the argument of vv 12–19. If, he goes on, v 6 is in its proper place, then its content in relation to vv 2–5 states a consequence (see Heinrici: "In that case however"); but this, he holds, νῦν δέ cannot mean.

29 Weiss finds that the logic of the second conditional clause is not entirely unexceptionable: we have to supply "instead of that." It is true that ἐὰν μὴ κτλ., "if I do not, etc.," depends on ὠφελήσω, "what good shall I do?" and does not by any means stand parallel to ἐὰν ἔλθω, "if I come"; yet the logic is in order: for indeed Paul is not rejecting speaking with tongues as such, but only the isolated phenomenon unaccompanied by intelligible language.

30 In 2 Cor 12:1, 7 the ἀποκάλυψις, "revelation," is ecstatic; here, on the contrary, it belongs to speaking ἐν νοΐ, "in one's senses"; Albrecht Oepke, *TDNT* 3:585; Lührmann, *Offenbarungsverständnis*, 39–44. Incidentally, 2 Cor 12 is the oldest evidence for the meaning "vision."

31 Heinrici and others understand v 9 to be a further example, and vv 7–11 thus to be an uninterrupted series (the analogies building up a climax).

32 Eur., *Ion* 881f (the seven-voiced lyre, ἑπτάφθογγος

■ **9** The application to speaking with tongues is presented.[33] The mode of expression is awkward: for to speak in tongues intelligibly is a contradiction in itself. But in the context it is clear what Paul means: if the interpretation is not added,[34] it is speaking into the air[35] —a proverbial phrase.[36]

■ **10–11** The multiplicity of languages is understandably enough a much–discussed theme in literature.[37] Paul would have chosen the word φωνή to designate language, because γλῶσσα has already another meaning in the context.[38] Is γένη φωνῶν, "kinds of languages,"

formulated on the lines of γένη γλωσσῶν, "kinds of tongues"?[39] ἄφωνος here means "void of language."[40]

Verse 11 is a comparison, not a description of speaking with tongues. It is idle to ask whether οὖν, "then," refers to v 10a or 10b; for the thought of v 10 is unified. δύναμις: "meaning."[41] ἔσομαι κτλ., "I shall be, etc.": the Vulgate turns it the other way round: *cui loquor*, "the man to whom I speak." ἐν ἐμοί: "in my eyes";[42] cf. 6:2. The passage is an excellent piece of evidence for the basic meaning of βάρβαρος, "foreigner," lit. "gibberish talker."[43]

κιθάρα); Plut., *Lib. educ.* 9c.

The flute is played at the symposium by professional flute–girls. It is the accompanying instrument in tragedy and comedy; for flute and lyre cf. the pictorial representation of the flute–player Marsyas and the lyre–player Apollo. Literature: Pauly–W. under the pertinent terms; Curt Sachs, *The History of Musical Instruments* (New York: Norton, 1940) (*Musik des Altertums* [Breslau: Hirt, 1924]); Max Wegner, *Das Musikleben der Griechen* (Berlin: De Gruyter, 1949); Friedrich Behn, *Musikleben im Altertum und frühen Mittelalter* (Stuttgart: Hiersemann, 1954); Thrasybulos Georgiades, *Musik und Rhythmus bei den Griechen* (Hamburg: Rowohlt, 1958).

φωνή of instruments is general; in the Bible, *3 Ezra* 5:63.

φθόγγος: Plat., *Leg.* 812d; M. Aur. Ant., *Medit.* 11.2: ᾠδῆς ἐπιτερποῦς . . . καταφρονήσεις, ἐὰν τὴν μὲν ἐμμελῆ φωνὴν καταμερίσῃς εἰς ἕκαστον τῶν φθόγγων . . ., "Thou wilt think but meanly of charming songs . . . if thou analyze the melodious utterance into its several notes . . ." (Loeb, 295). The σάλπιγξ, "bugle," is the signal instrument, see on 15:52; as a musical instrument ("trumpet") Rev 18:22. Gerhard Friedrich, *TDNT* 7:71–88. For ἄδηλον, "unclear," cf. the antithesis εὔσημον, "plain," in v 9. πόλεμος, "battle," 1 Macc. 2:41.

33 Weiss, Lietzmann. The "tongue" is here the organ of speech. Weiss observes that in order to avoid confusion with "tongues" in the technical sense, Paul puts διά in place of ἐν and adds the article, which is regularly omitted in the case of speaking "with tongues." Bachmann and Heinrici take v 9 not as the application but as a third illustration of unclear speech, because of διά and the article; οὕτως, they argue, places it in *one* line with the foregoing illustrations.

34 λόγον διδόναι, "utter words"; cf. φωνὴν διδόναι, v 8. εὔσημος, "plain" (with λόγος, Artemid., *Oneirocr.* 2.44): cf. ἄσημος, Plut., *Ser. num. pun.* 564b: φωνὰς ἵεσαν ἀσήμους οἷον ἀλαλαγμοῖς θρήνου καὶ φόβου μεμιγμένας, They "uttered inarticulate sounds,

mingled with outcries as of lamentation and terror" (Loeb 7:275). Luc., *Alex.* 13: ὁ δὲ φωνάς τινας ἀσήμους φθεγγόμενος, οἷα γένοιντο ἂν Ἑβραίων ἢ Φοινίκων, ἐξέπληττε τοὺς ἀνθρώπους . . ., "Uttering a few meaningless words like Hebrew or Phoenician, he dazed the creatures . . ." (Loeb 4:193).

35 Periphrastic conjugation; 2 Cor 2:17; 9:12.

36 Instances in A. Otto, *Die Sprichwörter und sprichwörtlichen Redensarten der Römer* (Leipzig: Teubner, 1890), 364; Ovid., *Am.* 1.6.42: *dare verba in ventos*, "talk to the winds." Bachmann holds that εἰς ἀέρα λαλεῖν, "talk into the air," does not suit speaking with tongues, since the latter is after all a form of speaking with God. But *here* it is of course merely a question of the reference to the community, of edification; cf. v 2: οὐκ ἀνθρώποις λαλεῖ ἀλλὰ θεῷ, "he speaks not for men, but for God."

37 Arno Borst, *Der Turmbau von Babel*, vol. 1 (Stuttgart: Hiersemann, 1957).

38 Wholly different Xenoph., *Mem.* 1.4.12: only the tongue of man can ἀρθροῦν τε τὴν φωνὴν καὶ σημαίνειν πάντα ἀλλήλοις ἃ βουλόμεθα, "articulate the voice and express all our wants to one another" (Loeb, 61).

39 Bachmann is too subtle when he says that the languages divide up into different kinds inasmuch as each embraces different dialects. But Paul means simply that there is a great variety of languages.

40 Paronomasia with φωνή. Many commentators interpret ἄφωνος in the light of v 11 as "unintelligible." But the unintelligibility does not arise until the next sentence. The phrase καὶ οὐδὲν ἄφωνον merely underlines τοσαῦτα . . . .

41 Plat., *Crat.* 394b; instances in Bauer.

42 Soph., *Oed. Col.* 1214: "in my judgment."

43 Rom 1:14; Col 3:11; Aristoph., *Av.* 199f: The hoopoe has taught the birds to understand the language of men, ἐγὼ γὰρ αὐτοὺς βαρβάρους ὄντας πρὸ τοῦ ἐδίδαξα τὴν φωνήν, "For I have taught them the language, before which they were barbarians" (cf. Loeb 2:147). On this the scholion comments: ἀντὶ τοῦ ἀφώνους ἢ ἀνηκόους ἀνθρώπων καὶ μὴ εἰδότας

■ **12** The application of the examples to the *phenomena* is followed by their application to the Spirit–inspired *church*.[44] ἐπεὶ ζηλωταί κτλ., "since you are eager, etc.": cf. v 1, ζηλοῦτε, "strive."[45] πνευμάτων, "spirits," here stands for πνευματικῶν, "spiritual gifts."[46] Where does the emphasis lie? Does Paul mean: "Strive for spiritual gifts, that the church may be edified by them" (Lietzmann); or: "Strive for the edification of the church, that is, not self–edification" (Weiss)? In the context οἰκοδομή, "edification," is the critical principle, namely, the community principle. We have accordingly to adopt the second interpretation.[47]

■ **13–19** These verses elucidate the principle laid down in v 12.[48] Here it becomes completely clear that the accent there lies on πρὸς τὴν οἰκοδομήν, "with a view to edification." The gift of interpretation is itself a charisma (12:10), hence an object of prayer—and this, too, on the part of the speaker with tongues himself (see v 5). The prayer is here not ecstatic, but conscious prayer.[49]

■ **14** Is γάρ, "for," part of the original text?[50] The important thing is the contrast between πνεῦμα/state of ecstasy and νοῦς, "mind." Here Paul is taking over existing views of inspiration,[51] but he subjects them to criticism by setting νοῦς above ecstasy—relatively, in the same sense as he sets prophecy above speaking with tongues. The "spirit" is subordinated to a rational, theological judgment.

■ **15** Verse 15 paves the way for this. To begin with it is only stated that in the case of ecstatic prayer the νοῦς is ἄκαρπος, "barren," which, in view of προσεύξομαι νοΐ, "I will pray with my understanding," means unoccupied, and hence unfruitful for the edification of the

---

τὴν φωνήν, "Instead of 'inarticulate or deaf toward men and ignorant of their language.' " Ovid., *Trist.* 5.10.37, on his relationship to the natives of Tomis, his place of exile: *barbarus hic ego sum, qui non intelligor ulli,* "Here I am a barbarian, understood by nobody" (cf. Loeb, 249). Strabo, *Geog.* 14.661f. Julius Jüthner, *Hellenen und Barbaren,* Das Erbe der Alten, 2, 8 (Leipzig: Dieterich, 1924); Hans Windisch, *TDNT* 1:546–553; Harald Riesenfeld, "Accouplements de termes contradictoires dans le Nouveau Testament," *CN* 9 (1944): 1–21.

44 Weiss observes that οὕτως καὶ ὑμεῖς, "so it is also with you," presupposes that it has previously been said of someone else that he strives after charismata which serve edification;·which, he goes on, was the case in vv 5a, 6. This is surely too subtle an observation. Verse 12 is immediately understandable as a piece of application.

45 See on 12:31. ζηλωτής of the relationship of a disciple: Epict., *Diss.* 1.19.6, etc.

46 There is not necessarily any animistic idea behind the plural πνεύματα, such as is assumed by Lietzmann: "as if it were each man's wish that a πνεῦμα [προφητικόν] would take up its abode in him as a separate supernatural being." There is certainly a glimpse of an animistic background here and there, cf. v 32. But the animistic idea never actually becomes realistic. The plural is explained simply as a reference to the multiplicity of workings.

47 Robertson and Plummer: "Let it be for the edifying of the Church that ye seek to abound." περισσεύειν: see on 8:8; 15:58; Rom 15:13; 2 Cor 1:5; 3:9; 4:15;

8:7; 9:8; 1 Thess 3:12; 4:1, 10. Cf. also the "growth" of 2 Cor 10:15, and the προκοπή, "progress," of Phil 1:25. For the notion of the "movement" of faith cf. Phil 3:12–14.

48 According to Weiss the connection by means of διό is an unhappy one: οὖν would be better, since of course it is being explained how one can περισσεύειν πρὸς τὴν οἰκοδομήν, "be rich for the edification (of the church)." This is in itself correct; but we have always to reckon with a loose use of particles in Paul. The logical strictness of classical usage is no more.

49 Verse 14 is no objection to this; there Paul's topic is precisely the different forms of prayer. A certain synthesis is found in Rom 8; 8:26 describes ecstatic prayer in tongues, but according to vv 15f the Spirit works also the understandable cry of prayer to the "Father."

50 Omitted in p[46] B G. Weiss finds again that γάρ is out of place: "Paul is thinking very fast." Just so; that deserves more attention than formal logic; see n. 48 above.

51 Philo, *Rer. div. her.* 265; *Spec. leg.* 1.65; 4.49; Lucan, *Bell. civ.* 5.161–197: the spirit of Apollo expels the soul of the Pythia and dwells in her instead of it. Reitzenstein, *Hellenistische Mysterienreligionen,* 308–333.

church.[52] Prayer[53] and psalm–singing, as parts of the service of worship, were taken over from the synagogue.[54] The future tenses are best taken with Weiss neither in a purely temporal nor a purely logical sense, but as loosely as in v 5a. θέλω, "I should like."[55] The fact that the statements on praying and singing (a) in the Spirit, (b) with full consciousness, are set side by side gives expression to the theological relativization of the momentary state of the man in question: if v 14 paved the way for the relative preeminence of the νοῦς, it is nevertheless made plain that the preeminence is only relative. The *ratio* does not as such become a theological value. Above all it is not itself the principle of knowledge.[56] The criterion is still, as before, the contribution to edification.[57] The sequence corresponds to the situation of

the discussion: the πνεῦμα is recognized in Corinth, whereas the validity of the νοῦς has still to be brought out.

■ **16** Having in v 15 established the rightness of praying and singing both in a state of ecstasy and in one of full consciousness, Paul now once more discusses the preeminence of the νοῦς. εὐλογεῖν is, like προσεύχεσθαι, a term belonging to the liturgical language of Hellenistic Judaism,[58] as is also εὐχαριστεῖν.[59] Both word groups are used in a practically synonymous sense.[60] We cannot argue from the choice of words to different forms of prayer.[61] The proof is adduced from the effect of ecstatic prayer upon the ἰδιώτης:[62] the noninitiated; this means either the hearer who is not seized by ecstasy (Lietzmann) or the non-Christian participant or cate-

52 Schlatter observes that in contrast to Hellenism Paul sees in the absence of the understanding not an enhanced spirituality but a defect. This means the rejection of enthusiasm. The human subject is not extinguished. This is correct. Only, we must not oversimplify the antithesis to the Greek world or to Hellenism. Enthusiasm is only *one* current. In philosophy the rationalistic tradition is asserted. Paul, of course, is not a rationalist either.

53 Instead of the first προσεύξομαι, ℵ A D G have -ξωμαι; instead of the second προσεύξομαι, A D G have -ξωμαι. The confusion of future indicative and aorist subjunctive has advanced rather a long way as compared with the classical language, see Blass–Debrunner §363.

54 προσεύχομαι in the LXX is usually a translation of הִתְפַּלֵּל; the compound form begins to supplant the simple εὔχομαι which is more frequent in secular Greek; Heinrich Greeven, *TDNT* 2:800–808. ψάλλω usually stands for זָמַר, also for נִגֵּן. For τῷ νοΐ we have only a seeming parallel in 1QS X, 9: אזמרה בדעת; the latter means the art of the practised singer (cf. דעת in Ex 31:3); Braun, *Qumran* 1:195.

55 Weiss, 329, goes on to say that the first clause has a "concessive air": I may—but I should like also.

56 Paul is not constructing a systematic anthropology. Anything of this kind would necessarily make a specific human state the presupposition of salvation, and would thus not be in keeping with the understanding of faith. The ontological structures of human nature are neutral as far as salvation is concerned.

57 Bachmann, 413, shifts the accent under the impression of the context: in both double sentences, he says, the first clause expresses the presupposition "on which the second is asserted as one that is then valid

and ought to be valid." The fact is rather that the two clauses stand side by side on equal terms: δὲ καί.

58 The word is hardly ever used in a religious sense in secular Greek. In the LXX the word group εὐλογ– is almost exclusively a translation of ברך; frequent in Philo: *Leg. all.* 1.18; *Migr. Abr.* 70; *Plant.* 135; Jos., *Ant.* 4.318, etc. Hermann W. Beyer, *TDNT* 2:754–765.

59 See the excursus to 11:25. In the writings of the Hebrew canon the word group is not found (except in the unimportant passage Prov 11:16). Aquila renders תּוֹרָה by εὐχαριστία. The word group is frequent in Philo.

60 Compare 1 Cor 11:24 (εὐχαριστήσας) with Mk 14:22 (blessing of the bread, εὐλογήσας); Lk 22:19 (εὐχαριστήσας); Mk 14:23 (blessing of the cup, εὐχαριστήσας, with which cf. 1 Cor 10:16, τὸ ποτήριον τῆς εὐλογίας); *Did.* 9:1–3 (εὐχαριστεῖν); further the different forms of the Synoptic and Johannine feeding narrative(s); in Paul the alternation between εὐχαριστεῖν and εὐλογητός in the proemium (2 Cor 1:3; cf. Eph 1:3; 1 Pet 1:3); compare Rev 4:9 with 7:12. For the synonymity see Jean-Paul Audet, *La Didaché*, Études bibliques (Paris: Gabalda, 1958), 386–393.

61 Nor to older or more recent stages of an internal Christian development; so Betz, *Eucharistie* 2.1:16f; James M. Robinson, "Die Hodajot–Formel in Gebet und Hymnus des Frühchristentums," in *Apophoreta: Festschrift für Ernst Haenchen*, BZNW, 30 (Berlin: Töpelmann, 1964), 194–235, here esp. 221f (see on 1:4–9).

62 The logic rests on the fact that the amen is a necessary part of the prayer; it can be spoken only when the prayer is understood; there is a full awareness of the meaning of the word amen as being assent to the content.

chumen (Weiss, Bauer). The word ἰδιώτης itself provides no help toward a decision.[63] It is simplest to think of all nonecstatics, Christians and non-Christians. For of course Christians cannot understand the speaker with tongues either. And in the sequel the presence of non–Christians is presumed.[64] If by ἰδιώτης we understand a proselyte or suchlike, then we shall take the expression ὁ ἀναπληρῶν κτλ. literally: the man who fills the place appointed for laymen.[65] Yet it can also be understood in a figurative sense: the man who has the standing of a layman, that is, who does not have the gift of speaking with tongues or interpreting.[66] ἀμήν is a pointer to established forms which have their place in the liturgy; the expression amen, too, is evidence for the dominating influence of the synagogue on the Christian service of worship.[67]

■ **17** This verse, too, agrees in tendency with v 15: the criticism is once more followed by recognition of the fact that ecstasy, too, is valid in principle.

■ **18** Paul can use himself as an illustration. He does so in loose style: "Thank God,"[68] followed by loose coordination instead of subordination.[69]

The observation has no polemical point. In Corinth it has apparently not yet been called in question that he is a genuine pneumatic, as was to happen later (2 Cor 10–13). On the other hand, he lets it be understood that he is not arguing in his own interests when he relatively degrades ecstasy. Again, he does not bind the community to his own person and his own abilities. He does not exploit these in order to kindle religious experiences.[70] Verse 18 is, along with 2 Cor 12:1ff, one of the few allusions to the psyche of Paul.[71]

■ **19** This statement presents the verdict on the use of his abilities,[72] a sober verdict determined by the criterion of his commission. ἐν ἐκκλησίᾳ: "in the assembly."[73]

63 ἰδιώτης is a formal concept: the nonexpert. It is defined from one case to another by the context, or by the closer definition, cf. 2 Cor 11:6: τῷ λόγῳ, "in speech." Weiss would interpret it in the light of v 23: the ἰδιῶται, he holds, take a place in between the church members and the ἄπιστοι, "unbelievers," and are accordingly proselytes who come more or less regularly to church and for whom seats are reserved. But in view of the formal sense of ἰδιώτης v 23 is no argument for v 16.

64 Lietzmann; Heinrich Schlier, *TDNT* 3:217, points out that ἰδιώτης is in fact explicitly characterized: ἐπειδὴ κτλ., "For of course, etc."

65 See on vv 22f. So Bauer, *s.v.* ἀναπληρόω, and Weiss. This would be in keeping with the scrupulous order of seating in Qumran.

66 τόπος in this sense: Philo, *Som.* 1.238 (τὸν ἀγγέλου τόπον, "the standing of an angel"); Jos., *Ant.* 16.190; *Bell.* 5.88: ἀππληροῦν τάξιν, "to act the part"; Plut., *Herod. malign.* 855e; *Comm. not.* 1070d; Ps.–Cl., *Hom.* 3.60. Epict., *Diss.* 2.4.5: If you are an adulterer, οὐδεμίαν χώραν δύνασαι ἀποπληρῶσαι ἀνθρωπικήν, e.g., φίλου οὐ δύνασαι τόπον ἔχειν, "you cannot fill a man's place," e.g., "you cannot hold the place of a friend" (Loeb 1:235).

67 1 Chr 16:36; Neh 5:13; 8:6 (LXX 2 Esd 15:13; 18:6); at the close of a doxology (concluding a covenant) *3 Macc.* 7.23; *4 Macc.* 18.24; Rom 1:25, etc.; 2 Cor 1:20; Rev 1:7; 22:20. Str.-B. 1:242f; 3:456–461. Amen in the OT is in the first instance the confirmation of a commission received: 1 Kgs 1:36 (LXX: γένοιτο). In the synagogue it is the commu-

nity's response to benedictions, etc.; 1QS I,18–20. In the present passage, too, it is an acclamation on the part of the community; Rev 5:14.

68 See on 1:14. It can be seen how free the use of εὐχαριστεῖν is.

69 ℵ "corrects" by transposing into the participle; p⁴⁶: λαλεῖν. The participle as extension of verbs of emotion has almost died out in the NT, Blass–Debrunner §415; still preserved in Acts 16:34; 2 Pet 2:10. The seeming asyndeton has the effect of emphasis, Kühner–Blass–Gerth 2:339–347. It is here bound up with the preference for the form of direct speech, Blass–Debrunner §471(1).

70 Again: if he does not present himself as an ecstatic, then this is a conscious renunciation for theological reasons, 2 Cor 12:1ff.

71 "Paul as a pneumatic" (Reitzenstein). Apparently he possesses further gifts as well (2 Cor 12:12); but he does not make them the object of his preaching and teaching.

72 θέλω ἤ, "I would rather": Epict., *Diss.* 3.22.53. For the omission of μᾶλλον, "rather," cf. Lk 15:7, etc.; Kühner–Blass–Gerth 2:303; Blass–Debrunner §§245(3), 480(4).

73 Karl Ludwig Schmidt, *TDNT* 3:506, observes that with ἐκκλησία there is often no difference between the presence and absence of the article, cf. vv 4, 5, 12, 28, 35. "Obviously ἐκκλησία is almost a proper name," Blass–Debrunner §257(2).

"Five" is a typical number. [74] $\kappa\alpha\tau\eta\chi\epsilon\hat{\iota}\nu$, "instruct,"
is a late and rare word. Paul uses it only of "dogmatic"
instruction (Rom 2:18; Gal 6:6).

---

20   Brothers, do not be children in discernment, but be babes in evil, yet in discernment mature! 21 / In the law it
is written: "By men of strange tongues
and by the lips of strangers will I speak
to this people, and yet they will not
listen to me, says the Lord."[1] 22 / The
speeches in tongues are accordingly
signs—not for believers, but for unbelievers, whereas prophecy is not for
unbelievers, but for believers. 23 / If,
then, the whole church is assembled[2]
and all are speaking in tongues, and lay
people or unbelievers come in, will
they not say you are mad? 24 / But if all
are prophesying and an unbeliever or
a layman comes in, then he is convinced[3]
by all, examined[4] by all. 25 / The secrets
of his heart are laid bare; and so he
will fall on his face and worship God and
confess: God is truly in your midst.
26 / What does this imply, brothers?
When you come together each has a
hymn, a piece of instruction, a revelation, a speech in tongues, an interpretation. It should all serve edification.
27 / If someone speaks in tongues, then
it should be two or at most three on
each occasion, and one after the other,
and someone should interpret. 28 / But if
there is no interpreter present (or:
But if he is not an interpreter[5]), then he
should remain silent in church and
speak only for himself and God. 29 / In
the case of prophets, however, two
or three should speak, and the others
should test what is said. 30 / But if
someone else who is sitting by receives
a revelation, let the first speaker be
silent. 31 / You can surely all prophesy
one after the other, so that all may learn

---

74   A round number for "several": Lk 12:6; 14:9. Gerhard Kittel, "Die fünfzahl als geläufige Zahl und
als stilistisches Motiv," in his *Rabbinica*, ARGU, 1, 3
(Leipzig: Hinrichs, 1920): 39–47; Eberhard Hommel, "Ein uralter Hochzeitsgebrauch im Neuen
Testament," *ZNW* 23 (1924): 305–310; Str.–B.
3:461.

1   "Says the Lord" is treated as part of the quotation.
2    $\epsilon\pi\grave{\iota}$ $\tau\grave{o}$ $\alpha\dot{\upsilon}\tau\acute{o}$: see on 11:20.
3    $\epsilon\lambda\acute{\epsilon}\gamma\chi\epsilon\iota\nu$ Jas 2:9; Herm., *Vis.* 1.1.5; outside the NT
also "test," and thus synonymous with $\dot{\alpha}\nu\alpha\kappa\rho\acute{\iota}\nu\epsilon\iota\nu$;
Friedrich Büchsel, *TDNT* 2:473–476.

4   2:14f. Weiss says that $\epsilon\lambda\acute{\epsilon}\gamma\chi\epsilon\iota\nu$ and $\dot{\alpha}\nu\alpha\kappa\rho\acute{\iota}\nu\epsilon\iota\nu$
form a *hysteron proteron*. But the two verbs cannot be
sharply distinguished at all.
5   D* G have the article before $\epsilon\rho\mu\eta\nu\epsilon\upsilon\tau\acute{\eta}s$ (sic! B D*
G have $\epsilon\rho\mu\eta\nu\epsilon\upsilon\tau\acute{\eta}s$, not $\delta\iota\epsilon\rho\mu\eta\nu\epsilon\upsilon\tau\acute{\eta}s$); on this see
Blass–Debrunner §252: individual–indefinite article
($\epsilon\sigma\tau\iota\nu$ $\dot{o}$ $\sigma\acute{\omega}\zeta\omega\nu$, "the needed or expected one, who,
however, is not known or not named").
6   The plural—as being objectionable—is replaced by
the singular in D G.
7   The text is confused:
1) $\dot{o}$ $\theta\epsilon\acute{o}s$ stands before $\dot{\alpha}\kappa\alpha\tau\alpha\sigma\tau\alpha\sigma\acute{\iota}\alpha s$ in A.
2) The article is missing in p[46] G.

and all be exhorted. **32**/ The spirits[6] of the prophets are under the prophets' control. **33**/ For God is not a God of disorder, but of peace.[7]

As (is customary) in all the churches of the saints,[8] **34**/ women should be silent at the meetings. For they are not permitted to speak, but should subordinate themselves, as the Law also says. **35**/ But if they want to know anything, they should ask their (own) husbands at home. For it is unseemly for a woman to speak at the meeting.[9] **36**/ Or was it from you that the word of God first went forth, or to you alone that it came?

37 If anyone thinks he is a prophet or pneumatic, then he must recognize that what I have written to you is (a command) of the Lord.[10] **38**/ If anyone does not know, then he will not be known.[11] **39**/ In short, my brothers, strive after prophecy and do not forbid speaking with tongues. **40**/ But let everything be done in a seemly and orderly way.

■ **20** The new section begins, as is often the case, with a new allocution. For the antithesis $\pi\alpha\iota\delta\iota\sigma\nu$, "child" ($=\nu\eta\pi\iota\sigma s$, "babe")—$\tau\epsilon\lambda\epsilon\iota\sigma s$, "perfect, mature," see 13:11; cf. 3:1. $\phi\rho\epsilon\nu\epsilon s$ is found in the New Testament only here: understanding, discernment.[12] The form of expression is purposely paradoxical: $\tau\hat{\eta}$ $\kappa\alpha\kappa\iota\alpha$ $\nu\eta\pi\iota\alpha\zeta\epsilon\tau\epsilon$, "be babes in evil."[13] $\kappa\alpha\kappa\iota\alpha$ is used in a general, moral sense; cf. 5:8. Perfection is not defined by an abstract ideal; it is a practically attainable state; cf. 3:1–3.[14] In regard to this passage it is permissible to read between the lines that Paul is indirectly characterizing the activities in Corinth as childish.

■ **21** Paul adduces a Scripture proof from the "Law," Isa 28:11f. According to Jewish usage, the whole Old

---

3) $\dot{o}$ $\theta\epsilon\dot{o}s$ is missing in Marcion, Tertullian. Hence Adolf von Harnack, "Über I. Kor. 14,32 ff. und Röm. 16,25 ff. nach der ältesten Überlieferung und der Marcionitischen Bibel," *SAB* (1919): 527–536, now in his *Studien zur Geschichte des Neuen Testaments I: Zur neutestamentlichen Textkritik*, Arbeiten zur Kirchengeschichte, 19 (Berlin and Leipzig: De Gruyter, 1931), 180–190 (cf. his *Marcion*, TU, 45 [Leipzig: Hinrichs, ²1924; Darmstadt; Wissenschaftliche Buchgesellschaft, 1960], 155*, n. 1): "For they are not inimical, but peaceable spirits, as in all the churches of the saints." But this is artificial; see below.

8 Harnack takes this passage with the foregoing, see the previous note. It is taken with the foregoing also by Robertson and Plummer, who point to Eph 5:22ff; Col 3:18ff. Others put $\dot{o}\dot{v}$ $\gamma\dot{\alpha}\rho$ $\dot{\epsilon}\sigma\tau\iota\nu$ $\kappa\tau\lambda.$, "for God is not, etc.," in parentheses.

9 On the use (or omission) of the article with $\dot{\epsilon}\kappa\kappa\lambda\eta\sigma\iota\alpha$ see Karl Ludwig Schmidt, *TDNT* 3:506.

10 Lietzmann considers the form in D * G (without $\dot{\epsilon}\nu\tau o\lambda\dot{\eta}$, "commandment") to be the original text.

Variants include:

1) (a) $\ddot{o}\tau\iota$ $\kappa\upsilon\rho\iota o\upsilon$ $\dot{\epsilon}\sigma\tau\iota\nu$ D * G; Orig^pt.
   (b) $\ddot{o}\tau\iota$ $\theta\epsilon o\hat{\upsilon}$ $\dot{\epsilon}\sigma\tau\iota\nu$ Orig., *Cat.* 277.32; 280.29, 32.

2) $\ddot{o}\tau\iota$ $\kappa\upsilon\rho\iota o\upsilon$ $\dot{\epsilon}\sigma\tau\iota\nu$ $\dot{\epsilon}\nu\tau o\lambda\dot{\eta}$ p^46 ℵ^c 33; with transposition ℵ*; plural and modifications D^c ℜ. Zuntz, *Text*, 139f: "Clearly $\dot{\epsilon}\nu\tau o\lambda\dot{\eta}$ is the intruder that caused this turmoil. $\kappa\upsilon\rho\iota o\upsilon$ $\dot{\epsilon}\nu\tau o\lambda\dot{\eta}$ is not a Pauline term, nor is the plural."

11 $\dot{\alpha}\gamma\nu o\epsilon\hat{\iota}\tau\omega$ p^46 B, "let him not be known," is easier.

12 For the content cf. Rom 16:19.

13 Misguided is Robert M. Grant's contention, "Like Children," *HTR* 39 (1946): 71–73, here esp. 71, that the Corinthians appeal to the fact that they are permitted to behave as newborn children. Kümmel rightly points out that speaking with tongues is nowhere characterized as baby language; cf. rather Rom 16:19. Another variant: Philo, *Leg. all.* 2.53 (on Gen 2!): $o\hat{\iota}o\nu$ $\dot{\eta}$ $\tauo\hat{\upsilon}$ $\nu\eta\pi\iota o\upsilon$ $\pi\alpha\iota\delta\dot{o}s$ $\psi\upsilon\chi\dot{\eta}$ $\dot{\alpha}\mu\epsilon\tau o\chi os$ $o\dot{\upsilon}\sigma\alpha$ $\dot{\epsilon}\kappa\alpha\tau\epsilon\rho o\upsilon$, $\dot{\alpha}\gamma\alpha\theta o\hat{\upsilon}$ $\tau\epsilon$ $\kappa\alpha\dot{\iota}$ $\kappa\alpha\kappa o\hat{\upsilon}$, "just as the soul of an infant, since it is without part in either good or evil" (Loeb 1:257).

14 Perfection: P. J. du Plessis, ΤΕΛΕΙΟΣ: *The Idea*

Testament can be so designated.[15] Paul follows neither the Hebrew text nor the LXX,[16] but another translation.[17] The transposition into the first person presumably stems from his own hand.[18] The train of thought is this:[19] Scripture predicts speaking with tongues as a God–given sign, but this sign has no attention paid to it. Thus the tone is first of all critical, and does not agree with the previous train of thought. For Paul's argument so far had been based on the fact that men *cannot* understand speaking with tongues,[20] whereas in the quotation it is based on the fact that they *will* not understand. The application which follows operates once more with the idea of inability. Thus the quotation is made use of only for the *one* thought, that speaking with tongues is a "sign" (namely, for unbelievers, see v 23).

■ **22** Here is a completely new aspect: Speaking with tongues is a sign for *unbelievers*. It is presupposed that "signs" are intelligible only to faith.[21] While ecstasy had thus far been treated esoterically, as a process within the community and in view of its effect upon the community, now it is considered in regard to its missionary effect.[22] This change of thought is apparently due to the quotation in conjunction with the example that follows, the glance at the community meeting. The wording of v 22 is overdone for the sake of rhetoric (parallelism between the statements on speaking with tongues and on prophecy): naturally, speaking with tongues is a sign *also* for believers, though not, of course, in the sense that it is unintelligible to them as a *process*. They know that it is a working of the Spirit; what is unintelligible to them is its content.

And prophecy has an effect *also* on unbelievers: v 24.[23] Apparently the phrasing is affected by the circumstance that (unlike 1:22) the element of unintelligibility is felt to be contained in the word σημεῖον, "sign."

■ **23–24** Verse 23 corresponds to v 22a, vv 24f to v 22b.[24] In view of the scarcity of material on primitive Christian worship, this glimpse of the activity at a church meet-

---

of *Perfection in the New Testament* (Kampen: Kok, 1959); review by Karl Prümm, "Das neutestamentliche Sprach– und Begriffsproblem der Vollkommenheit," *Biblica* 44 (1963): 76–92; Béda Rigaux, "Révélation des mystères et perfection à Qumrân et dans le Nouveau Testament," *NTS* 4 (1957–58): 237–262, here esp. 249–252.

15 Rom 3:19; Jn 10:34; see Str.–B. *ad loc.*

16 The LXX links up with the previous verse: θλῖψιν ἐπὶ θλῖψιν προσδέχου, ἐλπίδα ἐπ' ἐλπίδι, ἔτι μικρὸν ἐτὶ μικρὸν διὰ φαυλισμὸν χειλέων διὰ γλώσσης ἑτέρας, ὅτι λαλήσουσιν τῷ λαῷ τούτῳ λέγοντες αὐτῷ . . . καὶ οὐκ ἐθέλησαν ἀκούειν, "Take affliction upon affliction, hope upon hope, here a little and there a little with contemptuous lips and an alien tongue, that they will speak to this people saying to it . . . . and they would not hear." Hebrew: "Nay, but by men of strange lips and with an alien tongue the Lord will speak to this people" (RSV).

17 That he is not simply altering the text freely is shown by the relation to Aquila, who may have known the same translation, see Orig., *Philocal.* 9.2 (*The Philocalia of Origen*, ed. Joseph Armitage Robinson [Cambridge: University Press, 1893], 55): εὗρον γὰρ τὰ ἰσοδυναμοῦντα τῇ λεξει ταύτῃ ἐν τῇ τοῦ Ἀκύλου ἑρμηνείᾳ κείμενα, "for I found the equivalent of this reading in Aquila's interpretation" [Trans.]. Hans Vollmer, *Die alttestamentliche Citate bei Paulus* (Freiburg and Leipzig: J. C. B. Mohr [Paul Siebeck], 1895), 27f; but cf. Alfred Rahlfs, "Über Theodotion–Lesarten im Neuen Testament

und Aquila–Lesarten bei Justin," *ZNW* 20 (1921): 182–199; Michel, *Paulus und seine Bibel*, 64f.

18 So also does οὐδ' οὕτως, "and yet [they will] not" (literally, "and not even so will they"); ὅτι has a counterpart in the Hebrew (כִּי).

19 Lietzmann rightly warns us: "From the wording of the quotation it is naturally not permissible to draw any conclusions as to the nature of speaking with tongues." Yet the thought of unintelligibility is present as a linking motif.

20 ἑτερογλώσσοις, "men of strange tongues," can still be felt to be in keeping with this.

21 Karl Heinrich Rengstorf, *TDNT* 7:259, warns against overinterpretation of σημεῖον, "sign."

22 For forms and motives of conversion see Arthur Darby Nock, *Conversion* (Oxford: Oxford University Press, 1933); Kurt Aland, *Über den Glaubenswechsel in der Geschichte des Christentums* (Berlin: Töpelmann, 1961).

23 According to Weiss, v 22b is "an incidental idea which does not really contribute to the clarity." Heinrici says we have to supply not simply ἐστίν, "is" (then the thought would be: only believers are to be spoken to prophetically), but εἰς σημεῖόν ἐστιν, "is a sign for"; cf. v 24. Weiss finds that this expansion creates unnecessary difficulties. And that the sequel contradicts it: unbelievers are the very people who are shaken by prophecy.

24 Weiss thinks v 23 is rendered ambiguous by the quotation in v 21; without it the train of thought would be clear. Weiss probably overestimates the consistency with which the quotation is applied and is still

ing is invaluable, even if the high tension of spiritual inspiration here cannot be presumed to be normal.[25] The service of worship gives the impression of a "mania."[26] The ἰδιώτης is here, unlike v 16, a complete newcomer, who as yet knows nothing of the phenomenon of speaking with tongues.[27] No difference of meaning is perceptible between ἰδιώτης, "layman," and ἄπιστος, "unbeliever."[28] The passage is important also for the Pauline understanding of prophecy:[29] it is not prediction of the future, but unmasking of man.[30] The circle of those who may be awakened is the same as in v 23, in inverse order. For the effect—ἐλέγχειν, "convince, convict," and ἀνακρίνειν, "examine"—cf. 2:14f; 4:3f.

■ **25** τὰ κρυπτὰ κτλ., "the secrets, etc.": for the content cf. 2 Cor 4:2 (preaching as unveiling of the truth).[31] Conversion[32] is strictly speaking a work of the Spirit; it becomes manifest in adoration.[33] The inward factor of being convinced emerges in ἀπαγγέλων κτλ., "con-

25 We shall have to beware of generalizations. For the ancient ideas of ecstasy, see on vv 1 and 11. Plut., *Def. orac.* 437: the πνεῦμα works in the Pythia like wine. Lucan, *Bell. civ.* 6.169–174, 190–197, 211–218; list of the effects in Poll., *Onom.* 1.15; *Corp. Herm.* 9.4: διὰ τοῦτο οἱ ἐν γνώσει ὄντες οὔτε τοῖς πολλοῖς ἀρέσκουσιν οὔτε οἱ πολλοὶ αὐτοῖς· μεμημένοι δὲ δοκοῦσι, καὶ γέλωτα ὀφλισκάνουσιν, μισθούμενοί τε καὶ καταφρονούμενοι καὶ τάχα που καὶ φονευόμενοι, "Hence it is that those who have attained to the knowledge of God are not pleasing to the many, nor the many to them. They are thought mad, and are laughed at; they are hated and despised, and perhaps they may even be put to death" (Scott 1:181). Naturally the relatedness between ecstasy and intoxication is one of the most important elements in the interpretation of ecstatic phenomena; Philo, *Ebr.* 145–152; Hans Lewy, *Sobria Ebrietas: Untersuchungen zur Geschichte der antiken Mystik*, BZNW, 9 (Giessen: Töpelmann, 1929); Herbert Preisker, *TDNT* 4:545–548.

26 The reader naturally thinks of the ecstatic cults, see on 12:2.

27 With Lietzmann, despite Bauer's observation that ἰδιώτης can be a technical term of the cultic system, see Ditt., *Or.* 1:165 (no. 90, line 52); Ditt., *Syll.* 3:150 (no. 1013, line 6); 2:403 (no. 736, lines 16–19, mystery–inscription from Andania), and that in the religious guilds it denotes the participant in the sacrifice who is not a member of the guild, see Poland, *Geschichte des griechischen Vereinswesens*, 247, n. 1, and 422.

28 With Heinrich Schlier, *TDNT* 3:217. Neither ἤ, "or," nor v 24 is proof of a difference. The order is appropriate: the reference is first of all to his inexperience. In v 24 the order is reversed: because the topic is conversion.

29 According to H. Krämer and Gerhard Friedrich, *TDNT* 6:781–794, 828–861, the word group as such is ceremonious, but in content it is indeterminate and indifferent as far as the question of inspiration is concerned. Its content is derived on each several occasion from the context. For the Christian use, the OT Jewish tradition is decisive.

Plat., *Tim.* 71f: in Delphi the μαντικὴ ἔνθεος, "inspired priestess," is subject to the judgment of the ἔμφρων, the priest "in his normal mind." It is customary τὸ τῶν προφητῶν γένος ἐπὶ ταῖς ἐνθέοις μαντείαις κριτὰς ἐπικαθιστάναι (72a), "to set the tribe of prophets to pass judgment on these inspired divinations" (Loeb 7:187).

30 Philo, *Spec. leg.* 4:192: προφήτῃ δ᾽ οὐδὲν ἄγνωστον, ἔχοντι νοητὸν ἥλιον ἐν αὐτῷ καὶ ἀσκίους αὐγάς, "To a prophet nothing is unknown since he has within him a spiritual sun and unclouded rays" (Loeb 8:127). Entirely different is 1QpHab VII, 1–8: the prophet himself does not understand what he has to write at God's command. The meaning is revealed only to the teacher of righteousness.

31 This unveiling is a gift of the God who sees into the inward parts, who is καρδιογνώστης, a "knower of the heart," Rom 8:27; 1 Thess 2:4. Insight into another is held to be a gift of the θεῖος ἀνήρ, "divine man," Jn 4:29, etc.; Rudolf Bultmann, *The Gospel of John*, tr. G. R. Beasley-Murray et al. (Oxford: Blackwell; Philadelphia: Westminster, 1971), 102, n. 1 (*Das Evangelium des Johannes*, KEK, 2 [Göttingen: Vandenhoeck & Ruprecht, 18 1964], 71, n. 4); Philostr., *Vit. Ap.* 1.19; Ludwig Bieler, Θεῖος ἀνήρ: *Das Bild des "göttlichen Menschen" in Spätantike und Frühchristentum* (Vienna: Höfels, 1935–36; Darmstadt: Wissenschaftliche Buchgesellschaft, 1967) 1:89–94; Hans Windisch, *Paulus und Christus*, UNT, 24 (Leipzig: Hinrichs, 1934), 27f, 54.

32 See n. 22 above.

33 1 Kgs 18:39: καὶ ἔπεσεν πᾶς ὁ λαὸς ἐπὶ πρόσωπον αὐτῶν καὶ εἶπον· ἀληθῶς κύριος ὁ θεός, "And all the people fell on their faces and said, 'Truly the Lord is God.'" Wilhelm Michaelis, *TDNT* 6:163. In προσκυνεῖν, "worship," the dominant note is that of homage; Heinrich Greeven, *TDNT* 6:758–766. In the LXX it usually stands for הִשְׁתַּחֲוָה. Paul is leaning upon the OT, cf. Isa 45:14: the men of

in mind here.

fessing, etc.,"[34] yet in such a way that the psychological element does not come to stand on its own: the object of the statement is not the person convinced, but the power that convinces him.[35] A regulated process of conversion is not envisaged.[36]

■ **26** τί οὖν ἐστιν, "what does this imply?": a question inserted in diatribe style to quicken the interest, as in v 15; anaphora.[37] Paul returns again from examples to instructions; he sets out from the actual situation in the community. The statement ἕκαστος ἔχει, "each has," naturally must not be pressed to the effect that every single individual has one of the gifts mentioned, but means: one has this—another has that.[38] Paul apparently expresses himself in this way because the gifts are present in superabundance, so that orderliness is thereby threatened. The order in which he lists them is arbitrary.[39] The criterion is again the principle of οἰκοδομή, "edification," cf. v 12; it is immediately explained in more precise terms.[40]

■ **27** The introductory εἴτε, "whether," is not followed up afterwards. From the point of view of content, the continuation is v 29: προφῆται δὲ κτλ., "the prophets, however, etc." Paul presupposes that the inspired man remains master of himself. This is surprising: inspiration surely means transportation, ecstasy.[41] But for Paul the criterion of orderliness is apparently effective not only when it comes to the *content* of the inspired speech (this is treated in 12:1–3), but already in the case of the phenomenon itself. The Spirit does not bring about the extinguishing of the subject. Accordingly, the matter–of–fact rule is: "by turns,"[42] and not more than the community can stand. The demand for the interpretation of the otherwise fruitless speaking with tongues was already grounded in vv 13ff. The observations there made are now being turned into rules for the ordering of the service of worship.[43]

■ **28** To be sure, the relation between the speaker with tongues and the interpreter is not clear: who interprets?

Saba will come καὶ προσκυνήσουσίν σοι καὶ ἐν σοὶ προσεύξονται, ὅτι ἐν σοὶ ὁ θεός ἐστιν, "and will bow down before you and entreat you, because God is among you."

34 The word has here the nuance: to bear testimony to a fact, to honor the truth; 1 Thess 1:9; Mt 11:4; 28:8ff.

35 For the sense of ἐν ὑμῖν, "in your midst," cf. Isa 45:14 (n. 33 above). It does not mean: God is in you, as individuals—although God does in fact speak out of the inspired persons. But they work as exponents of the community. Misguided is the pietistic, legalistic shift of the thought by Schlatter, 382: "The picture which Paul draws here fosters the assumption that he often began his evangelization by uncovering the consciousness of guilt."

36 Against Robertson and Plummer, who see here a division of the process of conversion into three stages: "1) he is convinced of his sinful condition; 2) he is put upon his trial, and the details of his condition are investigated; 3) the details are made plain to him." The ἀνάκρισις is "the scrutiny in the court of conscience."

37 Bachmann: "The anaphoristic little principal clauses with ἔχει take over against πάντα . . . γενέσθω the place of protases (in the sense of εἴτε—εἴτε . . .)." On the repetition of ἔχειν see Bengel, *Gnomon, ad loc.*: it "elegantly expresses the distributed abundance of gifts."

38 This results from v 27: εἴτε γλώσσῃ τις λαλεῖ "if someone speaks in tongues." Paul is of course convinced that every Christian has a charisma, his par-

ticular charisma; but this does not have to be a liturgical gift. According to Lietzmann, v 26 "sketches the ideal state [*viz.* of the community] . . . and is thus surely an indirect expression of the wish, 'so it should be.' " But he leaves open the possibility that Paul is expressing himself ineptly, i.e. that he means to say: each of you who wants to bring forward a psalm, etc. . . . , and that ἕκαστος is accordingly taken up again by πάντα.

39 As is also their emergence in the service of worship. Schlatter assumes that the hymn stands first because the service was introduced with one. For the subject matter cf. Col 3:16; Eph 5:19; examples of Jewish psalmody are provided by the Qumran writings, especially the hymn scroll (*Hodayoth*); for Christian psalms see Lk 1:46ff, 68ff. An idea of the style of primitive Christian poetry is provided by the hymns of the Revelation of John, even if they are literary constructions by the author, and are not hymns taken over from the service of worship. On the style forms, see Martin Dibelius, "Zur Formgeschichte des Neuen Testaments (ausserhalb der Evangelien)," *ThR*, n.s. 3 (1931): 207–242, here esp. 219–225.

40 See on v 40, also for the style: πάντα. . . .

41 *Mart. Pol.* 7.3 (of Polycarp): ὥστε ἐπὶ δύο ὥρας μὴ δύνασθαι σιγῆσαι, "so that for two hours he could not be silent" (Loeb 2:321).

42 Instances in Bauer, *s.v.* ἀνά 2. τὸ πλεῖστον, "at most," Bauer, *s.v.* πολύς III 2 b β; Diod. S., *Bibl. hist.* 14.71.3: πεμπταῖοι ἢ τὸ πλεῖστον ἑκταῖοι, "the fifth day or the sixth at the latest" (Loeb 6:207).

One of the speakers with tongues themselves (v 13)? We can render: "But if no interpreter is present" (Lietzmann) or: "But if he is not an interpreter" (Weiss);[44] cf. on the one hand v 5, on the other 12:10. The rule that he should speak in tongues "at home" (ἑαυτῷ, "for himself") is in harmony with v 2.

■ **29–30** For the prophets the same rule is given, with a slight nuance,[45] as for the speakers with tongues. Here a difficulty seems to arise: the demand that speaking with tongues should be interpreted was understandable. But how should it be necessary, and possible, for prophecy to be "examined," when it is surely understandable in itself and provides its own authority? Who are οἱ ἄλλοι, "the others"? All the members of the community, or the rest of the prophets?[46]

The need for examination is shown by 12:1–3 and the gift of the distinguishing of spirits, 12:10.[47] Incidentally, v 30 shows it is customary for the speaker to stand.[48]

■ **31** This is an argument in favor of taking οἱ ἄλλοι in

v 29 as the rest of the *prophets* (see n. 46). For καθ' ἕνα πάντες, "all one by one," cannot mean simply everybody, but all who are to be considered here, all upon whom the spirit of prophecy comes.[49] The emphasis naturally does not lie on πάντες, "all," but on "singly," i.e., that you may be understood.

■ **32–33a** The phrasing is ambiguous here too: (a) The prophet is the master of his spirit, i.e., his inspiration. This sense fits well into the framework of the rules given here.[50] (b) It is also possible that the contrast is not between a self and a talking spirit, but between a prophet who is speaking and one who is rising to his feet.[51] In that case ἀκαταστασία is not the disorder in the community, but the disturbance that would arise if the Spirit were at variance with himself. Verse 40 points

---

43 Heinrici and Weiss hold that εἷς,, "one," is emphatic: "not several!" But in view of v 28 εἷς is better taken in the sense of τις, "someone," as opposed to οὐδείς, "nobody."

44 In that case ᾖ, "is," and σιγάτω, "remain silent," have the same subject. Yet this is not a conclusive argument.

45 τὸ πλεῖστον, "at most," is omitted. Does this indicate that Paul is here readier to make concessions in the direction of a greater number because the value toward edification is higher?

46 Heinrich Greeven, "Propheten, Lehrer, Vorsteher bei Paulus. Zur Frage der 'Ämter' im Urchristentum," *ZNW* 44 (1952–53): 1–43. According to Gerhard Friedrich, *TDNT* 6:851, it refers to the rest of the prophets as the court of decision. Allo takes it in a wider sense of all who have the gift of the distinguishing of spirits; and here a Roman Catholic intrusion enters: "chiefly the leaders of the congregation."

47 The criterion is formulated in principle in Rom 12:6: prophecy must conform to faith. Entirely different standards are provided by *Did.* 11.7–11: καὶ πάντα προφήτην λαλοῦντα ἐν πνεύματι οὐ πειράσετε οὐδὲ διακρινεῖτε· πᾶσα γὰρ ἁμαρτία ἀφεθήσεται, αὕτη δὲ ἡ ἁμαρτία οὐκ ἀφεθήσεται. οὐ πᾶς δὲ ὁ λαλῶν ἐν πνεύματι προφήτης ἐστιν, ἀλλ' ἐὰν ἔχῃ τοὺς τρόπους κυρίου. ἀπὸ οὖν τῶν τρόπων γνωσθήσεται ὁ ψευδοπροφήτης καὶ ὁ προφήτης. καὶ πᾶς προφήτης ὁρίζων τράπεζαν ἐν πνεύματι, οὐ φάγεται ἀπ' αὐτῆς, εἰ δὲ μήγε ψευδοπροφήτης ἐστί. πᾶς δὲ προφήτης διδάσκων τὴν ἀλήθειαν, εἰ ἃ διδάσκει οὐ ποιεῖ, ψευδοπροφήτης ἐστί. πᾶς δὲ προφήτης δεδοκιμασμένος, ἀληθινός, ποιῶν εἰς μυστήριον κοσμικὸν ἐκκλησίας, μὴ διδάσκων δὲ ποιεῖν, ὅσα αὐτὸς ποιεῖ, οὐ κριθήσεται ἐφ' ὑμῶν· μετὰ θεοῦ γὰρ ἔχει τὴν κρίσιν, "Do not test or examine any prophet who is speaking in a spirit; 'for every sin shall be forgiven, but this sin shall not be forgiven.' But not everyone who speaks in a spirit is a prophet, except he have the behaviour of the Lord. From his behaviour, then, the false prophet and the true prophet shall be known. And no prophet who orders a meal in a spirit shall eat of it; otherwise he is a false prophet. And every prophet who teaches the truth, if he do not what he teaches, is a false prophet. But no prophet who has been tried and is genuine, though he enact a worldly mystery of the Church, if he teach not others to do what he does himself, shall be judged by you; for he has his judgment with God" (Loeb 1:327).

48 Acts 13:16. The Jewish preacher sits (Lk 4:20) (but cf. Philo, *Spec. leg.* 2.62).

49 Greeven, "Propheten, Lehrer, Vorsteher" (see n. 46 above); he thinks προφητεύειν comprehends both λαλεῖν and διακρίνειν; this is too schematic.

50 Lietzmann. Weiss says: "Here Paul's ethical personality appears in the plainest light." This is to mistake the regulative principle. τάξις, "order," and οἰκοδομή, "edification," are *ecclesiastical* criteria. It is true, however, that Paul is opposed to the enthusiastic dissolution of the self.

51 Heinrici; Schlatter; Greeven, "Propheten, Lehrer, Vorsteher," 12–15.

rather to the first interpretation.[52]

■ **33b–36** This self–contained section upsets the context: it interrupts the theme of prophecy and spoils the flow of thought. In content, it is in contradiction to 11:2ff, where the active participation of women in the church is presupposed. This contradiction remains even when chaps. 11 and 14 are assigned to different letters. Moreover, there are peculiarities of linguistic usage,[53] and of thought. And finally, v 37 does not link up with v 36, but with v 33a. The section is accordingly to be regarded[54] as an interpolation.[55] Verse 36, which is hardly very clear, is meant to underline the "ecumenical" validity of the interpolation.[56] In this regulation we have a reflection of the bourgeois consolidation of the church, roughly on the level of the Pastoral Epistles: it binds itself to the general custom.[57] Those who defend the text as original are compelled to resort to constructions for help.[58]

■ **37** Verse 37[59] continues v 33a, or, in the present form

of the text, returns to the subject: prophecy and its criteria. ἢ πνευματικός, "or a pneumatic," expands the circle of persons concerned, yet not to all Christians as such, but to all ecstatics. It is not clear how Paul grounds his assertion that his exposition is a command of the Lord himself: with the help of the intermediate idea that everything that is generally valid in the church is a command of the Lord? Yet this idea is better suited to the interpolation than to Paul, and is suggested by it. Is Paul himself speaking as a prophet, with the same authority as accrues to the judicial statement in v 38?

■ **38** For the style and content of v 38, see on 3:17.[60] The statement proclaims in apodictic form the future divine talion. ἀγνοεῖσθαι, "not to be known," is the opposite of γινώσκεσθαι, which is equivalent to "to be chosen" (see 8:3). An object of ἀγνοεῖ is not required, since the reference to the knowledge of salvation is plain from the very form of such statements.[61]

■ **39–40** This concluding recognition[62] of the phe-

---

52 Cf. also v 37.

53 ἐπιτρέπεσθαι, "be permitted," is found in this sense only in 1 Tim 2:12. According to Weiss, "The passive points back to an already valid regulation, such as we find in 1 Tim 2:12." ὑποτάσσεσθαι, "subordinate oneself," is a typical catchword especially in the tables of household duties (Col 3:18; Eph 5:22); notice the absolute use.

54 The transposition of vv 34f to follow v 40 in D G is of course no argument for the assumption of an interpolation; it is a secondary simplification. Its compass does not coincide with that of the interpolation which is to be assumed. All the same, there is a sense of the difficulty of the passage.

55 As a comment on the term σιγᾶν? and with an eye on 1 Tim 2:11f?

56 ὡς ἐν πάσαις . . ., "as [is customary] in all the churches," according to 4:17; 7:17; and 11:16. Lietzmann (who accepts the genuineness of the passage) observes that apparently the active participation was defended from the Corinthians' side as a "custom of their own."

57 Thuc., *Hist.* 2.45.2; Val. Max., *Fact. et dict. mem.* 3.8.6: *Quid feminae cum contione? Si patrius mos servetur, nihil,* "What have women to do with a public assembly? If old-established custom is preserved, nothing" [Trans.]. Literature: Gerhard Delling, *Paulus' Stellung zu Frau und Ehe,* BWANT, 56 (Stuttgart: Kohlhammer, 1931), 110–114; Gottfried Fitzer, *Das Weib schweige in der Gemeinde,* Theologische Existenz heute, n.s. 110 (Munich: Kaiser, 1963); S. Aalen, "A Rabbinic Formula in I Cor. 14,34," in *Studia*

Evangelica, ed. F. L. Cross, vol. 2, pt. 1, TU, 87 (Berlin: Akademie–Verlag, 1964), 513–525

58 According to Lietzmann, Paul had in chap. 11 apparently only "conceded unwillingly" the speaking of women; here he gives his real opinion. Against this, Kümmel observes that there was no trace of this in chap. 11. Kümmel thinks it possible that Paul is *here* not thinking of women speaking under inspiration. But the whole context tells against this assumption. Kümmel has to tone down the argument: "Paul is seeking only to restrict as much as possible (*sic*) the public activity of women, without prejudice to the freedom of the Spirit." This is a very different thing from what stands in the text. Against Lietzmann: if Paul is here presenting his real opinion, then he was not able to make the concession of chap. 11 at all. Heinrici finds "in principle" in both passages the same basic rule. One would like to know how, and which rule. Schlatter says: "Blind obedience is . . . not asked of the women." But absolute silence is. Robertson and Plummer go on to worry about the unmarried women too: These can turn for information on questions of doctrine to the married women, who can apply to their husbands, who can apply to the church.

59 Erik Sjöberg, "Herrens bud 1 Kor. 14:37," *SEÅ* 22–23 (1957–58): 168–171.

60 ἀγνοεῖται, "will not be known," is to be read with A* ℵ*. The reading ἀγνοείτω, "let him not be known," (p⁴⁶ B) arose when the original sense (divine talion) was no longer understood; Käsemann, *NT Questions of Today,* 69 [71f].

homena brings the thought back again to the beginning, v 1 (*inclusio*). There is added a concluding statement of the governing standpoint—here, in accordance with the context, expressed in practical bourgeois terms: εὐσχημόνως, "seemly" (cf. Phil 4:8) and κατὰ τάξιν, "in an orderly way."[63]

---

61 The connection between knowing (God) and being known (8:1–6) has also to be borne in mind.

62 On the text, Zuntz, *Text*, 29–31, declares: the text of p[46] (with ἐν before γλώσσαις) is original. The impression that p[46] here supports a "Western" reading arises only through the splitting up of the texts in the critical apparatus. ἐν before γλώσσαις has to be taken along with the presence or absence (p[46]) of the article before λαλεῖν and with the position of κωλύετε. The alterations took place under the influence of the standing phrase λαλεῖν γλώσσαις. The process has the following appearance:

1) λαλεῖν μὴ κωλύετε ἐν γλώσσαις
2) Omit ἐν   1739
3) τὸ λαλεῖν μὴ κωλύετε γλώσσαις   ℵ A
4) τὸ λαλεῖν γλώσσαις μὴ κωλύετε   𝔐
4a) τὸ λαλεῖν ἐν γλώσσαις μὴ κωλύετε   D* F G

63 Kümmel finds the phrasing "remarkably secular." Secular it is, yet not remarkable but good Pauline style. And cf. the mystery-inscription from Andania, Ditt., *Syll.* 2:406 (no. 736, lines 41f): ῥαβδοφόροι . . . ἐπιμέλειον ἐχόντω, ὅπως εὐσχημόνως καὶ εὐτάκτως ὑπὸ τῶν παραγεγενημένων πάντα γίνηται, "Let the attendants . . . take care that everything is done by those present in a seemly and orderly way" [Trans.]. Jos., *Bell.* 2.132. For τάξις, "order," as a paraenetic term cf. *Test. N.* 2.9. Herbert Braun, *Spätjüdisch–häretischer und frühchristlicher Radikalismus* (Tübingen: J. C. B. Mohr [Paul Siebeck], 1957) 1:69, n. 5, compares תכון in 1QS V, 7 and מעמד in II, 22f. On the concept of order, etc., see W. C. van Unnik, "Is 1 Clement 20 Purely Stoic?" *VigChr* 4 (1950): 181–189; Jervell, *Imago Dei* 29f.

15

The Resurrection of the Dead

1 But I make known to you, brothers, the gospel which I preached to you, which you also received (or: accepted), in which you also stand, **2 /** by which you are also saved, with what form of words I preached (the gospel) to you, if you hold it fast,[1] unless[2] it was to no purpose[3] that you became believers.[4] **3 /** For I passed on to you above all[5] what I also received:

that Christ died for our sins
according to the Scriptures,
  4 / and that he was buried,
and that he was raised on the third day
according to the Scriptures,
  5 / and that he appeared to Cephas,
then to the Twelve.

6 / Then he appeared to more than five hundred brothers at once, of whom the majority are still alive, but some have fallen asleep. **7 /** Then he appeared to James, then to all[6] the apostles. **8 /** Last of all—as if to an abortive creature—he appeared also to me. **9 /** For I am the last of the apostles, who am not fit to be called an apostle, because I persecuted the church of God. **10 /** But by the grace of God I am what I am, and his grace toward me has not been in vain, but I have labored more than all of them, yet not I, but the grace of God that was with me.[7] **11 /** Whether then I or they, this is what we preach, and this is what you believed.

---

1   D G simplify by substituting ὀφείλετε κατέχειν, "you ought to hold it fast," for εἰ κατέχειν, "if you hold it fast."

2   ἐκτὸς εἰ μή: see on 14:5.

3   On the orthography, εἰκῆ or εἰκῇ, see Blass–Debrunner §26.

4   Verse 2 can be translated only with reservations. The following constructions and interpretations are possible:
    1) The indirect question is parallel to the relative clauses (as in the translation above). Against this construction it can be objected that the conditional clause has no apparent sense; cf. the fact that Kümmel, who advocates this construction, renders it "have held fast," without giving any reason.
    2) The indirect question is dependent on εἰ κατέχετε (Weiss): "if you hold fast the wording in which I delivered it to you, unless . . ."; this construction has a harsh effect.
    3) Blass–Debrunner §478 suggest putting a full stop after σῴζεσθε and deleting εἰ; then it is a case of the subordinate clause preceding the principal clause: "Hold fast the wording in which I preached the gospel to you." This construction, apart from requiring a conjecture, is over-artificial.
    4) It is possible to put a full stop after σῴζεσθε and take τίνι λόγῳ as a *direct* question (Lietzmann): "With what sort of words did I preach the gospel to you?" On which Weiss observes: "this would be a fit of bombastic rhetoric."
    5) The indirect question is dependent on γνωρίζω τὸ εὐαγγέλιον. In cases 4 and 5, τίνι λόγῳ is better rendered: "with what arguments," "on what grounds."
    6) τίνι λόγῳ is a closer definition of τὸ εὐαγγέλιον (Heinrici): "namely, in what way I proclaimed it to you—if, namely, you hold fast. . . ." The structure of the sentence and the order of words are against this.

5   Plat., *Resp.* 522c: ὃ καὶ παντὶ ἐν πρώτοις ἀνάγκη μανθάνειν, "and which is among the first things that everybody must learn" (Loeb 2:151).

Paul introduces the new theme without a transition. It is occasioned, unlike the preceding themes, not by a direct inquiry from Corinth,[8] but by rumors which have reached Paul.[9] The abrupt appearance of the new theme has here, too, given rise to operations of literary criticism.[10]

More important is the question of content raised by Karl Barth: the question whether, despite the looseness with which the various themes are strung together, there is not a unity of content throughout the whole epistle, namely, that which comes to light in chap. 15; whether eschatology has not already dominated the whole epistle so far, and the latter was accordingly planned with chap. 15 as its goal. Bultmann agrees that the whole epistle is oriented toward the Last Things. But the *sense* of eschatology, he holds, emerges in untrammelled form in chap. 13: love is the manifestation of the Ultimate. In chap. 15, he maintains, the sense is obscured by apocalyptic ideas.

Chap. 15 is a self–contained treatise on the resurrection of the dead. To be sure, it is only from v 12 onward that the topic becomes plain to the reader.[11] Looking back, we can then see how vv 12ff were prepared for by vv 1–11: the foundation is the traditional confession of faith, recognized without question both by Paul and by the Corinthian community, which is quoted in vv 3–5.

This method of argumentation is not a matter of arbitrary choice.[12] It is in harmony with Paul's understanding of theology: it is exposition of the faith as contained in propositions. These propositions, in turn, are "open": they are for their part propounded with a view to constant actualization, and require exposition. It is only when they encounter man that they go into action, so to speak—and this, too, by their own very nature: they mediate the event of salvation. Here the idea of tradition is fundamental.[13] Faith is dependent upon the transmitting of faith, and therewith upon the witnesses and preachers. On the other hand it is true that a doctrinal proposition concerning Christ is understood only when its soteriological reference is understood. Every statement concerning Christ contains a determination of the believer. Hearing the message of faith and understanding oneself on the basis of this message are not to be separated.

Thus Paul's method of proving the reality of the resurrection of the dead on the basis of the creed is vastly more than a formal proof. Rather, it is grounded in the fact that the resurrection itself is posited "in Christ." Christ is not merely the first to be raised, but is constitutive for our being raised: the dead will be made alive "in him." The result of this strictly Christological starting point is that Paul considers only the destiny of those who have died "in Christ." For it is only this destiny that he can derive from Christ himself—or, to put it otherwise, it is only in this way that he does not go beyond the creed and find himself in the realm of free speculation. The apocalyptic problem of a universal resurrection is not this concern, not at least in 1 Cor 15. Resurrection is for him not a question of the world picture, but of faith in Christ.[14]

For the exposition of the chapter we must keep consistently in view that Paul is here pursuing the task of

---

6 πᾶσιν, "all," is emphatic by reason of its position, Blass–Debrunner §575(5).

7 συν ἐμοι is to be taken not with ἐκοπιασα but with ἡ χάρις τοῦ θεοῦ, in the sense of ἡ συν ἐμοι χάρις, "the grace that was with me." The expansion in p[46] A ℝ is correct in point of content. For the omission of the article see Winer–Moulton, *Grammar*, 169.

8 The otherwise typical περι κτλ., "concerning, etc.," is missing. Not so 1 Thess 4:13, where Paul has been asked about the same, or a related, theme (during his sojourn in Corinth!).

9 Verse 12; cf. 5:1: ἀκούεται 11:18: ἀκούω.

10 According to Schmithals, *Gnosticism in Corinth*, 91f [85f], chap. 15 breaks the connection between 12—14 and 16:1. 15:1 links up well with 11:34. The chapter belongs to letter A. Paul, as distinct from chap. 9, does not yet require to defend his standing as an apostle; he can still designate himself without

11 Up to that point one is rather inclined to expect an exposition on the tradition and the apostolate.

12 There is already an external indication of this in the fact that in the parallel passage 1 Thess 4:13ff Paul proceeds in the same way: the foundation is laid by the creed (v 14), then follows the anthropological consequence.

13 Kümmel, *Kirchenbegriff*, 2–25; Wegenast, *Verständnis der Tradition*, 52–70.

14 According to Schwantes, *Schöpfung der Endzeit* (below, p. 250, n. 15), 83, Paul is not teaching a general resurrection of the dead. His thesis is that Paul knows only the notion of a "creation of the last days."

It is true that Paul can draw an analogy between creation and new creation. Both are the work of the one God (2 Cor 4:6). The fundamental question, however, is his Christology: it is the work of the God

---

any harm as the least of the apostles.

theology in the form of exposition of the creed. The dominant note is not that of apologetics. This can be seen from the fact that Paul's theses are in essence understandable even if we cannot reconstruct with certainty the views prevailing in Corinth on this world and the next, on death and an afterlife.[15]

■ **1** With considerable ceremoniousness,[16] the basis of the ensuing exposition, a basis known to the readers, is stated: the gospel[17] transmitted to them.[18]

■ **2** Complicated as the construction is, the essential elements can nevertheless be discerned.

a) The positive assertion of the "power" (cf. Rom 1:16f) of the gospel, our "salvation" (cf. 1:21).

b) The condition, holding fast, i.e., faith in its movement (which includes the possibility of "falling," 10:12).

The sense of παραλαμβάνειν, "receive," is given by its conjunction with παραδιδόναι, "pass on," in v 3; the Corinthians are characterized (as in 11:23) as receivers of the tradition.[19] For the commendation ἐστήκατε, "you stand," cf. 11:2 (Rom 5:2); on the other hand there is a note of warning against losing the truth. The assertion "you stand" implies that the authority and content of the creed are validly recognized in Corinth. This provides a common basis of argument. In other words: (a) in Corinth there is no support for a docetic Christology;[20] (b) Paul is not seeking to prove that Christ is risen. He can take this belief for granted. What he intends to elaborate is rather the expression "from the dead"; along with this he takes the anthropological consequences. He does not for a moment regard

who has reconciled the world to himself in Christ (2 Cor 5:19). God is he who raised Christ from the dead: 1 Cor 6:14; 2 Cor 4:14; Gal 1:1; Rom 8:11. Even when on one occasion Paul speaks in general of God as the God who brings the *dead* to life (Rom 4:17), his theological starting point is nevertheless not in the general notion of God, not in statements on the being of God, but in the sentence in the creed that God has raised Christ from the dead, Rom 10:9; 1 Thess 1:10. It is the man who is "in Christ" who is a "new creature" (2 Cor 5:17). The assertion of the resurrection of the dead as in the strict sense a statement of faith (where faith is related *a priori* to Christ) and is nothing else but a concretization of faith. What function is thereby exercised by certain elements in the world picture remains to be seen. There is a consistent absence of any psychologico-subjective reflection on death. Human existence is not in a structural sense being toward death. That it is so in actual fact is its perversion. Death is the last enemy. This is a statement of the *objective* relationship between man and death: it annihilates me—it can do so because of sin. This brings to light the connection between hope of eternal life and liberation from sin. There are indications of this connection running through the whole chapter, from v 3 via v 17 to v 56.

15   See the excursus on v 12. Literature: still of high value is Karl Barth, *The Resurrection of the Dead*; review article by Rudolf Bultmann, *Faith and Understanding* 1:66–94 [38–64], originally in *ThB* 5 (1926): 1–14; Karl Stürmer, *Auferstehung und Erwählung*, BFTh, 2, 53 (Gütersloh: Bertelsmann, 1953); Heinz Schwantes, *Schöpfung der Endzeit*, Arbeiten zur Theologie, 1, 12 (Stuttgart: Calwer, 1963), also issued as Aufsätze und Vorträge zur Theologie und Religionswissenschaft, 25 (Berlin: Evangelisches Verlagsan-

stalt, 1963); Franz Mussner, " 'Schichten' in der paulinischen Theologie, dargetan an 1 Kor 15," *BZ*, n.s. 9 (1965): 59–70; David M. Stanley, *Christ's Resurrection in Pauline Soteriology*, Analecta Biblica, 13 (Rome: Pontifical Biblical Institute, 1961); G. Brakemeier, *Die Auseinandersetzung des Paulus mit den Auferstehungs–Leugnern in Korinth* (dissertation, Göttingen, 1968).
On vv 1–11: Jacob Kremer, *Das älteste Zeugnis von der Auferstehung Christi*, Stuttgarter Bibelstudien, 17 (Stuttgart: Katholisches Bibelwerk, 1966); Ehrhardt Güttgemanns, *Der leidende Apostel und sein Herr*, FRLANT, 90 (Göttingen: Vandenhoeck & Ruprecht, 1966), 53–94; Hans–Werner Bartsch, "Die Argumentation des Paulus in I Cor 15,3–11," *ZNW* 55 (1964): 261–274; Josef Blank, *Paulus und Jesus*, SANT, 18 (Munich: Kösel, 1968), 133–183; see the literature cited on vv 3–5 (n. 54 below).

16   For γνωρίζειν as a ceremonious introduction see 12:3; Gal 1:11; 2 Cor 8:1.

17   Combination of noun and verb also in 2 Cor 11:7; Gal 1:11. It shows that the sense is formal and technical: preaching, message. The full sense of "good news" is provided by the context, the indication of the effect of the gospel.

18   See on v 3; 11:23; for the idea of tradition cf. also 1 Thess 2:13.

19   Kümmel. Lietzmann understands παραλαμβάνειν to mean *active* acceptance; otherwise, he argues, there would be a tautology with the foregoing; καί, "and," requires that the thought proceed. This is too subtle. Besides, the train of thought can also be the very reverse: that Paul first points in v 1 to the active acceptance, and now to the "receiving"; this fits in even better (with "in which you also stand").

20   This holds even if a limitation is found in εἰ κατέχετε, "if you hold it fast." But εἰ, "if," can also be

the raising of Christ as an isolated fact, but from the very start as saving event, that is, in its soteriological reference—which means, however, in its conjunction with death/cross.[21]

■ **3** The fact that the following statements are introduced by παραλαμβάνειν/παραδιδόναι, "receive/pass on," means that here established elements of the tradition are being quoted.[22] ἐν πρώτοις, "above all," is best understood as referring to order: "in the first instance." In contrast to 11:23, the receiving of the tradition is not explicitly traced back to the Lord. This is not necessary in the present instance, since of course Paul, having quoted the tradition, goes on to explain how he himself is involved in it, namely, through Christ's appearing to him.[23]

For the following analysis it is necessary, because of Paul's thus being included in the fundamental events, to distinguish two questions: (1) What is the extent of the formula quoted by him? (2) What is the extent of the truth which he asserts in face of the Corinthians to be authoritatively valid? The latter extends further than the former: its close is marked by the statement οὕτως κηρύσσομεν καὶ οὕτως ἐπιστεύσατε, "this is what we preach and this is what you believed."[24]

Excursus: The Christ Formula, vv 3–5[25]

The fact that vv 3–8 contain a formula which Paul has taken over from the church tradition is proved not only by his own explicit statement, but also by an analysis. The following are indications: similar formulations in other, non-Pauline passages;[26] the style, particularly the non-Pauline linguistic usage; the content, which goes beyond the immediate occasion (proof of the resurrection of the dead) and is self-sufficient.[27]

Opinions differ as to the *extent* of the quoted text. Linguistic considerations indicate that it extends as far as v 5. For in v 6 the grammatical construction begins anew.

Harnack does not agree. According to him, two competing statements have been combined: one on the appearance to Peter and the Twelve[28] and one on the appearance to James and all the apostles.[29] These, he says, are documents belonging to rival groups, each of which asserts the appearance

---

understood as a phrase used purely for purposes of the discussion.

21 Ernst Käsemann, "The Saving Significance of the Death of Jesus," in *Perspectives on Paul*, 32–59 [61–107], originally in *Zur Bedeutung des Todes Jesu*, ed. Fritz Viering (Gütersloh: Mohn, 1976), 13–34: "Paul only spoke of the resurrection of Christ in connection with, and as the beginning of, the resurrection of the dead in general. It is not for him the individual event of the revivification of a dead person. . . . As the overcoming of death it is for him rather the beginning of the rule of the one with whom the kingdom of divine freedom begins . . ." (p. 55).

22 See on 11:23. ὁ καὶ παρέλαβον is omitted by Marcion; for the tendency see Adolf von Harnack, *Marcion*, TU, 45 (Leipzig: Hinrichs, ²1924; Darmstadt: Wissenschaftliche Buchgesellschaft, 1960), 91*. Ulrich Wilckens, "Der Ursprung der Überlieferung," (n. 54 below), 62, thinks that ὁ καὶ παρέλαβον, "which I also received," merely emphasizes that there is no other gospel, but does not stress the idea of tradition as such. Against this is 11:23.

23 Lietzmann is of a different mind: because Paul is here stating the knowledge of the primitive church and adding his own.

24 Bartsch, "Argumentation" (n. 15 above).

25 For the literature see the end of this excursus (see also n. 15 above).

26 2 Tim 2:8; Acts 10:42; 1 Pet 2:21ff; 3:18ff; Mk 8:31; 9:31; 10:32ff; W. Kramer, *Christ, Lord, Son of God*, 19ff [15ff].

27 For the proof, the simpler form of the creed—that God raised Jesus from the dead (Rom 10:9), or that Christ died and came alive again (Rom 14:9)—would have sufficed. But in v 17 it comes to light why Paul here chooses the expanded form. Eduard Schweizer, *Lordship and Discipleship*, SBT, 1, 28 (London: SCM, 1960), 52 (*Erniedrigung und Erhöhung bei Jesus und seinen Nachfolgern*, AThANT, 28 [Zurich: Zwingli, ²1962], 89f), finds a certain tension between the formula and the context: the formula, he thinks, stresses the *death* ("for our sins"), the context the *resurrection* of Jesus. But Paul is stressing precisely the notion "from the dead." For the formula itself, death and resurrection are presumably equally important, much as in Rom 4:25.

28 Harnack emphasizes that before τοῖς δώδεκα there is no ὤφθη. He contends that the sentence ὅτι ὤφθη Κηφᾷ, εἶτα τοῖς δώδεκα, "that he appeared to Cephas, then to the twelve," is a single statement.

29 Here, too, ὤφθη occurs *once* only. Harnack's thesis on the twofold tradition has been variously taken up and modified, e.g. by Bammel, Winter, and Bartsch

to its master as the first one.[30] But the list does not contain a polemical note.[31]

All further attempts at analysis are methodologically unprovable.[32]

The *structure* is plain:

The foundation is constituted by two double statements:

a) ἀπέθανεν, ἐτάφη, "he died, he was buried";

b) ἐγήγερται, ὤφθη "he was raised, he appeared."

Two of the four verbs are marked out by the allusion to Scripture as being fundamental: ἀπέθανεν, ἐγήγερται. These are the two which constitute the foundation of the Christological "work" formula.[33] The expansions ἐτάφη, ὤφθη, are added as verifications on the two statements on salvation. Thus the two fundamental statements (dead – raised) are each provided with a twofold proof: from Scripture and from a verifying fact.[34]

The *language* shows peculiarities in comparison with Paul's usage elsewhere:[35] ὑπὲρ τῶν ἁμαρτιῶν ἡμῶν,[36] κατὰ τὰς γραφάς, ὤφθη,[37] ἐγήγερται.[38] Since there are echoes of the LXX (see below),

the formula originated in a Greek–speaking, Jewish–Christian community. More than this we cannot say.

Jeremias,[39] on the ground of Semitic coloring in the language, assumes a Semitic source.[40] But the form we now have before us is at all events a thoroughly Greek composition.

The individual arguments for a Semitic (presumably Aramaic) origin are:

1) The parallelism of the members. But apart from the fact that it is only relative, it is merely a general indication that a Jewish stylistic tradition prevails. This is true of everything that primitive Christianity has to offer in the way of set forms.

2) Adversative use of καί at the beginning of the third line. An adversative sense of καί would be good Greek; but it does not occur here at all.

3) The paraphrasing of the divine name by means of the passive (ἐγήγερται, "he was raised"). This, too, proves nothing in regard to the original language.[41]

4) ὤφθη Κηφᾷ is supposed to be a variant translation for Lk 24:34 (ἠγέρθη . . . καὶ ὤφθη Σί-

---

(literature, nn. 15, 54). If it is accepted, then at all events it ought to be complicated.

30 According to Harnack, "Verklärungsgeschichte" (n. 54 below), 65f, in actual fact the first appearance took place in Galilee, the appearance to James in Jerusalem and, moreover, not till after Pentecost, which is the appearance to the five hundred brethren. Historical consequences: pp. 68–70 ("The displacing of Peter as the first witness of the resurrection").

31 This note is a postulate based on a specific picture of the history of the primitive church. Against Harnack: Kümmel; von Campenhausen, *Ablauf der Osterereignisse* (n. 54 below), 10, n. 12; *Tradition and Life*, 45, n. 5 [53, n. 12]; Grass, *Ostergeschehen*, 97, according to whom Harnack's thesis is already ruled out by the chronological order. "Apart from this, the combining of rival traditions is a matter for people of the second generation"; cf. *ibid.*, 297f.

32 Héring would find the end of the formula at the end of v 4 already; Michaelis, Bammel, Bartsch (literature, nn. 15, 54) after ὤφθη. Then, so it is argued, we have a formally regular text. And then the formula has nothing to do with appearance narratives. But the argument with formal regularity is a pure postulate; Grass, *Ostergeschehen*, 94, n. 2. Wilckens would conclude a number of formulas from the repetition of ὅτι; see on v 3.

33 1 Thess 4:14; Rom 14:9; 2 Cor 5:15; expanded in Rom 4:25. The formula dead–raised also constitutes the foundation of Rom 6:3–5; Niklaus Gäumann, *Taufe und Ethik*, BEvTh, 47 (Munich: Kaiser, 1967),

61–102.

34 Lichtenstein, "Die älteste christliche Glaubensformel" (n. 54 below), 7. The structure is mistaken by Gerhardsson, *Memory and Manuscript*, 299f: "Each individual part is a short, heading-like designation for some passage of the tradition about Jesus."

The creed is not an abbreviated form of the narrative.

35 Jeremias, *Eucharistic Words*, 101–105 [95–99].

36 In the genuine Pauline epistles the plural of ἁμαρτία is found only in connection with traditional material: v 17; Gal 1:4; Rom 4:7.

37 Also 1 Tim 3:16 (in a quotation).

38 Apart from 1 Cor 15 only in 2 Tim 2:8, where there is likewise an underlying formula; see Martin Dibelius and Hans Conzelmann, *The Pastoral Epistles*, tr. Philip Buttolph and Adela Yarbro, Hermeneia (Philadelphia: Fortress, 1972), *ad loc.* (*Die Pastoralbriefe*, HNT, 13 [Tübingen: J. C. B. Mohr (Paul Siebeck), ⁴1966]).

39 Jeremias, *Eucharistic Words*, 101–105 [95–99]; modified in his "Artikelloses Χριστός: Zur Ursprache von I Cor 15,3b–5," *ZNW* 57 (1966): 211–215.

40 Jeremias, "Artikelloses Χριστός," 215: "To sum up, I should like to abide by the cautious statement that there are, 'if not indeed strict proofs, nevertheless certainly signs' (so *Abendmahlsworte*, 96) that the confession in 1 Cor 15:3–5—at all events in its original form—goes back to a Semitic original text." More bluntly Berthold Klappert, "Zur Frage des semitischen oder griechischen Urtextes von 1. Kor. xv.3–5," *NTS* 13 (1966–67): 168–173, here esp. 173.

μωνι, "he is risen . . . and has appeared to Simon"). This would presuppose a source cut and dried even to the individual wording. Nowhere in the New Testament, however, is there such a source for formulas.[42] It is a case of a variant *tradition*.

5) ὤφθη in the sense of ἐφάνη is supposed to be explained by the dual meaning of the Hebrew נִרְאָה, or rather the Aramaic אִיתחמי: "he was seen" and "he appeared." But this use of ὁράω, "see," can have been mediated by the LXX. It is moreover also Greek.[43] This is true also of the dative with the passive.[44] Owing to the proximity of the LXX elsewhere, it is a simple matter to see its influence also here.[45]

6) The ulterior position of the numeral (τῇ ἡμέρᾳ τῇ τρίτῃ) is presumably also to be explained in this way; cf. Hos 6:2 LXX: ἐν τῇ ἡμέρᾳ τῇ τρίτῃ ἀναστησόμεθα.[46] Moreover, it is traditional in Christian texts.[47]

7) Jeremias is presumably right (see below) in assuming that the formula is dependent on Isa 53. He thinks, however, that the source is not the LXX text but the Hebrew text. In the LXX, he argues,

we have no ὑπέρ. Yet we do have περί; and this is closer than the Hebrew מן. The two prepositions ὑπέρ and περί are interchangeable in kerygmatic formulations.[48] Jeremias [48a] and Klappert point also to the Targum Isa 53:5: אתמסר בעוונתנא. This corresponds to Rom 4:25, ὅς παρεδόθη διὰ τὰ παραπτώματα ἡμῶν, "who was delivered up for our trespasses" (RV), but is no proof that the original text of the formula was Semitic,[49] as indeed this very passage shows.

Positive arguments against an original Semitic form are the following:

1) "Christ" as subject at the beginning of the sentence, if not indeed impossible in Aramaic, is nevertheless unusual.[50] Incidentally, with the customary use of Χριστός as subject in the language of Chris-

---

41 Cf. Mt 16:21, an altered version of the Greek model in Mk 8:31.

42 For this reason all manipulations which reckon with literal adoption of specific statements are methodologically mistaken.

43 Already indicated in Eur., *Ba.* 914 (Dionysus calls Pentheus out of the house): ἔξιθι πάροιθε δωμάτων, ὄφθητί μοι, "Come forth before thine halls; be seen of me" (Loeb 3:77). Ael. Arist., *Or.* 27.351: ὤφθη τοιάδε, "appeared thus." Vulgar Greek in *PGM* 4.3090 (procedure to make the god appear): λαβὼν ἁλὸς χοίνικας δύο ἄληθε τῷ χειρομυλίῳ λέγων τὸν λόγον πολλάκις, ἕως ὁ θεός σοι ὀφθῇ, "Take two choenixes of salt and grind it in the hand-mill, saying the word many times, until the god appears to you" [Trans.]. Harnack, "Verklärungsgeschichte," 70, distinguishes two levels of meaning: originally, he says, ὤφθη means pure seeing, then secondarily ἐφάνη or ἐφανερώθη, "which leaves open all the possible kinds of experience of Christ that are now recounted." Mk 16:9, 12, 14; Jn 21:1, 14. Incidentally, the word ὤφθη is a motif of the kerygma (see on v 5), so that no conclusions can be drawn from it regarding an original language.

44 See previous note.

45 Gen 12:7: καὶ ὤφθη ὁ θεὸς τῷ Ἀβραάμ, "and God appeared to Abraham," cited by Philo, *Abr.* 77, also 80: διὸ λέγεται, οὐκ ὅτι ὁ σοφὸς εἶδε θεόν, ἀλλὰ ὅτι "ὁ θεὸς ὤφθη" τῷ σοφῷ, "That is why we are told not that the Sage saw God, but that God was seen by him [appeared to him]" (Loeb 6:45).

46 The Lukan recension has substituted the smoother

form τῇ τρίτῃ ἡμέρᾳ.

47 Mk 10:34 καὶ μετὰ τρεῖς ἡμέρας ἀναστήσεται is transposed in Lk 18:32 into the form καὶ τῇ ἡμέρᾳ τῇ τρίτῃ ἀναστήσεται; cf. further Jn 2:1 (redactional); Acts 13:33.

48 Cf. the alternation already between Isa 53:4 περί and 53:5 διά. Compare Mt 26:28 with Mk 14:24. A law according to which an original ὑπέρ was displaced by περί cannot be discovered; general reflections on the predilection of the NT for περί are of no avail; it is enough that the interchange also takes place in the opposite direction. In the kerygmatic phrase ὑπὲρ τῶν ἁμαρτιῶν, and suchlike, there is no rule at all. Cf. 1 Pet 3:18 (περί alongside of ὑπέρ); Heb 10:26 (περί); 1 Jn 2:2 (περί; but 3:16 ὑπέρ). ὑπέρ: Tit 2:14; 1 Pet 2:21; 3:18; Heb 10:12. In Gal 1:4 περί is testified by p[46] ℵ* A D G 𝕾.

48a See above n. 40.

49 A conclusion from the Greek prepositions is impossible in any case; cf. also Isa 53:12 LXX: καὶ διὰ τὰς ἁμαρτίας αὐτῶν παρεδόθη. It is methodologically mistaken to ask whether Rom 4:25 and 1 Cor 15:3 go back to Isa 53:5 *or* 53:12. There is no literal acceptance at all, but a general dependence on the whole passage. The Tg (אתמסר בעויתנא) can be appealed to only when these two words are totally isolated from their context. παραδιδόναι: Wiard Popkes, *Christus traditus*, AThANT, 49 (Zurich and Stuttgart: Zwingli, 1967), 27–36; mysteries: *ibid.*, 94–96; Josef Ranft, *Der Ursprung des katholischen Traditionsprinzips* (Würzburg: Triltsch, 1931), 181ff.

50 "Messiah" without the article is found in Judaism

253

tian formulas,[51] the titular sense of Χριστός, while it is not forgotten, is nevertheless the specifically Christian sense, which takes its bearings not on the general concept of the messiah, but on the person of Jesus.[52]

2) For κατὰ τὰς γραφάς, "according to the Scriptures," there is no exact Aramaic equivalent; one would have to be content to assume a free rendering.[53]

That the formula comes from early times is shown also by the fact that the decisive authority is still the immediate authority of the witnesses, not yet that of the church. The idea of tradition is not yet guaranteed by the idea of the church.[54]

The introduction of the formula by means of ὅτι, "that,"[55] is normal style; the repetition of ὅτι within the formula, however, is a peculiarity.[56] Χριστός (without the article) frequently appears as subject in kerygmatic statements in which Jesus is presented as the

---

above all in the Babylonian Talmud, see Str.-B. 1:6. The instances given by Rengstorf, *Auferstehung* (n. 54 below), 130f, are not really stylistic parallels to the primitive Christian use of Χριστός as *subject* (that is the decisive point!): *Sifre* 1 to Deut 1:1 (ed. Horovitz–Finkelstein, 7, line 4; explanation of Zech 9:1: "This is the Messiah . . ." (זה משיח); *b. Sanh.* 97a Bar.: "Three come unawares: Messiah, a found article and a scorpion" (Epstein 2:657: משיח מציאה ועקרב). *b. Sanh.* 93b: Bar Koziba declares, "I am the Messiah" (אנא משיח). *b. Sanh.* 99a: "And thus a *Min* [heretic] said to R. Abbahu: 'When will the Messiah come?' " (Epstein 2:668: אמתי אתי משיח). Jeremias refers to instances with "Messiah" at the beginning of a (principal or subordinate) clause: CD XX,1; *b. Sanh.* 96b; 98a: "When will the Messiah come?" (Epstein 2:664: משיח על חמרא אתי); *b. Erub* 43b; *b. Sukk.* 52a; *Pesikt.* 149a. These are not genuine analogies either.

51 The place of the word varies. At the beginning of the principal clause, Gal 3:13; Heb 9:11; cf. 1 Pet 3:18, where the quotation begins with Χριστός; at the beginning of the subordinate clause, Rom 5:6; 6:9; 8:10; 14:15; 1 Cor 8:11; 15:12, 14, 17; 1 Pet 2:21. A different word order, without any difference of meaning as far as content is concerned; Rom 6:4; 14:9; Gal 5:1.

52 Nils A. Dahl, "Die Messianität Jesu bei Paulus," in *Studia Paulina*, 83–95; Kramer, *Christ, Lord, Son of God*, 19–44 [15–40].

53 Jeremias, "Artikelloses Χριστός," 214, for כדכתיב and the like.

54 Wegenast, *Verständnis*, 52–70 (esp. 60, n. 4), against Kümmel. Literature: Adolf von Harnack, "Verklärungsgeschichte Jesu," *SAB* (1922): 62–80; Kümmel, *Kirchenbegriff*, 2–25; Wilhelm Michaelis, *Die Erscheinungen des Auferstandenen* (Basel: Majer, 1944); Ernst Lichtenstein, "Die älteste christliche Glaubensformel," *ZKG* 6 (1950–51): 1–74; Ernst Bammel, "Herkunft und Funktion der Tradionselemente in 1 Kor 15,1–11," *ThZ* 11 (1955): 401–419; Paul Winter, "I Corinthians xv 3b–7," *NT* 2 (1957–58):

142–150; Hans von Campenhausen, *Der Ablauf der Osterereignisse und das leere Grab*, SAH, 1952, 4 (Heidelberg: Winter, [3]1966), 8–20, 57–61; 2nd ed., SAH, 1958, 2, ET in *Tradition and Life*, 42–89 [48–113], here esp. 43–54 [50–66]; Karl Heinrich Rengstorf, *Die Auferstehung Jesu*, (Witten–Ruhr: Luther-Verlag, [4]1960), 128–135; Klein, *Die zwölf Apostel*, 38–43; Hans Grass, *Ostergeschehen und Osterberichte* (Göttingen: Vandenhoeck & Ruprecht, [2]1962), 92–106, 297–299; Hendrikus W. Boers, *The Diversity of New Testament Christological Concepts and the Confession of Faith* (dissertation, Bonn, 1962), 107ff; Ferdinand Hahn, *The Titles of Jesus in Christology*, tr. Harold Knight and George Ogg (London: Lutterworth; New York and Cleveland: World, 1969), 175–189 (*Christologische Hoheitstitel*, FRLANT, 83 [Göttingen: Vandenhoeck & Ruprecht, [3]1966], 197–218); Ulrich Wilckens, "Der Ursprung der Überlieferung der Erscheinungen des Auferstanpenen," in *Dogma und Denkstrukturen*, ed. Wilfried Joest and Wolfhart Pannenberg (Göttingen: Vandenhoeck & Ruprecht, 1963), 56–95, here esp. 81–95; Eduard Lohse, *Märtyrer und Gottesknecht*, FRLANT, 64 (Göttingen: Vandenhoeck & Ruprecht, [2]1963), 113–116; Hans Conzelmann, "Zur Analyse der Bekenntnisformel I. Kor. 15,3–5," *EvTh* 25 (1965): 1–11; Klaus Wengst, *Christologische Formeln und Lieder des Christentums* (dissertation, Bonn, 1967); Karl Lehmann, *Auferweckt am dritten Tag nach der Schrift*, Quaestiones Disputatae, 38 (Freiburg: Herder, 1968); Willi Marxsen, *The Resurrection of Jesus of Nazareth*, tr. Margaret Kohl (Philadelphia: Fortress, 1970), 80–87 (*Die Auferstehung Jesu von Nazareth* [Gütersloh: Mohn, 1968], 84–90).

55 Sc. πιστεύω or πιστεύομεν ὅτι. . . . 1 Thess 4:14; Rom 10:9; 1 Jn 5:1, etc.

56 Ulrich Wilckens, *Die Missionsreden der Apostelgeschichte*, WMANT, 5 (Neukirchen: Neukirchener Verlag, 1961), 76, n. 1. It cannot, however, be concluded from this that ὅτι in the present passage introduces on each occasion what was originally an independent formula; Kramer, *Christ, Lord, Son of*

perfecter of the work of salvation.[57] ἀπέθανεν, "died," is likewise an established term.[58] The death of Jesus is interpreted by ὑπὲρ κτλ., "for, etc.," as an atonement sacrifice or as a vicarious sacrifice.[59] The expression κατὰ τὰς γραφάς, "according to the Scriptures," is deliberately general: Scripture is seen as a unity.[60] This is not to deny that a specific passage is in mind, in this case apparently Isa 53.[61] The general character of the allusion indicates an early stage of the Scripture proof.[62] What is proved is of course not the death as such, but its character as saving event.[63]

■ 4 καὶ ὅτι ἐτάφη, "and that he was buried," is not an independent statement, but underlines ἀπέθανεν, "he died." This is shown by the history of the creation of the formula, which arose from the twofold form (see above), as indeed can still be clearly seen from its present structure.[64] ἐτάφη is linked with the death, not with the resurrection. There is accordingly no allusion to the empty tomb.[65] The intention is rather to emphasize the reality of the death, not indeed in an apologetic sense in face of a docetic Christology (such a Christology is envisaged neither by the formula nor by Paul), but in a positive sense, in order to present the death as a saving event.[66] From this Paul can draw his conclusions directly (vv 12ff). καὶ ὅτι ἐγήγερται, "and that he was raised": this is the original statement of the creed,

---

God, 19, n. 9 [15, n. 9], against Wilckens: ὅτι is "introduced ad hoc in order to emphasize each separate item in turn."

57 See above, n. 51. Dahl, "Die Messianität bei Paulus," observes: "Christ" cannot be separated from Jesus; Kramer, Christ, Lord, Son of God, 19–44, 133–150 [15–40, 131–148].

58 Rom 5:6; 8:34; 14:9; 2 Cor 15:14, etc.

59 The expression "die for" is Greek, both "for" persons (lovers, friends): Plat., Symp. 179b; Epict., Diss. 2.7.3, and for a cause or an idea: Philostr., Vit. Ap. 7.13. Hellenistic Judaism takes it over: 2 Macc. inculcates the readiness to die for God's laws (ὑπέρ, περί, διά), 2 Macc. 7:9, etc.; cf. 3 Macc. 1.23; 4 Macc. 6.27 (διά); 13.9 (περί). The Jewish idea of atonement is then linked up with this form of expression, 2 Macc. 7:37f; 4 Macc. 6.27–29. See Wengst, Christologische Formeln, 61–66; Lohse, Märtyrer und Gottesknecht, 66–72. The idea is taken up by Paul, but not developed; his tendency is closer to substitution than to atonement, 2 Cor 5:14f; see on 1:13 and 11:24. Alike in the formula and in Paul atonement and substitution are not sharply distinguished. One notices at most intentions which result from the Jewish tradition. Both aspects can thus be derived from Isa 53. Cf. also Rom 3:24f and 4:25.

60 For the plural cf. Rom 1:2; 15:4. Singular: Gal 3:8, 22. According to Lichtenstein, "Die älteste christliche Glaubensformel," 10–15, the reference to the Scriptures has an eye to the controversy with the synagogue. But it has in the first instance merely the form of a statement, as a positive reference to prophecy.

61 And this too in the LXX, as is plain from the affinities in the form of expression, cf. Isa 53:4, 5 (διὰ τὰς ἁμαρτίας ἡμῶν), 6 (καὶ κύριος παρέδωκεν αὐτὸν ταῖς ἁμαρτίαις ἡμῶν), also 9 (caption ταφή),

10, 11, 12. Dependence on Isa 53 is accepted by most exegetes (e.g. Jeremias, Lohse). Not so Hahn, Titles, 177 (Christologische Hoheitstitel, 201): "Scriptural proof and the motive of expiation regarding the death of Jesus must at first have been developed and handed on to some extent independently of each other." Passages like Rom 4:25 tell against this: the tradition of the Lord's Supper with its idea of covenant. Hahn confuses the reference to Scripture as such and a technique of Scripture proof which developed in course of time.

62 And presupposes that the hearers of this confession know the Scriptures.

63 According to Lohse, Märtyrer und Gottesknecht, 220–224, κατὰ τὰς γραφάς, "according to the Scriptures," cannot be separated from ὑπὲρ τῶν ἁμαρτιῶν ἡμῶν, "for our sins." Not so Weiss: the Scripture proof, he says, relates perhaps only to ἀπέθανε, "died," and ἐγήγερται, "was raised"; this assumption Harnack, "Verklärungsgeschichte," 64, n. 1, finds incomprehensible.

64 Grass, Ostergeschichte und Osterberichte, 146–173. For θάπτω, "bury," cf. the later, narrative development in the Gospel accounts of the burial.

65 Schweizer, Erniedrigung und Erhöhung, 89, n. 353, observes that there is no OT formula ἀπέθανεν καὶ ἐτάφη either (so Rengstorf; Gen 35:8; Jdg 8:32; Lk 16:22; Acts 2:29); "the second member is hitched on." Nor does the juxtaposition of 1 Cor 15:4 and Rom 6:4f provide an argument for Paul's being aware of the tradition of the empty tomb.

66 Lohse, Märtyrer und Gottesknecht, 115, finds that this is already a transition to the second act; without the resurrection the death has no expiatory force, cf. v 17. M. Ex. 20:7: "Rabbi says: I might have thought that the day of death does not bring forgiveness. But when it says: 'When I have opened

which can stand on its own.[67] Paul and the formula are both agreed that the raising (or "resurrection") and exaltation are identical. "On the third day" is a standing date for the resurrection of Jesus.[68] How did it arise? The following are the possibilities:

1) It designates the time of the first appearance(s).

2) It was derived from the fact that the Christians were accustomed to assemble on the first day of the week. But the evidence for the third day is older than for the "Lord's day."[69]

3) Three is said to be a typical number, and one, moreover, which occurs in similar contexts in the history of religion.[70] But the analogies are vague.

4) It is argued that on this day the empty tomb was discovered (H. von Campenhausen). But the date is older than the tomb legends.[71]

So there remains a fifth possibility, alongside the first:

5) The date was derived from Scripture. The phrase κατὰ τὰς γραφάς, "according to the Scriptures," presumably again refers here, too, not only to ἐγήγερ-ται, "he was raised," but to the whole statement.[72] The allusion is indicated in the same general way as that to Isa 53. It can only be to Hos 6:2.[73]

■ 5 ὤφθη, "he appeared," is a traditional term.[74] The idea is that the exalted Lord appears on each occasion from heaven.[75] The first appearance, to Cephas (on the name see 1:12), is not recorded in the Gospels and only alluded to in one passage, Lk 24:34. Historically speaking, it was the reason for the status of Peter in the primitive church[76] and probably for the founding of the

your graves,' etc. [Ezek. 37.13], behold we learn that the day of death does bring atonement" (Lauterbach 2:251).

67 Rom 10:9. ἐγείρω active: Acts 3:15, etc.; Rom 4:24; Gal 1:1; 1 Thess 1:10; Col 2:12; Eph 1:20; Heb 11:19; 1 Pet 1:21. Passive: Mk 16:6; Jn 2:22; Rom 6:4, 9; 8:34, etc. The passive is equivalent to the phrase that God raised him. The perfect stands contrasted in sense with the aorist ἐτάφη; it denotes the aftereffect; Blass–Debrunner §342(1); cf. Mk 6:14.

68 Alongside the phrase "after three days." The two phrases are equivalent and mean on the third day, cf. Jos., Ant. 7.280f; 8.214; cf. 8.218. The Synoptics interchange them: Mk 8:31 μετά (v. l. τῇ τρίτῃ) par. Mt 16:21 τῇ τρίτῃ (v. l. μετά) and Lk 9:22 τῇ τρίτῃ (v. l. μετά); cf. Lk 24:7, 46. There is a corresponding relationship between Mk 9:31 and Mt 17:23; Mk 10:34 and Mt 20:19/Lk 18:33; Bauer, s.v. τρεῖς; Gerhard Delling, TDNT 2:948–950. Detailed discussion on the date in Lehmann, Auferweckt am dritten Tag; he discusses (262–290) whether Gen 22:4 has had an influence on the dating. The "binding of Isaac" has saving significance ascribed to it in Jewish texts; see also Hans–Joachim Schoeps, Paul, tr. Harold Knight (London: Lutterworth; Philadelphia: Westminster, 1961), 141–149 (Paulus [Tübingen: J. C. B. Mohr (Paul Siebeck), 1959], 144–152). But the evidence is late.

69 The latter apparently first established itself in the Hellenistic world. Willy Rordorf, Sunday, tr. A. A. K. Graham (London: SCM; Philadelphia: Westminster, 1968) (Der Sonntag, AThANT, 43 [Zurich: Zwingli, 1962]).

70 For three days the soul remains in the neighborhood of a dead person; Bousset–Gressmann, Die Religion des Judentums, 297, n. 1; Maurice Goguel, La foi à la résurrection de Jésus dans le christianisme primitif, Bibliothèque de l' École des hautes études, Sciences religieuses, 47 (Paris: Leroux, 1933), 157–171. History of religion: Carl Clemen, Religionsgeschichtliche Erklärung des Neuen Testaments (Giessen: Töpelmann, ²1924), 146–154; Grass, Ostergeschehen und Osterberichte, 133f.

71 And the discovery of the tomb would still not explain this dating of the resurrection and its adoption in the creed; Grass, Ostergeschehen und Osterberichte, 129.

72 Not so Bruce M. Metzger, "A Suggestion Concerning the Meaning of I Cor. xv.4b," JThSt, n.s. 8 (1957): 118–123: κατὰ τὰς γραφάς, he holds, stands parallel to τῇ ἡμέρᾳ τῇ τρίτῃ as a qualification of ἐγήγερται, cf. 1 Macc 7:16f: Verbum, then (1) ἐν ἡμέρᾳ μιᾷ, (2) κατὰ τὸν λόγον. Von Campenhausen, Tradition and Life, 45f [54], holds that κατὰ τὰς γραφάς refers also to the date and that it is only from this that the latter acquires its dogmatic interest. Yet von Campenhausen is of the opinion that it can hardly be derived from Scripture alone.

73 Grass, Ostergeschehen und Osterberichte, 134–138. Delling, TDNT 2:949, points out that the Targum has altered the text (on grounds corresponding to those in Isa 53?): "He will revive us in the days of consolation which shall come in the future; on the day of the resurrection of the dead he will raise us up that we may live before him." Jacques Dupont, "Ressuscité 'le troisième jour,' " Biblica 40 (1959): 742–761, holds that κατὰ τὰς γραφάς is more likely to refer to the date than to ἐγήγερται. The date, he notes, always stands in connection with the idea of the fulfilment of Scripture: Lk 23:44–47; 24:6f; Mk 8:31. A synthesis between the historical and the dogmatic explanation is sought by Lindars, NT Apologetic, 59–72. He reckons that the expression goes back to Jesus himself, who used it in the sense of

circle of the Twelve. The latter is then legitimized by a further appearance.[77] That the circle arose only after the death of Jesus is already plain from the number: that Jesus appeared to "the Twelve."[78] Where the appearances took place is a moot point. It is simplest—for all the appearances, including those added by Paul (except of course the one to himself)—to think of Jerusalem.[79] As in all the early credal formulas, the prospect of the parousia is missing.[80]

■ **6** The construction changes; the series of "thats" is not continued. The change is most simply explained by assuming that the formula has come to an end and that Paul is now supplementing its data. The point of this addition seems at first sight to be clear: by its means Paul creates an impressive series of witnesses, and therewith a proof of the resurrection of Jesus.[81] On the other hand we find ourselves asking what purpose all this display is meant to serve, if no one in Corinth doubts the resurrection of *Jesus*.[82] If the point is found to lie in a proof of the facticity of the resurrection of Jesus, then a certain discrepancy arises between vv 3–11 and vv 12ff.[83] Certain as it is that for Paul the resurrection is a historical

---

a short interval (Lk 13:32f; Jn 7:33ff; 16:16ff). The resurrection on the third day then led to the literal prophecy being discovered in the Hosea passage.

74 Lk 24:34; Acts 9:17; 26:16; 13:31. The appearances to Paul are for Luke not "Easter" appearances. For the epiphany style cf. Mk 9:4 par.; Acts 2:3. What is meant is a real visible manifestation (Rengstorf, *Die Auferstehung Jesu*, 117–127, as against Wilhelm Michaelis, *TDNT* 5:326–328, 331–333, 355–361). The "word" element lies in the fact that the manifestation at once makes the person concerned a witness and presses toward proclamation. This crystallizes on the one hand in the reports of the missionary command (Mt 28:16ff; Lk 24:44ff; Acts 1:8, cf. 10:42), and on the other hand in such kerygmatic statements as Tit 1:3: God has revealed τὸν λόγον αὐτοῦ ἐν κηρύγματι, "his word in the proclamation."

75 Michaelis, *Erscheinungen*, 103–109.

76 On this status see Hermann Strathmann, "Die Stellung des Petrus in der Urkirche. Zur Frühgeschichte des Wortes an Petrus Matthäus 16,17–19," *ZSTh* 20 (1943): 223–282; Oscar Cullmann, *Peter: Disciple, Apostle, Martyr*, tr. Floyd V. Filson (London: SCM; Philadelphia: Westminster, 1962), 34–70 (*Petrus: Jünger–Apostel–Märtyrer* [Zurich: Zwingli, ²1960], 35–77). Erich Dinkler, "Die Petrus–Rom–Frage: Ein Forschungsbericht," *ThR*, n.s. 25 (1959): 189–230, 289–335; 27 (1961–62): 33–64; here esp. 196f, observes that it was only on the ground of this appearance that Simon (Lk 24:34) first received the nickname "Cephas," which then takes concrete form also in the statement ὤφθη Κηφᾷ, "he appeared to Cephas."

77 Vielhauer, *Aufsätze*, 68–71.

78 οἱ δώδεκα, "the Twelve," is found in Paul only here. It must naturally be asked how a circle consisting of specifically twelve persons came together. If we doubt that this circle had already been assembled by Jesus, then it must have been founded by Peter on the basis of his vision. In this there is revealed an idea of the church: the believers constitute the es-

chatological Israel. The vision would then confirm the circle in their role and therewith confirm Peter in his view of the church. Not so Béda Rigaux, "Die 'Zwölf' in Geschichte und Kerygma," in *Der historische Jesus und der kerygmatische Christus*, ed. Helmut Ristow and Karl Matthias (Berlin: Evangelische Verlagsanstalt, ²1961), 468–486.

79 See Grass, *Ostergeschehen und Osterberichte*, 120–127. The Easter narratives in the Gospels know nothing of a "flight of the disciples to Galilee" (and nothing of a return to Jerusalem that has to be postulated as a result of it). The appearance to the five hundred is located in Jerusalem also by Karl Holl, "Der Kirchenbegriff des Paulus in seinem Verhältnis zu dem der Urgemeinde," *SAB* (1921): 921–947, now in his *Aufsätze* 2:44–67 (and in *Paulusbild*, 144–178), here esp. 46 (he identifies it with Pentecost); cf. also Kümmel, *Kirchenbegriff*, 8.

80 The latter has a different "Sitz im Leben." It does not belong to the content of the "Faith." The latter relates to the work of salvation that has taken place, and is defined by it. The parousia is *awaited*. In the Synoptic tradition, too, the prophecy of suffering and resurrection and the prophecies of the parousia are originally separate; see Vielhauer, *Aufsätze*, 68–71.

81 According to Lietzmann, the historical testimony is such as to "make sure the resurrection of Christ as a fact that is historically given and has to be theologically evaluated."

82 And the Corinthians know of Peter (1:12), the brothers of Jesus and the apostles (9:5).

83 Bultmann, *Faith and Understanding* 1:83f [54f], declares that Paul's historical apologetic brings him into contradiction with himself.

fact, it must nevertheless be asked whether the argument in chap. 15 cannot be understood as a unity.[84] A help is provided by the remark tacked on to the next appearance: to over five hundred brothers "at once."[85] It is mentioned only here. In the postscript the point of the allusion to this vision emerges: the accent apparently lies not on the fact that the majority are still alive,[86] but on the fact that some have already died.[87] At the same time a further intention is strengthened, that of using the long list of witnesses of the resurrection to maintain its temporal distance from the present and thereby to rule out the possibility of a direct appropriation of it. This is parallel to the consistency with which *our* resurrection is maintained to be future: we are now living in the intermediate period between the resurrection and the parousia of Jesus. And by pointing out that even witnesses of the resurrection have died, Paul provides in advance an argument for his thesis that believers who die during this period attain to life.[88]

The question as to whether the series of particles (εἶτα—ἔπειτα, "then—then,"[89] etc.) is temporal or logical in sense is not very important. In favor of a temporal significance it can be argued that the appearance mentioned last, to Paul, is in fact not only temporally but also substantially the last, as being the conclusive end of the appearances. And in the original sense of the formula the first appearance, to Cephas, is the constitutive one. But within the list the sequence appears, to Paul's mind, to be of no significance.[90]

■ **7** James is of course the brother of Jesus (Gal 1:19). His status in the church was also grounded by "his" appearance.[91] "Then to all the apostles": this sounds as if the circle of apostles was a closed one, and not identical with the circle of the Twelve.[92] Who is an apostle?[93] The important thing is that *all* apostles have seen the risen Christ. This is accordingly definitive for the concept of an apostle. If he is thinking of a single appearance before them all, then Paul of course was not present. But

84 With Bartsch and Brakemeier.

85 Ernst von Dobschütz, *Ostern und Pfingsten* (Leipzig: Hinrichs, 1903); Holl, *Aufsätze* 2:47, n. 1, identifies it with Pentecost; so also S. MacLean Gilmour, "The Christophany to More than Five Hundred Brethren," *JBL* 80 (1961): 248–252; "Easter and Pentecost," *JBL* 81 (1962): 62–66. Against this C. Freeman Sleeper, "Pentecost and Resurrection," *JBL* 84 (1965): 389–399.

86 This can be assumed to be known also in Corinth.

87 Bartsch; Brakemeier, *Auseinandersetzung*, 31, n. 148. κοιμᾶσθαι: see on 7:39; 11:30.

88 Brakemeier. Somewhat different is Bartsch: Paul is combating the prevailing conviction in Corinth that immortality is acquired through faith in the appearances. It is right enough that the Corinthians think they have—without the mediation of the preaching of the cross—direct access to the exalted Lord. But how exactly they conceive of this direct access cannot be gathered from the text.

89 εἶτα—ἔπειτα are frequently used without connectives; Blass–Debrunner §459(4).

90 According to Bammel and Bartsch, the sense cannot be chronological; for Paul cannot have meant that the appearance to James was later than the one to the five hundred brethren.—Why not?—Marxsen, *The Resurrection of Jesus of Nazareth*, 91–96 (*Die Auferstehung Jesu von Nazareth*, 94–99), would find help in a new approach to the question: ". . . that the starting point for the wording of our formula is not the event but the groups which were [later] to be found in the church . . ." (p. 92). The purpose is to

bring these into a unity by having them severally trace their origin to an appearance of the risen Lord.

91 For the thesis that this was also held originally to be one of the first appearances and that it derives from an independent formula, see above. This appearance is likewise not preserved elsewhere in the canonical Scriptures, but it is found in *Ev. Hebr.* fr. 7 (Hennecke–Schneemelcher–Wilson 1:165; Klostermann fr. 21). It is reflected in *Ev. Thom.* 12: "The disciples said to Jesus: We know that thou wilt go away from us. Who is it who shall be great over us? Jesus said to them: Wherever you have come, you will go to James the righteous for whose sake heaven and earth came into being" (Guillaumont *et al.*, 9).
Whether James is designated an apostle by Paul in Gal 1:19 is disputed; Schmithals, *The Office of Apostle*, 64f [54]; Klein, *Die zwölf Apostel*, 46, n. 190; see on 9:5. This vision is frequently understood as the *conversion* of James. Grass, *Ostergeschehen und Osterberichte*, 101, is rightly sceptical of this.

92 Whether we regard the phrase as Pauline or assume that in v 7b a tradition emerges (so Klein).

93 Harnack answers: the Twelve. This thesis is possible, if we assume parallel formulas with different phrasing. Holl, *Aufsätze* 2:48, says: the Twelve and James, but not for the missionaries, for these constitute an *open* group. Lietzmann: a circle of Jesus' disciples which extends beyond the circle of the Twelve but is strictly limited. According to Klein, *Die zwölf Apostel*, 41, the phrasing is influenced by tradition. If the expression came from Paul, it would have to be assumed that he imagines either that all the apostles

indeed he is the straggler.

■ **8** His own vision is apparently meant as the conclusive end of the appearances of the risen Lord.[94] In strange contrast to Paul's position here as the last of all, we have his designation of himself as an ἔκτρωμα. For this word means a premature birth, or abortion.[95] It is not possible to decide whether Paul is describing himself as stillborn, or as a monstrosity.[96] This alternative presumably must not be raised at all. Possibly he has passages from the Old Testament in mind.[97] The sense is clarified by vv 9–11.

■ **9** In vv 9–11, too, the prevailing tendency is to state the resurrection of Jesus as a *past* event. The present is not the age in which we have direct access to the risen Lord, but is the age of grace, which appears *sub specie contrarii*.

Since from the very beginning the creed alludes to witnesses of the resurrection, Paul can introduce himself into his own expanded version of the creed.[98] In v 8 he had already hinted at the conclusion to be drawn from the sequence of the visions. This he now develops. Humanly speaking, he is the last, i.e., the least of the apostles. But this does no prejudice to the validity of his status.[99] For that rests upon an absolute factor, grace, and becomes visible in his achievements. Psychological categories do not suffice to explain this duality.[100] For it is here not a case of an unaccountable vacillation in personal moods—between self-esteem and self-humiliation—but of a fact that can be rationally grasped: his authority is "his" in a dialectical sense. He cannot exploit it for his own ends. He has it only as a servant (3:5).

---

were assembled together on one occasion, or else that it is a question of a number of individual visions, but the expression tells against this. According to Schmithals, *The Office of Apostle*, 76–79 [66–69], there is no tradition here and the word ἐφάπαξ, "at once," is not used; so it is a question of a number of visions. With this explanation, to be sure, Schmithals cancels out the chronological order on which he had insisted. Oversubtle also is his declaration (*ibid.* 79 [69]) that if οἱ ἀπόστολοι πάντες really means *all* the apostles, then Peter and James are excluded from this circle because they already had their visions before this.

94 H. von Campenhausen, *Tradition and Life*, 53 [64f]; Grass, *Ostergeschehen und Osterberichte*, 105.

95 According to Lietzmann, the *tertium comparationis* is the abnormality of such a birth and the immaturity of the child as compared with the other sons. Johannes Schneider, *TDNT* 2:465–467, assumes with Harnack that Paul is taking up a term of abuse used by his opponents; cf. Anton Fridrichsen, "Paulus abortivus. Zu 1 Kor. 15,8," in *Symbolae philologicae O. A. Danielsson octogenario dicatae* (Uppsala: Lundequist, 1932), 79–85, according to whom Paul is said to be an abortion of the ἀναγέννησις ("rebirth"), an abortive Christian, and he now takes up this reproach and relates it to his *pre*-Christian life. But this is an improbable construction. According to G. Björck, "Nochmals Paulus abortivus," *CN* 3 (1939): 3–8, ἔκτρωμα as a term of abuse can mean: a monster from birth. It does not have to be taken of the way in which Paul became a Christian. Johannes Munck, "Paulus tamquam abortivus," in *New Testament Essays: Studies in Memory of Thomas Walter Manson*, ed. A. J. B. Higgins (Manchester: University Press, 1959), 180–193, agrees with Björck in regard to the meaning of the article before ἔκτρωμα:

as in ἡμεῖς οἱ Ἕλληνες, that is to say: "He revealed himself to me as an ἔκτρωμα"; see Blass–Debrunner §433(3)A: τῷ ὡσπερεὶ ἐκτρώματι ὄντι, "as being so to speak an abortion." The meaning "monster" assumed by Björck is only late, and not popular. Thus Munck sees only two possibilities: (1) if we look forward to v 9, we can render: Paul is the most wretched of men, comparable only with a stillborn child; in that case we have a reminiscense of the OT: Job 3:16; Eccl 6:3; (2) "something embryonic that needs to be formed" (p. 190); cf. Severian of Gabala (Staab, *Pauluskommentare*, 272): τὰ ἐκβαλλόμενα βρέφη πρὶν ἢ μορφωθῆναι ἐν τῇ γαστρὶ ἐκτρώματα καλεῖται, "Fetuses expelled before being formed in the womb are called ἐκτρώματα." That is to say, Paul was still fashioned by the law, not yet by Christ. This interpretation probably finds more in the text than it contains.

96 See previous note (Björck).

97 Esp. Num 12:12: μὴ γένηται ὡσεὶ ἴσον θανάτῳ, ὡσεὶ ἔκτρωμα ἐκπορευόμενον ἐκ μήτρας μητρός, "Let her not be as one dead, as an ἔκτρωμα coming out of her mother's womb."

98 Munck observes that the oldest exegesis of ἔκτρωμα is Eph 3:8, ἐμοὶ τῷ ἐλαχιστοτέρῳ, "to me, who am less than the least," cf. further 1 Tim 1:15; Ign., *Rom.* 9.2. According to Thorlief Boman, "Paulus abortivus (1. Kor. 15,8)," *StudTheol* 18 (1964): 46–50, now in his *Die Jesusüberlieferung im Lichte der neueren Volkskunde* (Göttingen: Vandenhoeck & Ruprecht, 1967), 236–240, Paul, the little one (*paulus*), is described in Corinth as a "dwarf." Paul takes this up playfully: Yes, I am the least of the apostles.

99 He is "called," see 1:1; Gal 1:1; the consequences for the validity of his gospel are stated in Gal 1:11f, 15f.

100 For example, the suggestion that it is due to psychical

For this very reason it is restricted only by his commission, not by any human rivals. For in it there appears the authority of the Lord himself.[101] His renunciation of glory is nothing else save his concrete understanding of the grace which was manifested in the cross as an act of God.[102]

His status is vigorously emphasized by ἐγὼ γάρ, "for I." How far does this contain active polemic? Weiss thinks that ἱκανός, "fit, adequate," could be a catchword of his opponents, since one would sooner expect ἄξιος, "worthy." It is a fact that the ἱκανότης, "adequacy," of Paul is the theme of 2 Corinthians, though apparently in a new situation (2 Cor 2:16; 3:5f). The strongly phrased relative clause naturally does not express renunciation of the apostolic dignity, but says the same as v 10 and must be read along with it. There is no doubt that here we can also detect a part of Paul's psychological makeup. But this does not exhaust the content; for Paul grounds his unworthiness not on his personality in general, but on his concrete past as a persecutor of the "church of God."[103] This expression seems for him to be more or less cut and dried in this context; cf. the parallel, Gal 1:13f.[104] The foil of this past emphasizes

the factor of grace.

■ 10 Grace is an absolute factor.[105] His being is not a thing he can place to his own credit. But he is responsible for the fact that God's grace is not "in vain."[106] This of all things contains no merit.[107] The result emerges visibly in his labors: περισσότερον, "more abundantly," is illustrated by 2 Cor 11:21ff. The accent lies not only on the laborious effort, but also on the result. To this extent Paul has his glory.[108] "More than all of them" naturally does not mean more than all of them together, but more than each of them.[109] And at once the reference to his own achievement has a brake put on it: the subject of his achievement is not he himself, but grace. His glory is no merit (see 9:16).

■ 11 In his own characteristic mode of expression[110] Paul relativizes the *human* differences[111] in favor of the essential thing, proclamation and faith. With this, he has returned to vv 1–3a.[112] He has established the foundation for the arguments that follow and underlines their authority: οὕτως, "so, this is what," points back both to the creed quoted and also to its expansion by Paul. Once again it is plain that the authority and content of the creed are not disputed in Corinth.

tensions. An explanation in terms of the psychology of religion with the help of an allusion to the split in the self–consciousness of the Gnostic is likewise unsatisfactory. Lietzmann says: "Breathtaking is the transition from this expression of profoundest humility to the proud καυχᾶσθαι ἐν Χριστῷ." But this explains nothing.

101 For authority and "qualification" see 2 Cor 2:14–17; for the criterion and the effect of the apostolic preaching, 2 Cor 4:5f; inseparable from it is the human lowliness, 2 Cor 4:7ff.

102 That psychological categories do not suffice is shown by the fact that Paul does not expound his nothingness by means of self–observation and self–representation. He does not make himself the object of his preaching on the negative side either. Even where he illustrates the working of the cross in his own person, he never actively intensifies his nothingness. He simply points to the fate to which he is exposed by his work (2 Cor 11:21ff)—exposed, moreover, as an apostle, and thus in sharing this fate with the others (4:9).

103 He makes good his past not in psychological terms (by a display of his regret or suchlike) but in theological ways—by pursuing the work of mission. For the theological style of self–analysis, see Phil 3:7–11.

104 Wolfgang Schrage, " 'Ekklesia' und 'Synagoge':

Zum Ursprung des urchristlichen Kirchenbegriffs," ZThK 60 (1963): 178–202, draws from this the conclusion that the word ἐκκλησία contains from the start the note of a critical attitude to the Law.

105 Otto Glombitza, "Gnade—das entscheidende Wort. Erwägungen zu 1. Kor. xv.1–11, eine exegetische Studie," NT 2 (1958): 281–290, compares Ex 3:14: καὶ εἶπεν ὁ θεὸς πρὸς Μωϋσῆν· ἐγώ εἰμι ὁ ὤν. καὶ εἶπεν· οὕτως ἐρεῖς τοῖς υἱοῖς Ἰσραηλ· ὁ ὢν ἀπέσταλκέν με πρὸς ὑμᾶς, "And God said to Moses, 'I am he who is.' And he said, 'Thus you will say to the sons of Israel, "He who is has sent me to you." ' " He takes Paul to mean: where I do not live from grace, I am not what I am. This fails to recognize that the statement has a specific aim.

106 κενός: v 58; 1 Thess 2:1; εἰς κενόν, "in vain": Isa 29:8; 65:23; Phil 2:16; 1 Thess 3:5. ἐγενήθη εἰς ἐμέ, "directed toward me."

107 σὺν ἐμοί is naturally not intended in a "synergistic" sense, but means ἡ χάρις τοῦ θεοῦ ἡ σὺν ἐμοί, "the grace of God that was with me."

108 The glory is eschatological; it is imparted by a declaration on God's part, see on 3:12ff; Phil 2:16.

109 An indication, too, of the outward significance of the Pauline communities in the church.

110 εἴτε—εἴτε, "whether—or": 2 Cor 5:9; Phil 1:20; 1 Thess 5:10.

The notion of the *resurrection of the dead* derives from Persian religion. From this source it found its way into Judaism, where it was taken over by apocalyptic and by Pharisaism. For Jesus and the whole of primitive Christianity it is a matter of course. This, to be sure, does not mean that in a pagan milieu it was not open to doubt, not only from the standpoint of an enthusiastic spiritualism, but also from that of the universal Greek reserve in face of hopes of the beyond. Why, then, do such sceptics become Christians? They can regard Christian soteriology (the practice of sacramental rites which impart a share in the fate of the God of the cult) in terms of the mysteries. The working of the latter is conceived as belonging to this world.[113] Without prejudice to the likewise testified belief that the mysteries confer immortality,[114] the fact nevertheless remains that it is first and foremost earthly happiness that is sought in them.[115] Indicative in this respect is the well–known Isis aretalogy, in which we look in vain for a word on the continuance

of life.[116] Thus Paul can conceive both of mystes who do not believe in a further life,[117] and also of Christians; indeed there are even Jews who have no such hope.

What, now, is the view really advanced by "some" in Corinth? The statement ἀνάστασις νεκρῶν οὐκ ἔστιν, "there is no resurrection of the dead,"[118] does not give such a clear answer to this question as at first sight. At first, it appears to be a question of good Greek scepticism concerning an afterlife. It sounds like it at all events.[119] And we cannot simply assert that scepticism of this kind is out of the question in a Christian church (see above). But it does not fit in with the remainder of the picture of the community as supplied by the rest of the epistle—with its enthusiasm, or with the practice of vicarious baptism (v 29). Lietzmann holds that the Corinthians advocate the Greek doctrine of the immortality of the soul, and consequently deny the resurrection of the body.[120] But Paul's argument is not in harmony with this interpretation. He does not emphasize the

---

111 We must not ask for a precise definition of the ἐκεῖνοι, "they." This is precisely the sense of the passage.

112 Weiss finds this return forced. On the contrary, it is logical, and is implied in the train of thought. For the latter is not meant to lead us in the end to Paul as a personality, but to Paul as the representative of this cause.

113 Josef Kroll, *Gott und Hölle*, Studien der Bibliothek Warburg, 20 (Leipzig and Berlin: Teubner; London: Cassell, 1932; Darmstadt: Wissenschaftliche Buchgesellschaft, 1963), 500f; according to Rohde, *Psyche* 539f [2:379f], the vast majority of the grave inscriptions say nothing of any hope, see the situation in Werner Peek, *Griechische Grabgedichte*, Schriften und Quellen der Alten Welt, 7 (Berlin: Akademie–Verlag, 1960). Ditt., *Syll.* 3:118 (no. 985; conditions of admission to a mystery with promise, lines 46–49): οἱ θεοὶ τοῖς μ[ἐν ἀκολουθοῦσιν ἔ]σονται ἵλεως καὶ δώσουσιν αὐτο[ῖς ἀεὶ πάντα τἀγα]θά, ὅσα θεοὶ ἀνθρώποις, οὓς φιλοῦσι, [διδόασαν], "The gods will be gracious to those who follow them, and they will always give them every good thing, as much as gods give to men whom they love" [Trans.].

114 For immortality as a result of initiation (in this instance initiation into astrology) see Vett. Val., *Anth.* 31.3–5; André–Jean Festugière, *L'idéal religieux des Grecs et l'évangile*, Études bibliques (Paris: Gabalda, 1932). *Ibid.*, 143–160: immortality in grave inscriptions (Kaibel) with the counter–reckoning *ibid.*, 153–157; Nilsson, *Geschichte* 2:220f, observes that on the whole prospects of the Beyond are extremely rare. On Eleusis see Nilsson, *Geschichte* 1:672–678;

Plat., *Symp.* 207d, 208b; *Leg.* 721c.

115 Diod. S., *Bibl. hist.* 5.49.5f (Samothrace): διαβεβόηται δ' ἡ τούτων τῶν θεῶν ἐπιφάνεια καὶ παράδοξος ἐν τοῖς κινδύνοις βοήθεια τοῖς ἐπικαλεσαμένοις τῶν μυηθέντων. γίνεσθαι δέ φασι καὶ εὐσεβεστέρους καὶ δικαιοτέρους καὶ κατὰ πᾶν βελτίονας ἑαυτῶν τοὺς τῶν μυστηρίων κοινωνήσαντας, "But the fame has travelled wide of how those gods appear to mankind and bring unexpected aid to those initiates of theirs who call upon them in the midst of perils. The claim is also made that men who have taken part in the mysteries become more pious and more just and better in every respect than they were before" (Loeb 3:235).

116 Cf. also the inscription from Cumae: Nilsson, *Geschichte* 2:353f.

117 Without prejudice to their cult of the dead! Nilsson, *Geschichte* 2:349.

118 Plat., *Phaed.* 71e: εἴπερ ἔστι τὸ ἀναβιώσκεσθαι, "if there be such a thing as coming to life again" (Loeb 1:249).

119 The merely formally similar passage in Aesch., *Eum.* 648f, has a wholly different sense: ἀνδρὸς δ' ἐπειδὰν αἷμ' ἀνασπάσῃ κόνις ἅπαξ θανόντος, οὔτις ἔστ' ἀνάστασις, "But when the dust hath drained the blood of man, once he is slain, there is no return to life" (Loeb 2:335).

120 How strange the doctrine of the resurrection appeared to the Greeks is indicated by Luke in Acts 17:32. According to Just., *Dial.* 80.4, there are "so-called Christians" οἳ καὶ λέγουσι μὴ εἶναι νεκρῶν ἀνάστασιν, ἀλλὰ ἅμα τῷ ἀποθνήσκειν τὰς ψυχὰς

bodily character of the resurrection.[121] H. von Soden considers that the Corinthians are enthusiastic also in their eschatology: they anticipate "in the Spirit" the resurrection and teach, like the false teachers attacked in 2 Tim 2:18: ἀνάστασιν ἤδη γεγονέναι, "that the resurrection has already taken place." This is in harmony with v 4a and the whole discussion of the epistle,[122] though not indeed with the wording of vv 19 and 32. Bultmann would do justice to the latter by assuming that the Corinthians had in actual fact adopted a gnosticizing view, but that Paul has misunderstood their teaching to mean that death is the end of everything.[123] If we assume a misunderstanding, then of course it is impossible to derive from chap. 15 any conclusions as to the eschatology of "some," but the latter must be deduced from the rest of the epistle—and this, too, with caution, since indeed Paul does not ascribe this teaching to the community, but apparently only to a small group.

Still noteworthy is Albert Schweitzer's thesis that the Corinthians are advocates of the old "ultraconservative" eschatology which Paul has to deal with in 1 Thessalonians: that salvation is attained only by those who are still alive at the parousia.[124] But once again the practice of vicarious baptism is not in harmony with this. Schweitzer's thesis can, however, be modified to the effect that Paul *thinks* this teaching has made its way into Corinth. We can hardly manage without the assumption of a certain misunderstanding on Paul's part. Then, however, there is much to be said for the assumption that he is attacking people who, as he thinks, believe only in a

αὐτῶν ἀναλαμβάνεσθαι εἰς τὸν οὐρανόν, "who say too that there is no resurrection of the dead, but that their souls ascend to heaven at the very moment of their death" (Williams, 170). Festugière, *L'idéal*, 143–160. Cerfaux, *Christ*, 77, n. 1 [63, n. 1], remarks with greater elegance than exactitude: the Corinthians do not doubt that God can raise a corpse, but as Greeks they ask, "To what end?"

121 Julius Schniewind, "Die Leugnung der Auferstehung in Korinth," in his *Nachgelassene Reden und Aufsätze*, ed. Ernst Kähler (Berlin: Töpelmann, 1952), 110–139, objects that in face of such a position vv 24–28 would be meaningless as an argument.

122 Von Soden, "Sakrament und Ethik," 23, n. 1. Schniewind, "Leugnung," thinks he can largely reconstruct the Corinthian position from Paul's argument: Paul's eschatology, he holds, had been misunderstood in Corinth in the sense of 2 Thess 2:2 ("The day of the Lord is now present"). Bartsch modifies this, arguing that it is not the bodily character of the resurrection which is disputed, but the different nature of this bodily character (cf. vv 35ff). And the Corinthians think they can enter into the new existence without death or, as the case may be, transformation. Paul, he maintains, is not seeking to prove the bodily character of the resurrection, but the necessity of passing through death. But we do not know so much about the Corinthian views.

Incidentally, Gnostics later appropriated the word "resurrection"; Iren., *Haer.* 1.23.5; *Act. Joh.* 98; *Ev. Phil.* 63; the *Epistle to Rheginos*, see Michel Malinine, Henri–Charles Puech, Gilles Quispel, Walter Till, *De resurrectione epistula ad Rheginum* (Zurich: Rascher, 1963); also Hans–Martin Schenke, "Zum gegenwärtigen Stand der Erforschung der Nag–Hammadi–Handschriften," in *Koptologische Studien in der DDR*, Wissenschaftliche Zeitschrift der

Martin–Luther–Universität, Sonderheft (Halle-Wittenberg: Martin–Luther–Universität, 1965), 124–135.

123 In 2 Cor (5:1ff), he goes on, Paul is better informed. It is then possible to discover the Corinthian teaching there. We have there indications of dualistic ideas. But there, too, caution is called for in the reconstruction, because Paul puts them forward as his own.

Schmithals, too, assumes a misunderstanding on Paul's part. He describes the Corinthian teaching as Gnostic dualism, cf. v 46: the pneumatical is older than the psychical. The σάρξ, "flesh," is not only perishable, but contemptible. And the Gnostic has no need for further hope. It is in this sense that the phrase arises: ἀνάστασις νεκρῶν οὐκ ἔστιν, "there is no resurrection of the dead." This is also in accord with the rejection of the σάρξ of Christ (12:3). But Paul's opponents do not attack the σάρξ of Christ and do not dispute his resurrection, nor the resurrection as such, but the resurrection "of the dead" (Güttgemanns, *Der leidende Apostel*, 67f). They attain to their teaching on salvation not by means of cosmological gnosis, but as a consequence of their enthusiastic connection with the exalted Christ. Against the assumption of a misunderstanding see Jack H. Wilson, "The Corinthians Who Say There Is No Resurrection of the Dead," *ZNW* 59 (1968): 90–107.

124 Albert Schweitzer, *The Mysticism of Paul the Apostle*, tr. William Montgomery (New York: Holt, 1931), 93 (*Die Mystik des Apostels Paulus* [Tübingen: J. C. B. Mohr (Paul Siebeck), ²1954], 94). This would harmonize well with the sacramentalism: one imbues himself with vital powers. Schweitzer's thesis is taken up by Güttgemanns, *Der leidende Apostel*, 74–81 (on the presupposition that Paul is precisely aware of the situation in Corinth).

transformation of the living at the parousia, but not in a raising of the dead. This was the point of certain remarks already in vv 3–11, as also of the argument that follows.

12	But if it is proclaimed that Christ has been raised from the dead,[1] how is it that some of you say there is no resurrection of the dead? 13/ If there is no resurrection of the dead, Christ has not been raised either. 14/ If Christ has not been raised, then our proclamation is vain, and vain, too, is your faith. 15/ We are also found to be false witnesses of God, because we have testified of God that he raised Christ, whom he did not raise, if indeed[2] the dead are not raised. 16/ For if the dead are not raised, Christ has not been raised either. 17/ But if Christ has not been raised, your faith is vain, you are still in your sins. 18/ Then, too, those who have fallen asleep in Christ have been lost. 19/ If it is only in this life that we have hope in Christ, then we are more pitiable than all men.
20	But now, Christ has been raised from the dead as the firstfruits of those who have fallen asleep. 21/ For since death (came) through a man, the resurrection of the dead also (comes) through a man. 22/ For as in Adam all die, so also in Christ will all be made alive.
23	But each in his own order: Christ as the firstfruits, then 24/ at his coming those who are Christ's, then the end, when he hands over the sovereignty to God, the Father, after having annihilated every authority and power and force. 25/ For he must reign until he has "put all his enemies under his feet."[3] 26/ As the last enemy, death will be annihilated. 27/ For "he has put all things in subjection under his feet." But when it says that all things have been put in subjection, then it is plain: all things except him who has subjected all things to him. 28/ But when all things are subjected to him, then the Son will also subject himself to him who has made all things subject to him, that God may be all in all.
29	For what shall they do who have themselves baptized for the dead? If the dead are not raised at all, why then do they have themselves baptized for them?

1   For the use of the article, see the commentary; Blass–Debrunner §254(2).

2   *Sc.* "as they say"; Blass–Debrunner §454(2).

3   $ἄχρι οὗ = ἄχρι χρόνου ᾧ$; Bauer, *s.v.* $ἄχρι$. Subjunctive without $ἄν$ (classical): Blass–Debrunner §382(2); aorist subjunctive: Moulton–Howard–Turner,

30 Why then do we stand in jeopardy every hour?[4] **31** / Day by day I die, by that glorying in you,[5] brothers,[6] which I have in Christ Jesus, our Lord. **32** / If after the manner of men[7] I fought with beasts at Ephesus, what benefit is it to me?[8] If the dead are not raised, "let us eat and drink, for tomorrow we die."[9] Do not be deceived: "Evil company corrupts good manners." **34** / Be honestly[10] sober and do not sin! For many live in ignorance of God. I say this to your shame.[11]

■ **12–13** The first stage of the proof embraces vv 12–19: *Christology and Resurrection*, or: *Creed and Hope*.[12] Verse 12 links up again explicitly with the quotation and in doing so points forward to what is to be proved by adding: "ἐκ νεκρῶν" ἐγήγερται, "has been raised 'from the dead.'"[13] The Christological character of the proof

---

Grammar 3:111.

4 Plural of epistolary style, cf. v 31. τί καί: cf. v 29. Robertson and Plummer assume that καί is here not as in v 29 intensive, but means "also"; not so Bauer, *s.v.* τίς.

5 Or: "by my glory that I have acquired because of you." νή with accusative (*sc.* ὄμνυμι) is classical; in the NT only here. Gen 42:15f: νὴ τὴν ὑγίειαν Φαραω, "by Pharaoh's health." ὑμετέραν for the objective genitive, cf. ἣν ἔχω.

6 Om. p46 D G ℵ.

7 Lietzmann says: "as an ordinary man, not in view of my divine task." Bauer, *s.v.* ἄνθρωπος 1 c: "like an ordinary man"; the antithesis is: as a Christian certain of the resurrection. Weiss is against both. Schlatter holds that Paul is thinking not of one condemned to the beasts, but of a gladiator: "for he is reflecting on how he is in a position to defy death of his own will and in free sacrifice."

8 τὸ ὄφελος: without the article (τί μοι ὄφελος;) Herm., *Vis.* 3.3.1; Charit., *Chaer. et Call.* 7.4.10.

9 Futuristic use of the present: Blass–Debrunner §323(1).

10 δικαίως, "really": Joachim Jeremias, "Beobachtungen zu neutestamentlichen Stellen an Hand des neugefundenen griechischen Henoch–Textes," *ZNW* 38 (1939): 115–124, here esp. 122; Bauer, *s.v.*: "upright."

11 ἐντροπή: 6:5; "shame": Diod. S., *Bibl. hist.* 40.5a; Ps 68:8, 20. Classical: "reverence," "respect"; so Jos., *Ant.* 2.46; 14.375.

12 According to Walter Grundmann, "Überlieferung und Eigenaussage im eschatologischen Denken des Apostels Paulus," *NTS* 8 (1961–62): 12–26, two lines of thought crisscross each other, one that is temporal and eschatological and one that is personal and communicative (Christ as corporate personal-

ity). After 1 Cor the apocalyptic pictures disappear. "Existence between death and the future of the parousia also becomes for him a 'being with Christ' [Phil 1:23]" (p. 20). "It is not that the futurity disappears, but it is no longer expressed in the apocalyptic form of division into periods" (pp. 20f). But in view of the uncertain chronology of the epistles (Phil: Ephesus? Caesarea? Rome?) we should be as cautious in asserting development as in drawing conclusions *e silentio*, i.e. from the absence of a topic in an epistle. And the categories suggested by Grundmann are not appropriate to the situation in Paul. On vv 12ff see Paul Hoffmann, *Die Toten in Christus*, NtlAbh., n.s. 2 (Münster: Aschendorff, 1966), 239–252.

13 The expression "ἐκ (τῶν) νεκρῶν" is standard; see Bauer, *s.v.* νεκρός, Hoffmann, *Die Toten in Christus*, 180–185. The νεκροί are the totality of the dead, not merely as a number but also as a realm: the world of the dead. The expression is to be understood in this light; cf. Mt 14:2, "ἀπό." For the phrasing cf. also Phlegon (Jacoby, *FGH* 2B:1174 [no. 257, fr. 36.3.3]): ἀνέστη ὁ Βούπλαγος ἐκ νεκρῶν ..., "Bouplagos rose from the dead. . . ."

According to Erhard Güttgemanns, *Der leidende Apostel und sein Herr*, FRLANT, 90 (Göttingen: Vandenhoeck & Ruprecht, 1966), 74f, the point in v 12a lies in the "Christological difference": *Christ* is risen, *sc.* not *we*. With this Paul lays his finger on the Corinthian view. But the (Greek) wording and its intention are plain: Christ is—truly enough—proclaimed as risen. The future rising of the dead is thereby established.

Kümmel, *ad loc.*: "This fact of faith's being bound to an event that can be fixed in history, and yet cannot be historically grasped in its essential nature—namely, to the raising of the crucified Lord—marks

has the result that only the question of dead *Christians* can be dealt with, not that of the dead as such.[14] The creed does not supply speculative theses of a general kind, but defines the existence of believers and discloses hope.[15] This results from its content as such.[16] Then logic is brought into play (linking up with v 11): εἰ δὲ Χριστὸς κηρύσσεται . . ., "But if Christ is proclaimed. . . ." "Christ" is defined by the reference to the creed. The proclaiming of his resurrection is not supplementary to some other kind of proclamation of Christ, but is identical with it. Faith is indivisible. This also makes the logic of v 13 intelligible. Here it becomes completely plain that the Corinthians recognize Paul's presupposition, the resurrection of *Christ*. The argument rests upon this: "If . . .,[17] then. . . ." This is no mere play with the conclusions of formal logic.[18] For theological reasons, Paul sets out not from the fact, but from proclamation and faith. The resurrection is not an isolable fact. Even if Paul has emphasized that it lies in the past and is distinct

from our own, yet it is directed as such to us.

■ **14** Thus Paul can draw the conclusion: to dispute one's own resurrection is to abrogate the presupposition of one's own existence,[19] the kerygma and therewith also faith. The resurrection of Christ cannot be isolated.[20] It is believed only when it is grasped as a saving event. In this way Paul can theologically enforce belief in the resurrection.[21] For we have faith only together with the understanding of ourselves.

■ **15** The argument of v 14 on the basis of the kerygma (which is of course itself a factor in salvation) goes on to embrace the "witness": his existence, too, would be null and void.[22] The word ψευδόμαρτυς, "false witness," has given rise to a violent controversy. Karl

---

the foolishness of the message of the cross in all its offensiveness." This statement alters the tenor of chap. 15. The problems involved in the chapter consist in part in the very fact that it does *not* discuss cross and σκάνδαλον, "offense," but seeks to remove doubts. The apocalyptic world picture may be offensive to Greeks; the frontier situation between history and suprahistory may be so for modern reason; but a σκάνδαλον in Paul's sense is still another matter.

14 Non–Christians are not merely factually not envisaged, but also for theological reasons. No positive statements on them can be arrived at from the creed, from Christ. The practice of vicarious baptism confirms this rule. Incidentally, it can be seen that for Paul "raising" and "rising" are synonymous.

15 The chapter is a commentary on πίστις and ἐλπίς.

16 Jeremias, *Abba*, 303f, argues that Paul consistently distinguishes between νεκροί (without the article, vv 12, 13, 15, 16, 20, 21, 29b, 32) and οἱ νεκροί (29a, 35, 42, 52). νεκροί, he holds, are the dead in general, οἱ νεκροί are dead Christians. The change in v 29, he maintains, is made purposely. Rather, the statements with νεκροί are the general ones, which declare: "There is a resurrection of dead people." To this the statements on "the dead" are added. The use of the article is the same as in English. For νεκροί without the article meaning "the dead" cf. Thuc., *Hist.* 4.14.5; 5.10.12; Luc., *Ver. hist.* 1.39. The expression ἀνάστασις νεκρῶν is explained by ἀναστῆναι ἐκ νεκρῶν; Acts 17:32; Rom 1:4; τῶν νεκρῶν: Mt 22:31. Blass–Debrunner §254(2): "In 1 C 15:15,

16, 29, 32 the article has to be omitted because the concept, not the collective dead, is under discussion (otherwise 52)."

17 εἰ with the indicative of reality in "logical reasoning in Paul": Blass–Debrunner §372(2b); cf. 11:6; Rom 8:10f.

18 So Weiss. Such an argument, incidentally, would not be conclusive. Were Paul merely to maintain in general terms that a general repudiation of the resurrection would declare also a single instance to be impossible, then it could be replied that Christ—as a heavenly being—is an exception. Heinrici and Robertson and Plummer are right: the causal connection between the resurrection of Christ and that of the Christians is here already in Paul's mind. Christ's resurrection is not a single instance of a general rule.

19 As a new creature! The argumentation presupposes the context of event of salvation/proclamation/office of proclamation/faith. Commentary: 2 Cor 5:16–21.

20 This is stated later in the interpretation of Christ as the second Adam. Braun, *Gesammelte Studien*, 198–201, observes: if the resurrection of Christ is isolated to become an individual case, then it is no longer the Christ event. We may add: then it is the first instance and as such set fundamentally on the same level as the resurrection of man.

21 According to Braun, he does not appeal to their experience of faith, but guides them to the understanding of faith itself.

22 Here, too, the argument is neither merely formal nor sentimental: you surely will not regard us as liars.

Holl[23] concluded from the striking genitive construction ψευδομάρτυρες τοῦ θεοῦ that there existed an expression μάρτυρες τοῦ θεοῦ: eyewitnesses of God's mighty act. The ψευδόμαρτυς would accordingly be the false witness of God.[24] It was objected to this, especially by philologists, that the meaning can only be making false statements about God.[25] The controversy is decided by the ὅτι–clause, "because . . .," in which Paul explains the concept:[26] he is opposed to God and the testimony God wishes to be made; God has manifested this by raising Christ.[27] The logic again corresponds to v 13: εἴπερ ἄρα, "if indeed." νεκροί, despite the absence of the article, has to be rendered: "the dead" (see n. 16 above).

■ 16 This verse explains the logic of v 15b by harking back to v 13.

■ 17 This explains v 14: κενός is replaced by μάταιος[28] (both rendered "vain"). That our faith is ineffectual is defined to mean that it does not secure us freedom from our sins, that is to say justification, if Christ has not risen.[29] This tacitly relativizes all the religious forces that are at work in Corinth: they do not reach beyond "this" world. The plural of ἁμαρτία, "sin," which is unusual for Paul, is evoked by v 3.

■ 18 Paul here draws the conclusion with regard to those who have already died:[30] ἀπώλοντο, "they have been lost." If they are not liberated from sin, they remain a prey to death. And for Paul this does not mean simply that they are not alive, but that they are at the mercy of the *power* of death (or, at the mercy of death as a

What Paul says here must be understood in the light of the full theological sense of witness and witnessing.

23   Karl Holl, "Der ursprüngliche Sinn des Namens Märtyrer. Eine Entegegnung," *NJbchKlAlt* 37 (1916): 253–259, now in his *Aufsätze* 2:103–109; "Ψευδόμαρτυς," *Hermes* 52 (1917): 301–307, now in his *Aufsätze* 2:110–114; cf. already his "Die Vorstellung vom Märtyrer und die Märtyrerakte in ihrer geschichtlichen Entwicklung," *NJbchKlAlt* 33 (1914): 521–566, now in his *Aufsätze* 2:68–102, here esp. 70.

24   Like ψευδόχριστος, ψευδαπόστολος, ψευδοπροφήτης.

25   Blass–Debrunner §119(5). Hermann Strathmann, *TDNT* 4:513f: "Whether a man is μάρτυς or ψευδόμαρτυς depends on whether or not he tells the truth" (513). And: "The reference of the observation is to the content of the witness" (513). A certain compromise is sought by Hans von Campenhausen, *Die Idee des Martyriums in der Alten Kirche* (Göttingen: Vandenhoeck & Ruprecht, ²1964), 28f (esp. n. 4):
1) Paul does not elsewhere call himself a "witness of God." "The concept has not necessarily been taken over."
2) With Holl, however, we have to accept the meaning: he who wrongly bears the title "witness" (not: a witness *concerning* God, and not: he who makes false statements).
3) But Holl does not rightly explain the genitive (namely, as "genitive of possession": the witness who belongs to God).
4) Holl *and* his opponents wrongly presuppose the Greek concept of truth. Rather, the dominating concept is the personal concept of truth deriving from the OT. "For the truth to which the 'false witness' here opposes himself is not the logical truth of a statement, but 'the conduct which ful-

fils a specific expectation, a specific claim, justifies a proffered trust' " (Hans von Soden, "*Was ist Wahrheit?*" *Vom geschichtlichen Begriff der Wahrheit*, Marburger Akademische Reden, 46 [Marburg: Elwert, 1927], 13; now in his *Urchristentum und Geschichte*, ed. Hans von Campenhausen, vol. 1 [Tübingen: J. C. B. Mohr (Paul Siebeck), 1951], 1–24, here esp. 9).

26   With Strathmann, von Campenhausen, against Holl, who presupposes a fixed concept and declares that the ὅτι clause twists the original meaning.

27   Thus in the last analysis the false witness presents God as a liar. Jos., *Ant.* 8.404 and frequently, speaks of a καταψεύσασθαι τοῦ θεοῦ; Philo, *Op. mund.* 7; *Vit. Mos.* 1.90.

28   μάταιος is in Hellenistic–Jewish polemic characteristic of the "vain," "dead," "deceitful" idols.

29   Braun, *Gesammelte Studien*, 203f: "The removing of Christ as a special category turns faith in forgiveness and the attempt to live under it into an immanent affair—which, however, means into a utopia both in faith and in life." Weiss says the argument is "aimed at the heart." Against this, Braun rightly maintains that Paul does not appeal to the *experience* of redemption, but summons his readers to reflect on the presuppositions of faith in forgiveness: if the latter is merely something we possess in our souls, then it is self–deception: "only its nature as grounded in the eschatological Christ event makes it into that which, as pure experience, it vainly pretends to be" (*Gesammelte Studien*, 204).

30   For the expression cf. 1 Thess 4:13ff; there—in view of the present state of the dead—the perfect participle is used (as here in v 20), here—in view of their fate—the aorist participle. On κοιμᾶσθαι, see Robert E. Bailey, "Is 'Sleep' the Proper Biblical Term for the Intermediate State?" *ZNW* 55 (1964): 161–

power, as the last enemy),[31] "lost" in the full sense of ἀπώλεια.

■ **19** Verse 19 is not unequivocal: how are we to relate μόνον, "only"? Does Paul mean: "If we have hope only in this life" or "if in this life we have only hope"?[32] Both the trend of the passage and also the Pauline use of ἐλπίς/ἐλπίζειν lead to the former interpretation; ἐλπίς is for a Paul a *positive* concept.[33] The notion of an "eternal" life, in the beyond, is taken over from apocalyptic;[34] the mode of expression is rhetorical.[35]

This way of arguing is embarrassing for modern exegetes.[36] Bousset objects that even without such a hope one would have to live a life of loyalty to the Spirit of Jesus and of sacrifice. But Karl Barth aptly points out that this situation (envisaged by Bousset) is a theoretical construction.[37] The construction, he says, ignores the fact that we are *today* brought to judgment and determined by the cross. *Such* reflections would be possible if the preceding verses were not there. For Paul, hope is not merely the prospect of a better beyond, but the working out of existence in this world (see Rom 5:3ff). And existence in sin is despair (not *experience* of despair). Paul is not arguing in timeless theoretical terms, without regard to the *real* situation, but is challenging the Corinthians in the light of their faith.[38]

■ **20–22** Christ and Adam

■ **20** Paul provides a connecting link for the new thought[39] by recurring once more to the creed, and interprets ἐγήγερται (again with the addition of ἐκ νεκρῶν, as in v 12) by saying: ἀπαρχὴ τῶν κεκοιμημένων,[40] "the firstfruits of those who have fallen asleep." The history of the concept ἀπαρχή, "firstfruits," is of little help in regard to the meaning.[41] Paul uses this word to describe the first converts of a community (or a country) who are held in special esteem (16:15; Rom 16:5). He uses it as an eschatological term: the Spirit is

---

167 (debate with Otto Michel, "Zur Lehre vom Todesschlaf," *ZNW* 35 [1936]: 285–290 and Oscar Cullmann); he aptly remarks that the idea of resurrection does not lie in the word κοιμᾶσθαι which is an ancient Greek euphemism, but in the specific context. Lietzmann thinks the expression κοιμᾶσθαι ἐν Χριστῷ is used *cum grano salis*. For if Christ were not risen, neither would there be such a thing as being in Christ. The correct thing to say would be: those who have fallen asleep are under the delusion of being in Christ. This is not so. Paul insists upon the fact that Christ is risen and that they "have fallen asleep in Christ."

31 To be sure, there is no attempt at a logical redressing of the balance by means of the expectation that death itself will be annihilated as the last enemy.

32 Weiss (on ἠλπικότες ἐσμέν) says: if we are only hopers, i.e. dupes; ἐσμέν is not an auxiliary verb, but a copula.

33 With Kümmel. A certain compromise is made by Bachmann and Allo, who hold that μόνον limits the whole sentence: if we are nothing else save people who hope in Christ in this life. But then justice is not done to the perfect participle. An interpretation similar to Kümmel's is adopted by Héring, and by Harald Riesenfeld, "Paul's 'Grain of Wheat' Analogy and the Argument of 1 Corinthians 15," *The Gospel Tradition*, 171–186, here esp. 174, n. 4 (originally in *Studien zum Neuen Testament und Patristik: Erich Klostermann zum 90. Geburtstag dargebracht*, TU, 77 [Berlin: Akademie–Verlag, 1961], 43–55, here esp. 45, n. 2).

34 *S. Bar.* 21.13: "For if there were this life only, which belongs to all men, nothing would be more bitter than this" (Charles, *APOT* 2:494).

35 ἐλεεινός alongside ταλαίπωρος, Rev 3:17.

36 See Weiss.

37 An example of the abstractness of idealistic ethics, as compared with the concreteness and actuality of Paul.

38 Schlatter, 407: "He presupposes that they have faith with its results, with acquittal from guilt and with the certainty of eternal life." This holds whether we see in v 19 an allusion to the doctrine advocated in Corinth (naturally once again: as Paul understands it) or only an extreme consequence which Paul draws from his own reflections. In point of fact it is meant by Paul as an allusion to the Corinthian position. This emerges from its relatedness to v 12. Verse 19 confirms that to his mind all hope of a beyond is rejected in Corinth.

39 νυνὶ δέ, "but now." For the content see M. Aur. Ant., *Medit.* 2.11: εἰ δὲ ἤτοι οὐκ εἰσὶν ἢ οὐ μέλει αὐτοῖς τῶν ἀνθρωπείων, τί μοι ζῆν ἐν κόσμῳ κενῷ θεῶν ἢ προνοίας κενῷ; ἀλλὰ καὶ εἰσὶν καὶ μέλει αὐτοῖς τῶν ἀνθρωπείων, "But if indeed there are no Gods, or if they do not concern themselves with the affairs of men, what boots it for me to live in a Universe where there are no Gods, where Providence is not? Nay, but there *are* Gods, and they *do* concern themselves with human things" (Loeb, 35).

40 Now we have the perfect, appropriately: in view of what they now are (see n. 30 above).

41 This applies also to the OT meaning: the firstfruits

ἀπαρχή.[42] Here Paul is stating in the first instance that Jesus is the first of a series. But this does not exhaust the meaning. This much is already plain from the fact that Paul, apparently on purpose, does not say: the first of those who have been raised, but: of those who have fallen asleep. This is a hint in the same direction as was already perceptible in v 6. And the explanation of the meaning of ἀπαρχή in v 22 shows that the first instance is constitutive for the others.[43] At the same time ἀπαρχή is used to ward off fanaticism: Christ is so far the only one.[44]

■ **21** Paul states the Adam–Christ idea in the form of a principle.[45] In the background stands the idea of a correspondence between the time of origin and the time of end (see on v 45). The designation of Adam and of Christ as ἄνθρωπος, "man,"[46] presupposes the idea of the "primal man," and likewise the view of the Fall as the cause of death.[47] But now, already in v 21 we have indications of a modification of the mythical schema.

It would be in keeping with the schema as such to draw the conclusion: if the second "man," the Author of life, is already here (or, has already been here), then life, too, must be here. But this conclusion (which leads directly to the Corinthian position) Paul wards off by speaking on Christ's side not simply of "life,"[48] but of the "resurrection"; this is in keeping with the use of the future in v 22. A distinction from the myth is contained also in δι' ἀνθρώπου, "by man":[49] Paul does not explain Adam's sin by a "cause" lying behind it.[50]

■ **22** Adam is not merely the ancestor of men, but the primal man. This applies likewise to Christ as the ἄνθρωπος-Redeemer.[51] This idea cannot be derived from the biblical creation story. It is introduced by Paul, however, as a matter of course,[52] and has thus been taken over by him from the tradition. In point of fact Adam in Jewish speculation had become the primal man,[53] in whom the whole of mankind is virtually contained.[54] Death proceeds from him because the whole

---

of the flock, or the crop, which are to be dedicated to God.

42   Rom 8:23; synonymous is ἀρραβών (2 Cor 1:22).

43   Cf. πρωτότοκος ἐκ τῶν νεκρῶν, "firstborn from the dead," Col 1:18 and the double meaning of ἀρχηγός: temporally the first, Acts 3:15: τῆς ζωῆς, "of life" (cf. Acts 26:23: πρῶτος ἐξ ἀναστάσεως, "first of the resurrection") and: the author, Heb 2:10: τῆς σωτηρίας, "of salvation").

44   This antifanaticist point is directed essentially against the whole of the Corinthian position. It has naturally to be asked whether we must not also conclude that Paul has thus after all rightly seen through the Corinthians' fanaticist eschatology when he here lays down his eschatological and Christological reservation. Yet this conclusion is not compelling. The reservation in question has a fundamental character in Paul. It appears also in passages where there is no actual polemic, such as Rom 6.

45   ἐπειδή: "it is recognized"; 1:21f.

46   For greater detail see on vv 45–47; Egon Brandenburger, *Adam und Christus*, WMANT, 7 (Neukirchen: Neukirchener Verlag, 1962), 157.

47   On the doctrines of the effects of sin in Jewish theology see Brandenburger, *Adam und Christus*, 15–67. The Fall does not have to be proved by Gen 3; Gen 6 is also possible (the Fall of the Angels). Death can also be derived from Eve: Sir 25:24. The relation between the fate of sin and the fate of death is not clear (*4 Ezra* 7.118f). At all events the notion of the fate of death is bound up with the apocalyptic world picture: *4 Ezra* 3.7; *S. Bar*. 17.3; 23.4; 54.15; 56.6;

alongside of this we find the view that death is the individual punishment for the sins of each individual, see Str.–B. 3:228f.

48   That is to say: ". . . καὶ δι' ἀνθρώπου ζωή," ". . . by man comes also life." Cf. the analogous twist in Rom 6:4, 5.

49   Not in the preposition διά as such, cf. Sir 25:24 (διά with accusative). The distinction lies in the avoidance of the mythological derivation of sin. Brandenburger, *Adam und Christus*, 71f, observes that Paul has altered a notion of correspondence that already lay to hand. This is plain from the two πάντες, "all," that correspond to the schema. In Paul's context they are superfluous—indeed, the second (v 22b) militates against his argument. It is true that a restitution of all could be read out of this. But Paul of course in the whole chapter has only believers in view. Apart from this, he can express himself so because Christ has died for all men and consequently salvation is ready for them all.

According to Hans–Alwin Wilcke, *Das Problem eines messianischen Zwischenreichs bei Paulus*, AThANT, 51 (Zurich: Zwingli, 1967), 75 (against Schmiedel), ὥσπερ—οὕτως, "as—so," does not set the two πάντες parallel to each other, but the results of the deaths of Adam and of Christ.

50   Neither from the working of Satan nor from the evil urge; cf. Rom 5:12; Bultmann, *Theology* 1:251 [251]; Joseph Freundorfer, *Erbsünde und Erbtod beim Apostel Paulus*, NtlAbh, 13, 1–2 (Münster: Aschendorff, 1927).

51   The conceptual material is not consistent. *Here*, for

of humanity is contained in him.[55] Yet this notion of "corporate personality" does not suffice to explain the Adam—Christ typology. The notion of the primal man reaches beyond this, and anyway Jewish interpretation of Adam as the primal man points us to a wider context in the history of religion:[56] the idea of the primal man is widespread. Instances are provided above all by Gnosticism.[57]

As in v 21, so also here Paul reshapes the mythical schema. The latter requires: "So in Christ all have been made alive." By putting the future, however, Paul avoids a fanaticist conclusion. The futurity of the life in question is for him constitutive: it is precisely as future that it exerts its influence in the life of this world, not in the nonhistorical form of the fanatical and Gnostic self–

consciousness, but in the historical form of the new way of life. The fact that Paul uses the future purposely is shown by the consistency with which he maintains it in Rom 6.[58] Since it is not the mythical schema that holds, but the Pauline transformation of it, "all" does not mean all men altogether, but all who are in Christ.[59]

■ **23–28** The Apocalyptic Order as an Argument for the Resurrection.[60]

This section shows us Paul in the tradition of apocalyptic. The latter's fundamental notion that the course of the world follows a predetermined plan, along with a concrete conception of this plan, of the stages of its development is here taken for granted.[61] "Christ" (thus v 23, following v 3) has been subsequently introduced into the schema, thereby modifying it. Paul sets out from

example, preexistence plays no part—indeed it does not fit at all.

52 For of course it serves the argument; in Rom 5, too, it is presupposed as familiar.

53 Benjamin Murmelstein, "Adam, ein Beitrag zur Messiaslehre," *WZKM* 35 (1928): 242–275; 36 (1929): 51–86; Arthur Marmorstein, "Paulus und die Rabbinen," *ZNW* 30 (1931): 271–285; Willy Staerk, *Soter I: Die biblische Erlösererwartung als religionsgeschichtliches Problem*, BFTh, 2, 31 (Gütersloh: Bertelsmann, 1933); *Soter II: Die Erlösererwartung in der östlichen Religionen* (Stuttgart: Kohlhammer, 1938); Brandenburger, *Adam und Christus*.

54 It is usual to speak of the idea of "corporate personality"; Davies, *Paul and Rabbinic Judaism*, 57; Ernest Best, *One Body in Christ* (London: SPCK, 1955), 203–207; Rudolf Schnackenburg, "Todes– und Lebensgemeinschaft mit Christus. Neue Studien zu Röm 6,1–11," *MThZ* 6 (1955): 32–53; Eduard Schweizer, *TDNT* 7:1072–74.

55 "In Adam" may have been coined by Paul in dependence on the formula "in Christ"; Joachim Jeremias, *TDNT* 1:141, n. 7.

56 According to Brandenburger, *Adam und Christus*, 68–157; 135, n. 2, the Adam speculations presented by Staerk (*Soter* 1:102, 156–160; 2:61–132) cannot shed any light on the background of 1 Cor 15 and Rom 5. He rightly warns against overestimating the idea of Adam as the *guph* of souls (Brandenburger, 141). We cannot read out of this idea that the soul is *determined* by its "being in Adam." The notion provides no concrete statement whatever concerning human existence.

57 See Jervell, *Imago Dei*; Colpe, *Die religionsgeschichtliche Schule*, 57–68; Hans-Martin Schenke, *Der Gott "Mensch" in der Gnosis* (Göttingen: Vandenhoeck & Ruprecht, 1962); Kurt Rudolph, "Urmensch,"

*RGG*³ 6:1196. See on v 45 below.

58 This is bound up with the orientation of existence on the parousia. Hermann, *Kyrios und Pneuma*, 120, seeks to link the notion of life with the πνεῦμα. Yet it is particularly significant that Paul can argue without the notion of the Spirit. It is not correct that only this notion is constitutive for the Adam–Christ parallel. Schnackenburg, "Todes– und Lebensgemeinschaft mit Christus," 45f, says the temporal distance (that Christ is already risen, his followers not yet) plays no decisive part. "This ability to disregard the temporal gap is also characteristic of the wholeness of Hebrew [*sic*!] thinking." The temporal distance is not forgotten, v 23. But the time coefficient "arises only in view of the effectual emergence of the result in the many. For the basic starting point of this kind of thinking the time factor is nonessential," see 2 Cor 5:14. This is a postulate on dogmatic premises, and one which is exploded by the exposition of the text.

59 See n. 49 above. With Heinrich Molitor, *Die Auferstehung der Christen und Nichtchristen nach dem Apostel Paulus*, NtlAbh, 16, 1 (Münster: Aschendorff, 1933), 42. Molitor provides an overview of the history of the exegesis. The opposite interpretation appeals to the scheme as such and fails to notice the Pauline *differentia specifica*. Cf. Rom 5:12ff. Wilcke, *Das Problem eines messianischen Zwischenreiches*, 69–72.

60 The apocalyptic outlook carries on the future ζωο-ποιηθήσονται, "will be made alive."

61 "Apocalypse of the Ten Weeks" in *Eth. En.* 93 and 91; *Sib.* 4.47–91; the genealogies of Jesus in Mt 1 and Lk 3; Volz, *Eschatologie*, 141. The further investigations of historians of religion into the genesis of the idea in Parsism are of no significance here.

the type of apocalyptic which expects the kingdom of the messiah before the onset of the new aeon.[62] Whereas the Johannine Apocalypse simply takes over the Jewish combination of the new aeon, or new world, and the messianic kingdom preceding it, Paul refashions the Jewish notion in such a way as to make it a means to the presentation of his own eschatological intention, the distinction between present and future. He takes over from the schema the notion that death is not annihilated until the end of the messianic kingdom. But he transposes this kingdom into the present. For Christ is risen. His kingdom fills up the period between the resurrection and the consummation of the work of salvation after the parousia. It is not the kingdom of visible peace. This period is determined by the cross. Here the cosmological apocalyptic notions of the messianic kingdom disappear. It is Christologically speaking the time of the subjection of the powers, anthropologically speaking the time of the church, of the proclaiming of the death of Christ, of faith, of hope.[63]

■ 23 $\tau\acute{\alpha}\gamma\mu\alpha$ can designate an orderly division, or the standing or rank.[64] $\dot{\alpha}\pi\alpha\rho\chi\acute{\eta}$, "firstfruits," here too, of course, designates not only the temporal, but also the inherent precedence,[65] and in Paul's sense the causal connection between the resurrection of Christ and that of believers (see on v 20).[66] The Christological orientation is shown by the fact that Paul, here as before, is concerned only with the resurrection of *believers*.[67] The word $\pi\alpha\rho o\upsilon\sigma\acute{\iota}\alpha$ is not frequent in Paul.[68] In the political world it is used of the arrival of the ruler,[69] in religious language of the epiphany of the deity.[70] Paul does not yet employ it in an absolute, technical sense.[71]

Is $\epsilon\hat{\iota}\tau\alpha$ $\tau\grave{o}$ $\tau\acute{\epsilon}\lambda os$, "then the end," a continuation of the series of $\tau\acute{\alpha}\gamma\mu\alpha\tau\alpha$, "orders"? That is, does it mean a third group of people who are raised? Then $\tau\acute{\epsilon}\lambda os$ would have to mean "the rest," namely, all the rest of the dead. In this case we should have evidence here of a doctrine of the *general* resurrection of the dead.[72] In favor

62   *4 Ezra* 7.26–30 (duration: 400 years); *S. Bar.* 30: the messiah's judgment of the survivors, then resurrection of the dead and last judgment; Rev 20:2f: the millennium. Albert Schweitzer, *The Mysticism of Paul the Apostle*, tr. William Montgomery (New York: Holt, 1931), 84–90 (*Die Mystik des Apostels Paulus* [Tübingen: J. C. B. Mohr (Paul Siebeck), ²1954], 85–90).

63   Schweitzer, *Mysticism*, 90f (*Mystik*, 90f), fails to recognize the transposition of apocalyptic into believing understanding. According to him Paul, like apocalyptic, reckons with two different kinds of blessedness, messianic and eternal. But the kingdom of the messiah does not lie in the future for Paul. And the present state of believers is determined by the presence of the Spirit as $\dot{\alpha}\pi\alpha\rho\chi\acute{\eta}$ of what is to come, by transformation into a new creation, by faith, hope and love as advance gifts of the eschatological existence.

64   Division: $\sigma\tau\rho\alpha\tau\iota\omega\tau\iota\kappa\grave{o}\nu$ $\tau\acute{\alpha}\gamma\mu\alpha$, "company of soldiers" (Loeb 1:233), Ign., *Rom.* 5.1. Rank: *1 Cl.* 37:3; 41.1. Pharisees, Sadducees are $\tau\acute{\alpha}\gamma\mu\alpha\tau\alpha$, Jos., *Bell.* 2.164: $\Sigma\alpha\delta\delta o\upsilon\kappa\alpha\hat{\iota}o\iota$ $\delta\acute{\epsilon}$, $\tau\grave{o}$ $\delta\epsilon\acute{\upsilon}\tau\epsilon\rho o\nu$ $\tau\acute{\alpha}\gamma\mu\alpha$, "and the Sadducees, the second group [order]." Incidentally, the difference is not so very great. Gerhard Delling, *ThWNT* 8:31f, tends to favor "rank," "standing." Schlatter, 412, puts forward the subtle argument on the basis of the meaning "division," which is surely the more natural one, that "Jesus is not also a $\tau\acute{\alpha}\gamma\mu\alpha$; an individual is no $\tau\acute{\alpha}\gamma\mu\alpha$. His church is one." But consider the wording and *1 Cl.* 41.1.

65   Scholion to Eur., *Or.* 96: $\dot{\alpha}\pi\alpha\rho\chi\grave{\eta}$ $\dot{\epsilon}\lambda\acute{\epsilon}\gamma\epsilon\tau o$ $o\dot{\upsilon}$ $\mu\acute{o}\nu o\nu$ $\tau\grave{o}$ $\pi\rho\hat{\omega}\tau o\nu$ $\tau\hat{\eta}$ $\tau\acute{\alpha}\xi\epsilon\iota$, $\dot{\alpha}\lambda\lambda\grave{\alpha}$ $\kappa\alpha\grave{\iota}$ $\tau\grave{o}$ $\pi\rho\hat{\omega}\tau o\nu$ $\tau\hat{\eta}$ $\tau\iota\mu\hat{\eta}$, " 'firstfruit' designates not only the first in succession, but also the first in honor" [Trans.].

66   The Persian source: *Bundahišn* 30.7 (cited after Colpe, *Die religionsgeschichtliche Schule*, 158): "First the bones of Gâyômard are raised, then those of Mâshya and Mâshyôî, then those of the rest of mankind" (the righteous and the godless). Gâyômard, incidentally, is only in a temporal sense the first; he is not the redeemer (Colpe, *Die religionsgeschichtliche Schule*, 158). On the appearing of the bringer of salvation in the apocalyptic drama see Volz, *Eschatologie*, 211f.

67   "Those that are Christ's," Gal 5:24; 1 Cor 3:23.

68   1 Thess 2:19; 3:13; 4:15; 5:23 and 2 Thess 2:1, 8, 9. Further, in a profane sense (presence) 1 Cor 16:17; 2 Cor 10:10; Phil 1:26; (arrival) 2 Cor 7:6f; Phil 2:12.

69   *3 Macc.* 3.17; Ditt., *Syll.* 1:740 (no. 495, lines 85f); 2:419 (no. 741, lines 21, 30).

70   Diod. S., *Bibl. hist.* 4.3.3: $\tau\grave{\alpha}s$ $\delta\grave{\epsilon}$ $\gamma\upsilon\nu\alpha\hat{\iota}\kappa\alpha s$ $\kappa\alpha\tau\grave{\alpha}$ $\sigma\upsilon\sigma\tau\acute{\eta}\mu\alpha\tau\alpha$ $\theta\upsilon\sigma\iota\acute{\alpha}\zeta\epsilon\iota\nu$ $\tau\hat{\omega}$ $\theta\epsilon\hat{\omega}$ $\kappa\alpha\grave{\iota}$ $\beta\alpha\kappa\chi\epsilon\acute{\upsilon}\epsilon\iota\nu$ $\kappa\alpha\grave{\iota}$ $\kappa\alpha\theta\acute{o}\lambda o\upsilon$ $\tau\grave{\eta}\nu$ $\pi\alpha\rho o\upsilon\sigma\acute{\iota}\alpha\nu$ $\dot{\upsilon}\mu\nu\epsilon\hat{\iota}\nu$ $\tau o\hat{\upsilon}$ $\Delta\iota o\nu\acute{\upsilon}\sigma o\upsilon$, "while the matrons, forming in groups, offer sacrifices to the god and celebrate his mysteries and, in general, extol with hymns the presence of Dionysus" (Loeb 2:347). Ditt., *Syll.* 3:320 (no. 1169, line 35); Jos., *Ant.* 3.80, 203 (God's $\pi\alpha\rho o\upsilon\sigma\acute{\iota}\alpha$, vacillating between arrival and presence); 9.55. Cf. also the use of $\dot{\epsilon}\pi\iota$-$\phi\acute{\alpha}\nu\epsilon\iota\alpha$, "appearing," (in Diodorus it stands shortly before the passage quoted) in the Pastoral Epistles. The language of the court and that of the sanctuary

of this interpretation one can point to the fact that the phrase appears in the course of a series. [73] Against it, however, is the fact that there is no evidence for this meaning of τέλος. [74] Apart from the meaning of the word τέλος, "end, conclusion," [75] it is decisive for the exposition that Paul himself explains the sense by means of the two ὅταν clauses: [76] ὅταν [77] παραδιδοῖ [78] . . ., ὅταν καταργήσῃ, "when he hands over . . ., after he has annihilated." The second is subordinate to the first: "after." That is to say: God has delegated his βασιλεία, "kingship," to Christ for a definite period, from the raising of Christ (which of course is his exaltation) to his parousia, and for a definite end, the annihilation of the hostile powers. Christ gives the sovereignty back to God, [79] "after" having annihilated all his enemies. [80] The annihilating begins with the exaltation; [81] this is indeed the purpose of his enthronement. [82] The wording is also in harmony with this. Now is already the time of the sovereignty of Christ, and therewith also of the subjecting of the powers. Believers are still exposed to the latter, but no longer subject to them (Rom 8:34–39).

Demonology is a standard part of the apocalyptic

---

are contiguous in the age of the Hellenistic ruler cult.

71 Literature: Bauer, *s.v.*; Albrecht Oepke, *TDNT* 5:858–871.

72 Judaism in part expects the resurrection only of the righteous (2 Macc 7:9, 23; *Ps. Sal.* 14.3–7: ὅσιοι κυρίου ζήσονται ἐν αὐτῷ εἰς τὸν αἰῶνα, "the pious of the Lord shall live by it forever" [v 7; Charles, *APOT* 2:645]) and in part of all (with judgment; *4 Ezra* 7.32; *S. Bar.* 50f; *Eth. En.* 51; *Test. B.* 10).

73 According to Lietzmann, the three members are homogeneous, τέλος answers to ἀπαρχή, and we have to supply: (1) ἐζωοποιήθη; (2) ζωοποιηθήσονται; (3) correspondingly: ζωοποιηθήσεται. Lietzmann tends to see in this third instance a resurrection not to judgment, but to salvation. Then, to be sure, he must go on to add the speculation that "those who die in unbelief are converted in the beyond before their resurrection."

74 Gerhard Delling, *TDNT* 8:49–59, *ad loc.* p. 55; Wilcke, *Probleme eines messianischen Zwischenreiches*, 85–101. Nor does Lietzmann's reference to an occasional "concrete" sense of τέλος support the meaning "rest": Isa 19:15, κεφαλὴν καὶ οὐράν, ἀρχὴν καὶ τέλος, "head or tail, beginning or end." This passage tells *against* him. Incidentally, in his translation he writes: "the end." Paul is not thinking of a double resurrection.

75 We have accordingly to supply: ἔσται. Héring *ad loc.*; see also his "Saint Paul a–t–il enseigné deux résurrections?" *RHPhR* 12 (1932): 300–320. Herm., *Vis.* 3.8.9: ἔχει τέλος, "the end comes" (Loeb 2:49); cf. *4 Ezra* 7.35.

76 Heinrici, who observes that Paul is saying no more than that "after overcoming of all his enemies, which precedes the τέλος, the handing over of the kingdom to God the Father takes place at once."

77 With present indicative? Blass–Debrunner §382(4): "like ἐάν"; Moulton–Howard–Turner, *Grammar*, subjunctive: v 28; see following note.

78 Variant reading παραδιδῷ, p[46], Alexandrians, D; παραδῷ ℵ; παραδιδοῖ B G. διδοῖ can be indicative, Blass–Debrunner §94(1). But Blass–Debrunner §95(2) regard διδοῖ as subjunctive: "The inflection of the subjunctive of ἔδωκα has entirely gone over to the pattern of verbs in –οῦν."

79 Weiss says of τῷ θεῷ καὶ πατρί: "With our article we cannot reconstruct the force of the Greek. It has in this instance something of the demonstrative +relative: 'to him who is God and Father.' Nor can there be any doubt that these predicates are expressed from the standpoint of the παραδούς—'his God and Father' [II 1:3]—and not, for example, in a didactic sense from the standpoint of the Christian."

80 καταργεῖν in an apocalyptic context: see on 2:6. The "subjecting" (vv 25, 27) is nothing else than the annihilation; this emerges in v 26. Paul is not thinking, for example, of a restoring of fallen angels to obedience, but of the removal of the "enemies." The twofold form of expression is caused by the taking over of Scripture.

81 It does not begin only with the parousia. Then it becomes manifest. Ulrich Luz, *Das Geschichtsverständnis des Paulus*, BEvTh, 49 (Munich: Kaiser, 1968), 343–352, assumes that Paul in vv 24–28 is linking together two pre–Pauline Christian traditions: a tradition of the subjection of the powers at Christ's exaltation (Phil 2:6ff; Eph 4:8ff; 1 Pet 3:22) and another tradition of the handing over of the kingdom to God at the end (Rev 20, where indeed death is annihilated at the end of the apocalyptically conceived messianic interregnum). In the first tradition, he argues, a temporal dimension extending into the future is absent. By means of the synthesis, he goes on, Paul makes such a dimension perceptible, and thereby achieves his antienthusiastic point.

82 The pre–Pauline hymn in Phil 2:6ff likewise combines the subjection of the powers with the enthronement, but the conception and perspective are different. There the subjection is considered already complete, and the goal is the acclamation of Jesus as κύριος by all the powers, whereas according to Paul Christ annihilates the powers and then subjects himself to God.

world picture.[83] The designations of the demons are Jewish: ἀρχαί, ἐξουσίαι, δυνάμεις, "authorities, powers, forces."[84] In themselves they can mean either good or evil spirits. The combining of synonyms[85] is standard style: Rom 8:38.[86] The nonmythological sense is evident from the fact that Paul combines demonological concepts of power with concepts of existence (Rom 8:38; see on 3:22).

■ **25** This statement provides the proof by means of a brief allusion to the apocalyptic order (δεῖ, "he must") and above all by means of Scripture, Ps 109 according to the LXX. This passage also plays a part elsewhere in the New Testament's Scripture proof.[87] It buttresses the view of the "exaltation" of Christ.[88] The text of the LXX[89] is shaped and applied in a free, *ad hoc* manner. The interpretation, to be sure, is disputed: What is it meant to prove? The answer is bound up with how we determine the subjects of θῇ, "he has put," and ὑπέταξεν in v 27, "he has put in subjection," and the

possessive pronouns in vv 25 and 27: ὑπὸ τοὺς πόδας αὐτοῦ, "under *his* feet." Whose?

First of all, to what does the proof refer?[90] There are essentially four suggestions:

1) to the whole of v 24 (Heinrici, Lietzmann)
2) to the two ὅταν–clauses (Bachmann)
3) to the second ὅταν–clause (Schmiedel)
4) the element of proof lies in ἕως (*sic!* Paul says ἄχρι οὗ, "until"; "the σύνθρονον εἶναι, "sharing of the throne," has accordingly its limits" (Weiss).

Maier seeks to find a solution by examining the structure of vv 24 and 25: there are the following parallels both in form and in content:

a) ὅταν παραδιδοῖ—δεῖ γὰρ αὐτὸν κτλ., v 26
b) ὅταν καταργήσῃ—ἄχρι οὗ θῇ κτλ., v 27.

The purpose is to show that the whole messianic prophecy and the whole fulfillment agree with each other. The purpose is not the temporal limitation of the sovereignty of Christ, but the fact that it is guaranteed by God and

83   Otto Everling, *Die paulinische Angelologie und Dämonologie* (Göttingen: Vandenhoeck & Ruprecht, 1888); Martin Dibelius, *Die Geisterwelt im Glauben des Paulus* (Göttingen: Vandenhoeck & Ruprecht, 1909); for Jewish demonlogy: Str.-B. 3:581–584; 4:501–535; Bousset–Gressmann, *Die Religion des Judentums*, 320–331; Bauer and *TDNT* under the relevant key words.

84   These terms are not found in a personal sense in profane Greek, see Werner Foerster, *TDNT* 2:571–573; Walter Grundmann, *TDNT* 2:295.

85   Paul, unlike Jewish demonology, has no interest in the differentiation of classes of angels and demons. If an archangel appears at the parousia (1 Thess 4:16), then that is a relic from the tradition. In the present chapter he says nothing of this figure (v 52). Incidentally, the Jewish classifications are purely speculative.

86   Col 1:16; 2:10; Eph 1:21, etc. *Test. L.* 3.8 knows θρόνοι and ἐξουσίαι, *Test. Sal.* 20.15, ἀρχαὶ καὶ ἐξ-ουσίαι καὶ δυνάμεις.

87   Mk 12:36 parallels; Acts 2:34; Heb 1:13. In earlier rabbinical literature the passage is not messianically interpreted, Str.-B. 4:452–465. Billerbeck assumes that an existing messianic interpretation has been suppressed; for the oldest messianic interpretation is found in an active opponent of Christianity, R. Ishmael (*ca.* A.D. 100–130, see pp. 458–460). This conclusion is uncertain. Mk 12:36f par. likewise does not prove that the Jews interpreted Ps 110 (109) messianically.

88   Yet it is not to be supposed that the "exaltation" of

Christ was first spun out of this passage; so Ferdinand Hahn, *The Titles of Jesus in Christology*, tr. Harold Knight and George Ogg (London: Lutterworth; New York and Cleveland: World, 1969), 129–135 (*Christologische Hoheitstitel*, FRLANT, 83 [Göttingen: Vandenhoeck & Ruprecht, ³1966], 126–132). The idea of the exaltation is older than the explicit Scripture proof, and for its part made possible the Christological application of this Psalm. It should be noted that Paul does not link an enthronement with the parousia.

The "kingdom" of Christ is temporally limited. This view is bound up historically with the Jewish view of the temporal limitation of the messiah's kingdom. Yet it is in Paul no mere relic of the history of religion, but indicates that his Christology is constructed on strictly soteriological lines. To put a point on it: Christ is nothing else save the saving work of God.

89   κάθου ἐκ δεξιῶν μου, ἕως ἂν θῶ τοὺς ἐχθρούς σου ὑποπόδιον τῶν ποδῶν σου, "Sit at my right hand until I make your enemies your footstool" (cf. Mt 22:44: ὑποκάτω τῶν ποδῶν σου, "*beneath* your feet").

90   Review: F. W. Maier, "Ps 110:1 (LXX 109:1) im Zusammenhang von 1 Kor 15:24–26," *BZ* 20 (1932): 139–156.

91   See Wilhelm Dittmar, *Vetus Testamentum in Novo* (Göttingen: Vandenhoeck & Ruprecht, 1903), 274 (on Rev 11:15).

92   Of God it naturally cannot be said that his sovereignty is limited in time. In the Psalm ἕως οὗ, "until," denotes the final state of victory. Paul makes it

attains its goal. δεῖ γὰρ αὐτὸν βασιλεύειν, "for he must reign," is also already phrased in dependence on Scripture: Ps 10:16, etc.[91]

We have to agree with Maier that we cannot narrowly specify what is to be proved. Furthermore we have to note that the thing to be proved and the "Scripture proof" cannot be abstractly separated. For one thing, the two Scripture passages go together, and secondly they are themselves a part of the *representation* of the events of the end. We have thus to enquire into vv 24–27 as a whole. We must begin by determining the subjects and the possessive pronouns.

The subject of ἄχρι οὗ θῇ, "until he has put," is fixed by δεῖ γὰρ αὐτὸν βασιλεύειν, "for he must reign": it is Christ.[92] This sheds light on the completely free use of Scripture. In the Psalm it is only God who acts. He enthrones the king and subjects his (the king's) enemies to him. Through the transposition of the verb into the third person, Christ becomes the agent. But to whom does he then subject the enemies, to himself[93] or to God? Verses 27b–28 decide: he subjects the enemies to himself, i.e., according to v 24: he annihilates them.[94]

■ **26** This formally isolated thesis[95] is strongly high-lighted by the two Scripture passages which frame it. It is proved by the preceding πάντας and the subsequent πάντα ("all his enemies—all things").[96] It remains unclear what is the temporal relation between the moment of the annihilation of death and the moment of the resurrection. If we set out from the mythological idea, then the annihilation of death is the *presupposition* of the resurrection. If we set out from the interpretation of existence, then the two coincide. For Paul, however, this is not a genuine alternative, since he contracts the whole of the end into a single instant: v 52.[97]

The conception of death as a person, the conception of the angel of death, is apocalyptic (Rev 6:8). In itself, such a personification can be oriental, poetic style (Isa 25:8). But in apocalyptic the conception is realistic.[98] Paul now reduces the mythological element by the very fact that it is not the devil, but death that is declared to be the last enemy.[99] This sets the whole weight upon the immediate interpretation of existence; the concept is hardly realistic any more; it is no longer an independent object of reflection.[100] If Paul nevertheless retains the mythological element, then it becomes a means of representation. It can express the facts (a) that

93   So Weiss: αὐτοῦ has the sense of αὐτοῦ.

94   The enthronement and *sessio ad dextram* (at the resurrection) is presupposed by Paul, but not explicitly mentioned. What is important is only the conveyance and execution of the work of salvation.

95   Weiss observes: "This brief statement would fit very well after v 24, and one is tempted to delete it as a marginal note that has intruded at the wrong place." But Weiss goes on to say that it can be justified as a return to the subject of the resurrection: if death belongs to the ἐχθροί and ἀρχαί, the "enemies" and "authorities," then it now becomes plain why the resurrection can take place only at the end. This observation is correct. Yet this idea is not the point of what is said here, see below.

96   Brandenburger, *Adam und Christus*, 71, thinks the accent lies on the fact that death will be annihilated as the *last* enemy—a hint to the fanatics. But the series of πᾶς, etc., "all," dominates from v 24 on. Verse 24 has already an eye to the thesis of v 26. The point is, that the "last" enemy, too—who does in actual fact rage to the last—is reached; thus the point is the positive promise of salvation. That in content it is antifanaticist is plain.

97   Jeremias, *Abba*, 299, n. 2, finds a contradiction in v 54, where death is already annihilated by the time

of the parousia. But there is nothing to be learned in regard to the dating, because the point is the "instantaneousness" of the whole event.

98   The roots in the history of religion go a long way back: Ex 12:23; 1 Chr 21:15ff. Usually Satan is regarded as the angel of death, see Str.–B. 1:144f; 1 Cor 10:10; cf. Heb 2:14: he is the Lord of death (and thus the last enemy).

      b. BB. 16a says that Satan, the evil urge and the angel of death are identical. *S. Bar.* 21.22f: "Bring to an end therefore henceforth mortality. And reprove accordingly the angel of death" (Charles, *APOT* 2:494). (For the text see Kautzsch, *Apkr. u. Pseudepigr.* 2:420, n. e.) For the end of death in the future see on v 54 below; Str.–B. 3:481f.

      The Greeks, too, personified death, see Rohde, *Psyche*, 433 [2:249]. While this, e.g. in Euripides (*Alcestis*), may be poetic form, yet in the figure of fettered Hades in Seneca (*Herc. fur.* 52–62) there are surely signs of a realistic note; Josef Kroll, *Gott und Hölle*, Studien der Bibliothek Warburg, 20 (Leipzig and Darmstadt: Teubner, 1932; Darmstadt: Wissenschaftliche Buchgesellschaft, 1963), 432–435.

99   Cf. Rom 5:12ff: not the devil, but sin is the cause of death's sovereignty; see on v 21 above.

100   This is sensed by Weiss when he asks whether Paul regarded death, like sin, more as a principle; cf. Rom

      into a temporal limitation: v 28.

death is primarily God's adversary before being man's enemy (cf. in vv 54f the connection between death and sin); (b) that it has to do with the whole existence of man (not, for example, merely with his body considered in isolation); (c) that it is a *historical* power;[101] (d) that the victory over death does not consist in man's escaping death and its (abiding) power, but in death itself being overcome.[102]

■ **27** Here is a further Scripture proof, in dependence on Ps 8:7.[103] This time, too, it is worked into the process of representation. Hence the question as to what it is meant to prove must take account of the proof itself in the same way as in v 25. The quotation must be seen in its relation with the first one. The clue is provided here, too, by the word $\pi\acute{a}\nu\tau\alpha$. It is a retrospective proof of v 26.[104] In view of the matter–of–fact way in which Ps 8 is messianically interpreted, it can be assumed that this interpretation is already familiar to Paul (whether from Christianity or from Judaism;[105] cf. above on Ps 110; cf. Heb 2:6–9). It is frequently supposed that this interpretation is due to Ps 8:4, namely, to the expression $\upsilon\acute{\iota}\grave{o}\varsigma\ \tau o\hat{\upsilon}\ \acute{a}\nu\theta\rho\acute{\omega}\pi o\upsilon$, "son of man," understood by the Christians as a messianic title.[106] This would then be a proof of

the fact that Paul was aware of this title although he does not use it. It would mean he had refined it to $\acute{a}\nu\theta\rho\omega\pi o\varsigma$, which he of course understood as "primal man." By this means the quotation could be firmly built into the whole train of thought of v 20. Yet serious doubts exist in regard to this argument from the title "son of man."[107]

What is the subject of $\acute{\upsilon}\pi\acute{\epsilon}\tau\alpha\xi\epsilon\nu$, "he has put in subjection"? Christ (Lietzmann), or God (Weiss)? The trend of thought suggests that Christ is the subject.[108] This is why it is so important now to ward off the misunderstanding that Christ is the final $\beta\alpha\sigma\iota\lambda\epsilon\acute{\upsilon}\varsigma$, "king." The fact is rather: you are Christ's, and Christ is God's (3:23). The way is prepared for this by v 27b. $\acute{o}\tau\alpha\nu\ \delta'$ $\epsilon\acute{\iota}\pi\eta$ can be taken impersonally (Lietzmann): "But when it is said,"[109] with the suggestion that the subject is $\acute{o}\ \theta\epsilon\acute{o}\varsigma,\ \acute{\eta}\ \gamma\rho\alpha\phi\acute{\eta}$, "God," "Scripture," or suchlike.[110] The conclusion is: $\delta\hat{\eta}\lambda o\nu\ \acute{o}\tau\iota$: "For it is plain that . . ."[111]

■ **28** Paul makes a rhetorical play on $\acute{\upsilon}\pi o\tau\acute{a}\sigma\sigma\epsilon\iota\nu$, "to subject." During the messianic age (the present) Christ accordingly exercises the sovereignty of God in a specific area. When this commission has been fulfilled ($\tau\acute{o}\tau\epsilon$, "then," in an emphatic position) God once more rules

---

6:23 and the personifying way of speaking of sin in Rom 6 and 7.

101 Here lies a fundamental difference from the Stoa's view of death as an isolated point; Bultmann, *TDNT* 3:11–14.

102 Luz, *Geschichtsverständnis*, 348–352.

103 Ps 110 and Ps 8 stand side by side also in Eph 1:20–22. Lindars, *NT Apologetic*, 50f.

104 Weiss and Lietzmann understand the progress of thought from v 26 to v 27 as follows: none may remain; for the fact really is: "all"; cf. Heb 2:8. Not so Heinrici, who declares that a proof that death must be abolished would be superfluous. Rather it is a question of the relationship between God and the bearer of his commission. Heinrici accordingly relates the Scripture passage to what follows. But this is not an alternative.

105 In Judaism Ps 8 in *b. RH* 21b is applied to Moses.

106 Weiss holds that Paul was able to interpret the Psalm messianically only if he applied the term "man/son of man" to Christ.

107 Anton Vögtle, "Die Adam–Christustypologie und 'Der Menschensohn,' " *TThZ* 60 (1951): 309–328 (a debate with Joachim Jeremias, *TDNT* 1:142f); " 'Der Menschensohn' und die paulinische Christologie," in *Studiorum Paulinorum Congressus* 1:199–218 (a debate with Oscar Cullmann, *The Christology of*

the New Testament, tr. Shirley C. Guthrie and Charles A. M. Hall [London: SCM; Philadelphia: Westminster, 1963], *Die Christologie des Neuen Testaments* [Tübingen: J. C. B. Mohr (Paul Siebeck), ²1958]). According to Vögtle the use of Ps 8 is no proof of a Pauline use of $\acute{a}\nu\theta\rho\omega\pi o\varsigma$ as a title of Christ (equivalent to $\upsilon\acute{\iota}\grave{o}\varsigma\ \tau o\hat{\upsilon}\ \acute{a}\nu\theta\rho\acute{\omega}\pi o\upsilon$). Nor can this be concluded from Eph 5:31f; 1 Tim 2:5; Heb 2:6. Else it could hardly be explained why this designation does not appear in the passages in question. The official title, in the name of which Ps 110 and Ps 8 are related to Jesus, is $X\rho\iota\sigma\tau\acute{o}\varsigma$. It is not possible to derive from Ps 8 an antithesis between the two Adams, least of all when it is combined with Ps 110. With this we must agree.

108 In favor of God as subject it can be argued that he is the $\acute{\upsilon}\pi o\tau\acute{a}\xi\alpha\varsigma$ in v 27b. In favor of Christ: if God is the subject, then the correction in v 27b is pointless (Lietzmann). Furthermore, we have to note the correspondence with $\theta\hat{\eta}$ in v 25.

109 Cf. $\tau\acute{\iota}\ \lambda\acute{\epsilon}\gamma\epsilon\iota$, Rom 10:8; $\phi\eta\sigma\acute{\iota}\nu$, 1 Cor 6:16, etc.

110 Blass–Debrunner §130(3). Heinrici takes the aorist subjunctive in the sense of a future perfect: "When he (*sc.* Christ) will have said. . . ." But despite the aorist there is no thought of a definite act of speaking. Rather, we have here a loose usage for $\acute{o}\tau\alpha\nu$ $\lambda\acute{\epsilon}\gamma\eta$. Instances of this go back into classical times:

alone and directly; for then there is no more struggle, but only pure sovereignty. Remarkable, and in Paul unique, is the emphatic, absolute use of ὁ υἱός, "the Son" (Mk 13:32; Mt 11:27; John *passim*); is this an aftereffect of the phrase τῷ θεῷ καὶ πατρί, "to God the Father"? ἵνα, "that," denotes, as often in the New Testament, the attained end. The final standing of God is defined in a phrase which in itself has a mystic sound: "all in all."[112] Paul knows and uses phrases of this kind also elsewhere;[113] in his context, however, the sense is no longer mystic. He does not say that God and the All (and therewith also the believers) are identical, but that God once more directly exercises his total sovereignty.[114] Here it makes little difference whether πᾶσι, "in all," is understood as neuter (which is more in keeping with what

we must suppose to be the language of a formula) or masculine. The neuter is to be preferred from the very fact of the preceding τὰ πάντα.

The church Fathers had their difficulties with the subjection of the Son to the Father.[115]

■ **29** This is one of the most hotly disputed passages in the epistle. The tone and the style (with the series of rhetorical questions) change abruptly.

The wording is in favor of the "normal" exposition in terms of "vicarious baptism": in Corinth living people have themselves vicariously baptized for dead people.[116] Paul does not criticize the custom, but makes use of it for his argument. This custom once again shows the sacramentalism prevailing in Corinth.

Paul's reference to this custom provides one of the most

Demosth., *Or.* 44.64. Just., *Dial.* 138.2: ὅταν οὖν εἴπῃ ὁ προφήτης, "When therefore the prophet says." The observation ὅταν εἴπῃ simply introduces an exposition of the quotation.

111 See the instances in Bauer, *s.v.* δῆλος.

112 Macrob., *Sat.* 1.20.11: *Herculem hunc esse* τὸν ἐν πᾶσι καὶ διὰ πάντων ἥλιον, "Hercules as the sun 'which is in all and through all.' " Dessau, *Inscr. Lat. Select.* 2:177 (no. 4362): *te tibi una quae es omnia, dea Isis,* "to thee, O thou who art all, goddess Isis." Ael. Arist., *Or.* 1.3: ἀρχὴ μὲν ἁπάντων Ζεὺς τε καὶ ἐκ Διὸς πάντα, "The beginning of all things is Zeus, and of Zeus all things are born" [Trans.]. Musaeus in Diog. L., *Vit.* 1.3: ἐξ ἑνὸς τὰ πάντα γίνεσθαι καὶ εἰς ταὐτὸν ἀναλύεσθαι, "All things proceed from unity and are resolved again into unity" (Loeb 1:5).

113 See on 8:6; Rom 9:5; 11:36. For such seemingly pantheistic phrases cf. Sir 43:27f: τὸ πᾶν ἐστιν αὐτός, "He [*sc.* God] is the all." In the next sentence it is explained in terms of the Jewish idea of the Creator: αὐτὸς γὰρ ὁ μέγας παρὰ πάντα τὰ ἔργα αὐτοῦ, "For he is greater than all his works" (RSV).

114 This is in harmony with the tradition of Jewish eschatology, see Str.–B. 3:472 on Zech 14:9 ("And the Lord will become king over all the earth; on that day the Lord will be one and his name one" [RSV]) in rabbinical literature; Tg. Zech 14:9: "And the sovereignty of Yahweh will be revealed over all who dwell on earth."

115 They found help in various ways: (*a*) Didymus of Alexandria (Staab, *Pauluskommentare*, 8): πρός τε τὴν Ἑλλήνων μυθολογίαν τε καὶ ἀπάτην εἰρῆσθαι ταῦτα εἰπόντες τῶν φασκόντων πατραλοίας εἶναι θεούς, "They say that this was said in view of the mythology and deceit of the Greeks, who allege that the gods are parricides" [Trans.]. (*b*) Chrys., *In Epist.*

I ad Cor. Homil. 39.5 (*MPG* 61:340; Cramer, *Catenae graecorum patrum in Novum Testamentum* [Oxford: Oxford University Press, 1848] 5:307): "...ὑποταγήσεται," τὴν πολλὴν πρὸς τὸν Πατέρα ὁμόνοιαν δεικνύς, " '...be subjected,' showing his great concord with the Father" (*NPNF* 1.12:239). (*c*) The subjection relates only to the human nature of Christ; Aug., *Trin.* 1.8; see Allo *ad loc.* For Pauline subordinationism see on 3:23. For the title υἱός, "Son," cf. Rom 1:3f; 8:3; Gal 4:4.

116 Plat., *Resp.* 364e–365a: βίβλων δὲ ὅμαδον παρέχονται Μουσαίου καὶ Ὀρφέως, Σελήνης τε καὶ Μουσῶν ἐγγόνων, ὥς φασι, καθ᾽ ἃς θυηπολοῦσιν, πείθοντες οὐ μόνον ἰδιώτας ἀλλὰ καὶ πόλεις, ὡς ἄρα λύσεις τε καὶ καθαρμοὶ ἀδικημάτων διὰ θυσιῶν καὶ παιδιᾶς ἡδονῶν εἰσι μὲν ἔτι ζῶσιν, εἰσὶ δὲ καὶ τελευτήσασιν, ἃς δὴ τελετὰς καλοῦσιν, αἳ τῶν ἐκεῖ κακῶν ἀπολύουσιν ἡμᾶς, μὴ θύσαντας δὲ δεινὰ περιμένει, "And they produce a bushel of books of Musaeus and Orpheus, the offspring of the Moon and of the Muses, as they affirm, and these books they use in their ritual, and make not only ordinary men but states believe that there really are remissions of sins and purifications for deeds of injustice, by means of sacrifices and pleasant sport for the living, and that there are also special rites for the defunct, which they call functions, that deliver us from evils in that other world, which terrible things await those who have neglected to sacrifice" (Loeb 1:135). Kern. *Orph. Fr.*, 245 (no. 232; vicarious celebration of the Dionysian orgies for uninitiated dead): ὄργια τ᾽ ἐκτελέσουσι λύσιν προγόνων ἀθεμίστων μαιόμενοι, "And they will carry out the rites, seeking the release of unconsecrated forebears" [Trans.]; see Rohde, *Psyche*, 358, n. 66 [2:128, n. 5]. Inscription in Josef Zingerle, "Heiliges Recht," *Oestr Jhft* 23 (1926): supplement 1–71, here esp. 23f (see Albrecht

important arguments *against* the assumption that he has misunderstood the Corinthian position. He shows himself here to be obviously well informed. And if he is aware of this custom, then he cannot well credit the Corinthians with the view that death is the end of everything. Yet he gives expression precisely to his surprise at the seeming inconsistency of the Corinthians: on the one hand they assert that ἀνάστασις νεκρῶν οὐκ ἔστιν, "there is no resurrection of the dead," while on the other hand they practice vicarious baptism. To this Paul says: here I no longer follow you. Only reflect on the consequences of your own custom.

Some of the church Fathers are familiar with vicarious baptism as a heretical practice; thus Chrysostom knows of it as a custom of the Marcionites.[117] On the other

hand, the Greek church Fathers are united in offering a different exegesis: the νεκροί, "dead," are the σώματα ὑπὲρ ὧν βαπτιζόμεθα, "the bodies because of which we are baptized."[118] Hence Staab assumes that the interpretation in terms of vicarious baptism first arose owing to a misunderstanding on the part of Ambrosiaster; only then, he argues, did the passage become the crux of the exegetes.[119]

Since then, at all events, the ingenuity of the exegetes has run riot.[120] In part they seek to arrive at a different understanding of the passage by taking ὑπέρ in a "final" sense: "for the sake of."[121] But the wording demands the interpretation in terms of vicarious baptism.[122] And it is idle to dispute that a magical view of the sacraments prevails in Corinth. The *train of thought* is

---

Oepke, *TDNT* 1:542): Μεγάλη Μήτηρ Ἀνεῖτις. Ἀπολλώνιος Μηνοδώρου ὑπὲρ Διονυσίου τοῦ ἀδελφοῦ, ἐπεὶ κατελούσετο καὶ οὐκ ἐτήρησε τὴν προθεσμίαν τῆς θεοῦ, ἀπετελέσετο αὐτόν, "Great Mother Aneitis! Apollonius of Menodorus on behalf of his brother Dionysus, when he ceremonially washed himself and did not keep the appointment of the goddess, rendered his due" [Trans.].

117 Chrys., *Hom. in Epist. I ad Cor.* 40.1 (=*Cat.* 10.378c Montfaucon; *MPG* 61:347; Cramer, *Catenae* 5:310f): ἐπειδὰν γάρ τις κατεχούμενος ἀπέλθη παρ' αὐτοῖς· τὸν ζῶντα ὑπὸ τὴν κλίνην τοῦ τελευτητόκος κρύψαντες, προσίασι τῷ νεκρῷ, καὶ διαλέγονται καὶ πυνθάνονται, εἰ βούλοιτο λαβεῖν τὸ βάπτισμα. εἶτα ἐκείνου μηδὲν ἀποκρινομένου ὁ κεκρυμμένος κάτωθεν ἀντ' ἐκείνου φησὶν ὅτι δὴ βούλοιτο βαπτισθῆναι· καὶ οὕτω βαπτίζουσιν αὐτὸν ἀντὶ τοῦ ἀπελθόντος, "When any Catechumen departs [this life] among them, having concealed the living man under the couch of the dead; they approach the corpse, and talk with him, and ask him if he wishes to receive baptism; then, when he makes no answer, he that is concealed underneath saith in his stead, that of course he should wish to be baptized; and thus they baptize him in the stead of the departed one" (NPNF 1.12:244). Epiph., *Haer.* 28.6.4, of the Corinthians. Tert., *Marc.* 5.10.

118 From Didymus of Alexandria through Chrysostom, etc.; collected in Karl Staab, "1 Kor 15,29 im Lichte der Exegese der griechischen Kirche," in *Studiorum Paulinorum Congressus* 1:443–450.

119 Schmiedel traces this interpretation back to Chrysostom's statement on the Marcionites; see below.

120 Many count up to 200 different explanations; see the overview in K. C. Thompson, "I Corinthians 15,29 and Baptism for the Dead," in *Studia Evangelica*, ed. F. L. Cross, vol. 2, part 1. TU, 87 (Berlin: Aka-

demie–Verlag, 1964), 647–659. Thompson joins in with the suggestion of Semler and others to punctuate as follows: ἐπεὶ τί ποιήσουσιν οἱ βαπτιζόμενοι; ὑπὲρ τῶν νεκρῶν; εἰ ὅλως κτλ., "For what shall they do who have themselves baptized? For the dead? [i.e., do they have themselves baptized for the dead?]. If, etc."

To this Thompson links other suggestions: (*a*) ἐπεὶ τί ποιήσουσιν οἱ βαπτιζόμενοι; ὑπὲρ τῶν νεκρῶν, εἰ ὅλως . . ., "For what will they do who have themselves baptized? They do it for the dead if. . . ." (*b*) He finds it still better (following Tertullian) to put a comma after βαπτιζόμενοι and a question mark after ἐγείρονται, cf. Tert., *Res.* 48.11; *Marc.* 5.10. He points to the fact that in ℵ and B, despite the different length of the lines, a line ends in both cases with βαπτιζόμενοι.

121 Noted in Robertson and Plummer. Taken up by Maria Raeder, "Vikariatstaufe in 1 Cor 15:29?" *ZNW* 46 (1955): 258–260: pagan Corinthians who have lost Christian relatives have themselves baptized for their sakes, because the Christian faith promises reunion with them. Similarly Jeremias, *Abba*, 303f; he appeals to the phrase ὑπὲρ τῶν ἁμαρτιῶν ἡμῶν, "for our sins"; Blass–Debrunner §231 (2). Blass–Debrunner, to be sure, do not count ὑπὲρ τῶν ἁμαρτιῶν under the final meaning. And altogether, the final use of ὑπέρ tells *against* this interpretation. Where it appears, it is always unequivocal, cf. Phil 2:13.

122 Rightly Kümmel. Heinrici characterizes his overview of "divergent expositions" by saying: "at the same time as an example of exegetical distress and caprice." The article before (οἱ) νεκροί is also no argument against this interpretation (contrary to Bachmann).

understood by M. Rissi[123] as follows: Those who have themselves baptized for the dead, what will they do in future, when they have considered my arguments? If the dead do not rise, they will in future be doing something absurd and themselves "signally" giving the lie to their unbelief. Yet we do not here have a continuous, logical train of thought at all, but a stringing together of different arguments; cf. vv 30–34. And the future tense is aphoristic.[123a]

The conclusiveness of the argument is given without more ado, once the Christological presupposition with which Paul argues is accepted—and recognized.

■ **30–31** The new argument has nothing to do with the one advanced so far. Paul is stringing different thoughts together, though not of course in a disorderly manner: (a) your practice; (b) my existence.[124] For "every hour," "day by day," cf. 2 Cor 4:10f; Rom 8:36ff.[125] καύχησις, "glorying": 2 Cor 7:4; 8:24.[126] ἐν Χριστῷ Ἰησοῦ, "in Christ Jesus," once again shows that "his"

glory is a glory that is "not his own" (see on 1:31).

■ **32** Two questions intersect here:

1) Is the conditional clause real or unreal?

2) Is θηριομαχεῖν, "to fight with beasts," meant in a literal or figurative sense?[127] If figurative, then it is an expression for his "dying daily"; if it is literal, then it is an example of this.

Lietzmann argues that θηριομαχεῖν cannot be meant literally, because in the catalogue of troubles in 2 Cor 11:23–29 there is no mention of fighting with beasts, nor in Acts either,[128] "and because it was not possible for the Apostle as a Roman citizen to be condemned *ad bestias* at all without losing his citizenship, whereas at his arrest in Caesarea (*sic*!) he is still in possession of it."[129] It is accordingly a question of a figurative expression for: "fighting for his life."[130] Then the conditional clause can be understood as real; Lietzmann's argument is: "because the real examples will not be followed by an imaginary one."[131] Weiss on the other hand, considers it

123 Mathias Rissi, *Die Taufe für die Toten*, AThANT, 42 (Zurich and Stuttgart: Zwingli, 1962), with an overview of the investigations. Rissi perceives that only vicarious baptism can be meant, but seeks to avoid a sacramentalistic interpretation: the vicarious baptism, he argues, is an "act of proclamation and confession" by which the hope of resurrection for specific dead persons is testified: "We believe in the resurrection of this dead person" (p. 89). The significatory view of baptism is neither Corinthian nor Pauline, but Barthian.

123a Lietzmann, see Kühner–Blass–Gerth 1:171, 3.

124 The plural is epistolary style. Weiss says that ἡμεῖς, "we," will include also his fellows; but in the principal clause Paul is thinking of himself. This view is only possible when θηριομαχεῖν, "fight with beasts," is understood figuratively.

125 Sen., *Ep.* 24.20: *cotidie morimur, cotidie enim demitur aliqua pars vitae*, "We die every day. For every day a little of our life is taken from us" (Loeb 1:177). Here death is a natural process. Philo, *Flacc.* 175.

126 Reciprocity as an element in the relationship of apostle and church: 2 Cor 1:4ff; 9:3 (καύχημα); Phil 1:26. ὑμετέραν: Thuc., *Hist.* 1.69.5: αἱ ὑμετέραι ἐλπίδες, "the hopes they have placed in you" (Loeb 1:115); Kühner–Blass–Gerth 1:560, n. 11.

127 Abraham J. Malherbe, "The Beasts at Ephesus," *JBL* 87 (1968): 71–80 (for θηριομαχεῖν used figuratively cf. 16:8f).

128 But cf. 2 Cor 1:8. The report in Acts tones down.

129 *Dig.* 28.1.8.4: *Hi vero, qui ad ferrum aut ad bestias aut in metallum damnantur, libertatem perdunt*, "Those, how-

ever, who are condemned to the sword or to the beasts or to the mines, lose [their] civil rights" [Trans.]; cf. *Dig.* 48.19.29; rebels: *Dig.* 48.19.38.2. Theodor Mommsen, *Römisches Strafrecht*, Systematisches Handbuch der Deutschen Rechtswissenschaft, 1. 4 (Leipzig: Duncker & Humblot, 1899), 925–928. It must, to be sure, be borne in mind that Paul's Roman citizenship is testified only by Acts and is in poor harmony with the catalogue of troubles in 2 Cor 11:23ff (see v 25).

130 Ign., *Rom* 5.1: ἀπὸ Συρίας μέχρι Ῥώμης θηριομαχῶ διὰ γῆς καὶ θαλάσσης, "From Syria to Rome I am fighting with wild beasts, by land and sea" (Loeb 1:231) is of course not real evidence for the figurative use. Here the choice of the word lies near to hand, because Ignatius has a real fight with beasts ahead of him. Cf. Philo, *Flacc.* 175: προαποθνήσκω πολλοὺς θανάτους ὑπομένων ἀνθ' ἑνὸς τοῦ τελευταίου, "I die in anticipation and suffer many deaths instead of the final one" (Loeb 9:397).

131 Similarly Josef Schmid, *Zeit und Ort der Paulinischen Gefangenschaftsbriefe* (Freiburg: Herder, 1931), 39–64 (59, n. 5: examples of transferred usage). Aristoph., *Nu.* 184; *Eq.* 273; *Pl.* 439; Philo, *Vit. Mos.* 1.43f; Vett. Val., *Anth.* 129.33; 130.21; *P. Ryl.* 15.6f: κακοῖς [θηρίοις νιν] μονομαχήσειν ἀνέπεισαν, "They have persuaded him to fight alone with evil beasts" (Arthur S. Hunt in *P. Ryl.* 1:25). Bodleian scholion to Epict., *Diss.* 4.1.159f: (γνώ)σῃ ὅτι Σωκράτης ἐθηριομάχησεν, "You will know that Socrates fought with wild beasts." Tert., *Res.* 48.12: *depugnavit ad bestias [Ephesi], illas scilicet bestias Asiaticae pressurae,*

to be unreal: if as far as the will of men was concerned (see below) it would have come to fighting with beasts. This view is grammatically possible. Schmid,[131a] however, objects that the decisive argument against the interpretation as unreal is not the absence of ἄν,[132] but the fact that ἐθηριομάχησα, "I fought with beasts," stands parallel to τί βαπτίζονται; "why do they have themselves baptized?" and to τί κινδυνεύομεν; "why do we stand in jeopardy?" It is a question of real dangers (cf. Lietzmann). The interpretation is made still more difficult by the unclarity of the phrase κατὰ ἄνθρωπον. Has it to be rendered, "after the manner of men" (Lietzmann)? What, in that case, does it mean?[133] Or have we to translate, "as far as the will of men is concerned" (Weiss)?[134] From the phrase "in Ephesus," many exegetes conclude that this remark—and therewith the epistle—cannot have been written in Ephesus itself. Why not? The phrase τί μοι τὸ ὄφελος; "what benefit is it to me?" belongs to the style of the diatribe.[134a] Heinrici rightly observes that v 32 must not be isolated; otherwise the thought would be opportunist. It has to be understood in the whole context of redemption, liberation from sin, and grounding of morality, and in the setting of

the picture drawn in vv 31–32 of the Apostle plunged into suffering (cf. vv 16–19). In the background stands the earlier reflection that faith could be vain. N.B. a reflection on the part of *faith*! It makes a difference whether a man speaks theoretically of the beyond or as one who is involved, who is objectively in the process of dying, who has his death no longer *ahead* of him but *around* him. In this situation the thought, "if there is no resurrection of the dead," leads with complete consistency to the conclusion which Paul has of course rejected in advance, the libertinistic conclusion:[135] if "this" life is *the* life, then the sensible way of living it is to enjoy it to the full.[136] This is expressed by means of the "rule" of Isa 22:13.[137] Paul's argument here is once again in the tradition of Jewish Wisdom.[138]

■ 33 For μὴ πλανᾶσθε, "do not be deceived," see on 6:9. The warning is a quotation from Menander.[139] The sense of ὁμιλίαι is naturally not narrow ("conversations"),[140] but general: "dealings, company."[141] It may be asked whether Paul is using this quotation in order to give a general warning against conformity with the world (Rom 12:2) or a particular warning against dealings with those who deny the resurrection. Verse 34

"he fought against beasts [at Ephesus], namely, those beasts of the Asiatic affliction" [Trans.].

131a Schmid, *Zeit und Ort*, 42f.

132 Radermacher, *Grammatik*, 157f. On the other hand it is true that "unreal periods are remarkably scarce in Paul (1 C 2:8, 11:31, 12:19, G 1:10, 3:21, 4:15)" (Blass-Debrunner §360[4]). Weiss appeals to Epictetus: there, too, ἄν is often omitted in an unreal apodosis more particularly with τί τὸ ὄφελος, see index to *Epicteti Dissertationes ab Arrianae digestae*, ed. Heinrich Schenkl, Bibliotheca Scriptorum Graecorum et Romanorum Teubneriana (Stuttgart: Teubner, 1968).

133 Schmiedel replies: after the manner of a man for whom there is no resurrection, according to vv 29b, 32c.

134 In the context of his interpretation as unreal. This does in fact provide a plain sense.

134a Epict., *Diss.* 3.7.31.

135 The conditional clause, εἰ νεκροὶ οὐκ ἐγείρονται, "if the dead are not raised," is to be taken with what follows, on the analogy of the preceding sentence. The omission of the article before νεκροί is appropriate; see on v 12.

136 And were it in terms of a heroic and ascetic view of the world.

137 *Epigr. Graec.* 344.3: γνῶθι τέλος βιότου. διὸ παῖζε τρυφῶν ἐπὶ κόσμῳ, "Know the end of life. Wherefore sport and revel on earth" [Trans.]. Hdt., *Hist.* 2.78; Eur., *Alc.* 780–789; Horat., *Carm.* 1.4; 2.3. Similarly worldly wisdom is found in inscriptions on drinking cups (Deissmann, *Light*, 129–131 [103–105, cf. 251]). Particularly well known was the alleged grave inscription of Sardanapal, Plut., *Alex. fort. virt.* 330f; 336c: ἔσθιε, πῖνε, ἀφροδισίαζε· τἄλλα δ᾽ οὐδέν, "Eat, drink, sport with love; all else is nought" (Loeb 4:439). Malherbe, "The Beasts at Ephesus," points to the motivational context (anti-Epicurean polemic). On Sardanapal see Franz Heinrich Weissbach, "Sardanapal," Pauly-W. 1 A:2436–75; Juvenal, *Thirteen Satires*, ed. J. E. B. Mayor, vol. 2 (London: Macmillan, ⁴1886), 178f.

138 Wisd 2:6ff; 3. But Paul is not expressly drawing on this passage, for in Wisd there is also another motif adduced which Paul could well have used: the violating of the righteous man who boasts of his knowledge of God. See Eduard Grafe, "Das Verhältnis der paulinischen Schriften zur Sapientia Salomonis," in *Theologische Abhandlungen Carl von Weizsäcker zu seinem siebzigsten Geburtstage*, ed. Adolf von Harnack et al. (Freiburg: J. C. B. Mohr [Paul Siebeck], 1892), 251–286, here esp. 281f.

139 Menander, *Thais* fr. 218 Kock. Conclusions in regard to Paul's literary education are not to be drawn.

points in the latter direction. But the one, of course, does not exclude the other.

■ **34** ἐκνήψατε,[142] "be sober," points back to πίωμεν, "let us drink." This figurative use of νήφειν is common; it is a standard term of eschatological paraenesis.[143] The enjoying of our earthly life is intoxication, and intoxication is ἀγνωσία, "ignorance."[144] This word

is to be understood in the context of the negation of which Hellenism is so fond. Bousset translates: "Certain people have really no inkling of God."[145] This is too weak. For ἀγνωσία is an actively pursued way of life,[146] as is shown by the connection of thought between ignorance and sin.

35	But, one may ask, how are the dead raised? With what kind of body do they come? **36/** You foolish one! What you sow does not come to life unless it dies. **37/** And what you sow—you sow not the body that is to be, but a bare grain, perhaps of wheat or of some other kind. **38/** But God gives it a body as he has chosen, and to each seed its own particular body. **39/** Not all flesh is the same flesh, but that of men is one thing, the flesh of beasts is another, the flesh of birds another, that of fish another. **40/** And there are heavenly bodies and earthly bodies. But the luster of the heavenly is one thing and that of the earthly another. **41/** The luster of the sun is one thing, the luster of the moon another, the luster of the stars another. For star differs from star in luster. **42/** So it

This saying was widely known as a familiar quotation, cf. Eur., *Fr.* 1013 (ed. Nauck) and for the content Diod. S., *Bible. hist.* 16.54.4 (on Philip of Macedon): πονηραῖς ὁμιλίαις διέφθειρε τὰ ἤθη τῶν ἀνθρώπων, "By his evil communications he corrupted the morals of the people" (Loeb 7:391). ἦθος χρηστόν: *Ep. Ar.* 230; Philo, *Det. pos. ins.* 38.

140 Vulg.: *colloquia.*

141 Bauer, *s.v.*; Xenoph., *Mem.* 3.7.5; Plat., *Resp.* 550b. Xenoph. *Mem.* 1.2.20: δι᾽ ὃ καὶ τοὺς υἱεῖς οἱ πατέρες, κἂν ὦσι σώφρονες, ὅμως ἀπὸ τῶν πονηρῶν ἀνθρώπων εἴργουσιν, ὡς τὴν μὲν τῶν χρηστῶν ὁμιλίαν ἄσκησιν οὖσαν τῆς ἀρετῆς, τὴν δὲ τῶν πονηρῶν κατάλυσιν, "For this cause fathers try to keep their sons, even if they are prudent lads, out of bad company; for the society of honest men is a training in virtue, but the society of the bad is virtue's undoing" (Loeb, 21).

142 The tenses of the imperative have to be observed. The aorist imperative can be taken ingressively or complexively, as an apodictic command; the present imperative is durational, or summons to the continuation of the present circumstances; cf. Mk 14:34: μείνατε ὧδε (do not go away) καὶ γρηγορεῖτε (watch continually) μετ᾽ ἐμοῦ; Blass–Debrunner §§335–337.

143 1 Thess 5:6ff; Philo writes *De ebrietate*, "On Drunk-

enness," and *De sobrietate*, "On Soberness"; Otto Bauernfeind, *TDNT* 4:937–939.

144 *Corp. Herm.* 1.27: ὦ λαοί, ἄνδρες γηγενεῖς, οἱ μέθῃ καὶ ὕπνῳ ἑαυτοὺς ἐκδεδωκότες καὶ τῇ ἀγνωσίᾳ τοῦ θεοῦ, νήψατε . . ., "Hearken, ye folk, men born of earth, who have given yourselves up to drunkenness and sleep in your ignorance of God; be sober . . ." (Scott 1:133); 8.1. Weiss asks: Is this remark aimed ironically at the γνῶσιν ἔχοντες, "those who have knowledge" (8:1)? Cf. the irony at the beginning of chap. 3: κατὰ ἄνθρωπον, "in human ways."

145 Barth, *Resurrection*, 123 [70], finds this rendering "frightfully apt." Schlatter, 430, declares it to be false, because the Corinthians have "a great deal more than an inkling of God." This psychological approach fails to recognize the objectiveness of the judgment: Paul is not speaking of subjective inklings, but of objective understanding or not understanding how to behave toward God.

146 Wisd 13:1; 1 Pet 2:15; cf. 1:13f; *1 Cl.* 59.2: ἀγνωσία θεοῦ. Dupont, *Gnosis*, 6–8; Reitzenstein, *Hellenistische Mysterienreligionen*, 293–298.

is with the resurrection of the dead.
It is sown in perishability, it is raised in
imperishability; 43/ it is sown in disgrace, it is raised in honor; it is sown in
weakness, it is raised in strength.
44/ Sown is a psychical body, raised is a
spiritual body. If there is a psychical
body, there is also a spiritual one.
45/ Thus indeed it is written: "The first
man, Adam, became a living soul, the
last Adam became a life-giving Spirit."
46/ It is not the spiritual, however, that
is first, but the psychical, then the
spiritual. 47/ The first man is of (the)
earth, earthy; the second man is from
heaven.[1] 48/ As[2] is the earthy, so are
they also that are earthy, and as is the
heavenly, so are they also that are
heavenly. 49/ And as we have worn the
image of the earthy, we shall also wear
the image of the heavenly.[3]

■ **35** In loose diatribe style[4] the new theme is introduced: "How?" The question is at once more precisely
defined: $\pi o \iota \hat{\omega}$[5] $\delta \grave{\epsilon} \sigma \acute{\omega} \mu \alpha \tau \iota$[6] $\check{\epsilon} \rho \chi o \nu \tau \alpha \iota$;[7] "With what
kind of body do they come?" To this a fourfold reply is
given: (1) vv 36–38; (2) vv 39–44; (3) vv 45–49 (or 50,
see below); (4) vv 50(51)–57. In spite of this precision,
the real situation at issue is not clear here either. Is
Paul taking up an objection that had really been raised in
Corinth ($\pi \hat{\omega} s$; "how?")?[8] At all events his exposition
of the question shows that existence without a body is a
thing he cannot conceive of at all.[9] Yet the corporeality of

the future existence is not the point of the exposition
here either, but its self–evident presupposition; it is a part
of Paul's world picture. It is not in itself theological;
it *becomes* theological *in actu* at particular moments, e.g.,
against spiritualistic narrowing down of our hope, against
exclusion of the world from the realm of God's sovereignty, and thus against every form of Gnosticism or
fanaticism, against direct desecularization of the way of
salvation, etc.

■ **36–38** The discussion style continues: $\check{\alpha} \phi \rho \omega \nu$, "fool-
ish one."[10] On $o \grave{\upsilon} \zeta \omega o \pi o \iota \epsilon \hat{\iota} \tau \alpha \iota$, "does not come to

---

1   For the absence of the article see Blass–Debrunner
    §253(3).
2   For the style of vv 42–44, see Blass–Debrunner §490.
3   p[46], the Alexandrians (excepting B), D G read ϕo-
    $\rho \acute{\epsilon} \sigma \omega \mu \epsilon \nu$; the context demands the indicative.
4   $\grave{\alpha} \lambda \lambda$' $\grave{\epsilon} \rho \epsilon \hat{\iota} \tau \iota s$, "but it may be asked": Jas 2:18.
5   $\delta \acute{\epsilon}$ does not mark an antithesis, but simply continues;
    cf. the introduction of an explanation by $\delta \acute{\epsilon}$ 10:11;
    15:56.
6   Joachim Jeremias, "Flesh and Blood cannot inherit
    the Kingdom of God (I Cor. XV.50)," *NTS* 2
    (1955–56): 151–159, now in his *Abba*, 298–307, here
    esp. 302–305, assumes it is a case of two different
    questions: (1) $\pi \hat{\omega} s$; how does the process of resurrec-
    tion take place? (2) $\pi o \acute{\iota} \omega \sigma \acute{\omega} \mu \alpha \tau \iota$; what is the na-
    ture of the new corporeality? The answer, he says, is
    given in reverse order, to the second question as far
    as v 49, to the first in vv 50ff. This distinction and

classification is probably too subtle; Eduard Schweizer, *TDNT* 7:128f. See on v 50.
7   The presents are best understood as having a future
    meaning, as happens more particularly with $\check{\epsilon} \rho \chi o \nu$-
    $\tau \alpha \iota$; 16:5f; Blass–Debrunner §323. Weiss takes them
    as the present of doctrinal statements.
8   Schmithals, *Gnosticism in Corinth*, 155f [147], observes:
    "On the other hand, it is seriously to be doubted
    that people in Corinth had posed the questions in vs.
    35. . . . Verses 35–36 thus say nothing about cir-
    cumstances in Corinth but only reflect Paul's view
    about those circumstances." Others (Julius Schnie-
    wind, "Die Leugnung der Auferstehung in Ko-
    rinth," in his *Nachgelassene Reden und Aufsätze*, ed.
    Ernst Kähler [Berlin: Töpelmann, 1952], 110–139,
    here esp. 130; Egon Brandenburger, *Adam und Chris-
    tus*, WMANT, 7 [Neukirchen: Neukirchener Verlag,
    1962], 73, n. 2) assume that here we catch a glimpse

life," Weiss remarks that Paul is already thinking of the real subject (no longer figuratively); for of course the grain of seed has not to be quickened, but to bring fruit. This is a modern misunderstanding of the thought. For Paul, the important thing is in fact the coming to life of the seed, as 37 shows. We have here an understanding of nature which conceives of nature after the analogy of human life, and sees the events of nature, like the life of man, as a cycle of death and growth. This is a view that is widespread in the ancient world.[11] Paul sharply emphasizes:

1) The necessity of death as the condition of life;[12]

2) The discontinuity between the present and the future life.

He expounds the natural process not with an eye to the organic connection between seed and development, to an "entelechy,"[13] but with an eye to the new creation by God. The extent to which nature is seen in analogy to man is shown by the expression "$\gamma\nu\mu\nu\grave{o}\nu$" $\kappa\acute{o}\kappa\kappa o\nu$,

" 'bare' grain." For of course this expression does not suit a seed at all, but it does fit a specific picture of man: 2 Cor 5:1ff.[14] Lietzmann is right: "It is not this earthly body that rises" (cf. v 50). But Paul does not, as Lietzmann thinks, regard the heavenly body as clothing the "naked" soul; for he has no concept of the soul at all, and furthermore no concept for the abiding element that constitutes the continuity. For the latter cannot be described in objective, anthropological terms at all.[15] The new life is a *new* creation,[16] a gift bestowed "as God will" (Gen 1:11), and it is not regarded in general, theoretical terms, but in terms of faith's understanding of it as in each several instance *my* life: $\check{\iota}\delta\iota o\nu$, "own particular."[17]

■ **39–41** With the help of the series of concepts $\sigma\acute{a}\rho\xi$—$\sigma\hat{\omega}\mu a$—$\delta\acute{o}\xi a$, "flesh—body—luster," Paul seeks to show that the resurrection from the dead is ontologically possible; that is, he answers the question $\pi\hat{\omega}\varsigma$; $=\pi o\acute{\iota}\omega$ $\sigma\acute{\omega}\mu a\tau\iota$; "how? = with what kind of body?"·

of the opponents' mockery at the idea of a bodily resurrection.

9 According to Lietzmann, the opponents argue that a body after death is inconceivable. According to Bultmann, *Theology* 1:192f [193f], Paul adopts his opponents' mode of argument and is thereby led into using $\sigma\hat{\omega}\mu a$ "in a way not characteristic of him elsewhere," i.e. in the sense of "the body–form which could be stamped upon various materials."

10 Ps 13:1; Lk 12:20. Schmiedel takes $\sigma\acute{\nu}$ with $\check{a}\phi\rho\omega\nu$. But $\check{a}\phi\rho\omega\nu$ stands emphatically in the *casus pendens*, in antithesis to $\acute{o}$ $\delta\grave{\epsilon}$ $\theta\epsilon\acute{o}\varsigma$ in v 38.

11 Jn 12:24. Åke V. Ström, *Vetekornet* (Stockholm: Svenska Kyrkans Diakonistyrelses Bokförlag, 1944), 416–423; Herbert Braun, "Das 'Stirb und werde' in der Antike und im Neuen Testament," in *Libertas Christiana, Friedrich Delekat zum 65. Geburtstag*, ed. Walter Matthias, BEvTh, 26 (Munich: Kaiser, 1957), 9–29, now in his *Gesammelte Studien*, 136–158. Under Stoic influence *1 Cl.* 24.

12 This is a new thought. It is lacking even in *1 Cl.* 24. It is pointedly explained by Harald Riesenfeld, "Paul's 'Grain of Wheat' Analogy and the Argument of 1 Corinthians 15," *The Gospel Tradition*, 171–186 (originally in *Studien zum Neuen Testament und Patristik: Erich Klostermann zum 90. Geburtstag dargebracht*, TU, 77 [Berlin: Akademie–Verlag, 1961], 43–55): it presupposes that the resurrection was not doubted in the community. The theme is not really "The Resurrection of the Dead," but "Death as the Presupposition of the Resurrection" (p. 173). This is impossible, for the simple reason that not all die.

Riesenfeld, however, rightly observes that the example of the grain of wheat has its own tradition: cf. Jn 12:24ff; *1 Cl.* 24.

13 Aristot., *Part. an.* 1.1.641b.29–37: "The seed is accordingly the principle that creates a thing out of itself (!). This comes about by nature. . . . The seed is the origin, and the substance is the end, but prior to both is the thing from which the seed comes" [Trans.].

14 Weiss observes that strictly speaking the motif of nakedness belongs to a platonizing anthropology; Plat., *Gorg.* 523c–e; cf. Luc., *Ver. hist.* 2.12. This may be true of its origin. But the conception is widespread in Hellenism; see e.g. Gnosticism, 2 Cor 5:1ff. Judaism: *b. Sanh.* 90b (R. Meir, *ca.* A.D. 150): "If a grain of wheat, which is buried naked, sprouteth forth in many robes, how much more so the righteous, who are buried in their raiment!" (Epstein 2:607). The question as to how the dead can be recognized, if they do not "wear" their old body, does not worry Paul. This question falls by the board because of the continuity of the promise in virtue of which the man who has died in Christ remains his own self.

15 The $\sigma\hat{\omega}\mu a$ is *not* the bearer of the continuity nor an element in it (against Bultmann); John A. T. Robinson, *The Body: A Study in Pauline Theology*, SBT, 1, 5 (London: SCM, 1952), 78.

16 Heinz Schwantes, *Schöpfung der Endzeit*, Arbeiten zur Theologie, 1, 12 (Stuttgart: Calwer, 1963), also issued as Aufsätze und Vorträge zur Theologie und Religionswissenschaft, 25 (Berlin: Evangelische Verlagsanstalt, 1963), 58f.

17 Aristot., *Part. an.* 1.1.641b.27–29: "For in fact we do

1) There are different kinds of σάρξ.[18] σάρξ is here the stuff of which the body consists. Have we now to conclude from v 38 (each seed receives its own σῶμα) that here σάρξ and σῶμα are synonymous, i.e., that σῶμα, too, designates the stuff of the body? In favor of this is the parallelism between vv 38–39. And the emphasis on ἄλλος—ἄλλος, "one—another," corresponds to that on ἴδιον σῶμα, "its own particular body"; cf. v 42.

2) If we accept this, then we certainly find ourselves in a difficulty. For then indeed a shift takes place. It is first of all a question of the difference between earthly types of σάρξ, but then between earthly and heavenly bodies. In spite of appearances, Paul does *not* use σάρξ and σῶμα synonymously. σάρξ stands on its own, σῶμα is combined with a new concept, δόξα. The moment this latter concept comes into play, σῶμα is not the stuff of the body, but the form, and δόξα is its state. σάρξ is thus a "substance," whereas there is no such thing as a σῶμα in itself; σῶμα always exists in a specific mode of being; it has in each several instance, if not a substance, then at least a substantiality.[19]

What, then, does Paul mean to prove? Kümmel answers:[20] "Paul is not seeking to show the possibility of a new bodily substance, but of a different body." But such a distinction cannot be made. σῶμα is here clearly the form, though not, indeed, in the sense of Greek philosophical ontology. The form is always at once related to its *concrete* mode of being, that is, it is always at once heavenly or earthly as the case may be. It exists on its own only as a concept; in actual fact it is existent only in its substantiality and individuality. σῶμα is not individual being as such, either, but only insofar as all individual being belongs to a mode of being. This of course raises in sharpest form the problem of continuity. The latter "is not, however, natural, substantial, but historical" (Kümmel).

In order to describe the new alternative (earthly—heavenly[21] bodies) Paul has to introduce a further concept; for he cannot use σάρξ to characterize the heavenly existences. So he says δόξα;[22] the stars are thought of as living creatures with a body of light.[23]

■ 42–44 These verses contain the application: "so it is with the resurrection."[24] Paul resorts once more to rhetoric. There follow four antitheses, then a thesis; the last member is the longest.[24a] The emphasis is again on the contrasts, that is, the discontinuity, the miraculous

---

not find any chance creature being formed from a particular seed, but each from its own; nor does any chance seed come from any chance body" (Loeb, 73, modified). It is plain how far Paul is from an organic thought of nature.

18 For the listing of the living creatures cf. Gen 1:20ff; Rom 1:23. For the sake of alliteration he chooses κτήνη (instead of τετράποδα) and πτήνη (instead of πετεινά). For the omission of ἐστίν, "there are," see Blass–Debrunner §127(5): "condensed logical demonstration." For the omission of the article in v 41 see Blass–Debrunner §253(1).

19 Lietzmann understands σάρξ as the matter, σῶμα as the form. Earthly creatures consist of the substance of flesh, heavenly beings consist of δόξα = the substance of light. To τῶν ἐπιγείων we have to supply σόξα—only, in an improper sense: "For earthly bodies have no δόξα, but σάρξ, cf. Phil 3:21." In that case σῶμα would be the factor of continuity. But this is the very thing it is not; Eduard Schweizer, *TDNT* 6:420f.

20 Werner Georg Kümmel, *Römer 7 und die Bekehrung des Paulus*, UNT, 17 (Leipzig: Hinrichs, 1929), 21–23.

21 He means, as is manifest at once, the stars, the *visible* heavenly creatures.

22 This may mean simply the luster of the stars, as in Sir 43:9: κάλλος οὐρανοῦ, δόξα ἄστρων, κόσμος φωτίζων ἐν ὑψίστοις κυρίου, "The glory of the stars is the beauty of heaven, a gleaming array in the heights of the Lord" (RSV). But Paul is thinking of light–*substance*.

23 Stars as animated beings: *Sl. En.* 29; *S. Bar.* 59.11; Philo, *Op. mund.* 73; *Gig.* 8; *Plant.* 12: ζῷα γὰρ καὶ τούτους (sc. τοὺς ἀστέρας) νοερὰ δι' ὅλων φασιν οἱ φιλοσοφήδαντες, "Those who have made philosophy their study tell us that these [sc. the stars] too are living creatures, but of a kind composed entirely of Mind" (Loeb 3:219); *Som.* 1.135; Bousset–Gressmann, *Die Religion des Judentums*, 322f. Kümmel disputes the fact that δόξα is the light–substance of the heavenly beings; Paul, he argues, is speaking only of the difference in luster between the manifold bodies of heavenly and earthly beings. Bachmann and Robertson and Plummer dispute the fact that Paul regards the stars as living creatures; σῶμα, they argue, simply denotes material character. Not so Werner Foerster, *TDNT* 1:503–505.

24 Paul is accordingly here replying to the question πῶς; "how?" (against Jeremias).

24a Blass–Debrunner §490.

character of the future life. In the antitheses Paul's intention appears in its pure form.

Both the figure of sowing[25] and also the antithetical conceptuality are in keeping with the, initially, general ontological content of the discussion. The first antithesis is fundamental: φθορά—ἀφθαρσία, "perishability—imperishability" (see on vv 47, 53f). There follows a play on the word δόξα, which now no longer means "luster" (although this sense still rings in our ears), but "honor." On ἀσθένεια—δύναμις, "weakness—strength," cf. 1:24f; 4:10; 2 Cor 12:10; 13:3, 9. The impersonal form of expression ("it" is sown) is abandoned when the goal is reached: "sown is a σῶμα ψυχικόν, raised is a σῶμα πνευματικόν." What is a σῶμα πνευματικόν?[26] Lietzmann replies: a body that consists of heavenly πνεῦμα.[27] Kümmel contradicts him: not a body consisting of πνεῦμα, but "a body corresponding to existence ἐν πνεύματι." What is the inference from the context? In the preceding verses it is clearly a question of substances: σάρξ is the substance of the earthly σῶμα. On the other hand, the new antithesis brings a modification, when the antithesis to the σῶμα πνευματικόν is not a σῶμα σαρκικόν, but a σῶμα ψυχικόν. This of course does not mean one consisting of the substance of psyche or soul, but an earthly one (see on 2:14). The word has naturally here been chosen because of Gen 2:7. But it leads automatically to a certain re-

pudiation of Greek thinking in terms of substance. On the other hand, there remains the fact that the πνεῦμα is *conceived* as substance (see on v 47), and v 44b has the *form* of a general, ontological reflection.[28] The difficulties of the passage are reflected in E. Schweizer's observations.[29] He rightly rejects Lietzmann's explanation that Paul is thinking of a pneumatic body concealed beneath the earthly one (see on v 46). σῶμα πνευματικόν is not simply a body consisting of πνεῦμα, but one determined by πνεῦμα (Bachmann, Kümmel).[30] Yet this, according to Schweizer, applies only to Paul's *aim*. His *terminology*, Schweizer maintains, is Hellenistic: Hellenism conceives of effective supernatural power, "Spirit," in the form of substance. "Paul's argument is thus in content Jewish, in terminology Hellenistic." This alternative is not satisfactory. For Paul's aim is to go beyond the *Jewish* idea also.

Perhaps the meaning would be clearer if one could discern a counter-position: is the phrasing of v 44b polemical? Does it pave the way for v 46, which has to be polemically understood? (See on v 46.)

■ **45–49** The train of thought follows. Verse 45 works out the antitypical argument of the first and the "last" man on the basis of Scripture. Verse 46 brings the ontological thesis providing the proof.[31] Verse 47 explains the antithesis ψυχικόν—πνευματικόν, "psychical—

---

25 In reference back to vv 36–38. Bauer, *s.v.* σπείρω 1 b δ: "The body after burial is compared to a seed-grain. . . ." This leads to the antithesis σπείρειν—ἐγείρειν, "sow—raise." But it is just this comparison that does not interest Paul. Bachmann argues that σπείρειν symbolizes deliverance into the hand of death. Rather, we have here *figurative* speech in accord with vv 36–38, see the combinations (not only with φθορά, "imperishability," but also with ἀτιμία, "disgrace," and ἀσθένεια, "weakness").

26 Henri Clavier, "Brèves remarques sur la notion de σῶμα πνευματικόν," in *The Background of the New Testament and Its Eschatology*, ed. W. D. Davies and David Daube in honor of Charles Harold Dodd (Cambridge: University Press, 1956), 342–362.

27 Lietzmann develops this further: "Since, however, the Christian already has the πνεῦμα since his baptism, he already bears the germ (!) of this pneumatic body in and under his fleshly body." It is in similar terms, he says, that we have to understand 6:13–17.

28 Lietzmann says: "Verse 44b is not a conclusion drawn from the foregoing, but a thesis that will be

proved in what follows." But a different understanding of the logic is also possible: on the premise that σῶμα has a purely formal sense, v 44a and 44b become a unity. In that case v 44b is not an isolated ontological principle, but still belongs, as elucidation, to the series of antitheses.

29 *TDNT* 6:420f; cf. 7:1060–80.

30 Cf. also σῶμα τέλειον, "perfected body," *PGM* 4.495, on which Erik Peterson, "La libération d'Adam de l'Ἀνάγκη," *RB* 55 (1948): 199–214, now in his *Frühkirche, Judentum und Gnosis* (Rome, Freiburg and Vienna: Herder, 1959), 107–128, here esp. 113, observes that the caller is Adam, who calls for his own σῶμα τέλειον, as in *PGM* 4.1174 he calls for his μορφή and his πνεῦμα.

31 Schmithals, *Gnosticism in Corinth*, 169f [159f], holds that this thesis is formulated against the Gnostic thesis of the Corinthians that the pneumatic is the older. According to Eduard Schweizer, *TDNT* 6:420f, v 46 relates to the thesis of v 44, not to v 45, for it proves only the thesis of v 44. Paul "is not refuting an idea which would replace the eschato-

spiritual," as meaning earthly—heavenly.[32]

■ **45** Gen 2:7 LXX serves as a proof text. It has again (see on vv 25, 27) been altered *ad hoc*,[33] and completely reinterpreted:

(1) By means of the introduction of $\pi\rho\hat{\omega}\tau\sigma s$, "first," "man" is given a typological interpretation.[34] (2) By means of the insertion of "Adam," his character as "primal man" is indicated.[35] (3) By means of the antithesis $\psi v\chi\acute{\eta}$—$\pi v\epsilon\hat{v}\mu a$, "soul—spirit,"[36] of which there is no indication in the Old Testament text, Adam appears as an *antitype*. This thought is then pursued, and accordingly constitutes the point. It must be noted that Paul adds v 45b as if it were a part of the Scripture passage.[37]

It is plain that he stands in a given exegetical tradition. For this exegesis cannot be derived from the Old Testament text, and on the other hand it has not been freely constructed by Paul. To be sure, he transforms his tradition independently, according to his own Christology and eschatology.

Excursus: Adam and Primal Man

If we enquire into the presuppositions of this exposition of Gen 2:7, then we light upon the widespread idea of the *primal man*,[38] and this, too, in a specific form: that two "men" stand antithetically over against each other,[39] a heavenly, pneumatic man, and an earthly, "psychical" man.

The scattered traces of the mythological notion of the primal man have been assiduously collected and examined since Reitzenstein. But we are no clearer than ever, nor indeed is clarity to be expected at all. For the confusing factor lies, firstly, in the material itself and the impossibility of ordering it by means of a uniform conceptuality.[40] And secondly, the *one* concept primal man is applied to heterogeneous things: the macrocosmos, the protoplast, the prototype, the redeemer ("redeemed redeemer"), to the God "Man" in Gnosticism, where "Man" mostly means the highest God, but then also the revealing power of the deity.[41] On the negative

---

logical coming of the Redeemer by a doctrine of a pre-existent primal man. . . . He is contending against a belief which regards the pneumatic $\sigma\hat{\omega}\mu a$ as original [*Urdatum*]" (p. 420); this is proper to man and does not still have to be bestowed on him. Verse 44b, to be sure, seems to presuppose that the Corinthians know nothing of such a $\sigma\hat{\omega}\mu a$, but cf. v 29; apparently they know of a (Gnostic) body which now already lives a hidden life and after death simply continues to exist.

32 Charles K. Barrett, *From First Adam to Last* (New York: Scribner, 1962), 68–91.

33 LXX: $\kappa a\grave{\iota}$ $\check{\epsilon}\pi\lambda a\sigma\epsilon v$ $\acute{o}$ $\theta\epsilon\grave{o}s$ $\tau\grave{o}v$ $\check{a}v\theta\rho\omega\pi\sigma v$ $\chi\sigma\hat{\upsilon}v$ $\grave{a}\pi\grave{o}$ $\tau\hat{\eta}s$ $\gamma\hat{\eta}s$ $\kappa a\grave{\iota}$ $\acute{\epsilon}v\epsilon\phi\acute{\upsilon}\sigma\eta\sigma\epsilon v$ $\epsilon\acute{\iota}s$ $\tau\grave{o}$ $\pi\rho\acute{o}\sigma\omega\pi\sigma v$ $a\grave{\upsilon}\tau\sigma\hat{\upsilon}$ $\pi v\sigma\grave{\eta}v$ (Philo: $\pi v\epsilon\hat{\upsilon}\mu a$) $\zeta\omega\hat{\eta}s$, $\kappa a\grave{\iota}$ $\acute{\epsilon}\gamma\acute{\epsilon}v\epsilon\tau\sigma$ $\acute{o}$ $\check{a}v\theta\rho\omega\pi\sigma s$ $\epsilon\acute{\iota}s$ $\psi v\chi\grave{\eta}v$ $\zeta\hat{\omega}\sigma av$, "And God formed man of the dust of the *earth*, and breathed into his nostrils the breath [Philo: spirit] of life, and man became a living soul." Here $\psi v\chi\acute{\eta}$, "soul [RSV: being]," is a positive factor. Robin Scroggs, *The Last Adam* (Philadelphia: Fortress, 1966), 86–89: rabbinical exegesis of Gen 2:7. This sets out from the first half of the verse, from the orthography וַיִּיצֶר (with two yods): the word relates to the nature of man first in this, and then in the future, world.

34 Weiss says that with $\pi\rho\hat{\omega}\tau\sigma s$ an anticipatory note is introduced.

35 Not as redeemer, but as representative ancestor. The commentary is provided by Rom 5:12ff.

36 See on 2:14; Brandenburger, *Adam und Christus*, 84–89. *Naassene Sermon*, see below. Book of Baruch of Justin the Gnostic: Hipp., *Ref.* 5.26.36 (exposition

of Isa 1:2): $\sigma\grave{\upsilon}\rho av\grave{o}v$ $\lambda\acute{\epsilon}\gamma\epsilon\iota$ . . . $\tau\grave{o}$ $\pi v\epsilon\hat{\upsilon}\mu a$ $\tau\grave{o}$ $\acute{\epsilon}v$ $\tau\hat{\omega}$ $\grave{a}v\theta\rho\acute{\omega}\pi\omega$ . . ., $\gamma\hat{\eta}v$ $\delta\grave{\epsilon}$ $\tau\grave{\eta}v$ $\psi v\chi\grave{\eta}v$ $\tau\grave{\eta}v$ $\acute{\epsilon}v$ $\tau\hat{\omega}$ $\grave{a}v\theta\rho\acute{\omega}\pi\omega$ $\sigma\grave{\upsilon}v$ $\tau\hat{\omega}$ $\pi v\epsilon\acute{\upsilon}\mu a\tau\iota$, "Heaven means, he says, the spirit which is in man . . . and earth the soul which is in man (together) with the spirit" (Legge 1:179). The introduction of $\psi v\chi\acute{\eta}$ as a negative factor results in an anthropological trichotomy that represents a specifically Gnostic picture of man; Jonas, *Gnosis* 1:212–214; Schweizer, *TDNT* 6:395f.

37 Weiss.

38 Literature: Reitzenstein, *Poimandres; Das iranische Erlösungsmysterium* (Bonn: Marcus & Weber, 1921); further see Colpe, *Die religionsgeschichtliche Schule*; Bousset, *Hauptprobleme*, 203–209; Willy Staerk, *Soter II: Die Erlösungserwartung in den östlichen Religionen* (Stuttgart: Kohlhammer, 1938); Kurt Rudolph, "Ein Grundtyp gnostischer Urmensch–Adam–Spekulation," *ZRGG* 9 (1957): 1–20; *Theogonie, Kosmogonie und Anthropologie in den mandäischen Schriften*, FRLANT, 88 (Göttingen: Vandenhoeck & Ruprecht, 1965); E. S. Drower, *The Secret Adam* (Oxford: Clarendon Press, 1960); Jervell, *Imago Dei*; Colpe, *Die religionsgeschichtliche Schule* (history of research, bibliography); Hans–Martin Schenke, *Der Gott "Mensch" in der Gnosis* (Göttingen: Vandenhoeck & Ruprecht, 1962); Brandenburger, *Adam und Christus*.

39 Brandenburger, *Adam und Christus*, 68–157.

40 See Colpe's reflections in *Die religionsgeschichtliche Schule*, 171–193.

41 Schenke, *Der Gott "Mensch,"* esp. 6–15. Particularly informative are two editions of the *Apocryphon of*

side, we can today establish the fact that an original, self–contained myth of the primal man, such as Reitzenstein sought to reconstruct, never existed. The figure in question belongs not so much to myth as to mythological speculation. Hence we must not attempt, either, to track down dependences and influences from the history of religion. More important is the establishing of types.[42]

One form of the primal man is the Iranian Gayô-mart.[43] Gnosticism is largely dominated by speculation on the primal man, whereby a few standard basic types are varied in confusing multiplicity. The climax and conclusion—after the Mandaean texts[44] —is the Manichaean system.

Of special importance for us is a series of texts in which Jewish influence is present,[45] but which at the same time make plain that the conception of the primal man is a pre–Jewish substratum. This applies to the Naassene Sermon:[46] The "inner man" ($\check{\epsilon}\sigma\omega$ $\check{\alpha}\nu\theta\rho\omega\pi\sigma$) is brought down "to that which is formed of forgetfulness, the thing made of clay" (14: $\epsilon\check{\iota}s$ $\tau\grave{o}$ $\pi\lambda\acute{\alpha}\sigma\mu\alpha$ $\tau\hat{\eta}s$ $\lambda\acute{\eta}\theta\eta s$, $\tau\grave{o}$ $\chi o\ddot{\iota}\kappa\acute{o}\nu$). Rebirth is "the spiritual birth, the heavenly birth from above" (27:

$\grave{\eta}$ $\gamma\acute{\epsilon}\nu\epsilon\sigma\iota s$ $\grave{\eta}$ $\pi\nu\epsilon\upsilon\mu\alpha\tau\iota\kappa\acute{\eta}$, $\grave{\eta}$ $\acute{\epsilon}\pi o\upsilon\rho\acute{\alpha}\nu\iota os$, $\grave{\eta}$ $\check{\alpha}\nu\omega$). The great, higher Man was given a "soul" ($\psi\upsilon\chi\acute{\eta}$), "so that he might experience through the soul" (2: $\check{\iota}\nu\alpha$ $\delta\iota\grave{\alpha}$ $\tau\hat{\eta}s$ $\psi\upsilon\chi\hat{\eta}s$ $\pi\acute{\alpha}\sigma\chi\eta$). The soul accordingly belongs to the earthly side: it is the principle of unfreedom.[47] In a Gnostic prayer[48] Adam is the exalted, highest God, who has been rescued from cosmic menaces, to whom his followers pray for liberation. Factually speaking the praying Self is identical with Adam, so that here, too, a heavenly Adam and an earthly Adam reduced to servitude—or "man" as a heavenly and as an earthly, banished and exiled being—stand over against each other.

Jewish influence is plain also in the alchemist Zosimus.[49] Here, too, as Reitzenstein points out in *Poimandres*, 103–106, we have a confrontation of the spiritual ($\pi\nu\epsilon\upsilon\mu\alpha\tau\iota\kappa\acute{o}s$, pp. 103f) = inward ($\check{\epsilon}\sigma\omega$, p. 104) = shining ($\phi\omega\tau\epsilon\iota\nu\acute{o}s$, p. 105) man and the outward man ($\check{\epsilon}\xi\omega$ $\check{\alpha}\nu\theta\rho\omega\pi os$, p. 105) = the earthly Adam ($\gamma\acute{\eta}\ddot{\iota}\nu os$ $^{,}A\delta\acute{\alpha}\mu$, p. 106) = the fleshly Adam ($\sigma\acute{\alpha}\rho\kappa\iota\nu os$ $^{,}A\delta\acute{\alpha}\mu$, p. 104).

The interest in these speculations lies in the connection between the being of the primal man and of

John (Schenke, *Der Gott "Mensch"*, 34–43): (a) *Cod. Berolinensis Gnosticus* (*BG* 8502) 47–76 (Walter Till, *Die gnostischen Schriften des koptischen Papyrus Berolinensis 8502*, TU, 60 [Berlin: Akademie–Verlag, 1955], 135–193); (b) Pahor Labib, *Coptic Gnostic Papyri in the Coptic Museum at Old Cairo*, vol. 1 (Cairo: Government Press, 1956), 62f. Here we have side by side God as "the first Man" and the "Man" Adam. Since there is an allusion to Gen 1:26f, Schenke presumes that "Man" as a designation for God was developed from this passage, or from the Jewish doctrine of man being in the image of God. But the point that calls for explanation is precisely how it was possible to find in the Genesis passage the idea of the primal man. The latter must have already existed. This is not to dispute the widespread influence of Jewish speculations, see below.

42   Colpe, *Die religionsgeschichtliche Schule*, 197, rightly advises caution in face of the concept "myth": the Gnostic myth is an artificial product. And he issues the warning (p. 195): "At all events these questions must not be decided in advance to the effect that all the conceptions can be derived from each other or that they are bound up with each other from the start. Not every analogy contains a genealogy."

43   Sven S. Hartman, *Gayômart. Étude sur le syncrétisme dans l'ancien Iran* (Uppsala: Almqvist & Wiksell, 1953); Colpe, *Die religionsgeshichtliche Schule*, 140–170. The instances are late (*Bundahišn*), but point back to older times. Gayômart will be the first to rise from the dead. But he does not have any redeeming function.

44   Rudolph, *Theogonie*, 273–281. The "hidden Adam" is identical with the soul (*mana*) which is brought to the Adam–body by the messenger of light. Adakas–Ziwa above corresponds to the hidden Adam below. In the light of the idea that is constitutive for Gnosticism—the notion of the substantial unity between God/redeemer and soul/redeemed or requiring to be redeemed—it is understandable that the hidden Adam himself becomes the messenger of light and the redeemer.

45   Jewish speculations on the cosmic dimension of Adam (see on v 22) cannot be regarded as material for comparison, since the antithetical figure is missing. The material has been collected by Jervell, *Imago Dei*, 96–107, and Brandenburger, *Adam und Christus*, 135–139. Furthermore in this passage Paul is not taking up the thought of man's being in the image of God—this least of all things. For indeed his concern is to work out the antithesis and the discontinuity. He does not appeal to the "primal state" of Adam as the perfect man; Scroggs, *The Last Adam*, 100.

46   In its pre–Christian basic form (see Reitzenstein, *Poimandres*, 83–98). It is cited here according to Reitzenstein's chapter divisions. Reitzenstein–Schäder, *Studien*, 161–173.

47   Cf. $o\check{\iota}$ $\psi\upsilon\chi\iota\kappa o\acute{\iota}$, chap. 24. Incidentally, in the *Apocryphon of John*, the $\psi\upsilon\chi\acute{\eta}$ is a negative factor.

48   In two recensions, *PGM* 4.195–222 and 1167–1226; on which see Peterson, "La libération d'Adam."

49   Reitzenstein, *Poimandres*, 103–106; André–Jean Festugière, *La révélation d'Hermès Trismégiste*, vol. 1

the Gnostic. The principle always obtains: first the pneumatic, then the earthly (psychical).

A special case is that of Philo. He sees himself confronted by the exegetical problem that in Gen 1 and 2 there are *two* accounts of the creation of man. He solves it by distinguishing between two men, in two variations.

1) He distinguishes two types of man, the heavenly and the earthly, *Leg. all.* 1:31f (on Gen 2:7): διττὰ ἀνθρώπων γένη· ὁ μὲν γάρ ἐστιν οὐράνιος ἄνθρωπος, ὁ δὲ γήϊνος. ὁ μὲν οὖν οὐράνιος ἅτε κατ᾽ εἰκόνα θεοῦ γεγονὼς φθαρτῆς καὶ συνόλως γεώδους οὐσίας ἀμέτοχος, ὁ δὲ γήϊνος ἐκ σποράδος ὕλης, ἣν χοῦν κέκληκεν, ἐπάγη· διὸ τὸν μὲν οὐράνιόν φησιν οὐ πεπλάσθαι, κατ᾽ εἰκόνα δὲ τετυπῶσθαι θεοῦ, τὸν δὲ γήϊνον πλάσμα, ἀλλ᾽ οὐ γέννημα, εἶναι τοῦ τεχνίτου. ἄνθρωπον δὲ τὸν ἐκ γῆς λογιστέον εἶναι νοῦν εἰσκρινόμενον σώματι, οὔπω δ᾽ εἰσκεκριμένον, "There are two types of men; the one a heavenly man, the other an earthly. The heavenly man, being made after the image of God, is altogether without part or lot in corruptible and terrestrial substance; but the earthly one was compacted out of the matter scattered here and there, which Moses calls 'clay.' For this reason he says that the heavenly man was not moulded, but was stamped with the image of God; while the earthly is a moulded work of the Artificer, but not His offspring. We must account the man made out of the earth to be mind mingling with, but not yet blended with, body" (Loeb 1:167).[50] This mind (νοῦς) is earthly! Only when God breathes the life force into it does it become ψυχὴ (ζῶσα), a "[living] soul."

It is plain that the conception of the two men is already given. Philo himself transforms it psychologically and morally by making of the two men two human *types*.[51]

2) He distinguishes the idea man from the historical Adam, *Op. mund.* 134 (likewise on Gen 2:7):[52] ὁ μὲν γὰρ διαπλασθεὶς αἰσθητὸς ἤδη μετέχων ποιότητος, ἐκ σώματος καὶ ψυχῆς συνεστώς, ἀνὴρ ἢ γυνή, φύσει θνητός· ὁ δὲ κατὰ τὴν εἰκόνα ἰδέα τις ἢ γένος ἢ σφραγίς, νοητός, ἀσώματος, οὔτ᾽ ἄρρεν οὔτε θῆλυ, ἄφθαρτος φύσει, "For the man so formed is an object of sense–perception, partaking already of such or such quality, consisting of body and soul, man or woman, by nature mortal; while he that was after the (Divine) image was an idea or type or seal, an object of thought (only), incorporeal, neither male nor female, by nature incorruptible" (Loeb 1:107). Here, too, it is plain at once that this exegesis is not derived from the text.[53] Here, too, the heavenly man is the first, the earthly—as a copy of him—the second. Bousset's observation still holds:[54] there is nothing to indicate that Philo distilled his view from Gen 1f. The matter–of–fact way in which he advances it proves the contrary.

The question now is: Does Paul set out from the tradition about the first and second man which appears in Philo and stand it on its head—or, as he thinks, on its feet? In that case his thesis does not provide us with any conclusive inferences in regard to the circumstances of the discussion in Corinth. For in that case Paul may be advancing his arguments in theoretical debate with his Jewish school Wisdom. It is of course also possible that influences of this Jewish speculation are at work in Corinth, in a protognostic form similar to that of Alexandria. Or is Paul's background already a tradition of a totally different order?[55] In that case everything is again open.

At all events he does not reckon with an antithesis between Gen 2:7 and 1:26f. He sees Gen 2:7 as an account of the creation; Gen 1:27 (v 49) is an interpretation not of the nature of man, but of the connection between primal man and man. It is fundamental that the relation between the first and the second man is reversed, as compared with all similar material provided by the history of religion.

A problem is raised by the question of time: When did the "last" Adam "become" a πνεῦμα ζωοποιοῦν,

---

(Paris: Lecoffre, 1944), 260–282; Schenke, *Der Gott "Mensch"*, 52–56.

50   [The original German footnote has been absorbed into the text (Ed.).]

51   Cf. Philo, *Leg. all.* 1.53–55, 88–90. Pascher, *Königsweg*, 129–131: Brandenburger, *Adam und Christus*, 124–131.

52   Philo, *Conf. ling.* 146: the Logos is ὁ κατ᾽ εἰκόνα ἄνθρωπος, "the Man after His image" (Loeb 4:91).

53   Here too, of course, not in the form of an original myth, but in that of mythological speculation. Esp. *Leg. all.* 1.31f shows that the antithetical schema was not developed by Philo. His own interest lies at this point precisely in the platonizing and moralizing transformation of it (with Brandenburger, *Adam und Christus*, 117–131).

54   Bousset–Gressmann, *Die Religion des Judentums*, 353.

55   Kümmel holds that Paul is not dependent on the view that arises in Philo, but interprets Gen 1:27 from the standpoint of the primal man myth understood in eschatological terms. But in what form does he find the "primal man" among his materials? A tradition independent of the Alexandrian one might be indicated by the fact that for Paul the twofold narrative in Gen 1 and 2 presents no problem whatever. Besides, Philo does not compare the heavenly

"life–giving Spirit"? At his creation before all time, or at his resurrection?[56] The context points to the resurrection.[57] Only then are the attributes ἔσχατος and δεύτερος, "last" and "second,"[58] in place, and likewise ζωοποιοῦν, "life–giving."[59]

■ **46** The thesis–like form of this statement can be explained in various ways.

a) It is a purely exegetical statement intended to carry on v 45a; the transition of thought leads from the statement in v 44a via the principle of v 44b and the Scripture verse to vv 47–49. Here Paul may have a different exegesis in mind, which he wards off in passing. But the thesis can be explained from his own ideas and his usage of πνευματικός and ψυχικός.

b) The thesis is intended polemically from the start, against an exegesis of Philo's type or against a Gnostic principle.

Once again we must assume that the positive thought is the primary thing and that its polemical effect is secondary.[60] Inferences in regard to the Corinthian position are as uncertain as in the whole of the chapter.[61]

■ **47** The antithesis is repeated in a varied form: ψυχικός is explained by χοϊκός, "earth[l]y," πνευματικός by ἐξ οὐρανοῦ, "from heaven."[62] And in accordance with the relation accorded to the two principles, the psychical and the pneumatic, in v 46 ἔσχατος, "last," is now replaced by δεύτερος, "second." There are of course only these two "men" in the sense described, namely, as representatives. The conception is explained by Rom 5:12ff.[63] That the important thing for Paul is the representative character is shown by v 48.[64]

■ **48–49** The basic concept is εἰκών, "image."[65] As the thought of representation is clarified by Rom 5:12ff, so contrariwise the concept εἰκών casts light on the latter

---

Man with Adam; see Scroggs, *The Last Adam*, 87, n. 30. For Philo see further Joachim Jeremias, *TDNT* 1:143; Eduard Schweizer, *TDNT* 6:420.

56 A third possibility would be theoretical: at the incarnation. But this plays no part in Paul.

57 Eduard Schweizer, *TDNT* 6:420 (against Weiss, who takes it of preexistence and appeals for this interpretation to the common ἐγένετο). In favor of the resurrection date is also Hermann, *Kyrios und Pneuma*, 62: "The idea that the earthly Jesus, through his participation in the 'être divin' [Allo], already possessed the life–giving Spirit, is foreign to Paul."

58 This reduces the force of the mythology. Primal man and resurrection do not fit together. And no account is taken of the pre–existence of Christ.

59 Jervell, *Imago Dei*, 286, observes that the question is not one of restitution, because the men of the first creation bore not God's image, but Adam's.

60 In deliberate polemic he would surely work rather with the antithesis spiritual—fleshly. Then, to be sure, he could not say that the fleshly was "the first." According to Jeremias, *TDNT* 1:143, Paul does not say that Adam was created first, but v 46 "— with σῶμα as the subject, cf. 1 C. 15:44b—is really dealing with the bodily nature of the Christian, who first bears the physical [literally psychical] body and will then receive the spiritual at the *parousia*."

61 With Weiss and others: we have to supply not σῶμα, but merely ἐστίν. The inference drawn by Jervell, *Imago Dei*, 260, n. 311, "then, however, we have to understand it in such a way that v 46 relates only to v 44b and not also to v 45," is not conclusive.

62 Robertson and Plummer would relate ἐξ οὐρανοῦ rather to the parousia than to the incarnation. But neither readily suggests itself, see on v 45.

63 This does not mean that ἄνθρωπος, "man," is here a title.

64 For the supra–individual nature of the heavenly man see Käsemann, *Leib*, 74–81, 87–94.

Barrett, *From First Adam to Last*, 76: "What we have not learned about it [*sc.* Paul's picture of the Second Man] in the present context is why the Man from heaven should first appear on earth in the image of the earthly Man to suffer and die." Here we have in fact the result of the mythological schema. On the other hand it has to be borne in mind that the interpretation of Christ as "Man" is already constructed in view of the work of salvation. The abbreviated form of 1 Cor 15 must be expanded in the light of Rom 5.

On the terminology (Brandenburger, *Adam und Christus*, 76, n. 1): χοϊκός in the NT only here; *Naassene Sermon* 14; ἐπίγειος: 2 Cor 5:1; Phil 2:10; Jn 3:12; Jas 3:15; ἐπουράνιος: Phil 2:10; *Naassene Sermon* 27; ἀθανασία: 1 Tim 6:16; ἀφθαρσία: Rom 2:7; Eph 6:24; 2 Tim 1:10; for τὸ φθαρτόν cf. 1 Pet 1:18, 23.

65 Jervell, *Imago Dei*, 268, observes: "The combination of anthropos–pneuma–eikon is thoroughly Gnostic and shows that Paul is here standing on a Jewish–Gnostic exposition of Gen 1:26f and 2:7," which he reshapes independently. But one must object that this combination is not *in itself* Gnostic. It can be-

passage: Adam and Christ[66] are representatives as being severally prototypes.[67] Once again Paul, consistently enough, maintains over against the underlying prototype–copy schema, which is timelessly conceived, the eschatological reservation[68]—namely, by the choice of the future φορέσομεν, "we shall wear."[69]

The underlying notion is that prototype and copy are in essence one. It is here applied to the relationship between the primal man and individual men. And indeed the unity consists in the fact that the primal man is in the copy, and the latter in turn is in the prototype as his

representative. The word "wear" suggests at once the association of thought with the garment that is ontologically equivalent to the εἰκών.[70] This is a self–contained complex of ideas. The unity of this complex of ideas is now shattered in Paul. This is bound up with the fact that he is no longer himself the object of the knowledge that brings salvation, but is an instrument for the interpretation of the historical work of salvation.[71]

---

50   **This I say, brothers: flesh and blood cannot inherit the kingdom of God, nor does perishability inherit imperishability.**
51 / Behold, I tell you a mystery: we shall not all fall asleep,[1] but we shall all be changed, 52 / in a moment, in the twinkling of an eye, at the last trumpet. For it will sound[2] and the dead will be raised imperishable, and we shall be

---

come so. But this is decided solely by the sense of the statement. Incidentally, how little Paul is concerned with the schemata as such and with the harmonizing of them is shown by the omission of δόξα (despite vv 40f and 11:2ff).

66   And here the distinction has to be duly taken into account; cf the way in which Rom 5:12ff emphatically says: "*Not* as ... so. ..."

67   εἰκών: see on 11:2ff. εἰκών is best translated "form"; but it must be clear that this does not mean the outward form; "rather, in the form the essence itself comes to expression" (Eltester, *Eikon*, 23). The notion of preexistence would go well with the concept εἰκών in vv 45 and 47. But of course there is considerable confusion between the schemata because the creed, i.e. death and resurrection, is constantly in mind.

68   Which in itself does not suit an εἰκών Christology: 2 Cor 3:18; Phil 3:21; Rom 8:29f. Weiss finds that in οἱ ἐπουράνιοι, "those that are heavenly," we have a "tremendous prolepsis." Yet the expression does not of course say that we are now already heavenly beings, but merely formulates the principle. The time is determined by the future φορέσομεν, "we shall wear."

69   Kümmel says: "Paul sees the connection between the earthly and the risen man in terms not of substance, but of history." This is true of Paul's intention. Yet it must be discovered all through his terminology.

70   On "wear" see Käsemann, *Leib*, 166: ". . . as in fact one 'wears' the εἰκών, according to Gnostic teaching." Only, in Gnosticism the εἰκών is the subject of the Gnostic. Paul, on the other hand, knows no "wearer" of the continuity who can be directly described as such. He knows no "pure" subject either: it exists only in this or that condition. On the affinity between "image" and "garment" in Philo, see Pascher, *Königsweg*, 51–60; the *Hymn of the Pearl* in *Act. Thom.* 108–113.

71   Thus to redress the balance he has to introduce the parousia, which does not suit the schema, and has to transpose into the unsuitable future tense. The limitations of the εἰκών terminology as a means of representation here emerge.

1   πάντες οὐ (by means of this word order the parallelism is established): cf. Xenoph., *An.* 2.5.35; Herm., *Sim.* 8.6.2: πάντες οὐ μετενόησαν, "not all repented" (Loeb 2:203–205, modified). Blass–Debrunner §433(2). To be sure, the text is transmitted in vacillating form:

1) πάντες (μὲν) οὐ κοιμηθησόμεθα, πάντες δὲ
   ἀλλαγησόμεθα   B (𝕽)
2) πάντες (μὲν) κοιμηθησόμεθα, οὐ
   πάντες δὲ ἀλλαγησόμεθα   (ℵ) C
3) πάντες (μὲν) οὐ κοιμηθησόμεθα, οὐ
   πάντες δὲ ἀλλαγησόμεθα   p⁴⁶ (Aᶜ)
4) οἱ πάντες μὲν κοιμηθησόμεθα, οἱ
   πάντες δὲ ἀλλαγησόμεθα   A*
5) πάντες (μὲν) ἀναστησόμεθα, οὐ
   πάντες δὲ ἀλλαγησόμεθα   D* (Marcion)

D has transposed into terms of the average Christian metaphysic: resurrection of *all*, judgment, transfor-

changed. 53 / For this perishable being must put on imperishability, and this mortal immortality. 54 / But when this perishable puts on imperishability and[3] this mortal immortality, then the saying will be fulfilled which is written: "Death is swallowed up in victory.[4] 55 / Death, where is your victory? Death,[5] where is your sting?"[6] 56 / The sting of death is sin, and the power of sin is the Law. 57 / Thanks be to God, who gives us the victory through our Lord Jesus Christ. 58 / Therefore, my beloved brothers, be steadfast, immovable, always growing in the work of the Lord. For you know that your labor in the Lord is not in vain.

■ **50** Verse 50 is introduced by τοῦτο δέ φημι, "This I say," (cf. 7:29) as a new thought. It is a doctrinal statement (present). The style and content indicate that Paul found it already to hand (it is expounded by him in v 50b): (a) "flesh and blood";[7] (b) "inherit the kingdom of God" (see on 6:9).

Context: The new thesis is introduced abruptly. Is it intended to guarantee the foregoing, namely, the application of the Adam–Christ antithesis? Usually v 50 is taken with the following section. In favor of this is the emphasis in the introduction. Weiss says that v 50 intro-

duces the new theme: the fate of those who survive. He must admit, to be sure, that the thought is not sharply separated from the foregoing, and that the transformation of the living is only a passing thought. Jeremias (see on v 35) interprets as follows: vv 50ff are the answer to the question "how?" Verse 50 leads to the question: How, then, can they see God at all? The answer stands in vv 51–53. The parallelism in v 50 is synthetic. The statement, "flesh and blood . . .," speaks not of the resurrection of the dead, but of the transformation of the

---

mation, sc. of the blessed. ℵ C also—in a different way—assimilate to the average view: "All men must die." p[46] A[c] leave the Pauline bipartite form, but likewise "correct" the reference to transformation (or have we in p[46] a simple mistake, the mingling of two variants?).

Genealogy: D is dependent on the text form of p[46] (not so P. Brandhuber, "Die sekundären Lesarten bei 1 Kor. 15,51. Ihre Verbreitung und Entstehung," *Biblica* 18 [1937]: 303–333, 418–438: The readings of p[46] and A* were early rejected or remained unnoticed. The reading of p[46] goes back to Marcion; it coincides with his views. p[46] of course does not understand it in Marcion's sense; it can also be understood in a chiliastic sense. The readings of ℵ C and D* were created to ward off Marcion).

According to Lietzmann, (1) is original. All the corrections remove Paul's (unfulfilled) expectation that he would still live to see the parousia.

2   Impersonal: classical; Xenoph., *An.* 1.2.17; Blass–Debrunner §129.

3   τὸ φθαρτὸν . . . καί om. p[46] ℵ* C* Marcion, Vulg. —as a result of homoioteleuton.

4   νεῖκος: p[46] B D*; Tert. Cyp. Hier. Aug.: *contentio*.

5   ℵ sy: ᾅδη—following LXX.

6   νῖκος and κέντρον are interchanged in D G ℵ.

7   Paul: Gal 1:16. For the expression in rabbinical writings see Rudolf Meyer, *TDNT* 7:116: "From the very outset, then, the idea of mortality and creatureliness seems to be especially bound up with the phrase"; cf. Sir 14:18 (Hebrew).
LXX:

ὡς φύλλον θάλλον ἐπὶ δένδρου δάσεος,
τὰ μὲν καταβάλλει, ἄλλα δὲ φύει,
οὕτως γενεὰ σαρκὸς καὶ αἵματος
ἡ μὲν τελευτᾷ, ἕτερα δὲ γεννᾶται.

"Like flourishing leaves on a spreading tree which sheds some and puts forth others, so are the generations of flesh and blood; one dies and another is born" (RSV).
Heb.:

.כן דורות בשר ודם נוע אחד ואחד גומל

"Thus are the generations of flesh and blood: one dies and another is weaned."
Sir 17:31 (text?); Wisd 12:5; Philo, *Rer. div. her.* 57; Mt 16:17; Eph 6:12 (reverse order). For v 50: Joa-

living at the parousia.[8] Against this interpretation, to be sure, is the wording of the sentence, also the wording of vv 53f and the whole train of thought. Here, too, the emphasis is on newness and contingency. The statement explains—to begin with on the negative side—both the future φορέσομεν, "we shall wear," and also the meaning of εἰκὼν (τοῦ ἐπουρανίου), "image [of the heavenly]."[9] What is the relation between the two halves of the statement? Are they synonymous, or does the second introduce a further thought? Since the doctrinal statement was already to hand and the second statement presents an exegesis of it, the thought is the same.[10] In the subsequent history of the passage an interesting point is its transformation into Gnostic meditation in the *Gospel of Philip*.[11]

■ **51** In v 51 we have a similar emphasis on the introduction of a new thought as in v 50. Now this thought is characterized as μυστήριον. That means here also: mystery *and* unveiling of the same.[12] If in v 50 Paul took his stand on a thought that was already given, now he imparts one of his own. Underlying what he says is the expectation that he will personally live to see the parousia, as in 1 Thess 4:17.[13] The second πάντες again means all believers.[14] The Jewish background (and the transformation of it) is shown by *2 Bar.* 50f:[15] The dead first arise unchanged (in order that they can be recognized). Then the sinners and the righteous will be changed into the form appropriate to them. One can see that there are worries which Paul does *not* share with this apocalypticist: the concern for perceptibility, continuity,

---

8 chim Jeremias, "Flesh and Blood cannot inherit the Kingdom of God (I Cor. XV.50)," *NTS* 2 (1955–56): 151–159, now in his *Abba*, 298–307. Jeremias tabulates as follows:—

V 50:	(a) σὰρξ καὶ αἷμα	βασιλεία
	(b) φθορά	ἀφθαρσία
V 52:	(b) οἱ νεκροί	ἄφθαρτοι
	(a) ἡμεῖς	
V 53:	(b) τὸ φθαρτόν	ἀφθαρσία
	(a) τὸ θνητόν	ἀθανασία
V 54:	(b) τὸ φθαρτόν	ἀφθαρσία
	(a) τὸ θνητόν	ἀθανασία

The coordination of the concepts is governed merely by the paronomasia. φθαρτός and θνητός are synonymous, as are ἀφθαρσία and ἀθανασία. If a deliberate coordination according to content were present, one would expect: νεκροί—θνητόν/ἀθανασία. For the terminology cf. Rom 8:10f.

Lietzmann says: "Verse 50 establishes as a result that the Jewish notion of a resurrection of this fleshly body is to be rejected." This may be the original point of the thesis.

9 From this standpoint the reading φορέσομεν is certain.

10 Eduard Schweizer, *TDNT* 7:128f, thinks a distinction could be made in Jeremias' sense if v 50 belonged together with vv 51–55, as an answer to the question, "how?" But he holds that the distinction between the living and the dead can no longer be made in vv 53f. And μυστήριον in v 51, he goes on, indicates a *new* mystery. In that case σάρξ and αἷμα, "flesh" and "blood," stand parallel to φθορά, "imperishability." Then the result is: v 50 belongs to vv 36–49 as their conclusion, and has to be interpreted in this light. This view is contrary to most of the commentaries, but is to be preferred.

11 *Ev. Phil.* 23:"Some are afraid lest they rise naked.

Because of this they wish to rise in the flesh, and they do not know that those who bear the flesh [it is they who are] naked; those who . . . themselves to unclothe themselves [it is they who are] not naked. 'Flesh [and blood shall] not inherit the kingdom [of God]'" (Wilson, 32). There follows the explanation that the flesh which cannot inherit is the flesh we bear upon us. The flesh and blood of Christ can inherit; Jn 6:53f is quoted: "His flesh is the Logos, and his blood is the Holy Spirit." Wilson, 87–89.

12 See on 2:6 (λαλεῖν); 13:2; 14:2; Rom 11:25; for the content also 1 Thess 4:15–17.

13 It is idle to dispute this, as Allo attempts to do (appealing to 6:14; 2 Cor 5:8; Phil 3:11). Kümmel rightly observes: it is not possible, either, to refer the statement to those who are alive at the parousia.

14 Weiss says: if this πάντες denotes all Christians, then it is in contradiction to v 52. Hence it must be taken in a narrower sense: those who then remain. The difficulty, he says, would be removed if πάντες οὐ were to be understood in the sense that from now on nobody more will die; "but I do not venture to explain it thus." There is only a seeming contradiction, since Paul uses the word ἀλλάσσειν in a variable sense.

15 Cf. *Eth. En.* 62.15: "And the righteous and elect shall have risen from the earth. . . . And they shall have been clothed with garments of glory" (Charles, *APOT* 2:228). This garment, to be sure, is a different thing from the Pauline εἰκών.

16 Jeremias, "Flesh and Blood," finds a development in Paul's conception: in 1 Thess, he holds, Paul as yet knows nothing of the transformation, but shares to begin with the Jewish conception that the dead will rise unchanged. Now, Jeremias goes on, Paul has gained the insight (μυστήριον) that the transformation of the living and the dead takes place im-

compensatory justice.[16]

■ **52** The question whether this statement[17] still belongs to the mystery, or provides an elucidation of it, is not a genuine alternative, since the mystery is a communication on Paul's own part. He now explains both the manner and the time of the transformation. He must of course, because of his personal expectation and his apocalyptic conceptions in general, distinguish between those who remain alive and those who have already died, i.e., before the parousia.[18] But it is not this distinction as such that constitutes the real object. Paul is concerned on the contrary (as in 1 Thessalonians) to establish the fundamental equality in the destiny of the two groups. This already emerges from the combination: the announcement of an exact point of time, and the suddenness of the whole proceeding. These are two elements in the structure of early eschatology, which are already combined in 1 Thess 4.

The σάλπιγξ, "trumpet,"[19] is a normal apoca-

lyptic requisite.[20] The "last" trumpet means not the last in a series of trumpet blasts, but "the eschatological one."[21] Paul indeed underlines the note of instantaneity: "it sounds, and . . ."[22] This signal is the end. The customary conceptions of time must now fail. There now follows the resurrection and the transformation—in *one* act: there is no advantage and no disadvantage.

This picture does not automatically agree with v 26 (q.v.).[23] At all events Paul's intention *here* emerges in purer form. The concentration of everything into a single instant expresses the miraculous character of the new creation, the note of contingency.[24]

■ **53** This verse provides an elucidation in didactic style: formally speaking, the parallelism is taken up once again.

δεῖ, "must," denotes the apocalyptic order, not a necessity of nature. The statement is in content a repetition and modification of v 42: cf. τὸ φθαρτόν, "the perishable," with φθορά, "perishability," ἐνδύεσθαι, "put on," with σπείρειν, "sow"; ἀφθαρσία, "im-

---

mediately at the parousia, cf. then 2 Cor 5:1–5; Phil 3:20f; Col 3:4; in this sense, Jeremias argues, we have also to understand Rom 8:11, 23. But already in 1 Thess the Jewish succession of events no longer prevails.

17 ἄτομος: Aristot., *Phys* 6.236a.6: ἐν ἀτόμῳ, " 'at' an indivisible moment" (Loeb 2:141). Isa 54:8 Symmachus in MS 86 (see *Isaias*, ed. Joseph Ziegler, Septuaginta: Vetus Testamentum Graecum, 14 [Göttingen: Vandenhoeck & Ruprecht, 1939]); ἐν ἀτόμῳ ὀργῆς, "in a moment of wrath"; yet the tradition is divided: Eusebius (according to the as yet unpublished Isaiah commentary of MS 49; cf. Ziegler, *Isaias*, 12) transmits: ἐν ὀξυσμῷ (LXX: ἐν θυμῷ μικρῷ), "in an instant" (LXX: "in a little anger"). Which tradition is genuine for Symmachus is difficult to decide, since the Heb. רֶגַע in Isa 54:8 is a *hapax legomenon*. ὀξυσμός seems to be authenticated nowhere else in the whole of the Greek world. This would tell in favor of, rather than against, its having originated with Symmachus. In favor of this is also the fact that ὀξυσμός seems rather to be an assimilation to the Hebrew text (cf. Prov 27:4 קֶשֶׁף ~ ὀξύς). [Hint provided by R. Hanhart].

For ῥιπή, "casting," p[46] D* G have the variant reading ῥοπή, "inclination downwards," which (though without ὀφθαλμοῦ, "of an eye") is also found with the meaning "twinkling of an eye," see Bauer, *s.v.*

18 Cf. the trouble which this problem causes to Jewish apocalypticists. They are driven to speculative combinations, with the help of the kingdom of the mes-

siah and the assumption of a dual blessedness: the righteous of the last generation enjoy the blessedness of the messianic kingdom, after the end of which *all* the righteous enjoy the blessings of the coming aeon.

19 σάλπιγξ, "trumpet," is both the instrument itself and also its sound. 1 Thess 4:16; Mt 24:31. See on 1 Cor 14:8.

20 Rev 8:2–21; 11:15–19; *4 Ezra* 6.23; *Sib.* 4.173f. Theophany: Heb 12:19. Gerhard Friedrich, *TDNT* 7:71–88.

21 With Lietzmann; Friedrich, *TDNT* 7:87f. Matters are different in Rev. 1 Thess 4:16 says: ἐν σάλπιγγι θεοῦ, "with the trumpet of God." This naturally does not mean that God himself blows the trumpet, but that he gives the order to blow it.

22 Lietzmann is too subtle in reading out of ἄφθαρτοι, "imperishable": "i.e. already transformed at (!) the sounding of the trumpet."

23 Jeremias, *Abba*, 299, n. 2 (see above on v 26).

24 So Weiss who, to be sure, remarks that σαλπίσει κτλ. "sounds almost like a quotation." The repetition would "not be in place unless Paul were seeking to appeal to an established statement."

perishability," is repeated and varied: ἀθανασία, "immortality."[25] Here, too, the parallelism is synonymous: τὸ φθαρτόν = τὸ θνητόν, ἀφθαρσία = ἀθανασία. The statement of course provides a ground for v 52. The important thing is still the equality of the two groups.[26] ἐνδύεσθαι, "put on," is still more plain than the above–used expression "wear," an allusion to the conception of the heavenly garment,[27] without expanding this idea.[28] In ἐνδύεσθαι there lies a pointer to the identity of the believer with his future existence. But this identity is not objectified in Gnostic ways. Paul does not define an identical subject,[29] however seductively this may be suggested by the conception of the heavenly garment, which is the heavenly Self.[30] He remains content with the verbal expression.[31]

■ **54–55** The same tendency as in v 53 obtains in vv 54f.[32] The advance lies in the ὅταν—τότε, "when—then,"[33] which is derived from the Scripture proof. The latter not only proves what has been said thus far, but also leads over from the formal statement (the mortal puts on immortality) to the apocalyptic conception. Here the confrontation of mortal and immortality is now related to the act of the annihilation of death: cf. v 26 (cf. νῖκος, "victory," with ὑποτάσσειν, "subject"). Two Scripture passages are combined: Isa 25:8 and Hos 13:14.

1) Isa 25:8. The state of the textual tradition is as follows:

a) Hebrew: בִּלַּע הַמָּוֶת לָנֶצַח,
"He will swallow up death forever" (RSV).

b) LXX: κατέπιεν ὁ θάνατος ἰσχύσας,
"Death in his strength has devoured."

c) Aquila:[34] καταποντίσει τὸν θάνατον εἰς νῖκος,
"He will drown death in *victory*."

d) Symmachus: καταποθῆναι ποιήσει τὸν θάνατον εἰς τέλος,
"He will cause death to be swallowed up to the *uttermost*."

e) The text of Theodotion is uncertain:[35] Codex March has κατεπόθη, "has been swallowed up." Syrohexapla has an equivalent for κατέπιεν, "has devoured."[36] There follows ὁ θάνατος εἰς νῖκος, "death in victory." Thus in Paul a "pre–Theodotian" text becomes visible.[37]

Judaism appeals to this passage for the expectation that death will cease (Str.–B. 3:481–483).

2) For Hos 13:14, on the other hand, the rabbinical situation provides no assistance (Str.–B. 3:483). The textual tradition:

a) Hebrew: אֱהִי (=אַיֵּה) דְּבָרֶיךָ מָוֶת
אֱהִי קָטָבְךָ שְׁאוֹל

"O Death, where are your plagues?
O Sheol, where is your destruction?" (RSV).

b) LXX: ποῦ ἡ δίκη σου, θάνατε;
ποῦ τὸ κέντρον σου, ᾅδη;

"O death, where is your penalty?
O Hades, where is your sting?"

The fact that Paul puts νῖκος, "victory," in place of δίκη "penalty," is manifestly due to the Isaiah passage. Here, too, death is personified; but the personification again remains vacillating. καταπίνειν (cf. 2 Cor 5:4; 1 Pet 5:8) can mean not only "drink," but also in a general sense "devour." κέντρον is the drover's goad,[38] an

25 The word is taken over from Hellenistic Judaism: Wisd 3:4; 15:3; *4 Macc.* 14.5.

26 Jeremias once again interprets the parallelism "synthetically." The use of the verbal adjective already tells against this. See on v 50 (Schweizer, *TDNT* 7:128f).

27 *Od. Sal.* 15.8: "I have put on incorruption through His name, And I have put off corruption by His grace" (Harris–Mingana 2:281). *Asc. Is.* 4.17: "And afterwards they will turn themselves upward in their garments, and their body will be left in the world" (*The Ascension of Isaiah*, ed. and tr. R. H. Charles [London: Black, 1900], 35).

28 Plainer in 2 Cor 5:1ff.

29 In Gnosticism this is indispensable: the light–Self which is identical with the garment or image.

30 Cf. the "definition" of the subject: "this perishable," "this mortal."

31 In v 49 he had gone a step further; but even there the identity lies merely in the subject of "wear."

32 Cf. the repetition. The first member of the parallelism is omitted by p⁴⁶ ℵ* C*.

33 Cf. v 28. Bachmann's argument that ὅταν, "when," transposes us to the time of vv 26ff, when death as the last enemy is abolished, is artificial.

34 Schlatter, 445, says: "The text given for Aquila, καταποντίσει τὸν θάνατον εἰς νῖκος, is damaged, for Aquila did not render בלע by καταποντίζειν." But he did! Isa 3:12 and frequently.

35 Alfred Rahlfs, "Über Theodotion–Lesarten im Neuen Testament und Aquila–Lesarten bei Justin," *ZNW* 20 (1921): 182–199.

36 Thus Rahlfs for Theodotion.

37 Rahlfs, to be sure, points out that the rendering of נצח by νῖκος suggests itself so readily to an Aramaic-speaking Jew that εἰς νῖκος is no proof of such de-

instrument of chastisement, torture,[39] the sting of an animal;[40] it is the symbol of tyranny and force.[41]

The tone and sense of the passage are clear, apart from the textual question. Paul here sets his concluding note. Once again it is plain that he takes his bearings not on existence, but on death in the light of the victory over it.

■ **56** This verse interrupts the train of thought; it looks like a gloss.[42] Yet it can be explained in the context[43] as an exegetical remark. Hence the compressed style, the multiplication of characteristic Pauline keywords. They emerge here completely unexpectedly. ἀμαρτία, "sin," to be sure, is prepared for (vv 3, 17); but νόμος, "law," is a surprise. Yet this is no reason to exclude the statement as pre–Pauline.[44] For the connection between sin and law is for Paul a systematically established relationship. He expounds it in Romans, where we have repeated echoes of 1 Corinthians. Much the same applies to the connection between sin and death.[45]

Only after this expansion is the statement on the over-

throw of death shown to be relevant to present existence. How harshly the statement intrudes is significant. Paul is absolutely determined to express this thought.

■ **57–58** The block comprising chap. 15 is concluded by a thanksgiving, as in Rom 7:7ff.[46] Again the keyword νῖκος, "victory," is taken up. The point of the thanksgiving is the actualizing of hope for our present faith: τῷ διδόντι, "who gives," present tense. The thanksgiving is rounded off by a short expression of thanks appropriate to the style. What in itself sounds like a good Stoic notion of progress[47] is, in a wholly non–Stoic sense, a good Pauline thought:[48] that of progressing toward work.[49]

It is significant that, following the paraenesis, the participial clause gives a last, promising conclusion to this thematically eschatological chapter. εἰδότες, "knowing," appeals not to the readers' inner experience of themselves, but to the experience to be had with the kerygma; and οὐκ ἔστιν κενός, "is not in vain," is a final confirmation of the argument (see v 14) begun in v 12.

---

pendence. The LXX has νῖκος for נצח, derived from נצח, "be victorious," e.g. Job 36:7; Amos 1:11; 8:7.

38 Hom., *Il.* 23.387; so also in the saying about the "goad" in Acts 26:14; Eur., *Ba.* 794f and frequently.

39 Hdt., *Hist.* 3.130 with μάστιγες, "whips"; cf. Plat., *Leg.* 777a.

40 Scorpion: Aristot., *Part. an.* 4.6.683a.12.

41 Soph., *Fr.* 683: κωτίλος δ' ἀνὴρ λαβὼν πανοῦργα χερσὶ κέντρα κηδεύει πόλιν, "While a babbler directs the state, with the goad of mischief in his hands" (*The Fragments of Sophocles*, ed. A. C. Pearson [Cambridge: University Press, 1917] 2:300).

42 According to Weiss, it shows exact knowledge of Pauline theology, may have been written by Paul himself, but if so, then only subsequently. According to Walter Grundmann, "Gesetz, Rechtfertigung und Mystik bei Paulus. Zum Problem der Einheitlichkeit der paulinischen Verkündigung," *ZNW* 32 (1933): 52–65, here esp. 54f, Paul is acquainted with rabbinical traditions like "Yahweh's might is the Torah." Grundmann is more cautious in *TDNT* 2:308: "adopting the Jewish expression for the Torah (עוז יהוה)." It is in actual fact a question only of an expression, not of a statement. But the evidence is not at all sound. The most important instance is *M. Ex.* 15.13 (50b): "*Thou Hast Guided Them in Thy Strength.* For the sake of the Torah which they were destined to receive, for 'Thy strength' here [עֻזְּךָ] is but a designation for the Torah, as in the passage: 'The Lord will give strength [עֹז] unto His people' (Ps. 29.11)" (Lauterbach 2:70).

43 In content it is prepared for by vv 3–5; the hearer,

when it is read out, hears the creed in the background; then v. 17.

44 Heinrici says that vv 56f show "the firm dogmatic foundation" upon which the certainty of victory rests. In this authentication the whole of his gospel is summed up. Yet Heinrici concedes that formally speaking it could be a case of a subsequent addition.

45 Rom 5:12–21; 6:23; 7:7–20. For sin and death see Bultmann, *Theology* 1:246–249 [246–249]. He finds in Paul three conceptions side by side without being harmonized: (*a*) the juristic view of death as punishment; (*b*) the idea that death grows organically out of sin; and finally (*c*) the notion that man as a creature is earthly and mortal. This is correct. Bultmann also asks whether it is not possible to discern a unified understanding of existence.

46 Rom 7:25 (if this passage is not a gloss).

47 Note the use of προκόπτω. For ἑδραῖος, "steadfast," see 7:37. ἀμετακίνητος, "immoveable," in the NT only here; Plat., *Ep.* 7.343a; Jos., *Ap.* 2.169, etc. Inscription from Nazareth in Raphael Tonneau, "L'Inscription de Nazareth sur la violation des sépultures," *RB* 40 (1931): 544–564, here esp. 544, line 5.

48 14:12; Rom 15:13; Phil 1:9. *Proficere*, "making progress," is not for Paul a *semper incipere*, "continually beginning." But it is not a question of a psychologically apprehensible process; the man who makes progress does not make himself the object of consideration and proclamation. He is oriented toward the work *of the Lord*. 2 Cor 8:7 (χάρις).

49 2 Cor 9:8. The work of the Lord: 16:10.

16

Information and Greetings

1 Now concerning the collection for the saints, you should do as I have appointed for the churches in Galatia. 2/ On the first day of the week[1] let each of you put aside and store up whatever he can spare,[2] so that collections be not made only when I come. 3/ After my arrival I shall send people of your choice[3] with letters[4] to bring your gift to Jerusalem. 4/ If it is your mind[5] that I should also go, then they shall go with me.

5 I shall come to you when I have passed through Macedonia. I shall (only) pass through Macedonia, 6/ but if possible I will stay with you, or even spend the winter. Then you can send me on my way[6] wherever I wish to go. 7/ For I do not wish to see you only just in passing. I hope to spend some time with you, if the Lord permits. 8/ I will remain in Ephesus until Pentecost. 9/ For a great and effectual door has opened to me, and there are many adversaries.

10 But when Timothy comes, then see to it that he can be with you without fear. For he is engaged in the work of the Lord as I am. 11/ So let no one despise him. Send him on his way in peace, that he may come to me. For I am waiting for him together with the brothers. 12/ As regards the brother Apollos, I have often urged him to go to you with the brothers.[7] But it was not at all the will[8] that he should go now; but he will come as soon as he finds an opportunity.

13 Be alert, stand fast in the faith, be manly and strong. 14/ Let everything among you be done in love.

The final chapter brings, as usual, correspondence, concluding exhortation, and greetings.

Schmithals[8a] disputes the literary unity of the chapter.

He argues that between vv 12–13 there is a break; that v 13 is better in place after 15:58 than after 16:12; that exhortations at the close of an epistle always begin else-

---

1   For the expression cf. Mk 16:2 par.; Acts 20:7. It is not normal Greek, but probably Hebraizing; cf. Num 1:1: ἐν μιᾷ τοῦ μηνὸς τοῦ δευτέρου, "on the first day of the second month" (RSV); Jos., *Ant.* 1.29; Blass–Debrunner §247(1). σάββατον: Singular and plural both mean "Sabbath" and also "week."

2   εὐοδοῦσθαι: "have good success"; Lietzmann understands it here as "acquire."

3   The word can be used technically for the recognition of suitability for an official function; Bauer and Moulton–Milligan, *s.v.*

4   δι' ἐπιστολῶν: "provided with." It is presumably not a case of the plural of category ("by letter").

5   This is usually understood to mean: "if it is worthwhile." In that case the decision would be in Paul's hands. But the above rendering suits the context better, cf. v 6. ἄξιόν ἐστιν with the genitive of the substantival infinitive ("as classical"): Blass–Debrunner §400(3).

6   προπέμπειν: v 11; 2 Cor 1:16; Rom 15:24. Here the meaning is not "accompany."

7   Should the rendering be: "urged him along with the brothers"?

8   Of God or of Apollos? For θέλημα used absolutely of the will of God see Ign., *Eph.* 20.1; *Rom.* 1.1; cf. Paul in Rom 2:18.

where with direct address: 2 Cor 13:11; 1 Thess 5:14; Rom 15:30; 16:17; Phil 3:1. Thus Schmithals' conclusion is: vv 13–24 belong (following 15:58) to letter A. Letter B is preserved only as far as v 12. This explains the fact that Paul says nothing of Stephanas in 1:11, and nothing of Chloe's people in chap. 16: letter A was delivered by Stephanas, letter B was occasioned by Chloe's people.

The following considerations tell against this division. The absence of the direct address is not a conclusive argument; the material basis for this argument is too narrow: moreover, e.g., in using Phil 3:1, it already pre-supposes further hypotheses on the part of literary criticism. Although in the particular instance these are probable, yet it is surely a dubious method to ground a hypothesis on hypotheses. Furthermore, if v 13 had directly followed 15:58, it would probably be separated from it by Schmithals as a doublet. Much the same applies to v 15, which according to Schmithals' rule must *introduce* a paraenesis, and would therefore have to be separated from vv 13f.

■ 1 περί, "concerning": see on 7:1; here it cannot with certainty be inferred that Paul is taking up a point in the letter from Corinth. λογεία can designate a tax,[9] but also simply a money collection, e.g., the collection at worship.[10] The choice of this word at all events does not prove that in Paul's well–known collection for Jerusalem (see below) we have to do with a church tax imposed upon him. For εἰς, "for," instead of the dative of advantage cf. 2 Cor 8:4; 9:1, 13.[11]

From the sequel it emerges that preparations for the collection have already been made in Corinth. Its further progress after the writing of 1 Corinthians can be learned from 2 Cor 8 and 9.[12] The reference to Galatia makes it plain that the collection takes place throughout the whole of Paul's missionary territory. This is in harmony with the agreement at the Apostolic Council; see Gal 2:10.[13]

The designation "the saints" is here a standard designation for the original church (2 Cor 8:4; 9:1, 12).[14] Since Karl Holl, the nature of this collection has been a matter of dispute.[15] Holl sees in it an official church tax paid by the Pauline churches to the original church. Its point, he argues, is not really the support of the needy. "Poor," he says, is a technical designation for the church in Jerusalem, describing a primarily religious, not a primarily social status. The point is the recognition of Jerusalem's judicial status as headquarters, which anticipates the later status of Rome. In favor of this interpretation one can point to the example of the Jewish temple tax. But this temple tax is a regular duty that is payable annually, not one that is paid only once. Nor is it a special arrangement for the Diaspora. It is paid to the sanctuary, not to a community. The designation "the saints" implies no *judicial* claim.[16] And it is in actual fact a case of the support of the (socially) poor.[17] The whole mode of expression, especially in Rom 15:25–28, shows that it is a question of a *freewill* offering. Kittel rightly points out that Paul uses as synonyms of λογεία not technical fiscal terms, but devotional expressions: χάρις, "gift," v 3; 2 Cor 8:44ff; κοινωνία, "fellowship," Rom 15:26; 2 Cor 8:4; διακονία, "ministration," Rom 15:31; 2 Cor 8:4; 9:1; εὐλογία, "blessing," 2 Cor 9:5; cf. also

---

8a Schmithals, *Gnosis in Corinth*, 93f [87f].

9   Papyri. According to Gerhard Kittel, *TDNT* 4:282f, it is apparently the word preferably used for the extraordinary assessment, see *P. Oxy.* 239.5–9: ὀμνύω . . . μηδεμίαν λογείαν γεγονέναι ὑπ' ἐμοῦ ἐν τῇ αὐτῇ κώμῃ, "I swear . . . that I have levied no contributions . . . . in the said village" (*P. Oxy.* 2:183). But this conclusion is too subtle.

10 Deissmann, *Light*, 105 [84].

11 Bel 6: οὐχ ὁρᾷς ὅσα εἰς αὐτὸν δαπανᾶται καθ' ἑκάστην ἡμέραν; "Do you not see how much he [the god Bel] eats and drinks every day?" (RSV).

12 The question whether these two chapters belong to two different letters can here be left out of account.

13 In Gal we find no concrete instructions. An explanation of this negative circumstance is undertaken by Dieter Georgi, *Die Geschichte der Kollekte des Paulus für Jerusalem*, ThF, 38 (Hamburg–Bergstedt: Reich,

1965), 30–37. He assumes that the collection had been suspended for the time being.

14 Karl Holl, "Der Kirchenbegriff des Paulus in seinem Verhältnis zu der Urgemeinde," *NJbchKlAlt* 33 (1914): 521–556, now in his *Aufsätze* 2:44–67; Kümmel, *Kirchenbegriff*, 16f. In Gal 2:10 in a similarly phrased statement we have "the poor," which Holl likewise explains as a technical term; but in Rom 15:26 οἱ πτωχοί means those in Jerusalem who are really poor. Against the technical use of οἱ πτωχοί see Kümmel, *ibid.*, 16.

15 Holl, "Der Kirchenbegriff des Paulus"; Kittel, *TDNT* 4:282f; Kümmel, *Kirchenbegriff*, 53f, n. 85; Georgi, *Die Geschichte der Kollekte*.

16 Kümmel, *Kirchenbegriff*, 16f.

17 Rom 15:26: οἱ πτωχοὶ τῶν ἁγίων, "the poor among the saints"; so the materially poor are meant.

the plural in v 2. This confirms the picture of Gal 2; it is a question of a voluntary agreement. Its point is to document the unity of the church.

■ **2** Paul's arrangement is informative in regard to the state of organization, or nonorganization, in his communities at that time: there is obviously as yet no organized system of finance.[18] Not even a collection at the service of worship is envisaged, if each is to "lay by him in store" his own contribution.[19] κατὰ μίαν σαββάτου, "on the first day of the week": Paul abides by the Jewish calendar, with one modification; even if the collection is not made during the community meeting, it may be concluded from this statement of date that the Sunday is already the day of meeting. Why this day was chosen, there is no knowing.[20]

■ **3–4** The brief anticipation of the coming visit is made clear in vv 5ff. χάρις, "gift," describes the contribution as a free act; cf. 2 Cor 8:4ff.[21] The plan to have it delivered by delegates of the churches was fulfilled: Acts 20:1ff. This is in harmony with the intention (to display the unity of the church), but is also a precautionary measure on Paul's part: he must avoid the reproach of using this gift to enrich himself.[22] Hence he provides for controls: 2 Cor 8:18f. δι' ἐπιστολῶν, "with letters," is a genuine plural: Paul is thinking of a number of letters of introduction.[23] This is in harmony with the needs and customs of the time.

■ **5–9** As these verses[24] indicate, Paul finds himself in Ephesus. The plans for his journey are plain and understandable.[25] The plan to spend the winter follows from

---

18   This should be noticed in assessing the early view of office; von Campenhausen, *Ecclesiastical Authority*, 55–75 [59–81].

19   This point is then reached in Just., *Apol.* 1.67.6.

20   It is usually assumed that it was because this was the day of the resurrection of Jesus. Not so Harald Riesenfeld, "Sabbat et Jour du Seigneur," in *New Testament Essays: Studies in Memory of Thomas Walter Manson*, ed. A. J. B. Higgins (Manchester: Manchester University Press, 1959), 210–217 [see also *The Gospel Tradition*, 111–137]. According to Riesenfeld Sunday was chosen from rational considerations. In the beginning the Christians took part in the Jewish service. To this the supplementary, Christian meeting in the evening was added. *Then* there comes the symbolism of the resurrection, in early morning meetings. With this, the "Lord's Day" is constituted: Rev 1:10; *Did.* 14.1. Against this hypothesis: the wording points not to the Saturday evening, but to a day. Willy Rordorf, *Sunday*, tr. A. A. K. Graham (London: SCM; Philadelphia: Westminster, 1968), 179f, 193–196 (*Der Sonntag*, AThANT, 43 [Zurich: Zwingli, 1962], 176f, 190–193).

21   Georgi, *Die Geschichte der Kollekte*, 58–67.

22   2 Cor 12:14–18. Lietzmann suggests that he is perhaps warding off a possible suspicion that he wishes to enjoy alone the harvest of gratitude in Jerusalem.

23   Letters to different addressees and for different delegations; 2 Cor 9:1; see Bauer, *s.v.* ἐπιστολή. πέμπειν with infinitive: Blass–Debrunner §351; Weiss calls this the easygoing language of the NT. Letters of introduction: 2 Cor 3:1; Rom 16:1; Phlm. See Bauer, *s.v.* συστατικός; Wendland, *Literatur–formen*, 415, n. 2; Clinton W. Keyes, "The Greek Letter of Introduction," *AJPh* 56 (1935): 28–44. For the theory of this *Gattung* see Ps.–Demetr., *Form. ep.* 2 (ed. Weichert, p. 3, line 16—p. 4, line 4), and Ps.–Lib.,

Charact. ep. (ed. Weichert, p. 22, lines 12–14). Examples in Deissmann, *Light*, 170f [137f] (*BGU* 37), 197–200 [163–166] (*P. Oxy.* 32). Hans Lietzmann, *Griechische Papyri*, KlT, 14 (Bonn: Marcus & Weber, ²1910), no. 3 (= *P. Oxy.* 292).

24   On the language:

1) ὅταν with aorist subjunctive: anticipation; see on 15:27.

2) διέρχομαι: as usual with ἔρχομαι, the present with the sense of the future, Blass–Debrunner §323(1). When Weiss doubts whether the sense is future, this is bound up with his literary criticism: he asks whether v 5 was written in Macedonia.

3) τυχόν, "perhaps," "possibly"; Bauer, *s.v.* τυγχάνω 2 c; Blass–Debrunner §424.

4) Text: Lietzmann prefers the reading καταμένειν; παρα–, he says, is an assimilation to παραχειμάζειν. παρα– is supported also by p⁴⁶. There is no difference of meaning, see Bauer, *s.vv.*

5) ποῦ, "whither": the distinction between "where?" and "whither?" has disappeared; Bauer, *s.v.*; Blass–Debrunner §103.

6) ἀνοίγω intransitive, "open"; see Bauer, *s.v.*: used in this sense only in the second perfect; 2 Cor 6:11; Jn 1:51.

7) πρός with the accusative answering the question "where?" see Blass–Debrunner §239(1); Mt 13:56.

25   Weiss finds that ὅταν κτλ., "when, etc.," is surprising if the Corinthians do not as yet know anything of Macedonia. The simplest explanation is, according to Weiss, that they know that he is in Macedonia, and feel he is staying there too long. The opponents are triumphant, Paul speaks calmingly. This is a complicated assumption. The brevity with which the plan to pass through Macedonia is mentioned has nothing startling about it: travelers are passing to and fro between Ephesus and Corinth and the

the conditions of travel in those days: the winter is no time for journeys, above all not by sea. This is illustrated by the account in Acts of Paul's journey to Rome (Acts 27:9–12).

Paul stresses the fact that he will only pass through Macedonia, but that in Corinth he will *remain*. What is the meaning of ἄρτι[26] in v 7 (tr. "only just")? Weiss says it points to an earlier occasion on which he saw them only briefly, that is, an intermediate visit between his first, long sojourn and the composition of this epistle (or the pending visit). Heinrici holds that the emphasis is on ὑμᾶς, "you." ἄρτι accordingly does not mark the antithesis to an earlier visit, but to his sojourn in Macedonia. But this explanation does not hold up (with Robertson and Plummer).

ἐὰν ὁ κύριος ἐπιτρέφῃ, "if the Lord permits": the celebrated *conditio Jacobaea* (Jas 4:15) is fundamentally a Greek (not a Jewish) phrase.[27]

The figure of the opening of a door for the presenting of an opportunity is one Paul uses again in 2 Cor 2:12.[28] But he quickly drops the figure: (μεγάλη καὶ) ἐνεργής, "[great and] effectual." ἀντικείμενοι, "adversaries": see 15:32.

How the plans were actually carried out is told by 2 Corinthians. According to 2 Cor 1:15 Paul would have changed his plan: traveling direct to Corinth, and from there to Macedonia. But this new plan was not carried out. Paul went to Macedonia after all (2 Cor 2:12), then to Corinth, and from there via Macedonia to Jerusalem (Acts 20) along with the delegation from the churches.

■ **10–11** The meaning of ἐάν is close to that of ὅταν, "when."[29] Regarding the sending of Timothy, in 4:17 it was possible to ask whether ἔπεμψα, "I sent," was an epistolary aorist. Here we see that Timothy will not arrive in Corinth along with the epistle; he is already on the way (cf. Acts 19:22). For fellow–workers "in the work of the Lord" cf. 15:58. The phrase is explained by the idea of church and mission. What lies behind the emphatic recommendation, we do not know.[30] For προπέμψατε, "send on his way," cf. v 6. Is μετὰ τῶν ἀδελφῶν, "together with the brothers," to be taken with αὐτόν, "him," (Lietzmann), or with ἐκδέχεσθαι, "wait for"?

■ **12** For Apollos see on 1:12; 4:6. May we conclude from the tense of οὐκ ἦν θέλημα, "it *was* not the will,"[31] that at the moment he is absent? In view of the beginning of the epistle it should be noticed that the matter–of–fact way in which Paul speaks of Apollos counteracts the division of the community into groups.

■ **13–14** The paraenesis comes unexpectedly. And afterwards v 15 begins again as if vv 13 and 14 were not there.[32] Yet this circumstance is not sufficient reason for operations of literary criticism. It is a case of the customary, loose formation of the conclusion of an epistle; cf. 1 Thess 5:12ff: Phil 4;[33] Col 4:2ff; Eph 6:10ff. γρηγορεῖν, "be alert," is a well–known keyword in paraenesis, especially in an eschatological context.[34] στήκετε, "stand fast": cf. 15:1, 58; Gal 5:1; Phil 4:1. There follows an allusion to Ps 30:25 LXX.[35] πάντα κτλ., "let everything, etc.": 14:40.

---

bearers of the epistle know the facts and can answer questions. Weiss' doubts as to whether vv 5–7 and 8f belong to the same letter are also unnecessary.

26 Weiss finds that the indefinite statement in v 7 following the definite one in v 6 is surprising. This, too, is too subtle.

27 Ps.-Plat., *Alc.* 1.135d: Ἐὰν βούλῃ σύ, ὦ Σώκρατες. —Οὐ καλῶς λέγεις, ὦ Ἀλκιβιάδη.—Ἀλλὰ πῶς χρὴ λέγειν; —Ὅτι ἐὰν θεὸς ἐθέλῃ, " 'If it be your wish, Socrates.' 'That is not well said, Alcibiades.' 'Well, what should I say?' 'If it be God's will.' " (Loeb 8:221). Min. Fel., *Oct.* 18.11, describes it as *vulgi naturalis sermo*, "the natural language of the crowd" (Loeb, 365).

28 Not so Acts 14:27, where God opens to the Gentiles a door of faith.

29 Moulton–Howard–Turner, *Grammar* 3:114. γίνεσθαι with adverb: Blass–Debrunner §434(2).

30 Weiss: Paul's attitude is no longer unshaken. Lietz-

mann: "The authority of the young assistant [1 Tim 4:12] is weak."

31 Schmiedel adds: and the absence of a greeting from Apollos.

32 Lietzmann: "Verses 13–14 give the impression that Paul had here meant to begin the conclusion. Then afterthoughts follow."

33 In Phil 4, to be sure, there is the question of the findings of literary criticism.

34 1 Thess 5:6; 1 Pet 5:8; Mk 13:35, 37. Evald Lövestam, *Spiritual Wakefulness in the New Testament*, (Lund: Gleerup, 1963), 58–60.

35 ἀνδρίζεσθε καὶ κραταιούσθω ἡ καρδία ὑμῶν, "Be manly and let your heart be strong." Cf. Ps 27:14: חֲזַק וְיַאֲמֵץ, "Be strong, and let your heart take courage" (RSV); 1QM XV,7: חזקו ואמצו והיו לבני חיל, "Be strong! Be hardy! Show yourselves men of valour!" (Dupont–Sommer, 192).

15 I exhort you, brothers: you know that the household of Stephanas is the first-fruits of Achaea, and that they have set themselves[1] to service for the saints. **16/** Be subject[2] also to such people and to everyone who helps in the work and who labors. **17/** I rejoice at the coming of Stephanas and Fortunatus and Achaicus, for they have supplied what was lacking on your part. **18/** For they have set at ease my spirit and yours. Such people you must recognize.[3]

19 The churches of Asia greet you. Aquila and Prisca send you many greetings in the Lord, along with the church in their house. **20/** All the brothers greet you. Greet one another with the holy kiss. **21/** Greetings with my own hand, Paul. **22/** If anyone does not love the Lord, let him be accursed! Marana tha! **23/** The grace of the Lord Jesus be with you. **24/** My love is with you all in Christ Jesus.

■ **15** For Stephanas and his household[4] see on 1:16.[5] That those who were first baptized enjoy special esteem is seen also from Rom 6:5.[6] The Roman Province of Achaea comprises what is now central and southern Greece, a senatorial province since A.D. 44. Corinth was the capital from A.D. 27. On διακονία, "service," Lietzmann observes: "Here lie the roots of the office of the διάκονοι, 'deacons' "; cf. Rom 16:1; Phil 1:1. It must, however, be emphasized that for Paul there are indeed as yet no "offices" (as there is also no real organization), but functions, services; cf. v 16: help in the work,

labor. This is the same picture as in v 2 (q.v.) and in chap. 12: they are all χαρίσματα (12:5: διακονίαι). The voluntary character is underlined.

■ **16** καί, "also," should not be all too strongly emphasized.[7] The picture remains the same: there is no organization, but voluntary subordination.[8] "Help in the work": v 6; 3:9; Rom 12:8; 16:3. "Labor": 15:10. For the whole see 1 Thess 5:12f.

■ **17** The difficulty of this passage lies, as noticed above, in the fact that the presence of these three delegates is overlooked in chap. 1, while here, on the other hand,

1   τάσσειν ἑαυτόν, "set oneself": Plat., *Republic* 371c; Xenoph., *Mem.* 2.1.11.
2   ἵνα with the subjunctive is a vernacular substitute for the imperative; cf. 1 Cor 7:29; 2 Cor 8:7; Eph 5:33; Blass–Debrunner §387(3).
3   ἐπιγινώσκειν, "recognize": Mt 17:12; Ruth 2:10, 19.
4   For the prolepsis see Moulton–Howard–Turner, *Grammar* 3:325.
5   The passage is occasionally cited in the dispute on infant baptism. Since "the house" plays a role in the church, it is adults who are meant. For literature, see on 1:16. παρακαλεῖν, "exhort," see on 1:10.
6   In *1 Cl.* 42 this status is already institutionalized.
7   Schmiedel, Heinrici, Robertson and Plummer emphasize καί: "you also," *sc.* as a suitable return. This is surely overloading the word. Lietzmann is probably right: be also subordinate to such people (*sc.*

"also" with "subordinate").
8   In the sense of 14:40: πάντα κατὰ τάξιν, "everything in an orderly way" (cf. v 18: "recognition").
9   But why should they not have only now arrived? And the others already have left! The letter was not written in *one* day, and the sojourn of a delegation costs money. Fortunatus and Achaicus are unknown. The context shows that παρουσία here means "arrival" (not "sojourn").
10 ἀναπληροῦν, "make up for": Bauer, *s.v.*; Gerhard Delling, *TDNT* 6:305f. Commentators are fond of comparing a Jewish word of consolation: "God make up for your shortcomings!" יְמַלֵּא חֶסְרוֹנֵךְ, Str.–B. 3:485f. But Paul is not speaking of a compensation by God. Jos., *Bell.* 4.198: ἀναπληροῦν τὰ λείποντα, "supply deficiencies."

nothing is said of the presence of Chloe's people.[9] The allusion in v 17b was understandable only to the readers. Verse 18 gives a certain pointer to the meaning, though not an adequate one: "because they have made up for[10] your[11] failings," that is to say: "they have given me what you failed to give."[12] But does Paul really wish to find fault, and not simply to say: they were a substitute for you?[13]

■ **18** ἀνέπαυσαν,[14] "have set at ease": 2 Cor 7:13. πνεῦμα, "spirit," represents the person (Gal 6:18; Phil 4:23; Phlm 25).

■ **19** The greeting[15] is a standard part of the conclusion of an epistle.[16] O. Roller[17] maintains that Paul goes his own way. Before him, greetings are found in letters only exceptionally. But they are by no means unusual.[18] We miss the greeting indeed, when it is not there.[19]

Asia is the Roman province in the West of Asia Minor with Ephesus as the residence of the procurator (but not the capital).[20] "Churches":[21] cf. v 9. Ephesus is a missionary center. For Aquila[22] and Prisca (Acts: Priscilla) see Rom 16:3 (in Ephesus?). According to Acts 18 Paul made the couple's acquaintance in Corinth. From there they moved to Ephesus. Acts 18 is also aware of close relations with Apollos. A "house church" can be a church which assembles in their house, or their household as a church.

■ **20** All the brothers: this once again highlights the standing of Paul: he represents the community; cf. Gal 1:2.

The holy kiss: 1 Thess 5:26; Rom 16:16; 2 Cor 13:12.[23] This summons is an indication that the epistle is read at the community meeting. We can indeed discover even

---

11   For the position of the possessives in vv 17f see Blass–Debrunner §284(2).

12   Delling: "what you left undone," *sc.* in the resolving of the tensions between you and me.

13   Cf. v 18: καὶ τὸ ὑμῶν, "and yours"; Weiss, Bauer. Phil. 2:30; Col 1:24; 2 Cor 8:14; 9:12; 11:9. What cannot be meant is material support, because of chap. 9.

14   According to Schmiedel the meaning "refresh" would not suit τὸ ὑμῶν, "yours," hence: "set at ease," by supplying the arrears. They have been at work for Paul in Corinth and have brought better news than Chloe's people. The whole state of the discussion is against this.

15   The basic meaning of ἀσπάζειν seems to be "embrace" (*embrasser*); it is used of erotic desire in Plat., *Symp.* 209b; Hans Windisch, *TDNT* 1:496–502.

16   The greeting is very short in 2 Cor 13:12 (because the Epistle was subsequently edited?). Specially detailed in Rom 16.

17   Roller, *Formular*, 66–78.

18   The oldest instances, if they are genuine, would be the letters of Plato. Ps.–Plat., *Ep.* 13.363d: καὶ τοὺς συσφαιριστὰς ἀσπάζου ὑπὲρ ἐμοῦ, "and greet for me your comrades at the game of ball" (fellowspherists"; Loeb 7:627). For the rest see the list in Roller, *Formular*, 472f. Deissmann, *Light*, 179–183 [145–150].

19   *P. Grenf.* 1.53.8–12: Ἀλλοῦς πολλά σοι ἀπειλ[εῖ]· ἐπὶ γὰρ πολλάκις γράψας καὶ πάντας ἀσπασάμενος αὐτὴν μόνον οὐκ ἠσπάσου, "Allous breathes many threats against you; for although you have

often written and greeted everyone, her alone you did not greet" [Trans.]. In Plaut., *Pseudol.* 998–1016, the greeting is lacking in the letter from the officer Polymachaeroplagides to the pimp Ballio—typical of the unlearned soldier. Ferdinand Ziemann, "De epistularum Graecarum formulis sollemnibus quaestiones selectae," [dissertation, Halle, 1910] *Diss. phil. Hall.* 18 (1911): 253–369, here esp. 325–333. Lietzmann, *Griechische Papyri*, nos. 7–11, 13–15. For πολλά (adverbial accusative) cf. P. Oxy. 1067.25–27: κἀγὼ Ἀλέξανδρος ὁ π[α]τὴρ ὑμῶν ἀσπάζομαι πολλά, "I also, your father Alexander, send you many salutations" (P. Oxy. 7:222). BGU 822: ἀσπάζεται . . . . ἀσπάζου . . . . ἀσπάζεται . . . . καὶ πάντες, ἀσπάζονταί σε οἱ φιλοῦντες, "(He) greets . . . . (do you) greet . . . . (he) greets . . . . and everyone. Those who love you greet you."

20   Bauer, *s.v.*; C. G. Brandis, "Ephesos," Pauly-W. 2:1538–1562; Josef Keil, *Ephesos* (Vienna: Österreichisches Archäologisches Institut, ³1957); Franz Miltner, *Ephesos* (Vienna: Denticke, 1958).

21   The churches in the Lycus valley, Col 4:13.

22   Instances of the name: *MAMA* 7:5, 79, 114f (nos. 22, 324, 547).

23   August Wünsche, *Der Kuss in Bibel, Talmud und Midrasch* (Breslau: Marcus, 1911); Karl–Martin Hofmann, *Philema Hagion*, BFTh, 2, 38 (Gütersloh: Bertelsmann, 1938); Spicq, *Agapé* 2:338–341. In the papyri there stand assurances of love (see Moulton-Milligan, *s.v.* φιλεῖν) but not the word φίλημα. For greeting with a kiss cf. Ps.–Luc., *Asin.* 17: φιλή-

more about the course of the meeting.[24] At the close of 2 Corinthians there follow in succession, reading of the epistle, kiss, blessing. We find ourselves reminded of the elements of the liturgy, as they appear in *Did.* 9f;[25] cf. further Just., *Apol.* 1.65. May we conclude that the epistle was read at the community meal? Is the latter opened or closed with the φίλημα, "kiss"?[26]

■ **21** There follows Paul's own greeting with his own hand: Gal 6:11ff; Phlm 19; imitated in 2 Thess 3:17; Col. 4:18.[27]

■ **22** εἴ τις κτλ., "if anyone, etc.," is striking in style and content. The solemn phrase comes wholly without preparation. Apparently it is a question of a statement of sacral law, and one that is an element in the liturgy.[28] Unique in Paul is the word φιλεῖν, "love"[29]—and this

too with κύριος as object. οὐ φιλεῖν, "not to love," is in a cultic and judicial sense the negative relation to the Lord. Those who adopt it stand under the wrath of the Lord.[30] The latter is pronounced over them in the formula of curse: *anathema.*[31] This consigns the transgressor to God as his Judge.[32] Does the formula in the service of worship mark the separating of the baptized and the unbaptized before the eucharist?

The Aramaic cry *maranatha*, too, is an element in the liturgy. It can be rendered as "Our Lord, come!" or "Our Lord has come."[33] Yet it must be noticed that the purely formal rendering as *marana tha* or *maran atha* does not in itself decide the sense.[34] For (1) "Our Lord" is both *maran* and also *marana*; (2) the imperative "come!" is both אתא and also תא. A negative finding is that if אתא

μασιν ἠσπάζοντο ἀλλήλους, "they greeted each other with kisses" (cf. Loeb 8:77).

24 Lietzmann, *Mass and Lord's Supper*, 186f [229f].

25 For the analysis of *Did.* 9f see Bornkamm, *Early Christian Experience*, 170 (*Das Ende des Gesetzes*, 124), who holds (with Lietzmann) that in *Did.* 10.6 we have a liturgical dialogue, but (against Lietzmann) that nothing has been transposed: the end of the Supper is followed by the introduction to the Eucharist, which is not itself described.

26 Lyder Brun, *Segen und Fluch im Urchristentum* (Olso: Dybwad, 1932), 68, warns against hasty conclusions as to the place in the service. The situation on the arrival of a letter is unusual.

27 The word ἀσπασμός, "greeting," is very rarely found in the papyri; see Moulton–Milligan, *s.v.*

An example of an autograph greeting (change of handwriting) is provided by *BGU* 37; text and plate in Deissmann, *Light*, 170f [137f].

28 For the conditional style cf. *Did.* 10.6.

29 Relating to men, Tit 3:15. Ceslaus Spicq, "Comment comprendre φιλεῖν dans 1 Cor. xvi.22?" *NT* 1 (1956): 200–204, holds that v 22 is a quotation (from the Aramaic). Paul is thinking of people who under inspiration cry out ἀνάθεμα Ἰησοῦς, "Jesus is accursed," because they feel themselves oppressed like the Sibyl, like Cassandra; see on 12:1–3.

30 Bornkamm, *Early Christian Experience*, 170f (*Das Ende des Gesetzes*, 124).

31 ἤτω, "let him be": Jas 5:12; Blass–Debrunner §98. ἀνάθεμα: see on 12:3.

32 And is the curse conditional? Namely, a warning against the participation of unholy people in the Supper, because they would become guilty of the Lord? Not so Bornkamm, *Early Christian Experience*, 171 (*Das Ende des Gesetzes*, 125). According to him the dividing line does not run betweeen the baptized

and the unbaptized. Unbaptized persons can also be admitted. The explicit regulation in *Did.* 9.5 that only the baptized may participate shows that this was not a matter of course. This explanation of the regulation is not one that readily suggests itself.

33 The orthography of the word in the MSS (Nathaniel Schmidt, "Μαραναθα 1 Cor. xvi.22," *JBL* 13 [1894]: 50–60) naturally yields no conclusions.

34 Karl Georg Kuhn, *TDNT* 4:466–472. Hans Peter Rüger, "Zum Problem der Sprache Jesu," *ZNW* 59 (1968): 113–122, here esp. 120f, declares: "From the grammatical standpoint, however, the division of μαραναθά—מרנאתא into μαρὰν ἀθά—מרן אתא is the only one that can be taken into consideration. For (unlike the Aramaic of the Babylonian Talmud and the Syriac) in the dialects of the Pseudo–Jonathan Targum, the Fragment Targum and the Palestinian Pentateuch Targum, as also in the Aramaic of Samaria and of Christian Palestine, not only does the third person masculine singular of the perfect pe'al of אתא, "come," retain its א, but the second person masculine singular of the imperative pe'al does so also, so that for "our Lord" only מרן remains. And in point of fact the first person plural suffix with a noun ending in a consonant is, in the idiom of the Palestine Pentateuch Targum and in the Aramaic of Samaria and of Christian Palestine, always ־ן, in the dialects of the Pseudo–Jonathan Targum and the Fragment Targum, sometimes ־ן and sometimes ־נא."

35 Charles F. D. Moule, "A Reconsideration of the Context of *Maranatha,*" *NTS* 6 (1959–60): 307–310, advises caution in making statements on the place of the *maranatha* in the service of worship.

36 Erik Peterson, Εἷς Θεός, 130f, holds that the *maranatha* is itself anathema and the "Amen" is exorcistic reinforcement. For criticism of this interpretation

is taken as perfect (not imperative), then a future interpretation is not possible; see Kuhn: in Aramaic there are no instances of the prophetic perfect. The only possible rendering is then: "Our Lord has come (and is here)." The function of the cry in the service of worship[35] can be inferred from *Did.* 10.6 only in the form of a conjecture: does it serve as a warning to the nonholy: "The Lord is here"?[36] It is more probable, however, that the cry is addressed to the Lord: "Come!"[37]; and in this case it remains an open question whether it invites the Lord to the supper, or prays for his parousia—or whether a petition that was originally eschatological later became eucharistic.

■ **23–24** The concluding blessing is expressed in twofold form: with $\chi\acute{\alpha}\rho\iota\varsigma$ and $\dot{\alpha}\gamma\acute{\alpha}\pi\eta$, "grace" and "love." The latter is unusual.[38] As with the opening greeting, it should be noted that such a "blessing" is not an edifying phrase, but an effectual communication of grace and love.

---

see Kuhn, *TDNT* 4:471f; Bornkamm, *Early Christian Experience*, 171 (*Das Ende des Gesetzes*, 125).

37 Rev 22:20: $\ddot{\epsilon}\rho\chi ou$, "come," is manifestly a translation of *maranatha*. 1 Cor 11:26 is probably also an allusion to the formula: $\ddot{\alpha}\chi\rho\iota$ o$\hat{u}$ $\ddot{\epsilon}\lambda\theta\eta$, "until he comes"—a piece of evidence for the fact that it was eschatologically understood by Paul, as by the apocalypticist; this is certainly the original sense. Siegfried Schulz, "Maranatha and Kyrios Jesus," *ZNW* 53 (1962): 125–144, would distinguish between the meaning of "Lord" in this cry and in other acclamations. In detail: Paul–Émile Langevin, *Jésus Seigneur et l'eschatologie*, Studia, 21 (Bruges and Paris: Desclée de Brouwer, 1967); for v 22 see pp. 168–208. Langevin, too, interprets it of the parousia, but emphasizes that already at the pre–Pauline stage the sovereignty of Jesus is not merely future. We must "love" him now already, if we would participate in his Supper. A good example of a ceremony similar to the one to be presupposed here is found in Luc., *Alex.* 38:

a) $\pi\rho\acute{o}\rho\rho\eta\sigma\iota\varsigma\cdot$ $\epsilon\ddot{\iota}$ $\tau\iota\varsigma$ $\ddot{\alpha}\theta\epsilon o\varsigma$ $\ddot{\eta}$ $X\rho\iota\sigma\tau\iota\alpha\nu\grave{o}\varsigma$ $\ddot{\eta}$ $'E\pi\iota-\kappa o\acute{u}\rho\epsilon\iota o\varsigma$ $\ddot{\eta}\kappa\epsilon\iota$ $\kappa\alpha\tau\acute{\alpha}\sigma\kappa o\pi o\varsigma$ $\tau\hat{\omega}\nu$ $\dot{o}\rho\gamma\acute{\iota}\omega\nu$, $\phi\epsilon\upsilon\gamma\acute{\epsilon}\tau\omega\cdot$ o$\dot{\iota}$ $\delta\grave{\epsilon}$ $\pi\iota\sigma\tau\epsilon\acute{u}o\nu\tau\epsilon\varsigma$ $\tau\hat{\omega}$ $\theta\epsilon\hat{\omega}$ $\tau\epsilon\lambda\epsilon\acute{\iota}\sigma\theta\omega\sigma\alpha\nu$ $\tau\acute{u}\chi\eta$ $\tau\hat{\eta}$

$\dot{\alpha}\gamma\alpha\theta\hat{\eta}$.

b) $\dot{\epsilon}\xi\acute{\epsilon}\lambda\alpha\sigma\iota\varsigma$: 1. Alexander: $\ddot{\epsilon}\xi\omega$ $X\rho\iota\sigma\tau\iota\alpha\nu o\acute{u}\varsigma$.
　　　　　　　 2. Crowd: $\ddot{\epsilon}\xi\omega$ $'E\pi\iota\kappa o\upsilon\rho\epsilon\acute{\iota}o\upsilon\varsigma$.

"*a)* Proclamation [cf. the Eleusinians]: 'If any atheist or Christian or Epicurean has come to spy upon the rites, let him be off, and let those who believe in the god perform the mysteries, under the blessing of heaven.'

b) Expulsion: 1. Alexander: 'Out with the Christians!'
　　　　　　　 2. Crowd: 'Out with the Epicureans!' " (Loeb 4:225).

See Betz, *Lukian*, 7. Cf. also Kern, *Orph. Fr.* 245: $\phi\theta\acute{\epsilon}\gamma\xi o\mu\alpha\iota$ o$\hat{\iota}\varsigma$ $\theta\acute{\epsilon}\mu\iota\varsigma$ $\dot{\epsilon}\sigma\tau\acute{\iota}\cdot$ $\theta\acute{u}\rho\alpha\varsigma$ δ' $\dot{\epsilon}\pi\acute{\iota}\theta\epsilon\sigma\theta\epsilon$ $\beta\acute{\epsilon}\beta\eta\lambda o\iota$ $\pi\acute{\alpha}\nu\tau\epsilon\varsigma$ $\dot{o}\mu\hat{\omega}\varsigma$ (*v.l.* $\beta\epsilon\beta\acute{\eta}\lambda o\iota\varsigma$ $\pi\hat{\alpha}\sigma\iota\nu$), "I shall proclaim to them that it is a law: Run for the doors, you profane, all together (variant reading: to all the profane)" [Trans.].

38 Spicq, *Agapé* 2:121f.

**Bibliography
Indices**

1. Commentaries

Older Works

Cramer, J. A.
Catenae graecorum patrum, vol. 5 (Oxford: University Press, 1844).

Staab, Karl
Pauluskommentare aus der griechischen Kirche aus Katenenhandschriften, NtlAbh, 15 (Münster: Aschendorff, 1933); on 1 Cor:
1. Didymus of Alexandria, 6–14
2. Theodore of Mopsuestia, 172–196
3. Severian of Gabala, 225–277
4. Gennadius of Constantinople, 418f
5. Oecumenius of Tricca, 432–443
6. Photius of Constantinople, 544–583
7. Arethas of Caesarea, 659f

Origen
Claude Jenkins, "Origen on I Corinthians," *JThSt* 9 (1908): 231–247, 353–372, 500–514; 10 (1909): 29–51.

John Chrysostom
MPG 61:9–382.

Cyril of Alexandria
MPG 74:855–916.

Theodoret
MPG 82:225–376.

Ambrosiaster
MPL 17:183–276.

Pelagius
Alexander Souter, *Expositions of Thirteen Epistles of St. Paul*, Texts and Studies, 9, 1–3 (Cambridge: University Press, 1922–31); on 1 Cor, 2:127–130.

Thomas Aquinas
Opera omnia (Parma: Fiaccadori, 1862) 13:157–248.

Faber Stapulensis
Epistolae divi Pauli apostoli cum commentariis (Paris, 1512, ²1515).

Zwingli, Ulrich
Huldrici Zwinglii Opera, ed. M. Schuler and J. Schulthess, vol. 6, pt. 2 (Zurich: Schulthess, 1838), 134–188.

Melanchthon, Philip
CorpRef 15:1053–1192.

Calvin, John
CorpRef 77:293–574.

Modern Works

Bengel, Johann Albrecht
Gnomon of the New Testament, tr. Charlton T. Lewis and Marvin R. Vincent (Philadelphia: Perkinpine & Higgins; New York: Sheldon, 1864), 2 vols.; reprinted as *New Testament Word Studies* (Grand Rapids: Kregel, 1971), 2 vols.
Gnomon Novi Testamenti (Stuttgart: Steinkopf, ⁸1887).

Schmiedel, Paul W.
Die Briefe an die Thessalonicher und an die Korinther, Hand–Commentar zum Neuen Testament, 2, 1 (Freiburg: J. C. B. Mohr [Paul Siebeck], ²1892).

Heinrici, C. F. G.
Der erste Brief an die Korinther, KEK, 5 (Göttingen: Vandenhoeck & Ruprecht, ⁹1896).

Weiss, Johannes
Der erste Korintherbrief, KEK, 5 (Göttingen: Vandenhoeck & Ruprecht, ⁹1910, ¹⁰1925).

Robertson, Archibald, and Plummer, Alfred
A Critical and Exegetical Commentary on the First Epistle of St Paul to the Corinthians, ICC (Edinburgh: T. & T. Clark, ²1914).

Bousset, Wilhelm
"Der erste Brief an die Korinther," in *Die Schriften des Neuen Testaments*, ed. Wilhelm Bousset and Wilhelm Heitmüller, vol. 2 (Göttingen: Vandenhoeck & Ruprecht, ³1917), 74–167.

Billerbeck, Paul
Die Briefe des Neuen Testaments und die Offenbarung Johannis erläutert aus Talmud und Midrasch, in Kommentar zum Neuen Testament aus Talmud und Midrasch, 3 (Munich: Beck, 1926, ³1961), 321–494.

Allo, E.–B.
Première Épître aux Corinthiens, Études Bibliques (Paris: Gabalda, 1934).

Schlatter, Adolf
Paulus der Bote Jesu (Stuttgart: Calwer, ²1956).

Bachmann, Philipp
Der erste Brief des Paulus an die Korinther, with additions by Ethelbert Stauffer, KNT (Zahn), 7 (Leipzig and Erlangen: Deichert, ⁴1936).

Kuss, Otto
Die Briefe an die Römer, Korinther und Galater, Regensburger Neues Testament, 6, 1 (Regensburg: Pustet, 1940), 112–196.

Héring, Jean
The First Epistle of Saint Paul to the Corinthians, tr. A. W. Heathcote and P. J. Allcock (London: Epworth, 1962).
La première Épître de Saint Paul aux Corinthiens, Commentaire du Nouveau Testament, 7 (Neuchâtel: Delachaux & Niestlé, 1949, ²1959).

Lietzmann, Hans

    An die Korinther, rev. Werner Georg Kümmel, HNT, 9 (Tübingen: J. C. B. Mohr [Paul Siebeck], ⁴1949).

Grosheide, F. W.

    Commentary on the First Epistle to the Corinthians, NIC (Grand Rapids: Eerdmans, 1953).

Barrett, C. K.

    A Commentary on the First Epistle to the Corinthians, Black's/Harper's New Testament Commentaries (London: Black; New York: Harper & Row, 1968).

Wendland, H. D.

    Die Briefe an die Korinther, NT Deutsch, 7 (Göttingen: Vandenhoeck & Ruprecht, ¹²1968).

Studies

Barth, Karl

    The Resurrection of the Dead, tr. H. J. Stenning (New York: Revell, 1933).

    Die Auferstehung der Toten (Munich: Kaiser, 1924).

Betz, Hans Dieter

    Lukian von Samosata und das Neue Testament, TU, 76 (Berlin: Akademie–Verlag, 1961).

Betz, Johannes

    Die Eucharistie in der Zeit der griechischen Väter, vol. 2, part 1 (Freiburg: Herder, 1961).

Bömer, Franz

    Untersuchungen über die Religion der Sklaven in Griechenland und Rom, AAM 1957, 7; 1960, 1; 1961, 4; 1963, 10 (Wiesbaden: Steiner, 1957–63), 4 vols.

Bonsirven, Joseph

    Exégèse rabbinique et exégèse paulinienne (Paris: Beauchesne, 1939).

Bornkamm, Günther

    Early Christian Experience, tr. Paul L. Hammer (London: SCM; New York: Harper & Row, 1969). Translations from *Das Ende des Gesetzes* and *Studien*.

Idem

    Das Ende des Gesetzes. Gesammelte Aufsätze Band I, BEvTh, 16 (Munich: Kaiser, ⁵1966).

Idem

    Geschichte und Glaube. Erster Teil. Gesammelte Aufsätze Band III, BEvTh, 48 (Munich: Kaiser, 1968).

    Geschichte und Glaube. Zweiter Teil. Gesammelte Aufsätze Band IV, BEvTh, 53 (Munich: Kaiser, 1971).

Idem

    Die Vorgeschichte des sogenannten Zweiten Korintherbriefes, SAH 1961, 2 (Heidelberg: Winter, 1961). Reprinted in *Geschichte und Glaube* 2:162–194.

Bousset, Wilhelm

    Die Hauptprobleme der Gnosis, FRLANT, 10 (Göttingen: Vandenhoeck & Ruprecht, 1907).

Idem

    Kyrios Christos. A History of the Belief in Christ from the Beginnings of Christianity to Irenaeus, tr. John E. Steely (New York and Nashville: Abingdon, 1970).

    Kyrios Christos. Geschichte des Christusglaubens von den Anfängen des Christentums bis Irenäus, FRLANT, 22 (Göttingen: Vandenhoeck & Ruprecht, 1913, ²1921, ⁵1965).

Idem

    Jüdisch–christliche Schulbetrieb in Alexandria und Rom, FRLANT, 23 (Göttingen: Vandenhoeck & Ruprecht, 1915).

Idem

    Die Religion des Judentums im späthellenistischen Zeitalter, rev. Hugo Gressmann, HNT, 21 (Tübingen: J. C. B. Mohr [Paul Siebeck], ⁴1966).

Bouttier, Michel

    En Christ. Étude d'exégèse et de théologie paulinienne, Études d'Histoire et de Philosophie Religieuse, 54 (Paris: Presses Universitaires, 1962).

Brandenburger, Egon

    Adam und Christus. Exegetisch–religionsgeschichtliche Untersuchung zu Röm. 5, 12–21 (1. Kor. 15), WMANT, 7 (Neukirchen: Neukirchener Verlag, 1962).

Braun, Herbert

    Gesammelte Studien zum Neuen Testament und seiner Umwelt (Tübingen: J. C. B. Mohr [Paul Siebeck], 1962).

Idem

    Qumran und das Neue Testament (Tübingen: J. C. B. Mohr [Paul Siebeck], 1966), 2 vols.

Bultmann, Rudolf

    Faith and Understanding, vol. 1, tr. Louise Pettibone Smith, ed. Robert W. Funk (London: SCM; New York: Harper & Row, 1969), ET of *GuV* 1.

Idem

    Glauben und Verstehen. Gesammelte Aufsätze I–IV (Tübingen: J. C. B. Mohr [Paul Siebeck], 1933–65), 4 vols.

Idem

    Primitive Christianity in Its Contemporary Setting, tr. Reginald H. Fuller (Cleveland and New York: World/Meridian, 1956).

    Das Urchristentum im Rahmen der antiken Religionen (Zurich: Artemis, 1949, ²1954).

Idem

    Der Stil der paulinischen Predigt und die kynisch–stoische Diatribe, FRLANT, 13 (Göttingen: Vandenhoeck & Ruprecht, 1910).

Idem

    Theology of the New Testament, tr. Kendrick Grobel (London: SCM; New York: Scribner, 1952–55), 2 vols.

    Theologie des Neuen Testaments (Tübingen: J. C. B. Mohr [Paul Siebeck], 1948–53, ⁶1968).

von Campenhausen, Hans

    Die Begründung kirchlicher Entscheidung beim Apostel Paulus, SAH 1957, 2 (Heidelberg: Winter, 1957).

Idem

    Ecclesiastical Authority and Spiritual Power in the Church of the First Three Centuries, tr. John A. Baker

(London: A. & C. Black; Stanford: Stanford University Press, 1969).

Kirchliches Amt und geistliche Vollmacht in den ersten drei Jahrhunderten, BHTh, 14 (Tübingen: J. C. B. Mohr [Paul Siebeck]. ²1963).

Cerfaux, Lucien

Christ in the Theology of St. Paul, tr. Geoffrey Webb and Adrian Walker (Freiburg and New York: Herder & Herder, 1959).

Le Christ dans la théologie de saint Paul, Lectio Divina, 6 (Paris: Cerf, ²1954).

Idem

The Church in the Theology of St. Paul, tr. Geoffrey Webb and Adrian Walker (New York: Herder & Herder, 1959).

La théologie de l'église suivant saint Paul, Unam Sanctam, 54 (Paris: Cerf, ²1948).

Colpe, Carsten

Die religionsgeschichtliche Schule, Darstellung und Kritik ihres Bildes vom gnostischen Erlösermythus, FRLANT, 78 (Göttingen: Vandenhoeck & Ruprecht, 1961).

Cumont, Franz

The Oriental Religions in Roman Paganism, authorized translation, with an introductory essay by Grant Showerman (Chicago: Open Court, 1911; New York: Dover, 1956).

Les religions orientales dans le paganisme romain, Annales du Musée Guimet, Bibliothèque de vulgarisation, 24 (Paris: Leroux, ³1929).

Daube, David

The New Testament and Rabbinic Judaism, School of Oriental and African Studies, University of London, Jordan Lectures in Comparative Religion 2 (London: Athlone, 1956).

Davies, W. D.

Paul and Rabbinic Judaism. Some Rabbinic Elements in Pauline Theology (London: SPCK, ²1955).

Deissmann, Adolf

Light from the Ancient East, tr. Lionel R. M. Strachan, new and completely rev. ed. (London: Hodder & Stoughton; New York: Doran, 1927).

Licht vom Osten (Tübingen: J. C. B. Mohr [Paul Siebeck], ⁴1923).

Idem

Paul. A Study in Social and Religious History, tr. William E. Wilson (New York: Harper, ²1957).

Paulus. Eine kultur- und religionsgeschichtliche Skizze (Tübingen: J. C. B. Mohr [Paul Siebeck], ²1925).

Dinkler, Erich

"Korintherbriefe," *RGG*³ 4:17–23.

Idem

Signum Crucis. Aufsätze zum Neuen Testament und zur christlichen Archäologie (Tübingen: J. C. B. Mohr [Paul Siebeck], 1967).

Dupont, Jacques

Gnosis. La connaissance religieuse dans les épîtres de S. Paul, Universitas Catholica Lovaniensis, Dissertationes in Facultate Theologica, 2, 40 (Louvain: Nauwelaerts, ²1960).

Ellis, E. Earle

Paul's Use of the Old Testament (Edinburgh: Oliver & Boyd; Grand Rapids: Eerdmans, 1957).

Eltester, Friedrich Wilhelm

Eikon im Neuen Testament, BZNW, 23 (Berlin: Töpelmann, 1958).

Feuillet, André

Le Christ Sagesse de Dieu d'après les Épîtres pauliniennes, Études Bibliques (Paris: Gabalda, 1966).

Fowler, H. N., ed.

Corinth (Athens: American School of Classical Studies, 1929–   ), 16 vols. to date.

Georgi, Dieter

Die Gegner des Paulus im 2. Korintherbrief. Studien zur religiösen Propaganda in der Spätantike, WMANT, 11 (Neukirchen–Vluyn: Neukirchener Verlag, 1964).

Gerhardsson, Birger

Memory and Manuscript. Oral Tradition and Written Transmission in Rabbinic Judaism and Early Christianity, tr. E. J. Sharpe (Lund: Gleerup; Copenhagen: Munksgaard, 1961).

Grass, Hans

Ostergeschehen und Osterberichte (Göttingen: Vandenhoeck & Ruprecht, ²1962).

Güttgemanns, Erhardt

Der leidende Apostel und sein Herr, FRLANT, 90 (Göttingen: Vandenhoeck & Ruprecht, 1966).

Hermann, Ingo

Kyrios und Pneuma. Studien zur Christologie der paulinischen Hauptbriefe, SANT, 2 (Munich: Kösel, 1961).

Hurd, John C., Jr.

The Origin of I Corinthians (London: SPCK; New York: Seabury, 1965).

Jeremias, Joachim

Abba (Göttingen: Vandenhoeck & Ruprecht, 1966).

Idem

The Eucharistic Words of Jesus, tr. Norman Perrin (London: SCM; New York: Scribner, 1966).

Die Abendmahlsworte Jesu (Göttingen: Vandenhoeck & Ruprecht, ⁴1967).

Jervell, Jacob

Imago Dei. Gen 1,26f. im Spätjudentum, in der Gnosis und in den paulinischen Briefen, FRLANT, 76 (Göttingen: Vandenhoeck & Ruprecht, 1960).

Jonas, Hans

Gnosis und spätantiker Geist, vol. 1 (Göttingen: Vandenhoeck & Ruprecht, ³1964); vol. 2, pt. 1 (²1966).

Käsemann, Ernst

Essays on New Testament Themes, tr. W. J. Montague, SBT, 1, 41 (London: SCM, 1964). ET of essays from *Exegetische Versuche und Besinnungen* 1.

Idem

New Testament Questions of Today, tr. W. J. Montague (London: SCM; Philadelphia: Fortress, 1969). ET of essays from *Exegetische Versuche und Besinnungen* 2.

Idem

    Exegetische Versuche und Besinnungen (Göttingen: Vandenhoeck & Ruprecht, ²1960–65), 2 vols.

Idem

    Leib und Leib Christi. Eine Untersuchung zur paulinischen Begrifflichkeit, BHTh, 9 (Tübingen: J. C. B. Mohr [Paul Siebeck], 1933).

Idem

    Perspectives on Paul, tr. Margaret Kohl (London: SCM; Philadelphia: Fortress, 1971).
    Paulinische Perspektiven (Tübingen: J. C. B. Mohr [Paul Siebeck], 1969).

Klein, Günter

    Die zwölf Apostel. Ursprung und Gehalt einer Idee, FRLANT, 77 (Göttingen: Vandenhoeck & Ruprecht, 1961).

Kramer, Werner

    Christ, Lord, Son of God, tr. Brian Hardy, SBT, 1, 50 (London: SCM, 1966).
    Christos Kyrios Gottessohn, AThANT, 44 (Zurich: Zwingli, 1963).

Kümmel, Werner Georg

    Introduction to the New Testament, by Paul Feine and Johannes Behm, rev. Werner Georg Kümmel, tr. A. J. Mattill, Jr., from the 14th German ed. (New York and Nashville: Abingdon, 1966).
    Einleitung in das Neue Testament (Heidelberg: Quelle & Meyer, ¹⁴1965).

Idem

    Kirchenbegriff und Geschichtsbewusstsein in der Urgemeinde und bei Jesus, SBU, 1 (Uppsala: Seminarium Neotestamenticum Upsaliense; Zurich: Niehaus, 1943; Göttingen: Vandenhoeck & Ruprecht, 1968).

Lidzbarski, Mark

    Mandäische Liturgien, AGG, n.s. 17, 1 (Berlin: Weidmann, 1920; Hildesheim: Olms, 1962).

Lietzmann, Hans

    Mass and Lord's Supper, tr. Dorothea H. G. Reeve (Leiden: Brill, 1953–   ).
    Messe und Herrenmahl, Arbeiten zur Kirchengeschichte, 8 (Bonn: Marcus & Weber, 1926).

Lindars, Barnabas

    New Testament Apologetic. The Doctrinal Significance of the Old Testament Quotations (London: SCM; Philadelphia: Westminster, 1961).

Lohse, Eduard

    Märtyrer und Gottesknecht. Untersuchungen zur urchristlichen Verkündigung vom Sühntod Jesu Christi, FRLANT, 64 (Göttingen: Vandenhoeck & Ruprecht, ²1963).

Idem, ed. and tr.

    Die Texte aus Qumran (Darmstadt: Wissenschaftliche Buchgesellschaft, 1964).

Lührmann, Dieter

    Die Offenbarungsverständnis bei Paulus und in paulinischen Gemeinden, WMANT, 16 (Neukirchen–Vluyn: Neukirchener Verlag, 1965).

Mattern, Lieselotte

    Das Verständnis des Gerichtes bei Paulus, AThANT,

    47 (Zurich and Stuttgart: Zwingli, 1966).

Metzger, Bruce M.

    Index to Periodical Literature on the Apostle Paul, NTTS, 1 (Leiden: Brill, 1960).

Michaelis, Wilhelm

    Einleitung in das Neue Testament (Bern: Haller, ³1961).

Michel, Otto

    Paulus und seine Bibel, BFTh, 2, 18 (Gütersloh: Bertelsmann, 1929; Darmstadt: Wissenschaftliche Buchgesellschaft, n.d.).

Moore, George Foot

    Judaism in the First Three Centuries of the Christian Era (Cambridge, Mass.: Harvard University Press, 1927–30), 3 vols. Reprinted in 2 vols. (New York: Schocken, 1971).

Munck, Johannes

    Paul and the Salvation of Mankind, tr. Frank Clarke (London SCM; Richmond: John Knox, 1959).
    Paulus und die Heilsgeschichte, Acta Jutlandica, 26, 1 (Aarhus: Universitetsforlaget; Copenhagen: Munksgaard, 1954).

Neuenzeit, Paul

    Das Herrenmahl. Studien zur paulinischen Eucharistieauffassung, SANT, 1 (Munich: Kösel, 1960).

Neugebauer, Fritz

    In Christus. ΕΝ ΧΡΙΣΤΩΙ. Eine Untersuchung zum paulinischen Glaubensverständnis (Göttingen: Vandenhoeck & Ruprecht, 1961).

Norden, Eduard

    Agnostos Theos. Untersuchungen zur Formengeschichte religiöser Rede (Leipzig and Berlin: Teubner, 1913; Darmstadt: Wissenschaftliche Buchgesellschaft, ⁵1971).

Pascher, Joseph

    Η ΒΑΣΙΛΙΚΗ ΟΔΟΣ. *Der Königsweg zu Wiedergeburt und Vergottung bei Philon von Alexandreia*, Studien zur Geschichte und Kultur des Altertums, 17, 3–4 (Paderborn: Schöningh, 1931; New York and London: Johnson, 1968).

Peterson, Erik

    Εἷς Θεός: *Epigraphische, formgeschichtliche und religionsgeschichtliche Untersuchungen*, FRLANT, 41 (Göttingen: Vandenhoeck & Ruprecht, 1926).

Reitzenstein, Richard

    Die hellenistischen Mysterienreligionen nach ihren Grundgedanken und Wirkungen (Stuttgart: Teubner, ³1927; Darmstadt: Wissenschaftliche Buchgesellschaft, 1966).

Idem

    Poimandres. Studien zur griechisch–ägyptischen und frühchristlichen Literatur (Leipzig and Berlin: Teubner, 1904; Darmstadt: Wissenschaftliche Buchgesellschaft, 1966).

Idem and Schäder, Hans Heinrich

    Studien zum antiken Synkretismus aus Iran und Griechenland, Studien der Bibliothek Warburg, 7 (Leipzig and Berlin: Teubner, 1926; Darmstadt: Wissenschaftliche Buchgesellschaft, 1965).

Rohde, Erwin

Psyche. The Cult of Souls and Belief in Immortality among the Greeks, tr. W. B. Hillis (London: Kegan Paul, Trench, Trubner; New York: Harcourt, Brace, 1925; New York: Harper & Row, 1966).

Psyche. Seelencult und Unsterblichkeitsglaube der Griechen (Tübingen: J. C. B. Mohr [Paul Siebeck], 5,61910; Darmstadt: Wissenschaftliche Buchgesellschaft, 1960), 2 vols. in 1.

Roller, Otto

Das Formular der paulinischen Briefe, BWANT, 58 (Stuttgart: Kohlhammer, 1933).

Schlier, Heinrich

Der Brief an die Epheser. Ein Kommentar (Düsseldorf: Patmos, 1957, 51965).

Idem

Christus und die Kirche im Epheserbrief, BHTh, 6 (Tübingen: J. C. B. Mohr [Paul Siebeck], 1930).

Idem

Die Zeit der Kirche. Exegetische Aufsätze und Vorträge I (Freiburg: Herder, 1956).

Schmithals, Walter

Gnosticism in Corinth. An Investigation of the Letters to the Corinthians, tr. John E. Steely (New York and Nashville: Abingdon, 1971).

Die Gnosis in Korinth. Eine Untersuchung zu den Korintherbriefen, FRLANT, 66 (Göttingen: Vandenhoeck & Ruprecht, 1956, 21965, 31969).

Idem

The Office of Apostle in the Early Church, tr. John E. Steely (New York and Nashville: Abingdon, 1969).

Das kirchliche Apostelamt, Eine historische Untersuchung, FRLANT, 79 (Göttingen: Vandenhoeck & Ruprecht, 1961).

Idem

Paul and the Gnostics, tr. John E. Steely (New York and Nashville: Abingdon, 1972).

Paulus und die Gnostiker Untersuchungen zu den kleinen Paulusbriefen, ThF, 35 (Hamburg: Reich, 1965).

von Soden, Hans

"Sakrament und Ethik bei Paulus," in *Marburger theologische Studien (Rudolf–Otto Festgruss)*, ed. H. Frick, Vol. 1 (Gotha: Klotz, 1931), 1–40; reprinted in von Soden's *Urchristentum und Geschichte* 1:238–275; and in *Das Paulusbild in der neueren Deutschen Forschung*, ed. Karl Heinrich Rengstorf, Wege der Forschung, 24 (Darmstadt: Wissenschaftliche Buchgesellschaft, 1969), 338–379.

Idem

Urchristentum und Geschichte. Gesammelte Aufsätze und Vorträge, vol. 1, ed. Hans von Campenhausen (Tübingen: J. C. B. Mohr [Paul Siebeck], 1951).

Spicq, Ceslaus

Agapé dans le Nouveau Testament, Études Bibliques (Paris: Gabalda, 1958–59), 3 vols.

Thyen, Hartwig

Der Stil der Jüdisch–Hellenistischen Homilie, FRLANT, 65 (Göttingen: Vandenhoeck & Ruprecht, 1955).

Ulonska, Herbert

Die Funktion der alttestamentliche Zitate und Anspielungen in den paulinischen Briefe (dissertation, Münster, 1963).

Volz, Paul

Die Eschatologie der jüdischen Gemeinde im neutestamentlichen Zeitalter (Tübingen: J. C. B. Mohr [Paul Siebeck], 1934).

Wegenast, Klaus

Das Verständnis der Tradition bei Paulus und in den Deuteropaulinen, WMANT, 8 (Neukirchen–Vluyn: Neukirchener Verlag, 1962).

Weiss, Johannes

Beiträge zur paulinischen Rhetorik (Göttingen: Vandenhoeck & Ruprecht, 1897); first published in *Theologische Studien. B. Weiss zu seinem 70. Geburtstag dargebracht* (Göttingen: Vandenhoeck & Ruprecht, 1897), 165–247.

Wendland, Paul

Die urchristliche Literaturformen, HNT, 1, 3 (Tübingen: J. C. B. Mohr [Paul Siebeck], 31912). Usually bound with his *Die hellenistisch–römische Kultur* (HNT, 1, 2) and paged continuously with it, i.e., pp. 257–448.

Wetter, Gillis Petersson

Charis. Ein Beitrag zur Geschichte des ältesten Christentums, UNT, 5 (Leipzig: Hinrichs, 1913).

Wilckens, Ulrich

Weisheit und Torheit. Eine exegetisch–religionsgeschichtliche Untersuchung zur 1 Kor 1 und 2, BHTh, 26 (Tübingen: J. C. B. Mohr [Paul Siebeck], 1959).

Wiles, Maurice F.

The Divine Apostle, The Interpretation of St. Paul's Epistles in the Early Church (Cambridge: University Press, 1967).

Zuntz, Günther

The Text of the Epistles, Schweich Lectures 1946 (London: British Academy/Oxford University Press, 1953).

Indices*

1. Passages

a / Old Testament and Apocrypha

Gen

1:26f	286
1:27	186
2:7	283
	284
	286
2:18	188
2:22	188
5:1	187
6:1f	189
12:7	253(45)
42:15f	264(5)

LXX Gen

2:7	284

Ex

3:14	260(105)
12:14	198
12:16	22(32)
13:21	165
14:21ff	165
17:6	166
19:6	22(33)
24:8	199(73)

LXX Ex

32:6	167

Lev

7:6, 15	172

LXX Lev

24:7	199(65)

Num

1:1	294(1)
8:15	156(1)
12:8	227
12:12	259(97)
14:16, 30	167
20:7–11	166
25:1ff	168
26:62	168

Deut

17:7	102(85)
18:1–4	172
21:12	186(46)
21:23	204(10)
25:4	154
28:36	206(15)
32:17	173

1 Kings

18:39	243(33)

1 Macc

1:27	53(10)
3:19	93(29)

Ps

8:7	274
10:16	273
24:1	177
27:14	297(35)
77:18	168(34)
98:6	23(36)

LXX Ps

30:25	297
93:11	80
104:39	165
109:1	272
111:6	199(63)

Prov

3:7	89(42)
10:7	199(62)

Job

5:13	80

Sir

14:18	289(7)
17:1ff	187
43:9	282(22)
43:27f	275(113)

Hos

6:2	256
13:14	292

LXX Hos

6:2	253

Amos

4:11	77(85)

Zech

12:1	66
14:9	275(114)

Isa

1:16	107(44)
4:3	23(33)
19:11f	42
19:15	271(74)
22:13	278
25:8	292
28:11f	241
33:18	43
40:13	69
45:14	243(33)
53	255
53:4f	253(48)
53:4ff	255(61)
53:5	253
54:8	291(17)

LXX Isa

29:14	42
53:12	253(49)

Jer

8:13—9:24	44
9:22f	52

LXX Jer

38:31	199

Bar

3:9—4:4	44
3:14	41(15)
3:16ff	61(47)
3:23	43(31)

Dan

3:39	93(31)
4:1 Θ	19(6)

Bel

6	295(11)

Wisd

2:6ff	278(138)
2:23	187
7:22ff	187
	218(11)
7:25	220(18)

b / Old Testament Pseudepigrapha and Other Jewish Literature

Ab.

1	196(31)
6.6	224(56)

Asc. Is.

4.17	292(27)
11.34	64

AZ

2.3	139(6)
	176(14)

2 Bar.

50f	290

b.BB.

16a	273(98)

b.Ned.

30b	185(39)

b.Sanh.

90b	281(14)
93b	254(50)
97	254(50)
98a	254(50)
99a	254(50)

---

* Numbers in parentheses following
page citations refer to footnotes.

P. Ryl.			Plutarch	
15.6f	277(131)		*Aud. poet.*	
2:154.24f	120(18)		21f	167(30)
PGM			*Alex.*	
1.90	68(116)		330f	278(137)
4.495	283(30)		332ab	92(16)
4.1139	134(28)		336c	278(137)
4.1174	283(30)		*Amic. mult.*	
4.1247f	97(37)		94b	230(119)
4.3090	253(43)		*Apophth.*	
12.188	232(7)		200f	181(2)
Phaedr.			*Apophth. Lac.*	
Fab.			232c	185(40)
4.16.5	214(32)		*Cons. ad Apoll.*	
Philostratus			110d	43(28)
Vit. Ap.			*Def. orac.*	
4.22	106(32)		437	243(25)
8.7	134(28)		*Fort. Rom.*	
Phlegon			320b	75(58)
	264(13)		*Is. et Os.*	
Plato			371b	187
Ap.			382a	227
21b	83(18)		*Phoc.*	
Crito			21	224(63)
48b	231(127)		*Praec. coniug.*	
Leg.			140c	117(21)
873e	103(5)		*Quaest. conv.*	
958c	78(94)		729c	176(12)
Phaed.			*Quaest. Plat.*	
71e	261(118)		1001c	144(46)
Resp.			*Quaest. Rom.*	
364a	50(13)		267a	185(40)
364e–365a	275(116)		*Ser. num. pun.*	
411d	55(23)		564b	236(34)
484d	27(31)		*Solon*	
487e	187(57)		18.5(88c)	214(38)
522c	248(5)		*Them.*	
Soph.			27	187(58)
250b	171(18)		*Tranq. an.*	
Symp.			472a	87(28)
188b	171(20)		Poll.	
197c–197e	219		*Onom.*	
Tim.			3.131	169(45)
71b	227(94)		Polyb.	
71f	243(29)		*Hist.*	
92c	187		1.15.11	130(3)
Plaut.			4.86.5	177(15)
Pseudol.			Porphyr.	
998–1016	299(19)		*Abst.*	
Pliny			1.42	109(11)
Hist. nat. praef.			*Marc.*	
25	221(29)		13	228(97)
Panegyr.			24	229
33.3	88(36)			

Preisigke	
Sammelbuch	
7172	25(2)
7912	36(45)
Ps.–Aristot.	
Mund.	
6	144(46)
Ps.–Callisthenes	
Hist. Alex. Magn.	
2.21.21	103(4)
3.28.4	76(73)
Ps.–Demetr.	
Eloc.	
298	85(8)
Ps.–Luc.	
Asin.	
17	299(23)
Syr. Dea	
6	198(58)
Ps.–Plat.	
Alc.	
1.135d	297(27)
Ep.	
13.363d	299(18)
PSI	
166.11f	120(18)
Quint. Curt. Ruf.	
Hist. Alex.	
4.2.14	197(49)
10.6.8	211(7)
10.9.2	211(7)
Sallust.	
Jug.	
14.23	88(36)
Sallust. Neoplat.	
Deor. et mund.	
21	105(18)
Seneca	
Benef.	
7.3.2	80(17)
Const.	
17.1	147(14)
Ep.	
24.20	277(125)
27.2	226(84)
66.12	65(87)
95.52	211(8)
104.1	13(102)
Ouaest. nat.	
1.5.1	227(94)
1.15.7	227(94)
Sextus	
Sent.	
52	177(15)
190	187(53)

2. Greek Words

3. Subjects

Achaicus
298(9)
Adam
267,268,284,285,286,288
Adscriptio
20
Aphrodite
12
Apion
25(13)
Apocalyptic
43,58,59,62,64,76,105,
168(40),269,270,271,272,273,
274,275,291,292
Apollos
33,88(34),297
Apostle, apostles
19,215,258
Apostleship
151,152
Aquila
13,299
Asceticism
115,116
Authority
7,73,82

Baptism
35,36,36(46),107,165,275,276
Barnabas
154
Body of Christ
35,36,111,112,172,188,202,
211,212,213,214,215,216
Building
74,75,141(15)

Catalogues of Virtues and Vices
100,101,106
Chloe
32
Christ
21,33,34,35,47,92,183,249,
253,265,267,268
Christ, Body of
35,36,111,112,172,188,202,
211,212,213,214,215,216
Christology
11,15,24,34,38(56),145,188,
190,249(14),255,264
Church
21,104
Claudius
12,13

Collection
295,296
Conscience
83,137,147,148,176,178
Corinth
11,12,298
Covenant
99,199
Crispus
36(43)
Cross
11,40,41,51,63
Curse
204,204(10)
Cynics
10,87,108,152

Demonology
173,189,271
Diatribe
5,49,72,73,79,86,104,108,
126,162,270,280
Divorce
120,121,123

Ecstasy
16,60,204,206,237,239,242
Enthusiasm
14,57,137,185(41),204
Ephesus
296,299
Epistle to the Romans
4,6
Eschatology
11,11(79),11(81),28,43,87,
93,101,104,111,132,133,168,
202,225,230,249,291
Ethics
10,95,100

Faith
15,16,79,229,230,231
Flesh
72
Florilegium
42,44
Fortunatus
298(9)
Foundation
75
Freedom
10,14,16,38,109,126,127,
137,138,140,148,149,150,
152,160,178

Gaius
36(43)
Gallio
12,13
Gayômart
285
Gnostic, Gnostics
87(28),138(7),140,167(30),
194(20)
Gnosticism
14,15,61,67,141,188,269,285
God, Kingdom of
93,106,270,271,289
Gospel
9,15,27,39,41,91,157,250
Grace
21,24,26,27,64,87,126,260

Holiness
21,22,97,107,121,122,134
Hope
229,230,231,267

Imitation
92,179

James
258
Judaists
14
Judgment
28,75,78,83,84,85,88,102,
104,105,202
Justification
11,40,77,107

Kingdom of God
93,106,270,271,289
Knowledge
14,46,54,62,65,138,140,141,
143,169,222

Law
160,161,241,293
Libertinism
14,15,96
Lord's Supper
166,170,171,172,174,192,194,
195,196,197,198,199,200,201,
202,203
———, Tradition of
200,201
Love
141,149,217,218,219,220,221,
222,223,224,225,226,227,228,
229,230,231

Marcion
2
Marriage, marriages
96,114,116,118,119,121,184
Martyrdom
222
Menenius Agrippa
211(7),212(22),214(36)
Meristai
35(32)
Mirror
226,227,228
Muratorian Canon
2
Mystery, mysteries
36,58,59,62,65,206,261,290,
291
Mystes
206,261

Office
72,73,74,82,215,298
Opponents
14

Paraenesis
6,8,31,95,102,297
Parousia
28,29,88,202,262,270,290
Party
14,32,33,34,72,73,194
Passover
99
Peter
33,153,153(25),256,258
Philosophy
10,141(18),142
Planting
73,74
Pneumatic, pneumatics
55,57,69,72
Preaching
37,46,53,54
Preexistence
145(49),166,183
Primal man
268,284,285,286
Prisc(ill)a
13,299
Proemium, proemia
25,26,27,28,54,93
Prophecy
209,215,221,222,232,233,234,
235,236,237,238,239
Psychic
67,68

4. Modern Authors

In the design of the visual aspects of *Hermeneia*, consideration has been given to relating the form to the content by symbolic means.

The letters of the logotype *Hermeneia* are a fusion of forms alluding simultaneously to Hebrew (dotted vowel markings) and Greek (geometric round shapes) letter forms. In their modern treatment they remind us of the electronic age as well, the vantage point from which this investigation of the past begins.

The Lion of Judah used as a visual identification for the series is based on the Seal of Shema. The version for *Hermeneia* is again a fusion of Hebrew calligraphic forms, especially the legs of the lion, and Greek elements characterized by the geometric. In the sequence of arcs, which can be understood as scroll-like images, the first is the lion's mouth. It is reasserted and accelerated in the whorl and returns in the aggressively arched tail: tradition is passed from one age to the next, rediscovered and re-formed.

"Who is worthy to open the scroll and break its seals . . ."
Then one of the elders said to me
"weep not; lo, the Lion of the tribe of David,
the Root of David, has conquered,
so that he can open the scroll and
its seven seals."
Rev. 5:2, 5

To celebrate the signal achievement in biblical scholarship which *Hermeneia* represents, the entire series will by its color constitute a signal on the theologian's bookshelf: the Old Testament will be bound in yellow and the New Testament in red, traceable to a commonly used color coding for synagogue and church in medieval painting; in pure color terms, varying degrees of intensity of the warm segment of the color spectrum. The colors interpenetrate when the binding color for the Old Testament is used to imprint volumes from the New and vice versa.

Wherever possible, a photograph of the oldest extant manuscript, or a historically significant document pertaining to the biblical sources, will be displayed on the end papers of each volume to give a feel for the tangible reality and beauty of the source material.

The title page motifs are expressive derivations from the *Hermeneia* logotype, repeated seven times to form a matrix and debossed on the cover of each volume. These sifted out elements will be seen to be in their exact positions within the parent matrix. These motifs and their expressional character are noted on the following page.

Horizontal markings at gradated levels on the spine will assist in grouping the volumes according to these conventional categories.

The type has been set with unjustified right margins so as to preserve the internal consistency of word spacing. This is a major factor in both legibility and aesthetic quality; the resultant uneven line endings are only slight impairments to legibility by comparison. In this respect the type resembles the hand written manuscript where the quality of the calligraphic writing is dependent on establishing and holding to integral spacing patterns.

All of the type faces in common use today have been designed between 1500 A.D. and the present. For the biblical text a face was chosen which does not arbitrarily date the text, but rather one which is uncompromisingly modern and unembellished so that its feel is of the universal. The type style is Univers 65 by Adrian Frutiger.

The expository texts and footnotes are set in Baskerville, chosen for its compatibility with the many brief Greek and Hebrew insertions. The double column format and the shorter line length facilitate speed reading and the wide margins to the left of footnotes provide for the scholar's own notations.

Kenneth Hiebert, Designer

Category of biblical writing,
key symbolic characteristic,
and volumes so identified

1
Law
(boundaries described)
  Genesis
  Exodus
  Leviticus
  Numbers
  Deuteronomy

2
History
(trek through time and space)
  Joshua
  Judges
  Ruth
  1 Samuel
  2 Samuel
  1 Kings
  2 Kings
  1 Chronicles
  2 Chronicles
  Ezra
  Nehemiah
  Esther

3
Poetry
(lyric emotional expression)
  Job
  Psalms
  Proverbs
  Ecclesiastes
  Song of Songs

4
Prophets
(inspired seers)
  Isaiah
  Jeremiah
  Lamentations
  Ezekiel
  Daniel
  Hosea
  Joel
  Amos
  Obadiah
  Jonah
  Micah
  Nahum
  Habakkuk
  Zephaniah
  Haggai
  Zechariah
  Malachi

5
New Testament Narrative
(focus on One)
  Matthew
  Mark
  Luke
  John
  Acts

6
Epistles
(directed instruction)
  Romans
  1 Corinthians
  2 Corinthians
  Galatians
  Ephesians
  Philippians
  Colossians
  1 Thessalonians
  2 Thessalonians
  1 Timothy
  2 Timothy
  Titus
  Philemon
  Hebrews
  James
  1 Peter
  2 Peter
  1 John
  2 John
  3 John
  Jude

7
Apocalypse
(vision of the future)
  Revelation

8
Extracanonical Writings
(peripheral records)